GENERATIONS

GENERATIONS

The History of America's Future,
1584 to 2069

WILLIAM STRAUSS
and NEIL HOWE

Quill
William Morrow
New York

It is the policy of William Morrow and Company, Inc., and its imprints and affiliates,
recognizing the importance of preserving what has been written, to print the books we
publish on acid-free paper, and we exert our best efforts to that end.

Library of Congress Cataloging-in-Publication Data

Strauss, William.
    Generations : the history of America's future, 1584 to 2069 / Willaim Strauss and
Neil Howe. — 1st. ed.
      p. cm.
    Includes bibliographical references and index.
    ISBN 0-688-11912-3 (pbk.)
    1. Unites States—History. 2. Generations—United States— History. I. Howe,
Neil. II. Title.
[E179.S89 1992]
973—dc20   92-8222
                                                      CIP

Printed in the United States of America

First Quill Edition

1 2 3 4 5 6 7 8 9 10

*To our grandparents and grandchildren,
whose lives will touch parts of four centuries*

Preface

In a recent survey, new college graduates listed history as the academic subject whose lessons they found of *least* use in their daily affairs. In part, this reflects the show-me pragmatism of today's rising generation. Yet as America embarks on the 1990s, people of all ages feel a disconnection with history. Many have difficulty placing their own thoughts and actions, even their own lives, in any larger story. As commonly remembered, history is all about Presidents and wars, depressions and scandals, patternless deeds done by people with power far beyond what the typical reader can ever hope to wield. If history seems of little personal relevance today, then what we do today seems of equal irrelevance to our own lives (and the lives of others) tomorrow. Without a sense of trajectory, the future becomes almost random. So why not live for today? What's to lose?

During the 1970s and 1980s, this today fixation has rumbled throughout American society, top to bottom. Our Presidents and Congresses have expressed a broad-based preference for consumption over savings, debt over taxes, the needs of elders over the needs of children. In our private lives, we have seen the same attitude reflected in parents-come-first family choices, adults-only condos, leveraged Wall Street buy-outs, and the live-fast, die-young world of inner-city drug dealers. All these actions are more of a piece than many of us may feel comfortable admitting.

We offer this book as an antidote. More fundamentally, we hope to give our reader a perspective on human affairs unlike anything available in the usual history and social science texts. Once you have read this book, we expect you will reflect differently on much that you see in yourself, your family, your community, and the nation. You may understand better how the great events of American history, from wars to religious upheavals, have affected the lifecycles of real people, famous and common, in high political offices and in ordinary families. You may also gain a better sense of how you and your peers fit into the ongoing story of American civilization—a long and twisting human drama that offers each generation a special role. Appreciating the rhythm of this drama will enable you to foresee much of what the future holds for your own lifecycle, as well as what it holds for your children or grandchildren after your own time has passed.

This book presents the "history of the future" by narrating a recurring dynamic of generational behavior that seems to determine how and when we participate as individuals in social change—or social upheaval. We say, in effect, that this dynamic repeats itself. This is reason enough to make history important: For if the future replays the past, so too must the past anticipate the future.

We retell a favorite old tale in a brand-new way: the full story of America from the Puritans forward, presented along what we call the "generational diagonal"—the lifecycle course, childhood through old age, lived by the discrete birthyear groups we define as "generations." We identify eighteen such generations through four centuries of American history, dating back to the first New World colonists. Among these generations, we find important recurring personality patterns—specifically, four types of "peer personalities" that have (in all but one case) followed each other in a fixed order. We call this repeating pattern the "generational cycle." The cycle lies at the heart of our story and offers, we believe, an important explanation for why the story of America unfolds as it does. Read together, our eighteen generational biographies present a history of the American lifecycle and a history of cross-generational relationships. These relationships—between parents and children, between midlife leaders and youths coming of age, between elders and their heirs—depict history as people actually live it, from growing up in their teens to growing old in their seventies.

One of these eighteen American generations, of course, is yours. All but the very oldest or very youngest of our contemporary readers belong to one of the following four generations:

- "G.I." elders, born 1901–1924, age 66 to 89 as 1991 begins;

- "SILENT" midlifers, born 1925–1942, age 48 to 65;

- "BOOMER" rising adults, born 1943–1960, age 30 to 47;

- "13ER" youths, born 1961–1981, age 9 to 29.

In this book, we describe what we call the "peer personality" of your generation. You may share many of these attributes, some of them, or almost none of them. Every generation includes all kinds of people. Yet, as we explain in Part I, you and your peers share the same "age location" in history, and your generation's collective mind-set cannot help but influence you—whether you agree with it or spend a lifetime battling against it.

For the moment, let's suppose you share your peers' mind-set. If so, here is how you might respond to the message of this book.

If you are a G.I., your own collegial identity is so powerful—and has left such a colossal lifelong imprint on America's political, social, and economic institutions—that you tend to see older and younger generations as ineffectual facsimiles of your own. You may therefore resist our contention that other living generations are intrinsically different. But make no mistake: G.I.s have a distinct character. Of all four of our basic peer personalities, your "Civic" type is probably the most crisply defined, and the boundaries separating G.I.s from the Lost and the Silent are among the most compelling in American history. As firm believers in public harmony and cooperative social discipline, many of you might read into this book's plural title a disturbing message of discord. Possessed of a hubris born of youthful optimism fulfilled, perhaps you will puzzle over one of our core premises: that generations, like people, can relate to one another in ways which may not be mutually beneficial. Collectively, you G.I.s grew up so accustomed to being looked upon (and rewarded) as good, constructive, and deserving that you have had trouble, later in life, understanding how others might be viewed and treated differently—and how others might *view themselves* differently. All aging Civic generations have had this trouble, including the peers of Cotton Mather and James Blair in the late 1720s and the peers of Thomas Jefferson and James Madison in the early 1820s.

Yours is a rationalist generation. In the tradition of the eighteenth-century patriot-scientist Benjamin Rush, Civics have always come of age believing that history does (or should) move in orderly straight lines. For much of your lifecycle, this attitude brought you hope; in old age, it brings you mostly despair. Over the last two decades, you have recognized that younger generations do not display the friendliness, optimism, and community spirit you remember in your own peers at like age. Your perceptions are correct. Younger generations do not share your strengths. Instead, they are preparing to leave behind endowments of a less visible and secular nature, endowments that G.I.s have difficulty appreciating. As your generation loses energy, you may fear that not only your own unique virtue but perhaps all virtue will fade with you. But there is cause for hope. Our cycle suggests your special strengths will rekindle, thanks ultimately to a values-laden nurturing style associated with much of what you dislike (and what the elder Mather and Jefferson similarly disliked) in younger parents and leaders. If you can resist measuring others against your own standard, you may find our "generational diagonal" and nonlinear cycle to be comforting ideas. So too might the cycle revive your interest in the nurture of today's preschoolers. Their early childhood is beginning to resemble what you may remember of your own, seventy or eighty years ago.

If you are a SILENT, you are part of an other-directed generation that comes more easily to an appreciation of the mind-sets, virtues, and flaws of those born before or behind you. You need less persuasion than others to accept a typology of generations, a theory of historic oscillation, and the need for balance and diversity in any story of progress. Then again, since generations of your "Adaptive" type tend to respond ambivalently to anything they confront, you may well quarrel with our general conclusions and inquire into detail. Like the fiftyish managers of Teddy Roosevelt's "melting pot" America, you may dislike the majoritarian elements of our theory—doubting whether any diverse group numbering in the tens of millions can possibly fit into a single peer personality or a single generation. As Henry Clay once did with slave emancipation, you might try patching our new theory together in your mind with other competing theories to yield a consensus or "compromise" perspective. In the manner of Woodrow Wilson at Versailles, you might remain undecided until you hear what the experts have to say. And in the spirit of the aging William Ellery Channing or John Dewey, you might search for evidence to support your intuition that civilized man can, in the end, produce happy endings—as long as everyone remains open to new ideas and allows a little give and take.

We can picture you puzzling over what it means to be "Adaptive" as we define it—and debating over where we set our generational boundaries. You may at times sound or feel like a G.I. or a Boomer, but you are reaching the cusp of elderhood having shared neither the outer triumph of your next-elders nor the inner rootedness of your next-juniors. Sixty-five years after your first birthyear, no member of your generation has yet been elected President. That bothers you—though you would be the first to admit that an instinct for leadership may not be your generation's strong suit. Like the midlife peers of William Byrd II and Alexander Spotswood in their rococo Williamsburg drawing rooms, your generation has a highly refined taste for process and expertise that ties other people in knots. Yet in your very humility, your sense of irony, even the creative tension of your elusive hunt for catharsis, your generation has done more than any since Louis Brandeis' to bring a sense of nonjudgmental fairness and open-mindedness to American society. Your pluralist antennae, so generously directed everywhere else, have yet to focus on your own offspring, who have so far been mostly a source of disappointment and worry, much as Trumanesque children were to Wilsonesque parents. You had hoped your 13er children would grow up kind and socially sensitive; instead their generation is turning out too hardened for your taste. You suspect maybe your peers did something wrong as parents—but you're not about to give up searching for ways to make amends.

If you are a BOOMER, you know yours is, beyond doubt, an authentic generation. You will recognize the generational boundaries separating you from others (and, if born from 1943 through 1945, you are probably delighted that someone finally put you where you always knew you belonged). Unlike the G.I.s, you have no trouble recognizing how other generations have personalities very different from your own. Unlike the Silent, you have never imagined being anything other than what you are. But the great comfort you derive from your own identity is precisely what makes your generation troubling in the eyes of others. Like the peers of John Winthrop or Ralph Waldo Emerson, you perceive that within your circle lies a unique vision, a transcendent principle, a moral acuity more wondrous and extensive than anything ever sensed in the history of mankind. True, like a Herman Melville or an H. L. Mencken, you often loathe the narcissism and self-satisfaction of your peers. But that too is an important trait of your "Idealist" generational type. Possessing unyielding opinions about all issues, you judge your own peers no less harshly than you judge your elders and juniors. Either way, you may well appreciate that the time has come to move the Boomer discussion beyond the hippie-turned-yuppie, Boomer-as-hypocrite theme. Stripped to its fundamentals, your generation of rising adults is no more hypocritical than Thoreau at Walden Pond, or Jefferson Davis during his seven-year retreat into the Mississippi woods.

You may feel some disappointment in the Dan Quayles and Donald Trumps who have been among your first agemates to climb life's pyramid, along with some danger in the prospect of Boomer Presidents and Boomer-led Congresses farther down the road. Watching Franklin Pierce and Stephen Douglas, the peers of Lincoln and Lee felt much the same trepidation about their own generation— with reason, as history soon demonstrated. You may see in your peers a capacity for great wisdom, terrible tragedy, or perhaps just an insufferable pomposity. Over the centuries, Idealist generations like yours have produced more than their share of all three. Having lived just half a lifecycle, you probably find it hard to imagine that your generation may someday produce strong-willed leaders on a par with a Sam Adams or a Benjamin Franklin, a Douglas MacArthur or a Franklin Roosevelt. That's not surprising. Idealist generations—quite the reverse of Civic generations—typically exert their most decisive influence on history late in life. To understand how this happens, you need to step outside your inner-absorption, take a look at like-minded ancestors, and understand the fateful connection between the Idealist lifecycle and the larger flow of events. Perhaps you already sense that your Boomer peers, for all their narcissism and parallel play, will someday leave a decisive mark on civilization quite unlike anything they have done up to now. Your intuition is correct. History suggests they will.

If you are a 13er, we can imagine a cautious reception. Here we are, two writers from a generation you don't especially like, laying bare your generation's problems and affixing a label with an ominous ring. Back in the 1920s, Gertrude Stein, then in her mid-forties, did much the same to her thirtyish juniors, and the name she chose (the "Lost Generation") was just perverse enough to catch on with the rising cultural elite. You may not like being lumped in with mall rats, drug gangs, and collegians who can't find Chicago on a map—but you will grudgingly admit that's how others often see you. No doubt you have already noticed the recent barrage of books and articles declaring that people your age are dumb, greedy, and soulless. You may find solace in learning that several earlier American generations have also been perceived negatively almost from birth—for example, the peers of George Washington, John Hancock, and Patrick Henry. Along with Ulysses Grant or George Patton, you might not mind striking others as "bad," knowing full well that low expectations is a game you can play to your advantage. You know the odds. Maybe, like John D. Rockefeller, you will hit the jackpot—or else, like a Gold Rush 49er, you will go bust trying. Win or lose, you're not looking for testimonials—or, for that matter, any grand collective mission. When you notice that we've made your generation an equal partner to all the others in our saga, you might be half pleased, half alarmed: To be an equal partner means history might be counting on you, and you're not quite ready for that.

Our 13er reader knows perfectly well what your elders seldom admit: Yours is an ill-timed lifecycle. You experienced the "Consciousness Revolution" of the late 1960s and 1970s from a child's perspective—and, like Louisa May Alcott, you had to grow up fast to survive in a world of parental self-immersion or even neglect. You're tired of gauzy talk about Woodstock, born-again ex-hippies, and TV shows full of Boomers too busy whining about problems to solve them. Your generational consciousness is on the rise. You may already sense that it is just a matter of time before you and your peers snap into cultural focus and, as Sinclair Lewis did with snooty 'Babbitts,'' start trimming the sails of your smug next-elders. You take justifiable pride in your pragmatism, but watch out: It has its limits. A popular 13er putdown is "That's history," translated to mean "That's irrelevant." Wrong. We urge you to look eyeball to eyeball with other "Reactive" types—especially at those generations (like Captain Kidd's, Benedict Arnold's, William Quantrill's, and Al Capone's) whose entire lifecycle was spent dodging the criticism and mistrust of others. They produced many of America's toughest leaders, most effective warriors, most scathingly perceptive artists, and (of course) most successful entrepreneurs. But so too did many of their members burn out young, turn traitor, endure heaps of blame, and suffer a difficult old age.

Regardless of your generation or current phase of life, chances are you share the commonly held view that your own peers' recent lifecycle experiences are the norm. In each case, you may believe that other generations could *or should* think and behave like you at whatever phase of life you have recently completed. If a G.I., you probably regard retirement as a natural opportunity to stay active within your own community and reap the economic rewards of a lifetime of purposeful labor. If a Silent, you may believe that reaching the age of forty or

fifty inevitably triggers a midlife "passage," an abrupt and liberating personality
shift. If a Boomer, you may see spiritual self-discovery as the very essence of
being a 25-year-old. If a 13er, you may find it hard to imagine how any teenager
would not instinctively reduce such issues as courtship, schooling, and career
choice to their practical, matter-of-fact essentials. Whatever your peer group,
you feel that something is out of joint when your next-juniors turn out differently.
Let us reassure you: Americans have felt much the same sense of generational
warp for centuries. By nature, we all want to believe in an unvarying lifecycle;
this makes life more predictable and hence more manageable. That is not, however, how generations work. It isn't true in the early 1990s, it wasn't true during
the circa-1970 "generation gap," nor was it true in 1950 or 1930—nor, for that
matter, in 1830, 1730, or 1630.

Much of the stress in cross-generational relationships arises when people of
different ages expect others to behave in ways their peer personalities won't
allow. Plainly, this happened between G.I.s and Boomers in the late 1960s. It
has recently started happening again, albeit with less noise and fanfare, this time
between Boomers and 13ers. Poll today's collegians and ask them which generation they like the least; then ask fortyish professionals which generation they
think has the least to offer. The answer, in each case, will be the other. Boomers
and 13ers are coming to recognize how unlike each other they are; as yet, neither
side realizes that this personality clash will endure, and almost certainly sharpen,
over the next decade. This is nothing new. For centuries, "Idealist" generations
have invariably come of age mounting a highly symbolic attack against their
aging "Civic" elders—and have later entered midlife engaging in a bitter conflict
with their "Reactive" next-juniors. No other generational type shares this
lifecycle pattern of conflict. "Civics," for instance, have typically found late-
in-life battles with their twentyish children so difficult because they could recall
nothing like it from their own youth, while "Adaptives" have been spared from
overt generational conflict throughout their lives—often to their inner frustration.

One of our purposes in writing this book is to dispel the illusion of generational
sameness. In doing so, we hope to promote more reciprocal understanding and
more mutual respect among the very unalike generations alive today.

The timing and authorship of this book may indeed reflect the workings of
the cycle we describe. Many have told us this book could only have been written
by Boomers, which indeed your authors are (from the 1947 and 1951 cohorts).
True, some of the finest generational biographies ever published—including
Passages and *Private Lives*—have been written by Silent authors. Yet Boomers
remain the twentieth century's most generation-conscious peer group, one that
has overwhelmed all thinking about the subject over the past few decades. As
Boomers come to dominate the media, the word "generation" is today being
heard more often in news, entertainment, and advertising than at any time since
the late 1960s.

We attribute this, in part, to renewed stirrings of Boomer spiritualism in public life—and to the present location of Boomers at the center of multigenerational family trees. Your authors know that feeling quite well. At one end of our own families, we see surviving parents and stepparents, all G.I.s, all faring very well in comparison with what we remember of the (Lost) elders of our youth—and all looking upon the current drift of America with a mixture of public concern and private detachment. At the other end are our Millennial Generation children, born in the mid-1980s, about whose future adult Americans of all ages are beginning to worry. Between us, we have four children: two 13ers, two Millennials, perhaps more to come. Like many of our peers, we recognize that an instinct for teamwork and cooperation—something G.I.s have always had and Boomers came of age rejecting—may well make sense for the new Millennials just now coming onstage.

Both of us have separately written on generational topics for many years. In quite different ways, we each came across what we call the "generational diagonal." Our earlier books focused mainly on Boomers and G.I.s—Strauss' on the Vietnam War, Howe's on federal entitlements programs. We wondered why these two generations developed such entirely different ways of looking at the world: G.I.s seeing themselves (even in old age) as uniquely productive, Boomers seeing themselves (even in youth) as uniquely sagacious. We were fascinated by the curious 1970s-era resolution of the generation gap between them—an implicit deal in which G.I.s achieved economic independence (and spent the post-Vietnam fiscal "peace dividend" almost entirely on themselves) while Boomers asserted their social independence. In each case, this came at a cost: Aging G.I.s gave up cultural and spiritual authority, and Boomers abandoned any realistic prospect of matching their elders' late-in-life economic rewards. We wondered what it was about the very different growing-up experiences of G.I.s and Boomers that prompted such behavior, and whether any earlier American generations had ever acted along the same lines. We discovered that they had.

As we stretched our search for analogues back through the centuries, the panoramic outline of our generational saga began emerging. Again and again, this lifecycle approach to history revealed a similar and recurring pattern, one that coincided with many of the well-known rhythms pulsing through American history. We found ourselves with new answers to old riddles that have puzzled historians: why, for example, great public emergencies in America seem to arrive every eighty or ninety years—and why great spiritual upheavals arrive roughly halfway in between.

If we had in fact discovered a cycle, we knew the proof had to lie in its predictive possibilities. We decided then and there to write a last chapter on the future. Not many academicians take well to crystal-ball theories of history, but without predictions (what Karl Popper once called "falsifiability") any road map of history ends just where the reader begins to find it interesting. In advancing his own cycle theory about alternating eras of liberal activity and conservative quiescence, Arthur Schlesinger, Jr., has made some very date-specific predictions—for example, that America is now poised for a sharp pivot back toward 1960s-style activism. While we harbor doubts about that prognosis (for reasons we explain in Chapter 6), we credit Schlesinger for pioneering the cycle approach to American history and for giving his reader the measure by which his theory can be tested. The same is true for our forecasts: Time will surely tell. The events of the next few years will not explain much. Ten years will reveal something, twenty years quite a bit, and forty years will close the case, one way or the other.

Anyone who claims to possess a vision of the future must present it with due modesty, since no mortal can possibly foresee how fate may twist and turn. Readers who encounter this book fifty years from now will no doubt find Chapter 13 odd in much of its detail. But it is not our purpose to predict specific events; rather, our purpose is to explain how the underlying dynamic of generational change will determine which sorts of events are most likely. No one, for example, can foretell the specific emergency that will confront America during what we call the "Crisis of 2020"—nor, of course, the exact year in which this crisis will find its epicenter. What we do claim our cycle can predict is that, during the late 2010s and early 2020s, American generations will pass deep into a "Crisis Era" constellation and mood—and that, as a consequence, the nation's public life will undergo a swift and possibly revolutionary transformation.

The sum total of our predictions does not present an idealized portrait of America's future, but rather an honest depiction of where the generational cycle says the nation is headed. When reading Chapter 13, most readers will feel mixed emotions about what we foresee happening over the next several decades. Whatever your values or politics, you will surely find some things that please you and others that do not. You may also be surprised to find only passing mention of many subjects—from space-age technology to the shifting fortunes of political parties—that weigh so large in most speculations about the future. In our view, the timeless dynamic of human relationships comes first and matters most. While others may describe the technology with which America will send a manned spacecraft to the planet Mars, for example, we tell you something else: When America's leaders and voters will want this flight to happen; why; which generation will fly it; and how the nation will feel about it at the time and afterward.

We acknowledge this to be an ambitious book, with wholly new interpretations of important moments in American history—from the persecution of Salem witches to the rise of Wall Street yuppies. We admit, of course, that the generational cycle cannot explain everything. Were history so easily compartmentalized, it would lose not just its mystery, but also much of its hope, passion, and triumph. What we do insist is that generations offer an important perspective on human events, from the great deeds of public leaders to the day-to-day lives of ordinary people. We urge those who believe in other theories of history (or in no theory at all) to consider how ours can at times help explain the otherwise unexplainable. Many readers may well remain unpersuaded about the cycle, at least until more time passes. To skeptical historians in particular, we suggest you suspend your disbelief long enough to take a hard look at the generational diagonal. Historians seldom write biographies—and, all too often, recount events without the lifecycle perspective of what we call "people moving through time." Generations and history share an important two-way relationship—not just in America, and not just in the modern era.

In Part II, where we describe the peer personalities of America's eighteen generations, we could not always feature a totally representative sample of the population. Sometimes, for example, we had to limit the attention given to women and minorities—either because not as much is known about them or because we wanted to refer to actors and events that most readers would recognize. Yet while the generation is, almost by definition, a majoritarian social unit, the concept has much to say both about sex roles and about issues of class or race. No comparison of G.I.s with Boomers (or the Glorious with Awakeners) can overlook the stunning contrasts in their respective attitudes toward femininity and masculinity. Likewise, no comparison of the Silent with 13ers (or Progressives with the Lost) can make sense without mentioning their contrasting opinions about ethnic and racial pluralism.

The generational cycle indeed raises important questions about when and how certain racial, ethnic, and women's issues arise. Every major period of racial unrest—from the Stono Uprising of 1739 to Nat Turner's Rebellion of 1831, from W.E.B. DuBois' black consciousness movement of the early twentieth century to the long hot summers of the late 1960s—has started during what we call an "Awakening" constellation of generational types. Similarly, the widest gaps between acceptable male and female sex roles have taken place during an "Outer-Driven" constellation. Where we consider these issues especially important to our story, we discuss them. But this book is mainly about generations as units, not subgroups within them. We encourage specialists among our readers, whatever their backgrounds, to shed more light on the component pieces of the generational puzzle. We would be delighted to see others write on the generational history of any ethnic group, for example—or about the generational dynamic behind changes in technology, the arts, or family life. In fact, the biography of any single generation could easily be expanded to book length. Apart from our own capsule summary of the G.I.s, no one has ever written even a short biography of that generation. Is there a G.I. somewhere who will?

Much work remains to be done in this barely tapped field. We invite debate about our interpretation of social moments, our generational boundaries, and our peer personality descriptions. This book may be the first word on many of these subjects; we hope it will not be the last. In particular, we encourage experts familiar with other nationalities—from China to Eastern Europe, the Middle East to Latin America—to examine the dynamic of generational change in societies other than our own. Such inquiry might identify deviations in the generational cycle (like America's Civil War anomaly) and suggest how our theory of generations might be refined to account for the full range of human experience.

We hope to persuade specialists among our readers that the study of generational (and lifecycle) behavior is of major importance. Those who assemble data can help by sorting them around birth cohorts as well as around fixed age brackets, and by repeating old polls taken one or more generations earlier, to update cohort and age-bracket responses. Historians can similarly help the study of generations by offering cohort-specific information whenever possible. To aid the research of others, we are providing extensive bibliographic notes and (in Appendix B) a summary of new data we have compiled on each generation's numerical representation in Congress and state governorships.

Each of the eighteen generational biographies required substantial research into not just the history, but also the *historiography* of each era—not just what happened, but how and why historians have interpreted events as they did. Accordingly, this book posed unique research problems. There were no shortcuts. Our efforts to piece together separate generational lifecycles were impeded by the way many historians tend to blur cohort experiences. The typical chapter on the history of childhood, for instance, focuses mainly on linear change, blending together experiences over time spans as long as a century. To discover what happened to specific cohort groups required laborious detective work—sometimes poring through many articles or books just to confirm an observation covered here in less than a sentence. Whatever our challenge, we were aided immeasurably by the many fine social histories published over the past two decades—especially the phase-of-life histories about childhood, adolescence, or old age. We have also been blessed by the recent research findings of a small but growing number of historians and social scientists who concentrate specifically on cohort analysis. Had we or anyone else written this book as recently as 1970, it would have been far poorer in texture and detail.

We ask our reader to approach this book in the same manner we came to the subject—*inductively*, as a gradual discovery of something very new. Yes, we sometimes use terms you may find unfamiliar at first, like "cohorts" and "spiritual awakenings." When necessary, we even invent our own terms, including typologies of generations and of "constellational" eras. Our glossary defines all these terms, for easy reference. We urge our reader to enliven these concepts with your own experience and imagination. Whether or not you agree with our vision of America's future, we hope you will find our approach useful in clarifying your own view of the next decade and century.

Whatever your generation—G.I., Silent, Boom, 13th—you will learn, as we have, how every generation has its own strengths and weaknesses, its own opportunities for triumph and tragedy. Yes, there are implicit messages here—for example, about how each generation should apply its unique gifts for the benefit of its heirs. But our object here is less to judge than to understand. In the words of the great German scholar Leopold von Ranke, who weighed so many Old World generations on the scales of history, "before God all the generations of humanity appear equally justified." In "any generation," he concluded, "real moral greatness is the same as in any other. . . . "

Acknowledgments

"Historical generations are not born," Robert Wohl once said. "They are made." Surely the "making" of *Generations* involved far more than just the work of two coauthors. We consider this book to be an interpretive gathering of many disciplines, each reflecting the important achievements of a number of scholars, journalists, pollsters, and friends—several of whom deserve mention.

On the concept of the generation itself, we were aided immeasurably by the writings of Julián Marías, himself a disciple of José Ortega y Gasset. We also must credit Anthony Esler, who has kept the "generations approach" alive in American academic circles over the last two decades. On cycles, we acknowledge the pioneering work of the two Arthur Schlesingers, who have demonstrated that an oscillating political and social mood can coincide with American-style progress. We have William McLoughlin to thank for his discovery of important parallels between periodic "awakenings" and Samuel Huntington for being the first to see the relationship between awakenings and what we call secular crises.

In our depiction of historical cycles through the nineteenth century, we are indebted to those modern social historians who have uncovered so many important clues about cohort and age-bracket behavior. On matters of childhood, we especially thank Oscar Handlin, Mary Cable, Ray Hiner, Joseph Hawes, Peter Gregg Slater, Robert Bremner, and David Nasaw; for education, Bernard Bailyn, Frederick Rudolph, Carl Kaestle, and Lawrence Cremin; for adolescence, the work of Joseph Kett stands out; and for old age, David Hackett Fischer,

David Stannard, and Andrew Achenbaum. In identifying generational shifts in family life, we should mention John Demos, Barbara Welter, Edmund Morgan, Daniel Blake Smith, Jan Lewis, Nancy Cott, and Carl Degler; in community life, Philip Greven, Christine Heyrman, Richard Bushman, Michael Zuckerman, Robert Gross, and Mary Ryan; in spiritual life, Perry Miller, Sydney Ahlstrom, Alan Heimert, Ernest Lee Tuveson, Cushing Strout, and Nathan Hatch; and in the new perspectives of what we might call "psychohistorical themes of generational conflict," Emory Elliott, Jay Fliegelman, Peter Shaw, Pauline Maier, Michael Kammen, Michael Paul Rogin, and George Forgie. We commend Peter Charles Hoffer for his expert and pathbreaking application of a formal lifecycle model (Erik Erikson's) to a historical generation (Republican).

We also credit those historians (especially J. C. Furnas, William Manchester, Daniel Boorstin, Carl Bridenbaugh, Wade Smith, Robert Remini, Richard Hofstadter, Henry Steele Commager, Franklin Frazier, and Frederick Lewis Allen) who gave as much attention to private as to public lives—and, in doing so, revealed important phase-of-life information. We should give special praise to historian Ann Douglas, who in *The Feminization of the American Culture* provides exactly the kind of birthyear and cohort-focused information that generational analysis requires. And, of course, anyone writing a book like this needs a standard historical reference, and for that we thank the incomparable Samuel Eliot Morison.

For modern generations, we thank Paula Fass, William Manchester, William O'Neill, Todd Gitlin, and Landon Jones for their histories; Malcolm Cowley, F. Scott Fitzgerald, Benita Eisler, Annie Gottlieb, Cheryl Merser, and Wanda Urbanska for their generational biographies; Gail Sheehy, Daniel Levinson, and Betty Friedan for their lifecycle observations; Robert and Alice Lynd for their keen-eyed observations on American town life in the early twentieth century; and Harold Stearns and Huston Smith for compiling the best single written records of the national mood and generational relationships of the 1930s and 1950s, respectively. For the separate phases of life, we have Marie Winn, Vivian Zelizer, and Neil Postman to credit for their inquiries into modern childhood; Kenneth Keniston, Lewis Feuer, and Kett again for adolescence; and Bernice Neugarten, William Graebner, Samuel Preston, Alan Pifer, and Fischer again for old age. We are grateful to *Atlantic* and *Esquire* magazines for their penetrating essays on generational mind-sets; to Leonard Cain, whose cohort analysis is the best defense of a generational boundary ever written; and to Nancy Smith, Shann Nix, and Patrick Welsh for the most probing accounts to date of the 13er mood.

For our modern data, we owe a great debt to two fine 1980s-era magazines, *Public Opinion* and *American Demographics* (and, especially, to Karlyn Keene and Cheryl Russell for their helpful familiarity with opinion polls); to the Gallup, Harris, Roper, and Yankelovich polling organizations; to the quarter-century of work at UCLA (Alexander Astin) and the University of Michigan (Jerald Bachman) for their ongoing youth surveys; to Warner Schaie of Pennsylvania State

ACKNOWLEDGMENTS 21

University and his one-of-a-kind Seattle Longitudinal Study; to John Keane, Bill Butz, and their many colleagues at the U.S. Census Bureau; and to the many other helpful individuals in the Bureau of Justice Statistics, National Center for Health Statistics, Public Health Service, Social Security Administration, National Taxpayers Union, and Children's Defense Fund.

This book has been aided by innumerable conversations, probably reaching into the thousands, with members of each of the four major living generations. We extend our thanks to Doug Lea of American University, who has been our principal link with 13er students from dozens of colleges around the nation. We particularly thank our own 13er-on-the-job, Kelly Stewart, for tabulating some 15,000 Congressmen, governors, and justices by birthyear and thereby reducing mountains of data into usable form. We are likewise grateful to the well-equipped libraries of Georgetown University and of Arlington and Alexandria, Virginia.

We owe special credit to our editor, Adrian Zackheim, for his patience throughout a long and difficult project; our agent and partner-in-planning, Rafe Sagalyn, whose confidence in our task kept us hard at it; Pete Peterson and Jim Sebenius, for introducing us to each other; the Honorable Albert Gore, Charles Percy, and John Porter, for their encouragement and advice; Jim Davidson, Paul Hewitt, David Keating, and Phil Longman, for their counsel in the early stages of this project; Tipper Gore and Marilyn Ferguson, for their counsel in its late stages; and the helpful readers of raw manuscript—Alan Crawford, Peter d'Epiro, Robert Horn, Richard Jackson, Jeremy Kaplan, William Lane, Doug Lea, Robert Quartel, David Werner, Richard Willard, and Ernest Wilson. We are also grateful to Elaina Newport, Jim Aidala, and other good friends and colleagues with the Capitol Steps for the kind of social commentary you can get nowhere else.

Finally, we thank our special G.I. consultants *en famille* (Suzy Strauss, Margot Howe, Mary Kamps); our Canadian repository of insights on European generations (Carla Massobrio); our wives, Janie and Simona, for their tireless critiques of endless drafts; and our children, Melanie, Victoria, Eric, and Rebecca—who, along with the rest of our families, have cheerfully accepted a years-long invasion of tall stacks of books and photocopies, the clickety-clack of word processors, constant chatter about Transcendental this and Silent that, and the many other perils of living with the sort of people who would write this sort of book.

We also thank our reader, for taking the time.

Bill Strauss
Neil Howe
October 1990

Contents

PART III: THE FUTURE

There is a mysterious cycle in human events. To some generations much is given. Of other generations much is expected. This generation has a rendezvous with destiny.

—*Franklin Delano Roosevelt, 1936*

Chapter 1

PEOPLE MOVING THROUGH TIME

Twenty-eight years had passed, but the message to other generations remained the same. George Bush's inaugural parade, like John Kennedy's in 1961, featured a full-scale model of his vehicle of valor: in Bush's case a Grumman Avenger fighter plane, in Kennedy's a PT-class torpedo boat. When Bush bailed out over ChiChi Jima, Michael Dukakis was a fifth-grader in Brookline, Massachusetts. Dukakis later served in Korea, but when he sat atop a tank in his Presidential campaign, people laughed. It just wasn't the same. Back in 1944, Illinois Governor Jim Thompson had been in the second grade, three years behind Dukakis. ''You don't need to be shot down from the sky to know the world is a dangerous place,'' Thompson remarked about Bush, ''but my guess is it sure helps.''

Marching alongside these two parade floats, both times, were saluting veterans—with one important difference. At Kennedy's inaugural, the float-bearers were men of ''vigor'' in their late thirties and forties, celebrating their arrival into national leadership. At Bush's, the vets were in their late sixties and seventies, evoking more remembrance than hope. Time marches on. The aging paraders had to realize that 1989 would be the last time America would salute the triumphant Presidential arrival of a World War II combat hero. At age 20, George Bush had been among the Navy's youngest fighter pilots when he was shot down over the Pacific. Almost certainly, the next American President will walk down Pennsylvania Avenue having known that war through a child's eyes— or, perhaps, through nothing more than history books and film clips. When that happens, Americans of all ages will feel something missing.

In the thirty years from 1961 through 1990 (and counting), the American Presidency has been the exclusive preserve of men who ranged in age from 17 to 34 on Pearl Harbor Sunday, men belonging to what we call the G.I. Generation. Never before in the nation's history has one generation held the White House so long. Few others have exercised such massive power over public events in each phase of life. From youth to old age, the G.I.s have been the confident and rational problem-solvers of twentieth-century America, the ones who knew how to get things done—first as victorious soldiers and Rosie the Riveters, later as builders of rockets and highways, lastly as aging Presidents in the era of democracy's economic triumph over communism.

The G.I. lifecycle bears the imprint of the threshold moments that catapulted America into its modern superpower era. The first G.I. babies were born in 1901, and the last will turn 75 in the year 1999—a span exactly coinciding with the "American Century" of economic growth, technological progress, and (mostly) military triumph. Following a debauched and dispirited "Lost Generation," they brought cheerfulness, public spirit, and collective muscle to every problem they encountered. Older generations once looked upon them as good scouts with a mission of civic virtue. Decades later, younger generations came to see them as powerful and friendly, if also culturally complacent and overly "macho." From childhood on, G.I.s have defined what contemporary America means by *citizenship,* that two-way symbiosis between man and government. In the person of George Bush, America clings to one last dose of that old war-hero "right stuff," uncertain about what the future will be like without G.I.s at the helm.

Contemplating this generation's inevitable passing from power, we have been waving it goodbye much as we would a beloved family member whose train is pulling out of a station—a station we could call midlife. But let's walk down the track a bit. For some time now, this same train has been pulling into *another* station: elderhood.

The expression "senior citizen" is so much a part of our modern vocabulary that we forget how new it is—and how it did not come into wide use until the first peers of these seven G.I. Presidents started to reach old age. As with every other life phase, G.I.s have infused old age with uncommon collective energy. In the early 1960s, the elderly were America's unhappiest, loneliest, and poorest age bracket. Politically, they tended to be unorganized, Republican-leaning, and hostile to government. Yet over the last quarter century, all these attributes have reversed direction. Polls now show most people over age 65 to be happy and socially assertive, members of an exploding list of senior clubs, condo associations, and lobbying groups. They are no longer fixed-income, thanks to inflation-indexed government benefits. Meanwhile, the elderly poverty rate has fallen from the highest of any age bracket (in the mid-1960s) to well below the rate for children and young adults (today). Of all circa-1990 age groups, these elders are the heaviest-voting and by far the most Democratic-leaning, with polls show-ing them overwhelmingly supportive of big government. Yes, we can still find an elder age bracket whose members are substantially lonely, poor, and Repub-lican. But they are not G.I.s. These very old people, mostly in their nineties, are the dwindling survivors of the Lost Generation.

How do we explain this dramatic change in what it means to be old in America, this sudden transformation both in the behavior of people past their middle sixties and in the treatment they receive from their juniors? We could, on the one hand, attribute it to a variety of complex, apparently unrelated factors: public policy, demographics, social and economic trends, changing family attitudes, and so on. Alternatively, we could attribute it to the gradual replacement of one gen-eration by another in the elder age bracket. Let's put it schematically: Is it easier to explain why 75-year-olds transformed from Type X in 1965 to Type Y in 1990, or to explain how the Y-like 50-year-olds we remember from 1965 aged into the Y-like 75-year-olds of 1990? The latter is by far the better explanation. *Separate generations are aging in place.*

Over the last quarter century, G.I.s have moved up the age ladder a notch, transforming elderhood the way they once did every other phase of life. Seldom do we draw any connection among America's first Boy Scouts and Girl Scouts, Charles Lindbergh, CCC tree-planters and TVA dam-builders, D-Day troops, Levittowners, Stan "the Man" Musial, Jim and Betty Anderson of *Father Knows Best,* Kennedy's "best and brightest," General Westmoreland, Reagan-Shultz-Weinberger, and the American Association of Retired Persons. We greet the G.I. train (and, later, bid it farewell) at each station, but not many of us recognize it as the same train.

Is this an isolated case? To consider this question, let's extend our railroad analogy. Picture one long lifecycle *track,* with birth the place of origin and death the destination. Imagine phase-of-life *stations* along the way, from childhood to elderhood. Now picture a series of generational *trains,* all heading down the track at the same speed. While the G.I. train is moving from one station to the next, other trains are also rolling down the track. If we picture ourselves sitting at any given station watching one train go and another arrive, we notice how different each train looks from the next.

Replacing the G.I.s at the midlife station, and overdue for a turn at Presidential leadership, is the Silent Generation train—carrying men and women who came of age too late for World War II combat and too early to feel the heat of the Vietnam draft. These were the unobtrusive children of depression and war, the conformist "Lonely Crowd," Grace Kelly and Elvis Presley, young newlyweds with bulging nurseries, Peace Corps volunteers, the "outside agitators" of the Mississippi Summer, the middle managers of an expanding public sector, di-vorced parents of multichild households, makers of R-rated movies, Hugh Hefner and Gloria Steinem, space-shuttle technocrats and supply-side economists, Gary Hart and Mike Dukakis, litigators and arbitrators, Jim Henson, the MacNeil-

Lehrer NewsHour, and the less colorful cabinet officials in the Bush administration. Back in the 1960s, we used to think of 55-year-olds as homogeneous and self-confident—clingers to worn marriages and brittle proponents of a bland culture under siege from the young. In 1990, 55-year-olds dance to rock music and wink at unmarried kids who bring a date home for the night. They are sentimental pluralists, easy touches for charity, inclined to see two sides to every issue—and not especially surefooted. Today's midlifers dominate the helping professions and have provided late-twentieth-century America with its most committed civil rights advocates and public interest lawyers—and most of its best-known sexual swingers, feminists, and out-of-the-closet gays. A quarter century ago, we would never have associated a crowd like this with the peak years of adult power. Now we do.

At the rising-adult station, behind the Silent, comes the best-known of all American generations: the Boomers, who came to college after Eisenhower and before the Carter malaise of 1979. These were the babies of optimism and hubris, Beaver Cleaver and Mouseketeers, the post-Sputnik high school kids whose SAT scores declined for seventeen straight years, student strikers, flower-child hippies and draft resisters, Hamilton Jordan and Jody Powell, yuppie singles avoiding attachment, Gilda Radner and Oprah Winfrey, grass-roots evangelicals, Lamaze parents, Oliver North and William Bennett, oat-bran eaters and Perrier drinkers, Earth Firsters, and antidrug crusaders. This Boom Generation has totally transformed its current phase of life. Reflect back on a typical man-woman couple approaching age 40 around 1970. They had been married for almost two decades, with children nearing college age. Their family income was rising swiftly. They emulated their elders, envied their juniors, and disliked the suggestion that any one set of values was superior to another. Contrast that picture with the typical "thirtysomething" couple of today. The woman has worked since college. Possibly they are married, and just as possibly they are not. Possibly their income is rising, and just as possibly it is stagnating or falling behind inflation. At most, they have two children, none beyond elementary school. They firmly believe in values. Intensely self-immersed, they neither emulate nor envy people older or younger than themselves. A quarter century ago, such a couple would have stood out as hard-luck misfits. But don't tell Boomers that. Polls show their level of self-satisfaction is quite high and remarkably unrelated to their income or family status.

The next generational train rolls into the coming-of-age station wearing shades, averting the critical glare of the adult world. We have seen this generation before. These were the first babies American women took pills *not* to have, *Rosemary's Baby,* the children of sharply rising divorce and poverty rates, pupils in experimental classrooms without walls, latchkey kids, precocious Gary Coleman and Tatum O'Neal, pubescents of the sex-obsessed 1970s, Valley girls, college students criticized by one blue-ribbon commission after another, young singles of the post-AIDS social scene, inner-city drug entrepreneurs, "boom-erang" children living at home after college, the best-qualified recruits in military history, the hard-nosed invaders of Panama, and the defenders of Persian Gulf oil. In the late 1960s, 21-year-olds were considered radicals, the conscience of America, and they drew the respect of the adult world they were attacking. Today, kids in their early twenties comprise America's most Republican-leaning age bracket. They associate smoothly and compliantly with elders—who, for their part, express disappointment in how they are turning out. To date, this generation has no consensus name. We label it the 13th Generation—partly for the gauntlet its members see in its "bad" reputation, also in recognition that it is the thirteenth to know the American nation and flag.

Last comes a train still taking on passengers, with adult America heralding its departure. These tots are entering a childhood today's collegians would hardly recognize. Check out their brief lifecycle, and you will find the first test-tube babies, "Everybody's Baby" Jessica McClure rescued from a Midland well, Superbabies, the diapered stars of *Raising Arizona* and *Three Men and a Baby*, KinderCare Kids, "Baby M" and Hilary Morgan at the center of custody dis-putes, inner-city kindergartners in uniform, little "Dooney" saved from the crack house, George Bush's Hispanic grandchildren, and the high school Class of 2000 whom President Bush, former Surgeon General C. Everett Koop, and numerous others have already targeted as a smarter, better-behaving, and more civic-spirited wave of American youth. Any community trying to treat its children this way in the late 1960s would have been condemned as culturally totalitarian. But in the early 1980s, adults began to look upon childhood quite differently—spawning a new Millennial Generation, the first of whom will indeed come of age around the year 2000.

As Millennials keep climbing aboard, adding close to four million new pas-sengers every year, two trains are reaching the end of the line: the very old Lost, peers of Eisenhower, Truman, and F. Scott Fitzgerald; and a smattering of supercentenarians from Franklin Roosevelt's Missionary Generation. One other train we would have seen in the 1960s, Woodrow Wilson's Progressive Gen-eration, has disappeared entirely.

In Figure 1-1, we list the schedule of generational trains, in 1969 and now. Over this twenty-two-year period, seven have been alive at any one time.

Leaving aside the very old and very young, America today has four generations that form what we call a generational "constellation," the lineup of living generations ordered by phase of life. The constellation is always aging, always shifting, moving up one lifecycle notch roughly every twenty-two years. Youths come of age, rising adults reach midlife, midlifers reach elderhood, elders pass on (or reach advanced old age)—and a new set of babies enters youth. *Whenever the constellation shifts up by one notch, the behavior and attitudes of each phase of life change character entirely.* Unmistakably, this happened between the late

FIGURE 1-1
Living American Generations

GENERATION	BIRTHYEARS	AGE IN 1969	AGE IN 1991
Progressive	1843–1859	109+	(*not alive*)
Missionary	1860–1882	86–108	108+
Lost	1883–1900	68–85	90–107
G.I.	1901–1924	44–67	66–89
Silent	1925–1942	26–43	48–65
Boom	1943–1960	8–25	30–47
Thirteenth	1961–1981	0–7	9–29
Millennial	1982– ?	(*not alive*)	0–8

1960s and now. It also happened between World War II and Vietnam, between World War I and II, between the Gay Nineties and World War I—and, indeed, through all of American history.

The generational constellation establishes our snapshot impression of the American lifecycle of the moment, from the seventeenth century through the present day. If, in any one year or decade, we were to picture what it was then like to be a child, a young adult, middle-aged, or old, our composite impression would be a hodgepodge of segments from very different generational lifecycles. Piece together these constellational snapshots in a decade-by-decade newsreel of an evolving American lifecycle, and the picture becomes hopelessly confusing.

In this book, we suggest looking at the American lifecycle as it has actually been lived by each generation, from childhood through old age. Using our earlier analogy, we suggest looking at the lifecycle from the perspective of *trains* rather than *stations*. At any given moment, we can see as many different lifecycle stories, as many different trains, as the number of generations then alive.

We treat generations as *people moving through time,* each group or generation of people possessing a distinctive sense of self. We look at history just as an individual looks at his own life. We explain how a generation is shaped by its "age location"—that is, by its age-determined participation in epochal events that occur during its lifecycle. During childhood and, especially, during the coming-of-age experiences separating youth from adulthood, this age location produces what we call a "peer personality"—a set of collective behavioral traits and attitudes that later expresses itself throughout a generation's lifecycle trajectory.

Because the peer personality of each generational type shows new manifestations in each phase of life, and because it is determined by the constellation into which it is born (a pattern that is forever shifting), the ongoing interplay of peer personalities gives history a dynamic quality. How children are raised affects how they later parent. How students are taught affects how they later teach. How youths come of age shapes their later exercise of leadership—which, in turn, substantially defines the coming-of-age experiences of others. This push and pull between generations moves synchronously with other alternating patterns in American history: for example, between periods of public action and private introspection, secularism and spiritualism, cultural suffocation and liberation, fragmentation and consensus, overprotective and underprotective nurture of children.

As we examine these pendular movements, a startling pattern emerges: *a recurring cycle of four distinct types of peer personalities, arriving in the same repeating sequence.* From the sixteenth century forward, this cycle has been constantly turning. It has shown only one aberration, following the Civil War, when it skipped a beat and omitted the hubristic G.I. type. Each generation has its own unique story, of course, but when we strip away gradual secular trends (rising living standards, improving technology, expanding population, shifting geography), we see similar human dramas, repeating again and again.

If generations come in cycles, moreover, so do constellations. Each constellational *era*, each of the four possible layerings of peer personalities, possesses its own recognizable *mood*. As generations layer themselves and age in place, one after the other—Lost, G.I., Silent, Boom, 13th, and so on—the mood of a constellation itself shifts over time. A constellation with outer-focused doers in midlife and inner-focused moralists in youth, for instance, will set a national mood quite different from one with inner- and outer-focused generations in the opposite positions. Some constellations produce a national mood of staleness, others of rejuvenation. Some fight wars well, others badly. Some defer crisis, others congeal it.

Looking back over American history, we find a correspondence between recurring patterns in generational constellations and recurring types of historical events. Consider, first, the four great periods of crisis in American history: the colonial emergencies culminating in the Glorious Revolution of 1689; the American Revolution; the Civil War; and the twin emergencies of the Great Depression and World War II. All but one began at almost exactly the same constellational moment, just as the first Boom-type midlifers were entering elderhood and the first G.I.-type youths were coming of age. (The Civil War occurred nearly on schedule, but roughly a half generation early.) Now reflect on America's five great spiritual awakenings, from the Puritans' "City on a Hill" in the 1630s to the Boomers' "Consciousness Revolution" that began in the late 1960s. Without exception, all five began at the same constellational moment, just as the first G.I.-type midlifers were entering elderhood and the first Boom-type children were coming of age.

This recurring cycle of generational types and moods helps us not only to understand the past, but also to forecast how the future of America may well unfold over the next century. The cycle delivers no specific timetable about wars, stock-market crashes, or scientific discoveries. It does offer an approximate calendar and itinerary of major changes that America can expect in the next decade and century—and important predictions about how today's children will grow up, today's adults will grow old, and today's elders will be remembered.

Our theory of generations is, in effect, two related theories, the merging of two separate traditions of scholarship. First, building on the "generations approach" (a mostly European school of sociology pioneered by Karl Mannheim, José Ortega y Gasset, and others), we propose what we call an "age-location" perspective on history. Most historical narratives treat each separate age group, especially the midlife or leadership age group, as a continuous, living entity over time. The reader rarely learns how earlier events, experienced at younger ages, influence later behavior at older ages. Examining history by age location, however, we can see how events shape the personalities of different age groups differently according to their phase of life, and how people retain those personality differences as they grow older. Since we stress the link between age and events, the concept of a "cohort-group" (a group of all persons born within a limited span of years) is central to our theory. *We define a generation as a special cohort-group whose length approximately matches that of a basic phase of life,* or about twenty-two years over the last three centuries.

Intuitively, everyone recognizes the importance of age location. A generation's place in history affects everything from the nurture it receives from elders to the nurture it later gives its young. Today's fiftyish and sixtyish Silent can recall the smothering style of their own upbringing in the 1930s and 1940s, in sharp contrast to the "hurried" children they raised in the 1960s and 1970s. Everyone also recognizes how the same event can have a very different meaning for generations in different phases of life. Consider the Great Depression and its Pearl Harbor sequel. For children (Silent), it meant tight protection; for rising adults (G.I.s), teamwork and challenge; for midlifers (Lost), a new sense of responsibility; for elders (Missionaries), an opportunity to champion long-held visions. But the pattern is not the same for every event. Compare the depression 1930s, for example, with the counterculture 1970s. This latter time, we saw children (13ers) grow up quickly and on their own; rising adults (Boomers) fragment and turn inward; midlifers (Silent) speed up to a new sense of adventure; and elders (G.I.s) defend institutions under siege from the young.

The lesson? There is no such thing as one universal lifecycle. To the contrary, neighboring generations can and do live very different lifecycles depending on their respective age locations in history. While observing (or trying to predict) phase-of-life behavior, we must remember that the age of each generation is *rising* while time moves *forward.* Thus, we can visualize age location along what we call the "generational diagonal." Tracing this diagonal allows us to connect the event, the age, and the behavior of the same generation over time.

Yet this approach alone tells us little about how generations shape history. So we turn now to our second proposition, related to the first: *Generations come in cycles. Just as history produces generations, so too do generations produce history.* Central to this interaction are critical events that we call "social moments"—which alternate between "secular crises" and "spiritual awakenings." Because a social moment hits people in different phases of life, it helps shape and define generations. And because generations in different phases of life can together trigger a social moment, they help shape and define history—and hence, new generations. Throughout American history, social moments have arrived at dates separated by approximately two phases of life, or roughly forty to forty-five years. Most historians look upon this rhythm as, at most, a curious coincidence. We look upon it as key evidence that a generational cycle is at work, ensuring a rather tight correspondence between constellations and events. The correspondence is not exact—but the average deviation from what the cycle would predict is only three or four years. That, we think, is a small margin of error for a theory applied over four centuries.

We label the four generational types Idealist, Reactive, Civic, and Adaptive. With one exception, they have always recurred in a fixed order. During a spiritual awakening, Idealists are moving into rising adulthood while Reactives are appearing as children; during a secular crisis, Civics are moving into rising adulthood while Adaptives are appearing as children. Later in life, these generations trigger another social moment and thus keep the cycle turning. Among today's living generations, the centenarian Missionaries and rising-adult Boomers are Idealists; the very old Lost and coming-of-age 13ers are Reactives; the senior-citizen G.I.s and baby Millennials are Civics; and the midlife Silent are Adaptives. The first and third types are what we call "dominant" in public life—Idealists through redefining the inner world of values and culture, and Civics through rebuilding the outer world of technology and institutions. The other two types are "recessive" in public life, checking the excesses of their more powerful neighbors—Reactives as pragmatists, Adaptives as ameliorators.

The passage of four generations, Idealist through Adaptive, completes one full generational cycle over the course of four twenty-two-year phases of life (a total duration of roughly ninety years). From the 1584 Puritan birthyear forward, we can trace five such cycles through American history—of which three (Colonial, Revolutionary, and Civil War) are fully ancestral, a waning fourth (Great Power) comprises the eldest 28 percent of the American population at the beginning of 1991, and an emerging fifth (Millennial) includes the youngest 72 percent. Within these cycles, we identify eighteen generations, from John Winthrop's Puritans to Jessica McClure's Millennials—and a recurring pattern of awakenings and crises. While each era has produced its special variations, the basic pattern has persisted unchanged since the late sixteenth century, when the peers of Sir Philip Sydney, Francis Bacon, and William Shakespeare–men the age of the Puritans' fathers—triumphed in war, glorified science, and praised the order of the universe.

We leave our cycle prophecies for later. At this point, we focus on one demographic fact we can project for certain. Twenty-two years from now, the generational constellation of 1991—the one we listed in Figure 1-1—will have moved up a notch, as shown in Figure 1-2. (We assume the Millennial Generation will be of average length.)

This projection reminds us not just of our own personal mortality, but also of the mortality of our generation. Like a person, a generation is allotted a limited time in each phase of life. Ultimately, most of what we associate with our generation—styles, habits, and artifacts—will disappear. We leave behind no more than what we persuade or oblige younger generations to take from us. Thus will all of us someday join the heritage of American civilization.

America offers what may be mankind's longest and best case study of generational evolution. Since the eighteenth century, observers the world over have found this country unique for the freedom enjoyed by each successive generation to develop, and act upon, its own personality. When Alexis de Tocqueville visited America in the 1830s, he observed how generations mattered far more here than in Europe, how in America "each generation is a new people." Tocqueville may have overstated the case. As we shall see, generational change in the Old World played a key role in triggering the Colonial cycle in the New World—back when most settlers still believed themselves, culturally and socially, part of Europe. Since then, generations in America have often shared a similar mind-set, a sort of sympathetic vibration, with their transatlantic peers. Like America, Western Europe also had its romantic radicals in the 1840s; its

FIGURE 1–2
Future Generational Constellation

GENERATION	BIRTHYEARS	AGE IN 1991	AGE IN 2013
Missionary	1860–1882	108 +	(*not alive*)
Lost	1883–1900	90–107	112 +
G.I.	1901–1924	66–89	88–111
Silent	1925–1942	48–65	70–87
Boom	1943–1960	30–47	52–69
Thirteenth	1961–1981	9–29	31–51
Millennial	1982–2003	0–8	9–30
Unnamed	2004– ?	(*not alive*)	0–8

Blut und Eisen realists in the 1860s; its disillusioned *génération du feu* of World War I soldiers; and its *nouvelle résistance* student movements in 1968. Tocqueville's main point, however, remains sound. Far more than the Old World—with its tradition-shaped culture, hereditary elites, hierarchical religion, and habits of class deference—America has always been unusually susceptible to generational flux, to the fresh influence of each new set of youth come of age.

In recent decades, as other societies have grown more open and mobile, this distinction between America and other societies may be disappearing. Were Tocqueville to travel through today's world, he might find many countries with generations born "new." Shifts in peer personality have recently coursed through modern societies in all continents. From Eastern Europe to the Pacific Rim, from the Middle East to Latin America, new generational waves are breaking. In Poland, Lech Walesa was born too late to remember the World War II atrocities committed there by German and Soviet armies. Today's emerging "Thaw Generation" of Soviet leaders can recall the 20th Soviet Congress in 1956, when Khrushchev first challenged the memory of Joseph Stalin. They often cite this event as a critical coming-of-age experience. To place them in our own cultural artifacts, we could point to the opening and closing scenes in the movie *Doctor Zhivago,* where the old revolutionary (Alec Guinness) asks a twentyish hydroelectric worker (Rita Tushingham) to remember the turmoil and sacrifice of 1917. He draws blank stares from the obliging young woman, who then would have been roughly the same age as Raisa and Mikhail Gorbachev. In Beijing, the ruling octogenarians of Deng Xiaoping's "Long March" generation offer a powerful if chilling example of how history can shape a generation in ways that cause it, decades later, to force a new set of youths to come of age through a bloody gauntlet. In Bucharest, meanwhile, this shaping process backfired on Nicolae Ceausescu, who launched a nationalist campaign in 1967 to raise a large and patriotic generation of Romanians. These late-1960s babies matured into the implacable student revolutionaries who, in 1989, sparked the very uprising that sealed Ceausescu's demise.

These may be isolated phenomena—or they may reflect generational cycles in these other societies. If the latter, our theory would not reflect anything uniquely American, just human nature working itself out in a world relatively unbound by tradition.

So what's going on in America, and where are we today?

Reflect on the national life of the late 1830s, just after Tocqueville had written *Democracy in America.* The last of the great civic heroes of 1776—the Patriots of Bunker Hill, the Constitution framers in Philadelphia, the Caesarlike creators of *E Pluribus Unum*—were passing away. Thomas Jefferson and Eli Whitney had both died a decade earlier, James Monroe and John Marshall within the last five years. James Madison was in his mid-eighties, Noah Webster and Aaron Burr in their late seventies. Their passing was already being lamented by the likes of the fiftyish Daniel Webster, who wondered how America could cope without these men of "massive solidity" whom the "iron harvest of the martial field" had united "happily and gloriously" in a "great and common cause." Others in their fifties and sixties—Andrew Jackson's Democrats and Henry Clay's Whigs—complained about a gridlocked Congress and gestured nervously over mechanistic compromises and issues of character. On the great unresolved issues of the day—from slavery to western settlement—America drifted without direction.

Meanwhile, a rising younger generation of evangelicals, utopian reformers, and transcendentalists (the likes of Ralph Waldo Emerson, William Lloyd Garrison, Elizabeth Cady Stanton, Brigham Young, Frederick Douglass, and John Brown) were redefining American culture according to fresh, self-discovered values. Abraham Lincoln and Jefferson Davis, both reaching age 30, were showing signs of stern principle. Farther down the age ladder, hardscrabble children—Ulysses Grant, Stonewall Jackson, Andrew Carnegie, and Mark Twain—showed far less interest in philosophy than in action. Their peers were beginning to come of age amid criticism from older adults, who found them shallow and reckless. Does this all sound familiar? It should. In the late 1830s, generational types were lining up in just about the same constellation (from elderly Civics to teenage Reactives) that we see in present-day America.

We find much the same pattern back in the late 1740s, as memories of the young patriots of the Glorious Revolution—by then dead or quite old—gave way to confusion about the future. Midlife leaders and parents lacked their elders' sense of collective purpose. Gripped by a refined, highly analytical mind-set, they saw life as complicated, political choices as burdensome. Colonial society wobbled along, no one knowing exactly where. At that same moment, an introspective cadre of preachers and moralists ranging in age from their late twenties to mid-forties (including Jonathan Edwards, John Woolman, Benjamin Franklin, and Samuel Adams) were drawing spiritual zeal from their peers' recent "Great Awakening." And a pugnacious, liberty-loving troop of kids was just setting out to explore, fight, and strike it rich. Daniel Boone, Patrick Henry, Ethan Allen, and Benedict Arnold were on the edge of puberty. John Adams and George Washington, both teenagers, were burning with personal ambition. Sound familiar? Here again, it should. Here again, the constellation was turning to a position much like today's.

Americans alive in those two past eras, just like Americans today, felt themselves living off the achievements of the past. They saw their present world as comfortable but lacking direction, perhaps crumbling in its foundations. They looked forward to their own future and the future of their children with a mixture of guilt and anxiety. In the late 1980s, an American could pick up a journal and read a serious-minded essay entitled "The End of History" and tune to a pop radio station chanting lyrics like "no new tales to tell," the lyrics of boredom. When history loses urgency, people tend to live at the expense of the future despite their better judgment. What we find, today, are splintered families, downwardly mobile 20-year-olds, razor-thin savings rates, threats to the global environment, an eroding sense of national mission, and pyramiding entitlements for older generations crowding out investments needed by their heirs. As was true around 1750 and 1840, Americans in the early 1990s have only the vaguest sense of what the future holds—for their society as a whole, and for each living generation.

Here is where the cycle can help. The story of civilization seldom moves in a straight line, but is rich with curves, oscillations, and mood shifts. The ebb and flow of history often reflect the ebb and flow of generations, each with a different age location, peer personality, and lifecycle story. By viewing history along the generational diagonal, by searching the cycle for behavioral clues, we can apply the mirror of recurring human experience to gaze around the corner of current trends and say something instructive about the decades to come.

The lifecycle experience of ancestral generations tells us, in particular, that the peer personality of each generational type expresses itself very differently from one phase of life to the next. For example, Idealist generations (like Samuel Adams') typically come of age attacking elder-built institutions before retreating into self-absorbed remission, but later mature into uncompromising "Gray Champion" moralists. Reactive generations (like George Washington's) bubble over with alienated risk-taking in their twenties, but age into mellow pragmatists by their sixties. Civic generations (like Cotton Mather's) are aggressive institution-founders when young, but stolid institution-defenders when old. Adaptive generations (like Theodore Roosevelt's) are elder-focused conformists early in life, but junior-focused pluralists later on. With fourteen generational lifecycles already completed, we can draw on a rich source of analogues to help us understand how the peer personalities of today's four youngest generations—Silent, Boom, 13th, Millennial—are likely to express themselves as they age in place. And looking back over four full generational cycles, we can also project how the national mood will evolve over the next half century as the generational constellation clicks up one, two, and three notches.

History does not guarantee good endings. The American saga is replete with good and bad acts committed by generations no less than by individuals. Our national liturgy reminds us how ancestral generations provided helpful *endowments* that made progress possible, from the clearing of land to the building of infrastructure, from the waging of wars against tyrants to the writing of great literature. Yet ancestral generations have also, at times, inflicted terrible harms on their heirs—from instituting slavery to exterminating Indian tribes, from exploiting child labor to accumulating massive public debts. A lesson of the cycle is that *each generational type specializes in its own unique brand of positive and negative endowments*. Each of today's adult generations—G.I., Silent, Boom, and 13th—has its own special way of helping or hurting the future. Each, collectively, has choices to make that will determine what sort of world its heirs will someday inherit, and how those heirs will remember its legacy. We shall return, at our story's end, to what history suggests those choices will be.

We opened with an account of inaugural parades celebrating the heroism of aging G.I.s. Today's babies are being nurtured under conditions that could someday make them, like the G.I.s, a dominant generation of can-doers, victors in great struggles, and builders of great things. Around the year 2050, when the first Millennial Generation President is inaugurated, his or her peers may indeed have as many heroic memories to celebrate as the peers of John Kennedy and George Bush had in 1961 and 1989.

With four centuries of history as a guide, we can see how today's small children lie not at the end, but near the *beginning* of a new generational cycle. And they will have many new tales to tell.

Part I
THE CYCLE

Chapter 2

LIFE ALONG THE GENERATIONAL DIAGONAL

"At last, this is your story. You'll recognize yourself, your friends, and your lives," reads the book jacket of *Passages*. In her best-selling book about "the predictable crises of adulthood," Gail Sheehy describes a human lifecycle with common mileposts. We "do what we should" through our twenties, marrying around age 21, making babies, baking brownies. We often suffer our first divorce between the ages of 28 and 30—and, upon reaching our mid-thirties, watch our last child head off to kindergarten. Around ages 38 to 42, we experience an all-out midlife crisis. After making fundamental life changes, often including a switch in spouse and career, we feel "a mellowing and a new warmth" through our forties—after which her book trails off. Sheehy published *Passages* in 1976, when she was 39 years old. Her Silent Generation peers then ranged in age from 34 to 51.

In the year *Passages* first hit the shelves, a 25-year-old publishing assistant bought Sheehy's book, looking for guideposts to her own life. "The problem was," Cheryl Merser later recalled, "I couldn't find my life anywhere in *Passages*." Eleven years went by. Upon reaching age 36, Merser published her autobiography, *"Grown-ups,"* in which she described how she and her Boomer friends were embarking on a lifecycle which kept them curiously on hold through their mid-thirties. Almost none of her friends was doing what they "should." Few had gotten married by the age Sheehy said they should already be divorced. No one she knew had experienced a midlife crisis. "Finally, after umpteen readings, *Passages* began to make sense to me," Merser wrote in 1987. "I realized in amazement that what I was reading, down to the details of the deadline-decade divorce and the subsequent rebirth, was the story of my parents' lives."

To understand her same-age male friends, Merser might have paged through *The Seasons of a Man's Life,* a 1978 lifecycle road map by Daniel Levinson. In it, he sorted the post-adolescent male lifespan into six segments, three of them "transitional" in the manner of Sheehy's various passage points. Decade after decade, adult crises of self-definition dominated the lifecycle of the forty men Levinson studied—all roughly Sheehy's age, born from the mid-1920s through the mid-1930s. Yet the two major impulses Levinson found in young men, the twin search for a "Loved One" (a woman to marry) and for a "Stronger One" (an older mentor), would have been wholly foreign to men in Merser's circle. Male or female, her peers were remaining socially and professionally noncommittal—entirely unlike Levinson's early-marrying careerists.

So where could Merser turn for a guide to her own Boomer peers? She could have studied Erik Erikson's "Eight Ages of Man" in his 1950 book *Childhood and Society.* Working from what he described as his "clinical experience" (mostly observations of his own G.I. peers), Erikson emphasized how people reject maternal authority and forge permanent ties with the community soon after a major coming-of-age trial. By the time a person reaches Merser's age, according to Erikson, the social, economic, and family direction of life is fixed in concrete. For thirtysomething Boomers—still experimenting with life—this model works no better than Sheehy's. Moving back further, Merser could have read Malcolm Cowley's 1934 Lost Generation autobiography, *Exile's Return,* and seen a young-adult world of alienation, unromantic toughness, and pleasure-seeking binges. No Boomer connection there, either. But going back a fourth notch to Jane Addams' peers, well captured in Ellen Lagemann's *A Generation of Women,* Merser might well have recognized a lifecycle resembling her own: the late- or never-marrying women of the Missionary Generation, comfortable with themselves and firm in their values, but uncertain where the world might someday lead (or leave) them.

Something seems out of joint here. Why should Merser and her Boomer peers have to go back almost a century to find a lifecycle they recognize?

To understand, we have to start with the building-block of generations: the "cohort." Derived from the Latin word for an ordered rank of soldiers, "cohort" is used by modern social scientists to refer to any set of persons born in the same year; "cohort-group" means any wider set of persons born in a limited span of consecutive years. The answer to Cheryl Merser's confusion is that Sheehy, Erikson, and Cowley (but not Jane Addams) each belong to a cohort-group whose phase-of-life experiences were very different from her own.

The Cohort-Group Biography

Plainly, Gail Sheehy did something important when she wrote *Passages*. Her book has remained enormously popular with readers and critics because it offers a rare and compelling example of a cohort-group biography—a persuasive rendering, in Sheehy's case, of the collective personality of American men and women now in their fifties. Sheehy tells *human* history, history from the inside out, life as her peers have known and lived it, in stages. The same could be said for all good cohort-group biographies. They make us understand ourselves as groups of like-aged friends with a distinctive collective story, as fraternities or sororities that have grown up and matured in ways that are, in some sense, special.

This is not always how we are taught to look at people. Picture the classic image that greets children when they first open a history book: a series of portraits of America's forty-one Presidents, constituting (upon first election) a twenty-eight-year age bracket ranging from their early forties to their late sixties. Adjust the hairstyles and clothing, and they would all look like midlife members of the same club, gazing at life with identical emotions. From this collage, we find no inkling that when Grover Cleveland became a 47-year-old mutton-chopped President, Harry Truman was a baby, Herbert Hoover an adolescent, Woodrow Wilson a book-writing young professor—and the retired Ulysses Grant was dying of cancer. Each had a fundamentally different relationship with the world around him. Most history books are filled with fiftyish leaders and parents depicted over time as an endless continuum—an entity with its own memory, its own habits, its own inertia, its own *self-perpetuation*. At historic moments, such as the signing of the Declaration of Independence, we get occasional glimpses of generational layering. Even then, we seldom learn about the different lifecycle prisms through which the peers of the 33-year-old Jefferson, of the 44-year-old Washington, or of the 70-year-old Franklin understood such moments.

Likewise, read any of the histories about individual phases of life—about childhood, adolescence, courtship, or old age. You'll see mostly the same thing: one age bracket reified, fixed across time as a story unto itself. A 10-year-old Boy Scout in the 1920s somehow grows out of a 10-year-old "newsie" from the 1890s, or a 70-year-old senior activist in the 1980s out of a 70-year-old doughboy widow from the 1960s. Since no one actually grows this way, we call this perspective the "age-bracket fallacy," the mistake of endowing a life phase with an anthropomorphic identity over time. You could indeed create a genuine cohort-group biography from pieces of such histories. But it would be arduous work. To learn about the lifecycle Abraham Lincoln's peers actually experienced, to give one example, you would have to read the 1800s-to-1810s chapter in a childhood book, the 1820s chapter in a coming-of-age book, the 1830s-to-1840s chapter in a book about family life, the 1850s-to-1860s chapter in a regular history book, and the 1870s chapter in a book about old age. You would have to puzzle your way through a maze of disconnected clues and fragments.

Another way to look at life is through direct observation. To learn how people grow older, your first impulse might be to observe how people in different age groups think and behave. In one day, you could interview people at age 10, 30, 50, and 70, and then patch together your findings into one lifecycle snapshot. The trouble is, people don't travel from infancy to old age in just one day. Imagine what you would have found around the year 1970: hurried children, adolescent mystics, playboys in their mid-thirties, "square" 55-year-olds, and reclusive elders. Such life phases could never fit together into a single and integrated human experience. Then check your findings for 1990: adored babies, cynical college kids, self-immersed yuppies, ambivalent midlifers, and busy senior citizens. Again, try to imagine people actually traveling through such a lifecycle. You can't. And for good reason: No one ever lived it. Sociologist Matilda White Riley calls this the "life-course fallacy," the mistake of describing a lifecycle simply by tacking together all the different age brackets alive at the same time.

Because Sheehy and Levinson approach human experience from the perspective of people moving through time, they successfully dodge both the phase-of-life and the lifecycle fallacies—and therefore say something important. But they do not guard against a third fallacy, what Riley calls the "fallacy of cohort-centrism," the assumption that the lifecycle experience of one's own cohort-group offers a single paradigm for all others. Sheehy calls the crises in *Passages* "predictable," its lifecycle (quoting Jorge Luis Borges) a "web" of "what will be, is, and was." Similarly, based on interviews with men who all came of age in the late 1940s and early 1950s, Levinson declares his "seasons" to have existed "in all societies, throughout the human species . . . for the past five or ten thousand years." Yet a lifecycle alleged to have lasted since the days of ancient Babylon somehow became unrecognizable to Cheryl Merser's peers just one decade later.

You can search further back into American history for an invariant and universal lifecycle. You won't find it. To the contrary, every American life phase has encountered frequent and major shifts over the last four centuries. New Englanders born when Boston was founded in 1630 emerged as teenagers with a collective personality their patriarchal elders found utterly alien. The youths of the 1680s preferred teamwork over spiritual conversion; their sons in the 1730s preferred the reverse. The twentyish soldiers of the French and Indian War grew up distrusting authority, while the twentyish patriots of 1776 came of age infatuated with public order. In the mid-1830s, young adults tried to fire the passions of the old; three decades later, young adults doused old men's fires. Following America's two world wars, midlifers extended very different welcomes to homecoming young soldiers: after World War I, cracking down on their wildness and drinking; after World War II, showering them with tax-supported benefits. Take any phase of life, move forward or backward a quarter century, and you will invariably discover profound changes in what it meant to be that age in America.

To be sure, the human lifecycle has many timeless denominators. The biological phases of aging—growth, puberty, menopause, senescence—always affect roughly the same age brackets in a similar and highly visible manner. Basic social roles also follow a relatively fixed age schedule: infancy, childhood, coming of age, marriage, midlife leadership, and elderly withdrawal. But within this general and slowly changing matrix, human behavior can be anything but invariant from one era to the next. Indeed, to fall into the trap of cohort-centrism is to commit, implicitly, both the other two fallacies at once. If the lifecycle were in fact universal, then fifty-fiveish people truly would be a seamless panorama, and we could tape together same-day phase-of-life snapshots into a coherent montage. American life would then be essentially premodern, and parents could expect their children to behave little differently from how they themselves (or their grandparents) once behaved.

Taken together, these three fallacies lead to a world that most Americans would hardly recognize: a society having little connection to our history and no connection at all with the complicated phase-of-life changes we notice over time in friends, family, and neighbors.

A lifecycle must be lived to be genuine, and to understand the behavior of any phase of life we must look at the special story of the flesh-and-blood people traveling through it. This is the important insight of *Passages* and other cohort-group biographies. However, no law of nature decrees that all cohort-groups must live the same lifecycle. The most cursory glance at history confirms that they do not. Because they do not, we must look at each cohort-group's unique age location in history to uncover the inner logic of its own story. This is the important insight of the generational diagonal.

The Generational Diagonal

When reflecting on our own lives, especially on our college years, many of us can recall unusual cohort-groups coming of age as young adults—perhaps a few years younger, perhaps a few years older than ourselves. In the memory of the living, this has happened four times. In the early 1920s, an upbeat, collectivist batch replaced the cynics and individualists. In the late 1940s, a risk-averse batch replaced the can-do war heroes. In the mid-1960s, a fiery batch replaced the adult emulators. And around 1980, a smooth batch replaced the complainers. Whichever side of the line they were on, college alumni commonly remember these breakpoints. Others can recall less dramatic shifts: the rising drug use among successive college freshmen cohorts in the late 1960s and early 1970s, for example, or the growing popularity of military and entrepreneurial careers among those who came to campus in the early 1980s. As each of us grows older, we look at people of other ages and wonder whether we are changing or they are changing. The answer, quite often, is neither: We were both different to begin with. We were born at different times. We belong to different cohort-groups.

What exactly does it mean to belong to a cohort-group? Unlike many group definitions (like neighborhood or career), cohort-group membership is *involuntary*. Then again, so is age. But unlike age, cohort-group membership is *permanent*. And unlike sex or race (also involuntary and permanent), it applies to a finite number of identifiable individuals. After its last birthyear, a cohort-group can only shrink in size. Fixed in history, it must eventually disappear. What makes the cohort-group truly unique is that all its members—from birth on— always encounter the same national events, moods, and trends at similar ages. They retain, in other words, a *common age location in history* throughout their lives. Since history affects people very differently according to their age, common age location is what gives each cohort-group a distinct biography and a distinct lifecycle.

We have no trouble appreciating age location when thinking of momentous historical events like war, depression, revolution, and spiritual prophecy. How these events affect people depends on their age at the time. The same cataclysm that a 10-year-old finds terrifying a 30-year-old may find empowering, a 50-year-old calming, a 70-year-old inspiring. Once received, such impressions continue to shape the personality people take with them as they grow older. Today's seventy-fiveish G.I.s, for instance, came of age with the New Deal, World War II, and collective heroism. They retain their taste for teamwork—and often wonder why self-obsessed yuppies never had it. Thirty-fiveish Boomers, on the other hand, came of age with Vietnam, Watergate hearings, and "Consciousness III" euphoria. They retain their taste for introspection, and often wonder why bustling senior citizens never had it. The 75-year-old had no Woodstock, the 35-year-old no D-Day—nothing even close. This coming-of-age contrast will continue to influence both groups' attitudes toward the world—and toward each other—for as long as they live. Likewise, a very different contrast will always separate those who were children at the time of D-Day and Woodstock. If D-Day empowered young-adult G.I.s, it intimidated Silent children. And if Woodstock brought inner rapture to 25-year-old Boomers, it made 5-year-old 13ers feel that the adult world was turning hysterical.

Age location also shapes cohort-groups through historical shifts in society-wide attitudes toward families, schooling, sex roles, religion, crime, careers, and personal risk. At various moments in history, Americans have chosen to be more protective of children, or more generous to old people, or more tolerant of unconventional young adults. Then, after a while, the mood has swung the other way. Each time this happened, the social environment changed differently for each cohort-group. Take "open classrooms" in the early 1970s; or A-bomb drills for elementary students in the mid-1950s; or the huge rise in Social Security benefits in the mid-1970s. All were passing fads, but fads that forever changed the lives of the specific cohort-groups affected by them. The first permanently if subtly altered how today's twenty-fiveish adults feel about parental authority; the second, how today's fortyish adults feel about nuclear deterrence; the third, how today's seventy-fiveish adults feel about their social status relative to people of other ages. Trees planted in the same year contain rings that indicate when they all met with a cold winter, wet spring, or dry summer. Cohort-groups are like trees in this respect. They carry within them a unique signature of history's bygone moments.

Almost by design, America's present-day social institutions accentuate the power of age location. The more tightly age-bracketed the social experience, the more pronounced the ultimate cohort identity. From kindergarten through high school, almost all pupils in any one classroom belong to the same birthyear. In nonschool activities like Little League and scouting, children participate within two- or three-year cohort-groups. College-age students date, study, and compete athletically within cohort-groups seldom exceeding five years in length. As modern adults age into midlife, their friendships typically widen into longer birthyear zones. But their cohort bonds remain strong. Most retain contact with "Big Chill" circles of like-aged friends, with (or against) whom they measure progress at each phase of life. High school and college reunions remind alumni of their cohort bonds—how each class remains, in important respects, different from those a few years younger or older. Over the last few decades, cohorts have even been retiring together in their early to mid-sixties. Like all status designations (including sex, race, and profession), cohort-group membership forges a sense of collective identity and reinforces a common personality.

Quantitative research on cohorts is still a young science. The very term "birth cohort" was not coined until 1863 (by the French sociologist Émile Littré), and the concept attracted little attention over the next hundred years. Since the early 1960s, the interest has grown more serious—especially in America. Intrigued by lifecycle shifts, a few historians have begun to pore over town archives, gravestones, and census records to study cohort-groups in small communities. Social scientists have also begun to look more carefully at modern behavioral data from a birthyear perspective. All this could not happen at once. The number-crunchers first had to wait until they could obtain age-bracketed data for the American population at large. Then they had to wait still longer until time could sort out the independent effect of cohort membership from other behavior-shaping variables such as phase of life (the "age effect") and historical change (the "period effect"). But as the widespread collection of age-bracketed data enters its third decade, the results are finally arriving. More often than not, they show that cohorts matter a great deal.

Survey analysis of voting behavior is a classic case in point. In the early 1960s, researchers discovered that Americans age 65 to 80 voted heavily Republican, while younger Americans voted Democratic. At that time, three explanations seemed equally plausible: People always tend to vote Republican when they get old (the age effect); elders were the leading wave of a national trend toward Republicanism (the period effect); or the 1890s cohort-group leans Republican (the cohort effect). Most experts opted for the first answer—the age effect. "Aging seems to produce a shift toward Republicanism," concluded one study in 1962. "The pattern appears to be linear." Wrong. Two decades passed, enabling survey researchers to isolate and measure the influence of each effect. Cohorts won, hands down. The post-1970 arrival of a new and increasingly Democratic batch of 65-to-80-year-olds made cohorts the only possible explanation. So, a decade later, did the arrival of a new and increasingly Republican batch of young voters.

Further confirmation of the power of cohorts comes from longitudinal tests of intelligence and educational aptitude. For the last third of a century, psychologist K. Warner Schaie has measured the "psychometric intelligence" of a long series of seven-year cohort-groups—born from 1886 through 1962—living in Seattle, Washington. Schaie's original purpose was to trace universal lifecycle trends (the age effect) in aptitude scores. In this, he has been successful. His surveys show that measured intelligence rises most steeply in the twenties, begins to level off during the thirties, and enters a gradual decline around the middle fifties. What Schaie was not looking for—but found—was a powerful correlation between his aptitude scores and his specific cohort-groups. In each case, the cohort effect remained strong even after Schaie isolated it both from the influence of age and from the influence of historical changes such as better schooling. Among subjects under age 70, in fact, *most measures of aptitude vary far more across cohort lines than across age brackets*. For example:

- The 1886–1892 cohort-group scored the highest of all groups in "word fluency" (vocabulary), but the lowest in everything else.

- The 1907–1927 cohort-groups have done very well in overall "intellectual ability" and have clearly outperformed all other groups in "numbers skills." The last of these three groups (1921–1927) appears, on balance, to be the highest-scoring group thus far tested.

- The 1935–1941 cohort-group has scored highest of all groups in "space" (geometry) reasoning, second in "reasoning" (logic), but last in "word fluency."

- The 1942–1948 cohort-group has beaten all the others in "verbal meaning," but has done little better than average in "numbers skills" and "space" reasoning.

- More recent cohort-groups (born 1949–1962) have shown progressively declining scores across the board.

Such marked contrasts between cohort-groups prompt us to ask searching questions about the age location and collective biography of each group. As yet, however, research on cohort effects remains in its infancy, and seldom are such questions ever addressed. Even when birthyear information is available, most experts do not bother to isolate it from data presented under other labels. A typical table shows age on the vertical axis, calendar year on the horizontal. Thus, by implication (though not by label), the cohort lies along the *generational diagonal*. Unless you are looking diagonally for the cohort effect, you will not see it. And unless you are willing to wait many years, you cannot rule out that what you see is simply due to aging or to historical trends affecting all age brackets.

To see how this diagonal can work where other approaches fail, consider the 1970s-era debate over declining Standard Aptitude Test (SAT) scores among U.S. high school seniors. For seventeen straight years, from 1964 through 1980, the average SAT score declined. In 1976, the federal Wirtz Commission attributed roughly half the fall to the growing share of all high school seniors who chose to take the test and the rest to such vague period effects as permissiveness and less homework. But in 1988, the Congressional Budget Office (CBO) looked again at the SAT numbers and compared them with the standardized test scores of younger students. CBO researchers discovered a very close *diagonal* match— at all grades—between scores and birth cohorts. In other words, *the SAT trend could have been predicted, in each year, by looking at the lower-grade test scores in earlier years for each cohort*. Even as the Wirtz Commission agonized in 1976 over the SAT decline, 12-year-olds were already scoring higher than their next-elders—which (had anyone been looking) could have foretold an SAT reversal five years in the future. Test scores in the third grade showed improvement by the early 1970s; in the sixth grade by the mid-1970s; and in junior high school by the late 1970s. Once these same kids (the 1964 and 1965 cohorts) reached twelfth grade in the early 1980s, SAT scores did indeed begin rising again.

Are these aptitude scores linked to any other important cohort shifts? Let's hunt down the "generational diagonal" among a handful of age-bracketed indicators for violent crime, substance abuse, and drunk driving. These indicators, of course, always show a marked lifecycle pattern—rising sharply through adolescence, peaking in the early twenties, and falling at higher ages. If we tabulate these rates by age, however, we can control for the age effect and focus on how the rate changes, year by year, at any given age. In Figure 2-1, we summarize data on average grade-school test scores (from ages 8 to 17); per capita consumption of alcohol (17- and 18-year-old students only) and marijuana (17-year-old students only); per capita arrest rates for arson, robbery, and assault (from ages 15 to 24); and per capita arrest rates for drunk driving (from ages 18 to 24). In a format we use throughout this book, we show age on the vertical axis, calendar year on the horizontal. For each age, we mark the calendar year at which the indicator reached its *negative extreme* (the lowest test score or the highest rate of crime or substance abuse) since such statistics have been compiled.

No one will have any trouble identifying the diagonal.

The portrait that emerges of the 1961–1964 cohort-group is vivid and unflattering. Over the postwar period, at each age through 24, this group has generated all of America's lowest aptitude-test scores; the highest high school senior drug and alcohol abuse; all but one of America's highest drunk-driving rates; and most of America's highest rates for three violent crimes. Very likely (though detailed age-bracketed data remain unavailable), it has also generated record rates for many other social pathologies, including suicide. Since most of the high-crime years cluster around the late 1970s and early 1980s, we might at first glance suspect that part of the story is a historical trend affecting all age groups. Yet the behavior of older age brackets rules this out. From the mid-1970s to the mid-1980s, while the rates for drunk driving, suicide, and most violent crimes were accelerating swiftly for 15-to-24-year-olds, they were stabilizing or falling for all age brackets over age 35.

By 1991, the men and women born from 1961 through 1964 have reached their late twenties. They are no longer taking aptitude tests and have left their high-crime and high-drinking ages behind them. We would be naive, however, to assume that the collective personality of these individuals will simply disappear as they grow older. Plainly, America is dealing with a troubled cohort-group. To know why, we must again ponder age location. Individuals born in 1962, for example, were year-old infants when Jack Kennedy was assassinated; age 5 during the "long hot summer" of urban rioting; age 7 at the time of anti-Vietnam marches, the moon landing, Chappaquiddick, and a sudden leap in divorce rates; age 13 when the Watergate trials ended and the poverty rate for youths rose steeply (just when it was plummeting for the elderly); and age 17 when Americans parked in gas lines and saw angry Iranian mobs cursing America every evening on TV. We might reflect on what these youngsters saw in their elder brothers and sisters, heard from their teachers, or sensed from their parents.

FIGURE 2–1

**Aptitude Tests, Substance Abuse, Violent Crimes,
and Drunk Driving: The Cohort Diagonal**

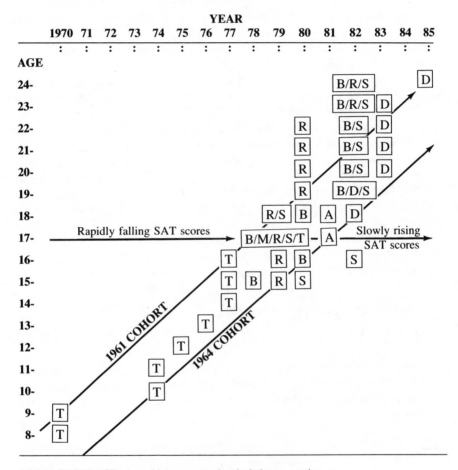

FOR A GIVEN AGE: **A** = highest per capita alcohol consumption
B = highest per capita robbery conviction rate
D = highest per capita drunk-driving arrest rate
M = highest per capita marijuana consumption
R = highest per capita arson conviction rate
S = highest per capita assault conviction rate
T = lowest average aptitude test score

From Cohorts to Generations

Reading along the generational diagonal shows us that history does not always move in a straight line. It also prompts us to ask *why*. What differences in parental nurture, schooling, adult expectations, economic trends, or cultural tone might explain why the early-1960s cohorts scored so low on aptitude tests? Or why the early-1920s cohorts (if Seattleites are any guide) grew up scoring so high? The closer we look, the more interesting such questions become. Why, for example, did the schoolchildren of the 1930s develop such strong number skills, and then raise their own children (the "Jack and Jill" readers of the 1950s) to have such a commanding grasp of verbal meaning? What was it about the nurture of the 1886–1899 cohort-groups that produced such precocious talent at word play—culminating in memorable slang, brilliant mystery fiction, the invention of crossword puzzles, five of America's nine Nobel Prizes for literature, and the greatest elder elocutionists (from Adlai Stevenson to Sam Ervin) of the twentieth century?

Countless such questions lie unanswered among the myriad cohort-groups of the past four centuries. How and at what age did history shape them? And how and at what age did they in turn shape history? A few other examples:

- During the fifteen years from 1633 to 1647 were born the most berated and abused children in colonial history, the most notorious seventeenth-century American pirates and rebels, and about half of all women ever tried and executed for witchcraft in New England.

- During the three years from 1721 to 1723 were born all Americans age 18 at the height of the colonial "Great Awakening," the most energetic evangelicals and antislavery activists of the entire eighteenth century—and half of all delegates over age 50 who attended the First Continental Congress in 1774.

- During the nine years from 1767 to 1775 were born all Americans who watched the Revolutionary War only as children; all 44 of the methodical and well-behaved members of the Lewis and Clark expedition; and all three members of the antebellum "Great Triumvirate" (Clay, Webster, and Calhoun), known in midlife for hair-splitting oratory, procedural compromises over the issue of slavery, and twelve failed attempts to run for the Presidency.

- During the thirteen years from 1809 to 1821 were born the vast majority of the best-known reformers, abolitionists, feminists, self-proclaimed prophets, and commune founders of the nineteenth century—and nearly two-thirds of the Congress in session (plus the President and Vice President) at the outbreak of the Civil War.

- During the eight years from 1822 to 1829 were born most of the Gold Rush '49ers, the most colorful and effective Civil War generals, the leading postwar "scalawag" southern governors, the most notorious machine bosses of the Gilded Age, and every American age 64 to 71 during the Crash of '93—the first recession that forced a categorical retirement of elder workers to what was then known as the "industrial scrap heap."

- During the eleven years from 1869 to 1880 were born nearly all the fiery young journalists whom Theodore Roosevelt called "muckrakers," nearly half the Congress that approved Prohibition in 1919, and the leading public figures (Herbert Hoover, Douglas MacArthur, George Marshall, Bernard Baruch, and Herbert Lehman) who established, by midcentury, America's global reputation as a crusading defender of civilized morality.

- During the eleven years from 1911 to 1921 were born nearly all the Depression-era high school graduates whose first job was in a New Deal relief program, all but one of President Kennedy's leading "best and brightest" advisers, two-thirds of all Americans ever awarded the Nobel Prize for economics— and the most aggressive (and effective) elderly lobbyists for public retirement benefits in American history.

- During the eight years from 1925 to 1932 were born most of the "Li'l Rascals," the kids of the Great Depression, the core "beatniks" of the 1950s, and the vast majority of the most popular social and political satirists during the entire postwar era, from the 1950s to the present day.

- During the two years of 1941 and 1942 were born the children of the *Brown v. Board of Education* school desegregation case in 1954, the majority of the Greensboro lunch-counter sit-in protesters in 1961, the best-known "black power" advocates of the late 1960s and 1970s, and Jesse Jackson.

- During the single year of 1943 were born World War II's home-leave "goodbye babies"—and a vastly disproportionate number of the most inner-driven and judgmental figures of the last several decades, including: Bob Woodward, Gracie Slick, Jim Morrison, Bobby Fischer, Robert Crumb, Randy Newman, Mitch Snyder, Oliver North, Newt Gingrich, William Bennett, Richard Darman, and Geraldo Rivera.

- During the four years of 1967 to 1970 were born all the children conceived during the flower-child summers of "love" and antiwar protest, nearly everyone who first heard about the space shuttle *Challenger* disaster while sitting in a high school classroom, and two-thirds of all U.S. soldiers killed during the American invasion of Panama in December of 1989.

So far we have only focused on narrow birthyear spans. What we need is a way to simplify age location for all cohorts, to aggregate all Americans into a larger pattern of distinct biographies.

FIGURE 2–2

**The History of the American Lifecycle
in the Twentieth Century**

	1920	1942	1964	1986
ELDER Age 66–87	sensitive	visionary	reclusive	busy
MIDLIFE Age 44–65	moralistic	pragmatic	powerful	indecisive
RISING Age 22–43	alienated	heroic	conformist	narcissistic
YOUTH Age 0–21	protected	suffocated	indulged	criticized

To begin, let's build a simple lifecycle framework out of four life phases of equal twenty-two-year lengths. Accordingly, we define "youth" as lasting from ages 0 to 21, "rising adulthood" from ages 22 to 43; "midlife" from ages 44 to 65; and "elderhood" from ages 66 to 87. Now picture a chart with this lifecycle on the vertical axis and calendar years on the horizontal axis. We mark the calendar years at twenty-two-year intervals, so that Americans located in any one life phase (such as "youth") in one marked year will be in the next life phase ("rising adulthood") in the next marked year. At each intersecting point, we place an adjective that reflects how contemporaries regarded the personality of Americans in that phase of life and in that year. We describe midlife adults in 1920 as "moralistic," for example, since that is how their juniors and elders perceived them; they were in fact the major proponents of Prohibition. Filling in all these adjectives, we get the mosaic shown in Figure 2-2.

Reading history horizontally along any single row is to commit the age-bracket fallacy. No entry seems to have any intrinsic connection to whatever comes before or after it. If we read along the midlife row, for example, we see life as political historians usually portray it—as a seamless ribbon of eternal 55-year-olds. Reading vertically up any single column is to commit the life-course fallacy. Pick any column, and try to imagine how someone could grow older that way. You can't. Yet if we ignore rows and columns and just look at all the adjectives one by one, the history of the modern American lifecycle becomes hopelessly complicated. Everything seems to be changing all the time.

FIGURE 2–3

The Generational Diagonal in the Twentieth Century

	1920	1942	1964	1986
ELDER Age 66–87	sensitive	visionary	reclusive	busy
MIDLIFE Age 44–65	moralistic	pragmatic	powerful	indecisive
RISING Age 22–43	alienated	heroic	conformist	narcissistic
YOUTH Age 0–21	protected	suffocated	indulged	criticized

There's a third approach: *to read history along the generational diagonal,* just as we did with SAT scores. Consider Figure 2-3.

Let's start at the bottom of the 1942 column and move diagonally up and to the right, following the same cohort-group: from "suffocated" youths to "conformist" rising adults to "indecisive" midlifers. This is the story told by Gail Sheehy in *Passages*. Switching to the next diagonal to the right, we see Cheryl Merser's path. Switching in the other direction, we see the "protected" then "heroic" then "powerful" then "busy" diagonal of the peers of Erik Erikson (and John Kennedy). Tracing along these diagonals in sequence, we can avoid the fallacy of cohort-centrism and monitor how each set of peers has traveled a separate path through life, from youth to elderhood. With a little imagination, we can appreciate how each era looked and felt to the people who lived these different lifecycles.

Each of the diagonals depicted in Figure 2-3, of course, represents more than just a randomly selected cohort group. Each diagonal represents *a generation* possessing its own distinct age location and peer personality. Although smaller cohort-groups often reveal telling links over time between experience and behavior, only *generational* cohort-groups encompass all individual cohorts and organize them by *peer personality* into basic building blocks of social change. By inquiring into generations—what creates them, how long they are, how their boundaries can be identified, and how they align in constellations—we can begin to understand their powerful relationship with history over the centuries.

Chapter 3

BELONGING TO
A "GENERATION"

"**Y**ou belong to it, too. You came along at the same time. You can't get away from it. You're a part of it whether you want to be or not." What is this "it" in Thomas Wolfe's dialogue in *You Can't Go Home Again*? His own "Lost Generation." To Wolfe, Fitzgerald, Hemingway, Cowley, and other like-aged writers of the 1920s, membership in this generation reflected a variety of emotions and mannerisms: weary cynicism at a young age, risk-taking, bingelike behavior, disdain for a pompous "older generation." Wolfe's peers stood across a wide divide from moralistic midlifers and across another divide from straight-arrow teenagers who had never known the lethal futility of trench warfare. To belong, you had to be combat-eligible during World War I and a rising adult when Prohibition started. No one formally defined it that way. You just knew.

A half century later, demographers tried to define a later generation—Boomers—as all cohorts born during the high-fertility years of 1946 through 1964. But this statistical definition fails Wolfe's "you belong to it" test. Does a 1944 baby "belong to it"? Absolutely. What about a 1964 baby? Not a chance. Just ask a few of today's 46-year-olds or 26-year-olds. Clearly, Wolfe understood something that demographers didn't.

To be sure, people are born all the time—an argument often used to dismiss the "generation" as a meaningful concept. How can we draw any distinctions between babies born a day, a year, even a decade apart? Likewise, feet, yards, and miles are everywhere. But sometimes a foot crosses a national boundary or a continental divide. The Spanish sociologist Julián Marías, writing in 1967, used this analogy to liken generational mapping to "social cartography." Examining consecutive cohorts is like tracing land across wide river basins occasionally "creased" by ridges. "In this analogy," Marías suggested, "each generation would be the area between two mountain chains, and in order to determine whether a certain point belonged to one or the other, it would be necessary to know the relief. Two widely separated points could belong to the same generation, or two close points, on the other hand, might belong to different generations. It would depend on whether the points were on the same slope or on different sides of a slope." Sometimes Marías' "creases" would be a jagged peak, other times a low rise. Water flows down a low rise less swiftly than down a jagged peak, but it flows down just as surely in opposite directions.

Like most other social categories—religion, political party, income, occupation, race—generations can be imprecise at the boundaries. We define generational boundaries (Marías' "creases") by calendar year—and, of course, some people born just on one side may really belong on the other. But a little ambiguity does not keep us from distinguishing Catholics from Protestants, Democrats from Republicans, or the middle class from the poor. Nor should it keep us from distinguishing Silent from Boom. "Specifying generations," notes historian Alan Spitzer, "is no more arbitrary than specifying social classes, or ideologies, or political movements where there is inevitably a shading off or ambiguity at the boundaries of categories."

Then again, even small amounts of time can be decisive in binding—and separating—generations. In today's era of age gradations, a one-minute delay in birth (most often at the stroke of the New Year) can mean the difference between kindergarten and first grade six years later. That decision, in turn, can mean the difference between wartime draft and schoolroom comfort twelve or thirteen years farther down the road. (A Ph.D. candidate born on December 31, 1942, had an excellent chance of gliding through graduate school on student deferments; one born the next day found it much harder to avoid Vietnam.) In this respect, a generational boundary is like the federal definition of poverty. A family whose income is $1 below the income limit for child support will think, behave, be perceived, and be treated differently from another family whose income is $1 above the limit. As years pass, the $1-under and $1-over families will probably grow less alike, thanks to what was at first an arbitrary distinction. Likewise with generations.

For centuries, the power of the generation has not escaped the eye of philosophers and poets, historians and sociologists. Writing in the early twentieth century, José Ortega y Gasset called the generation "the most important conception in history." Many others have shared that view. Since the days of the Old Testament and ancient Greece, the word "generation" and its various roots have connoted the essence of life—birth and death, the maturing of youth and the letting-go of old age, the rise and fall of dynasties and nations. In Appendix

A, we summarize briefly what has been written over the millennia about what Karl Mannheim once called the "generations problem." We explain how the dynamics of generational definition and cyclical change can be inferred from sources ranging from the *Iliad* and the Book of Exodus to the writings of several nineteenth-century Europeans. We attempt to go beyond our predecessors by not just talking about "generations" in the abstract, but by defining the term precisely enough to batch real-life cohort-groups into generations—and fix them in history. Once we do this, we can understand the relationships among them—and, especially, how and why they occur in cycles.

We begin with the following definition:

- *A GENERATION is a cohort-group whose length approximates the span of a phase of life and whose boundaries are fixed by peer personality.*

This definition includes two important elements: first, the *length* of a generational cohort-group, and second, its *peer personality*.

The Length of a Generation

Let's begin with the question of *length*. Although social philosophers over the last two centuries have often (like ourselves) defined a generation as a cohort-group, they have had difficulty explaining how long it should be. Many have wrongly suggested that the length be based on the average age of parenthood— that is, the average span of years that pass between being born and giving birth. This rhythm of genealogy makes sense when applied to an individual family over a few decades, but not to an entire society, nor even to many families over a longer period. The reason is simple: Parents give birth to children at widely differing ages (typically from their mid-teens to early forties), and children intermarry with other families with equally wide birth distributions. Each chain of parent-to-child lineage produces a single thread of *family time*, but combining millions of such threads produces no single rope of *social time*.

We choose instead to base the length of a generational cohort-group on the length of *a phase of life*. We define life phases in terms of central social roles. Returning to the twenty-two-year phases we used in Chapter 2, let's outline what these roles might include:

- ELDERHOOD (age 66–87). Central role: *stewardship* (supervising, mentoring, channeling endowments, passing on values).

- MIDLIFE (age 44–65). Central role: *leadership* (parenting, teaching, directing institutions, using values).

- RISING ADULTHOOD (age 22–43). Central role: *activity* (working, starting families and livelihoods, serving institutions, testing values).

- YOUTH (age 0–21). Central role: *dependence* (growing, learning, accepting protection and nurture, avoiding harm, acquiring values).

These central role descriptions are only suggestive. All we require is that each role be different and that the age borders for each role be well defined. Practically every society recognizes a discrete coming-of-age moment (or "rite of passage") separating the dependence of youth from the independence of adulthood. This moment is critical in creating generations; any sharp contrast between the experiences of youths and rising adults may fix important differences in peer personality that last a lifetime. Most societies also recognize a midlife transition when an adult is deemed qualified for society's highest leadership posts, and an age of declining physiological potential when adults are expected or forced to retire from strenuous social and economic life. In America over the last two centuries, our twenty-two-year intervals reflect these divisions. Ages 21–22 have approximated the age of legal majority, the end of apprenticeship, the first year after college, the release of noncollege men from the armed forces, and (from around 1820 until 1971) first suffrage; ages 43–44, the youngest age of any successful Presidential candidate; and ages 65–66, a typical age (and, since the 1940s, often an official age) for retirement.

Now suppose a decisive event—say, a major war or revolution—suddenly hits this society. Clearly, the event will affect each age group differently according to its central role. In the case of a major war, we can easily imagine youths encouraged and willing to keep out of the way (dependence), rising adults to arm and meet the enemy (activity), midlifers to organize the troops and manage the home front (leadership), and elders to offer wisdom and perspective (stewardship). We can also imagine how most people will emerge from the trauma with their personalities permanently reshaped in conformance with the role they played (or were expected to play but didn't). The decisive event, therefore, creates four distinct cohort-groups—each about twenty-two years in length and each possessing a special collective personality that will later distinguish it from its age-bracket neighbors as it ages in place. If future decisive events arrive when all of these cohort-groups are well positioned in older life phases, then those events will reinforce the separate identities of older cohort-groups and create new and distinct twenty-two-year cohort-groups among the children born since the last event.

The result over time is a series of distinct cohort-groups that includes everyone ever born. Each of these we call a "generation," and each of these possesses what we call a "peer personality."

We cannot, of course, expect that the length of every generation must always be twenty-two years—or any other precise number. The world is far too complicated to follow our simple model like clockwork. The effective length of each phase of life is always shifting a bit from one era to the next. Throughout American history, we can find some eras when youths became scrappy adventurers or valiant soldiers in their late teens, and others in which they waited well into their twenties before leaving home. During the 1960s and 1970s, for example, the coming-of-age division between youth and rising adulthood drifted upward in age and the division between midlife leadership and elder stewardship drifted downward. During the 1930s and 1940s, with very different peer personalities occupying each phase of life, these two divisions drifted in the reverse directions. Large and sudden changes, however, are quite rare. When have most Americans come of age? Not always at age 22, but not often many years sooner or later.

Even though generational membership does not depend at all on family lineage (brothers and sisters or husbands and wives may fall anywhere with respect to cohort-group boundaries), the special bonds—emotional, biological, social, economic—connecting parents to their own children clearly matter. In fact, family relationships follow a pattern that offers three important corollaries to our cohort-based definition of a "generation":

• *A generation's parents (or children) are distributed over the two preceding (or two succeeding) generations;*

• *A generation's early or "first-wave" cohorts are likely to have an earlier parent generation than late or "last-wave" cohorts; and*

• *Each generation has an especially strong nurturing influence on the second succeeding generation.*

The first rule reflects the link between the age distribution of childbearing (with the average age of mothers and fathers typically ranging from 20 to 45) and the average length of successive generations (twenty-two years). Consider parents belonging to the Silent Generation, the 1925-to-1942 cohort-group. With a few stray exceptions, their earliest children appeared in the mid-1940s, born to young parents themselves born in 1925; their latest children appeared in the early 1980s, born to midlife parents themselves born in 1942. The total birthyear span from the eldest to the youngest children of Silent parents thus approximates the combined 1943-to-1981 birthyear span of the Boom and 13th Generations. The distribution, moreover, is bell-shaped—meaning that most of these children were Boomers born in the 1950s and 13ers born in the 1960s. Continuing down the family tree, we would find that each generation spreads its grandchildren roughly over three later generations—the second, third, and fourth successors.

The second rule, the distinction between what we call a generation's "first wave" and "last wave," helps us understand differences in the nurture received by early as opposed to late cohorts in any single generation. Boomers are a good example: Their first wave (born in the mid-1940s) includes mostly children of confident G.I.s, their last wave (born in the late 1950s) mostly children of the more ambivalent Silent. This distinction, in turn, can produce differences in the behavior later expressed by a generation's two waves. Among Boomers, for instance, the last wave came of age showing more pathologies (crime, drug use, suicide, low aptitude scores) than the first wave.

Finally, the crucial nurturing relationships between generations two apart reflect the greater social influence of older over younger parents. By 1960 (the last Boom birthyear), G.I. and Silent parents were raising Boomer children in roughly equal numbers. But the fortyish and fiftyish G.I.s—from Dr. Spock and Walt Disney to school principals and scout leaders—had much greater influence in 1960 over the childhood environment than did the twentyish and thirtyish Silent. Similarly, the 1970s were a decade in which Silent and Boom parents together raised 13er children, but the fortyish Silent set the tone—from *Sesame Street* and open classrooms to rising divorce rates and the decline of G-rated movies. Now, as the 1990s dawn, Boomers (not 13ers) are asserting control of the world of Millennial children. Between any two parenting generations, the one in midlife naturally exercises a greater cultural and institutional influence than the one in rising adulthood.

Peer Personality

So far we have established, in the abstract, something about how generations are created, how long they are, and how they relate to family genealogy. But how do we actually identify one? For that, we have to focus our attention on "peer personality"—the element in our definition that distinguishes a generation as a cohesive cohort-group with its own unique biography. The peer personality of a generation is essentially a caricature of its prototypical member. It is, in its sum of attributes, a distinctly personlike creation. A generation has collective attitudes about family life, sex roles, institutions, politics, religion, lifestyle, and the future. It can be safe or reckless, calm or aggressive, self-absorbed or outer-driven, generous or selfish, spiritual or secular, interested in culture or interested in politics. In short, it can think, feel, or do anything an individual might think, feel, or do. Between any two generations, as between any two neighbors, such personalities can mesh, clash, be attracted to or repelled by one another.

As a social category, a generation probably offers a safer basis for personality generalization than such other social categories as sex, race, region, or age. We can more easily fix a consensus personality for the Lost (or for Boomers) than we ever could for women, or Hispanics, or Californians, or all the 30-year-olds of a given century. The reason, in the words of Italian historian Giuseppe Ferrari, is that a generation "is born, lives, and dies." Like any individual—and unlike other social groups—a generation collectively feels historical urgency and finality, conscious of the unrepeatable opportunities offered by whatever phase of life it occupies. It understands that work left undone at each phase of life may never be done by others—or at least not in a way an aging generation might wish it done. In contrast, a sex, an age bracket, and (probably) a race will endure as long as the human species survives.

Like any group, a generation includes all kinds of people. Yet individual divergences from peer personality, and how those divergences are perceived, can explain much about a generation. In some respects, a peer personality gives heavy focus to the attitudes and experiences of the generational elite—what Ferrari called *i capi della società, i re del pensiero, i signori della generazione* ("the heads of society, the kings of thought, the lords of the generation"). But while they commonly express the tone of a generation's peer personality, the personality itself is often established by non-elites. In particular, the attitudes of women and mothers toward their own sex roles and family roles are central to a generation's peer personality. Likewise, groups which are (or feel) at the social periphery—immigrants, blacks, fundamentalists—often play a major role in fixing or revealing their generation's peer personality.

We can use peer personality to identify a generation and find the boundaries separating it from its neighbors. To do so, we need a working definition—one that will tell us what evidence we need and how to evaluate it. We offer the following three-part test:

• *A PEER PERSONALITY is a generational persona recognized and determined by (1) common age location; (2) common beliefs and behavior; and (3) perceived membership in a common generation.*

To assess the peer personality of any cohort-group, we look first at its chronology: its common age location, where its lifecycle is positioned against the background chronology of historic trends and events. Second, we look at its attributes: objective measures of its common beliefs and behavior, identifying which cohorts share common personality traits. Third, we look at awareness: how society perceives membership in a common generation—that is, who is generally considered a member and who is not.

Chronology: Common Age Location in History

Practically all generations writers have agreed that members of a generation feel the ebb and flow of history from basically the same age or phase-of-life perspective. To find a generation, we look for a cohort-group whose members "came along at the same time" (as Wolfe put it)—who are nurtured as children, enter adulthood, and pass through subsequent life phases during eras that show no sudden discontinuities. Studying his tempestuous (Hitlerian) peers from abroad, the German sociologist Karl Mannheim invented the term *Generations-*

lagerung ("generational setting") to refer to the sense of common historical location shared by a well-defined cohort-group. He described it as "a community of date and space" and "a common location in the historical dimension of the social process" in which a generation encounters "the same concrete historical problems." Mannheim's Spanish peer José Ortega y Gasset similarly defined a generation as a set of "coetaneous" cohorts, born within "zones of dates" which make them "the same age vitally and historically."

Within each generation, a sense of social community—reinforced by the expectations of elders—can create something akin to gravity and pull outlying cohorts into a common peer personality. At any one time, a generation of average length can stretch from newborn babies to graduate students or, alternatively, from 19- to 40-year-olds. Any major event will touch its youngest and oldest members in dissimilar ways, even when they belong to the same phase of life. But the experiences of a few important cohorts can strongly influence the lifelong reflections of a much larger cohort-group. Austrian historian Wilhelm Pinder wrote of "decisive clusters of births" which develop a "generational entelechy," a social and emotional center of gravity pulling at a larger group of slightly older or younger peers.

Consider, as a modern example, the World War II combat cohorts born between 1915 and 1924. They pulled on older (but not younger) cohorts, who saw themselves participating in the same collective struggle—taking the same risks and earning the same rewards. Or consider the draft-influenced Vietnam-era cohorts born between 1943 and 1949. They pulled on younger (but not older) cohorts who identified with their experiences. Cheryl Merser recalls that, for many Boomers born in the 1950s, their "sixties took place in the seventies." Merser uses the word "sixties" to identify not a date-fixed era, but a sense of generational setting. Her classmates came of age with something everyone would recognize as a "sixties" experience, albeit dislocated and not quite authentic. No one had his "sixties" in the fifties or eighties. Likewise, it would be meaningless to speak of anyone having his "seventies" in the eighties. People born in 1944 and 1954 are, by this definition, part of the same *Generationslagerung*. Those born in 1964 are not.

To find boundaries between generations, we look closely at the history surrounding two moments: birth and coming of age. Some boundaries arise in years when older generations, especially parents, change their nurturing attitudes toward children. As we shall see, such shifts in child nurture typically occur during or just after eras of exceptional spiritual fervor (for example, the 1741–1742, 1842–1843, or 1981–1982 shifts) or during or just after major crises in public life (the 1859–1860 or 1942–1943 shifts). Generational boundaries can also result from sudden differences in how war hits members of adjacent cohorts (1842–1843, 1900–1901, or 1924–1925) or in how the ebbing of spiritual enthusiasm closes a door of communication between coming-of-age youngsters of successive cohorts (1723–1724, 1882–1883, or 1960–1961). There is no single rule for locating a decisive shift in age location that divides adjacent generations. Usually, many historical trends are at work, most of them pointing to the same boundary.

Attributes: Common Beliefs and Behavior

As a generation ages, its inner beliefs retain a certain consistency over its lifecycle, much like the personality of an individual growing older. Writing in the nineteenth century, Auguste Comte noted how each generation develops a "unanimous adherence to certain fundamental notions." Wilhelm Dilthey spoke of a generational *Weltanschauung*, a web of beliefs and attitudes about ultimate questions that each generation carries with it from rising adulthood through old age. Certain important behavioral traits also offer important clues about generational boundaries. Sometimes we notice a boundary when we observe social pathologies peaking and then receding in frequency—as, for example, across the troubled cohorts of the early 1960s that we examined earlier. Almost any kind of data can offer evidence about peer personalities: data on marriage, crime, fertility, suicide, education, aptitude, accidents, divorce, drug consumption, alcoholism, voting, work habits, and ambition. Telling contrasts often appear in famous personages born across adjacent cohorts (for example, across the 1723–1724, 1821–1822, 1859–1860, and 1924–1925 cohort pairs).

The beliefs and behavior of a generation never show up uniformly across all of its members. As Ortega observed, the generational experience is a "dynamic compromise between the mass and the individual." But even those who differ from the peer norm are generally *aware* of their noncomformity. Within each generation, we find examples of what the German sociologist Julius Peterson called "directive," "directed," and "suppressed" individual personalities. The "directive" individual helps set the overall tone, the "directed" follows and legitimizes his peers' mind-set, and the "suppressed" either withdraws from his peers or spends a lifetime struggling against them. A "directive" in one generation might have been a "suppressed" in another, or vice versa—but any individual is well aware of the difference between reality and might-have-beens. Among G.I.s, for example, Walt Disney was a "directive" tone-setter, Walter Cronkite a "directed" tone-follower, and Jack Kerouac a "suppressed" rebel who struggled against his generation. Among G.I. Presidents, we might describe Kennedy, Johnson, and Reagan as "directive"; Nixon, Ford, and Bush as "directed"; and Carter as "suppressed." (Carter's fixation on fair process, "malaise," and "small earth" rhetoric aligned him with his juniors, in clear opposition to his own hubristic G.I. peers.)

Consider one present-day example of "directive" and "suppressed" types: the findings of the annual UCLA survey of college freshmen. From the late 1960s to the late 1980s, the share of all students giving high priority to "developing a philosophy of life" has fallen, roughly, from 80 percent to 40 percent—while the share that prefers "being very well off financially" has risen commensurately. In both eras, clearly, plenty of young people have been in both camps. But, also in both eras, people in the minority have been acutely aware that they are running against the tide of their peer consensus. In 1970, any college senior who interviewed for a job with Dow Chemical (maker of napalm) had heavy explaining to do when he came back to his dorm room. In 1990, by contrast, any youngster who picketed a Dow recruiter was looked upon as a throwback by peers who generally agreed that "Dow Lets You Do Great Things." A one-third-to-two-thirds electoral victory is usually considered a colossal landslide that lets both winners and losers know exactly where they stand. The same holds for peer personality. As Thomas Wolfe warned, "You can't get away from it."

We can apply no reductive rules for comparing the beliefs and behavior of one cohort-group with those of its neighbors. Social science data, though vital, must be interpreted in the proper historical context. We always have to ask what each statistic tells us about the total person—about the balance between inner and outer life, or risk-taking, or individual self-esteem, or collective self-confidence. Trends in alcohol and drug consumption data generally do reflect the same personality traits over the centuries: High rates of substance abuse have always indicated an attraction to risk, a passion for self-discovery, and defiance of institutional norms. The rise in drug and alcohol consumption during the 1890s says much the same about generations alive in 1910 as the rise during the 1960s and 1970s says about generations alive today. Average marriage age, on the other hand, must be interpreted differently from decade to decade depending on social conventions. In the early 1700s, coming-of-age men who wanted to conform to elders' expectations and reduce lifetime risks tended to delay marriage and stay with their parents. In the 1950s, by contrast, young men and women pursued the same goals by accelerating marriage and moving out early.

Awareness: Perceived Membership in a Common Generation

"Each of us moves with the men of our generation," Julián Marías observed two decades ago. "To ask ourselves to which generation we belong is, in large measure, to ask who we are." Most people know their own generation. And they usually have a good intuitive feeling for the generational membership of their next-elders and next-juniors.

Awareness of generational membership helps us most with boundary cohorts possessed of Pinder's "entelechy." Even when these cohorts reveal few *objective* clues about where they belong, they often cry out with unambiguous *subjective* perceptions. The hardboiled Lost novelists born in 1898–1899 (like Fitzgerald and Hemingway) made it clear that they felt hugely different from what Fitzgerald called the "bright and alien" youngsters (like Lindbergh and Disney) born in 1901–1902. The lifelong media ripple that has accompanied the 1943 cohort offers an even better example of how awareness can nail down a generational boundary. These Americans were the first toddlers to be labeled "Dr. Spock" children; the first high school debaters to include self-described "extremists"; the first college class (1965) to be called "radical"; the first Vietnam-era draft-card burners; the eldest among the "Americans Under 25" whom *Time* magazine named its "1967 Man of the Year"; and among the last 29-year-olds (in 1972) who still heard the phrase "under-30 generation" before its sudden disappearance. Today, find a person born in 1943. Ask him whether he identifies with those a bit older or younger than himself. Probably, he will say the latter. Find someone born in 1942, and the answer will just as probably be the opposite.

Generational awareness applies not only to where a cohort-group finds itself today, but also to where it is expected to go tomorrow. Ortega likens a fully come-of-age generation to "a species of biological missile hurled into space at a given instant, with a certain velocity and direction," on a "preestablished vital trajectory." Mannheim calls this a generation's "essential destiny." For some generations, this sense of destiny is very strong; for others it is nonexistent. The cohesion of postwar G.I.s reflected a keen generational consensus about the world they wanted and expected to build—adding to the sense of collective triumph when John Kennedy brought his peers to power in 1961. Two earlier American generations also shared a strong sense of Mannheim's "essential destiny" in reconstructing the outer world: the peers of Thomas Jefferson and the peers of Cotton Mather. In all three cases, elders and juniors alive at the time reinforced this expectation: They too expected greatness from these generations.

A generation, like an individual, merges many different qualities, no one of which is definitive standing alone. But once all the evidence is assembled, we can build a persuasive case for identifying (by birthyear) eighteen generations over the course of American history. All Americans born over the past four centuries have belonged to one or another of these generations. To paraphrase Wolfe, they belonged whether they wanted to or not.

Our next and deeper challenge is to identify recurring elements in these peer personalities, suggestive of a relationship between the sequence of generations and the larger pattern of history. We now turn to the cycle.

Chapter 4

THE FOUR-PART CYCLE

Virtually every American in his fifties or older in 1991 remembers where he was, what he was doing, and *how old he was* when the Japanese attacked Pearl Harbor on December 7, 1941. Pearl Harbor Sunday was unquestionably a generation-shaping event. To mobilize America for total war, each generation suddenly defined (or redefined) itself according to its phase-of-life role: aging Missionaries as stewards of national purpose, midlife Lost as on-the-scene managers, rising-adult G.I.s as soldiers and workers, and Silent children as stay-out-of-the-way dependents. Move forward a half century and picture how the principal generations alive today look back on (and remain associated with) World War II. The G.I.s fought it, the Silent saw it through a child's awestruck eyes, Boomers were nurtured in its exuberant aftermath, and 13ers know it only as ''history.''

Now repeat this exercise with the headline events that marked the month between July 18 and August 18, 1969: the first Apollo moon landing, Chappaquiddick, and Woodstock. Much like Pearl Harbor Sunday, the midsummer of 1969 anchored a pivotal era of generational definition. Once again, Americans of all ages played out their respective phase-of-life roles—though this time, of course, the collective result was maximum convulsion rather than maximum cooperation. Speaking for the aging G.I.s, now the all-powerful stewards of national direction, Richard Nixon announced after the moon landing: ''This is the greatest week in the history of mankind since the Creation.'' By now feeling

69

frustrated, the Silent began to break away from their rising-adult conformism and to find fault with G.I. constructions. Anthony Lewis complained that the Apollo mission gave him "a guilty conscience"—and Ted Kennedy's ill-fated adventure signaled the traumatic, divorce-plagued future awaiting Silent-led families. Meanwhile, at Woodstock, coming-of-age Boomers established a generational community that was as defiantly anti-G.I. as anything they could possibly have concocted. And in the newly self-absorbed culture of the late 1960s, child 13ers found themselves emotionally uninvited in a world that expected kids to grow up fast. Over the next decade of social upheaval, each generation would again define (or redefine) itself, and in so doing would entirely recast the phase of life it was entering: G.I.s (elderhood), Silent (midlife), Boomers (rising adulthood), and 13ers (youth).

These two events—and the eras surrounding them—clearly made a strong impression on the generations participating in them. And by reading along their separate diagonals, we can imagine how each of these generations constitutes an active, living bridge between the mood of D-Day and the mood of the moon landing, divorce epidemic, and Woodstock several decades later. World War II empowered G.I.s as America's greatest twentieth-century collection of civic doers and rationalists. So too did it encourage them to overreach as they approached elderhood—a hubris that appeared arrogant and soulless to their juniors. The Silent, painfully aware of their own lack of catharsis, came of age emulating their war-hero next-elders—and then, on the edge of midlife, began to compensate by engaging in high-risk personal behavior. Among Boomers, the postwar G.I. dogma of science and optimism planted the seeds of spiritual rebellion and defiance. A still-younger generation of 13ers, disconnected from the focal event that had influenced all three of their generational elders, passed through childhood without an adult-perceived mission.

Since 1969, the span of roughly one more generation has passed. Everyone has moved up one lifecycle notch, and Millennials are now replacing 13ers in youth. Yet memories of World War II and the late 1960s still define generational mind-sets. In January 1989, in his last speech to the nation as President, G.I. Ronald Reagan regretted the fading memory of World War II heroism and urged Americans to teach what he termed "civic ritual" to Millennial schoolchildren. A baby born on the day Reagan gave that speech had more personal distance from Pearl Harbor Sunday—a span of just over forty-seven years—than the forty-six-year distance Reagan himself had, as a newborn, from Lee's final Civil War surrender to Grant at Appomattox. Similarly, the echoes of the 1960s live on in countless ways in our public and private lives—for example, in the campaigns of Boomer William Bennett (first as Education Secretary and next as "Drug Czar") to protect children from the lingering detritus of his peers' coming-of-age years, and of Senator Albert Gore to challenge the global environmental harms wrought by G.I. science. Just as 5-year-old Boomers grew up amid the giddy optimism of secular achievement, 5-year-old Millennials are being nurtured in the sober aftermath of spiritual discovery.

What we see in this unfolding tale is part of a generational cycle—and the importance of what we call "social moments" in directing its evolution. Were we to back up to the years around 1910, we would find ourselves at a similar position in a prior cycle. And we would sense the influence of a comparable pair of prior social moments (the Civil War and the tumultuous 1890s) in defining the American generations alive at that time and reinforcing similar differences in their peer personalities at each phase of life.

- *A SOCIAL MOMENT is an era, typically lasting about a decade, when people perceive that historic events are radically altering their social environment.*

How do we know a social moment when we see it? The best way is to live through one, or to listen to someone who has. It is an era when everyone senses—at the time and afterward—that history is moving swiftly, that the familiar world is disappearing and a new world is emerging. One such moment arrived with Franklin Roosevelt's election in 1932 and stretched through VJ-Day in 1945. Those thirteen years visibly rearranged nearly every feature of the American social landscape, from the function of government and the organization of the economy to man's relationship with technology and the U.S. role in world affairs. The next such moment arrived in the late 1960s and lasted through the 1970s. During that "Consciousness Revolution," Americans again experienced a re-shuffling of national life, an amalgam of radical changes in attitudes toward family, language, dress, duty, community, sex, and art. Pick any cultural artifact created in this century—from novels to slang to clothing—and even if you could say nothing else about it, you could probably tell whether it came along before, during, or after this "revolution." As these two examples suggest, social moments can be very different from one another. In fact:

- *There are two types of social moments: SECULAR CRISES, when society focuses on reordering the outer world of institutions and public behavior; and SPIRITUAL AWAKENINGS, when society focuses on changing the inner world of values and private behavior.*

Social moments do not arrive at random. For example, a secular crisis and a spiritual awakening never occur back to back. Nor does half a century ever pass without a social moment of either type. Instead, social moments arrive on a rather regular schedule.

- *Social moments normally arrive in time intervals roughly separated by two phases of life (approximately forty to forty-five years), and they alternate in type between secular crises and spiritual awakenings.*

In Appendix A, we explain in some detail how and why this timing of social moments tends to occur in nontraditional societies like America, and how it is linked to a cyclical creation of generations and generational types. At the heart of our explanation lies the premise that each generation tries to redefine the social role of older phases of life as it matures through them. After a social moment has reinforced a "dependent" social role in children, for example, that cohort-group will later try to redefine rising adulthood in terms of that dependence. (Picture the Silent peers of Michael Dukakis and Gary Hart, the passive children of depression and war who came of age during the culturally quiescent 1950s.) Likewise, rising adults in whom an "active" role was reinforced will try to retain that role as they move into midlife. (Picture the G.I. peers of John Kennedy and Ronald Reagan, who reached adulthood in World War II, then chafed impatiently until they surged to power around 1960.)

Such redefinitions sustain themselves through one phase-of-life transition. They cannot, however, work through two such transitions. A dependent role cannot be transferred into midlife, nor an active role into elderhood. At that point—roughly two phases removed from the earlier social moment—the growing incongruity between peer personality and age must induce a new social moment and realign social roles back into their original life phases. The midlife Silent, for instance, could not retain their dependency role—prompting the sudden emphasis on personal redefinition (and risk-taking) that Gail Sheehy labeled "passages." The new social moment represents a reaction against the ossifying and dysfunctional roles forged by each generation during the earlier social moment. As a result, the new social moment will be *opposite in type* from the one that came before. Fueling the secular changes of the Depression and World War II, for example, were rising-adult G.I.s who helped steer America away from what they considered to be futile moralisms left over from turn-of-the-century reform movements. Likewise, fueling the spiritual changes of the late 1960s and 1970s were rising-adult Boomers who prodded America away from postwar secularism and back toward a fresh commitment to moral passion.

This two-life-phase pattern means that the age location of successive generations, relative to any social moment, falls into an alternating rhythm. If the first generation (say, the G.I.s) is entering rising adulthood during one social moment, then the second generation (Silent) is entering youth during the same moment, the third (Boom) entering rising adulthood during the second moment, the fourth (13th) entering youth during the second moment, and so on. We label generations with the first and third age location (Boom and G.I.) as "dominant" generations; those with the second and fourth (Silent and 13th) as "recessive." In other words:

- *During social moments, DOMINANT generations are entering rising adulthood and elderhood.*

• *During social moments, RECESSIVE generations are entering youth and midlife.*

We display the pattern schematically in Figure 4-1, again with phases of life on the vertical and calendar years on the horizontal. (Since social moments normally arise as each generation is entering a phase of life, with each moment typically culminating when the generation has fully entered it, we show them appearing somewhat before each twenty-two-year interval.) Read along the generational diagonal, and notice how dominant and recessive generations pass through social moments at alternating life phases.

FIGURE 4–1

The Generational Diagonal:
   Dominant and Recessive Generations

SOCIAL MOMENT

	Secular Crisis		Spiritual Awakening	
YEAR	**Year 0**	**Year 22**	**Year 44**	**Year 66**
ELDER Age 66–87	Recessive	Dominant	Recessive	Dominant
MIDLIFE Age 44–65	Dominant	Recessive	Dominant	Recessive
RISING Age 22–43	Recessive	Dominant	Recessive	Dominant
YOUTH Age 0–21	Dominant	Recessive	Dominant	Recessive

Each generation shown in Figure 4-1 has a unique age location relative to each type of social moment. Of the two dominant generations, one enters rising adulthood during a crisis and enters elderhood during an awakening, the other the opposite. Of the two recessive generations, one enters youth during a crisis and enters midlife during an awakening, the other the opposite. Thus, every generation has a unique phase-of-life position before and after each type of social moment, a unique set of generational neighbors, and (recalling our genealogical discussion in Chapter 3) a unique combination of parents and children. Consequently, *each of the four generations develops its own unique type of peer personality.*

These four generational types recur in a fixed order. Moving up vertically from the youths in year 44 of Figure 4-1, their lifecycles can be described as follows:

1. A dominant, inner-fixated IDEALIST GENERATION grows up as increasingly indulged youths after a secular crisis; comes of age inspiring a spiritual awakening; fragments into narcissistic rising adults; cultivates principle as moralistic midlifers; and emerges as visionary elders guiding the next secular crisis.

2. A recessive REACTIVE GENERATION grows up as underprotected and criticized youths during a spiritual awakening; matures into risk-taking, alienated rising adults; mellows into pragmatic midlife leaders during a secular crisis; and maintains respect (but less influence) as reclusive elders.

3. A dominant, outer-fixated CIVIC GENERATION grows up as increasingly protected youths after a spiritual awakening; comes of age overcoming a secular crisis; unites into a heroic and achieving cadre of rising adults; sustains that image while building institutions as powerful midlifers; and emerges as busy elders attacked by the next spiritual awakening.

4. A recessive ADAPTIVE GENERATION grows up as overprotected and suffocated youths during a secular crisis; matures into risk-averse, conformist rising adults; produces indecisive midlife arbitrator-leaders during a spiritual awakening; and maintains influence (but less respect) as sensitive elders.

The dominant generational types encounter their first social moment entering rising adulthood—for (Boomer) Idealists, an awakening; for (G.I.) Civics, a crisis. Taking their social roles with them into midlife, they tend to monopolize the style of adulthood in the public world—the Idealists dominating rhetoric and culture, the Civics technology and institutions. The recessive types—(13er) Reactives and (Silent) Adaptives—encounter their first social moment as children. They compensate for their diminished public role by exercising a commensurately greater influence on the private world of human relationships. Raising their own children, for example, Reactives have a tendency to restore protectiveness, Adaptives to allow greater freedom. Recessive generations also play critical midlife roles in social moments—Adaptives as flexible mediators in spiritual awakenings, Reactives as pragmatic managers of secular crises.

In sum, Idealist generations tend to live what we might label a *prophetic* lifecycle of vision and values; Reactives a *picaresque* lifecycle of survival and adventure; Civics a *heroic* lifecycle of secular achievement and reward; and Adaptives a *genteel* lifecycle of expertise and amelioration. When we reach Chapter 12, we will return to these lifecycle paradigms in much greater detail. For now, let's take Figure 4-1 one step further, by labeling each of these four types.

In Figure 4-2, we see the generational cycle. These four generational types recur in fixed order, given one important condition: that society resolves with reasonable success each secular crisis that it encounters. When this condition does not hold, the cycle experiences an interruption—in effect, skipping a beat.

FIGURE 4–2

From the Diagonal to the Cycle: Four Generational Types

SOCIAL MOMENT

		Secular Crisis		Spiritual Awakening
YEAR	**Year 0**	**Year 22**	**Year 44**	**Year 66**
ELDER Age 66-87	Adaptive	Idealist	Reactive	Civic
MIDLIFE Age 44-65	Idealist	Reactive	Civic	Adaptive
RISING Age 22-43	Reactive	Civic	Adaptive	Idealist
YOUTH Age 0-21	Civic	Adaptive	Idealist	Reactive

If a secular crisis weakens instead of strengthens the confidence of rising adults, then a Reactive generation can be followed by an Adaptive rather than a Civic. This has happened once in American history, in the nineteenth century. We cannot say for sure whether other beats could be skipped. We can only say that in America, so far, they have not been.

If this four-type cycle revolves in a fixed sequence, so too must the shifting age location of all four types as they layer themselves from one era to the next. Each time one type is entering rising adulthood, for instance, the other types entering other phases of life will all line up in a predictable pattern. We call each of these four recurring patterns a generational "constellation," each with its own "era" and "mood." The two-apart eras when Idealists and Civics come of age have moods reflecting the social moments (spiritual awakenings or secular crises) that occur largely within those eras. The intervening eras when Reactives or Adaptives come of age have moods reflecting a period of transition from one social moment to the next.

Picture the cycle of shifting constellations as you might imagine the seasonal transformation of nature: alternating between the heat of summer and the cold of winter, the germination of spring and the harvest of autumn. Through the generational seasons of social history, beginning with a spiritual awakening, we see the following four constellational eras and moods:

• An AWAKENING ERA (Idealists coming of age) triggers cultural creativity and the emergence of new ideals, as institutions built around old values are challenged by the emergence of a spiritual awakening.

• In an INNER-DRIVEN ERA (Reactives coming of age), individualism flourishes, new ideals are cultivated in separate camps, confidence in institutions declines, and secular problems are deferred.

• A CRISIS ERA (Civics coming of age) opens with growing collective unity in the face of perceived social peril and culminates in a secular crisis in which danger is overcome and one set of new ideals triumphs.

• In an OUTER-DRIVEN ERA (Adaptives coming of age), society turns toward conformity and stability, triumphant ideals are secularized, and spiritual discontent is deferred.

We define the chronological end of each era by locating the specific year of what we call an "aligned" constellation: the moment at which the last cohort of a new generation is born and each older generation has fully moved into a new phase of life (years 0, 22, 44, and 66 in Figure 4-2). Aligned constellations arrive as often as new generations arrive—about once every twenty-two years. An Awakening era ends, for example, in the year when the last cohort of a new Reactive generation is born; this will roughly coincide with the year when the last cohort of an Idealist generation has entered rising adulthood, and similarly when older Adaptive and Civic generations have fully moved into midlife and elderhood. (The most recent such year would be 1981; before that, 1900.) At this point, the cycle reaches an aligned Awakening constellation. The following Inner-Driven era will then last until an aligned Inner-Driven constellation, and so on.

While all four generational types contribute to the nature of each constellational era, the two dominant types—Idealist and Civic—are key. Coming of age into rising adulthood, these two types recast society's new "active" agenda, either from secular to spiritual or vice versa. The G.I.s did this in the years between 1932 and 1945, Boomers during the late 1960s and 1970s. Entering midlife, with recessive generations behind them, they continue to set the social agenda until the next social moment, whether a crisis or an awakening.

Thus, during both types of social moments, *history shapes generations;* yet at the same time, by congealing crises and sparking awakenings, *generations shape history.*

How can this cycle exist in a complicated world? To be sure, history has its good and bad surprises and accidents, its good and bad actors: the rise of perestroika or the killing of the Austrian archduke; the emergence of a Churchill or a Saddam Hussein. Some would say instinctively that history is too cluttered to allow for our kind of cycle. But such a prejudice focuses too closely on events without sufficient attention to *the response those events generate*. It is the response that determines the social moment. Compare, for example, the American response to World War I and World War II. Both wars were preceded by aggressive foreign acts (the sinking of the *Lusitania,* the air attack on Pearl Harbor). In one case, Congress waited two years before declaring war; in the other case, it declared war the next day. In one case, the war helped propel divisive movements like Prohibition; in the other, the nation mobilized as a single organism. Both wars ended in total victory—but in one case, soldiers came home to moral nagging and vice squads; in the other, they came home to ticker-tape parades. Both wars strengthened America's influence overseas—but in one case, that influence was quickly squandered; in the other, it was consolidated over the next two decades.

Why? When a society is in the midst of a Crisis era, as America was in 1941, generational forces tend to congeal a secular crisis from whatever exogenous events arise. Had the world not drifted into global depression and war, the cycle suggests that some other historic emergency would have gripped the nation, given the age location of the respective peer personalities: inner-fixated Missionary prophets in their sixties, plucky Lost pragmatists in their forties, outer-fixated G.I. doers in their twenties, and the undemanding Silent in childhood. America was poised for decisive and effective action. Compare 1941 with 1967—the year of the Tonkin Gulf incident. At that point, America was entering an Awakening era. The doers were reaching elderhood, and a new set of prophets reaching combat age. Both generations filled their war-waging roles awkwardly, and each displeased the other with its behavior. Indeed, the generational cycle has significantly influenced how Americans have acted during and after every major war in their history. Which wars occurred in comparable constellational moods? The Revolution and World War II (Crisis eras). The War of 1812 and Korea (Outer-Driven eras). The French and Indian War and World War I (Inner-Driven eras). What many historians consider the nation's most misguided wars— the Spanish-American and Vietnam—were waged during the social turmoil of Awakening eras. These parallels are instructive. They suggest how fortunate America may have been that the world's hour of fascist peril came when it did, and not a quarter century earlier or later.

Wars and other secular crises are triggered from without, spiritual awakenings from within. Less dependent on outside events, spiritual awakenings are almost entirely endogenous to the generational cycle. The specific year of their emergence may hinge on political events (as in 1621), economic conditions (1886), a war (1967), or simply an overdose of heroic fathers (1734 and 1822). The examples of the Awakeners in the 1730s and Transcendentals in the 1820s show how, sooner or later, these awakenings will arise even in the absence of specific historical sparks. We can reasonably conclude that the Puritans would eventually have erupted without their ostracism (though not necessarily by sending offshoots to America), Transcendentals without abolitionism, Missionaries without Haymarket and agrarian revolt, and Boomers without Vietnam and urban riots. Put simply, Idealist generations are nurtured to burst forth spiritually upon coming of age. When they do, they awaken other generations along with them.

The generational cycle is deterministic only in its broadest outlines; it does not guarantee good or bad outcomes. Each generation has flaws, and each constellational mood comes with dangers. The Missionary generation could have produced a zealot President (Mitchell Palmer, for instance) who, in turn, might have touched off a socialist insurrection. Instead, it produced the principled if inflexible Herbert Hoover and later—for the darkest hour—Franklin Roosevelt. And notwithstanding all the deserved admiration Americans bestow on the memory of Lincoln, his generation triggered the one major crisis in American history for which it is easy to imagine a better outcome for everyone—Union, Confederate, and slave. In its tragedy, the Civil War offers an important normative lesson for all generations alive today. The cycle provides each generation with a location in history, a peer personality, and a set of possible scripts to follow. But it leaves each generation free to express either its better or its worse instincts, to choose a script that posterity may later read with gratitude or sorrow.

Recall our discussion in Chapter 2 where we first discovered the generational diagonal. In Figures 2-2 and 2-3, the eras between the first two and last two columns (1920–1942 and 1964–1986) roughly encompass America's most recent moments of secular crisis (1932–1945) and spiritual awakening (1967–1980). Note that the adjectives match those in our four-part typology of generations. When we combine all the generational names, types, and adjectives, we see the diagonals shown in Figure 4-3. Note also that the "aligned" dates shown here, each exactly twenty-two years from the next, do not coincide perfectly with actual generational boundaries. As we shall see in the next chapter, the actual aligned dates (when the last cohort of each new generation is born) are 1924, 1942, 1960, and 1981. Remember, neither a generation nor a constellational era is always precisely twenty-two years long.

This is the generational cycle as it has unfolded during the first eight decades of the twentieth century. In the second and fourth columns, we see the Crisis and Awakening constellations with which we began the chapter. Reading along the diagonal, lower left to upper right, we can identify the connections between social moments and peer personality.

What would we see if we extended this chart to the left, through four centuries? The dynamics of the generational cycle suggest we should find much the same pattern—of constellational eras and generational types both. Let's now take a look at what actually has happened in American history—with eighteen generations in five cycles. We shall find that, in all but the Civil War Cycle, the pattern has held.

FIGURE 4–3

The Generational Diagonal in the Twentieth Century

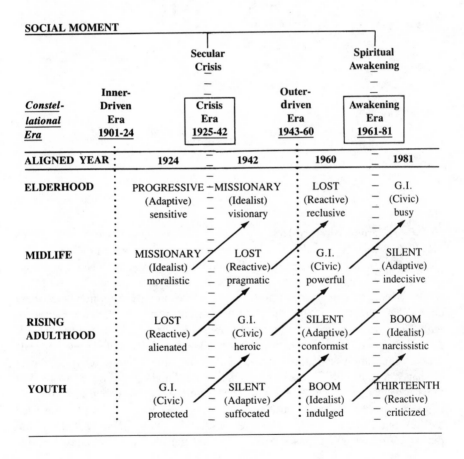

SOCIAL MOMENT				
		Secular Crisis		Spiritual Awakening
Constel- lational Era	Inner- Driven Era 1901-24	Crisis Era 1925-42	Outer- driven Era 1943-60	Awakening Era 1961-81
ALIGNED YEAR	1924	1942	1960	1981
ELDERHOOD	PROGRESSIVE (Adaptive) sensitive	MISSIONARY (Idealist) visionary	LOST (Reactive) reclusive	G.I. (Civic) busy
MIDLIFE	MISSIONARY (Idealist) moralistic	LOST (Reactive) pragmatic	G.I. (Civic) powerful	SILENT (Adaptive) indecisive
RISING ADULTHOOD	LOST (Reactive) alienated	G.I. (Civic) heroic	SILENT (Adaptive) conformist	BOOM (Idealist) narcissistic
YOUTH	G.I. (Civic) protected	SILENT (Adaptive) suffocated	BOOM (Idealist) indulged	THIRTEENTH (Reactive) criticized

Chapter 5

THE CYCLE
IN AMERICA

One afternoon in April 1689—as the American colonies boiled with rumors that King James II was about to shackle them into slavery—the King's hand-picked governor of New England, Sir Edmund Andros, marched his troops menacingly through Boston to let the locals know their place. The future of America looked grim. Yet just at that moment, seemingly from nowhere, there emerged on the streets "the figure of an ancient man," a "Gray Champion" with "the eye, the face, the attitude of command." The old man planted himself directly in front of the approaching British soldiers and demanded they stop. His dress, "combining the leader and the saint," and "the solemn, yet warlike peal of that voice, fit either to rule a host in the battlefield or be raised to God in prayer, were irresistible. At the old man's word and outstretched arm, the roll of the drum was hushed at once, and the advancing line stood still." Inspired by that single act, the people of Boston roused their courage and acted. Within the day, Andros was deposed and jailed, and the liberty of colonial America was saved.

"Who was this Gray Champion?" asks Nathaniel Hawthorne at the end of this story in *Twice-Told Tales*. No one knew, except that he was once one of the fire-hearted young Puritans who first settled New England a half century earlier. Later that very evening, just before he disappeared, he was seen embracing the 85-year-old Simon Bradstreet, a kindred spirit and one of the very few original Puritans still alive. "I have heard," adds Hawthorne, "that whenever the descendants of the Puritans are to show the spirit of their sires, the old man appears again.''

One such moment arrived, of course, during the revolutionary summer of 1775—when elder Americans once again appealed to God, called the young to war, and dared the hated enemy to fire. And indeed, notes Hawthorne, ''when eighty years had passed,'' the Gray Champion walked once more. ''When our fathers were toiling at the breastwork on Bunker's Hill, all through that night the old warrior walked his rounds. Long, long may it be ere he comes again! His hour is one of darkness, and adversity, and peril. But should domestic tyranny oppress us, or the invaders' step pollute our soil, still may the Gray Champion come. . . .''

Hawthorne did not say who the next Gray Champion would be or when he would return—though perhaps he should have been able to tell. Hawthorne wrote this stirring legend in 1837 as a young man of 33. Had he counted another eight or nine decades forward from Bunker Hill, he might have guessed that the next Gray Champions would come from among his own peers—a generation seared young by God and destined late in life to face an hour of ''darkness, and adversity, and peril.'' Hawthorne would someday learn their names: John Brown, damning the unrighteous from his scaffold and condemning them to rivers of blood; General William Tecumseh Sherman, scorching the earth of Georgia with ''the fateful lightning of His terrible swift sword'' while ''His truth is marching on''; or Robert E. Lee, thrusting out his authoritative baton and sending thousands of young men to die before Cemetery Ridge.

Moving ahead yet another eight or nine decades, America once again saw the Gray Champion return—an aging, principled generation pursuing its ''Rendezvous with Destiny.'' Many Americans alive today can recall the unflinching demeanor of Douglas MacArthur, Henry Kaiser, George Marshall—and, above all, Franklin Delano Roosevelt.

In each of America's decisive moments of secular crisis—the Glorious Revolution of 1689, the American Revolution, the Civil War, and the twin emergencies of the Great Depression and World War II—this society has witnessed the cyclical return of a special breed of elder, a very different type from the outer-focused, bustling ''senior citizens'' of the 1970s and 1980s. At each of these four history-turning moments, America turned for guidance to aging Idealists, spiritual warriors possessed of strong inner vision, patriarchs commanding the respect and obedience of their juniors. *All four* of these generations of patriarchs had previously been young adults during an era of spiritual awakening; *none* of them had come of age facing a secular crisis even remotely similar to the one they faced as grandparents.

In Chapter 4, we demonstrated how Idealist elders arrive once every generational cycle, in what we call a ''Crisis constellation.'' We also described how the three other constellations produce very different moods and events. In this chapter, we trace this cycle through four centuries of American history, from the 1580s through the 1980s. The model fits: From the first New World colonies to the present day, with only one interruption, American history has pulsed to the rhythm of the generational cycle.

Eighteen American Generations

All things have a beginning, and so must the story of American generations.

We start with the European cohort-group of 1584 through 1614. We call it the "Puritan Generation." This group amounts to about 25,000 persons (almost all of them English, plus a few Dutch settlers) and includes the vast majority of the first Old World immigrants to the Atlantic seaboard, the edge of what would someday become the United States.

To be sure, a scattering of earlier-born immigrants came to this territory. But their number was small—certainly fewer than a thousand—and the majority were fishermen, explorers, and adventurers who had no intention of staying. Of the earlier-born immigrants who did plan to settle permanently, most were soon massacred (at Roanoke), forced by hardship to flee back home (from Kennebec, Maine), or killed in a few months by disease (in early Jamestown). The scant evidence suggests that no more than one hundred persons born before 1584 came, settled, and survived more than five years—of whom perhaps only two or three dozen were lucky enough to find spouses and bear children. The 25,000 members of the Puritan Generation, on the other hand, consisted almost entirely of permanent settlers—of whom between 7,500 and 10,000 survived and bore children in the New World, often in large families. Quite simply, the numerical contrast between all pre-1584 cohorts and the Puritan Generation is overwhelming.

Demographic importance is not the only reason we fix our first birthyears around these dates. The Puritan Generation also possesses all the striking attributes of an *Idealist-type* generation. As an English-born cohort-group, it came into the world just after a secular crisis (a great war with Spain), grew up as children under the midlife tutelage of Civic-like Elizabethans, came of age triggering one of the most awesome spiritual awakenings known to Europe or the New World, and, after several decades in America, aged into the elder persona of the "Gray Champion."

Raised in the Old World, the Puritan Generation assumed much of its distinct personality through self-selecting emigration to America. Yet even their peers who stayed in Europe displayed a stunning concentration of radical, inner-fixated hilosophers—the likes of Thomas Hobbes (born in 1588, the same year as John Winthrop) and René Descartes (born eight years later). Entirely apart from any consideration of America, the Spanish generations writer José Ortega y Gasset identifies precisely these two birthyears as the center of what he considers a "decisive generation," the very first generation of "the Modern Age" in western civilization.

Starting with the Puritans and applying the methods discussed in Chapter 3 to all later cohorts in American history, we locate a total of eighteen generations, their birthyear periods stretching in an unbroken series from 1584 to the present day. We group them into five generational cycles—each beginning with an Idealist-type generation and concluding with an Adaptive type. The first four American generations, comprising the Colonial Cycle, remained literally "colonial" throughout their lifecycles. All four included large proportions of immigrants and were significantly influenced by the shifting personalities of their Old World contemporaries. Only when we reach number five—the "Awakeners," the Idealist trigger of the new Revolutionary Cycle—do we encounter the first truly American generation whose parents were mostly native-born and whose personality took shape without much assistance from social or cultural forces from abroad. This Awakening Generation was also the first to include a significant number who, late in life, became citizens of the United States.

Next come the remaining generations of the Revolutionary Cycle and Civil War Cycle, all fully ancestral. Then, in the Great Power Cycle, we find our first present-day survivors, including all Americans who reached age 48 by the dawn of 1991. Lastly, we arrive at the Millennial Cycle, whose members are still arriving by birth and immigration. Altogether, some 440 million American nationals (or colonists) have ever lived, four-sevenths of whom are alive today. The population of each cycle is as follows:

Colonial Cycle: 600,000 people
Revolutionary Cycle: 8,000,000 people
Civil War Cycle: 50,000,000 people
Great Power Cycle: 200,000,000 people
Millennial Cycle: 180,000,000 people (340,000,000 projected by 2025)

Figure 5-1 lists the eighteen American generations by cycle, type, and birthyear cohorts, along with the name of one of the generation's best-known public figures.

Looking carefully at Figure 5-1, we can recognize the patterns we identified in Chapters 3 and 4:

• *Generational boundaries*. The first cohort of each of the five Idealist generations was born during or immediately after a secular crisis. For the Puritans, the birthyears start four years prior to the culminating English victory over the Spanish Armada; for the Awakeners, twelve years after the Glorious Revolution; for the Transcendentals, three years after the ratification of the U.S. Constitution; for the Missionaries, one year before the start of the Civil War; and for the Boomers, just after the turning point of World War

FIGURE 5–1
Eighteen American Generations

CYCLE	GENERATION	TYPE	BIRTHYEARS	SAMPLE MEMBER
Colonial:	Puritan	Idealist	1584-1614	John Winthrop
	Cavalier	Reactive	1615-1647	Nathaniel Bacon
	Glorious	Civic	1648-1673	Cotton Mather
	Enlightenment	Adaptive	1674-1700	William Shirley
Revolutionary:	Awakening	Idealist	1701-1723	Benjamin Franklin
	Liberty	Reactive	1724-1741	George Washington
	Republican	Civic	1742-1766	Thomas Jefferson
	Compromise	Adaptive	1767-1791	Andrew Jackson
Civil War:	Transcendental	Idealist	1792-1821	Abraham Lincoln
	Gilded	Reactive	1822-1842	Ulysses Grant
	Progressive	Adaptive	1843-1859	Theodore Roosevelt
Great Power:	Missionary	Idealist	1860-1882	Franklin Roosevelt
	Lost	Reactive	1883-1900	Dwight Eisenhower
	G.I.	Civic	1901-1924	John Kennedy
	Silent	Adaptive	1925-1942	Walter Mondale
Millennial:	Boom	Idealist	1943-1960	Newt Gingrich
	Thirteenth	Reactive	1961-1981	Tom Cruise
	Millennial	Civic (?)	1982-	Jessica McClure

II. Similarly, we can link the first birthyear of each Civic generation with the completion (or afterglow) of historic eras of spiritual awakening: 1648, 1742, 1901, and 1982.

• *Length of generations.* The cohort lengths of all seventeen completed American generations range from 17 to 33 years and average 23.4 years. The first two Colonial Cycle generations were 31 and 33 years long, respectively, and were shaped mostly by irregular bursts of immigration to small and isolated American settlements. Afterward, only one generation is longer than 26 years, and the average length drops to 22.3 years. This average roughly matches the 22-year span we postulated (in Chapter 3) between birth and the typical coming-of-age moment.

• *The two-stroke rhythm.* All generations appear in an alternating sequence of dominant (Idealist or Civic) and recessive (Reactive or Adaptive) lifecycles with only one exception: the two back-to-back recessives (Gilded and Progressive) during the Civil War Cycle.

- *The four-type cycle.* The four generational types appear in a fixed sequence: from Idealist to Reactive to Civic to Adaptive—again with the single exception of the Civil War Cycle, where a Civic type is missing.

- *Cycles and history.* Timed to the alternating rhythm of awakenings and crises, each cycle roughly matches a discrete historical epoch in American history, with a crisis era at its approximate midpoint. When we move from the dawn of one awakening to the dawn of the next (a period roughly extending from the coming-of-age of first-wave Idealists through the coming-of-age of last-wave Adaptives), we traverse a well-defined period. Four of these periods have already been completed: Colonial (1621–1733), Revolutionary (1734–1821), Civil War (1822–1885), and Great Power (1886–1966). The fifth— Millennial—cycle began in 1967 and is still underway. The first four cycles have averaged eighty-nine years in length. The three-generation Civil War Cycle, only sixty-four years long, is considerably shorter than the average.

To our knowledge, we are the first to define, locate, and name the entire sequence of American generations. Beginning with the Lost, the reader may recognize several generations whose consensus names we have adopted. Except for one well-known case, no generation has ever been given precise cohort boundaries. That one exception, of course, is the so-called "Baby Boom" generation, which demographers often define as a cohort-group spanning the high-fertility years of 1946 through 1964. We fix its boundaries a few years earlier— to fit our criteria for peer personality, not the fecundity of the Boomers' parents. Also, we toss out the "Baby" and leave the "Boom," a more appropriate name for a generation now entering midlife.

We are not the first to claim that a generational sequence is an effective means of interpreting American history. Working separately, four scholars have suggested loose generational divisions that closely approximate the boundary lines we set. In 1925, historian Arthur Schlesinger described eight generations, from Liberty to Missionary, where we find seven. In 1976, Daniel Elazar, a political scientist at Temple University, found eleven generations over the Awakener-to-13er span, where we identify thirteen. In 1978, Harvard government professor Samuel Huntington listed eight generations that roughly match our eight from Republicans through G.I.s. And in a superb capsule summary of American political generations written in 1976, Brandeis historian Morton Keller identified eleven generations where we see eleven, stretching from the Liberty through the Boom.

Despite this close fit, there remains an important difference between our approach and what others have written about American generations. Most scholars have defined generations largely in terms of *public activity* during rising adulthood and midlife. Instead, we look at their entire lifecycles, examine their peer personality during each phase of life, and evaluate their private as well as public behavior.

In Chapter 4, we explained how social moments—secular crises and spiritual awakenings—lie at the core of the generational cycle. Now that we have identified five cycles of American generations, let's see how they line up with the sequence of crises and awakenings that have in fact occurred. Figure 5-2 shows this rhythm for the past five centuries. The first two social moments (the Reformation Awakening and the Armada Crisis) shaped the peer personalities of the immediate English-born ancestors of the Puritan Generation. The next nine (beginning with the Puritan Awakening) have all occurred during the lifecycles of the eighteen American generations.

As Figure 5-2 indicates, social moments can run from about one to two decades in length. Toward the end of each, there typically occurs a climactic event, a specific episode when the social moment reaches maximum emotional impact. During secular crises, this may be an event that energizes (Pearl Harbor Sunday in 1941, or the colonial Glorious Revolution in 1689), turns the tide (Gettysburg in 1863), or culminates an epoch of institution-building (the ratification of the U.S. Constitution in 1789). During spiritual awakenings, this climax is typically an event that marks a decisive reaction against a euphoric tide of truth-seeking and values experimentation: the sudden end of the radical Great Migration to New England in 1640; the orthodox counterattack against the Great Awakening in 1743; the economic Panic of 1837; or the election of Ronald Reagan in 1980. When such peak events occur, a social moment can suddenly shape cohort-groups into well-defined generations according to their respective phases of life. Alternatively, since the entire duration of a social moment can make a deep impression on youths in their late teens and mid-twenties, it can shape the entire generation as it comes of age.

Figure 5-2 shows the intervals between the end of one social moment to the end of the next. The intervals are not identical, partly because the generational bonding process can widen or narrow the exact length of the intervals between social moments. For example, the powerful influence of last-wave G.I.s (on earlier-born peers) and first-wave Boomers (on later-born peers) helped to narrow the interval between the World-War-II-era crisis and the Boom Awakening. The average interval is forty-four years, matching the forty-four-year span for two phases of life. The somewhat longer intervals come early, where we notice somewhat longer generations. The single and telling exception is the twenty-eight-year interval before the Civil War Crisis, precisely where we observe a truncated, three-generation cycle.

Now let's take a closer look at these two kinds of social moments.

Secular Crises

An important coincidence lies at the heart of American history, a coincidence familiar to most historians. The timespans separating the four pivotal events of

FIGURE 5-2
Social Moments in American History

Years from End of Crisis to End of Awakening	SPIRITUAL AWAKENING	Years from End of Awakening to End of Crisis	SECULAR CRISIS
	(1517-1539)	49 years	(1580-1588)
Pre-Colonial Period			
	Reformation Awakening		Defeat of Spanish Armada
52 years	(1621-1640)	52 years	(1675-1692)
Colonial Cycle			
	Puritan Awakening		Glorious Revolution
51 years	(1734-1743)	46 years	(1773-1789)
Revolutionary Cycle			
	Great Awakening		American Revolution
48 years	(1822-1837)	28 years	(1857-1865)
Civil War Cycle			
	Transcendental Awakening		Civil War
38 years	(1886-1903)	42 years	(1932-1945)
Great Power Cycle			
	Missionary Awakening		Great Depression & World War II
35 years	(1967-1980)		
Millennial Cycle			
	Boom Awakening		

American history almost exactly match. *Exactly eighty-five years passed* between the first Confederate shot on Fort Sumter and Pearl Harbor Day. Back up the story, and note that *eighty-five years also passed* between Fort Sumter and the Declaration of Independence. (Or, as President Lincoln noted, "Four score and seven years" separate the first Fourth of July from the Battle of Gettysburg.) Back up still further, and note that *another eighty-seven years passed* between the Anglo-American "Glorious Revolution" of 1689 and Independence Day. Preceding the Glorious Revolution by a slightly longer period—*ninety-nine years*—was the epochal victory of the English navy over the Spanish Armada.

All five events marked the culmination of swift and sweeping change in the secular world. Each surrounding era witnessed widespread fear for personal and social survival, collective unity in the face of peril, and sudden institutional change or innovation. Apprehension about the future reached a climax—and was followed (in all but the fourth case) by a sense of victory and the dawning of a bright new era. We list these five secular crises as follows:

- *The Armada Crisis* (1850–1588), in England, extended from the first overt hostilities between England and Spain through Drake's epic voyage in the *Golden Hind,* and ended with the English destruction of the Spanish invasion Armada. Sample rising-adult leaders: Sir Walter Raleigh, Francis Bacon, Sir Philip Sydney.

- *The Glorious Revolution Crisis* (1675–1692), in the American colonies, extended from King Philip's War and Bacon's Rebellion through the American rebellions against James II, and ended about the time of the Salem witch trials. Sample rising-adult leaders: Cotton Mather, John Wise, Peter Schuyler.

- *The American Revolution Crisis* (1773–1789), in the American colonies and states, extended from the Boston Tea Party through the Declaration of Independence and ended with the ratification of the United States Constitution and the inauguration of President Washington. Sample rising-adult leaders: Thomas Jefferson, James Madison, John Marshall.

- *The Civil War Crisis* (1857–1865), in the United States, extended from the *Dred Scott* decision, the great Kansas debates, and the fragmentation of the Democratic Party, and ended with Lee's surrender and Lincoln's assassination. Sample rising-adult leaders: Ulysses Grant, Stonewall Jackson, Andrew Carnegie.

- *The Great Depression–World War II Crisis* (1932–1945), in the United States, extended from the bleakest depression year and Franklin Roosevelt's election and ended with VJ-Day. Sample rising-adult leaders: John Kennedy, Robert Oppenheimer, Walt Disney.

FIGURE 5-3
Crisis Constellations

PHASE OF LIFE	SECULAR CRISES			
	GLORIOUS REVOLUTION (1675–1692)	**AMERICAN REVOLUTION** (1773–1789)	**CIVIL WAR** (1857–1865)	**GREAT DEPRESSION WORLD WAR II** (1932–1945)
ELDER:	PURITAN (Idealist) *Simon Bradstreet*	AWAKENING (Idealist) *Samuel Adams*	COMPROMISE (Adaptive) *James Buchanan*	MISSIONARY (Idealist) *Franklin Roosevelt*
MIDLIFE:	CAVALIER (Reactive) *Increase Mather*	LIBERTY (Reactive) *George Washington*	TRANSCENDENTAL (Idealist) *Abraham Lincoln*	LOST (Reactive) *Dwight Eisenhower*
RISING:	GLORIOUS (Civic) *Cotton Mather*	REPUBLICAN (Civic) *Thomas Jefferson*	GILDED (Reactive) *Ulysses Grant*	G.I. (Civic) *John Kennedy*
YOUTH:	ENLIGHTENMENT (Adaptive) *Elisha Cooke, Jr.*	COMPROMISE (Adaptive) *Dolley Madison*	PROGRESSIVE (Adaptive) *Booker T. Washington*	SILENT (Adaptive) *Sandra Day O'Connor*
CYCLE:	Colonial	Revolutionary	Civil War	Great Power

In each of these periods of secular crisis, public institutions suddenly strength-ened—sometimes with the help of emergency powers—as people of all ages banded together and gave absolute priority to the protection and survival of their larger community. During and shortly after these periods, leaders reshaped public institutions beyond earlier recognition. History turned, decisively.

Figure 5-3 identifies the generational constellations of each Crisis era, ex-cluding the precolonial Armada Crisis.

The constellational pattern is unmistakable. In every secular crisis except the Civil War, America had old Idealists, midlife Reactives, rising-adult Civics, and child Adaptives. Picture the peer personalities of each generational type, at its respective phase of life:

- *Idealist elders* providing principle and vision;
- *Reactive midlifers* understanding how the real world functions, and leading accordingly;
- *Civic rising adults,* smart and organized, doing their duty; and
- *Adaptive youths* emulating adults and making relatively few demands.

This is the optimal generational lineup for overcoming social emergencies, attacking unsolved problems, waging whatever war may be deemed necessary, and achieving a brighter future for the soon-to-be-born (Idealist) children of the next cycle. Elders bring wisdom, midlifers savvy, rising adults cooperation, and children silence. The resolute order-givers are old, the dutiful order-takers young. This is a constellation of action, not reflection. People become pragmatic, community-oriented, and more risk-averse in public and private life. The dis-tinctions between sex roles widen, and the protection of children grows to max-imum intensity. The crisis leaves a heavy footprint on the remaining lifecycle of every generation then living—especially the Civic, who thereafter assume a hubris born of triumph, a belief in community over self, and a collective con-fidence in their own achievements that their elders and juniors can never match.

To propel the generational cycle in this manner, *a secular crisis must end with triumph*. This happened in every cycle but one: the Civil War. By no means does this anomaly contradict the cycle; instead, it offers important lessons about how generational history can turn out well—or badly.

The Civil War Anomaly

We have already observed that the Civil War Cycle lacks a Civic-type gen-eration. At sixty-four years, this cycle is fully seventeen years shorter than any other. A mere twenty-eight years separate the end of the Civil War Crisis from the end of the preceding (Transcendental) awakening. What happened?

First, the crisis came early. The initial year of the crisis came fifty-one years after the middle birth cohort of the Transcendental (Idealist) generation. The other crisis periods began seventy-six, sixty-two, and sixty-one years after the middle Idealist birthyear. This ten-to-fifteen-year difference (the equivalent, roundly, of half a phase of life) is quite significant. Consider the 1920s, when Franklin Roosevelt's midlife Missionary Generation was still crusading for its great Prohibition "experiment" and the rising-adult Lost had yet to emerge from alienation and pleasure-seeking. Suppose a combination of depression and global fascism had hit then. Very likely, the national mood would have been more fragmented, public action less decisive. Likewise, imagine what form the American Revolution might have taken had it occurred before the Stamp Act riots of 1765—and what sort of Constitution might have been written by midlife Awakener zealots or hard-luck Liberty young adults, rather than by confident and public-minded Republicans. In effect, these odd hypotheticals point to what happened in the Civil War, when a still-zealous Transcendental generation congealed a crisis in midlife. Picture some facsimile of the Civil War waged fifteen years later—with Transcendentals more self-controlled as elder stewards, the Gilded less daring as midlife leaders, and Progressives more effective as rising-adult order-takers. The generational cycle suggests that the crisis would have been resolved with far less tragedy.

Second, the three adult generations allowed their more dangerous peer instincts to prevail. Following the failed efforts of Henry Clay, Daniel Webster, and John Calhoun to avert war, the elderly Compromisers of the Buchanan era were unable to rise above empty process and moral confusion. The Transcendental Generation split not just into two competing factions, but into two self-contained, mutually exclusive societies. Transcendental leaders—the likes of Abraham Lincoln, William Sherman, Thaddeus Stevens, Jefferson Davis, and Julia Ward Howe—were, as a generation, unable to resist waging war (and peace) with ruthless, apocalyptic finality. The younger Gilded never outgrew an adventurer's lust for battle or an easily bruised sense of personal honor—never, that is, until the war was over. These three adult generations steered a very dangerous constellation, and together produced the nearest approximation of holocaust America has ever experienced. Place the Civil War Cycle alongside the generational calendar of its two neighboring cycles—Revolutionary and Great Power—and notice how the Civil War occurred roughly a decade before the Revolution and World War II, a decade after the French and Indian War and World War I. It combined the worst features of both: the colossal scale of the former two with the lasting bitterness of the latter two.

Third, the crisis came to an untriumphant end. Was the Civil War a failure? We need not answer the question yes or no, but simply observe that for each of the other secular crises on our list, we find it difficult to imagine a more uplifting finale than that which actually occurred. For the Civil War, we can easily imagine a better outcome. Yes, the Union was preserved, the slaves emancipated, and the industrial revolution fully unleashed. But consider the enormous cost: deep-rooted sectional hatred, the impoverishment and political exile of the South, the collapse of Reconstruction into the era of lynchings and Jim Crow, and the long delay that postwar exhaustion later imposed on most other social agendas, everything from antitrust policy and labor grievances to temperance and women's rights.

The political reaction of those alive at the time, moreover, indicates that many Americans did indeed attribute the painful finale (at least in part) to calamitous miscommunication between young and old. The Civil War was followed by the largest generational landslide in American history, in 1868, when voters tossed out aging Transcendental zealots for the fortyish Gilded. Afterward, no rising generation emerged to fulfill the usual Civic role of building public institutions to realize the Transcendentals' visions. Instead, the Gilded aged into a unique Reactive-Civic hybrid—and, in midlife, presided over a period of unusual cultural and spiritual staleness. Likewise, although the Progressives had been raised with a protective prewar nurture that prepared them to come of age as a Civic generation, they emerged from the Civil War scarred rather than ennobled. Acquiring little collective confidence as young adults, they left their future in the hands of the Gilded and developed a distinctly Adaptive peer personality.

Spiritual Awakenings

Having seen that America encounters a secular crisis roughly every ninety years, we now turn to the other kind of social moment that arrives roughly halfway in between: the spiritual awakening. Stepping ahead forty-two years from the Armada victory of 1588 brings us to 1630—a year of peaking religious enthusiasm in England when John Winthrop and his fellow zealots set sail to found a New Jerusalem in America. Moving forty-five years past the colonial Glorious Revolution of 1689 takes us to 1734—the year Jonathan Edwards touched off the Great Awakening in the Connecticut Valley. Similar intervals separate each of the remaining three secular crises from later episodes of widespread and tumultuous spiritual fervor.

Over the past two decades, several social and religious historians have explored the importance of these episodes. In his 1978 book *Revivals, Awakenings, and Reform,* William McLoughlin identifies five American "awakenings" roughly conforming to the intervals our cycle would suggest. McLoughlin defines awakenings as "periods of culture revitalization that begin in a general crisis of beliefs and values and extend over a period of a generation or so, during which time a profound reorientation in beliefs and values takes place." Building from anthropologist Anthony Wallace's theory of "revitalization movements," McLoughlin describes how, in a modern society, a spiritual awakening can "alter the world view of a whole people or culture." Over the intervening span of six to eleven decades, "times change; the world changes; people change; and therefore institutions, world views, and cultural systems must change." He also notes that each awakening episode was, in its own time, an update of the "individualistic, pietistic, perfectionist, millennarian ideology" which "has from time to time been variously defined and explained to meet changing experience and contingencies in our history."

Unlike an episode of secular crisis, when a real-world threat triggers disciplined collective action and sudden institutional change, an awakening is driven by sudden value changes and a society-wide effort to recapture a feeling of spiritual authenticity. The focus is not on institutions, but on the spirit. And the moment is not essentially public or collective (though it may spark crowds, hysteria, and violence), but personal and individual. An awakening brings to rising-adult Idealists what Robert Bellah has called "a common set of moral understandings about good and bad, right and wrong, in the realm of individual and social action." During the Reformation and Puritan Awakenings, these new "understandings" arose almost entirely in terms of religious dogma. Ever since, the focus has shifted by degrees toward the radical "isms" of the modern age. The underlying psychology of the awakening conversion, however, has remained much the same through subsequent centuries.

Like a crisis, an awakening leaves a permanent impression on the remaining lifecycle of every generation then alive and shapes the rising-adult generation with special force. Whereas a crisis empowers the rising-adult generation, an awakening endows it with a spiritual or ideological mission that stays with its members for life. Among the vanguard of an awakening, we always notice isolated or ambivalent midlife Adaptives (Desiderius Erasmus, William Brewster, Thomas Foxcroft, William Ellery Channing, John Dewey, and Charles Reich) who are quite aware that the movement's center of gravity is located in a younger generation. Yet the best-known leaders are typically first-wave Idealists, preaching to younger Idealists just coming of age—peer leaders like Martin Luther, John Winthrop, Jonathan Edwards, Ralph Waldo Emerson, William Jennings Bryan, and Angela Davis.

McLoughlin's five American "awakenings" correspond closely to the five "spiritual awakenings" as we define them. Other historians have located and named eras of historic spiritual upheaval at similar dates. Starting with the first surge of Reformation enthusiasm in the precolonial period, we list them as follows, naming each after the Idealist Generation whose coming-of-age youths were largely responsible for pushing it forward.

• *The Reformation Awakening* (1517–1539) in Europe, universally known as the "Reformation" and no doubt the best known of all awakenings in western history. Sample rising-adult leaders: Martin Luther, John Calvin, John Knox.

- *The Puritan Awakening* (1621–1640) in England, Scotland, and America, often called the "Puritan Awakening," also known as the era of "Puritan Enthusiasm" or "Revolutionary Puritanism." Sample rising-adult leaders who came to America: John Winthrop, John Cotton, Anne Hutchinson.

- *The Great Awakening* (1734–1743) in the American colonies, known at the time as "the Great and General Awakening" and referred to ever since as the "Great Awakening." Sample rising-adult leaders: Jonathan Edwards, George Whitefield, William Tennent.

- *The Transcendental Awakening* (1822–1837) in the United States, a loosely dated period known to most historians (and McLoughlin) as the "Second Great Awakening," also called the era of "Romantic Evangelicalism" and "Transcendental Idealism." Sample rising-adult leaders: Ralph Waldo Emerson, Nat Turner, Charles Finney.

- *The Missionary Awakening* (1886–1903) in the United States, called the "Third Great Awakening" by McLoughlin and a few others, also known as the age of "Reform," "Revivalism," and "Labor Radicalism." Sample rising-adult leaders: William Jennings Bryan, Jane Addams, W.E.B. DuBois.

- *The Boom Awakening* (1967–1980) in the United States, called the "Fourth Great Awakening" by McLoughlin, at times termed the "new transcendentalism," now generally referred to as the recent "Sixties," "Counterculture," or (especially) "Consciousness Revolution." Sample rising-adult leaders: Arlo Guthrie, Mark Rudd, Rap Brown.

Figure 5-4 identifies the generational constellations of each Awakening era, excluding the precolonial Reformation Awakening.

Once again, we see a repeating constellational pattern in all but the Great Power Cycle (which followed the Civic-less Civil War Cycle)—a pattern consisting of old Civics, midlife Adaptives, rising-adult Idealists, and young Reactives. Picture the peer personalities of each generational type, at its respective phase of life:

- *Civic elders* confidently running or overseeing institutions they once built around an earlier set of values;

- *Adaptive midlifers* feeling pulled in competing directions by more powerful generations on either side;

- *Idealist rising adults* experiencing spiritual conversion near the coming-of-age moment and cultivating implacable moral conviction; and

- *Reactive youths* too young to participate, left alone, urged to grow up quickly, and criticized as "bad."

FIGURE 5-4
Awakening Constellations

SPIRITUAL AWAKENINGS

PHASE OF LIFE	PURITAN AWAKENING (1621–1640)	GREAT AWAKENING (1734–1743)	TRANSCENDENTAL AWAKENING (1822–1837)	MISSIONARY AWAKENING (1886–1903)	BOOM AWAKENING (1967–1980)
ELDER:	Peers of William Shakespeare	GLORIOUS (Civic) James Blair	REPUBLICAN (Civic) James Monroe	GILDED (Reactive) John D. Rockefeller	G.I. (Civic) Richard Nixon
MIDLIFE:	Peers of John Donne	ENLIGHTENMENT (Adaptive) Cadwallader Colden	COMPROMISE (Adaptive) William Ellery Channing	PROGRESSIVE (Adaptive) Theodore Roosevelt	SILENT (Adaptive) Gloria Steinem
RISING:	PURITAN (Idealist) John Winthrop	AWAKENING (Idealist) Jonathan Edwards	TRANSCENDENTAL (Idealist) Ralph Waldo Emerson	MISSIONARY (Idealist) William Jennings Bryan	BOOM (Idealist) Jim Morrison
YOUTH:	CAVALIER (Reactive) Increase Mather	LIBERTY (Reactive) George Washington	GILDED (Reactive) Louisa May Alcott	LOST (Reactive) Harry Truman	THIRTEENTH (Reactive) Tom Cruise
CYCLE:	Colonial	Revolutionary	Civil War	Great Power	Millennial

This lineup of elder doers and rising-adult thinkers—very different from the Crisis constellation—rarely does well at large public undertakings. The trained order-takers are old, while the instinctive order-givers are young. Any collective effort (such as a major war) faces strong social obstacles. On the other hand, this constellation can generate great spiritual energy and unusual creativity in religion, letters, and the arts. During each Awakening era, we witness mounting frustration with public institutions, fragmenting families and communities, rising alcohol and drug abuse, and a growing tendency to take risks in most spheres of life. Sex-role distinctions decline, and the protection accorded children reaches a low ebb. Afterward, maturing Idealists retain the inner convictions borne of their awakening experience and (after a period of political dormancy) attempt to project and enforce their principles on the world around them. Where post-crisis rising-adult Civics exude confident optimism and rationality as they move into midlife, post-awakening Idealists steer the national mood toward pessimistic and portentous spiritualism.

To comprehend the generational cycle is to foresee where the cycle will turn as the future unfolds. It is to anticipate who the next "Gray Champion" will be—and when his next "hour of darkness, and adversity, and peril" will arrive. "Long, long may it be ere he comes again!" wrote Hawthorne. One purpose of this book is to help the reader foresee *how* long—and understand why.

Chapter 6

FROM PURITANS
TO MILLENNIALS
AND BEYOND

The year 1968 was not exactly the Year of the Baby. But amid the assassinations, riots, student strikes, Vietnam buildup, and rise of Richard Nixon, one of the highest-grossing movies of the year featured a baby: *Rosemary's Baby*. Watching Daddy sell a soon-to-be-born child to a witch's coven, many in the audience had to be thinking, "Please don't have this baby, abort it!" Over the next ten years, child demons proliferated across American movie screens: *The Exorcist, Exorcist II, Damien, Omen, Omen II, Omen III, It's Alive!, It Lives Again, Demon Seed*. Even when the film children of the 1970s were not slashing and hexing parents, they were pictured as hucksters (*Paper Moon*), prostitutes (*Taxi Driver*), molls and racketeers (*Bugsy Malone*), arsonists (*Carrie*), spoiled brats (*Willy Wonka and the Chocolate Factory*), or abandoned articles (*Kramer vs. Kramer*). Never in the age of cinema have producers and audiences obsessed over such a thoroughly distressing image of childhood. Compare this with the children featured in the Disney *Shaggy Dog* films of the 1950s: bright, well-meaning kids whom adults respected, kids any filmgoer knew would grow up to be interesting people. Or compare those 1970s-era child images with the cuddly-baby antidotes that began to appear in the mid-1980s—*Raising Arizona, Three Men and a Baby, Baby Boom,* and *Parenthood*—all featuring tots audiences felt like bundling in their arms and protecting.

Who occupied the early-childhood age bracket when these films were being made and viewed? Boomers during the smart-kid movie era of the 1950s; 13ers

97

during the witch-kid movie era of the 1970s; and Millennials during the precious-baby movie era that began in the mid-1980s. This was no coincidence. The 13er childhood years, roughly from the mid-1960s through the early 1980s, defined an era of unremitting hostility toward children. One of every four rental apartments banned children, a 50 percent increase over the Boomer child era. The homicide rate against children under age four more than doubled. Adults of fertile age doubled their rate of surgical sterilization. The number of legal abortions per year rose tenfold. Birth-control technology became a hot topic—as did the cost and bother of raising a child, seldom an issue when Boomers were small. Net tax rates for childless households remained steady, while rates for families with children rose sharply. The child poverty rate grew, while the poverty rate for those in midlife and elderhood fell. Tax revolts cut school funding substantially in California and other states, which made public-school teachers suffer seven consecutive years of reduced purchasing power. The proportion of G-rated films fell from 41 to 13 percent, and Walt Disney Studios laid off cartoonists. The nation financed a growing share of its consumption by piling up federal debt and other unfunded liabilities whose greatest burdens, adults realized, would someday fall on small children. Then, during the 1980s, many of these trends began stabilizing—and, in some cases, turning around.

The English language has no single word to describe what happened to the child's world in America through the Consciousness Revolution of the late 1960s and 1970s. The Germans do. They call it *Kinderfeindlichkeit*—a society-wide hostility toward children.

Has *Kinderfeindlichkeit* ever happened before in America? Yes, several times—though not in precisely the same ways, of course. These other "bad-child" eras came before movies, birth-control pills, and weekly U.S. Treasury auctions. But earlier generations of adults had ample ways of declaring a child generation unwanted. In the 1640s, Cavalier children were routinely "kidnapped" off the streets of London and sold in the Chesapeake colonies as quasi-slaves. In the late 1730s, most American colonists left Liberty kids to their own "wildness" and generally agreed with Jonathan Edwards that they were "infinitely worse than young vipers." During the Age of Jackson, Gilded youth were commonly regarded as self-seeking and savage, and were packed off to America's first "reform schools." In circa-1900 America, Lost children struggled to make their own way as streethawking vagabonds while elders expressed horror over their "juvenile delinquency." *All these were, like the 13th, Reactive generations.* In each case, adults considered the children who came before (Idealists) smarter and more worthy of freedom, and those who came after (Civics) better-behaved and more worthy of protection.

Over the past four centuries, Reactive generations have always been children at the worst possible times. Why? They have had the bad luck to be born during Awakening eras, years of young-adult rapture, self-immersion, and attacks on elder-built culture. Home and hearth are assaulted, not exalted. The generational constellations of these Awakening eras feature angry two-way dramas between Civic elders and Idealist rising adults, with Adaptives mediating between them. None of these older generations offers much comfort to society's Reactive newcomers.

Conversely, during the Crisis eras at the *other* end of the cycle, the constellation produces the opposite form of nurture: the suffocating overprotection of Adaptive children. Older generations exalt family and community over self, sternly guard the home, and deny children independence or adventure coming of age. The most recent such era occurred during the war years of the 1940s, when the last-wave Silent were kids. Back in the 1690s, 1780s, and 1860s, three earlier generations of Adaptive children were told to behave, be quiet, and be thankful to their elders for sacrifices made on their behalf.

The two dominant generational types spend their childhood years midway between these extremes of underprotection and overprotection. Civics grow up during eras when adult control is increasing, Idealists when it is decreasing. Figure 6-1 illustrates how, over time, childhood nurture oscillates with the rhythm of the generational cycle. The trends are not always as gradual as this sine wave might suggest. From time to time, abrupt shifts occur from one era to the next, often marking a generational division between one cohort-group and the next. As America moved into an Inner-Driven era in the early 1750s, for example, colonial towns suddenly moved to protect small Republican children from the violent, even deadly Halloween mischief practiced by Liberty kids in the 1740s.

FIGURE 6–1

Tendency in Child Nurture,
by Generational Type and Constellational Era

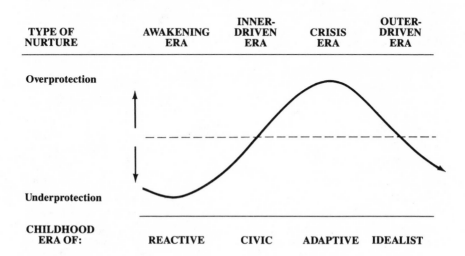

Around 1900, speeding wagons and streetcars were a leading cause of death among Lost city kids. Few adults tried to do much about it. But starting around 1905, as America again entered an Inner-Driven era, angry urban crowds began threatening to lynch drivers who ran over child G.I.s—and reformers began pulling children off the dangerous streets and into households and supervised playgrounds.

In Chapter 4, we described the pattern by which society's second-elder (mid-life) parental generation sets the nurturing style for any given generation of youth. Since the passage from youth to midlife takes a generation through two phases of life (half a cycle), midlife generations tend to raise the current generation of youth in *a manner opposite to that in which they themselves were raised*. Figure 6-2 clarifies this compensatory dynamic. Listing the two-apart parental and child generations in capital letters, we show how underprotected Reactives (say, the Lost) produce overprotected Adaptives (Silent), who then in turn raise underprotected Reactives (13ers). Civics (G.I.s), themselves raised under a tightening parental grip, relax the grip for Idealists (Boomers), who later retighten it around their own Civic (Millennial) children. Much the same pattern can be found in prior centuries—as, for example, in the tendency of Compromisers, themselves suffocated as children, to widen parental boundaries with their own later-born children, ultimately spawning the wild Gilded.

FIGURE 6–2

The Four Generational Types:
Child Nurture Relationships

	IDEALIST	REACTIVE	CIVIC	ADAPTIVE
Phase of Life during Awakening:	rising	youth	elder	midlife
Phase of Life during Crisis:	elder	midlife	rising	youth
TYPE OF PARENTS:	CIVIC & Adaptive	ADAPTIVE & Idealist	IDEALIST & Reactive	REACTIVE & Civic
TYPE OF CHILDREN:	Reactive & CIVIC	Civic & ADAPTIVE	Adaptive & IDEALIST	Idealist & REACTIVE
How It Is Nurtured:	relaxing	under-protective	tightening	over-protective
How It Nurtures:	tightening	over-protective	relaxing	under-protective

It would be misleading to attribute this compensating pattern of nurturing styles to deliberate parental intent. Instead, the pattern reflects the entire peer personality of the midlife parental generation—as well as the shifting mood of the constellational era. Reactives may well have their own laissez-faire upbringing in mind when they try to overprotect their Adaptive young. But they are also influenced in midlife by their exhausted and risk-averse outlook toward life in general and by the high priority that Crisis-era society places upon protecting the family at all cost. Opposite motives govern Adaptive parents. In part, their nurturing style reflects intended compensation for memories of their own dark-closet childhood, but midlife Adaptives are also enmeshed in a quest for personal liberation and are constantly reminded (by other Awakening-era generations) that everyone needs more social autonomy—small children included.

Childhood nurture plays a major role in shaping a generation's peer personality. Even as children, peer groups begin to create attitudes and expectations (within themselves and among elders) that determine how they will later fulfill social roles. By tracing any set of children forward along the generational diagonal, we can often observe how these attitudes and expectations later manifest themselves in adulthood. Recall the contrast between the castaway 10-year-olds of the 1740s and the precious 10-year-olds of the 1750s. Following these two groups forward to the 1780s, we can discern an equally stark contrast later on: between an independent and sometimes cynical or untrustworthy cadre of fiftyish Liberty leaders (from George Washington and John Adams to Ethan Allen and Benedict Arnold) and a cooperative, cheerful, and rational cadre of fortyish Republicans (from Thomas Jefferson and James Madison to Benjamin Rush and John Jay). Likewise, put the 4-year-olds of 1900 and 1915 on fast forward until the late 1960s. Among eminent leaders in the first group, we find shrewd seventyish Lost curmudgeons like Everett Dirksen and Sam Ervin; among the second, we recognize confident mid-fiftyish G.I. optimists like Hubert Humphrey and Ronald Reagan.

Childhood nurture alone does not stamp a generation for life. To define its peer personality and fix its cohort boundaries, a generation needs further contact with history, especially as it comes of age into rising adulthood. Other behavioral and attitudinal patterns—in youth and later phases of life—match the timing of our generational cycle. Like the different brands of child nurture received in youth and dispensed in midlife, these patterns all oscillate between extremes at opposite (two-apart) eras in the generational cycle.

Youths of the two dominant types (Idealist and Civic), for example, reveal the widest contrast in their symbolic affinity to mothers versus fathers. Young Idealists typically show the strongest attachment to mothers and the most conflict with fathers. Scholars have long illustrated the dynamics of oedipal behavior by drawing most of their examples from notable Idealists—Martin Luther and Oliver Cromwell, Abraham Lincoln and Franklin Roosevelt, even the "young radicals" studied by Kenneth Keniston and Lewis Feuer in the late 1960s. Again and again, from Puritans to Boomers, rising Idealists have given spiritual awakenings an anti-masculine flavor. Later in life, Idealist leaders commonly ascribe greater influence to their mothers. By contrast, the sharpest attacks on elder mother figures have come from rising Civics—from the anti-witch diatribes of James I and Cotton Mather to Philip Wylie's tirade against "momism" and "she-popery." Later in life, Civic leaders typically ascribe greater influence to their fathers.

Moving beyond youth, we see other striking patterns coincident with the generational cycle. For each of them we could draw a sine curve like the wave in Figure 6-1. For example:

- COMING OF AGE, Idealists are the most attracted to spiritual self-discovery and the least attracted to teamwork; Civics, the reverse. Reactives display the strongest desire for early independence and adventure; Adaptives, the weakest.

- In RISING ADULTHOOD, Idealists narrow the distinction between acceptable sex roles; Civics widen them. Reactives are the most risk-prone; Adaptives, the most risk-averse.

- In MIDLIFE, Idealists feel a growing pessimism about worldly affairs; Civics a growing optimism. Reactives tire from earlier bingeing and slow down; Adaptives break free from earlier conformity and speed up.

- In ELDERHOOD, Idealists are preoccupied with moral principle; Civics with secular achievement. Reactives typically live least comfortably relative to younger generations; Adaptives, most comfortably.

We spell out these phase-of-life oscillations in greater detail in Chapter 12, where we connect them with constellational eras and moods. Our point here is simply to demonstrate the breadth of life experience encompassed by the generational cycle. It is not just about the "history" of elections and wars. The cycle has at least as much to do with children and parents as it does with Presidents and generals.

Cycle Theories of American History

We are by no means the first to observe cycles in American history. Over the years, many scholars have been struck by the recurrent timing of certain kinds of trends or events. A few have explicitly connected these cycles with the concept of generational change; most have at least remarked that they coincide with a generational rhythm. Perhaps the two best-known modern American cycle theories are those advanced by Frank Klingberg and by the two Arthur Schlesingers, father and son. Both the Klingberg and the Schlesinger theories describe a two-stroke pendular movement between periods of activity and calm in public life.

In 1951, Klingberg suggested that American foreign policy since 1776 has alternated between "extroversion" (interventionism) and "introversion" (isolationism). Each period, he observes, lasts about twenty-three years—which makes the timing of his foreign policy cycle closely match the timing of our own cycle of generations and social moments. But where his two-part cycle registers two oscillations, our four-part cycle registers only one. For example, Klingberg takes the period of American interventionism extending from the Spanish-American War (1898) through World War I (1918) and equates it with the interventionism of the 1940–1965 "Pax Americana." Because Klingberg sees both spiritual awakenings and secular crises as *periods of activity,* his cycle does not differentiate between them. We, on the other hand, interpret these two periods in terms of very different generational constellations. The first, beginning at the end of an Awakening era, was a moralistic crusade urged by rising-adult Idealists and managed by equivocating Adaptives. The second, beginning at the end of a Crisis era, was an institutional framework for peace and prosperity urged by rising-adult Civics and managed by pragmatic Reactives. The purpose of interventionism, the nature of national leadership, and indeed the entire public mood differed substantially on each occasion.

The Schlesinger cycle is much like Klingberg's. In *Paths to the Present,* published in 1949, the elder Schlesinger suggested that American history follows a pendular movement between two public or political moods, later defined by Arthur, Jr., as a period of "public activity" and a period of "private interest" (or "conservative retrenchment"). Each period lasts about sixteen years, on average (with wide variations before 1900). In certain respects, the Schlesinger cycle has successfully predicted how popular attitudes toward government did in fact twist and turn over the postwar era: the mid-1940s surge toward conservatism, the late-1950s tilt toward liberalism, and the reemergence of Reagan-style conservatism in the mid-1970s. More recently, however, their cycle has stumbled. In the spring of 1988, Arthur Schlesinger, Jr., published an article entitled "Wake Up, Liberals, Your Time Has Come," predicting a resurgence of sixties-style liberalism over the next few years. To date, Schlesinger's prediction seems wide of the mark. One problem, in our view, is that a sixteen-year pendulum is too exact—and (unlike Klingberg's twenty-three-year pendulum) speeds the clock too fast.

A more basic limitation of the Schlesingers' approach is that, like Klingberg's, it focuses on a bipolar index of the national mood: the presence or absence of public activism. But what *kind* of activism? According to Arthur Schlesinger, Jr., the New Deal and the Great Society initiated two equivalent eras of hope and energy. According to our four-part generational cycle, we see two constellational eras that were in many ways the *opposite* of each other. The New Deal era invited outer-fixated rising adults (Civic G.I.s) to propel America to build a better world. That is just what they did—obediently and with great collective enthusiasm. The Great Society era, by contrast, invited inner-fixated rising adults (Idealist Boomers) to move the nation toward introspection and spiritual rebirth—certainly not toward building anything or obeying anybody. Consider what happened to the names themselves. "New Deal" became a symbol of elder vision and youthful achievement that G.I.s later spoke of with pride. "Great Society" became a symbol of elder hubris and youthful revolt that Boomers today recall with irony or even ridicule. After the fact, 25-year-old Boomers never came away from LBJ's "guns and butter" with anything like the community-spirited energy that 25-year-old G.I.s brought away from FDR's fireside chats. These are fundamental differences, the kind that cast a long shadow on history.

In *The Cycles of American History,* published in 1986, Arthur Schlesinger, Jr., agrees that "it is the generational experience that serves as the mainspring of the political cycle." But the formative experiences of politically active Americans around 1965 in no way resemble those when Roosevelt was first elected in 1932. Nor do the constellations during the two most recent conservative periods identified by Schlesinger. The first (the late 1940s and 1950s) was a time of conformist immersion in community, the second (the late 1970s and 1980s) of nonconformist immersion in self. If generations are indeed the "mainspring" for his cycle, Schlesinger is saying, in effect, that the rising generation of the 1980s (the Boomer "yuppies") were the political and social equivalent of Schlesinger's own generation of postwar G.I. heroes. Two more dissimilar sets of rising adults can scarcely be imagined.

The logical problem faced by two-stroke cycles, whether thirty-two or forty-six years in length, is that they imply that generations two apart will engage in very similar public behavior. That defies human nature. You can look through all of American history for an example of matching midlife-youth peer personalities, but you will not find any. This certainly did not happen between Missionaries and G.I.s, or between G.I.s and Boomers. Nor between the Lost and the Silent, or the Silent and the 13ers. Klingberg and the Schlesingers limit themselves to a two-stroke cycle (of dominant and recessive generations) perhaps because they focus exclusively on what are known as "political generations." Like Thomas Jefferson and so many others who have examined cycles and generations, they do not incorporate the entire lifespan into their theories.

There is nothing unprecedented about a historical cycle based, like our own, on the total lifecycle experience of cohort-group generations. As we explain in Appendix A, many have been there before us—with origins of our theory dating as far back as Homer and Ibn Khaldun. Over the last two centuries, eminent social philosophers from Auguste Comte and John Stuart Mill to José Ortega y Gasset and Karl Mannheim have endorsed a generational perspective on history that transcends politics alone. Nor are we the first to postulate a cycle revolving around four generational types. Two nineteenth-century writers, Émile Littré and Giuseppe Ferrari, identified such a cycle in modern European history. In the twentieth century, a Spanish sociologist and an American historian, Julián Marías and Samuel Huntington, have also identified elements of a four-part cycle.

Huntington's theory, designed specifically to explain the American experience, is an especially important antecedent to our own. What he calls his "IvI" ("Institutions versus Ideals") cycle lines up social moments exactly as we do—between eras of "creedal passion" in which new ideals emerge and periods of secular action in which ideals are institutionalized in public life. Within this sixty-to-ninety-year cycle, Huntington sees a sequence of "idealistic," "cynical," "complacent," and "hypocritical" attitudes—social moods that roughly describe our four constellational eras and reflect the coming-of-age personalities of our four generational types.

While these four writers reach what we consider to be essentially correct definitions of the cycle, none (including Huntington) has much to say about *why* it occurs, beyond general references to the rejuvenative nature of social change. Like Klingberg and the Schlesingers, they limit their discussion to political generations and focus on just two generations at a time (those occupying what we term the rising adulthood and midlife phases of life). They give little or no attention to the importance of a generation's nurturing and coming-of-age experiences, or to its behavior in old age. Accordingly, these writers have succeeded more in describing what the cycle is than in explaining its connection with the larger currents of social history.

The Predictive Record of the Generational Cycle

According to an ancient Chinese legend, two astronomers named Hi and Ho once failed to predict an eclipse of the sun—and were thereupon beheaded by the emperor. In 1989, the California earthquake caught Joan Quigley, Nancy Reagan's astrologer, completely by surprise in her San Francisco apartment—an oversight for which she was pummeled by sarcastic columnists. Fair enough. The acid test of any theory is its ability to forecast.

Unlike other cycle theorists, we make no claim that our generational cycle can predict which party will win what election, or whether a stock crash or war will occur in this or that year. Cycles that aim at such accuracy never work over time. Sooner or later, they don't even come close, because the historical observer who obsesses over accuracy typically refuses to examine the underlying (though imprecise) dynamics of social causation. The person who tries to predict when each ocean wave will break on the shore gets nowhere, but the person who thinks about high and low tides—well, he just might come up with a theory of considerable predictive power. We liken our theory more to the tide analogy.

FIGURE 6–3
The Timing of Social Moments and Cohorts

CYCLE	FIRST REACTIVE COHORT	SPIRITUAL AWAKENING	FIRST CIVIC COHORT	FIRST ADAPTIVE COHORT	SECULAR CRISIS	FIRST IDEALIST COHORT
Colonial	1615	1621–1640	—	—	1580–1588	1584
Revolutionary	1724	1734–1743	1648	1674	1675–1692	1701
Civil War	1822	1822–1837	1742	1767	1773–1789	1792
Great Power	1883	1886–1903	(no Civic)	1843	1857–1865	1860
Millennial	1961	1967–1980	1901	1925	1932–1945	1943

That is why we phrase our conclusions about the past (and visions of the future) not in terms of specific years, but in terms of constellational eras and generational phases of life.

Although we resist calibrating our conclusions to the exact year, our cycle does reveal a four-century record of strikingly consistent timing. In Figure 6-3, we show that every social moment has begun shortly after the first birthyear of a recessive-type generation—that is, shortly after the beginning of the matching (awakening or crisis) constellational era. We also show that every social moment has ended near the first birthyear of a dominant-type generation.

Each of the nine social moments has started between 0 and 14 years after the first recessive (Reactive or Adaptive) birth. On average, they have started 6 years afterward, with an average margin of error of 3.0 years. At the other end, each social moment has ended between 9 years before and 5 years after the first dominant (Idealist or Civic) birth. On average, they have ended 1 year afterward, with an average margin of error of 4.1 years. This is remarkable timing, considering that each type of social moment (and the first birthyear of each generational type) occurs only once every 89 years.

Just as the timing of social moments is linked with the arrival of the first recessive birth cohort, so too is it linked with the aging of the dominant generations that propel and preside over them. Plotting the midpoint of Idealist and Civic generation birthyears against the arrival of social moments, Figure 6-4 reveals another consistent pattern.

Here we see the two-stroke dynamic underlying the rhythms Klingberg and the Schlesingers have seen in American history. Both types of dominant generations occupy roughly the same lifecycle stage when social moments begin. One is partway into rising adulthood, still straddling its coming-of-age "rite of passage." The other is partway into elderhood, still exercising its final leadership role before the ebb of old age. On average, social moments begin 18 years (and end 33 years) after the mid-cohort births of the younger dominant generation, with an average margin of error of 2.8 years. They begin 64 years (and end 77 years) after the mid-cohort births of the elder dominant generation, with an average margin of error of 7.7 years. As we would expect, the two types of dominant generations (Idealist and Civic) have exactly opposite phase-of-life relationships with the two types of social moments.

We can foresee future historians someday filling in the Millennial Cycle blanks in Figure 6-4 with numbers roughly comparable to those above it. Such prophecies are an important part of the message of this book. Again, projecting the future range of such numbers does not allow us to predict social moments with to-the-year accuracy. Since generational boundaries remain imprecise while a cohort-group is still young (especially when a social moment has yet to shape its peer personality), we cannot make calculations about the future as precisely as about the past. Still, the generational cycle shows a powerful recurring rhythm—and, with it, a powerful two-way relationship with history.

FIGURE 6–4

Age of Dominant Generations
at Start of Social Moments

CYCLE:	Mid-Idealist Births to Awakening	Mid-Civic Births to Awakening*	Mid-Civic Births to Crisis	Mid-Idealist Births to Crisis
Colonial	22 years	74 years	15 years	76 years
Revolutionary	22 years	68 years	19 years	62 years
Civil War	16 years	(no Civic)	(no Civic)	51 years
Great Power	15 years	55 years	20 years	61 years
Millennial	16 years	——	——	——
Average	18 years	65 years	18 years	66 years**

*Awakening of the next cycle
**Not including the Civil War Cycle

Looking for Analogues

Analogues are familiar to anyone who has ever talked about generations. We recall that the rise of John Kennedy in the early 1960s was heralded, by his admirers, as the dawn of a new "Augustan Age." In the late 1960s, college-age utopians were sometimes labeled "New Transcendentals"—and nowadays, values-obsessed 40-year-olds are often called "New Puritans." We hear some of today's fiftyish liberals labeling themselves "Progressives." Thirteeners are sometimes described as a "Lost" (or "New Lost") generation. Eras have analogues as well. Some of the most common decade pairings coincide with our matching constellations—the 1960s with the 1890s or 1830s, to mention one example.

Searching for analogues—recognizing which ones apply and understanding why—is precisely what makes history enjoyable and important. Its reader often wants to ask: How does *that* character or situation compare to any that *I* have come across? Over the next five chapters, where we present capsule biographies for America's eighteen generations, we expect the reader will want to ask such questions and to ponder how these collective life stories compare with his or her own life story and the life story of older or younger acquaintances. We urge our reader, when immersed in an ancestral generation, to recall its modern analogue (Puritan-Boomer or Lost-13th, for example) and, when reading about a modern generation, to reflect on its ancestral analogues.

Part II is organized by generational cycle, one chapter per cycle. We begin each chapter by showing how the social moments of a given cycle helped define the generational drama. We illustrate the age location of each generation with a diagram of "diagonals," whose geometry brings to mind how French sociologist François Mentré once likened generations to "tiles on a roof." These diagrams remind us that generational history is essentially three-dimensional—and that a chronological date is not a point, but rather a line that intersects evolving peer personalities at different phases of life. A single event in time, writes historian Wilhelm Pinder, is like "a depth sounding that we drop vertically through life developments"—a sounding that registers vast differences between how the world appears at a "depth" of age 10, 30, 50, or 70.

Within each chapter, we offer capsule biographies of the generations themselves. In describing lifecycles, we give equal weight to each phase of life (plus the critical coming-of-age experience between youth and rising adulthood). These biographies are suggestive sketches, not histories. We offer them to clarify the cohort boundaries, peer personality, age location, and lifecycle trajectory of each generation.

After traversing eighteen generations, we shall return in Part III to the patterns of the cycle. By then, we expect, the reader will have gained a deeper, more intuitive feel for what it means to belong to an "Adaptive" or "Idealist" generation or to live in an "Outer-Driven" or "Crisis" era. In Chapter 12, we construct analogues—for constellational moods, generational types, and endowment behavior. Finally, in Chapter 13, *we project these analogues into the future*. We explain what four centuries of generational history have to say about how the national mood will evolve in the decades to come, how each of today's living generations will mature through later phases of life, and what kinds of endowments each can be expected to leave for its heirs.

To stimulate thinking about analogues, we sort generations by type in Figure 6-5.

These analogues identify historical examples of generational types that match those alive today. They can help us answer questions like the following:

• What do the legacies of the Glorious and Republicans tell G.I.s about how they will ultimately be remembered—and tell all of us about what sense of community today's Millennial infants are likely to feel upon coming of age?

FIGURE 6–5
Generations, By Type

CYCLE	IDEALIST	REACTIVE	CIVIC	ADAPTIVE
Colonial	Puritan	Cavalier	Glorious	Enlightenment
Revolutionary	Awakening	Liberty	Republican	Compromise
Civil War	Transcendental	Gilded	——	Progressive
Great Power	Missionary	Lost	G.I.	Silent
Millennial	Boom	Thirteenth	Millennial	

• What do the old-age experiences of Enlighteners, Compromisers, and Progressives tell the Silent about the sense of connection with history they will feel at the end of their lives?

• What do the completed lifecycles of Puritans, Awakeners, Transcendentals, and Missionaries tell "draft-dodging" Boomers about whether (and why) they may someday send younger generations into battle?

• What do the stories of America's "bad child" Reactive generations—Cavaliers, Liberty, Gilded, and Lost—tell 13ers about what they can expect from a mistimed lifecycle?

• How does the endowment behavior of other Awakening eras compare with the narcissism associated with the recent Boom Awakening?

• What can the constellational moods of other Inner-Driven eras tell us about whether the consensus vision of the future will brighten or darken as America approaches the year 2000?

Historian Anthony Esler has commented how "the generational approach may, in fact, provide one of the royal roads to total history." Take a look at the fold-out chart preceding this chapter. In it, you will find a complete road map of the journey we are about to take—a journey through American history along the generational diagonal, from Puritans to Millennials and beyond.

Part II

THE
GENERATIONS

Chapter 7

THE COLONIAL CYCLE

"What a piece of work is man! How noble in reason! How infinite in faculties! In form and moving, how express and admirable! In action, how like an angel! In apprehension, how like a god!" So wrote William Shakespeare, whose creative life—from his first child in 1583 to his death in 1616—almost perfectly matches the birthyears of the Puritans, the first generation of Americans. Along with Shakespeare, such titanic peers as Francis Bacon, Walter Raleigh, Robert Cecil, Philip Sydney, and Christopher Marlowe represented the pantheon of midlife Elizabethans who raised the Puritans as children. They celebrated order, rationality, optimism, and expansion. As young soldiers, the fathers had triumphed over the most monstrous empire on earth, the Spanish Hapsburgs. In trade, they had transformed England into a global entrepôt of commerce. And in culture, they had brought the glory of the Renaissance north to their "Sceptred Isle."

The world of their fathers was not the only generational layer the young Puritans inherited. Most of these children could also look up at the less stolid, more picaresque world of their grandparents—peers of daring seadogs like Francis Drake and John Hawkins, and of the wily Queen Elizabeth and her master sleuth, Francis Walsingham. In the children's eyes, their Shakespearean fathers may have lost something by comparison. Looking farther up, many Puritans recognized great-grandparents who had come of age alongside Martin Luther and John Calvin and who had been burned at the stake as Protestant heretics.

Young Puritans heard these stories by word of mouth or read them in the gruesome *Book of Martyrs* by John Foxe, a best-seller for children in the early seventeenth century. Here we can be certain that the fathers suffered by comparison. Consider how the Puritans saw their fathers: worldly burghers and optimistic clerics, sliding comfortably into their fifties along with their witch-hating midlife peer King James I. Then consider how they might idealize their earlier ancestors: hundreds of world-rejecting prophets, piously refusing to recant as the smoke wafted up into their eyes. As they matured, the Puritans were fated to live a lifecycle having far more in common with such ancestors than with their own parents.

The style of nurture which produced the Puritans and the mood of the world in which they came of age were substantially determined by the generational constellation into which they were born. That constellation, in turn, was shaped by the social moments that occurred during the lifecycles of the Puritans' parents, grandparents, and great-grandparents. The first (a spiritual awakening) was the initial floodtide of Reformation enthusiasm in Europe; the second (a secular crisis) was a dramatic and epochal shift in the European balance of power, hinging on the English sea victory over the Hapsburg Armada.

Participating in these events were individuals who, taken collectively, reflect the four peer personalities of a precolonial "Reformation Cycle" of generations.

Preparing for the Puritans: The Reformation Cycle

The Reformation Cycle was triggered by an Idealist-like cast of rising adults, what many historians call "the Reformation generation." Nearly all of them were born between 1483 and 1509—including Martin Luther, John Calvin, Ulrich Zwingli, Ignatius Loyola, John Rogers, Nicholas Ridley, Thomas Cranmer, and John Knox. Next came the Reactive-like generation of Drake and Queens Elizabeth and Mary, born between 1510 and 1541, whose late wave reached midlife during the Armada Crisis. That historic struggle arrived just as Shakespeare's generation—confident, Civic-like youths born between 1542 and 1565—were coming of age. Describing the contrast between these second and third English peer groups, historian Anthony Esler calls the peers of Drake and Elizabeth "a burned-out generation" of risk-takers who "grew up in an age of ideological ferment" and later aged into "cool, cautious, and *politique* elders." By contrast, the younger peers of Shakespeare and Raleigh were "born at a uniquely favorable time," undertook "ambitious projects of breath-taking scope and grandeur," and ultimately aged into a "generation of overreachers." Esler has named them the "Generation of 1560"—which, in turn, was followed by a fourth, Adaptive-like generation born between 1566 and 1583—the anxious, sentimental (and upwardly mobile) peers of John Donne, Ben Jonson, and Sir John Davies.

Aligned with these four very different generations were two social moments representing the most significant turning points of English history during the sixteenth century:

- *The Reformation Awakening* (1517–1539), often regarded as the final curtain on the European Middle Ages, began in 1517 when Martin Luther tacked on the church door at Wittenberg his famous protest against Papal doctrine. Thus began two decades of religious and social upheaval—peasant uprisings, fanatical Anabaptist heresies, the sack of Rome, and the Protestant conversion of many German and Scandinavian princes. The uproar culminated with the anarchist Münster Rebellion of 1535 and John Calvin's arrival in Geneva the next year (after feeling what he called a "sudden conversion" at age 24). In England, the enthusiasm peaked at about the same time. King Henry VIII broke with the Papacy in 1534, and a "Reformation Parliament" confiscated vast Catholic estates through the late 1530s. The fervor ebbed after 1539, though dynastic wars and unrest continued throughout Europe. Many rising-adult leaders of the English Reformation, after maturing into midlife as dour and uncompromising prophets, were later executed by Henry VIII in the 1540s and by Queen Mary in the 1550s.

- *The Armada Crisis* (1580–1588) marked the climax of a long rivalry between the Spanish Hapsburg emperor Philip II and the Protestant queen of England Elizabeth. The crisis began in 1580, with England's alliance with the Netherlands, Philip's acquisition of Portugal, and Drake's return from a daring three-year voyage around the world—in a ship loaded with pirated Spanish treasure. In 1588, led by the fiftyish Drake and Hawkins, the English fleet destroyed Philip's invasion "Armada" and thereby established England as a growing naval and colonial power. During the following era of security and optimism, those who had celebrated heroic victory as coming-of-age soldiers—the younger courtiers, poets, merchants, scientists, and explorers serving their elder queen—ushered in the Elizabethan Renaissance, today remembered as the "Age of Shakespeare." By midlife, they set a prosperous stage for their "chosen" generation of disaffected children—some of whom would seek spiritual exile in the New World.

The Puritan Awakening in England would begin eighty-seven years after the Reformation's peak year of 1534—and forty-one years after Queen Elizabeth decided to test Spain's naval power in 1580.

The Colonial Cycle

Atop Gallows Hill near Salem, Massachusetts, on the morning of September 22, 1692, eight middle-aged New Englanders, seven women and one man, stood on a scaffold with nooses around their necks. Their crime: witchcraft. Near the foot of the scaffold gathered a crowd of persons of all ages. They ranged from 89-year-old Simon Bradstreet (the recent governor), to 61-year-old William Stoughton (the presiding judge at the witch trials), to 29-year-old Cotton Mather (the brilliant and energetic clergyman), to the "possessed" children in their early teens whose jerking and shrieking reminded everyone why the witches had to die. No one in the crowd was surprised by the horrible spectacle. Over the prior decade, New Englanders had lived through revolution, anarchy, war, and pestilence—all signs that their chosen community had broken its sacred "Covenant with God." Their ministers had warned them that witches would come next, and now the four generations of the COLONIAL CYCLE could witness the fulfillment of that prophecy.

- For Bradstreet's patriarchal PURITAN GENERATION (Idealist, then age 78 and over), the scene on Gallows Hill represented God's culminating judgment on His "Chosen Remnant"—and on the Puritans' own life mission. Over a half century earlier, working alongside such "visible saints" as John Winthrop and John Cotton, Bradstreet and his peers had forsaken their Elizabethan fathers, left England, and founded a holy community of love and reform in the New World. More recently, their utopia had been punished for its wayward offspring. By purging the witches, the handful of Puritans still alive hoped that God would finally put an end to these tribulations— and raise up a younger generation to greatness and glory. So it happened. The hangings that day turned out to be the last judicial executions for witchcraft in America. By the end of the century, calm had returned to the colonies, and the ancient tail of the Puritan Generation passed on in peace. Simon Bradstreet died in 1697—after residing in America for sixty-seven years, and after outliving his friend Winthrop by forty-eight years and his poetess wife Anne by twenty-five years. With him expired a legend.

- Stoughton's CAVALIER GENERATION (Reactive, age 45 to 77), having no such memories or hopes, watched with resignation. The witches about to die were their own age, as were the leading magistrates who condemned them. In their hearts, Cavaliers knew they all shared the guilt. Since childhood, they had always been told they were a "lost generation," that their spirit was "corrupt" and "unconverted." Their only escape was the stick

FIGURE 7–1
Colonial Cycle: Age Location in History

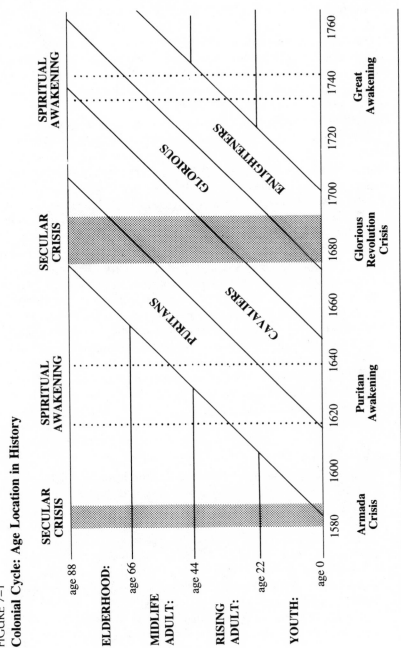

of silver, piece of land, or ship passage that could separate them from Puritan judgment. But when they were caught, this generation of traitors and rebels, predators and prey, rarely protested the punishment. More their style was the response of a Cavalier Virginian, William Drummond, when Puritan Governor William Berkeley informed him he would be hanged in half an hour: "What your honor pleases." No excuses. No righteous denial. Cavalier leaders like Stoughton, Increase Mather, and Joseph Dudley— men of brutal realism—would later take America over the threshold of the next century and into a new era of caution and stability. Chastened and mellowed, most Cavaliers were about to enter old age unthanked, forgiving their juniors as they had never been forgiven by their own elders.

• Cotton Mather's GLORIOUS GENERATION (Civic, age 19 to 44) looked on with impassive approval—a few of them, like young Cotton himself, scientifically inspecting the witches for damning, last-minute evidence of "maleficium." The Glorious were not suspected of sorcery and, unlike their next-elders, never imagined suspecting themselves. They had always lived up to the principles of their holy Puritan fathers, just as they had always shared their community's doubts about the shifty Cavaliers. They looked upon the aging (and mostly female) witches as irrational threats to their future. The solution: Get rid of them. With the path thus cleared, many Glorious who witnessed the hangings could later excel in their generational mission to bring confidence, reason, and good works to the colonies. Over the next quarter century, Thomas Brattle would write on celestial mechanics while his brother William would help found a new church dedicated to a "reasonable" God; John Leverett, as president of Harvard, would encourage the "most useful discoveries"; and Cotton Mather, pitiless witch-baiter in his youth, would help found Yale College and conquer "ignorant" prejudice by introducing the smallpox vaccine to America.

• The young ENLIGHTENMENT GENERATION (Adaptive, age 18 and under), paralyzed by the pervasive dread, understood it was for their sake that the Cavalier witches had to die—just as so many other adults had recently died to protect them from the ravages of riot and war. Most of the "possessed" children would later lose any recollection of the witches who had victimized them. Remembered or not, the trauma shaped all these children. It was their destiny to come of age as colonial America's most sensitive and conformist generation. Almost certainly, one or two of the young Enlighteners present on Gallows Hill survived long enough to hear news of another epochal event in their extreme old age: the signing of the Declaration of Independence. The last witch hanging at Salem therefore became a unique generational focal point in American history, one of the very few moments when those who had raised John Winthrop's "City on a Hill" stood side by side those who would someday become citizens of James Madison's "United States."

The New England witch trials completed seventeen years of social emergency that erupted just as the Colonial Cycle had turned roughly halfway through its course. When the cycle began in the 1620s with the founding of Plymouth and Salem and with the first sizable tobacco export from Jamestown, the New World remained an untouched wilderness. When the cycle came to an end in the early 1730s, some 750,000 persons of European and African descent crowded the bays and river shores of the Atlantic seaboard. In slightly more than a century, the holy visions of the coming-of-age Puritans had been transformed into a prosperous, enterprising, and literate civilization, just then adding the last (Georgia) of its thirteen colonies. The Puritans conceived it; the Cavaliers sacrificed for it; the Glorious built it; and the Enlighteners improved it. America had become the proudest and fastest-growing member of the English empire—a peaceful and busy country, looking forward to a grand future. The colonists hardly imagined that their complacency was about to be shattered by Idealist youths of the next cycle.

The Colonial Cycle contained two social moments:

• *The Puritan Awakening* (1621–1640), a dramatic resurgence of radical Protestantism throughout Europe, triggered the Thirty Years War on the continent and boiled over in England in 1621 when the House of Commons denounced the "unholy" war and tax policies of James I. The awakening gained popular momentum with the succession of Charles I to the throne in 1625 and reached a hysterical climax with demands for social, spiritual, and religious "Reform" in 1629. Charles tried suppressing these demands by refusing to convene any more Parliaments. The next year, John Winthrop led a "saving remnant" of true believers to America. In Old England, the rising-adult enthusiasm turned inward in the early 1630s, soon to explode again during Cromwell's Puritan Revolution. In New England, the excitement did not subside until the end of the 1630s, when immigration stopped, families settled, and moral orthodoxy stiffened. *AGE LOCATION: Puritans in rising adulthood; Cavaliers in youth.*

• *The Glorious Revolution Crisis* (1675–1692) followed an era of growing anxiety about the future of colonial America. The crisis began in 1675 with King Philip's War (a deadly struggle between New England settlers and musket-armed Algonquin Indians) and Bacon's Rebellion (a brief civil war in Virginia). The mood of emergency peaked when England, led by King William of Holland, mounted the Glorious Revolution in the fall of 1688 against its Catholic Stuart king, James II. Before learning the outcome,

American colonists staged their own "Glorious Revolution" in the spring of 1689 by launching rebellions in New England, New York, Maryland, and the Carolinas. While still in the grip of political turmoil, the New England colonies staved off a determined French invasion from Canada. The crisis ended in 1692, the year of the Salem witch trials. The accession of William and Mary to the English throne put to rest the colonists' greatest fears: social unrest, tyrannical governors, and annihilation by Indians. As the fever subsided, the colonies began celebrating their membership in an affluent and constitutional empire. *AGE LOCATION: Puritans in elderhood; Cavaliers in midlife; Glorious in rising adulthood; Enlighteners in youth.*

PURITAN GENERATION

Born: 1584–1614
Type: Idealist

Age Location:
Puritan Awakening in rising adulthood
Glorious Revolution Crisis in elderhood

"We shall be as a city upon a Hill," 42-year-old John Winthrop told his assembled passengers aboard their flagship *Arabella* as it sailed for Massachusetts in 1630. "We must love brotherly without dissimulation; we must love each other with a pure heart fervently. . . . The end is to improve our lives to do more service to the Lord . . . that ourselves and posterity may be the better preserved from the common corruptions of this evil world." Winthrop's message was a generational clarion call. A quarter century earlier, he had been a moody 15-year-old at Cambridge University, trying his best to prepare for a squire's life of comfort on his father's English manor. He had not yet heard of John Endecott (age 14), Anne Hutchinson (age 12), Richard Mather (age 7), Oliver Cromwell (age 4), or Roger Williams and Simon Bradstreet (both in infancy). Young Winthrop would soon learn, through a soul-searing conversion experience, how God's grace was destined to push all of them to the forefront of history. Together, they would lead the PURITAN GENERATION, transatlantic vanguard of a European peer group that violently wrenched the West out of Renaissance complacency, founded a religious utopia in the New World, and comprised all but a handful of Europe's first colonists on the Atlantic seaboard of North America.

The Puritans belonged to an English-born generation of boundless spiritual ambition. As children, they encountered a culture grown overlarge and lifeless in the hands of their Elizabethan fathers. Coming of age, they were (as many Puritans put it) "ravished by the beauty of the Lamb." As rising adults, they experimented with novel lifestyles: odd combinations of education and piety, commerce and agitation, colony-founding and prophecy. Moving into midlife, they gravitated toward decisive action—laboring to reshape the world just as God had earlier reshaped their souls. Of the vast majority who never left England, many joined activists like Cromwell in launching the Puritan Revolution against King Charles I, or preachers like the Fifth Monarchists in advocating a dictatorship of God on earth, or poets like John Milton in recreating a universe of chaos in which each soul struggles personally toward grace.

But a few of these "Puritans," led by Winthrop himself, chose to leave home

PURITAN GENERATION (Born 1584 to 1614)

TYPE: Idealist

Total number: 25,000
Percent immigrant: 100%
Percent slave: 1%

SAMPLE MEMBERS, birth (death)

    1584 John Cotton (1652)*
    1584 Myles Standish (1656)*
    1585 John Rolfe (1622)*
    1588 John Winthrop (1649)*
    1589 John Endecott (1665)*
    1590 William Bradford (1657)*
    1590 William Pynchon (1662)*
    1591 Anne Hutchinson (1643)*
    1592 Peter Stuyvesant (1672)*
c. 1595 Pocahontas (1617)
    1596 Richard Mather (1669)*
    1597 John Davenport (1670)*
    1603 Roger Williams (1683)*
    1603 Simon Bradstreet (1697)*
    1604 John Eliot (1690)*
    1606 Sir William Berkeley (1677)*
    1606 John Winthrop, Jr. (1676)*
    1607 John Harvard (1638)*
    1609 Henry Dunster (1659)*
c. 1612 Anne Bradstreet (1672)*
* = immigrant

FAMILY TREE

Typical grandparents: born c. 1540
  (e.g., Francis Drake)
Parents: born c. 1550–1585
  (e.g., William Shakespeare)
Children: Cavalier and Glorious
Typical grandchildren: Enlightenment

PERIOD OF POLITICAL LEADERSHIP

First and last year of colonial governorship
  and total duration of officeholding
  (permanent immigrants only):

Massachusetts: 1629–1692, 53 years
Connecticut: 1639–1683, 44 years
Rhode Island: 1638–1686, 29 years
Virginia: 1609–1677, 37 years

PROMINENT FOREIGN PEERS

    1588 Thomas Hobbes (1679)
    1596 René Descartes (1650)
    1599 Oliver Cromwell (1658)
    1600 Charles I (1649)
    1608 John Milton (1674)

Age	Date	HISTORY AND LIFECYCLE
0– 4	1588:	England defeats Spanish Armada
0–19	1603:	Death of Queen Elizabeth
6–36	1620:	Pilgrim separatists land at Plymouth Rock
8–38	1622:	First massacre of Jamestown by Indians
16–46	1630:	"Great Migration" to New England begins
24–54	1638:	Anne Hutchinson tried and banished for heresy
27–57	1641:	"Great Migration" ends; Massachusetts separates from England
29–59	1643:	John Davenport persuades Connecticut to adopt Mosaic law
35–65	1649:	Charles I executed; rise of Oliver Cromwell in England
46–76	1660:	Restoration of Charles II; colonial persecution of Quakers peaks
61–91	1675:	Start of King Philip's War and Bacon's Rebellion
75 +	1689:	Glorious Revolution in America

SAMPLE CULTURAL ENDOWMENTS: *The Sincere Convert* (Thomas Shepard); *Bay Psalm Book*; *The Bloody Tenent of Persecution* (Roger Williams); *The Sum of Church Discipline* (Thomas Hooker); *The Tenth Muse* (Anne Bradstreet); *Of Plymouth Plantation* (William Bradford); *An Exposition upon the Thirteenth Chapter of the Revelation* (John Cotton); "Algonquin Bible" (John Eliot) and found a religious experiment they called New Jerusalem. Although a mere 12,000 of Winthrop's peers emigrated to Massachusetts during the 1630s, after just their first year they outnumbered all of the adult colonists who had yet settled in New England (including the tiny band of *Mayflower* pilgrims who had migrated ten years earlier). By the end of the decade, they outnumbered the combined adult population of all other English colonies in America, including the 33-year-old colony of Virginia.

When this entire English-born generation reached midlife, the Puritans knew they had changed the course of history. But in the Old World, the changes were mixed. The stay-at-home Puritans never budged England from the corrupting influence of world affairs, and many of their hopes for revolution and reform were ultimately disappointed by the Restoration of the Stuart throne in 1660. Not so across the Atlantic. The New England Puritans stopped at nothing short of perfection. Rather than be corrupted by the world, they pushed themselves into spiteful isolation from outsiders. Rather than tolerate weakness, they riveted every corner of their society to God's ideal template. By the Restoration, the Puritans had become America's first generation of patriarchs, uncompromising defenders of a perfect spiritual order. Maybe too perfect. In midlife, they closed ranks around their theocracy by punishing everyone who threatened it—especially the younger Cavaliers, whom they regarded as shallow and wasted, in every respect their moral inferiors. In elderhood, threatened by tyranny and war, they prayed that a still younger generation of Glorious might save their holy experiment after all.

The Puritan birthyears reflect the events that shaped their lifecycle. Their first wave (John Cotton, Myles Standish) came of age just as Queen Elizabeth was dying and a handful of elder reformers were raising new excitement about church reform. Their last wave (Anne Bradstreet, Henry Dunster) came of age during the late-1630s tyranny of Charles I, when twentyish men and women could hone a flinty idealism in years of suppressed expectation—not yet years of revolution. Last-wave Puritans were the youngest adults to join in the Great Migration to New England and experience the feverish enthusiasm of the Bay Colony in the 1630s. First wave or last, the Puritans' success at founding colonies grew with advancing age. Such was their peer personality: immature and narcissistic through a long adolescence, but implacably strong-willed and morally committed when older. The 12,000 Puritan settlers who came to New England in the 1630s were mostly married adults in their late twenties to early forties—at least three out of four of whom thrived. At least as many Puritans came to colonies south of New England, but most were single males in their late teens, and their survival rate was as abysmal as their age was young. Only one in six survived Indians, starvation, and malaria in time to bear children—not enough to shape the southern colonies in the face of the Cavalier hordes who came soon after.

Even the few southern Puritans who survived to become leaders of lasting importance, such as Governor William Berkeley in Virginia and Governor Leonard Calvert in Maryland, followed their generation's formula for success. They came to America past their mid-twenties, and they applied their leadership to a lofty moral purpose. Berkeley wanted Virginia to preserve true-blue English royalism. Calvert, steering his flagships *Ark* and *Dove* toward the northern shore of Chesapeake Bay in 1634, saw "Maryland" as a holy refuge for Catholics. Like Winthrop, both were men of tenacious and unyielding principle. The Puritans who made it in America did not include the helpless teenage servants writing home in tears from Jamestown. Rather, they were those who chose with mature and radical conviction to leave the world of their parents. They were likely to call out (as did several *Mayflower* passengers) "Farewell, Babylon! Farewell, Rome!" as their ship set sail from England. They were likely to pray (as did John Cotton) that "when a man's calling and person are free and not tied by parents, or magistrates, or other people that have an interest in him, God opens a door there and sets him loose here, inclines his heart that way, and outlooks all difficulties."

Puritan Facts

• Puritan emigrants to New England during the 1630s included roughly one university alumnus (Cambridge or Oxford) for every forty families, an educational level that towered above England's at the time and was not again reached by any later American generation until the Missionaries, nearly three centuries later.

• Throughout their lives, the English-born Puritan elite earned a reputation for radicalism. When they were students and teachers, Thomas Hobbes noted scornfully that the English universities had become "the core of rebellion" against the English throne. Later on, when the House of Commons approached the brink of war, they were far more likely than their next-juniors to advocate revolution. In 1642, Roundheads outnumbered Royalists two-to-one among all Members of Parliament in their fifties (Puritan cohorts), while the opposite ratio prevailed among all M.P.s in their twenties (Cavalier cohorts). By the 1650s, elder Puritans in London—some having returned from America—dominated the most violent religious sects; several were executed when the throne was restored to Charles II in 1660.

• Wherever the radicals of this English-born generation set up their "reformed" communities—in Amsterdam, Geneva, America, or London—women assumed roles of conspicuous activism and leadership. In the 1630s, several New England women became popular lay preachers, and the charismatic Anne Hutchinson gathered such a powerful Boston constituency that she nearly toppled Winthrop's leadership. Anne Bradstreet today remains the most celebrated American authoress born before the Transcendentals.

- Puritans held the governorship of Massachusetts for fifty-three years—the longest single-generation control of a major political entity in American history. The last Puritan governors stepped down from office in Virginia (1677), Connecticut (1683), Rhode Island (1686), and Massachusetts (1692) at an average age of 77.

- Town records indicate that the New England Puritans lived on average into their late sixties—making this (excluding the southern settlers) the longest-lived American generation born before the twentieth century. Of all thirty-five New England Puritan ministers whose birthdates are known, thirty-two preached until their death at a median age of 68; only three retired, at a median age of 73. Their longevity can be attributed to good nutrition; scattered settlements, which retarded the spread of disease; little crime or substance abuse; and a regular pattern of work and leisure, thanks to a strictly enforced Sabbath.

The Puritan Lifecycle

YOUTH: Puritans grew up in the brightening aftermath of political triumph. First-wavers had hardly been born by the Armada year of 1588 and were still in their teens when James I succeeded Queen Elizabeth to the throne. England was a confident, optimistic world—booming with trade and new colonies, teeming with art and construction, and well protected by their fathers' mighty fleet. It was also, their parents told them, an ordered world: Despite the rising bustle, every person and planet "knew" his rank. Puritan children—indulged, secure, and showered with new schools—should have settled happily into this friendly future. But they didn't. Instead, as they grew into adolescence, a striking number became introspective and morally demanding. Behind the new prosperity, these children saw moral chaos and spiritual drift. At an early age, they likened London to Sodom and Gomorrah. They were obsessed with the sinfulness of man apart from God—not, like their midlife elders, with man's potential for godliness on his own. In "Doomsday," young George Herbert prayed: "Come away,/Help our Decay./Man is out of order hurled,/Parcell'd out to all the world./Lord, thy broken consort raise,/And the music shall be praise." Elders ridiculed these touchy young souls by popularizing the very word "Puritan" to describe them—while also puzzling (in the words of one elder Elizabethan) over "whose child he is . . . for willingly his faith allows no father." Most leaders of this generation—including Cromwell and Winthrop, John Cotton and Thomas Shepard—later recalled a far closer relationship with their mothers. According to historian David Leverenz, the Puritan Generation expressed an extreme "ambivalence about the father's role," reflecting a "mixture of relatively good mothering and relatively anxious, distant, weak, or repressive fathers."

COMING OF AGE: Near the end of adolescence there arrived—full of pain, wonder, and joy—the threshold event of the Puritan lifecycle: the conversion experience, the moment when God "ravished" them. Tentative prayers became rushes of enthusiasm. Moral qualms became fervent principle. For years after their conversion, Puritans struggled to master this inner ecstasy by inventing regimes of personal piety, what historians call "precisionism": prayer, work, reading, spiritual diaries, and sporadic bursts of abstinence and political activism. Together, converted Puritans felt more kinship with peers than with parents, and used generational code words to identify each other ("churches" for groups, "saints" for individuals—as in "we have many saints among us in this town"). Alone, they often meditated on their faith with sublimated sexuality. "Spread thy skirt over us, and cover our deformity," Winthrop wrote to God in his diary, "make us sick with thy love: let us sleep in thine arms, and awake in thy kingdom." To the chagrin of their fathers, young men insisted on "faith" over "works" and celebrated a dependent and feminine relationship to God, as "brides of Christ." By the 1620s, conversion had pushed many of them into strident opposition to elder authority, and an apocalyptic strain began appearing in their writings. Reviling the "prodigious lusts" and "impudent sinning" he saw around him, Herbert wrote: "Religion stands on tiptoe in our land,/Ready to pass to the American strand." Pointing to "these so evil and declining times," Winthrop called upon his peers to leave home and establish in America a government of Christ in exile. Thus began the Great Migration to New England.

RISING ADULTHOOD: During a single decade, the 1630s, the young Puritan voyagers to New England founded nearly everything for which future Americans would remember them: the port of Boston, church-centered towns stretching from Connecticut to Maine, Harvard University, a printing press, schools for Indians, representative assemblies, and their own liturgy. These rising adults hardly heard the wolves still howling near their cabins as they labored—with minds as much as bodies—to create an entirely God-focused civilization. To account for their creative energy, Winthrop, Cotton, and Shepard spoke incessantly of "love." Church members laid "loving hands" on ministers. New towns held "loving conversations," agreed to unanimous covenants of "everlasting love," and kept a "loving eye" on neighbors. There was nothing liberal about their utopian communities. To Puritans, all society had to be a church and all behavior had to reflect perfect fellow feeling. Of "toleration," declared Cotton proudly, "we are professed enemies." Thus, when two group leaders disagreed over God's truth, compromise was unthinkable. Ego clashes typically ended in banishment—the fate of Anne Hutchinson (who conversed personally with God), Roger Williams (who deemed no one holy enough to take communion with him), and Samuel Gorton (whose "Family of Love" worshiped him as Jesus Christ). Group intolerance, not frontier spirit, propelled the wide geographic scattering of Puritan towns during the 1630s. A single settlement just couldn't accommodate so many infallible prophets, each playing "spiritual chemist" (said John Wheelright) in search of the perfect life.

MIDLIFE: The outbreak of the English Civil War in 1641 put a sudden stop to new voyages and thrust the American colonies into temporary isolation. It also marked a midlife turning point in the Puritan lifecycle—from inward enthusiasm to outward righteousness. During the 1640s and 1650s, Puritans abandoned fanciful dreams of world reform and labored to achieve a more realistic ideal: enforceable moral order at home. As geographic mobility declined and as customs congealed around the seasonal rhythms of agriculture, Puritans steered their institutions toward formalism. They replaced "loving" covenants with written compacts, enacted draconian punishments for religious apostasy, and insisted that all new church members offer public proof of their conversions. Puritan parents and leaders raged over the apathy of younger Cavaliers who seemed perversely reluctant to join their churches. "This was an alarming situation for a community which had been founded for religious purposes," observes historian Edmund Morgan. "It was one thing to create a church of saints; it was another to let those saints carry the church out of the world with them entirely when they died." But like their radical peers back in England (and like Berkeley in Virginia), advancing age made the Puritans less compromising toward any behavior that did not conform to the "pure heart." By 1645, Winthrop insisted that his fellow colonists had "a liberty to that only which is good, just, and honest" and urged them all to "submit unto that authority which is set over you . . . for your own good." By the late 1650s, the humorless Governor John Endecott (who hanged younger Cavalier Quakers who mocked the Puritan creed) completed this generation's midlife transition from the law of love to the love of law.

ELDERHOOD: They entered old age knowing their world was heading for crisis. Half the New England Puritans lived to learn of the restoration of the throne to Charles II in 1660, which shoved the colonies back under the heel of Stuart "tyranny." A quarter lived to witness their grandchildren go off to fight (many to die) in a gruesome war against King Philip's Indians in 1675. A handful, like Bradstreet, still presided in high office as late as 1689, when the colonies joined England in the Glorious Revolution against James II. Most of these ancients, looking down on the troubled souls of their grown children, feared the young would trade ideals for security and thereby destroy everything that mattered. Their last act, accordingly, was to set an unyielding example. The diehards included patriarchs like Massachusetts Governor Richard Bellingham, who (at age 75) scornfully burned letters from the English crown; John Davenport, who (at age 70) left his Mosaic "Kingdom of God" in New Haven to fulminate in Boston against youth who "polluted" the church; Indian apostle John Eliot, who (at age 72) protested seeing his life's work torn apart by younger soldiers more interested in killing Indians than in saving their souls; and Virginia Governor Berkeley, who (at age 71) hanged twenty-three younger leaders of Bacon's Rebellion. Confident that principle would triumph, most Puritans faced death with what historian Perry Miller has described as "cosmic optimism." Said a witness at John Eliot's deathbed: "His last breath smelt strong of Heaven." So often had the Puritans expected Christ's return that when death finally arrived they met it with composure—like travelers returning home after a pilgrimage.

*   *   *

Spiritual self-absorption was both the strength and the weakness of this generation. It gave the Puritans the confidence to plant the first successful colonies in the American wilderness. Yet it did so by making them think they were building the only perfect society since Adam's Fall. New Jerusalem was a project the next generation would not understand—and would secretly resent. As the Puritans grew older, they forgot that grace could be experienced only by the moment. They tried to freeze their church of peer-love and isolate it from every external corruption. Their punishment was to see, among the devils attacking Eden, the faces of their firstborn, their own Cavalier children. Their expiation was to pass away showing the later-born Glorious what it meant to believe in an idea. Insensible to the Puritans' inner fire, the Glorious later revered them as black-clothed statues of unfeeling rectitude. We can only guess how this image would have struck the Puritans themselves—a generation that had once forsaken all earthly dross to create the perfect society, a community of love. "As 'tis with woman when the fullness of the husband's love is seen, it knits the heart invincibly to him, and makes her do anything for him; so here." Thus did Puritan Thomas Shepard as a young minister describe the faith that motivated his coming-of-age peers. Later generations would rediscover this feeling. But the Puritans' own offspring could not possibly understand. They had not been there—at that moment of history and at that phase of life.

CAVALIER GENERATION

Born: 1615–1647
Type: Reactive

Age Location:
Puritan Awakening in youth
Glorious Revolution Crisis in midlife

"A wicked and perverse generation," the young Quaker Josiah Coale called his peers as he toured the American colonies at midcentury. He might also have called them the CAVALIER GENERATION, a peer group of pluck, materialism, and self-doubt. The Cavaliers followed the Puritans the way flotsam scatters after the crashing of a storm wave: skepticism following belief, egotism following community, devils following saints. At their worst, the Cavaliers were an unlettered generation of little faith and crude ambition—so they were told all their lives, and so many of them believed and behaved. Their roster includes more than the usual number of rogues: adventurers, witches, pirates, smugglers, Indian-haters, and traitors. Yet at their best, the Cavaliers were a generation whose perverse defiance of moral authority gave America its first instinct for individual autonomy, for the "rights" of property and liberty—concepts utterly foreign to their Puritan elders. William Penn, apostle of religious toleration, was a Cavalier, as were such unattractive and pugnacious defenders of colonial independence as Nathaniel Bacon, Increase Mather, Elisha Cooke, and Jacob Leisler.

The typical life experience of the 100,000-member Cavalier generation varied dramatically according to geography. Of the 40,000 in New England, nearly all were either born in America or brought over as children by their parents. They grew up in large families among towns and churches dominated by their long-lived Puritan elders. Of the 60,000 or so farther south, especially in the Chesapeake colonies of Virginia and Maryland, most were immigrants—perhaps two-thirds coming over as young, parentless, and indentured servants. The Chesapeake Cavaliers rarely saw a complete family. Most arrived unattached and perished before marrying. Throughout the seventeenth century, theirs was a frontier society of extreme youth and routine violence—"a people," scowled the old Puritan Governor Berkeley, "where six parts of seven at least are poor, indebted, discontented, and armed." Yet whatever the colony, Cavaliers everywhere met life on similar terms: discarded in a childhood without structure, shamed while coming of age, and pushed into adulthood with few hopes other than climbing fast and avoiding judgment. Later on, during years of war and

CAVALIER GENERATION (Born 1615 to 1647)

TYPE: Reactive

Total number: 100,000
Percent immigrant: 61%
Percent slave: 4%

SAMPLE MEMBERS, birth (death)

c. 1616 Mary Dyer (1660)*
   1619 Arent Van Curler (1667)*
c. 1620 John Carter (1669)*
c. 1620 Josias Fendall (1687)*
   1624 John Hull (1683)*
c. 1626 John Pynchon (1703)*
   1631 William Stoughton (1701)*
   1631 Michael Wigglesworth (1705)*
   1637 Elisha Cooke (1715)
   1638 Fitz-John Winthrop (1707)
c. 1638 George Keith (1716)*
   1639 Increase Mather (1723)
   1639 Benjamin Church (1718)
   1640 Jacob Leisler (1691)*
c. 1640 Samuel Willard (1707)
c. 1642 Metacomet, "King Philip" (1676)
   1643 Solomon Stoddard (1729)
c. 1645 William Kidd (1701)*
   1647 Nathaniel Bacon (1676)*
   1647 Joseph Dudley (1720)

* = immigrant

FAMILY TREE

Typical grandparents: born c. 1560
   (e.g., Shakespeare)
Parents: first-wave Puritan
Children: Glorious and Enlightenment
Typical grandchildren: Awakening

PERIOD OF POLITICAL LEADERSHIP

First and last year of colonial governorship
   and total duration of officeholding
   (permanent immigrants only):

Massachusetts: 1672–1715, 27 years
Connecticut: 1683–1707, 22 years
Rhode Island: 1657–1698, 22 years
Virginia: 1655–1690, 12 years

PROMINENT FOREIGN PEERS

1618 Aurangzeb (1707)
1630 Charles II (1685)
1632 John Locke (1704)
1638 Louis XIV (1715)
1644 William Penn (1718)

Age	Date	HISTORY AND LIFECYCLE
0–15	1630:	Great Migration to New England begins
0–20	1635:	Rapid growth in servant immigration to Chesapeake
0–29	1644:	Second massacre of Jamestown by Indians
2–34	1649:	Charles I executed; young royalists emigrate to the Chesapeake
8–40	1655:	First permanent settlements in Carolinas
13–45	1660:	Restoration of Charles II; theaters, brothels reopen in London
17–49	1664:	Duke of York captures New Amsterdam in second Dutch War
29–61	1676:	King Philip's War ends; Bacon rebels sentenced to death in Virginia
38–70	1685:	James II inherits throne, creates "Dominion of New England"
42–74	1689:	Glorious Revolution; Comte de Frontenac attacks from Canada
45–77	1692:	Salem witch trials
66–98	1713:	Queen Anne's War (1702–1713) ends with Treaty of Utrecht

SAMPLE CULTURAL ENDOWMENTS: *The Day of Doom* (Michael Wigglesworth); *A Character of the Province of Maryland* (George Alsop); *Pray for the Rising Generation* (Increase Mather); *Mercy Magnified on a Penitent Prodigal* (Samuel Willard); *Will and Doom* (Gershom Bulkeley); *The Danger of Speedy Degeneracy* (Solomon Stoddard); *Entertaining Passages Relating to King Philip's War* (Benjamin Church) rebellion, midlife Cavaliers managed to salvage their reputation for posterity—not by suddenly turning virtuous, but by fighting gamely according to their own rules.

The Cavalier character first took shape in the Old World. There, around the mid-seventeenth century, a new generation came of age—profoundly disillusioned by the chaos left behind by saintly next-elders. On the continent, three decades of holy war had succumbed to the realpolitik of hungry new superpowers: France, Sweden, and Holland. In England, religious revolution had given way to the brutality of Cromwell, the decadence of the Restoration, and the duplicity of Cavalier-age kings Charles II and James II. For this new generation, it was a time to repudiate failed dreams, to learn that self-interest is the secret of happiness and that power is the source of glory. Tired of bookish principle, Cavaliers avoided Puritan idealism, prompting English historian Lawrence Stone to note that "the old were more radical than the young in the 1640s." They grasped instead for what was tangible and grandiose—the fabled jewels of Aurangzeb, the Versailles splendor of Louis XIV, the sensuous curves of baroque art. The initial Cavalier birthyear, 1615, marks the first English-born cohort whose childhood environment began to disintegrate from the stable Elizabethan order known by Puritans at like age. In America, that year also draws a rough dividing line between the Great Migration to New England (ending in 1640 for adults in their late 20s) and the huge influx of English immigrants to Virginia (beginning about 1635 for servants in their late teens).

The English word "Cavalier" comes from a mixture of Romance words for "horse," "hair," and "knight" (in French; *cheval, cheveux,* and *chevalier*)—fitting images of the showy, arrogant, and predatory values this generation took to heart. Many historians, most recently David Hackett Fischer, have called this the "Cavalier wave" of American immigration. To be sure, only a few adorned themselves like Prince Rupert and fully *dressed* the part. But what matters is how many *played* the part—and not only in royalist Virginia. Fitz and Wait Winthrop, concludes their biographer, "grew up a couple of Cavaliers in Israel": "half-ludicrous, uncertain of their values, and always chiefly absorbed with fashion, status, and accumulation of real estate." "By the mid-1650s," writes historian Bernard Bailyn about New England, "the character of the rising generation was discernible, and to the entrenched oligarchy it seemed pitifully weak. The children of the Founders . . . knew nothing of the fire that had steeled the hearts of their fathers. They seemed to their elders frivolous, given to excess in dress and manners, lacking the necessary fierceness of belief." What they did not lack, these children would someday show their elders, was the necessary fierceness of action.

Cavalier Facts

- A young male servant coming to Maryland in the 1640s stood only a two-thirds chance of surviving the voyage. If he made it ashore, he faced a 57 percent chance of living out his indenture term, a 29 percent chance of ever owning enough land to support himself, a 6 percent chance of dying with an estate worth more than 1,000 pounds, and less than a 1 percent chance of ending up as a respected "planter-merchant."

- While the Puritan voyagers to Massachusetts came mainly from the east of England (Roundheads and short vowels), the Cavalier voyagers to the Chesapeake came mainly from the southwest of England (Royalists and wide vowels). These regional differences in England accentuated the contrast between the two peer personalities—and gave rise to regional differences in America that have persisted to this day.

- Throughout the colonies, the Cavaliers probably represent the largest one-generation decline in educational achievement from their next-elders in American history. In Massachusetts, no Harvard-trained Cavalier minister was ever regarded (or regarded himself) as the intellectual equal of the leading Puritans. In the Chesapeake, 60 percent of the young immigrants could not sign a name to their indenture contracts.

- From the 1640s through the 1660s, a majority of the first graduates of Harvard College left for England seeking escape or adventure—usually returning again to their native New England by midlife.

- A striking number of best-known Cavaliers died a violent death: Quaker Mary Dyer (hanged in Boston, 1660); the twenty-three captured leaders of Bacon's Rebellion (hanged in Virginia, 1677); Metacomet (the Indian leader "King Philip," shot in the back in rural New England, 1676); Jacob Leisler and Jacob Milbourne (drawn and quartered in New York City, 1691); most of the thirty-one convicted Salem witches (hanged in Salem, 1692); Thomas Tew (blown in half by Muslim merchants, 1695); and William Kidd (hanged in London, 1701).

- Among the thousands of young, poor, and solitary Cavaliers who emigrated from England to the Chesapeake, four—John Washington, Thomas Jefferson, James Maddison, and Andrew Munro—were great-grandfathers to four of the first five U.S. Presidents.

The Cavalier Lifecycle

YOUTH: During the 1630s through the 1650s, as adults grappled with messianic visions, children understood that no one cared much about their welfare. In England, revolution and war sent tens of thousands of these afterthought kids—orphaned and abandoned—scurrying toward cities like London and Bristol. There they scrambled for a living until poverty, arrest, defeat in battle, or "kidnapping" (a word first coined at midcentury) consigned them to disease-ridden ships bound for Virginia and Maryland. Unschooled but worldly-wise, youthful Cavalier servants fought bad odds and self-hatred to survive grueling seven-year slavelike indentures in the tobacco fields. "To wickedness I quickly was inclined," rhymed teenage convict James Revel in Virginia, "Thus soon is tainted any youthful mind." Childhood among the isolated and fanatical towns of Winthrop's "New Jerusalem" was safer, but hardly more conducive to self-esteem. Puritan parents frequently castigated youngsters for their palpable unsaintliness, and elder assemblies in Boston soon declared child misbehavior a capital crime. Perhaps more often, self-obsessed Puritans left kids on their own—to discover New England for themselves among the forests and Indians. "I have no confidence in my doings, O wretched worm that I am," wrote young Michael Wigglesworth in his Massachusetts diary. "What will become of this generation?" remarked Eleazar Mather several years later. "Are they not in danger to sink and perish in the waters?"

COMING OF AGE: "Early in the 1640s," notes historian Perry Miller, "ministers began to complain that sons and daughters were not exhibiting zeal." By midcentury, midlife New Englanders spoke routinely of a "corrupt and degenerate rising generation"—or, as Puritan Richard Mather put it, "the sad face of the rising generation." Unimpressed by these "heathenish" and "hard-hearted" 20-year-olds, Puritans accused them of "cruelty" and "covetousness," of living by "external considerations only, by a kind of outward force without any spiritual life or vigor or delight in them." In England, the mayor of Bristol echoed similar disgust at the "felons, runaways, and beggars" flowing through his port to the Chesapeake. And when they arrived in Virginia, Puritan Governor Berkeley picked up where others left off. "The wild beast multitude," Berkeley called them—"rude, dissolute, and tumultuous" youths who valued "pelts" over their lives. Young Cavaliers offered few rebuttals. "We, poor we, alas what are we!" lamented young William Stoughton. "It is a sad name to be styled 'Children that are Corrupters.'" Yet beyond blaming themselves, Cavaliers grew to resent the lies they were inheriting. Their Puritan elders had promised them a "New Jerusalem" (in Massachusetts) and a royalist "land of plenty" (in Virginia), but all they saw around them were miserable exiles and a howling wilderness. "In the eyes of the immigrants," concludes historian Oscar Handlin, "the second generation seemed a ruder, less cultivated, and wilder people." But in the eyes of the Cavaliers, what was ruder and wilder was the New World to which their elders had taken them.

RISING ADULTHOOD: Alienated by elder criticism, thirtyish Cavaliers struck out alone, trying (explained officer Fitz Winthrop, then a young expatriate in London) to stay away from "a city or place where I am known, and where every judgment will pass their verdict on me." They also hustled desperately to win wealth and respect. In the Chesapeake world of isolated plantations and contracted labor, rising planters like John Carter competed fiercely for what they called "the main chance," that one swift trade or promotion that would catapult them to the top. In New England, apprentices like John Hull became silversmiths and world traders, fur trappers like Benjamin Church wandered to the frontier, and the aspiring elite sought attractive posts back in England. Of all ways to the top, land became a Cavalier obsession. "Land! Land! hath been the Idol of many in New England," thundered Increase Mather at his peers. The odds were slim that an ex-servant could acquire enough land to merit a titled name ("mister" or "esquire"), but Cavaliers took their chances willingly. Besides, by bending a few rules—smuggling, bribing, faking "headright" documents—they could always get an edge. The truly bold joined Thomas Tew and William Kidd in the ultimate gamble and purest of Cavalier lifestyles: piracy and "buccaneering," a rising plague along the Atlantic coast from the 1650s forward. Why not go for it? Everyone kept telling the Cavalier he was a loser anyway. A dead loser, he would no longer have to listen. A rich loser, no one would dare tell him in his presence.

MIDLIFE: The crisis year of 1675 marked the Cavaliers' passage into midlife and inaugurated the darkest two decades in American history until nearly another century afterward. In New England, the bloody Indian rebellion known as King Philip's War killed more inhabitants per capita than any subsequent war in American history. In Virginia, Bacon's Rebellion similarly began as a war against Indians, but soon expanded into a vicious civil war between a Puritan governor (Sir William Berkeley) and a Cavalier rebel (Nathaniel Bacon). More adversity soon followed: epidemics, riots, the colonial Glorious Revolution, and global war against France. All eyes turned to the Cavaliers for leadership. Could this wild and pragmatic generation handle such adversity? Doubtful Puritan elders, still retaining symbolic authority into extreme old age, shook their heads. But Cavalier leadership prevailed, and did so thanks to talents their elders never possessed—realistic diplomacy (Increase Mather), cunning generalship (Benjamin Church), and reckless courage (Jacob Leisler). Outshining the Puritans in elemental altruism, midlife Cavaliers staged suicidal rebellions and bore crushing war-era taxation on behalf of their families without complaint or condescension. They treated the younger Glorious, moreover, with a gentleness they had been denied at like age. Exhausted and politically tainted once the crisis had passed, they hardly protested the numerous vendettas (such as the Salem witchcraft frenzy of 1692) that targeted their own peers.

ELDERHOOD: At the turn of the century, Cavaliers sank into old age marveling that perhaps the worst was over. They had survived the Indians, the Restoration, the Dutch, the rebellions, and (for the time being) the French. The colonies were again growing rapidly, thanks mainly to the younger and more industrious Glorious. Reminiscing over their lives, many Cavaliers no doubt attributed their success to dumb luck, the only sort of grace that most of them had ever prayed for. Even as elders, they never tried to hide their generation's faults, especially their vulgarity and irreligion. "This exile race, the Age of Iron," New Yorker Henricus Selyns described them in the 1690s, "living here among so many wild beasts and bulls of Bashan." Nor did Cavaliers ever stop blaming themselves for not measuring up to their elders. "If the body of the present generation be compared with what was here forty years ago," boomed Increase Mather, "what a sad degeneracy is evident in the view of every man." As Benjamin Tompson looked back in verse: "These golden times (too fortunate to hold),/ Were quickly sin'd away for love of gold." But Cavalier "gold" only landed on a handful: the few former apprentices who now owned Boston mansions or shares in a New York pirate ship, or the few former servants who now owned Tidewater estates with private river docks. Others were not so lucky. Most Cavaliers died before age 45; the rest entered old age without wealth or pretense— crusty, used up, and unaware of what they had given. In his late seventies, Boston merchant Joshua Scottow wrote a book entitled *Old Men's Tears for Their Own Declensions,* and the eightyish Jonathan Burt agreed that "the Lord is pleased with the Rod to visit me when Old."

*   *   *

Self-deprecating realism gave the Cavaliers special strengths: the ability to outwit evil, to survive in an ugly, no-second-chance world and later joke about their escapades in America's first adventure tales and travelogues. Unlike the Puritans (who could just as well have emigrated to the moon), Cavaliers felt a visceral affinity for the American wilderness—lonely and uncouth, like their own generation. "Dear New England, Dearest land to me!" wrote Michael Wigglesworth, painfully aware how many mountains and forests distanced him from civilization. Yet if the Cavaliers excelled in outgaming Satan—perhaps because they were "devils" themselves, as the elder Berkeley told Bacon and the younger Cotton Mather told the Salem witches—they remained helpless against the judgment of God and community. Early in the seventeenth century, Cavaliers grew up in a world that faulted children and hardly bothered to punish kidnappers (the official fine was one shilling) who "spirited" London waifs to the New World as quasi-slaves. Near the end of the century, they grew old in a world that faulted the elderly, that sermonized on old age with what historian John Demos calls "a note of distaste . . . almost of repulsion." The very sacrifices they made as mature adults to protect their families helped, sadly, to keep themselves a target of blame throughout their lifecycle.

GLORIOUS GENERATION

Born: 1648–1673
Type: Civic

Age Location:
Glorious Revolution Crisis in rising adulthood
Great Awakening in elderhood

"Be up and doing. Activity. Activity," preached Benjamin Colman in his thirties. "This will be most likely followed and rewarded, with triumphant satisfaction." Colman's message energized his young audience—and sums up the life story of the GLORIOUS GENERATION, the band of American heroes who came of age during the last quarter of the seventeenth century. Their dutiful valor won the Indian wars and repelled the French. Their cooperative discipline overthrew Stuart tyranny and quelled social disorder. Their rational minds planned harbors, charted the planets, and organized African slaves. In 1689, the colonial Glorious Revolution led them all, at ages 16 to 41, through a culminating rite of passage—stamping them for life as public persons, institution-founders, collective builders, and secular dreamers. Ever afterward, their diaries buzzed with nonstop activity: families, elections, trade, profits, roads, cultivation—all accomplished with only the rarest idle feeling. To Cotton Mather in Boston, who wrote 450 volumes over three decades, "sloth" was inexcusable; to Robert Beverley in Virginia, "laziness" the only sin. Not just any activity would do. It had to be "social," "useful," "serve the public" or "enrich the commonwealth."

Growing up in an increasingly protective adult world, coming of age at a moment of triumph, and entering adulthood programmed for achievement, the Glorious mapped out a lifecycle of enormous collective confidence. Those born before 1648 arrived too soon to experience what Cavalier Thomas Shepard, Jr., called the "more thorough, conscientious, religious, effectual care for the rising generation." Those born after 1673 came of age too late to participate in victory. As the Puritans' favored heirs, the Glorious revered the moral vision of elder patriarchs and never imagined improving it. Instead, from childhood on, they understood that their group mission was to champion that vision against growing worldly threats—to make it stable and orderly, to give it permanence and power and grandeur. After helping to topple the Cavalier-age Stuart James II from the throne of England, the Glorious effectively defended their "rightful" colonial liberties from later crown-appointed governors. Yet they also came to admire their like-minded peers in England and tried to bathe in the reflected glory of

GLORIOUS GENERATION (Born 1648 to 1673)

TYPE: Civic

Total number: 160,000
Percent immigrant: 42%
Percent slave: 12%

FAMILY TREE:

Typical grandparents: first-wave Puritan
Parents: Puritan and Cavalier
Children: Enlightenment and Awakening
Typical grandchildren: Liberty

SAMPLE MEMBERS, birth (death)

1649 Elihu Yale (1721)
1651 Sir William Phips (1695)
1651 William Randolph (1711)*
1651 William Fitzhugh (1701)*
1651 Francis Daniel Pastorius (c. 1720)*
1652 John Wise (1725)
1652 William Byrd (1704)*
1652 Samuel Sewall (1730)*
1655 James Blair (1743)*
1657 Hannah Dustin (c. 1730)
1657 Peter Schuyler (1724)
1658 Thomas Brattle (1713)
1659 Samuel Cranston (1727)
1663 Cotton Mather (1728)
1663 Robert ("King") Carter (1732)
1666 Gurdon Saltonstall (1724)
1669 Joseph Talcott (1741)
1671 Lewis Morris (1746)
1673 Robert Beverley (1722)
1673 Benjamin Colman (1747)
* = immigrant

PERIOD OF POLITICAL LEADERSHIP

First and last year of colonial governorship
and total duration of officeholding
(permanent immigrants only):

Massachusetts: 1692–1694, 2 years
Connecticut: 1707–1741, 34 years
Rhode Island: 1683–1740, 44 years
Virginia: 1705–1741, 11 years

PROMINENT FOREIGN PEERS

1650 King William III (1702)
1650 First Duke of Marlborough (1722)
1665 Queen Anne (1714)
1672 Joseph Addison (1719)
1672 Peter the Great (1725)

Age	Date	HISTORY AND LIFECYCLE
0–12	1660:	Restoration of Charles II
2–27	1675:	Start of King Philip's War and Bacon's Rebellion
4–29	1677:	Culpeper's Rebellion in the Carolinas
9–34	1682:	Quakers begin large-scale settlement of Pennsylvania and Jerseys
12–37	1685:	James II inherits throne, creates "Dominion of New England"
16–41	1689:	Glorious Revolution in America
17–42	1690:	King William's War (1690–1697) against French Canada begins
19–44	1692:	Salem witch trials; acceleration of slave imports to South
32–57	1705:	Omnibus slave code enacted in Virginia
40–65	1713:	Queen Anne's War (1702–1713) ends with Treaty of Utrecht
47–72	1720:	First paper money, insurance, stagecoaches; rising household wealth
61–86	1734:	Great Awakening begins in Connecticut Valley

SAMPLE CULTURAL ENDOWMENTS: *Good Order Established in Pennsylvania and New Jersey* (Thomas Budd); *The Revolution in New England Justified* (Samuel Sewall); *Essays to Do Good* (Cotton Mather); *The History and Present State of Virginia* (Robert Beverley); *Rulers Feeding and Guiding Their People* (Benjamin Wadsworth); *Gods Deals with Us as Rational Creatures* (Benjamin Colman)

Marlborough's brilliant victories, London's booming prosperity, Addison's "Augustan" odes, Purcell's martial trumpets, Van Brugh's Palladian facades—and, especially, King William's "Glorious" arrival. It pleased them to feel part of a worldwide effort to build a great empire.

The Glorious disliked spiritual heat—not because they felt unworthy (as did many Cavaliers), but because they deemed the gloomy enthusiasm of their elders antisocial and unproductive. Far better, they urged, to regard religion from a more optimistic and rational perspective. Benjamin Wadsworth called the covenant of grace "most reasonable." Colman affirmed that "a cheerful spirit is a happy and lovely thing." Worshipping Newton as "our perpetual dictator," Cotton Mather reminded his peers: "Our faith itself will not be found to be good and profitable if good works do not follow upon it." The Glorious infatuation with "good works" and useful reason made them distrust the wildness and self-doubt of their next-elders. It also shaped them into a decidedly male-focused generation. Striving (like "King" Carter) to "preserve the character of the father," Glorious authors like Beverley and Mather celebrated their male ancestors while admitting with Benjamin Wadsworth that "persons are often more apt to despise a mother (the weaker vessel, and frequently most indulgent), than a father." As the Salem trials demonstrated in 1692, the Cavalier and female "witch" was a natural target for a young generation of soldiers, scientists, and builders ready to remake the world.

The Glorious were America's first generation of secular optimists. As children, they looked upon the passion and poverty of their parents as an embarrassment to be transcended. As adults, they set out not to save themselves personally, but to save their society collectively. They believed that social institutions could improve the "welfare of mankind," that science could be "useful," that prosperity could "advance" over time. Could such an ambitious life trajectory betray any disappointment? Not so long as the Glorious were still building and doing. Yet later on, after the church bells had pealed in 1713 for the peace of Utrecht and the Glorious had settled into midlife, many looked uneasily over the world they had created. By then, they had cause to worry that an era celebrating "Reason" might someday be despised as a cultural wasteland; that their spinning wheels of "Commerce" were wearing down the civic spirit they held so dear; and, most ominously, that chattel slavery—an institution this generation chiseled into law—might cost their heirs far more in hatred (and blood) than it would ever benefit them in wealth.

Glorious Facts

• The Glorious were America's first mostly native-born generation of colonists. From first cohort to last, immigrants declined steadily relative to natives, especially after Parliament ceased transporting convicts in 1670 and enacted the death penalty for "spiriting" children in 1671. The Glorious included most of the young Quakers who laid out Philadelphia's boxy street plan in the 1680s and were the first generation to include large numbers of non-English (German, French Huguenot, and African) members.

• Over the span of the active adulthood of the Glorious—from their first wave at age 30 (1677) to their last wave at age 60 (1733)—blacks rose from 4 to 15 percent of the total American population.

• Except for the first Puritan immigrants, the Glorious were elected to town offices at a younger age than members of any other generation during the colonial era. In the two colonies having elective governorships, Connecticut and Rhode Island, they also came to colonial office younger (at age 41 and 32) and served far longer (thirty-four and forty-two years).

• In the Chesapeake, the rising Glorious elite replaced an unstable government of immigrant adventurers with an enduring oligarchy of "native" planters. In the decades preceding the American Revolution, 70 percent of the 110 leaders of the Virginia House of Burgesses were drawn from families resident in Virginia before 1690.

• As America's first generation of veterans, the Glorious received the first war-service pensions—usually in the form of land grants issued after 1700 by Glorious-dominated colonial assemblies.

The Glorious Lifecycle

YOUTH: On the eve of the first Glorious births, Puritans entering midlife began changing their minds about how children should be raised. In 1647, lamenting the "great neglect of many parents" that had turned out so many jaundiced Cavaliers, the Massachusetts assembly ordered towns to provide primary schooling for children—a landmark statute soon copied elsewhere in New England. Also in 1647, Virginia required counties to "take up and educate" abandoned children and the next year opened its first "orphan's court." During the 1650s and 1660s, the trend toward protective nurture strengthened. For the first time, colonial parents came under attack for what Increase Mather labeled "cruel usage of poor children." "Do we not grievously neglect them? to instruct them, to cherish and promote any good in them?" worried Harvard president Urian Oakes in 1673. New England churches began teaching good works and civic duty ("preparation of salvation") rather than passive conversion. While sheltering young Glorious from material harm, Puritan and Cavalier elders also urged them to be cooperative achievers able to save their colonies from impending danger. Though telling young New Englanders they were "walled about with the love of God," Oakes also reminded them that "every true believer is a soldier, engaged in a warfare." Leaving instructions in 1669 for the care of his six-year-old son Robert, the dying Virginian John Carter instructed his guardians to "preserve him from harm" and educate him to be "useful for his estate." The double message worked. By the mid-1670s, a new sort of American began graduating from Harvard and taking over Virginia plantations: confident rationalists with a steady eye on their future.

COMING OF AGE: Their rite of passage offered few moments of lone introspection. Instead, it forced the coming-of-age Glorious to band together and prove their public spirit in the heat of action. For the first wave (the eldest in their late twenties), the trial began with the Indian wars of 1675–1676. For the last wave (the youngest in their late teens), it culminated in the terrifying riots and rebellions of 1689–1692 that expelled from America Europe's "Great Scarlet Whore," the alleged Catholic conspiracy of James II and Louis XIV. Cotton Mather called it "a happy revolution." And well might all of his peers, for the crisis "released long-suppressed generational tensions" (according to historian T. H. Breen) and triggered a seismic shift in political authority from old to young. In New England, young Glorious ousted elder militia commanders, set up Committees of Public Safety, voted themselves into public office, and supported the witchcraft frenzy against elders who victimized children. In the Chesapeake, the educated young elite who came to power from the 1670s to 1690s created the famous "planter oligarchy" of Byrds, Randolphs, Fitzhughs, Carters, Pages, Taneys, and Carrolls that would shun outsiders and rule the South for generations to come. Throughout the colonies, energetic young men began elbowing aside their seniors. Rather than "dishonor yourselves," the 27-year-old Mather boldly preached to aging Cavaliers in 1690, "look often into your coffins" and "let your *quietus* gratify you. Be pleased with the retirement you are dismissed into."

RISING ADULTHOOD: Once past the crisis, thirtyish Glorious labored to build new institutions that would promote social order and productive activity. Detesting the remnants of the anarchic Cavalier lifestyle, they helped the English rid the New World of piracy and replaced the predatory violence of Chesapeake planters with friendlier substitutes like gambling and horse racing. Unlike the Cavaliers at like age, they did not wander. Planter-statesmen in the South, or farmer-soldiers in the North, the Glorious stayed put, taking pride in their ethos of loyal community-building. Where young voters could empower their own governors (Samuel Cranston in Connecticut or Joseph Talcott in Rhode Island), they made their colonies peaceful and prosperous. Elsewhere, they closed ranks and enforced their will on crown-appointed governors through peer solidarity. Rising Glorious men and women encouraged an unprecedented division between sex roles. Men began wearing powdered periwigs, women the whalebone corset—new symbols of what John Cotton in 1699 celebrated as "the industry of the man" and the "keep at home" woman. Religion underwent a complementary transition from passion to "reason," from fanaticism to "cheer," from mysticism to "clarity." By pushing spiritual emotion toward domesticated mothers, Cotton Mather's "handmaidens of the Lord," the Glorious clergy left fathers free to build. The duty of "Man," announced Thomas Budd in Philadelphia, was "to bring creation into order."

MIDLIFE: In 1721, clergyman John Wise surveyed the busy coastal ports of America and announced: "I say it is the merchandise of any country, wisely and vigorously managed, this is the king of business for increasing the wealth, the civil strength, and the temporal glory of a people." Throughout the colonies, from "Bostonia" to the "idyllic gardens" of the Carolinas, midlife Glorious took pride in their worldly accomplishments. They had reason. Throughout their active adulthood, from the 1670s to the 1720s, they presided over colonial America's most robust era of economic growth, a 50 to 100 percent advance in living standards by most statistical measures: per capita imports from England, number of rooms per home, amount of furniture per family, estate size at death. The Glorious succeeded not with Cavalier risk-taking, but rather by establishing "orderly" markets, pioneering paper money, and building what they liked to call "public works." They also introduced new types of property rights, such as private ownership of communal town land—and of black Africans. When the Glorious came of age, a mere 6,000 blacks labored in America, primarily immigrants from other English colonies, many of whom exercised the same rights as indentured servants. This generation changed all that. In the 1690s, young planters began importing blacks directly from Africa by the thousands. By the 1700–1710 decade, Glorious-led assemblies were everywhere enacting statutes that fixed slavery as a monolithic racial and legal institution. Those few Glorious who objected found little support. Samuel Sewall, who wrote *The Selling of Joseph* to keep slaves out of Boston, acknowledged that his opinions elicited "frowns and harsh words" from his peers.

ELDERHOOD: Old age brought mixed blessings to a generation of builders and doers. True, the aging Glorious could look back on a lifetime of achievement. When they were children, the colonies had been a savage outpost of some 100,000 subjects, chained to a corrupt kingdom. Now they saw around them a wealthy colonial "jewel," with a population pushing one million, attached to the most prestigious empire on earth. They had earned and saved far more during their lifetimes than had the Puritans or Cavaliers ("Our fathers," Colman admitted, "were not quite enough men of the world for us"), and rising land prices gave them commanding bargaining power over their own land-poor children. Yet in their diaries, the elder Glorious complained of physical decline and regretted that their secularized religion offered so little solace. Upon death, they staged such gaudy last rites for old friends that in the 1720s Massachusetts led several other colonies in enacting laws to "restrain the extraordinary expense at funerals." Most of all, they wondered why the young did not show them the same warmth they remembered feeling for their own fathers. Celebrating each other with adjectives like "honored" and "ancient," they withdrew from the hostile and increasingly value-laden culture of young Awakeners. In his mid-sixties, Cotton Mather criticized the doctrine of spiritual rebirth gaining popularity among younger ministers by insisting that "going to heaven in the way of repentance, is much safer and surer than going in the way of ecstasy." But he also warned his aging peers: "Our patience will be tried by the contempt . . . among those who see we are going out."

* * *

By the end of their lives, the Glorious had overcome every major challenge they had faced coming of age. They had taken America, politically, from chaos to stability; materially, from poverty to affluence; and culturally, from fanaticism to science. From youth through old age, the Glorious knew they were gifted achievers—and they let their elders and juniors know it as well. If their Whig-and-wig legacy had a dark side, it lay not in deeds left undone, but in too many deeds done too well. Their sheer energy often eclipsed all reflection. Right up to his death, the tireless Cotton Mather, author of *Essays to Do Good,* never stopped marking "GDs" (for "Good Deeds") in the margin of his diary. A regimented instinct for social discipline limited them to the starkest of metaphors—the ant or bee colony—to describe their ideal society. "All nature is industrious and every creature about us diligent in their proper work," preached the sixtyish Colman. "Diligence is the universal example. Look through the whole creation, and every part it has a work and service assigned to it." By old age, many Glorious hoped that the two new colleges they had founded—Yale and William and Mary—might allow their children to aspire to something higher than "diligence." "Pray God," sighed the aging "King" Carter, "send the next generation that it may flourish under a set of better polished patriots." The colonies did indeed get "polish"—and much else besides.

ENLIGHTENMENT GENERATION

Born: 1674–1700
Type: Adaptive

Age Location:
Glorious Revolution Crisis in youth
Great Awakening in midlife

" 'Tis no small matter for a stripling to appear in a throng of so many learned and judicious seers," announced a William and Mary student to the Virginia Assembly in 1699 on behalf of his fledgling college. The next young speaker promised that every student would "kindly submit himself to the maternal and paternal yoke," and a third described his peers as the most "docile and tutorable" in the world. "O happy Virginia!" he concluded. "Your countenance is all we crave." Careful to avoid a misstep, the ENLIGHTENMENT GENERATION came of age eager to mature into the "better-polished generation" the Glorious had hoped for. And so they became. Growing up during an era of crisis, they witnessed the blood shed by elders on their behalf. Entering adulthood just as peace and prosperity dawned, they appreciated their good fortune and did not dare risk upsetting the status quo. Yet behind all the nice ornaments they added to colonial life—the minuets, carriages, and libraries; the lawsuits, vote counting, and purchased pews—lay an inner life of gnawing anxiety. The Enlighteners never stopped worrying that their refinement and sensitivity betrayed an absence of generational power and vision, that their nibbling reforms amounted to mere gesture, and that their leaders tended to defer rather than solve problems.

Tying together this record of outer polish and inner tension is the Enlighteners' lifecycle, best defined by the cataclysms they just missed coming of age: the Glorious Revolution and the Great Awakening. First-wavers arrived too early (at age 15–16) to take part in political triumph, while late-wavers arrived too late (in their mid-30s) to take part in spiritual revival. Too early or too late. Either way, the absence of coming-of-age catharsis robbed them of a visceral peer bond. It made them better mediators for other generations than confident leaders of their own—and it impelled them to hunker down early, a caution for which they paid by missing (though often seeking) release later on. Reaching midlife, when they had finally outgrown the shadow of their elders, Enlighteners took more risks in a society bursting open with enterprise and fashion, art and wit, social mobility and rising immigration. Yet hardly had they begun to enjoy this freshness when they heard younger moralists condemn them for moving in the wrong direction. Caught in a generational whipsaw, those who had once defended their civic muscle to elders spent their later years defending their moral purity to juniors. For the few Enlighteners who survived (in their eighties) until the American Revolution, proving themselves to the young was a rearguard battle they rarely won, but never gave up.

The Enlighteners produced the first American writers and aesthetes to compete in erudition with their European peers; the first credentialed professionals in science, medicine, religion, and law; the first printers and postal carriers; and the first specialist-managers of towns, businesses, and plantations. Yet for all their wit and learning, they had one common denominator: a fatal indecisiveness, a fear of stepping too far in any direction. In civic life, the strength of the next-elder Glorious, Enlighteners specialized in stalemating executive action through legislative process. Voicing the consensus of historians, William Pencak notes that "between Queen Anne's and King George's Wars"—precisely when Enlighteners began to dominate colonial assemblies—"two styles of politics prevailed in British North America: paralysis and procrastination." Nor could they wholly accept the inner-driven passion of spiritual life, the strength of younger Awakeners. "Zeal" is "but an erratic fire, that will often lead to bogs and precipices," warned Thomas Foxcroft, author of *An Essay on Kindness*. The function of a minister, according to Nathaniel Appleton, was "pointing out those middle and peaceable ways, wherein the truth generally lies, and guarding against extremes on the right hand and on the left."

Individual Enlighteners are sometimes referred to as "inheritor" or "transitional" figures. Together, they might also be called America's first "silent" generation. Without question, no other American peer group includes so few leaders (James Logan? Cadwallader Colden? Elisha Cooke, Jr.? William Shirley? William Byrd II?) whose names Americans still recognize. The same goes for their precious squabbles, resembling those of their peers in England—Walpole's vote-jobbing, Pope's mock epics, Butler's clockwork universe—full of post-heroic affectation, utterly forgotten today. Yet the very mood of anonymous stasis the Enlighteners brought to their initial years of power, the 1720s and 1730s, transformed that era into the Williamsburg prototype of colonial life. No other period fits. Earlier, we would have seen hogs instead of coaches on the streets of Boston; later, we would have heard fiery sermons about Antichrist instead of fulsome odes to a golden age of politeness. During the century and a half between Newton and Rousseau, this generation best reflects, at its adult apogee, what historians call the Age of Enlightenment, that delicate equipoise between certainty and doubt, order and emotion, gentility and candor. "Enlightenment" suggests perfect balance, the lifetime goal of a generation that always felt off-balance. It is a name they themselves would have relished.

ENLIGHTENMENT GENERATION (Born 1674 to 1700)

TYPE: Adaptive

Total number: 340,000
Percent immigrant: 34%
Percent slave: 17%

FAMILY TREE

Typical grandparents: Puritan
Parents: Cavalier and Glorious
Children: Awakening and Liberty
Typical grandchildren: Republican

SAMPLE MEMBERS, birth (death)

1674 William Byrd II (1744)
1674 James Logan (1751)*
1676 Alexander Spotswood (1740)*
1678 Elisha Cooke, Jr. (1737)
1679 Zabdiel Boylston (1766)
1685 Daniel Dulany (1753)*
1686 Andrew Bradford (1742)
1688 Cadwallader Colden (1776)*
1690 Thomas Lee (1750)
1690 Johann Conrad Beissel (1768)*
1691 Mann Page (1730)
1693 Nathaniel Appleton (1784)
1694 William Shirley (1771)*
1696 Samuel Johnson (1772)
1696 Sir William Pepperrell (1759)
1696 Ebenezer Gay (1787)
1697 Thomas Foxcroft (1769)
1697 James Franklin (1735)
1697 Peter Zenger (1746)*
1699 John Bartram (1777)
* = immigrant

PERIOD OF POLITICAL LEADERSHIP

First and last year of colonial governorship
and total duration of officeholding
(permanent immigrants only):

Massachusetts: 1715–1757, 28 years
Connecticut: 1741–1769, 28 years
Rhode Island: 1740–1758, 16 years
Virginia: 1710–1768, 58 years

PROMINENT FOREIGN PEERS

1676 Robert Walpole (1745)
1685 Bishop George Berkeley (1753)
1685 George Frederick Handel (1759)
1694 Voltaire (1778)
1696 James Edward Oglethorpe (1785)

Age	Date	HISTORY AND LIFECYCLE
0– 1	1675:	Start of King Philip's War and Bacon's Rebellion
0–15	1689:	Glorious Revolution and King William's War (1690–1697)
0–18	1692:	Salem witch trials; acceleration of slave imports to South
1–27	1701:	Yale College founded (after William and Mary in 1693)
13–39	1713:	Queen Anne's War (1702–1713) ends with Treaty of Utrecht
21–47	1721:	James Franklin begins printing New England Courant in Boston
28–54	1728:	George Berkeley visits Rhode Island (1728–1731) to public acclaim
40–66	1740:	Peak of Great Awakening; founding of separatist churches
45–71	1745:	Shirley and Pepperrell capture Louisbourg from French
63–89	1763:	French and Indian War (1754–1760) ends with Treaty of Paris
65–91	1765:	Stamp Act riots; leading elders plead for conciliation
76 +	1776:	Declaration of Independence signed

SAMPLE CULTURAL ENDOWMENTS: *Secret Diary* (William Byrd II); *The Reasonableness of Regular Singing* (Thomas Symmes); *Ministers Are Men of Like Passions with Others* (Ebenezer Gay); *Cato's Moral Distiches Englished in Couplets* (James Logan); *God Sometimes Answers* (Eliphalet Adams); *Flora Virginica* (John Clayton); *Journal of the Siege of Louisbourg* (William Shirley)

Enlightener Facts

• The Enlighteners include the first large population (over 50,000) of African-born Americans, about triple the total number of blacks in all previous generations combined. Primarily young slaves purchased by elder Glorious planters, these Enlighteners were the first of four large generations of African-Americans—extending through the Republicans—transported to America on slave ships.

• The Enlighteners were the least geographically mobile generation in American history. Among native-born New Englanders, only 23 percent died more than sixteen miles from their birthplace, less than half the share for every generation born before or after. In the southern colonies, they were the first landed planters whose marriages and inheritances were dynastically arranged by (mostly Glorious) parents.

• The Enlighteners ran America's first bar and clerical associations, managed America's first electoral machines (in Boston and Philadelphia), included the first significant number of doctors and scientists with European credentials, and gained more memberships in the prestigious London Royal Society than any other colonial generation.

• Founders of many church- and town-based charities, the Enlighteners were the most humanitarian of colonial generations. In the early 1730s, their English peer James Oglethorpe colonized Georgia as a haven for imprisoned debtors. He financed the venture entirely through private donations.

• As Anglophile rising adults, Enlighteners brought to America the Queen Anne style of dainty china, walnut cabinets, parquet floors, and what they termed "comfortable" furniture. They also adopted the new English fad of tea drinking, never imagining that their children and grandchildren would someday dump the stuff contemptuously into Boston harbor.

The Enlightener Lifecycle

YOUTH: Growing up in the midst of rebellion and war, Enlightener children learned to split the universe into two halves. On one side, recalled Samuel Johnson, lurked a gallery of "bogeymen"—dark forests filled with Indians, armies, and infant-hungry devils. On the other side lay the safety of the family, protected by the smothering embrace of midlife Cavaliers like Samuel Willard ("If others in a family suffer want, yet the children shall certainly be taken care for") and the confident energy of rising-adult Glorious like Cotton Mather ("restrain your children from bad company. . . . You can't be too careful in these matters''). In New England, towns appointed tithingmen ''to attend to disorders of every kind in the families under their charge'' and sent children to ''dame schools'' in nearby households rather than let them risk long walks outdoors. In the South, the vast influx of bonded young Africans traumatized youths of both races. With the first glimmers of peace at the end of the century, adults encouraged children to emulate emerging sex-role divisions. Girls privileged to become ''virtuous mothers'' were tutored in religion, music, and embroidery and learned to wear towering ''fontanelle'' hairstyles. Boys attired in wigs were sent to writing schools—or to the new colleges. Yale assured parents that the souls of their children were in safekeeping, while the charter of William and Mary promised that young gentlemen would be ''piously educated in good letters and manners.''

COMING OF AGE: Haunted through youth by fears of ''disorder,'' Enlighteners matured into compliant, immobile, and parent-respecting young adults. Seeking approval, their peer elite mastered structured and value-neutral subjects like botany (John Bartram), mapmaking (Lewis Evans), medicine (Zabdiel Boylston), and especially law (Jeremiah Dummer, Daniel Dulany, and Thomas Lee). Such achievements earned them respect more than admiration. By the late 1690s, the Glorious began complaining about youthful behavior that failed to meet their own super-straight standard at like age. Elders chafed at the snooty English mannerisms of youth—from coffeehouse etiquette to ribald verse—and suspected them of cowardice during Queen Anne's War (which ended in a stalemate in 1711). They fretted over the young generation's cardplaying, swearing, taverning, and premarital pregnancy—petty vices indicating post-adolescent tension release. Yet if the Cavaliers and Glorious considered them effete, coming-of-age Enlighteners felt perfectly justified in bringing a touch of wit and class to the dull conformity of post-crisis America. Here a handful of them stood their ground. In 1721, James Franklin set up a Boston newspaper and lampooned the fiftyish Cotton Mather (who, notes historian Perry Miller, ''appeared, for the first time, silly''). In 1723, Yale graduate Samuel Johnson shocked New England by announcing his conversion to the Anglican Church. Such tepid, isolated gestures amounted to the closest the Enlighteners ever came to generational rebellion.

RISING ADULTHOOD: ''The Golden Age succeeds the Iron,'' announced the *Rhode Island Gazette* in 1732, celebrating the ''erudition and politeness'' Enlighteners were bringing to colonial ''civilization.'' Outwardly, these rising adults were lucky, setting out in life in a new era of peace and prosperity. Seemingly without effort, their well-groomed elite could inherit or marry into upwardly mobile lifestyles—as town leaders (now versed in law), as genteel planters (now building symmetrical, Williamsburg-style mansions), as colonial agents (now riding in coaches), or as managers of trading empires (now familiar with luxuries). Inwardly, they compensated for their denied catharsis by obsessing guiltily over the rococo interior of their lives. "The Grandeur (ah, empty grandeur!) of New England," worried 26-year-old Thomas Paine. "Our apparel, how fine and rich! Our furniture and tables, how costly, sumptuous, and dainty!" William Byrd II studied the *Complete Gentleman* to improve on the manly virtue of his Glorious father, while hiding his sexual and poetic fantasies in a secret coded diary. Attracted to emotional privacy while inheriting a deep trust in institutions, Enlighteners gathered in "philosophical" associations, "virtuoso" societies, and humanitarian charities. They also embraced a new ethos of professionalism and dominated the explosive post-1720 growth in colonial law. Reaching office in the 1720s and 1730s, they became what historian Jack Greene has labeled "the new political professionals"—and their parliamentary bickering marks the dullest pages in colonial history. Compared to the like-aged Glorious, rising-adult Enlighteners were more apt to sue than vote, lobby than build, and advocate private process rather than collective action.

MIDLIFE: Enlighteners took a subversive pleasure in the looser and freer tone of colonial society in the 1730s. Past age 40, many took risks for the first time: speculating in land, launching new businesses, womanizing, poetizing. A few dabbled in skeptical philosophy (of Berkeley and Hume) or in mystical religion (Zinzendorf's Moravian Church). All this nervous joviality came to a sudden end around 1740, thanks to the youth-propelled Great Awakening. Midlife Enlighteners had sensed it coming; indeed, their clergymen had long urged "refreshed" emotion in church. Yet face to face with unbridled passion, they quickly realized how little regard the younger Awakeners showed for the Enlighteners' own strengths—credentials, politeness, pluralism, and deference. Condemned by Awakener Jonathan Edwards as "moral neuters," many sank into guilt. "I have studied to preserve a due moderation," admitted Edward Wigglesworth, "and if any expressions have happened to slip from me, that may seem a little too warm or harsh, I shall be sorry for it." While Samuel Niles feared "strife and contention" and Benjamin Doolittle warned of "too much boldness," most Enlighteners responded to their next-juniors with a sympathy, even an envy that revealed their own inner doubts. Nathaniel Appleton, said one observer, became "more close and affecting in preaching" after hearing the youthful enthusiasts. Admiring the passion of the younger George Whitefield, clergyman Samuel Dexter confessed: "ten thousand worlds would I give . . . to feel and experience what I believe that man does."

ELDERHOOD: "I don't think I know anything," said the aging Nathaniel Chauncy in 1756 after reading a popular book on religion. "Forty years have I been studying, and this book has told me more than I have ever known." Most Enlighteners entered old age with a remarkable capacity to rethink narrow childhood prejudices, admit failure, and try again. "The greatest and worst sorts of trouble and uneasiness," lamented Samuel Johnson shortly before his death in 1772, "are endless doubts, scruples, uncertainties, and perplexities of mind." Superseded as leaders by moralistic midlife Awakeners, many old Enlighteners tried, like Johnson, to be "yet further useful" as elders. When the stakes seemed limited, they behaved with imitative swagger—like William Shirley and William Pepperrell, gung-ho leaders of the colonial crusade against the French in the 1740s and 1750s. But later, as the stakes grew larger, they usually argued for compromise. Daniel Dulany and Thomas Lee supported "polite" and "friendly intercourse" with the English, and Ebenezer Gay (in the words of one admirer) tried "to point out that there was another side to every controversy." The handful who lived to see the outbreak of revolution typically hoped, like Daniel Perkins, for "that calmness, dispassionateness, and prudence that may prevent rage and acts of violence." Ultimately, the 79-year-old Perkins was forced by his juniors to sign a statement endorsing the American Revolution. Cadwallader Colden, New York governor and *philosophe,* struggled in vain to arrange a compromise in 1776. Watching every symbol of his beloved mother country smashed in fury, he died that same year, at age 88, not knowing how the crisis would be resolved.

                                                        *   *   *

The Enlighteners were the most decent, accommodating, and pluralist—if also the most colorless—of colonial generations. Their collective legacy can be inferred from their eulogies, which typically reflect a painful struggle for equilibrium. Clergyman Thomas Greaves was remembered as "exact, but unaffected . . . grave, but not morose"; Nathaniel Appleton as "impartial yet pacific, firm yet conciliatory"; William Byrd II as "eminently fitted for the service and ornament of his country," yet "to all this were added a great elegance of taste and life." As mediators between the civic hubris of their elders and the inner fire of their juniors, Enlighteners prevented the colonial world from twisting too far in either direction. They pioneered "freedom of the press," used their relative affluence to adorn colonial culture, and cultivated a respect for "due process" that their grandchildren later incorporated into a national Constitution. Yet for all the balance they brought to public life, their own personal lives took them on a zigzag path of overcompensation. As rising adults, they knuckled under too easily to rulebook conformity. In midlife, dazzled by the younger Awakeners and left with anxious memories of their own smothered youth, they veered so far toward personal adventure and hands-off parenting that they failed to protect an emerging crop of Liberty children. No one called the Enlighteners a great generation, but then again they did not try to be. They sought approval from others and tried to be helpful in great struggles that—often to their secret frustration—never seemed to hit them full force.

Chapter 8

THE REVOLUTIONARY CYCLE

"O may our camp be free from every accursed thing! May our land be purged from all its sins! May we be truly a holy people, and all our towns cities of righteousness!" Thus did the gray-haired president of Harvard Samuel Langdon lead 1,200 soldiers in twilight prayer on the Cambridge Common. Early the next morning, on June 17, 1775, William Prescott guided these Patriot troops to a rise near Bunker Hill overlooking the British army that occupied Boston. Prescott, who would slay redcoats with his sword before the day was over, was a gritty Indian-war veteran in his forties. He had little of Langdon's flair for elevated words. "Don't fire until you see the whites of their eyes," he advised his men, before adding with a smile, "Then aim at their waistbands; and be sure to pick off the commanders, known by their handsome coats." The twentyish soldiers obediently did as they were told. Seeing the redcoats fall in piles before them, they knew they had won not just a battle, but glory in the eyes of all posterity. Meanwhile, a young mother led her 8-year-old child "Mr. Johnny" (John Quincy Adams) to a nearby hill where he could watch the cannons thunder at a safe distance. The stage was set. All four generations of the REVOLUTIONARY CYCLE were present at an epochal moment that signaled the birth of a new nation.

• For Langdon's AWAKENING GENERATION (Idealist, then age 52 to 74), the Battle of Bunker Hill tested a vision that had first inspired them decades ago as coming-of-age youngsters. Back then, an upwelling of godly euphoria had incited them to rage against their fathers. "Many such instances there were of children condemning their parents" and calling them "old hypocrites," young Charles Chauncy had written of his twentyish peers in 1743. Much later, by the time of the Revolution, that ideal had matured into stern principles of civic virtue which leading Awakeners—from Sam Adams to Benjamin Franklin—preached entirely to their juniors. It was time for the old to think and the young to act. "Love itself is a consuming fire with respect to sin," Joseph Bellamy told the Connecticut volunteers who came to Boston. Joseph Hawley likewise inspired the Minutemen under Prescott by reminding them of their Puritan ancestors: "You will show by your future conduct whether you are worthy to be called offspring of such men." The elder Awakeners had raised these "republican" youth for worldly valor—and praised them warmly when they displayed it against General Howe.

• Prescott's LIBERTY GENERATION (Reactive, age 34 to 51) shrugged off this dialogue between next-elders and next-juniors. The Awakeners' inner fire was something they had learned to avoid, something that had scorched them once as berated children and again, during the 1750s, as despised foot soldiers in a murderous crusade against the French. Colonel Prescott was not alone in his wry wit. From George Washington to Daniel Boone, from Francis Marion to Benedict Arnold, the French and Indian War had left its mark of devilry and cynicism on their entire generation. "Rifleman" Daniel Morgan even had the scars of 499 British lashes on his back to prove it. (His punishment called for 500, but when the quartermaster miscounted, Morgan joked, "I got away with one.") As for the younger soldiers on Bunker Hill, Prescott and his peers did what they could to teach them the grim realities of life and war. The Liberty entered the Revolution without counting on a good outcome for themselves. No matter which side they chose or which side won, these hardbitten peers of John Adams—a generation whom historian Cecilia Kenyon has called "men of little faith"— fully expected to be blamed. Most of them would indeed reach elderhood getting just what they expected: little thanks and precious little reward.

• For the eager soldiers of the REPUBLICAN GENERATION (Civic, age 9 to 33), waiting in their trenches for the redcoats to charge, Bunker Hill began the most exhilarating rite of passage in American history. " 'Tis but the morning of the world for us," Princeton student Hugh Henry Brackenridge had announced a year earlier. "Nations shall be taught lessons of heroism and grow great by our example," exulted Israel Evans to his peers six years later, after their epic victory at Yorktown. To most elder Liberty (like John Adams) the war marked the end of Revolution. But to younger

FIGURE 8-1
Revolutionary Cycle: Location in History

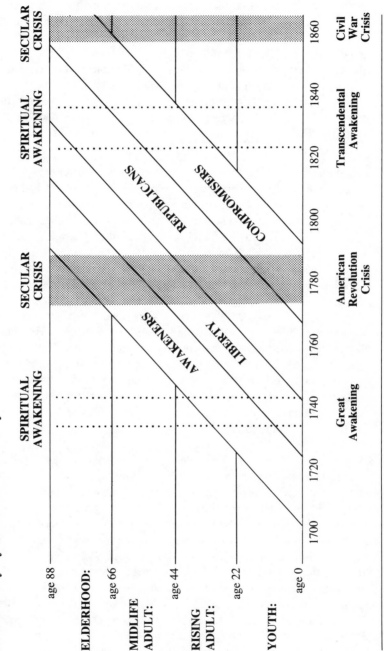

Republicans (like Benjamin Rush) it "was nothing but the first act of a great drama"—a drama that would not end until this mighty generation had built a new Constitution, acquired vast new territories, and seen (as Timothy Dwight once predicted) "Round thy broad fields more glorious Romes arise/ With pomp and splendor bright'ning all the skies." Where the elder Awakeners who loved and praised these youngsters had been a more godly generation than most, so would the Republicans become more worldly than most. Historian Edmund Morgan sums up the contrast: "In the 1740s America's leading intellectuals were clergymen and thought about theology; in 1790 they were statesmen and thought about politics."

• To John Quincy Adams' COMPROMISE GENERATION (Adaptive, age 8 and under) came the frustration of watching the war without fighting it— and then growing up realizing that their gigantic next-elders had completed all the great deeds just ahead of them. Their own role, they soon discovered, was simply to be good and dutiful—and to avoid mistakes. John Quincy himself, careful not to disappoint his fussy mother Abigail, graduated from college feeling a "useless and disgraceful insignificancy." The like-aged Andrew Jackson later declared that his fellow soldiers must not forget "the blessings which the blood of so many thousands of heroes has purchased for them." As a Dartmouth student, Daniel Webster declaimed: "For us they fought! For us they bled! For us they conquered!" Webster, only an infant when the war ended, would consecrate a Bunker Hill monument forty-three years later by acknowledging his generation's "gratitude" to Republican "heroes." Only as these "heroes" began passing away in the 1820s would the Compromisers, now reaching midlife, emerge from their elders' intimidating shadow. By then, Webster's peers would have to turn their attention in a new direction—this time toward a loud younger generation just coming of age.

Bunker Hill was the first full-scale battle in a crisis whose origins stretch back decades, to the very beginning of the Revolutionary Cycle. The cycle began with the soul-shattering conversions that greeted Jonathan Edwards' Northampton sermons in 1734, the first genuine thunder of the eighteenth-century "Great Awakening." It reached forward through the French and Indian War, the Revolutionary War, the Constitutional Convention, and the War of 1812, and closed with James Monroe's outwardly calm but inwardly turbulent "Era of Good Feeling" in the mid-1820s. This cycle left behind a shining legacy of nation-building that Americans will always cherish. But having solved so many problems, these four generations could hardly help allowing others to fester. Most notably, they failed to act on the issue of southern slavery, an omission which would figure fatefully in the next awakening—and in the next crisis.

The Revolutionary Cycle contained two social moments:

• *The Great Awakening* (1734–1743) began as a series of isolated spiritual revivals in the Connecticut Valley. It spread quickly, especially in the northern
and middle colonies, and reached a peak in 1741 during the rousing American tour of the English-born evangelist George Whitefield. After mass
gatherings and "concerts of prayer" in the early 1740s, the fervor receded
in most areas—but not without reshaping the temperament of most rising
adults who had lived through it. They would later reach midlife setting a
tone of spirituality and public principle utterly unknown during their fathers'
"Glacial Age of Religion." *AGE LOCATION: Glorious in elderhood; Enlighteners in midlife; Awakeners in rising adulthood; Liberty in youth.*

• *The American Revolution Crisis* (1773–1789), broadly defined, stretched from
the Boston Tea Party through the ratification of the Constitution and the
swearing-in of the first President and Congress in 1789. Amid all the brave
moments, especially that dark Valley Forge winter of 1778, lurked the very
real fear that these "rebels" might fail and that the leaders of the Continental
Congress would be hanged as traitors. The crisis ended with the ratification
of the new Constitution and the inauguration of President George Washington and Vice President John Adams. Over the next twelve years, Washington and Adams steered the infant nation with protective caution while
watching a younger, more optimistic cadre of veterans rise to power and
plan for the Republic's glorious future. *AGE LOCATION: Awakeners in
elderhood; Liberty in midlife; Republicans in rising adulthood; Compromisers in youth.*

AWAKENING GENERATION

Born: 1701–1723
Type: Idealist

Age Location:
Great Awakening in rising adulthood
American Revolution Crisis in elderhood

"You would be apt to think him a madman just broke from his chains, but especially had you seen him . . . with a large mob at his heels, singing all the way through the streets, he with his hands extended, his head thrown back, and his eyes staring up to heaven," reported the *Boston Evening Post* in 1741 of James Davenport. During a tour of New England, this 25-year-old messiah was "attended with so much disorder" that his followers "looked more like a company of Bacchanalians after a mad frolic, than sober Christians who had been worshipping God." For colonial newspapers, the frenzy marked yet one more riotous episode in America's "Great and General Awakening." For hundreds of radical preachers like Davenport—and for the young crowds smitten by their prophetic thunder—it was a coming-of-age moment for the AWAKENING GENERATION. The moment brought truth, euphoria, and millennial vision to America. It also brought hysteria, shattered families, and split towns. What did it feel like to be there? Writing in 1742, an elder Salem minister declared: "It is impossible to relate the convulsions into which the country is thrown." Writing in the 1970s, historian Richard Bushman likened the fervor to "the civil rights demonstrations, the campus disturbances, and the urban riots of the 1960s combined . . . a psychological earthquake that reshaped the human landscape."

The Awakener lifecycle reads like a prophecy: at first straining to see God through a glass darkly and at last breaking through to a purifying fire. Born into secure and slowly loosening families, Awakener children grew up seeking, but not finding, spiritual comfort in the secular world of Glorious midlifers. Coming of age, they discovered it—inside themselves. In a burst of passion, these converts to a "religion of the heart" shattered the ossified social discipline of their fathers. When the Great Awakening expired in mid-1740s, rising Awakeners drifted off into quieter avenues of self-perfection and paid little attention to the worldly troubles enveloping the colonies. Only later, as they entered midlife worrying about the dissolute younger Liberty, did Awakeners find a substitute for the old order they had wrecked. Theirs was an entirely new vision—of an America destined by Providence to play a millennial role in the salvation of the world. It would be a land where all souls stood on an equal footing, where social union depended on principle rather than convenience, where education aimed at virtue rather than utility, where grace and union took precedence over laws and rights. The Awakeners championed this spiritual agenda so persuasively that on the threshold of old age, they presided over a society of patriots ready to die for independence.

Any roster of famous Awakeners is top-heavy with moral prophets: "sons of thunder" like Jonathan Edwards, George Whitefield, and William Tennent, tearing down the "do-good" orthodoxy of their elders; flinty rationalists like Jonathan Mayhew and Charles Chauncy, insisting from their pulpits that death was preferable to the "slavery" and "corruption" of England; missionary educators like Eleazar Wheelock, John Witherspoon, and Anthony Benezet (who, according to one observer, "carried his love of humanity to the point of madness"); radical slavery-abolitionists like "Visions of Hell" Jacob Green and John Woolman (clad in white as Jesus Christ). The same image fits the best-known Awakener patriarchs who later stewarded the American Revolution: Samuel Adams and Benjamin Franklin. Still radical, still cerebral. In Boston, the austere Adams was said by one biographer to "preach hate to a degree without rival" in quest of his "Christian Sparta." In Philadelphia, Franklin believed so fervently in higher causes that he abandoned a prospering printing business in his mid-forties to devote his life to reflection and moral uplift. Careless of orthodox religion, Franklin left his soul to the evangelical prayers of his good friend Whitefield. But years earlier, at age 16, Franklin wrote in his diary that he "conceived the bold and arduous project of arriving at moral perfection" and concluded it with the self-aimed injunction to "Imitate Jesus and Socrates."

The "Puritan" label has always come easily to this generation. Contemporaries called Samuel Adams "the last of the Puritans," Roger Sherman "an old Puritan," Edwards a "Puritan" Calvinist. Even the arch-Tory Thomas Hutchinson has been described by his biographer as a "neo-Puritan ascetic." Like the Puritans, the Awakeners refused to compromise over principle or separate politics from religion. Mayhew said he had a duty to "preach politics." Patriot leader Joseph Hawley announced himself an "enthusiast in politics." Hebrew scholar and Patriot governor Jonathan Trumbull sprinkled his war correspondence with the phrase "The Lord Reigneth." In exile, Peter Oliver blamed the Revolution on what he called America's "black regiment." By that he meant old Awakeners preaching upheaval in their churches—ministers like 72-year-old Samuel Dunbar, who read the entire Declaration of Independence from his pulpit. Not all elderly Awakeners, of course, became Patriots during the Revolution. Some became Tories and sailed away to pass their twilight years in Canada or England. But few Tory Awakeners ever felt much affinity with their generation, even decades before the Revolution; virtually none had shared their peers' euphoria during the Great Awakening. The Tory Awakener was a self-confessed outcast,

AWAKENING GENERATION (Born 1701 to 1723)

TYPE: Idealist

Total number: 550,000
Percent immigrant: 19%
Percent slave: 18%

SAMPLE MEMBERS, birth (death)

```
     1703  Jonathan Edwards (1758)
     1703  Gilbert Tennent (1764)*
     1706  Benjamin Franklin (1790)
     1710  Jonathan Trumbull (1785)
     1710  Richard Bland (1776)
     1711  Thomas Hutchinson (1780)
     1711  Jupiter Hammon (c. 1800)
     1713  Anthony Benezet (1784)*
     1714  George Whitefield (1770)*
     1720  John Woolman (1772)
     1720  Pontiac (1769)
     1721  Peyton Randolph (1775)
     1721  Roger Sherman (1793)
     1721  Samuel Hopkins (1803)
c.   1722  Eliza Pinckney (1793)
     1722  Samuel Adams (1803)
     1723  William Livingston (1790)
     1723  Crispus Attucks (1770)
     1723  Samson Occom (1792)
     1723  John Witherspoon (1794)*
```
* = immigrant

FAMILY TREE

Typical grandparents: Cavalier
Parents: Glorious and Enlightenment
Children: Liberty and Republican
Typical grandchildren: Compromiser

PERIOD OF POLITICAL LEADERSHIP

First and last year of colonial governorship
   and total duration of officeholding
   (permanent immigrants only):

Massachusetts: 1760–1774, 14 years
Connecticut: 1769–1776, 7 years
Rhode Island: 1755–1776, 17 years
Virginia: 1750–1776, 13 years

Presidency of Continental Congress: 1774–
   1775, 1781–1782

PROMINENT FOREIGN PEERS

1703 John Wesley (1791)
1707 Henry Fielding (1754)
1712 Jean Jacques Rousseau (1778)
1712 Frederick the Great (1786)
1717 Maria Theresa (1780)

Age	Date	HISTORY AND LIFECYCLE
0–12	1713:	Treaty of Utrecht; longest peace in colonial era begins
0–19	1720	Appearance of grand Georgian buildings; growing household opulence
11–33	1734:	First outbreak of youth conversions in Connecticut River Valley
17–39	1740:	Peak of Great Awakening; many slaves convert to Christianity
31–53	1754:	Albany Congress adopts Franklin's "Plan of Union"
42–64	1765:	Stamp Act riots; leading midlifers preach civic revival
50–72	1773:	Adams and Molineux organize Boston Tea Party
52–74	1775:	Continental Congress proclaims Thanksgiving Day prayer and fasting
60–82	1783:	Slave ownership abolished in most northern states
64–86	1787:	Franklin, Sherman, and Livingston attend Constitutional Convention
67–89	1790:	Franklin dies, huge funeral in Philadelphia, eulogies in France
70–92	1793:	Samuel Hopkins publishes *Doctrines Contained in Divine Revelation*

SAMPLE CULTURAL ENDOWMENTS: *Autobiography, Poor Richard's Almanac* (Benjamin Franklin); *Sinners in the Hands of an Angry God* (Jonathan Edwards); *Spiritual Travels of Nathan Cole* (Nathan Cole); *Christian Sobriety* (Jonathan Mayhew); *The Danger of an Unconverted Ministry* (Gilbert Tennent); *Christ Triumphing and Satan Raging* (Samuel Finley); *Some Considerations on the Keeping of Negroes* (John Woolman); *The Duty of Self Examination* (Roger Sherman) bewildered by what the exiled Samuel Curwen termed the "imprudence . . . even madness" of his peers. "I must own I was born among the saints and rebels," explained New York Tory Samuel Auchmuty just before his death in 1777, "but it was my misfortune."

Awakener Facts

- The Great Awakening has been credited with 250 new churches and 200,000 religious conversions, "chiefly" or "especially" (according to contemporary observers) the work of "young people." Among Presbyterians in 1740, "New Side" revivalists averaged 25 years of age; defenders of the "Old Side" orthodoxy averaged 59 years of age. From 1730 to 1745, the average age of joining a New England church plummeted from the late thirties to the mid-twenties, and the share of new church members joining before age thirty rose from one-fifth to two-thirds.

- More American colonists graduated from Harvard in the 1730s (nearly all of them twentyish Awakeners) than in any other decade until the 1760s. The colonists published more books on the Antichrist and Last Judgment during the 1750s (written mostly by Awakeners entering midlife) than in any other decade before the Revolution. Awakeners Jupiter Hammon and Samson Occom were the first black and Indian, respectively, to write for publication in America.

- Awakener women assumed positions of visibility unprecedented in colonial society: religious leaders (like Sarah Osborn in Rhode Island), Indian missionaries (like the Moravian "single sisters" in Pennsylvania), and planters (like Eliza Pinckney, who ran three plantations in South Carolina and became the first American to cultivate indigo).

- Awakeners entering elderhood were America's leaders of choice at the outset of the American Revolution. From 1774 to 1776, the average age of officeholding in New England towns rose from the low forties to the low fifties. In 1776, eleven of the thirteen new "states" were in effect led by Awakeners. In five colonies, the Revolution threw out younger (Liberty) Tories and replaced them with elder (Awakener) Patriots. Awakeners Peyton Randolph and Henry Middleton were the first two presidents of the Continental Congress.

- Awakener clergyman John Witherspoon, president of the recently founded Princeton College for twenty-six years, was the beloved schoolmaster to an entire generation of rational Republican statesmen (including Madison, Burr, Marshall, ten future cabinet leaders, and sixty future members of Congress).

The Awakener Lifecycle

YOUTH: Raised in secure communities and largely spared from war or violence, Americans born after 1700 grew up as the best-fed, best-housed, and best-educated generation of children their elders had ever seen. At home, these kids listened to the happy discipline of *A Family Well Ordered,* in which Cotton Mather taught that "our submission to the rules of reason is an obedience to God." In school, their standardized *New England Primer* drummed the same message with the "Dutiful Child's Prayer." Yet soon these children began turning away from their distant, busy fathers—and toward their mothers, whom the Glorious had entrusted with piety and emotion. Many Awakeners later vowed with George Whitefield "to make good my mother's expectations" or chose with Samuel Adams to abandon worldly careers to please their mothers' "religious principles." A striking number (including Benjamin Franklin, Richard Bland, and Roger Sherman) became bookish loners. Others were hit by dreamlike visions. Young Jonathan Edwards walked off to "solitary places, for meditation" where he could reflect on "the divine glory in almost everything." Young John Woolman imagined "past ages" in which people "walked in uprightness before God in a degree exceeding any that I knew, or heard of, now living." By the 1720s and 1730s, teenagers began crowding into colleges seeking spiritual callings or sparking town riots against such perceived agents of immorality as brothels, market houses, smallpox inoculators, and immigrants. The Boston press in 1734 called them "a new sort of reformers, vulgarly called the mob." According to historian Gary Nash, these youths were "antirational, antiscientific . . . and moralistic"—rejecting the secular world their Glorious fathers were about to hand them.

COMING OF AGE: With the Great Awakening, the raging inner life of these indulged young Americans exploded in a spiritual firestorm. In 1734, wrote Edwards, the firestorm first struck his own town like "a flash of lightning upon the hearts of the young people." By the late 1730s and early 1740s, it had spread through most of the colonies. In colleges, young Awakeners banded together in clubs of "saints"; from pulpits, they fulminated against the "spirit-dead"; in open-air gatherings, they exhorted each other to leave their parents, if necessary, to join Christ. Where the like-aged Glorious had once stressed cheerful teamwork, young Awakeners preached spiritual perfection, demanding "New Light" faith over "Old Light" works, mixing "kisses of charity" with what Charles Chauncy called "a censuring and judging spirit." Denouncing elders who kept "driving, driving to duty, duty!" Gilbert Tennent assaulted "those of another generation" who "imagine happiness is to be had in wealth and riches." As for the pliable Enlighteners, Samuel Finley roared: "Away with your carnal prudence!" When the enthusiasm faded in the mid-1740s, the orthodoxy mounted a reaction that expelled many students from college and punished with special vengeance Awakener slaves who had staged rebellions during the frenzy. Inwardly, however, the young knew their triumph was complete. Americans of all ages would never again preach or pray or feel as they had before. And for most Awakeners themselves, a special memory would linger—of that day or week or season when they had created a spiritual community. Many, like Edwards, declared that America in 1740 was inaugurating the reign of God on earth, a "New Jerusalem . . . begun to come down from heaven." Decades later, Franklin would fondly recall Philadelphia in that same year: "It was wonderful to see the change. . . . It seemed as if all the world were growing religious."

RISING ADULTHOOD: After their explosion of self-discovery, thirtyish Awakeners entered adulthood with a mixture of outer detachment and inner principle. In Boston, Samuel Adams drifted through menial jobs ("I glory in being what the world calls a poor man"). In New York, William Livingston dabbled in law and wrote best-selling poems like *Philosophic Solitude.* In Virginia, Landon Carter saw fit "to cultivate the inward man." Meanwhile, young spiritual prophets hit the road—converting Indians, denouncing slavery, gathering separatist churches, and founding communes. Rising Awakeners made poor citizens. Most avoided voting or running for office, and many left home at an early age to join newer, younger towns. In effect, they reversed their parents' lifecycle: Values first, they insisted, then worldly things. "What can all the world afford us," asked Ebenezer Pemberton, "beyond a competent supply of our bodily wants?" Young men understood that born-again innocence (becoming "again like a child," to use Edwards' phrase) meant rejecting their fathers' interest in prestige and power. Young women likewise understood that they need not become one of Mather's "hidden ones." Although Awakeners recognized America's growing military and economic problems, they were obsessed primarily with moral dramas. Frontier preachers like Samuel Finley saw the French and Indian War as a replay of Armageddon, Virginia reformers like Bland attacked "the least flaw" in colonial rights, and rising Pennsylvania Quakers resigned en masse from public office in the late 1750s rather than compromise their pacifism by fighting Indians. "If the potsherds of the earth clash together," said Samuel Fothergill on behalf of his scrupulous peers, "let them clash."

MIDLIFE: "Let sin be slain!" boomed theologian Joseph Bellamy in 1762 as he addressed his late-fortyish peers in the Connecticut assembly while decrying the "luxury, idleness, debauchery" of the rising generation. Entering midlife, Awakeners at last began turning their principles toward the outer world. In the early 1760s, far from delighting in the victorious end of the French and Indian War, they expressed horror over America's growing moral decadence, especially the "gangrene" and "vice" of the wild young Liberty. In 1765, they responded to Britain's Stamp Act by organizing popular crusades of economic austerity and breast-beating virtue. As assembly leaders, they founded Committees of Correspondence to bind America into what Mayhew termed a "communion of colonies." As town leaders and educators, they sparked what historian Michael Kammen calls "an awakening of civic consciousness"—a new passion for public-spirited clubs and colleges. As printers, they used Franklin's "Join or Die" slogan to roar out the rhetoric of unity. As popular leaders, they led the Boston Massacre (Crispus Attucks) and the Boston Tea Party (Samuel Adams, William Molineux). Watching colonial resistance to Britain quicken toward the point of no return, Awakeners never lost sight of the moral issue. John Witherspoon, president of Princeton College, vowed "to prefer war with all its horrors, and even extermination, to slavery." Clergyman Jonathan Parsons promised that if the British did not relent, "the spirit of Christian benevolence would animate us to fill our streets with blood." In 1774, to the thunderous applause of the First Continental Congress, Joseph Hawley proclaimed, "It is evil against right."

ELDERHOOD: "We shall succeed if we are virtuous," Samuel Adams insisted. "I am infinitely more apprehensive of the contagion of vice than the power of all other enemies." As generals or administrators, aging Awakeners had little talent. But as inner-driven chieftains of virtue and wisdom ("Let us act like . . . wise men," said Adams in 1772), Americans of all ages preferred them to younger men during the moment of trial. Their moralistic leadership dominated the initial revolutionary movement. In the Continental Congress, old Awakeners enacted blue laws to make "true religion and good morals" the national credo. In local Patriot committees, they led the ideological radicals— insisting on unanimous votes, requiring Tories to "confess" to their conversion, or invoking (like the sixtyish Bellamy) the "Curse of Meroz" against cowardice. During the war, they relinquished political power to make room for the much-younger Republicans whom they trusted and loved. But even in the 1780s and 1790s, elderly Awakeners retained a voice of authority, a voice the young took seriously. Many of their political leaders favored a new Constitution that would empower the rising Republican elite, and many of their clergymen continued to agitate against the "sin of slavery," forcing the legal or de facto emancipation of northern slaves by the end of the century. Facing death, the Awakener instinct was not to reach back for the world, but to transcend it—writing about the Last Judgment (Sherman), philosophizing in salons (Franklin), or requesting no show of mourning at their funerals (Samuel Mather, Cotton's son). Samuel Adams, still penniless in his eighties, insisted that a man certain of his own virtue always dies "with dignity." Claimed the elderly Landon Carter ("King" Carter's son) just before his death, "In spite of my merits, I have only inward satisfaction."

*   *   *

The Awakeners may be America's least understood and most underestimated generation. Historians agree that the spiritual fury of the Great Awakening fed directly, decades later, into the political fury of the American Revolution. According to Nathan Hatch, "few would doubt that the piety of the Awakening was the main source of the civil millennialism of the Revolutionary period." "What the colonists awakened to in 1740," agrees Alan Heimert, "was none other than independence and rebellion." Yet no historian has left us with a clear picture of the single peer group whose adult lives bridged both events. Above all, this was a generation of crusaders: the first young zealots since the Puritans to rebel against their fathers; and the last elder moralists until the Transcendentals to urge political independence and demand freedom for slaves. Shortly before his death in 1790, 84-year-old Benjamin Franklin signed a memorial to Congress for the abolition of slavery. Three years earlier, he had been one of four Awakeners to sign the Constitution. Fourteen years earlier, he had been one of eleven Awakeners to sign the Declaration of Independence. A half century earlier, Jonathan Edwards (born only three years before Franklin) had predicted that the millennium would begin in America and make the world "a kingdom of holiness, purity, love, peace, and happiness to mankind." Although Edwards never lived to see the Revolution, Franklin had their common generation in mind when he was asked what image should adorn the national seal of the United States. With little hesitation, he answered: the fatherly image of Moses, hands extended to heaven, parting the waters for his people.

LIBERTY GENERATION

Born: 1724–1741
Type: Reactive

Age Location:
Great Awakening in youth
American Revolution Crisis in midlife

He became a daredevil colonel of the Virginia militia at age 22, and when he first heard "bullets whistle," he found "something charming in the sound." He read little, never prayed to God, and meted out brutal discipline to his own like-aged soldiers. George Washington was not alone. In 1758, while this young Virginian begged his superiors to rank him above "the *common* run of provincial officers," most of his LIBERTY GENERATION peers were coming of age with similar pluck and ambition. Daniel Boone (age 24) was checking out land bargains along the Alleghenies. John Adams (age 23) was studying hard in Boston while daydreaming about "fame, fortune, and personal pleasure." Isaac Sears (age 28) was captaining an eighteen-gun privateer in search of French merchant prey. Robert Morris (age 24) was angling to make a fortune selling war supplies. The Liberty yearned to join the worthy causes led by their elders, holy reform and the war for empire. But they soon learned that their elders did not like them. Not the British officers: General James Wolfe blasted them as "the dirtiest, most contemptible, cowardly dogs that you can conceive." Nor the Awakeners: God bless "the *small* number of saints that appear among us," prayed an older chaplain who accompanied them into battle. So, instead, the Liberty punched and tricked their way into adulthood—resenting their elders, hating themselves for their own wickedness, and doing everything by extremes.

Their lifecycle drove many of them to the brink of madness. Raised in an era of spiritual upheaval and economic dislocation, Liberty children hardly knew the care and protection of close family life. First-wavers arrived too late to share in their elders' inner euphoria, last-wavers too early to feel the sympathetic nurture that welcomed a younger generation in the late 1750s. Still in their teens, the Liberty rushed from their homes—just in time to bear the full brunt of the French and Indian War, the colonies' last and largest imperial struggle. Here they tasted bitterness and death, and learned a brutal coming-of-age lesson: Get what you can grab, keep what's yours, and never trust authority. Until their mid-forties, they cut an unparalleled swath of crime, riot, and violence through American history. Whatever the mob—Vermont's "Green Mountain Boys" or

Pennsylvania's "Paxton Boys" or New York's "Liberty Boys"—the Liberty "acted where others talked" (as one historian says of Sears). Whatever their army—whether led by "Swamp Fox" Francis Marion or "Game Cock" Robert Sumter or "Rifleman" Daniel Morgan—they always performed best as plucky warrior bands. Hit by the Revolution just as they were entering midlife, the Liberty responded with characteristic frenzy. They mixed heroism with treachery, scrapped with each other, and ended up distrusted by everybody. No other generation so eagerly risked their lives for the Declaration of Independence. Nor did any other "turn Tory" in such massive numbers.

The Liberty knew they were a black sheep among generations. When young, they felt the horrified dismay of elders who saw in them so few principles and so much cynicism. "That such a monster should come from my loins!" declared Landon Carter of his profligate gambler son Robert ("Wild Bob") Wormeley. "Nothing has ever hurt me so much," cried Benjamin Franklin of his Tory son William, "a man of deep deceit and light vanity" whom he later disinherited. Thereafter, a sense of inner worthlessness haunted them. "We are a crooked and perverse generation," lamented Josiah Bartlett to the Continental Congress, "longing for the fineries and follies of those Egyptian task masters from whom we have so lately freed ourselves." John Adams confessed on the eve of war: "We have not men fit for the times. We are deficient in genius, in education, in travel, in fortune—in everything. I feel unutterable anxiety." In midlife, most Liberty deferred thanklessly to their gifted and confident juniors. General Washington trusted his youthful Republican aides far more than his own peers. "I am obnoxious, suspected, and unpopular," admitted John Adams to Thomas Jefferson before agreeing to let this younger man draft the Declaration of Independence because "you write ten times better than I do." Still suffering the early scars of alienation, the Liberty aged into pessimistic "fogies" and "codgers"—epithets that gained their scornful meaning just when this generation was entering elderhood. Later in life, Washington wondered if the republic would outlive him; Adams suspected an American monarchy might better suit the "self-seeking" darkness of the human heart.

"Give me liberty or give me death!" roared 39-year-old Patrick Henry in 1775, invoking the one word that always intoxicated his generation, from a castaway childhood to a leave-me-alone old age. When Henry's peers sang, they sang the name: *The American Liberty Song* by John Dickinson, *The Massachusetts Song of Liberty* by Mercy Warren, and *My Days Have Been So Wondrous Free* by Francis Hopkinson. When they acted, they acted in the name, organizing as "Sons of Liberty," planting Liberty trees, and parading around "Liberty" poles. Where Awakener elders preached "Unite or Die!" this generation had a more anarchic battle cry: "Don't Tread on Me!" or simply "Liberty or Die!"—the motto emblazoned on the shirts of Morgan's riflemen. They came to be known (and remembered) as "Yankees," a derisive nickname for young Amer-

LIBERTY GENERATION (Born 1724 to 1741)

TYPE: Reactive

Total number: 1,100,000
Percent immigrant: 24%
Percent slave: 19%

SAMPLE MEMBERS, birth (death)

1725 James Otis (1783)
1725 George Mason (1792)
1727 Ezra Stiles (1795)
1728 Mercy Warren (1814)
1731 Robert Rogers (1795)
1731 Martha Washington (1802)
1732 Francis Marion (1795)
1732 John Dickinson (1808)
1734 Daniel Boone (1820)
1734 Robert Morris (1806)*
1735 Paul Revere (1818)
1736 Patrick Henry (1799)
1737 John Hancock (1793)
1737 Thomas Paine (1809)*
1737 Charles Carroll (1832)
1737 Francis Hopkinson (1791)
1738 Benjamin West (1820)
1738 Ethan Allen (1789)
1739 George Clinton (1812)
1741 Benedict Arnold (1801)

* = immigrant

FAMILY TREE

Typical grandparents: Glorious
Parents: Enlightenment and Awakening
Children: Republican and Compromiser
Typical grandchildren: Transcendental

PERIOD of POLITICAL LEADERSHIP

Plurality in House: —
Plurality in Senate: —
Majority of Supreme Court: —

U.S. PRESIDENTS: 1789–1801

1732 George Washington (1799)
1735 John Adams (1826)

Presidency of Continental Congress: 1775–
  1778, 1779–1781, 1782–1783, 1784–1788

PROMINENT FOREIGN PEERS

1727 John Wilkes (1797)
1729 Edmund Burke (1797)
1729 Catherine the Great (1796)
1735 Saint-Jean de Crèvecoeur (1813)
1738 George III (1820)

Age	Date	HISTORY and LIFECYCLE
0–11	1735:	Ten-year diphtheria epidemic begins in northern colonies
4–21	1745:	Halloween violence worsens; half of militia die at Louisbourg
6–23	1747:	"Knowles Riot," worst in Boston's history
15–32	1756:	French and Indian War declared; "privateering madness" in ports
22–39	1763:	Pontiac uprising; George III bans trans-Appalachian settlements
24–41	1765:	England imposes Stamp Act; rising adults organize "Liberty" mobs
34–51	1775:	Patrick Henry's speech; Paul Revere's ride; Battle of Bunker Hill
35–52	1776:	Paine publishes Common Sense; Declaration of Independence signed
40–57	1781:	Washington defeats Cornwallis at Yorktown; fighting stops
46–63	1787:	Shays' Rebellion crushed; George Clinton opposes new Constitution
55–72	1796:	Washington refuses to run for third term, gives "Farewell Address"
59–76	1800:	Nation mourns Washington's death; Adams fails to win reelection

SAMPLE CULTURAL ENDOWMENTS: *Battle of the Kegs* (Francis Hopkinson); *Pontiac; or the Savages of America* (Robert Rogers); *Death of Wolfe* (painting, Benjamin West); *The Rights of the British Colonies* (James Otis); *Letters from a Farmer* (John Dickinson); *Novanglus* papers (John Adams); *Common Sense, The Rights of Man* (Thomas Paine); Fairfax Resolves, *Virginia Declaration of Rights* (George Mason); Farewell Address (George Washington) icans that first became popular in the 1760s. A "Yankee" was a hick or fop, and "Yankee Doodle Dandy" a scornful British song about idiotic provincials. True to form, the Liberty adopted both the name and song as their own—sticking "a feather in their caps" (or a twig or piece of cloth) to identify themselves in battle and announce to the world that, yes, we are bastards and scoundrels. Leave martyrdom for the Awakeners. For the Liberty, there was no transcendence. It was victory or suicide. Either way, they heaped upon themselves the guilt of rebellion and left their own children to start fresh.

Liberty Facts

- During the late 1730s and early 1740s, while parents were preoccupied with the Great Awakening, Liberty children were victimized by the deadliest child-only epidemic in American history, the "great throat distemper" (diphtheria), which killed an estimated one child in fifteen throughout most of New York and New England.

- The Liberty were by far the most war-ravaged generation of the colonial era. Describing casualties during the French and Indian War, historian Gary Nash estimates that by 1760, "Boston had experienced the equivalent of two twentieth-century world wars in one generation." One-third of all Liberty men in Massachusetts enlisted for at least one season between 1754 and 1759. Stockade and ship records indicate that disease and bad nutrition killed an estimated 5 to 10 percent of all recruits during each year of service.

- Having grown up during an era of falling rum prices and rising public disorder, the Liberty matured into a notorious generation of drinkers, thieves, and rioters—to the dismay of elder Awakener moralists. The Liberty consumed more alcohol per capita than any other colonial generation. Between 1760 and 1775, they led more violent mobs than the cumulative total for all prior generations. They coined both the words "regulator" (for vigilante) and "lynch" (after the Liberty Virginian Colonel Charles Lynch).

- The Liberty accounted for the largest wave of colonial immigration—most notably the poor, fierce (and anti-English) Scots-Irish, who typically disembarked in Philadelphia and then sped south, west, and north to the frontier.

- Though comprising only half of all members to the Continental Congress, the Liberty accounted for all five delegates accused of complicity with the British; the two most famous military traitors (Benedict Arnold and Benjamin Church); the most famous near-traitors (including Ethan Allen, who secretly considered selling Vermont to the British); and the most notorious Tory writers (from Hugh Gaine to Samuel Seabury).

- The Liberty included nearly two-thirds (thirty-five of fifty-six) of the signers of the Declaration of Independence in 1776. Eleven years later, they included only one-third of the signers of the U.S. Constitution. In fact, a list of leading "Anti-Federalist" opponents of the Constitution in 1788 reads like a Liberty Who's Who: Patrick Henry, George Mason, Richard Henry Lee, George Clinton, Mercy Warren, John Lamb, David Rittenhouse, and Herman Husbands (average age, 57).

- During the 1780s, midlife Liberty leaders were statistically more likely to be what historian Jackson Turner Main defines as political "localists" (less educated and more suspicious of ideas and large institutions) than either their juniors or their elders.

The Liberty Lifecycle

YOUTH: During the 1730s and 1740s, while William Hogarth drew pictures of abused London waifs, the thawing trend in American child-rearing approached wholesale neglect. Colonial newspapers noted the rising number of children abandoned as "bastards," turned over to wetnurses, fed liquor to shut them up, or just left free to run around on their own. For most first-wave Liberty kids, the new nurturing style reflected the midlife Enlightener dash toward personal autonomy. "We should think of little children to be persons," insisted the pedagogue Samuel Johnson. For most last-wavers, watching young Awakener parents grope for holiness and rage against authority, childhood was an awkward by-product of the Great Awakening. The specter of adults crying out in church, noted Awakener Charles Chauncy, "frequently frights the little children, and sets them screaming." First wave or last, Liberty kids quickly learned that self-immersed adults at best ignored them, and at worst reviled their streetwise realism. Jonathan Edwards warned them that children "out of Christ" are "young vipers, and are infinitely more hateful than vipers." His Bostonian peer Andrew Eliot condemned them as an "evil and adulterous generation." Franklin wrote *Poor Richard's Almanac* to lecture them on prudence and thrift. But all in vain. Reaching their teens at a time of economic bust, land pressure, and rising immigration, the daunted Liberty set off on their own in quest of fame and fortune. Soon young losers began turning up underfoot everywhere—gambling, begging, stealing in the towns, "strolling" aimlessly on back roads, and sparking America's first Halloween mayhem in Boston.

COMING OF AGE: The colonies fought both of their midcentury struggles against France—King George's War (1744–1748) and the French and Indian War (1754–1760)—primarily with Liberty muscle and guts. At first, nothing so thrilled these plucky teenagers as news that armies were marching. War meant freedom from moralizing elders and penny-pinching masters, boom wages in the ports, and the glittering prospect of soldiers' bounties, pirate shares, and enemy booty. But as the campaigns wore on, the dreams turned into nightmares. Smitten by "privateering fever" ("almost a kind of madness," remarked New York Awakener James DeLancey), thousands enlisted onto French-hunting gunboats. Only a handful made fortunes; nearly half ended up killed, crippled, or captured. Royal Navy impressment gangs dragged away many of the young port workers, who responded with the most violent town riots in colonial history. Young militiamen heard themselves called wild "dogs" and selfish "riffraff" by British officers, who used martial-law punishment (including 500-lash whippings) to cow them into compliance. The war brought horrible youth suffering. While sixtyish Enlighteners sipped tea with the visiting officialdom and while fortyish Awakeners preached and prayed, the twentyish Liberty paid the physical price. They were "young people with nothing to do and nowhere to go," writes historian William Pencak, and "war took care of them—in both the literal and colloquial senses—during the forties and fifties."

RISING ADULTHOOD: From 1750 on, the colonies registered the onset of Liberty adulthood with a seismic jump in every measure of social pathology—from drinking, gambling, and crime to begging, poverty, and bankruptcy. After the wars, during the wild and depressed 1760s, it only got worse. Debtor prisons bulged with young spendthrifts. Veterans and immigrants raised havoc on the frontier, especially against Indians (some of whom, under the elder Pontiac, punished the white settlers with violent fury). Young planters partied far beyond their means, doubling the colonial debt to Britain between 1760 and 1775. Elders were aghast, and towns cut relief payments to the burgeoning numbers of young poor. "The only principle of life propagated among the young people is to get money," complained the old Enlightener Cadwallader Colden. "They play away, and play it all away," lamented Awakener Landon Carter of younger Virginians who preferred "bewitching diversions" to "solid improvements of the mind." With the Stamp Act riots of 1765, the Liberty's anti-British agitation increased—but everyone knew their mob leaders mixed self-interest with patriotism. Many of the leading Liberty Patriots were smugglers (John Hancock), hopeless debtors (Thomas Nelson), renegade settlers (Ethan Allen), or disgruntled office-seekers (Richard Henry Lee). Fiftyish Awakeners thundered against the thirtyish Liberty for their greed and selfishness—for being a generation of "white savages," as Benjamin Franklin called the Paxton boys. Samuel Adams' remarks, said a contemporary, "were never favorable to the rising generation." But the Liberty took a nihilistic pleasure in their elders' discomfort. "Virginians are of genuine blood—they will dance or die," they laughed back. Reflecting his peers' implacable hostility to Awakener holiness, Daniel Boone declared his secret of happiness to be "a good wife, a good gun, and a good horse."

MIDLIFE: When the Continental Congress crowded up to sign the Declaration of Independence, the fiftyish (and very corpulent) Benjamin Harrison elbowed a (thin) younger delegate. When the signers are all hanged, Harrison quipped, "I shall have all the advantage over you. For me it will be all over in a minute, but you will be kicking in the air half an hour after I am gone!" For the Liberty, now entering midlife, the Revolution was a moment of truth. Unlike their elders, they expected no miracles ("I think the game is pretty near up," wrote Washington during his retreat across New Jersey). Unlike their juniors, they had families and reputations at stake and less future to look forward to. But they never lost their practical and defensive goal: to prevent "tyranny" and to protect individual "liberties," as George Mason put it in his Virginia Bill of Rights. Nor did they lose their cunning and ferocity. These 50-year-olds excelled at the dirty work: privateering (Sears again, this time owning shares in fifteen ships), requisitioning supplies ("Sumter's Law"), raising money (Morris, the "Financier of the American Revolution"), and guerrilla tactics ("this damned old fox" Francis Marion, whom the British charged "would not fight like a Christian or a gentleman"). The Liberty also accounted for most of the war-era treachery—confirming elder judgments that they were not to be trusted. When the struggle was over, most of them fell into exhaustion, and a suspicious realism replaced their once-wild ardor. In 1788 they provided the leading opponents to the ambitious new Constitution concocted by younger Republicans. "All checks founded on anything but self-love will not avail," warned 52-year-old Patrick Henry, now a self-confessed "old-fashioned fellow," skeptical of the work of "young visionaries." But in the end, the fast-aging Liberty barked without biting. They were not about to stand in the way of the energy of their juniors—or the dreams of their elders. Their opposition relented, and by the fall of 1789 nearly all the states had ratified the Constitution.

ELDERHOOD: "Perhaps the strongest feature in his character was prudence," the younger Jefferson wrote of President Washington. With gruff words and tender manner, Washington protected the infant nation during its first eight years. He dealt mildly with the Indians and Tories who had once been his enemies, and (perhaps recalling how his own peers had once been treated) resisted younger calls for harsh action against the Whiskey Rebels. To avoid the risk of war, he avoided alliances abroad and warned against "interweaving our destiny with any part of Europe." His successor, President Adams, ruined his own chances for reelection by steering a similar course of caution and vigilance. Prudent, realistic, and self-effacing, the Liberty entered elderhood just when Americans were shifting from the veneration of age toward the celebration of youth. "The language of abuse for old men dates only to about 1800," writes historian David Hackett Fischer, noting that this was "the generation whose unhappy fate it was to be young in an era when age was respected, and old in a time when youth took the palm." In the 1790s, for example, New England churches eliminated age-ranked seating and a majority of states imposed mandatory retirement ages for judges. Many Liberty elders met with sad fates. Robert Rogers, their greatest war hero of the 1750s, was arrested for counterfeiting, turned Tory during the Revolution, and died an alcoholic in England. Thomas Paine died a lonely outcast on Long Island. Robert Morris died penniless, Daniel Boone landless. When old, John Adams despaired that the only "great men" were "aged men, who had been tossed and buffeted in the vicissitudes of life" and taught "by grief and disappointment . . . to command their passions and prejudices." Few of the Liberty expected to be thanked—so certain were they, like the eightyish Adams, that "mausoleums, statues, monuments will never be erected to me."

*   *   *

In the eyes of older and younger Americans who knew them, the Liberty were a generation of kinetic physicality. They played hard, spent wildly, wagered on cockfights and boat races, and danced the furious and competitive jig. They chose peer leaders of legendary size (including Henry, Arnold, Allen, Morgan, Boone, Harrison—and above all, George Washington, whose six-foot-three-inch physical presence towered above his peers). Discarded in childhood and punished coming of age, they chose lives of reckless abandon—not running toward holiness like their next-elders, but running away from it; not praying for grace but rather (like Allen and Harrison) swearing at the Bible. Ezra Stiles, their most learned scholar, once puckishly described the Great Awakening as a time when "multitudes were seriously, soberly, and solemnly out of their wits." No one expected this generation to sacrifice itself in America's hour of crisis. But that they did—with visceral (if corruptible) motives only they could understand: fury at the British "lobsterbacks" who had once tortured them, and hope that they might achieve some measure of security for their children. Afterward, they mellowed into risk-averse elders who were able to congratulate Republican heroism while also checking the naive ambitions of young "Hamiltonians." Having gambled and suffered quite enough for one lifetime, the Liberty reached old age with no illusions about human nature. Ralph Waldo Emerson later described a portrait of the sixtyish President Washington: "The heavy, leaden eyes turn on you, as the eyes of an ox in a pasture . . . as if this MAN had absorbed all the serenity of America, and left none for his restless, rickety, hysterical countrymen."

REPUBLICAN GENERATION

Born: 1742–1766
Type: Civic

Age Location:
American Revolution Crisis in rising adulthood
Transcendental Awakening in elderhood

"All human greatness shall in us be found,/ For grandeur, wealth, and reason far renown'd," announced 29-year-old David Humphreys to his peers after the American triumph at Yorktown. These young victors all knew who they were—and why they were special. In the 1760s, they were the precious boys and girls whom elders sheltered from Liberty "vice" and British "corruption." In 1775, they were the dutiful young Minutemen who stood their ground at Concord bridge. In the winter of 1778, they were the cheerful soldiers who kept faith with General Washington at Valley Forge. Seven years after Yorktown, in 1788, they became the rising-adult achievers—so many of them already famous—who celebrated the news of their new Constitution. Thus did the REPUBLICAN GENERATION come of age, performing deeds of collective valor that gave birth to a new nation. Thus too did worldly triumph forge them into lifelong builders and rationalists—single-minded creators of what they called "energy in government," "order and harmony" in society, "tranquillity" of mind, "usefulness and reason" in science, "abundance" in commerce. Like few other generations, young Republicans *expected* glory. Sang New York patriot recruits in 1776: "The rising world shall sing of us a thousand years to come/ And tell our children's children the wonders we have done." From the very beginning, notes historian Charles Royster, "the revolutionary generation knew that they would stand above all their descendants."

As protected colonial children in the 1750s and 1760s, Republicans grew up under the visionary tutelage of midlife Awakeners, who saw in them the future of "republican" virtue. As rising adults during decades of crisis, they fulfilled their special mission, winning independence and establishing political and social order. As midlife parents and community leaders during the Jefferson Presidency, they harnessed the growing nation to their enormous energy and collegial discipline. They never let their elders down. To list their leaders is to invoke a palladium of nation-builders: patriotic war heroes like Nathanael Greene, Henry Lee, Anthony Wayne, Molly Pitcher, and John Paul Jones; architects of "Columbia" like Benjamin Latrobe and Pierre Charles L'Enfant; organizers of knowledge like Benjamin Rush and Noah Webster; inventors of steamships and rational industry like Robert Fulton and Eli Whitney. Above all, the Republicans proved to be a fabled generation of statesmen: Thomas Jefferson, James Madison, James Monroe, Alexander Hamilton, John Jay, Albert Gallatin, Robert Livingston, John Marshall, Gouverneur Morris, James Wilson, Charles Cotesworth Pinckney, Timothy Pickering.

No generation since the Glorious attained public renown so early in life: Hamilton, famous political pamphleteer at age 17; Henry Knox, commander of the Continental Army's artillery at age 25; George Rogers Clark, wilderness Napoleon at age 27; Jefferson, author of the Declaration of Independence at age 33. Through midlife and old age, they should have delighted in the gathering political and economic might of their "Empire of Liberty." But instead—embarrassed in the War of 1812, challenged by spiritual youth, unable to control the Promethean energy they had unleashed—the aging Republican elite felt frustration and ultimately despair. As busy and outwardly "venerated" elders during President Monroe's "Era of Good Feeling," they feared that their massive worldly accomplishments might not survive the restive and emotional culture of their children. Self-discipline they practiced by instinct, but self-immersion they found incomprehensible. In all the volumes Jefferson wrote about politics and science ("a more methodically industrious man never lived," observes historian Edmund Morgan), he never kept a diary and hardly once mentioned his feelings. "We must go home to be happy, and our home is not of this world," Jay told a friend. "Here we have nothing to do but our duty."

Republicans saw themselves as tireless reasoners and builders, chosen by history to wrest order from the chaos. Their most famous statesman (Jefferson) won equal fame as a scientist and architect. Their most famous legislator (Madison) was hailed as "the master-builder of the Constitution." Of their two "geniuses" of public finance, one (Gallatin) likened himself to a "laboring oar" for American prosperity, while the other (Hamilton) deemed "the habit of labor in a people" to be "conducive to the welfare of the state." Their foremost jurist (Marshall), said one admirer, argued his opinions "as certainly, as cogently, as inevitably, as any demonstration of Euclid." In 1802, their leading poet (Joel Barlow) proudly authored *The Canal,* subtitled "A Poem on the Application of Physical Science to Political Economy," in which he predicted "science" would "raise, improve, and harmonize mankind." Projecting their personality into religion, leading Republicans worshiped a "Creator" or "Supreme Being"—a God of Reason deliberately expunged of spirituality. "Throughout Jeffersonian thought," notes historian Daniel Boorstin, "recurs this vision of God as the Supreme Maker. He was a Being of boundless energy and ingenuity who in six days had transformed the universal wilderness into an orderly, replete and self-governing cosmos. The Jeffersonian God was not the Omnipotent Sovereign of the Puritans nor the Omnipresent Essence of the Transcendentalists, but was essentially Architect and Builder."

All their lives, the word "republican" (from Latin *res publica,* literally "the

REPUBLICAN GENERATION (Born 1742 to 1766)

TYPE: Civic

Total number: 2,100,000
Percent immigrant: 17%
Percent slave: 17%

SAMPLE MEMBERS, birth (death)

1742 Nathanael Greene (1786)
1744 Abigail Adams (1818)
1745 John Jay (1829)
1745 Benjamin Rush (1813)
1747 John Paul Jones (1792)
1750 Kunta Kinte (c. 1815)*
1752 Gouverneur Morris (1816)
1752 Timothy Dwight (1817)
1754 Pierre L'Enfant (1825)*
1754 Joel Barlow (1812)
1754 "Molly Pitcher" (1832)
1755 Nathan Hale (1776)
1755 John Marshall (1835)
1757 Alexander Hamilton (1804)*
1758 Noah Webster (1843)
1761 Albert Gallatin (1849)*
1763 John Jacob Astor (1848)*
1765 Robert Fulton (1815)
1765 Eli Whitney (1825)
1766 "Uncle Sam" Wilson (1854)
* = immigrant

FAMILY TREE

Typical grandparents: Enlightenment
Parents: Awakener and Liberty
Children: Compromise and Transcendental
Typical grandchildren: Gilded

PERIOD OF POLITICAL LEADERSHIP

Plurality in House: 1789–1813
Plurality in Senate: 1789–1813
Majority of Supreme Court: 1791–1826

U.S. PRESIDENTS: 1801–1825

1743 Thomas Jefferson (1826)
1751 James Madison (1836)
1758 James Monroe (1831)

Presidency of Continental Congress: 1778–
1779, 1783–1784, 1788–1789

PROMINENT FOREIGN PEERS

1755 Marie Antoinette (1793)
1756 Wolfgang Amadeus Mozart (1791)
1757 Marquis de Lafayette (1834)
1758 Maximilien Robespierre (1794)
1758 Horatio Nelson (1805)

Age	Date	HISTORY AND LIFECYCLE
0–17	1759:	Last campaign of French and Indian War
4–28	1770:	Colonies outraged by death of youths in "Boston Massacre"
10–34	1776:	Jefferson drafts Declaration of Independence
19–43	1785:	Rising adults gain majority of seats in Continental Congress
23–47	1789:	States ratify U.S. Constitution
27–51	1793:	French Revolution widens "Federalist"-"Republican" rift
34–58	1800:	Jefferson elected President, promises to heal party divisions
37–61	1803:	Louisiana Purchase; Marshall Court decides *Marbury* v. *Madison*
48–72	1814:	British troops burn White House before War of 1812 ends
54–78	1820:	"Era of Good Feeling"; Monroe wins 231 of 232 electoral votes
57–81	1823:	Public hails Monroe Doctrine as anticolonial mood spreads abroad
60–84	1826:	Jefferson and Adams die exactly fifty years after Independence Day

SAMPLE CULTURAL ENDOWMENTS: Declaration of Independence, plan for the Virginia state capitol (Thomas Jefferson); United States Constitution (James Madison et al.); *The Federalist* (Hamilton, Madison, Jay); *American Dictionary of the English Language* (Noah Webster); *Modern Chivalry* (Hugh Henry Brackenridge); *The Columbiad* (Joel Barlow); plan for the "Federal City" (Pierre L'Enfant); *The Battle of Bunker Hill* (painting, John Trumbull); *The Conquest of Canaan* (Timothy Dwight).

public thing'') was central to their collective self-image and life purpose. "Republican" did not just refer to a form of government, nor to their radical agemates in France, nor even to the party label chosen by all three of their Virginia Presidents. For this generation, "republican" meant a classical paradigm of secular order—and an entire approach to social life—with which they so thoroughly reconstructed America that today we still live in their civic shadow. Without these *Res Publicans,* our public buildings and banks would not look like miniature Parthenons. We would not have cities named Rome, Ithaca, and Cincinnati, nor roads named Euclid Avenue and Appian Way. Our currency would not be metric, nor our money adorned with Roman images (eagles, fasces, and arrows) and lapidary inscriptions (*Novus Ordo Seclorum,* "the new order of the ages"). Our government would not sound as if it had been transplanted from the age of Augustus (with states, capitols, Presidents, and senators).

Most of all, this generation's unflagging devotion to the public good remains a standard to which all later generations must compare their behavior. "We want great men who, when fortune frowns, will not be discouraged," said Knox in his mid-twenties. "I only regret that I have but one life to lose for my country," declared the youthful Yale graduate Nathan Hale to his British executioners—in a voice so firm it brought tears to the eyes of the redcoats who heard it. Many years later Jefferson wrote, "When a man assumes a public trust, he should consider himself public property." The Republicans believed that the "happiness" and "order" and "security" of society took precedence over any private desire. They also believed in "equality"—as a working hypothesis about the uniformity of Nature, not as a moral imperative. While many in the Republican elite disapproved of slavery (and succeeded in ending the African slave trade), what they disliked worse was an angry debate about it. They feared any divisiveness that might imperil the great republic they had created. For this generation, some evils had to be accommodated for what they believed to be the greater good. They acted accordingly—and, late in life, often wondered why their children could not.

Republican Facts

- The vast majority of Republican political leaders (from Jefferson, Madison, and Monroe to Marshall, Webster, and Rush) were both native-born and college-educated in America—in contrast to the helter-skelter Liberty, whose leaders were more likely immigrant (Paine), native but educated abroad (Dickinson), or entirely without formal schooling (Washington).

- Between native cohorts born in 1730 and 1760, better child nutrition caused the average height of adult Americans to rise by more than half an inch—the most rapid one-generation climb recorded in America until the G.I.s.

In 1780, the typical Republican soldier was at least two inches taller than the typical English redcoat he was fighting.

- During the 1760s, when first-wave Republicans began graduating from college, the share of American graduates entering clerical careers fell from four-fifths to one-half. Many young men turned instead to radical Masonry, a male "brotherhood" dedicated to teamwork, good works, and secular progress. Masonic symbolism (the compass, plumbline, and carpenter's square) celebrated the builder; Masonic praise (to be "on the square") directness and utility; the Masonic icon (sunlight) the divinity of practical reason.

- Republicans assumed political power early in life. In the 1780s, they were elected to New England town offices at a younger age than members of any generation since the Glorious. From 1774 to 1787, their delegate share of the Continental Congress soared from 7 to 75 percent. During the three Liberty Presidencies (1789–1801), Republicans claimed over three-quarters of all members of Congress, two-thirds of all Supreme Court justices, one of the two Vice-Presidencies, nearly all the diplomatic posts, and all fourteen cabinet appointments—from Secretary of State to Postmaster General.

- The leading Federalist advocates of the Constitution were on average ten to twelve years younger than their Anti-Federalist opponents. At the Philadelphia Convention in 1787, thirtyish Republicans (Madison, Pinckney, Hamilton, Wilson, Martin, King, and Strong) were the most influential drafters and debaters.

- No other generation has ever matched the forty-seven-year tenure spanning the Republicans' first and last years of national leadership—from John Jay (in 1778 elected president of the Continental Congress at age 33) to James Monroe (whose second term as U.S. President expired in 1825 at age 67).

- Not until the G.I.s has any other generation of leaders been so aggressively secular in outlook. Most of the Republican candidates for President—especially Jefferson, Madison, Burr, Pinckney, and King—avoided any display of Christian piety and were widely regarded as atheists by their contemporaries. When asked by an elder clergyman why the Constitution did not mention God, the young Hamilton pertly replied: "I declare, we forgot."

- The political eclipse of the Republicans coincided with their humiliation in the War of 1812. On the eve of Jefferson's embargo of 1806, Republicans still constituted 71 percent of all congressmen and governors. By the first postwar election of 1815, their share had plunged to 37 percent.

- In the 1820s, Congress repeatedly raised pension benefits to elderly Revolutionary War veterans; by the end of the decade, nearly half of all federal spending consisted of interest and pension payments. In 1828, 70-year-old Noah Webster introduced the word "veneration" into the American vocabulary. In the 1830s and 1840s, Americans began to "venerate" the image of "Uncle Sam" in the person of the seventyish veteran Samuel Wilson, one of the last survivors of his generation.

The Republican Lifecycle

YOUTH: Around 1745, routine brutality among and against colonial teenagers aroused little adult sympathy. By 1770, the year of the "Boston Massacre," the violent death of one child was enough to spark vehement public outrage. Over the course of just twenty-five years, American attitudes toward the young reversed direction entirely—from neglect to protection, from blame to comfort. Despairing the wayward Liberty, midlife Awakeners wanted to ensure that this new crop of kids would grow up to be smart and cooperative servants to a dawning vision, a republic of virtue. During the war-torn 1750s, towns shielded children from the rowdiness of twentyish Liberty by tightening up on begging, gambling, and theaters. "By 1750," observes historian Jay Fliegelman, "irresponsible parents became the nation's scapegoat." The number of tutors per capita doubled as popular books reinforced the holy and protective role of the parent. In the 1760s, parents began avoiding "corrupt" English schools and sent their kids instead to Awakener-founded academies in the colonies. Here Republican teenagers could imbibe the new fever of "civic revival" and a new Scottish school of practical and optimistic curricula—now purged of skeptics like Hume and Berkeley (who, noted Awakener Witherspoon, "take away the distinction between truth and falsehood"). Between parents, Republican kids showed a marked preference for fathers over mothers. Marshall later confessed that "my father was a greater man than any of his sons"; many others, like Jefferson, cultivated a lifelong preference for male company. Historian Kenneth Lynn concludes that "certainly in no other period of our past can we find the top leaders of American society speaking as gratefully as these patriots did about the fathering they received."

COMING OF AGE: "Columbia, Columbia, to Glory Arise!" urged Timothy Dwight to his peers on the eve of revolution. In 1774, the oldest (age 32) were just young enough to have no childhood memories before the new rage of parental protection and civic fervor. The youngest (age 8) were just old enough to join the fight before it was over and reach full adulthood by the time of Washington's inauguration. Elder Americans had never before seen such competent, cheerful, and selfless youngsters. "All gaming, tricking, swearing, lying,/ Is grown quite out of fashion," intoned a popular ballad in 1779, "For modern youth's so self-denying,/ It flies all lawless passion." In war, young soldiers fought as a team, seldom asking why but always asking how. To elder eyes, they could do no wrong. Victimized by foul play (like the scalped Jane McCrea), they were lionized as "butchered innocents." Caught for treason (like Major John André), they attracted sympathy, even while the older Benedict Arnold was burning in effigy across the colonies. Unlike Liberty marauders and pirates, the more homogeneous Republicans—Greene, Wayne, Lee, Clark, and Jones—soon proved to be the ablest leaders of the conventional war effort. When aging Awakeners stepped down from their posts during the war, many Republicans leapfrogged their Liberty next-elders to fill the vacancies. Riding a dazzling reputation for genius and optimism, they swept into town offices and the Continental Congress, drafted state constitutions and policy treatises, and grabbed most of the new state and national offices. Assuming power just when (as Rush put it) "everything is new and yielding," their youthful confidence soon collided with the exhaustion and localism of their next-elders. Here these young heroes won their culminating victory: drafting a stronger Constitution and ratifying it over churlish Liberty opposition. In Virginia, the ringing words of 35-year-old Edmund Randolph ("Mr. Chairman, I am a child of the Revolution . . .") overwhelmed the fiftyish Patrick Henry. In New York, the genius of *The Federalist*—rapidly penned by Hamilton, Jay, and Madison (average age, 36)—outclassed the fiftyish Henry Clinton.

RISING ADULTHOOD: Elevated by their coming-of-age triumphs, they likened themselves to history's greatest empire-builders, from "Caesar" (Hamilton) to "Lycurgus" (Madison). In the 1790s, young Republicans lived and breathed worldly accomplishment. Their first priority was to secure public order by eradicating riotous Liberty atavisms. They crushed the Shaysites, Whiskey Rebels, and Ohio Indians; organized as "orderly" Federalists and "rational" Republicans; and ostracized wayward peers who refused to outgrow their coming-of-age sympathy with the French Revolution. Proud of the "mechanical courage" they had learned as soldiers, they behaved collegially and placed public interest over private gain. "Every engine should be employed to render the people of this country national," declared Noah Webster. Energetic builders, they founded "Societies for Advancement of Industry," designed a "Columbia" of colonnaded grandeur (L'Enfant), invented the cotton gin (Whitney), and launched steamboats (Fulton). They also began leading America toward much wider sex-role distinctions. Having proved themselves "men" to their beloved fathers, rising Republicans associated "effeminacy" (and "that old hag" Britain) with corruption and disruptive passion, "manliness" with reason and disinterested virtue. Federalists taunted Jefferson for his "womanish" attachments to France, while Jefferson contemptuously called the Adams Presidency "a reign of witches" and (notes one historian) "would have totally banished women from the public sphere." Republicans widely believed that sexual and political order were directly linked. "Society is composed of individuals," Enos Hitchcock remarked. "They are parts of a whole,—and when each one moves in his own orb, and fills his own station, the system will be complete." Their men would thereafter specialize as producers and rulers, their women as moral guardians of the family.

MIDLIFE: They all arrived together: a new century, a new capital, a new President, and a new generation. Taking office in Washington, D.C., on March 4, 1801, Jefferson asked his "fellow citizens" to "unite in common efforts for the common good" and to contemplate "a rising nation . . . advancing rapidly to destinies beyond the reach of mortal eye." Confident (versed Joel Barlow) in the "fair science of celestial birth" that "leads mankind to reason and to God," midlife Republicans deemed nothing to be beyond their collective power. So it often seemed. From Jefferson's Northwest Ordinance (1787) to Monroe's acquisition of Florida (1819), the Republicans quintupled the effective size of America's domain. "The United States take their place among powers of the first rank," exulted Robert Livingston in 1803 after the 500-million-acre Louisiana Purchase. Meanwhile, Livingston's peers presided over rapid material growth, awesome by any measure—dollars of exports, miles of turnpikes and canals, bushels of cotton, and numbers of banks, post offices, ships, patents, and corporate charters. Yet these very successes prompted growing uneasiness. As their once-compact "Republic of Virtue" expanded into a mighty "Empire of Liberty," midlife Republicans worried that something was dissolving the innocence and optimism they recalled from their youth. Perhaps it was the multiplying slave plantations, or the decimation of Indians; perhaps the vast and impersonal markets, or the westward rush of disorderly pioneers. Their frustration came to a head in the War of 1812—a conflict that disgraced six Republican major generals, nearly triggered the secession of New England, and humiliated Madison when the British effortlessly torched the White House. Their invincible self-image shattered, most Republicans thereafter retreated from public life—leaving only their Presidents in power.

ELDERHOOD: In the fall of 1823, the public watched in awe as three white-haired and magisterial Virginians (Monroe, Madison, and Jefferson—average age, 72) conferred over a declaration today known as the Monroe Doctrine. With this grand twilight moment of Republican statecraft, Americans of all ages sensed that a magnificent generation was passing. As living testimonials to the great institutions they had wrought, aging Republicans still exuded outward energy and confidence. "We must never forget that it is the *Constitution* we are expounding," urged Marshall proudly to younger justices. From stately Montpelier, Madison called America "the workshop of liberty to the civilized world"; from sunny Monticello, Jefferson saw "the great march of progress passing over us like a cloud of light," and his last public testament hailed "the general spread of the light of science." Inwardly, however, many despaired. No matter how hard they kept busy in their retirement ("It is wonderful how much may be done, if we are always doing," wrote Jefferson to his daughter), the prospect of death came hard to a secular-minded generation dedicated more to progress than to God. Having hoped for so much, elderly Republicans expressed frustration over their waning influence on public life. "How feeble are the strongest hands. How weak all human efforts prove," complained the aging Freneau, his upbeat poetry now unread. More often, they turned the blame around: they had not betrayed history; history had betrayed *them*. By history they meant their children—who were feminizing their once-manly "virtue," spurning their rational Masonic brotherhood, fragmenting into political faction, and celebrating feeling rather than teamwork. Many onlooking Republicans sensed a mocking repudiation of everything they had built. "We will leave this scene not for a tittering generation who wish to push us from it," fulminated David Humphreys. Beware "your worst passions," Gallatin presciently warned the young. After hearing the angry slavery debates of 1820, the 78-year-old Jefferson shocked two younger generations when he declared: "I regret that I am now to die in the belief that the useless sacrifice of themselves by the generation of 1776, to acquire self-government and happiness to their country, is to be thrown away by the unwise and unworthy passions of their sons."

*   *   *

Government is "instituted," observed Hamilton as a young man, "because the passions of men will not conform to the dictates of reason and justice, without constraint." All their lives, "passion" was the Republicans' most hated word. The young Pickering boasted that his Federalist peers "gave the reins not to . . . passions, but to reason." The young Jefferson hoped rational Deism might soon become the national religion. Yet, late in life, passion did indeed become their nemesis. For a few Republicans (including Webster, who decades earlier had proclaimed America "an empire of reason" and had tried to popularize the verb "happify"), born-again religion offered solace from despair in their extreme old age. For most, the passion of their children loomed as a threat they could neither accept nor understand. Ironically, this generation of "Founding Fathers" had far closer, more affectionate relationships *as children with their own fathers* than they ever had later on as fathers with their own children. In the 1760s, Republicans were handed a worldly mission by unworldly elders and as young adults achieved immortal greatness fulfilling it. A half century later, they tried to make their own young into replicas of themselves—to make them (as Rush described the purpose of education) into "Republican machines" able "to perform their parts properly in the great machine of government of state." It seemed a simple enough task for such powerful and heroic builders—the only "generation" of Americans praised throughout their lives (and ever afterward) for unequaled glory. But it was the single task at which they failed utterly.

COMPROMISE GENERATION

Born: 1767–1791
Type: Adaptive

Age Location:
American Revolution Crisis in youth
Transcendental Awakening in midlife
Civil War Crisis in elderhood

"We can win no laurels in a war for independence," insisted Daniel Webster as a young man. "Earlier and worthier hands have gathered them all." Henry Clay, John C. Calhoun, Meriwether Lewis, and William Clark would have agreed. Along with Webster, they had all been protected and thankful children during the glorious years of nation-founding. Also with Webster, and with many other notables among their COMPROMISE GENERATION, they were all fated to careers of secret turmoil and hidden frustration. In 1804, Lewis and Clark set out with forty-four young civil servants to inventory the vast territories acquired by their next-elders. They obeyed President Jefferson's request to observe "with great pains and accuracy" and to "err on the side of safety." (Only one man died en route.) But soon after returning, Lewis suffered from emotional depression and in 1809 died mysteriously—probably a suicide. Clark, for thirty years a kindly Indian Commissioner for the western territories, later regretted his complicity in the Jacksonian policy of Indian removal that led to the 1838 Cherokee "Trail of Tears." As for the learned and eloquent "Great Triumvirate" of Webster, Clay, and Calhoun, few Americans have ever groomed themselves so carefully for national leadership. Yet at critical moments they invariably stumbled; collectively, the Triumvirs were zero for twelve in runs for the Presidency. The members of what historians sometimes call America's "post-heroic" or "second" generation searched in vain for an authentic sense of collective accomplishment. "We may boast of our civil and religious liberties," Lyman Beecher modestly observed, "but they are the fruits of other men's labors."

They lived an awkward lifecycle. Outwardly, fortune blessed them: Compromisers were coddled in childhood, suffered little in war, came of age with quiet obedience, enjoyed a lifetime of rising prosperity, and managed to defer national crisis until most of them had died. But behind these outer blessings lay inner curses. Their birthyear boundaries reflect *non*participation in the major events of their era. Born in 1767, the eldest (Andrew Jackson, John Quincy Adams) watched the Revolution as children and came of age when the military and political triumphs of the Republicans were already complete. Born in 1791,

COMPROMISE GENERATION (Born 1767 to 1791)

TYPE: Adaptive

Total number: 4,200,000
Percent immigrant: 10%
Percent slave: 15%

FAMILY TREE

Typical grandparents: Awakening
Parents: Liberty and Republican
Children: Transcendental and Gilded
Typical grandchildren: Progressive

SAMPLE MEMBERS, birth (death)

1767 Denmark Vesey (1822)
c. 1768 Tecumseh (1813)
1768 Dolley Madison (1849)
1769 DeWitt Clinton (1828)
1773 John Randolph of Roanoke (1833)
1774 Meriwether Lewis (1809)
1775 Francis Cabot Lowell (1817)
1777 Roger Taney (1864)
1777 Henry Clay (1852)
1780 William Ellery Channing (1842)
1782 Daniel Webster (1852)
1782 John C. Calhoun (1850)
1783 Washington Irving (1859)
1785 John Audubon (1851)*
1786 Davy Crockett (1836)
1786 Winfield Scott (1866)
1787 Emma Willard (1870)
1788 Sarah Hale (1879)
1789 James Fenimore Cooper (1851)
1791 Samuel F. B. Morse (1872)
* = immigrant

PERIOD OF POLITICAL LEADERSHIP

Plurality in House: 1813–1835
Plurality in Senate: 1813–1841
Majority of Supreme Court: 1829–1860

U.S. PRESIDENTS: 1825–1845, 1849–
      1850, 1857–1861

1767 Andrew Jackson (1845)
1767 John Quincy Adams (1848)
1773 William Henry Harrison (1841)
1782 Martin Van Buren (1862)
1784 Zachary Taylor (1850)
1790 John Tyler (1862)
1791 James Buchanan (1868)

PROMINENT FOREIGN PEERS

1769 Napoleon Bonaparte (1821)
1769 Duke of Wellington (1852)
1770 Ludwig van Beethoven (1827)
1771 Sir Walter Scott (1832)
1783 Simón Bolívar (1830)

Age	Date	HISTORY AND LIFECYCLE
0–14	1781:	English Army surrenders at Yorktown; Revolutionary War ends
0–20	1787:	U.S. Constitution framed in Philadelphia
2–26	1793:	Fugitive Slave Act enacted; first use of cotton gin
13–37	1804	Lewis and Clark explore newly purchased Louisiana Territory
21–45	1812:	War of 1812 begins; ends in 1814 with Battle of New Orleans
29–53	1820:	Clay's Missouri Compromise; Channing organizes Unitarian Church
42–66	1833:	Compromise Tariff; Jackson begins second term
45–69	1836:	Crockett dies at Alamo; Congress gridlocked over "gag rule"
56–80	1847:	Generals Taylor and Scott invade Mexico
59–83	1850:	Compromise of 1850; Webster embraces new Fugitive Slave Law
61–85	1852:	Webster, Clay die; Whig Party disintegrates after electoral loss
66–90	1857:	Buchanan starts term; Taney Court issues *Dred Scott* decision

SAMPLE CULTURAL ENDOWMENTS: *The Legend of Sleepy Hollow* (Washington Irving); *The American Democrat, The Last of the Mohicans* (James Fenimore Cooper); *The Star-Spangled Banner* (song, Francis Scott Key); *Married or Single?* (Catherine Sedgwick); *A Visit from St. Nicholas* (Clement Clarke Moore); *The Old Oaken Bucket* (Samuel Woodworth); *The First Forty Years of Washington Society* (Margaret Bayard Smith); *The Value and Importance of Legal Studies* (Joseph Story) the youngest (James Buchanan, Samuel F. B. Morse) reached adulthood just ahead of new youth movements in religion and literature. The Transcendental Awakening of the 1820s and 1830s hit most of them at an unsettling time—squarely in midlife. Having spent their early years emulating their celebrated next-elders, Compromisers spent their later years trying to please or calm their next-juniors. History records little that is distinctly theirs. The stunning victories of Jackson, Oliver Perry, and Stephen Decatur late in the War of 1812 culminated a pointless and blundering conflict declared by elder Republicans. Two decades later, the social upheaval of their "Age of Jackson" was fueled mainly by younger Transcendentals.

Compromisers were content to split the difference. They sought what President Jackson called "the middle course"—between two regions (North and South), two parties (Whig and Democrat), and two neighboring peer personalities (confident manliness and moral passion). Their confusion spilled over into self-conscious cruelty toward slaves and Indians, chronic ambivalence about economic and territorial expansion, and—late in life—paralyzing irresolution over the approaching collision between abolitionism and King Cotton. At the same time, they humanized and stabilized the new institutions wrought by Promethean elders. Their political leaders (historian Matthew Crenson calls them the "administrative founding fathers") defended pluralism, due process, and two-party politics. Their professionals (Francis Cabot Lowell) methodized industry. Their artists (John Audubon) catalogued nature. Their writers (James Fenimore Cooper and Washington Irving) leavened American culture with "romantic" sensitivity. Their clerical elite, prodded by William Ellery Channing's Unitarian Church, was the first to suggest that "society itself" may be responsible for the ills of modern life.

All these efforts earned mixed reviews from other generations. Republican elders appreciated the Compromisers' earnest sense of professionalism, but resisted any attempt to substitute what historian John Ward calls the Jacksonian "power of the heart" for the Jeffersonian "power of the head." John Randolph, a young House leader at the time of the Louisiana Purchase, blamed America's obsession with new territory on leaders whom he emotionally denounced as "energy men." Randolph's elders considered him deranged—as indeed he eventually became. Two decades later, young Transcendentals looked to Compromisers for flashes of a crusading virtue they sensed was fading from the world. "Jackson's life," observes historian Michael Rogin, "gratified a softer generation living prosaic lives." But the young often found Compromiser eloquence more enervating than inspiring. "There are seasons," announced the fiftyish Channing, "when new depths seem to be broken up in the soul, when new wants are unfolded in multitudes, and a new and undefined good is thirsted for." Once Channing died, the thirtyish firebrand William Garrison noted scornfully that "his nerves were delicately strung. The sound of a ram's horn was painfully distressing to him."

"Life itself is but a compromise," observed the 73-year-old Henry Clay, the "Great Compromiser" himself, as he proposed the last of his famous balancing acts. "All legislation, all government, all society is formed upon the principle of mutual concession, politeness, comity, and courtesy." Clay's generation presided over America during the three decades that span the Missouri Compromise of 1820, the Compromise Tariff of 1833, and the Great Compromise of 1850. Every step of the way, an odd mixture of outer calm and emotional turmoil plagued them. Sensitized young to the feelings of others, they matured into parents and leaders who sought to preserve their "reputation" and the approval of "public opinion." At worst, their other-directedness blinded them to simple choices. "The world is nothing but a contradance," worried Webster to a friend, "and everything volens, nolens, has a part in it." Yet at best, their irrepressible instinct for openness and honesty ennobled even their failures. No generation of southerners ever felt so ill at ease with their "peculiar institution" of slavery; no generation of northerners ever agonized so earnestly over the plight of the "noble savage." Entering the White House in March of 1849, Zachary Taylor promised "to adopt such measures of conciliation as would harmonize conflicting interests. . . ." On his deathbed a year later, he confessed, "God knows I have tried to do my honest duty. But I have made mistakes."

Compromiser Facts

• The Compromisers came of age and married amid a floodtide of romantic literature. Between the American Revolution and the War of 1812, the number of "romance novels" rose tenfold—as did the number of magazine articles stressing the "glorification of personal emotions" and the "idealization of the loved one."

• During the War of 1812, the average age of U.S. major generals fell from 60 to 36. Nearly all the military leaders disgraced early in the war were midlife Republicans; nearly all the leaders victorious late in the war were rising-adult Compromisers. Yet the war ended in a stalemate—and, ironically, the greatest Compromiser-led victory (Andrew Jackson's at New Orleans) occurred two weeks after John Quincy Adams (then across the Atlantic) had concluded the treaty which ended the war. Twenty years later, Congressman Henry Wise explained why a Compromiser-led Congress refused to include a scene from Jackson's victory in the Capitol rotunda: "I would be content to confine the subjects to a date prior to 1783."

• From first cohort to last, Compromiser women enjoyed rising access to advanced education—beginning with the Philadelphia Academy, founded in 1787 by Republicans in order to produce "sensible, virtuous, sweet-tempered" wives and mothers. Among all biographical entries in *Notable*

American Women, less than one-quarter of those born before 1770 had an advanced education, versus nearly two-thirds of all entries born by the 1780s.

- The Compromisers were the first generation to invent a specialized vocabulary for politics, coining such words as "lobby," "logrolling," "spoils," "bunk," "filibuster," and "noncommittal" (first coined to describe Martin Van Buren).

- During the Compromisers' "log cabin" rising adulthood, the share of the American population living west of the Appalachians grew from 3 percent in 1790 to 28 percent in 1830. But while many sought fresh western soil, many also chose professional and commercial callings. The big losers were the New England farm and the Virginia plantation. During this generation's three prosperous midlife decades (1820 to 1850), the share of the American workforce engaged in agriculture fell from 79 to 55 percent—the most rapid decline in American history.

- By the 1810s, Compromiser parents in their thirties and forties began to avoid having children, initiating a long-term decline in U.S. fertility that would later accelerate with the Transcendentals. After liberalizing marriage and child-custody laws in the late 1820s and 1830s, Compromisers entering midlife became the first American generation to divorce in significant numbers.

- The Compromisers attained their peak share of Congressional seats and governorships in 1825, four years before the "Age of Jackson" began. In 1839, two years after Andrew Jackson had left the White House at age 69 (the oldest exiting President until Eisenhower), their share had fallen beneath that of the younger Transcendentals.

- Household tax data from 1850 suggest that Compromisers, in their sixties and seventies, were wealthier relative to young adults than any other elder generation over four centuries of American history.

The Compromiser Lifecycle

YOUTH: "Rocked in the cradle of the Revolution" was how Clay later described his childhood—a phrase that fits most of his young peers. First-wavers witnessed the worst of the mob and wartime violence. At age 12, Andrew Jackson (whose mother and two older brothers died during the war) was himself beaten and jailed by the British. At age 8, William Henry Harrison watched Benedict Arnold's redcoats use his father's cattle for target practice. Last-wavers grew up seeing less violence, but sensing comparable adult anxiety during the turmoil of the 1780s and the hysteria over the French Revolution during the early 1790s. Surrounded by political and economic crisis, Compromiser children toed the line, while protective midlife Liberty and buoyant rising-adult Republicans pulled in the boundaries of family life to maximum tightness. Parents urged boys and girls to emulate widening sex-role divisions. Hastily rewritten textbooks taught them to revere the mythic grandeur of their elder "Founding Fathers." Teachers strictly monitored their classrooms (and America's first Sunday schools) to prevent unruly behavior—and passed out black crepe for teenagers to wear when Washington died in 1799. Republican educators insisted that this first generation of "national children" be "molded" into serviceable and obedient patriots. It was not a good time for the young to draw attention to themselves. Attending disciplined colleges, the aspiring elite studied hard, worried about their "sober deportment," and looked forward to brighter times ahead.

COMING OF AGE: Their passage into adulthood was smooth and seamless. "We were indeed in the full tide of successful experiment," recalled John Randolph of the rising optimism—and conformism—of the Jefferson and Madison Presidencies. Shunning risk, the young Adams wrote of "our duty to remain the peaceable and the silent" in an essay that won him an appointment as ambassador. Webster observed his college chums "balancing," easing unobserved into the adult world. Single women worried about being dismissed as "old maids" at age 25, yet understood (like Eliza Southgate) that "reputation undoubtedly is of great importance to all, but to a female 'tis everything—once lost 'tis forever lost." Single men obeyed the law. After 1790, the youth-driven mob violence that had coursed through so much of colonial history since the 1730s suddenly abated. Even when defying authority, young Compromisers chose their rebellions with care. Fledgling authors (both men and women) indulged in syrupy romanticism, teasing stolid midlife Republicans with deep feeling. College teachers like Lyman Beecher challenged secularism with earnestly respectful religious movements. Backwoods lawyers like Clay and Jackson crossed the Appalachians in search of rowdy adventure, yet felt less like conquerors than mischievous "settlers" on Republican-designed land grids. Courtships were awkwardly sentimental. Webster's biographer describes him as "better at writing poetry than making love"—but unlike their elders at like age, Compromisers *expected* emotion to resemble poetry. Men compensated for their absence of catharsis by flamboyant gestures of dominance over women, slaves, and Indians—and by dueling. A few months after Clay and Randolph missed each other at a chivalric ten paces, Clay gushed (upon hearing of a friend's duel): "We live in an age of romance!"

RISING ADULTHOOD: "Let our age be the age of improvement," urged Webster, exulting in America's surging prosperity. In the 1790s, twentyish first-wavers embarked on prosperous careers during America's first export boom.

Around 1820, thirtyish late-wavers joined the rage of canal-building and cloth manufacture in the north, or migrated to the southwestern frontier, where they could make fortunes growing cotton. Yet behind the easy affluence lurked personal unease. Like William Wirt, rising Compromisers tried "to assume the exterior of composure and self-collectedness, whatever riot and confusion may be within." They knew their destiny lay in dutiful expertise, not heroism. Despite rousing victories (at New Orleans) and stirring words (*The Star-Spangled Banner*) during the War of 1812, these young men realized that this "Second War for Independence" hardly compared with the first. Where their elders had founded an "Empire of Liberty" and "stood" for office as citizen-statesmen, Compromisers talked of an "American System" and "ran" for office as political professionals. Nor could thirtyish women replay the young heroine role of their mothers; instead, they embraced the new romantic "cult of true womanhood"— emphasizing innocence, femininity, and domestic virtue. As they matured, both men and women felt a growing tension between duty and feeling, between the proper division of social labor and a subversive desire for personal fulfillment. They felt an ambivalence that they knew had never bothered their parents.

MIDLIFE: During the 1820s, as aging Republican executives passed out of power and the Transcendental Awakening erupted, midlife Compromisers turned their adaptive antennae from elders to juniors. Still believing (with Washington Irving) that "ours is a government of compromise," yet swayed by what Tocqueville termed a "faith in public opinion," they tried to overcome their youthful caution by taking greater risks. Their first three Presidents—the effete Adams, the swaggering Jackson, and the calculating Van Buren—accurately reflect the fragmenting jigsaw of their "post-heroic" midlife personality. By the late 1830s, Compromiser leaders vied to outposture each other with youth-oriented rhetoric of populism and reform. Even the Whigs, hyping "log cabin and cider" and their Alamo martyr Davy Crockett, learned to spar with the Democrats at their own game. Public debate fixated on process and gesture, what the despairing Cooper called "petty personal wranglings" and "intellectual duellos." During the 1820s, southern Compromisers founded dozens of antislavery societies, but their hopes for gradual emancipation were soon dashed by the polarizing rhetoric of rising Transcendentals. (By the late 1830s, all of these southern societies had been disbanded.) The younger Emerson began assailing "the timid, imitative, and tame" Compromiser leadership; Thaddeus Stevens came to scorn their "mercenary, driveling" congressmen, eager "to conciliate Southern treason." As America entered the 1850s, remarks historian Samuel Eliot Morison, "there seemed nobody left to lead the nation but weak, two-faced trimmers and angry young men." Meanwhile, as society raced toward urbanization and westward expansion, the American family drifted toward trouble, with rising divorce rates, budding feminism, and a disturbingly wild new batch of (Gilded) children. Sarah Hale, who had written "Mary Had a Little Lamb" as a young widow, joined midlife peers like Lydia Sigourney and Emma Willard in denouncing men's "cruelty" to women, "to which every female heart must revolt."

ELDERHOOD: Torn between the congealing fanaticism of the young and guilty memories of Republican discipline, Compromisers entered elderhood watching America drift toward painful outcomes: Indian removal, anti-immigrant riots, lawless frontiers, slave chases, and sectional hatred. As they struggled to remain accommodating, their leaders shied away from the venerable titles once accorded to old Republicans. They preferred chummier nicknames: "Old Hickory" (Jackson), "Old Fuss and Feathers" (Scott), "Old Rough and Ready" (Taylor), "Old Prince" (Clay), and "Old Man Eloquent" (Adams). Sensing tragedy approach, they feared the final judgment of history. Clay had earlier despaired how his generation might "ignobly die" with "the scorn and contempt of mankind; unpitied, unwept, and unmourned." Their last chance to mediate rising Transcendental passions—culminating in their Compromise of 1850— earned them (Webster especially) precisely what Clay feared, the "scorn and contempt" of their next-juniors. Later on, seventyish "Old Buck" Buchanan, John Crittenden, and Roger Taney persisted in fruitless efforts to defer or ignore the rush to war. "Say to the seceded states: 'Wayward sisters, depart in peace,'" wrote the white-haired General Winfield Scott to younger leaders who no longer cared for the advice of 1812 war heroes. Dying on the eve of crisis, Philip Hone voiced his "anxious thoughts" about how "time unhallowed, unimproved . . . presents a fearful void." A few years later, the dying Buchanan blamed the Civil War on both "the fanatics of the North" and "the fanatics of the South." Like Hone and Buchanan, most Compromisers died lamenting both sides, just as they had lived trying to accommodate both sides.

*   *   *

Compromiser eulogies were full of mixed phrasing. One scholar said of Webster: "With all the greatness and smallness, with all the praise and blame . . ." Ever since, historians have been unable to decide whether Jackson was a force for pettiness or progress, or whether the Clay-Webster-Calhoun "Great Triumvirate" moderated or worsened the ultimate ferocity of the Civil War. Behind so many of this generation's favorite schemes—transporting Indians, recolonizing Africa, granting sovereignty to territories—was a faith in fair play and pluralism. Unlike their next-elders, Compromisers realized that the bond of social discipline could no longer hold the pieces together; unlike their next-juniors, they refrained from forcing their own judgments on others. From the perspective of subsequent events, their choices can easily be criticized. But we often forget how few alternatives were open to them—given their own instinctive caution as well as the zeal and lawlessness of younger Americans. Some choices may have averted worse outcomes: Had Compromiser leaders not compelled the eastern Indians to migrate west, even their humanitarian peers conceded that the tribes would soon have been wiped out by land-hungry whites.

Other choices may have come closer to success than we realize: Until youth anger and rabid sectionalism broke out in the 1830s, Compromiser plans for the gradual abolition of slavery seemed perfectly feasible. (Similar plans had worked earlier in several northern states and were then being seriously discussed in Virginia.) Such is the painful, might-have-been legacy of a kind but confused generation sandwiched between two others of extraordinary power. The Compromisers inherited grandeur and tried to perfect it by adding humor, sensitivity, expertise, and fairness. They passed away fearing they had failed to preserve, much less perfect, the achievements of their forefathers. No American generation ever had a sadder departure.

Chapter 9

THE CIVIL WAR CYCLE

"There is nothing like it on this side of the infernal region," recalled one war veteran of the youthful "rebel yells" that screeched over the hills above Bull Run Creek near Manassas, Virginia (today a suburb of Washington, D.C.), on a sultry July afternoon in 1861. Among some 18,000 Union soldiers mostly in their twenties, the "peculiar corkscrew sensation" of this sound triggered panic and retreat. But it delighted another 18,000 Confederate soldiers—including a plucky 37-year-old brigadier general, Thomas "Stonewall" Jackson. For them, the yell seemed to herald a quick victory. The attention of all America was riveted on a battle that many believed would decide the war in a single day. From Richmond, 53-year-old Jefferson Davis sped toward the scene to witness the triumph of his new "Nation under God." In Washington, 52-year-old Abraham Lincoln warned the Union not to despair over this "Black Monday" and hurriedly signed a bill enlisting 500,000 more soldiers. Fiftyish congressmen who had journeyed to Manassas as spectators climbed out of their carriages and commanded the fleeing young bluecoats to return to the battle. "We called them cowards, denounced them in the most offensive terms, put out our heavy revolvers, and threatened to shoot them, but all in vain," explained Ohio Congressman Albert Riddle. "No man ever saw such a mass of ghastly wretches." That night, in Augusta, Georgia, 4-year-old Woodrow Wilson joined his parents in praying for the Confederacy—while in a house on West 20th Street, New York City, 2-year-old Theodore Roosevelt did likewise for the other side.

In the aftermath of Bull Run, the 75-year-old Winfield Scott would retire as commander of Union forces, his Anaconda Plan now in total disrepute, along with the Crittenden Compromise and all the other conciliatory measures suggested by Scott's aging generation. In the summer of 1861, the Compromisers had no senators, one governor, and only two congressmen in office—a historic nadir for the political influence of Americans in their seventies. The epic climax of the CIVIL WAR CYCLE would be a drama not of four generations, but three:

• Lincoln's TRANSCENDENTAL GENERATION (Idealist, then age 40 to 69) had, in their twenties, provided the original core of the 1830s-era evangelical and abolitionist movements. Ever since, the extremism of William Lloyd Garrison, the stridency of young plantation owners, and the memory of Nat Turner's violent slave rebellion had worked to snuff out any Compromiser hope of peacefully weaning the South from slavery. Now in their fifties, this generation of Massachusetts "Black Republicans" and South Carolina "Fire Eaters" was fully prepared to shed younger blood to attain what they knew was right. Preaching from pulpits and railing from Congress, the peers of John Brown, Harriet "Moses" Tubman, Julia Ward Howe, Alexander Stephens, and Robert E. Lee looked to war for what New Englanders heralded as "the glory of the coming of the Lord" and Virginians "the baptism of blood" for their newborn confederacy. The hand of God was felt in Richmond no less than in Washington—and, over the next four years, these two capitals of "His Truth" would be bisected by a hundred-mile scar of mud and blood. All their lives, Transcendentals were a generation others feared but followed—until their apocalypse ended. In their old age, as they watched Reconstruction disintegrate and other principled causes fall into scorn, many of them would look back on Bull Run as the moment their ideals began self-destructing.

• Stonewall Jackson's GILDED GENERATION (Reactive, age 19 to 39) comprised the "ghastly wretches" Congressman Riddle saw scrambling away across Bull Run Creek. They had signed up for what they had expected to be a quick adventure, with maybe a little glory and profit mixed in—not much different from the California gold fields to which many had rushed as teenagers. Most expected that their sheer energy and derring-do ("Always mystify, mislead, and surprise the enemy," advised Jackson) would end the war quickly and let them get on with life's practical challenges. For Gilded whites, any resolution at all to the thundering hatred between elder abolitionists and elder "Southrons" would at last allow them to settle the western frontier. For Gilded blacks, including the slaves who began fleeing northward on the "underground railroad," Bull Run marked a necessary first step (albeit a tactical setback) toward flesh-and-blood freedom. But as the war settled into its meaner, later years, the jaunty opinion of this generation would sour. The scrappy adventurers whom Oliver Wendell Holmes,

Jr., saw as "touched with fire" in their youth would later turn bitterly cynical about passionate crusades. The same 25-year-olds who had shrieked (or heard) the rebel yell would, much later in their sixties, remember Bull Run—and Antietam, Gettysburg, and Atlanta—and warn the young against the horrors of war. Few would listen.

- For Wilson's PROGRESSIVE GENERATION (Adaptive, age 2 to 18), the news of Bull Run signaled the beginning of a family trauma that was destined to pass over their childhood like a dark and cruel cloud. They would not see daylight again until 1865, when Abraham Lincoln's funeral train journeyed from Washington through New York to Illinois. The black-creped cortege would be seen by an astonishing seven million Americans, nearly one-fifth the population of the reunited nation. Witnessing the last act, the youngest in this most fatherless of American generations would sit hoisted on a mother's shoulder and hear elders talk of the sufferings they had endured to provide children with a better future. The eldest would help out in the war effort: teenage Thomas Edison stringing telegraph wires, Sergeant William McKinley serving hot meals to troops at Antietam. Later, they would pass from a smothered youth to a conformist young adulthood, concentrating on smallish tasks in a society where great things were built (or said) by others. Emancipated young, black Progressives like Booker T. Washington would reach midlife disinclined to provoke a white society that, over the four bloody years commencing with Bull Run, had shown its capacity for organized butchery.

In the Civil War, the midlife Transcendentals wrote the script and dominated the credits; the rising-adult Gilded did the thankless dirty work; and the child Progressives watched and worried. All three suffered the wreckage and became cohabitants of America's only three-part cycle—the one whose crisis came too soon, too hard, and with too much ghastly devastation. This cycle is no aberration. Rather, it demonstrates how events can turn out badly—and, from a generational perspective, what happens when they do.

The Civil War Cycle had its origin when the failed Presidential bid of Andrew Jackson in 1824 fired a fresh mood of radicalism among coming-of-age Transcendentals—an accelerating enthusiasm over spiritual conversion, social reform, "Manifest Destiny," abolitionism, and utopian communalism. The cycle extended through the pitched battles of the Civil War and came to an inglorious end with the conformism and spiritual decline of the "Gilded Age" of the 1870s and 1880s. Climaxing in tragedy, the cycle failed to produce a Civic-type generation. After swiftly elbowing aside Transcendental leadership in the years following the war, the Reactive Gilded transformed in midlife from a recessive to a dominant generation, assuming some of the traits (secularism, conformism, lengthy political tenure, and an indulgent style of child nurture) associated with

FIGURE 9-1
Civil War Cycle: Age Location in History

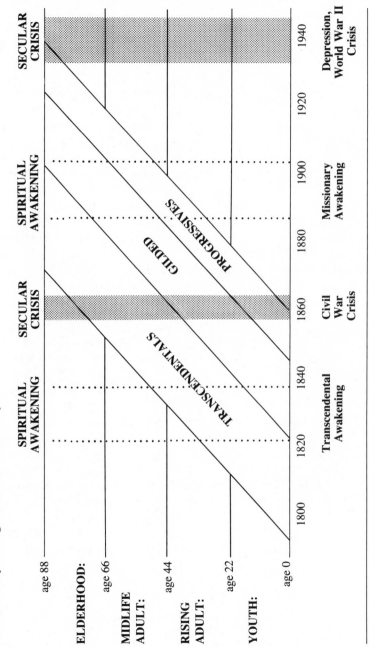

the Civic type at that phase of life—but without the hubris of crisis-era success. Though first-wave Progressives began life with a nurture similar to that of a Civic childhood, the trauma of war caused this generation to come of age smothered instead of empowered. Thereafter, its awkward connection with history and its other-directed peer personality would follow the pattern of an Adaptive type.

The Civil War Cycle contained two social moments:

• *The Transcendental Awakening* (1822–1837) was triggered by the evangelical preaching of Charles Finney and by widespread excitement over religious conversion, social reform, and radical idealism. Often merging with the popular "Jacksonian" movement, it peaked around 1831 with Nat Turner's rebellion, the founding of abolitionist societies, and the rise of labor parties and new religious sects. After giving birth to the "transcendentalist" school of philosophy and literature, the fervor subsided along with the collapse of Jacksonian prosperity in 1837. "The great years of the new revivalism were 1825 to 1837," notes historian Edward Pessen. Steeped in the awakening's radical call for Christian perfection, rising adults afterward took this agenda with them as they aged into the midlife leaders of the Civil War. *LOCATION IN HISTORY: Republicans in elderhood; Compromisers in midlife; Transcendentals in rising adulthood; Gilded in youth.*

• *The Civil War Crisis* (1857–1865)—"the Second American Revolution" according to Charles and Mary Beard—began in 1857, the year of Buchanan's inauguration, the "Bleeding Kansas" debates, and the *Dred Scott* decision. The crisis extended through the war itself and ended with General Robert E. Lee's surrender at Appomattox (on Palm Sunday) and the assassination of President Lincoln (five days later, on Good Friday). Graying preachers gloried in the religious symbolism. But unlike other crisis eras, the denouement of the Civil War produced less optimism than a sense of tragedy having run its course. At the end of the 1860s, a disillusioned "bloody shirt" generation of generals, officers, and older soldiers surged into political office—a position of power they would hold (but exercise cautiously) for a very long time. Meanwhile, the coming-of-age generation—traumatized, not energized, by the most destructive military conflagration yet witnessed in world history—meekly avoided asserting itself in public life. *LOCATION IN HISTORY: Compromisers in elderhood; Transcendentals in midlife; Gilded in rising adulthood; Progressives in youth.*

TRANSCENDENTAL GENERATION

Born: 1792–1821
Type: Idealist

Age Location:
Transcendental Awakening in rising adulthood
Civil War Crisis in midlife

"The young men were born with knives in their brain," recalled Ralph Waldo Emerson of his youthful peers in the 1830s. He once described them as an assortment of "madmen, madwomen, men with beards, Dunkers, Muggletonians, Come-Outers, Groaners, Agrarians, Seventh-Day Baptists"—utopians and sectarians of all stripe, whom the like-aged southerner Edgar Allan Poe mockingly labeled "frogpondium." They looked the part, too: their "anti-corset" women wearing mannish "Bloomers" and their young men at Brook Farm (to quote a fellow communard) wearing "their hair parted in the middle and falling upon their shoulders, and clad in garments such as no human being ever wore before." Nathaniel Hawthorne nostalgically looked back on Brook Farm as "our exploded scheme for beginning the life of Paradise anew" and on Emerson's Concord crowd as "a variety of queer, strangely dressed, oddly behaved mortals, most of whom took upon themselves to be important agents of the world's destiny." Early in life, they deemed themselves agents of the world's *inner* destiny. Only later did the men and women of this TRANSCENDENTAL GENERATION project their zeal onto the outer world and lead America toward the Last Judgment. In his thirties, Emerson wrote, "Beware when the great God lets loose a thinker on this planet." In his fifties, he greeted the bombardment of Fort Sumter by confessing in his journal that he found purification in "war"—which "shatters everything flimsy and shifty, sets aside all false issues. . . . Let it search, let it grind, let it overturn."

As post-crisis babies, Transcendentals took first breath in a welcoming new era of peace and optimism. As indulged children, they were assured by midlife Republican hero-leaders that every conflict had been won, every obstacle surmounted. But coming of age, these youngsters erupted in fury against the cultural sterility of a father-built world able to produce (charged Emerson in 1820) "not a book, not a speech, a conversation, or a thought worth noticing." They preached feeling over reason, community over society, inner perfection over outer conformity, moral transcendence over material improvement. The outburst defined the Transcendentals as a generation. First-wavers were just learning to

TRANSCENDENTAL GENERATION (Born 1792 to 1821)

TYPE: Idealist

Total number: 11,000,000
Percent immigrant: 20%
Percent slave: 13%

FAMILY TREE

Typical grandparents: Liberty
Parents: Republican and Compromise
Children: Gilded and Progressive
Typical grandchildren: Missionary

SAMPLE MEMBERS, birth (death)

1792 Thaddeus Stevens (1868)
1795 Dred Scott (1858)
1797 Sojourner Truth (1883)
1800 John Brown (1859)
1800 Nat Turner (1831)
1801 Brigham Young (1877)
1803 Ralph Waldo Emerson (1882)
1805 William Lloyd Garrison (1879)
1807 Robert E. Lee (1870)
1807 Henry W. Longfellow (1882)
1808 Jefferson Davis (1889)
1809 Edgar Allan Poe (1849)
1813 John Frémont (1890)
1815 Elizabeth Cady Stanton (1902)
1817 Frederick Douglass (1895)
1817 Henry David Thoreau (1862)
c. 1820 Harriet Tubman (1913)
1820 William Tecumseh Sherman (1891)
1820 Susan B. Anthony (1906)
1821 Mary Baker Eddy (1910)

PERIOD OF POLITICAL LEADERSHIP

Plurality in House: 1835–1869
Plurality in Senate: 1841–1873
Majority of Supreme Court: 1861–1889

U.S. PRESIDENTS: 1845–1849, 1850–
1857, 1861–1869

1795 James Polk (1849)
1800 Millard Fillmore (1874)
1804 Franklin Pierce (1869)
1808 Andrew Johnson (1875)
1809 Abraham Lincoln (1865)

PROMINENT FOREIGN PEERS

1795 Thomas Carlyle (1881)
1805 Alexis de Tocqueville (1859)
1813 Richard Wagner (1883)
1818 Karl Marx (1883)
1819 Queen Victoria (1901)

HISTORY AND LIFECYCLE

Age	Date	
0– 8	1800:	Jefferson elected to first term
0–20	1812:	War of 1812; elder generals disgraced
4–33	1825:	New Harmony community launches utopian movement
10–39	1831:	Nat Turner's slave rebellion; Garrison launches abolitionism
27–56	1848:	"Manifest Destiny" defeats Mexico; Women's Rights Convention
31–60	1852:	*Uncle Tom's Cabin* fuels abolitionism in North
38–67	1859:	John Brown's raid on U.S. arsenal at Harper's Ferry
42–71	1863:	Emancipation Proclamation; Union victorious at Gettysburg
44–73	1865:	Lee surrenders at Appomattox; Lincoln assassinated
47–76	1868:	Radical Republicans fail to impeach President Johnson
56–85	1877:	Reconstruction ends; U.S. troops leave South
61–90	1882:	Longfellow, Emerson die one month apart, eulogized for wisdom

SAMPLE CULTURAL ENDOWMENTS: *The Liberator* (William L. Garrison); *Walden*, "Civil Disobedience" (Henry D. Thoreau); Gettysburg Address (Abraham Lincoln); *Encyclopedia Americana* (Francis Lieber); *Leaves of Grass* (Walt Whitman); "The Transcendentalist" (Ralph W. Emerson); "The Raven" (Edgar Allan Poe); *Battle Hymn of the Republic* (song, Julia Ward Howe); *The Book of Mormon* (Joseph Smith); *The Scarlet Letter* (Nathaniel Hawthorne); *The Rise and Fall of the Confederate Government* (Jefferson Davis) talk when their dutiful Republican fathers were crushing the Whiskey Rebels, age 9 at Jefferson's first inauguration, and barely 30 when the initial clamor over revival and reform broke out during the twilight Monroe years. Last-wavers came of age just in time to join the furor before it receded in the late 1830s. First wave and last, they afterward embarked on self-immersed voyages—starting families and careers while founding communes, joining sects, dabbling in odd lifestyles, probing the soul with art. In the 1850s, the Transcendentals emerged again into public life, this time as midlife champions on both sides of what William Seward called their "irrepressible conflict." Summoning juniors to battle, they presided as leaders over four years of total war, which only ended when William Tecumseh Sherman vowed to punish the Confederacy to its "innermost recesses" and sixtyish Radicals like Thaddeus Stevens demanded a postwar "reconstruction" of the southern soul.

From Stevens to Lincoln, Whitman to Poe, Garrison to the Blackwell sisters, Transcendentals grew up notoriously estranged from their fathers. Many warned, like Garrison, of "the terrible judgments of an incensed God" that "will complete the catastrophe of Republican America"; or proclaimed, like Emerson, that "men are what their mothers made them"; or condemned, like Thoreau (whose mother brought home-cooked meals to his Walden retreat), "the mouldering relics of our ancestors." " 'Our fathers did so,' says someone. 'What of that?' say we," wrote Theodore Parker, described by a friend as "a man of Nature who abominates the steam-engine and the factory." But if young Transcendentals often joined Compromisers in sniping attacks on Republican social discipline, they reached midlife without their next-elders' instinctive caution. "Compromise—Compromise!" wrote William Herndon on the eve of war. "Why I am sick at the very idea."

Whether Abolitionists, "Southrons," Mormons, or Anti-Masons, they agreed that each person must act on an inner truth that transcends the sensory world—a credo immortalized by Emerson in 1842 as "Transcendentalism" and praised by Oliver Wendell Holmes as "our intellectual Declaration of Independence." Unlike their elders, Southern "fire-eaters" like Robert Barnwell Rhett and William Yancey refused to apologize for slavery, but instead found virtue in an aggressive empire of chivalry and bondage. Meanwhile, northerners like Seward declared the abolition of slavery to be "a higher law" than their father-drafted Constitution, and Garrison condemned the half-slave Union as "a covenant with death, an agreement with hell." Neither side questioned that God was on its side. While ax-wielding visionaries like John Brown and Nat Turner sanctified what Herman Melville heralded as their "meteor of war," Harriet Beecher Stowe demanded that the "wrath of Almighty God" descend on America, a day that "shall burn like an oven."

Throughout most of the nineteenth century, all Americans ridiculed, respected, or feared whatever age bracket the Transcendentals occupied as a moving repository of inner-driven passion and unbreakable principle. In the 1820s, the

age bracket was youth: fledgling preachers like Charles Finney and their adolescent followers who made up the elder-attacking core of what historians call
the Second Great Awakening. In the 1840s, it was rising adulthood: thirtyish
men and women, oblivious to any peer group but their own, who filled the ranks
of America's abolitionists, southern expansionists, feminists, labor agitators,
utopians, and reformers. In the 1860s, it was midlife: bearded fiftyish crusaders
who despised both the caution of their elders and the opportunism of their juniors.
In the 1880s, it was elderhood: craggy patriarchs and matriarchs—some starting
new causes (Wendell Phillips' socialism), others persisting in old movements
(Elizabeth Cady Stanton's feminism), and all warning the young not to back
down from truth and justice. At every age, Transcendentals mingled images of
nature, mother, love, redemption, and apocalypse. Few became great scientists;
Isaac Singer and Cyrus McCormick were their only celebrated inventors. But
as moral prophets, no generation ever paraded so many visions of godliness—
whether Lincoln's Union, Davis' Confederacy, Brigham Young's "Kingdom of
Zion," John O'Sullivan's "Manifest Destiny," John Humphrey Noyes' "perfectionism," Mary Baker Eddy's Christian Science, Albert Brisbane's utopian
communes, Orestes Brownson's Catholic socialism, or Dorothea Dix's severe
but redemptive penology.

From youth to old age, the Transcendentals celebrated the subjective like no
other generation before or since. While Garrison chastised his peers for their
"thralldom of self," Emerson preached "whoso would be a man must be a
nonconformist," Thoreau insisted on the "majority of one," and Whitman (in
his "Song of Myself") rhapsodized that "I dote on myself, there is that lot of
me and all so luscious." "All that we see or seem/ Is but a dream within a
dream," wrote Poe. French visitor Alexis de Tocqueville, encountering "a
fanatical and almost wild spiritualism that hardly exists in Europe," concluded:
"Religious insanity is very common in the United States." British visitor Frances
Trollope called them the "I'm-as-good-as-you-are population" and added, "I
do not like them." No matter. Transcendentals cared only for what they thought
of themselves. They valued inner serenity: "having a strong sphere" (Stowe);
being a person who "is what he is from Nature and who never reminds us of
others" (Emerson); or possessing a "perfect mental prism" (as a friend described
Lincoln). Only later in life did their narcissism mutate into an irreconcilable
schism between northern and southern peers, each side yearning for perfection
no matter how the violence might blast the young. Like a generation of Captain
Ahabs, Transcendentals from Boston to Charleston turned personal truth into
collective redemption. Crowding into churches while younger men died at Gettysburg, they sang the third verse of Julia Ward Howe's *Battle Hymn of the
Republic* with utter conviction: "I have read a fiery gospel writ in burnished
rows of steel:/ As ye deal with my contemners, so with you my grace shall deal;/
Let the hero, born of woman, crush the serpent with his heel,/ Since God is
marching on."

In his last public address, Lincoln declared: "Important principles may and must be inflexible." Yet after he died, many of his aging peers came to regret, like Dr. Holmes, the ravages of "moral bullies" who "with grim logic prove, beyond debate,/ That all we love is worthiest of hate." "One trembles to think of that mysterious thing in the soul," wrote Melville, pondering "the vindictiveness with which we carry on our wars, and the misery and desolation that follow in their train." The Transcendentals may have been America's most high-minded generation—but they also became, by any measure, its most destructive. Recalling Robert E. Lee, the younger Henry Adams bitterly remarked after the Civil War was over, "It's always the good men who do the most harm in the world."

Transcendental Facts

- Thanks to Republican science, Transcendentals were the first American babies to be yanked into the world by forceps-wielding male doctors rather than by midwives. Thereafter, mothers insisted that these infants be regarded as unique individuals: They were the first whose names were chosen primarily by mothers instead of fathers; the first whose names were actually used in family conversation (no longer "it" or "baby"); and the first not commonly named after parents. From the 1780s to the 1810s, the share of New England babies named after parents dropped from 60 to 12 percent. (It rose again for later generations.)

- The worst riots (then known as "breaking-ups") in the history of American universities occurred from 1810 through the mid-1830s. At Harvard in 1823, two-thirds of the senior class were expelled shortly before commencement. At Oberlin, abolitionist clubs held "revivals" in which students recounted the "sins" of their slaveholding fathers.

- From the 1810s to 1830s, rising Transcendentals fueled the most rapid expansion of evangelical religion in American history. In the West, youthful settlers flocked to new Baptist and Methodist churches. In the South, young preachers buried forever the cool rationalism of the Republican planter-statesmen. "By 1830," notes historian Russel Nye, "had Jefferson been still alive, he would undoubtedly have found his religious principles highly unpopular in his native Virginia."

- Coining the words "spiritualism," "medium," "rapping," "séance," "clairvoyance," and "holy roller," rising Transcendentals delighted in altered states of consciousness. From the 1840s on, a large share of this generation believed in psychic phenomena (séances with the dead, prophetic dreams)—including Abraham and Mary Todd Lincoln, reformers William Lloyd Garrison and Horace Greeley, and even many Transcendental feminists, from

Lucy Stone to Elizabeth Blackwell. "Consistently," claims historian Ann Braude, "those who assumed the most radical positions on woman's rights became Spiritualists."

- The Transcendentals were the first coming-of-age Americans to experiment with opium. By the time they ranged from their teens through their thirties (the early 1830s), U.S. alcohol consumption had climbed to its highest level ever—the equivalent of a quart of whiskey per week for every American over age 15. Entering midlife, however, this generation led a thundering campaign against "Demon Rum" which successfully reduced alcohol consumption to one-fourth its former level by 1850.

- In his *History of American Socialisms,* published in 1870, the aging Transcendental John Humphrey Noyes deemed seventy-four utopian communities worth mentioning and dating. Fifty-five were founded between 1825 and 1845. "All died young," Noyes observed, "and most of them before they were two years old."

- Over one six-year span, fortyish Transcendental authors published the best-remembered literature of the nineteenth century—including *The Scarlet Letter* (Hawthorne, 1850); *Uncle Tom's Cabin* (Stowe, 1852); *Walden* (Thoreau, 1854); *The Song of Hiawatha* (Longfellow, 1855); *Moby Dick* (Melville, 1855); and *Leaves of Grass* (Whitman, 1855). Formerly regarded by Europeans as literary primitives, American authors suddenly acquired a vast European following. By the late 1850s, Longfellow outsold Tennyson in England.

- When Transcendentals came of age, all America cherished the look and sagacity of youth; when they grew old, Americans respected the look and sagacity of age. The full beard—an enduring symbol of Transcendental wisdom—came into vogue among midlife men in the late 1850s (just about the time of John Brown's raid). Though the beard remained popular among elderly men in the 1880s, the next generation of midlifers began adding a mustache or rejecting it altogether in favor of bushy "sideburns" (named after the Gilded Union general Ambrose Burnside).

- Of the sixteen leading "Radical Republicans" in Congress who took the hardest line against the defeated Confederacy in 1867, fifteen were Transcendentals (average age, 57)—although Congress as a whole (average age, 49) was by now one-third Gilded.

- The Civil War years began with Transcendentals enjoying the greatest one-generation political hegemony in American history (a 90 percent share of governors and Congress in 1860) and ended with the largest generational rout in the election of 1868 (when the Transcendental share plunged from

63 to 44 percent). The period from 1865 to 1869 marked the steepest-ever decline in one generation's share of national leadership.

The Transcendental Lifecycle

YOUTH: "Our schools, our streets, and our houses are filled with straight, well-formed children," exulted David Ramsay in 1802, praising the offspring of midlife Republican nurture. Transcendentals missed the atmosphere of crisis that had smothered young Compromisers. They grew up instead in the orderly yet brightening climate of Jeffersonian America. "The elements added after 1790" to childhood, notes historian Joseph Kett, "were increasingly on the side of freedom." Many parents used their rising affluence to give their children expensive toys (including pastel-painted children's furniture) and to seat them in individualized family portraits. Pestalozzian tutors encouraged positive emotion, and schoolbooks like *Alphabet Without Tears* made learning more friendly. In 1818, a British visitor noted "the prominent boldness and forwardness of American children" who are "rarely forbidden or punished for wrong doing" and "only kindly solicited to do right." Transcendentals later felt nostalgia for their childhood, a friendly and preindustrial "Age of Homespun," as Horace Bushnell came to label it. Nevertheless, most recoiled at an early age from fathers whom they perceived as reserved and soldierly. While parents urged duty, activity, and society, these children preferred meditation, reading, and "solitude" (a word they would cherish throughout their lives). Cerebral and self-immersed, they avoided joining the adult world and turned their teenage years, notes Kett, into "a period of prolonged indecision." At work, they felt themselves "minds among the spindles" (as one visitor described the first Lowell factory girls). Attending college, they mixed a passion for God and nature with angry attacks on rotelike curricula. While Lyman Beecher, the Compromiser educator, reported effusively that the most radical youths had "the finest class of minds he ever knew," Emerson's description of his young peers struck an ominous note: "They are lonely; the spirit of their writing is lonely; they repel influence; they shun general society.... They make us feel the strange disappointment which overcasts every youth."

COMING OF AGE: The revolt against fathers warmed up during the outwardly placid late 1810s, when coming-of-age Transcendentals began rejecting what 22-year-old James Polk described as "a tedious enumeration of noble ancestors." Fashions celebrating age (powder and queues, waistcoats, knee breeches) swiftly gave way to those celebrating youth (short hair, shouldered jackets, pantaloons). Youngsters drawn to upstate New York to help build the Erie Canal, a region soon known as the "Burnt-Over District," launched an evangelical surge led by the young Charles Finney. Teenagers of both sexes (including Joseph Smith, the future Mormon prophet) experienced radical conversions and attacked elders as "sinners" and "hypocrites." By the late 1820s, as social and geographical mobility quickened with the first surge of industrialization, youths joined religion to a radical social agenda. Screaming "to wake up a nation slumbering in the lap of moral death," young William Lloyd Garrison proclaimed, "I will be as harsh as truth, and as uncompromising as justice." He launched the riotous abolitionist movement in 1831—the same year 28-year-old Nat Turner led his bloody insurrection against slave masters. By the mid-1830s, young radicals were sparking labor and "Locofoco" activism in the cities, joining the Anti-Masonic Party in the countryside, and rallying to new cultural and religious standards in the college towns—from Emerson's "Idealism" to John Greenleaf Whittier's antislavery lyrics to Mary Lyon's bold new college (Mount Holyoke Seminary) for women. "The Seventy"—an entourage of young lecturers who traveled the nation chastising their elders—featured women as well as men. "There is no purely masculine man, no purely feminine woman," observed Margaret Fuller. Henry Wadsworth Longfellow, deemed by Emerson "the universal poet of women and young people," urged his peers to "shake the vast pillars of this Commonweal, / Till the vast Temple of our liberties / A shapeless mass of wreck and rubbish lies."

RISING ADULTHOOD: Whitman called it "simmering," Emerson "metamorphosis," Thoreau the moment "when we have lost the world . . . and begin to find ourselves." For twentyish and thirtyish adults, it meant the transition from radical awakening to a mellower era that promised (declared Fuller's *Dial* magazine) "the unfolding of the individual man, into every form of perfection, without let or hindrance, according to the inward nature of each." This era of Transcendental remission was triggered by the Panic of 1837, an event that historian Sidney Ahlstrom says "darkened the dream" for young reformers and led them into "the Fabulous Forties." Institutionally, Republican-built (and now Compromiser-managed) America stood intact—but, culturally, rising adults were substituting an entirely new agenda. Pursuing separate paths, they mixed outward pessimism with inward confidence by secluding themselves (Thoreau at Walden, Davis on a Mississippi plantation), founding utopian communities (Brook Farm, Nauvoo, Fruitlands), establishing colleges as reform enclaves (Oberlin, Antioch), launching "spiritualist" fads (homeopathy, phrenology), and asserting women's rights (Seneca Falls). They turned the tide against substance abuse by advocating alcoholic temperance and natural-food diets like Sylvester Graham's fermented crackers. They challenged neoclassical architecture with a "Gothic revival"—asymmetrical houses with churchish gables and earth-tone colors. Their first political leaders displayed surprisingly sharp edges. President James Polk, an austere "born-again" Methodist, led a moralistic crusade against Mexico that shocked elders—and a 32-year-old congressman proposed a "Wilmot Proviso" that challenged the life work of the aging Compromiser Triumvirate. Down South, Transcendental preachers found godliness in slavery as fortyish "ultimatumists" began demanding secession. Foreign visitors in the early 1840s remarked on the "seriousness" and "absence of reverence for authority" of the "busy generation of the present hour." "All that we do we overdo," agreed Theodore Parker. "We are so intent on our purpose that we have no time for amusement."

MIDLIFE: "The age is dull and mean. Men creep, not walk," complained Whittier of the 1850s, a decade of stale Compromiser leadership that Stowe described as "an age of the world when nations are trembling and convulsed." The mood turned sour with the failure of European revolutions, the unpopular Compromise of 1850, frontier violence, and spectacular fugitive slave chases. In the mid-1850s, with lawless mayhem breaking out in "Bleeding Kansas," midlife Americans feared that the rapacious younger Gilded were about to shatter their visions and rip America to pieces. Fiftyish preachers warned of Apocalypse from their pulpits. Like-aged legislators began shouting at each other over principle—one brutally caning another on the Senate floor. In 1859, the "martyrdom" of John Brown after his raid on Harpers Ferry catalyzed the mood on both sides. "How vast the change in men's hearts!" cried Phillips. "The North is suddenly all Transcendentalist," exulted Thoreau. "Unborn deeds, things soon to be, project their shapes around me," mused Whitman of "this incredible rush and heat, this strange ecstatic fever of dreams." Once Lincoln's election answered Whitman's plea for a "Redeemer President," his peers grimly prepared for a Civil War that Lincoln insisted "no mortal could stay." As the young marched off to bloody battle, midlife Transcendentals urged them on with appeals to justice and righteousness. Garrison spoke of the "trump of God," while Phillips warned that the Union was "dependent for success entirely on the religious sentiment of the people." Around the time Atlanta was in flames, the words "In God We Trust" first appeared on U.S. coinage. Late in the war, though the devastation grew catastrophic, both sets of Transcendental Presidents and Congresses refused to back down. "Instruments of war are not selected on account of their harmlessness," insisted Thaddeus Stevens, beckoning Union armies to "lay waste to the whole South." And so the North did—finding redemption at Gettysburg, in Sherman's march, and in Emancipation. Afterward, Transcendentals felt spiritual fulfillment: a huge human price had been exacted from the young, but a new era was indeed dawning. Observed Melville, "The Generations pouring . . . / Fulfilled the end designed;/ By a wondrous way and glorious/ A passage Thou dost find. . . ."

ELDERHOOD: "Great is the art of beginning, but greater the art is of ending," wrote Longfellow, adding (in "Morituri Salutamus") how, "as the evening twilight fades away,/ The sky is filled with stars, invisible by day."

One contemporary remarked how Longfellow "grew more beautiful every year of his advancing old age—with his flowing white hair and beard and his grand face." Late in the nineteenth century, a generation that had once detested elderhood now found new powers in it. The young father-hater Theodore Parker grew old watching his peers mature into "a noble, manly life, full of piety which makes old age beautiful"; Sidney Fisher felt "a profound sense of the dignity and worth of our souls." The Gilded had their doubts. After blunting the postwar vengeance of aging Radicals, 30- and 40-year-olds moved swiftly in the late 1860s to purge the nation of Transcendental leaders—in Congress, governors' mansions, and the White House. In three straight Presidential elections (1868, 1872, and 1876), older Transcendental candidates fell to less reform-minded juniors. Meanwhile, old Confederates remained unrepentant (like Jefferson Davis), led younger white "Redeemers" (like Nathan Forrest, "Grand Wizard" of the postwar Ku Klux Klan), or aged into chivalric symbols of the "Lost Cause" (like Wade Hampton). In scientific circles, the amoral Darwinism that so enamored the Gilded drew heated criticism from old Asa Gray. Thus did Transcendentals transform into elders much like those in the novels of Hawthorne and Melville—stern-valued patriarchs, revered but feared (like Thaddeus Stevens) for "something supernatural" that "inhabits his weary frame." While the aging minister Albert Barnes assured his friends they would die *The Peaceful Death of the Righteous,* aging spiritualists likewise heralded the end with stoic confidence. For Lydia Child, "The more the world diminished and grew dark, the less I felt the loss of it; for the dawn of the next world grew even clearer and clearer." Versed Holmes to Whittier "On His Eightieth Birthday": "Look Forward! Brighter than earth's morning ray/ . . . The unclouded dawn of life's immortal day!"

*　*　*

With their passing, the Transcendentals left behind an enduring projection of their peer personality. Exalting inner truth, they brought spirit to America— lofty imperatives of heartfelt religion and moral justice unknown to the Jeffersonian world of their childhood. Contemptuous of earthly reality, so too did they wreak vast material devastation. They emancipated the slaves, wrote inspiring verse, and preserved the Union their fathers had created. But they also slaughtered the younger Gilded, thereby triggering a massive reaction that vaunted pragmatism over principle. For decades after the Civil War, the old Transcendental causes lay dormant (temperance), repudiated (feminism), even reversed (Jim Crow) by juniors who reached midlife despising the fruits of righteousness. Worse, the still younger generation of child Progressives, whom these elders might have empowered to lock in their grand visions, instead came of age in a wrecked world of spent dreams. The memory of Transcendentals would eventually grow warmer among a new generation of postwar babies who went to school staring up at portraits of what Booth Tarkington remembered as "great and good" old men—the likes of Longfellow, Holmes, Whittier, and

Emerson. In 1881, a fresh crop of young college men heard the seventyish Phillips warn them to "sit not, like the figure on our silver coin, ever looking backward." In 1892, a fresh crop of young college women heard the 77-year-old Elizabeth Cady Stanton remind them of "The Solitude of Self." A quarter century later, these inner-driven Missionaries would build a national monument to Lincoln, worship Susan B. Anthony, and celebrate the Transcendentals as a generation beloved for its principle and vision.

Yet among the most important Transcendental endowments is a terrible lesson. The generation of Lincoln was also that of John Brown, a man who summoned "a whole generation" to "die a violent death" and was elevated to sainthood by his most eminent peers. It was also the generation of Mary Baker Eddy, who insisted that "God is Mind, and God is infinite; hence all is mind," and of William Lloyd Garrison, who urged war in order to bring mankind "under the dominion of God, the control of an inward spirit, the government of the law of love." The peers of Lincoln, Brown, Eddy, and Garrison—born to heroic parents, indulged as children, fiery as youths, narcissistic as rising adults, and values-fixated entering midlife—ultimately chose to join technology and passion to achieve the maximum apocalypse then conceivable.

GILDED GENERATION

Born: 1822–1842
Type: Reactive

Age Location:
Transcendental Awakening in youth
Civil War Crisis in rising adulthood
Missionary Awakening in elderhood

"The *only* population of the kind that the world has ever seen," Mark Twain wrote of the Gold Rush 49ers, "two hundred thousand young men—not simpering, dainty, kid-gloved weaklings, but stalwart, muscular, dauntless *young* braves, brimful of push and energy," all having caught what Twain called the "California sudden-riches disease." Eight in ten were between age 10 and 30, making circa-1850 San Francisco the most monogenerational city ever seen in America—and among the most anarchic, with no families or laws, just vigilante justice enforced by hangings. The wildness of the western territories prompted the fortyish Horace Mann to ask disparagingly, "Why were they not colonized by men like the pilgrim fathers?" Back in eastern cities, meanwhile, unsupervised youths shocked elders—poor kids by roaming wild in the streets and organizing America's first urban gangs with names like Roach Guards; the better-off kids (whom Van Wyck Brooks later called *la jeunesse dorée* of the 1840s) by throwing books through college windows and striking cynical poses in fashionable clothing. Trying to make the best of a dangerous world and then getting damned for it—that was the life story of the GILDED GENERATION. Twain himself later memorialized the Gilded childhood in his adventures of Tom Sawyer and Huckleberry Finn—pranks and pluck in a world of Aunt Beckyish elders. It didn't change much with age.

The Gilded lived perhaps the most luckless lifecycle in American history. First-wavers grew up too late to share the euphoria of the Transcendental Awakening—but in time to feel its damage as children. Two decades later, last-wavers grew up just in time to maximize their risk of death and maiming in the Civil War. They all came of age in an era of economic swings, floodtide immigration, and a darkening national mood. In rising adulthood, they bore the human burden of Transcendental conscience, becoming what Henry Adams described as a "generation . . . stirred up from its lowest layers." Those who survived became what historian Daniel Boorstin calls "the Go-Getters" of the late 1860s, thirtyish buccaneers who had seen Union armies camp on Brook Farm and cannons annihilate the most decent of their peers. After Appomattox, writes Brooks, "the young men were scattering in all directions. Their imagination was caught by the West, and scores who might have been writers in the days of *The Dial* were seeking their fortunes in railroads, mines, and oil wells." Principle seemed pointless next to the confession of the "Plumed Knight," James Blaine: "When I want something, I want it dreadfully." Blaine's remark, notes historian Richard Hofstadter, "might have been the motto of a whole generation of Americans who wanted things dreadfully, and took them."

Inheriting the physical and emotional wreckage left behind by their elders, the Gilded entered midlife and reassembled the pieces—their own way. They muscled into political power, repudiated their elders' high-flown dreams, rolled up their sleeves, and launched a dynamo of no-holds-barred economic progress to match their pragmatic mood. They reached the cusp of old age during the 1890s, again an unlucky moment for their phase of life, when a rapidly growing share of all elderly landed in what Americans began calling an "industrial scrap heap." With few means of public or private support, that is where many of them eked out their twilight years. "Let the chips fall where they may," said Roscoe Conkling. By most indicators—wealth, higher education, lifespan—the Gilded fared *worse* at each phase of life than their next-elders or next-juniors, a sacrificial one-generation backstep in the chain of progress. No wonder they behaved, all their lives, like survivalists. Taking a cue from their laissez-faire guru William Graham Sumner, they learned to "root, hog, or die."

Throughout their lifecycle, and indeed ever since, the Gilded have been inundated by torrents of critical abuse. Before the Civil War, midlife Transcendentals like Horace Mann charged that "more than eleven-twelfths" of them could not read, and George Templeton Strong saw in them "so much gross dissipation redeemed by so little culture." Later on, Walt Whitman complained of their "highly deceptive superficial intellectuality," and Longfellow accused their generation of taking America "back to the common level, with a hoarse death-rattle in its throat." A younger Progressive, Henry James, accosted "that bright hard medal, of so strange an alloy, one face of which is somebody's right and ease and the other somebody's pain and wrong." By the 1890s, the righteous reformers of a still younger (Missionary) generation rediscovered the old Transcendental theme of Gilded soullessness. Historians Charles Beard despised their "cash nexus," Ralph Adams Cram their "mammonism," Vernon Parrington their "triumphant and unabashed vulgarity without its like in our history." Closer to our own time, Samuel Eliot Morison has written: "When the gilt wore off, one found only base brass." The Gilded seldom answered such charges; in fact, their leading writers mostly agreed. In 1873, with rumpled heroes like Ulysses Grant and John D. Rockefeller riding high, Twain and his 35-year-old coauthor Charles Dudley ("Deadly Warning") Warner published a popular satirical book,

GILDED GENERATION (Born 1822 to 1842)

TYPE: Reactive

Total number: 17,000,000
Percent immigrant: 28%
Percent slave: 10%

FAMILY TREE

Typical grandparents: Republican
Parents: Compromise and Transcendental
Children: Progressive and Missionary
Typical grandchildren: Lost

SAMPLE MEMBERS, birth (death)

1823 "Boss" Tweed (1878)
1824 "Stonewall" Jackson (1863)
1829 Roscoe Conkling (1888)
1829 Levi Strauss (1902)
1830 James G. Blaine (1893)
1830 Emily Dickinson (1886)
1830 "Mother Jones" (1930)*
c. 1831 Sitting Bull (1890)
1832 Louisa May Alcott (1888)
1832 Horatio Alger (1899)
1835 Andrew Carnegie (1919)*
1835 Mark Twain (1910)
1837 J. Pierpont Morgan (1913)
1837 "Wild Bill" Hickok (1876)
1838 John Wilkes Booth (1865)
1839 John D. Rockefeller (1937)
1839 George Custer (1876)
1840 Thomas Nast (1902)*
1841 Oliver W. Holmes, Jr. (1935)
1842 William James (1910)
* = immigrant

PERIOD OF POLITICAL LEADERSHIP

Plurality in House: 1869–1893
Plurality in Senate: 1873–1903
Majority of Supreme Court: 1890–1910

U.S. PRESIDENTS: 1869–1897

1822 Ulysses S. Grant (1885)
1822 Rutherford B. Hayes (1893)
1830 Chester A. Arthur (1886)
1831 James A. Garfield (1881)
1833 Benjamin Harrison (1901)
1837 Grover Cleveland (1908)

PROMINENT FOREIGN PEERS

1828 Henrik Ibsen (1906)
1832 Maximilian (1867)
1832 Lewis Carroll (1898)
1833 Alfred Nobel (1896)
1839 Paul Cézanne (1906)

Age	Date	HISTORY AND LIFECYCLE
0–15	1837:	Economic Panic of 1837; spiritual fervor recedes
3–23	1845:	Travel volume peaks along Oregon and Santa Fe trails
6–26	1848:	U.S. wins Mexican War; Irish immigration; California Gold Rush
13–33	1855:	Unofficial war in Kansas; Know-Nothing movement peaks
18–38	1860:	Pony Express riders hired; Lincoln elected; South Carolina secedes
21–41	1863:	51,000 soldiers killed, wounded, or missing at Battle of Gettysburg
27–47	1869:	Grant takes office; golden spike laid in Utah
29–49	1871:	Peak year for cattle drives along Chisholm Trail
34–54	1876:	Custer massacred at Little Big Horn; Centennial Exposition
35–55	1877:	Hayes wins "stolen" election; South throws out carpetbaggers
51–71	1893:	Panic of 1893; Columbian Exposition
69–89	1911:	Supreme Court breaks up Standard Oil; Carnegie starts foundation

SAMPLE CULTURAL ENDOWMENTS: *Little Women* (Louisa May Alcott); *The Adventures of Huckleberry Finn* (Mark Twain); political cartoons (Thomas Nast); *The Rise of Silas Lapham* (William Dean Howells); "The Checkered Game of Life" (Milton Bradley); "The Outcasts of Poker Flat" (Bret Harte); *The Gospel of Wealth* (Andrew Carnegie); *Luck and Pluck* (Horatio Alger); *The Oregon Trail* (Francis Parkman); *The Gilded Age* (Mark Twain and Charles Dudley Warner); Home Insurance Building skyscraper (Le Baron Jenney)

The Gilded Age, whose title perfectly described this generation of metal and muscle.

Hit by pain and hard luck that seemed to justify all the critics, the Gilded suffered from low collective self-esteem. "I'm Nobody! Who are you?/Are you—Nobody—too?" But Emily Dickinson's peers were nobody's fools. In their eyes, the central lesson of history was the devastation that inner passion can inflict on the outer world. They became skeptics, trusting principle less than instinct and experience. "As a rule we disbelieve all facts and theories for which we have no use," wrote William James, who popularized "pragmatism" as a philosophy based on "truth's cash value." The Gilded played for keeps and asked for no favors. Their motto, as General Grant put it, was to strike "as hard as you can and as often as you can, and keep moving on." When young, devilish raiders like Jeb Stuart delighted in cavalier foppery (black plumes and gold-threaded boots). When old, "robber barons" like Andrew Carnegie unabashedly proclaimed "the Law of Competition" as "the soil in which society so far has produced the best fruit." Midlife apostles of Darwin's "survival of the fittest," the Gilded did not mind becoming a generation of spectacular winners and losers. Their ranks included those who struck gold and those who died trying; fugitive slaves and the posses chasing them; war profiteers and war widows; Pullman millionaires and sweating "coolies"; Irish immigrants and nativist mobs; General Custer and Sitting Bull.

Twenty years after the young 49ers first reached San Francisco, Twain asked: "And where are they now? Scattered to the ends of the earth—or prematurely aged and decrepit—or shot and stabbed in street affrays—or dead of disappointed hopes and broken hearts—all gone, or nearly all—victims devoted upon the altar of the golden calf—the noblest holocaust that ever wafted its incense heavenward. It is pitiful to think upon." Yet Twain's "golden calf" peers dug the first oil, laid the golden spike, built the first business trusts, designed the first "skyscrapers"—and, most important, targeted most of their throat-cutting competition against their own peers. In so doing, the men and women of this self-demeaning generation gave chestiness to a modernizing nation and a much better life to their children.

Gilded Facts

- From youth to elderhood, the Gilded were more likely to die or fall into destitution than their parents at like age. They were also more likely to make a fortune starting out from nothing. According to C. Wright Mills, a larger share of their business elite came from lower- or lower-middle-class backgrounds than was the case in any earlier or later generation— including Andrew Carnegie, John D. Rockefeller, Jay Gould, James J. Hill, Leland Stanford, and Charles Crocker.

- With traditional apprenticeships dwindling in an era of rapid industrialization and cheap immigrant labor, many Gilded youth took to the streets and became the first generation of urban criminal gangs. By the 1840s, their violence prompted elders to organize the first big-city police forces and establish the first "reform" schools. "If the reform school differed at all from adult prisons," observes historian Joseph Kett, "it was because children could be shipped off to the former not just for crimes but for general vagrancy and stubbornness."

- The Gilded include a larger share of immigrants (28 percent) than any other American generation since colonial times. To the East Coast came the first large influx of Irish Catholics, triggered by the Irish potato famine of the late 1840s; to the West Coast came the Chinese, hired on as laborers for the Union Pacific Railroad.

- Suffering worsening nutrition as children, the adult height of the Gilded declined from first cohort to last. Later in life, the quest for protein became a generational obsession. The Gilded include America's best-known cannibals (Al Packer and the Donner Party survivors); the founder of the King Ranch; the first Texas-to-Abilene cattle drivers; the first large-scale meat-packers (Gustavus Swift and Philip Armour); and, by the 1880s, the midlife beneficiaries of plunging beef prices. Shunning the lithe (Transcendental) physique, the aging Gilded celebrated the rotund body and the Delmonico steak dinner as a mark of success. In 1907, when the youngest Gilded had entered elderhood, U.S. life expectancy at age 65 declined to the shortest span ever measured (under 11.5 years).

- Throughout their lifecycle, the Gilded defined today's image of the western adventurer: from the youthful 49er and Pony Express rider before the Civil War, to the midlife rancher, cowboy, "bad man," and Indian fighter of 1870s, to the grizzled old mountaineer of 1900.

- Gilded blacks include the first large population of American mulattoes (many, presumably, the children of white Compromiser fathers); the slave generation that suffered most at the hands of white owners increasingly fearful of rebellion; the most celebrated 1850s-era slave fugitives; and, during the Civil War, the soldiers and officers of the first black regiments in North America. In the Reconstruction years, fifteen Gilded blacks were elected to Congress, a greater number than from any later generation until the Silent.

- War hit the Gilded harder than any other American generation. They were the first American youths to be subject to conscription—and led the bloodiest antidraft riots in American history. Of the seven million Gilded men who reached combat age, roughly 10 percent died in the Civil War; one in fifteen in the Union states, nearly one in four in the Confederate states. Another

5 percent ended the war in disease-ridden prisoner-of-war camps. Altogether, the number killed in more than six thousand Civil War battles exceeded the cumulative total for all other American wars—a per capita casualty rate equal to eight World War IIs combined. Nearly half the Gilded war dead were buried in unmarked graves.

• In the generational landslide election of 1868, the median age of governors in the nine core Confederate states fell from 62 to 37. The Gilded include most of the postwar carpetbaggers and scalawags.

• As "Victorian" stewards of the late-nineteenth-century American economy, the Gilded set an unmatched record for prudence and thrift. From the late 1850s to the late 1890s, gross capital formation more than doubled as a share of GNP and the wholesale price index declined by one-third. From 1866 to 1893, Gilded leaders and taxpayers sustained twenty-eight consecutive federal surpluses—reducing the national debt by one-third and making theirs the only generation in American history to leave behind a smaller federal debt than it inherited.

The Gilded Lifecycle

YOUTH: "Children are commercial before they get out of their petticoats," remarked visitor David MacRae of America's Jacksonian-era children. "You will see a little girl of six show a toy to her companion, and say, gravely, 'Will you trade?' " William Dean Howells later recalled how he and his friends grew up fast at a time when "the lowest-down boy in town could make himself master if he was bold and strong enough." The young Gilded had little choice. Some were the casual offspring of experimental communities; others were hungry arrivals by boat. Nearly all of them, looking up at uncertain midlifers and self-absorbed rising adults, understood at an early age that they had better take care of themselves—if necessary, by scavenging in the cities or moving away to the frontier. Parents complained of their toughness, lawmakers decried the new flood of "street orphans" who mixed huckstering with crime, and in 1849 the New York police chief condemned "the constantly increasing number of vagrants, idle and vicious children of both sexes, who infest our public thoroughfares." One writer described them as *The Dangerous Classes of New York,* "friendless and homeless. . . . No one cares for them, and they care for no one." Hearing elders moralize, Gilded youths steered clear of adults and practiced what many parents referred to (favorably) as "self-dependence." Louisa May Alcott, likening her impractical father (a utopian reformer in Emerson's circle) to "a man up on a balloon," secretly resolved as a girl "to take Fate by the throat and shake a living out of her." Gilded students showed little of their next-elders' interest in the cerebral. In the 1830s, farmers' sons were grabbing get-rich manuals and bolting from their homes and schools at ever-earlier ages. By the 1840s and 1850s, college attendance sank—and those who did arrive on campus made sure to keep fortyish reformers at bay. When Garrison and Longfellow came to speak, these collegians jeered and hissed. When teachers ordered them to pray, writes historian Frederick Rudolph, they responded with "deliberate absenteeism, indifference, disrespect, by ogling female visitors, the writing of obscene doggerel on the flyleaves of hymnals, by expectorating in the chapel aisle." Boasted one student at Brown: "We live in a perfectly independent way."

COMING OF AGE: "Of all the multitude of young men engaged in various employments of this city," reported a Cincinnati newspaper in 1860, "there is not one who does not desire, and even confidently expect to become rich." In the 1840s and 1850s, the Gilded came of age pursuing what the aging Compromiser Washington Irving sarcastically called "the almighty dollar, that great object of universal devotion throughout our land." These were frenetic years for 20-year-olds. Many stayed in the East, where they mingled with crowds of new immigrants, found jobs in new factories, and rode a roller-coaster economy. Others, alienated by rising land prices and intolerant next-elders, followed the "Go West, Young Man" maxim of Horace Greeley—perhaps the only Transcendental advice they considered sensible. During the Mexican War, they proved eager to fight for new territory (and to learn how to handle the new Colt "six-shooter"). While Emerson chastised "young men" who "think that the manly character requires that they should go to California, or to India, or into the army," twentyish Gilded adventurers were crying "Eureka!" and chasing the newfound mother lodes. The lucky got rich panning for metal, the cunning (like 21-year-old Levi Strauss) by feeding and outfitting their desperado peers. Back across the still empty Great Plains, the Gilded added leather lungs to the polarizing debate over union—first as the core of the nativist "Young America" movement, next as "Know-Nothings" shouting their defiantly anti-Transcendental slogan "Deeds Not Words," and finally as unpropertied "Lincoln shouters" and "hurrah boy" Republicans. In the North, they agreed with Lincoln's argument that slavery posed a threat to free men everywhere—and were coaxed by the new party's promises to enact a homestead law and build railroads. In the South, cries for battle rose from those whom Sherman darkly referred to as "young bloods" and "sons of planters"—"brave, fine riders, bold to rashness, and dangerous subjects in every sense" who "must be killed or employed by us before we can hope for peace." Ranging in age from 19 to 39 in 1861, the Gilded were ready, in Twain's words, "to make choice of a life-course & move with a rush." Many volunteered for war, like Oliver Wendell Holmes, Jr., "because we want to realize our spontaneity and prove our power for the joy of it."

RISING ADULTHOOD: For the young Gilded, the first years of the Civil War were more dashing than bloody. Thirtyish commanders George McClellan and Stonewall Jackson enjoyed great popularity with their "Billy Yank" and "Johnny Reb" troops. Following the deadly battles of 1862–1863 and the first draft calls, however, the Gilded began to think twice about their prophetic next-elders. Ultimately, a bulldog Gilded general (Ulysses Grant) toughed out a reputation for slow wits and hard liquor by throttling "Gentleman Lee"—who surrendered just days before a self-loathing Gilded assassin (John Wilkes Booth) put an end to "Father Abraham." Afterward, while 55-year-olds declaimed over principle, 35-year-olds saw mostly ruined farms, starving widows, diseased prisoners, dead bodies, and amputated limbs (carried away from Gettysburg by the wagonload). In the South, poet Henry Timrod described the postwar landscape as "beggary, starvation, death, bitter grief, utter want of hope." No southerner of Timrod's generation would later emerge to prominence in any sphere of national life—business, science, letters, or politics. In the North, the Gilded went to work disarming the Transcendental leadership. After a 42-year-old senator, Edmund Ross, blocked the Radicals' plot to impeach President Johnson, Gilded leaders dismantled Reconstruction and left their southern black peers to fend for themselves. The feisty women of this male-short generation focused their postwar energy on family solidarity and matured into the durable Scarlett O'Hara matrons of the Victorian era. The men found it harder to adjust. Some became rootless "bums" and "hobos," wandering along newly built railways and evading postwar "tramp laws." Others burst forth with bingelike rapacity—notorious "bad guys" (Wild Bill Hickok, William Quantrill), Indian fighters (Phil Sheridan, George Custer), and "robber barons" (Jim Fisk, Jay Gould). After the war, the Gilded purged their memory of elder zealots by turning their regional focus away from New England and by looking instead toward the busier, less talkative Midwest—especially Ohio, home to four of the six Gilded Presidents. Rutherford Hayes wrote from Cincinnati: "Push, labor, shove—these words are of great power in a city like this."

MIDLIFE: In 1876, the Gilded celebrated their midlife dominion with the Philadelphia Centennial Exposition. The Hall of Machines stood for bigness, strength, and worldliness—and not a hint of the Transcendental inner life that most Gilded still associated with meanness and tragedy. During the 1870s, Gilded survivalism turned conservative. Seeking an ethos suitable for a generation of scoundrels, they found it first in Charles Darwin's "law of natural selection," next in Herbert Spencer's "social statics," and most fully in the "pragmatism" of Charles Peirce and William James. Amid what was known as the "Victorian crisis of faith," the Gilded played the game of life according to worldly measures of success. The first Wall Street financiers like John Pierpont Morgan and Anthony Drexel counted dollars; the first trust-builders like John D. Rockefeller and Andrew Carnegie counted sales; the first rail tycoons like Leland Stanford and James J. Hill counted miles of steel and tons of freight. The new wealth fortified a fiftyish up-from-nowhere elite that came to dominate both culture and politics, to the despair of their "Mugwump" critics. These new philistines eclipsed a succession of weak Presidents and tilted political power toward state and local governments. They crushed most dissenters, from genteel cosmopolitans like Henry Adams to rural populists like "Sockless Socrates" Simpson. And by the 1880s, they reconciled themselves to a prudish morality promulgated by Frances Willard's "Temperance" and "Social Purity" movements. The new standard stressed modesty, self-control, and a shameless reputation—requiring many of these fiftyish parents to hide (or at least leave unmentioned) their checkered personal histories. The Gilded midlife era ended in 1893 as it began— with a world's fair, this time in Chicago. But a few months before it opened, the worst panic in living memory plunged the nation into sudden depression. When the fair's opulence drew angry fire from the young, Charles Eliot Norton found a "decline of manners" and Mark Twain a "soul full of meanness" in an America now gripped by the Missionary Awakening.

ELDERHOOD: "A new America," complained Norton on the eve of the Spanish-American War, "is entering on the false course which has so often led to calamity." In 1898, as young zealots pressed for an invasion of Cuba, virtually all of America's aging Gilded luminaries (Twain, Cleveland, Carnegie, Sumner, James, Howells) urged peace and caution. But by now a new crop of Progressive leaders were listening to the zeal of youth, not the exhaustion of old-timers— and chose to "Remember the *Maine*," not Gettysburg. As the century ticked to a close, Gilded conservatism gave way to the attacks of younger reformers. Old Sumner lamented that the bonds of close family loyalty, a source of strength and comfort to his peers after the Civil War, now attracted ridicule from fashionable social critics. College students romanticized a bucolic preindustrial past—a past the old Gilded knew had been wild and dangerous. Meanwhile, according to historian Andrew Achenbaum, the new century unleashed an "unprecedented devaluation" of the elderly: "Instead of extolling the aged's moral wisdom"—as they had in the twilight years of Emerson and Longfellow— "commentators increasingly concluded that old people had nothing to contribute to society." In a widely reprinted 1905 lecture, the Progressive William Osler wrote of "the uselessness of men above sixty years of age" and stressed "the incalculable benefits" of "a peaceful departure by chloroform." Old Henry Adams complained that "young men have a passion for regarding their elders as senile." Many Gilded elders heard themselves reviled as "old geezers" and "old fogies"—their elite as "old guard" senators, "standpatter" House members, and reform-blocking Supreme Court justices. Where prior generations of elders had typically worked until death (or were cared for by younger relatives on farms), many now faced an involuntary, pensionless "retirement" in a rapidly urbanizing economy that substantially favored young adults. As inept "soldiering" became a new insult in the workplace, inflation began eroding the real value of federal pensions to "Grand Army" veterans. "There is now no place in our working order for old men," observed Edward Everett Hale in his seventies. Never asking for special favors, the old Gilded kept to themselves and rarely complained about their treatment. "I am seventy," confessed the otherwise acid-penned Mark Twain in 1905, "seventy and would nestle in the chimney corner . . . wishing you well in all affection."

*   *   *

The enduring images of this generation conjure up rapacity, nihilism, and ugliness: Know-Nothings and Ku Klux Klanners; Union "bummers" and Quantrill's raiders; Crédit Mobilier and the Salary Grab Act; gold spittoons and penny novels; carpetbaggers and scalawags; Boss Tweed's machine and Morgan's trust; "Half-Breed" James Blaine and "His Fraudulency" President Hayes. But low expectations and a negative self-image were all part of the Gilded game plan: to live according to their own pragmatic rules—and if that meant making massive lifecycle sacrifices, so be it. After all, their merciless competition favored fast-paced innovation; their city machines fed poor children; their business trusts and government surpluses favored huge investment in infrastructure and long-lived capital goods; their elder industrialists became fabled philanthropists; and their chromo culture protected the family—all benefits that would accrue not to themselves (aside from a handful of flashy winners), but to their children. Neglected and brutalized early in life, this "bad" generation reached midlife power with every opportunity to indulge itself and let its children waste among the postwar ruins. Instead, the Gilded rebuilt America while mainly wasting each other. They became loud proponents of Social Darwinism just as they reached the threshold of elderhood—precisely the phase of life when "survival of the fittest" would plainly work to their own disadvantage.

Few ever sought credit for lofty motives. Late in life, Justice Holmes admitted that he was a "Philistine" and "egotist." Likewise, at age 64, even William James excoriated his peers for their "exclusive worship of the bitch-goddess SUCCESS." Rather than be judged for how they felt, the Gilded preferred to be judged for what they built. Arriving in New York City in 1907, the elder James looked around at the commercial bustle and marveled: "in the center of the cyclone, I caught the pulse of the machine, took up the rhythm, and . . . found it simply magnificent." By refusing to look beyond the material world, the Gilded sacrificed themselves bodily for their "machines"—mechanical, commercial, and political. This self-deprecation resulted in a very real kindness: to ensure that younger Progressives and Missionaries would enjoy far more affluence than the Gilded had themselves ever known. Their greatest failure late in life was not to realize that the high tide of laissez-faire growth would hurt all

of society's dependents, not only themselves as elders, but also a still younger
(Lost) generation of children. The tots of the 1890s were about to embark on a
lifecycle much like their own—a fact that would have pained the old Twains
and Carnegies had they known it. The Gilded lifecycle thus deserves the same
warning that Twain's "Notice to the Reader" offered for *Huckleberry Finn:*
"Persons attempting to find a moral in it will be banished."

PROGRESSIVE GENERATION

Born 1843–1859
Type: Adaptive

Age Location:
Civil War Crisis in youth
Missionary Awakening in midlife

In the late 1860s, while Gilded railroad barons were building powerful lo-
comotives and designing luxurious Pullman cars, 22-year-old George Westinghouse invented an air brake to make trains *safe*. A few years later, at the 1876
Philadelphia Centennial, the delicate inventions of 29-year-old Thomas Edison
and 27-year-old Alexander Graham Bell drew more international acclaim than
the huge Gilded steam turbines. Where the midlife Gilded liked to build things
that rewarded society's strongest and richest, these young tinkerers targeted their
efforts toward the disadvantaged. Edison designed his arc light to assist the
visually impaired, Bell his crude telephone to audibilize voices for the deaf.
Westinghouse, Edison, and Bell lay at the vanguard of the PROGRESSIVE
GENERATION, a cadre of fledgling experts and social meliorators as attuned
to the small as their next-elders were to the big. Their leading figures, the fortyish
Theodore Roosevelt and the sixtyish Woodrow Wilson, liked to describe themselves as "temperate," their designs as "moderate." In politics as in family
life, their inclination was to make life gentler and more manageable; their global
credo (in Wilson's memorable words) was to make the world "safe for democracy." Like their inventor peers, Progressives believed that calibration and communication would eventually make America a nicer country.

For a generation to assume such an other-directed mission required unusual
sensitivity—and a collective identity of unusual malleability. Progressives acquired both, thanks to a lifecycle that located them in an odd warp of history.
They were born at the wrong time for authentic catharsis—too late for free-
wheeling adventure, too soon for the youth-fired movements of the late nineteenth
century. First-wavers were the keep-your-head-down teenagers of the Civil War;
last-wavers came of age during the thickening social consensus of the 1870s.
Through the 1880s, they became rising-adult partners to the Gilded in a fast-
growing nation still gripped in a survivalist mentality. Their social role soon
became clear: to apply their credentialed expertise toward improving what their
next-elders had pioneered. They added "organization" to new corporations,
"efficiency" to new assembly lines, "method" to new public agencies. Such

PROGRESSIVE GENERATION (Born 1843 to 1859)

TYPE: Adaptive

Total number: 22,000,000
Percent immigrant: 27%
Percent slave: 9%

SAMPLE MEMBERS, birth (death)

1843 Henry James (1916)
1843 Montgomery Ward (1913)
1844 Henry Heinz (1919)
1845 Mary Cassatt (1926)
1846 George Westinghouse (1914)
1846 Carry Nation (1911)
1847 Thomas Edison (1931)
1847 "Pitchfork" Ben Tillman (1918)
1849 Alexander Graham Bell (1922)*
1849 Crazy Horse (1877)
1850 Samuel Gompers (1924)*
1854 John Philip Sousa (1932)
1855 Robert La Follette (1925)
1855 Andrew Mellon (1937)
1856 Booker T. Washington (1915)
1856 Louis Brandeis (1941)
1856 Frederick Winslow Taylor (1915)
1857 Ida Tarbell (1944)
1857 Clarence Darrow (1938)
1859 John Dewey (1952)
* = immigrant

FAMILY TREE

Typical grandparents: Compromise
Parents: Transcendental and Gilded
Children: Missionary and Lost
Typical grandchildren: G.I.

PERIOD OF POLITICAL LEADERSHIP

Plurality in House: 1893–1909
Plurality in Senate: 1903–1917
Majority of Supreme Court: 1911–1923

U.S. PRESIDENTS: 1897–1921

1843 William McKinley (1901)
1856 Woodrow Wilson (1924)
1857 William Howard Taft (1930)
1858 Theodore Roosevelt (1919)

PROMINENT FOREIGN PEERS

1853 Vincent van Gogh (1890)
1854 Oscar Wilde (1900)
1856 Sigmund Freud (1939)
1859 Kaiser Wilhelm II (1941)
1859 Henri Bergson (1941)

Age	Date	HISTORY AND LIFECYCLE
0– 6	1849:	Horace Mann completes "Massachusetts model" for public education
4–20	1863:	Battle of Gettysburg; slaves emancipated
17–33	1876:	Ph.D. program at Johns Hopkins, "case method" law at Harvard
20–36	1879:	"Big Business" economy surges; Edison invents light bulb
29–45	1888:	Granger populism spreads; Frank Sprague invents electric trolley
37–53	1896:	McKinley overwhelms Bryan on high-tariff, "sound-money" platform
39–55	1898:	Sinking of *Maine* triggers Spanish-American War
42–58	1901:	McKinley assassinated; Theodore Roosevelt becomes President
47–63	1906:	Pure Food and Drug Act; Congress tightens regulation of railroads
53–69	1912:	Roosevelt founds "Progressive" (Bull Moose) Party, loses to Wilson
60–76	1919:	Treaty of Versailles; Wilson advocates the League of Nations
66–82	1925:	Andrew Mellon proposes tax cuts; Darrow defends John Scopes

SAMPLE CULTURAL ENDOWMENTS: *The Portrait of a Lady* (Henry James); *Babes in Toyland* (Victor Herbert); "The Man with the Hoe" (Edwin Markham); *The Reign of Law* (James Lane Allen); "Wynken, Blynken, and Nod" (Eugene Field); *Uncle Remus* (Joel Chandler Harris); *Up from Slavery* (Booker T. Washington); *The School and Society* (John Dewey); *History of the Standard Oil Company* (Ida Tarbell); *The Theory of the Leisure Class* (Thorstein Veblen); *The Rough Riders* (Theodore Roosevelt) value-free ideations would always define their life mission. John Dewey never ceased to delight in the "educative process," William Howard Taft in "interpreting" the law, Woodrow Wilson in "consulting the experts," and Booker T. Washington in "constructive compromise." Starting families at the height of the social and sexual conformism of the mid-Victorian era, they tried hard to take part in what they called "the progress of civilization"—progress that now required method over personality. "In the past the man has been first," declared Frederick Winslow Taylor in his world-famous *Principles of Scientific Management;* "in the future the system must be first."

Their lifecycle had a decisive turning point: the turbulent 1890s and 1900s, when they embarked on anxious midlife passages and shifted their attention from age to youth. Stifled by the narrowed purpose of their younger years, they envied the passion of younger Missionaries while expressing relief in a newfound "liberty" that Wilson defined as "a process of release, emancipation, and inspiration, full of a breath of life . . . sweet and wholesome." Past age 40, many Progressives embraced new causes with joyful vigor, from political reform (Robert La Follette) and organized feminism (Harriot Blatch) to world peace (David Starr Jordan), temperance (the WCTU), and health foods (John Harvey Kellogg). Thanks to their efforts, lonely dissenters found genteel protectors like Clarence Darrow and Governor John Altgeld; "The Social Question" (even socialism itself) became a subject of polite dinner conversation; anticorporate populism gave birth to officious "regulations" and "commissions"; and anti-Gilded students discovered charismatic leaders willing to join their attack on Rockefeller ("the greatest criminal of the age," cried La Follette) and Standard Oil ("bad capitalism," agreed Teddy Roosevelt). Reaching the age of leadership, Progressives often fretted over their next-juniors' passion for reforms at home and crusades abroad. Overwhelmed by events and pushed out of power during World War I, Progressives entered elderhood trying to stay involved while nudging America back toward tolerance and conciliation.

By the standards of their next-elders, the Progressives lived a lifecycle in reverse. They set out as sober young parents in the shadow of Reconstruction—attired in handlebar mustaches and tight corsets—and ended up as juvenating midlifers in an era of Rough Riders and gunboats, evangelism and trust-busting, Model Ts and hootchie-kootchie girls, Freud's "talking cure" and Bergson's *élan vital.* Taught young the importance of emotional self-control, they reached the new century probing desperately for ways to defy taboos, tell secrets, and take chances. In social life, the peers of Woodrow Wilson sought to expose scandal and "open up" the system by insisting that "there ought to be no place where anything can be done that everybody does not know about." In economic life, the peers of Thorstein Veblen satirized the Gilded obsession with self-denial and savings, turning their attention toward leisure and consumption instead. In personal life, most of all, these uneasy midlifers spawned what historian Jackson Lears calls the "therapeutic world view"—a fear of "overcivilization," a longing for the primitive, an obsession with releasing inner energies. While "TR" hunted elephants, Brooks Adams praised "barbarian blood," and Populist leaders like Tom Watson goaded younger mobs to racial violence, psychologist G. Stanley Hall spoke of his peers' "universal hunger for more life." It was, admittedly, awkward to discover life at 50. "Faculties and impulses which are denied legitimate expression during their nascent period," Hall explained, "break out well into adult life—falsetto notes mingling with manly bass as strange puerilities."

Mediators between two pushy generations, Progressives won respect for their intelligence and refinement. Yet so too did they make easy targets for their prissiness and indecision. Their academics were teased as "Professor Tweetzers" and "Doctors of Dullness," their frontier settlers as "tenderfeet" and "greenhorns," their good-government types as "goo-goos" and "Miss Nancys," and their guilty liberals (like Joseph Fels, who promised to spend his "damnable money to wipe out the system by which I made it") as "millionaire reformers" and "the mink brigade." Younger Missionaries scorned their caution, William Randolph Hearst belittling President Wilson as "a perfect jackrabbit of politics, perched upon his little hillock of expedience . . . ready to run and double in any direction." The older Gilded chided their midlife anxiety. During the 1880s, the Gilded Howells tweaked people who "now call a spade an agricultural implement" and wondered why "everyone is afraid to let himself go, to offend conventions, or to raise a sneer." Watching 40-year-olds take up youthful sports during the next decade, the sixtyish Henry Adams likened the Progressive to "the bicycle-rider, mechanically balancing himself by inhibiting all his inferior personalities, and sure to fall into the subconscious chaos below, if one of his inferior personalities got on top."

Progressives spent midlife seeking such a "mechanical balance"—patching together Gilded realism with Missionary principle, blending the rugged West with the effete East. While Theodore Roosevelt demanded (in his late forties) an overcompensating manliness he labeled the "strenuous life," his soft-life peers defined what came to be known as "genteel" *fin de siècle* American culture. The result was a self-conscious mixture of primness and toughness. At the close of the century, Charles Sheldon warned his peers to "be free from fanaticism on the one hand and from too much caution on the other."

"Neutral in fact as well as in name . . . impartial in thought as well as action." Spoken before the country was prodded into World War I by a younger Congress, Wilson's famous remark could be deemed the motto of this generation in public life. Exclude the young Missionary zealots, and circa-1900 "Progressivism" stood for what historian Samuel Eliot Morison describes as an "adaptation . . . to the changes already wrought and being wrought in American society," or what Robert Wiebe calls "the ambition of the new middle class to fulfill its destiny through bureaucratic means." Most Progressive leaders liked calling themselves "middle-class," just as they dreaded extremism and violence from either unions or corporations, Wobblies or Pinkertons. Far better, they thought, to push society forward through incremental consensus. "I do not believe you can do any good on an issue of this kind by getting too far in advance," Roosevelt said of Prohibition, explaining how the public "will ultimately come to the national suppression of the liquor traffic and I am heartily with them when they do." Even Wilson's "high ideals" had less to do with moral outcomes than with the fair process by which competing ideals are reconciled. "If my convictions have any validity," he declared, "opinion ultimately governs the world." So the Progressives behaved, spending a lifetime listening to—and adjusting to—others. "Tell me what's right," Wilson told his younger aides en route to Versailles, "and I'll fight for it."

Progressive Facts

- Emulating the new vogue of Gilded rotundity in the early 1880s, young Progressives read best-sellers like *How to Be Plump* and worshiped the chubby "Lillian Russell" female. Entering midlife, many slimmed down to look more youthful; others tried dieting but failed—including the 300-pound William Howard Taft, the fattest President in U.S. history.

- The Progressives include the first sizable number of Americans to attend black colleges, women's colleges, and land-grant colleges. They were also the first to earn graduate degrees in America and provided the Ph.D.-credentialed faculties that elevated American universities to their circa-1900 era of maximum prestige—culminating in the election of America's only Ph.D. President, Woodrow Wilson.

- Between 1883 and 1893, four 34-to-37-year-olds produced several of America's most stirring paeans to patriotism: the Pledge of Allegiance (Francis Bellamy); *America the Beautiful* (Katherine Lee Bates); *Semper Fidelis* (John Philip Sousa), and the inscription on the Statue of Liberty (Emma Lazarus). As Bates wrote "confirm thy soul in self-control" and Lazarus about "huddled masses yearning to breathe free," their rising peers cautiously steered clear of electoral politics. In 1893, fifty years after their first birthyear, Progressives held only 39 percent of all national leadership posts (versus, at like age, 64 percent for Transcendentals, 60 percent for Gilded, and 48 percent for Missionaries).

- What historian Joseph Kett calls "the burgeoning of certification requirements after 1880" made this the first generation of industrial leaders who rose "not from the workbench but through successive layers of management." The Progressives also accounted for the largest nineteenth-century expansion in lawyers, notably corporate legal experts who could advise Gilded tycoons. In 1860, America contained only nine law schools requiring more than one year of training; by 1880, fifty-six required three years of training.

• Progressives provided the initial memberships for an extraordinary number of enduring fraternal, labor, academic, and (to use a word they popularized) "professional" associations, including the Elks Club, Knights of Columbus, Daughters of the American Revolution, Modern Language Association, American Historical Association, American Economics Association, American Federation of Labor—and the first "professional" sports league, the National League of Professional Baseball Clubs.

• Obsessive organizers, the Progressives invented the cash register, adding machine, carbon paper, mimeograph, and first workable typewriter. They were the first generation to use time clocks at work and to carry timepieces on their person ("pocket" watches after 1870; "band" or "wrist" watches after 1900). In 1883, their young civil servants designed the federal system of four U.S. time zones. Later in life, Progressive Presidents founded the Bureau of Standards, the Bureau of Labor Statistics, and the first permanent Census office—and led the "Crusade for Standardization" during World War I. In 1928, an elderly Progressive founded the (Robert) Brookings Institute. Its purpose was "to collect, interpret, and lay before the country in clear and intelligent form the fundamental economic facts concerning which opinions need to be formed."

• Progressives included the large influx of Nordic immigrants who settled the upper Midwest and Great Plains late in the century. These states witnessed many of the Progressives' midlife experiments in "populist" government and "liberal" Republicanism.

• A Progressive (John Gates) invented barbed wire in the 1880s. The subsequent "battle of the barbed wire" between cattle ranchers and wheat farmers was typically a dispute between tough-as-nails midlife Gilded and law-abiding ("Let's elect a sheriff") rising-adult Progressives.

• At the turn of the century, the term "middle age" began to indicate a phase of life (roughly, age 40 to 60) and soon appeared frequently in popular periodicals. Much of the interest focused on feelings of disorientation, in such articles as "On Some Difficulties Incidental to Middle Age" (1900), "On Being Middle-Aged" (1908), and "The Real Awkward Age" (1911). In their forties and fifties, many of the best-known Progressives experienced what would now be described as "midlife crises" or "nervous depressions"—including Woodrow Wilson, Theodore Roosevelt, Josiah Royce, G. Stanley Hall, Brooks Adams, and Frederick Winslow Taylor.

• According to historian Nathan Hale, Jr., the Victorian ethos of continence and sexual purity weighed most heavily on Americans "born from the 1840s to the early 1860s"—making this a generation for whom the prim Anthony Comstocks set the early tone. The psychic cost of this smothering childhood first appeared in the late 1880s and 1890s—which, for fortyish Progressives, was an era of sharply rising divorce rates, and an epidemic of "neurasthenia" and female "hysteria" (often "treated" by uterectomies and hysterectomies). After the Spanish-American War, concern over "overstress" and "mental cancer" (what the *Atlantic Monthly* described as "our now universal disorder, nervous prostration") sparked a growing interest in mind-cure fads, from hypnotism and psychotherapy to dream analysis and rest cures. In 1909, the sixtyish psychologist G. Stanley Hall invited an eminent European peer to lecture in America. Sigmund Freud's tour was a media sensation.

The Progressive Lifecycle

YOUTH: "A hundred wills move at once simultaneously" with "an accuracy that was really amazing," observed one visitor to Civil War–era American schools. As the national mood veered toward war, youths understood that risky behavior could trigger adult rebuke—which, in turn, could bring lifelong penalties. Instead of describing American children as precocious or ill-mannered, as they had two decades before, foreigners began remarking how "the most absolute obedience and the most rigid discipline prevail in all American schools." Midlife Transcendentals demanded compulsory attendance laws (first enacted by Massachusetts in 1853 for all children under age 10), led the "high school movement" in the late 1850s, and generally insisted on more orderly child behavior than earlier teachers had demanded of the Gilded. They also popularized the custom of issuing report cards in order to bring parental authority to bear on child discipline. The leading parenting guide, written by Transcendental Horace Bushnell, described children as "formless lumps" equally capable of good and evil, requiring careful guidance within the "organic unity of the family." The child environment—already becoming more planned and protected—was abruptly pushed to suffocation by the Civil War. This implosion in family life reflected what historian Joseph Kett calls the midcentury "desire of middle-class Americans to seal their lives off from the howling storm outside." The storm raged worst for Confederate children, many of whom lived with the fear of marauding armies—or who, as teenagers, became the homesick and traumatized kid soldiers of bloody campaigns late in the war. The extended wartime absence (or death) of fathers gave mothers a stronger role in the child's world. As the Transcendental Catharine Beecher warned against turning over children to "coarse, hard, unfeeling men," many a war-era ballad idealized "Mother" as the embodiment of social order.

COMING OF AGE: The shell-shocked children of the Civil War reached their twenties eager to please adults, who advised them (in the words of one Sunday-school spokesman) to show "neither excesses nor defects in your character, but a harmonious blending, a delightful symmetry, formed of fitting proportions of every high quality." Progressives passed from youth to adulthood between the late 1860s and the early 1880s, a time of mounting social consensus in favor of Victorian rectitude in personal (and sexual) behavior. "Within my own remembrance," recalled an older YMCA official, boys had to "go through fermentation before they could afford to be good." But now, he observed, "they are to carry from the cradle to the grave an unblemished name, with unblemished morals." Kett notes how "the old idea that youth was a time for sowing wild oats, that an excess of prohibitions in youth merely produced an erratic adult, had no place in the thought of midcentury moralists." As colleges regained the popularity and discipline they had lost during the antebellum decades, Progressives became the nineteenth century's most docile students—preoccupied with grades, prizes, school spirit, and newly practical coursework. Arming themselves with impressive credentials, they hoped to make up in expertise what they obviously lacked in ruggedness. Whether as clerks in growing corporations or as dry-land farmers along a disappearing frontier, young Progressives generally failed to find authentic adventure—like Theodore Roosevelt, who arrived in the Dakota Territory "but little over half a dozen years since these lands were won from the Indians." Even the best-known Progressive outlaws, from Jesse James to Billy the Kid, were less loathed (and certainly less feared) than the original Gilded marauders. After the late 1860s, most indices of crime and disorder began falling well below their prewar levels. Few young Progressive men could bear a sullied conscience. After marrying at age 22, Theodore Roosevelt thanked heaven he was "absolutely pure. I can tell Alice everything I have ever done."

RISING ADULTHOOD: Through the 1870s and 1880s, the growing size and complexity of the industrial economy sparked a rising demand for the technical skills in which Progressives had been trained to excel. America was overrun with young lawyers, academics, teacher trainers, agronomists, and the first-ever cadre of "career" civil servants and Congressional staffers. Where the Gilded had gambled fortunes as rowdy miners, financiers, and self-made industrialists, the Progressives arrived as metallurgists, accountants, and "time and motion men" in the manner of Frederick Winslow Taylor. What Gilded young adults had achieved two decades earlier in capital goods, thirtyish Progressives achieved in retailing: H. J. Heinz' "57 varieties" of food, F. W. Woolworth's five-and-ten-cent stores, James Duke's dainty machine-rolled cigarettes, and Montgomery

Ward's 240-page catalogue for farmers (plus his new "money-back guarantee"). More alert to the risk of failure than the like-aged Gilded had been, Progressives became America's late-nineteenth-century bet-hedgers, definers of social conscience, and organizers of risk-spreading associations. "Grangers" founded the first rural co-ops. Samuel Gompers, after taking part in a failed strike, "began to realize the futility of opposing progress" and founded the modern trade union movement. Writers like Henry Demarest Lloyd (*Wealth Against Commonwealth*), Jacob Riis (*How the Other Half Lives*), and George Cable (*The Silent South*) exposed the costs of untamed economic growth and urged a weepy ethos of social cooperation—"a humane movement," wrote Edward Bellamy in *Looking Backward,* "a melting and flowing forth of men's hearts toward one another." In return, while proper young ladies suffered under stultifying sex-role definitions, dandified young men were accused of being what historian Geoffrey Blodgett calls the "Gelded Men" of the Gilded Age. Only when economic depression struck did the core of this fortyish and fiftyish generation directly challenge their war-veteran elders. They staged the realigning elections of 1894 and 1896, sweeping the McKinley Republicans—and his Progressive peers—into power.

MIDLIFE: Having spent half their lifecycle adapting to a Gilded-built world, Progressives entered midlife taking their cues from the young. In the mid-1890s, McKinley resolved to follow "the best aspirations of the people" by siding with young "jingoes" in a war against Spain. He and his three White House successors entangled themselves in position shifts by alternately urging and then hedging on subsequent Missionary causes, from child labor and woman's suffrage to Prohibition and immigration. Preoccupied with public opinion, they backed the genial procedural reforms of the "Progressive Era": initiatives and referenda, direct election of senators, the "open playing field" of antitrust, and expert-run regulatory commissions. Many Progressives, emerging as effete caricatures of late-Victorian manhood, continued to pursue what scientist Albert Michelson termed "the sixth place of the decimal"—or, like Melvil Dewey, precise systems for cataloguing knowledge. Others veered toward the other extreme. After leading younger "rough riders" up San Juan Hill, Theodore Roosevelt attacked the "men of soft life." Just after the turn of the century, he appointed a Commission on Country Life, led a youth-envying "cult of strenuosity," and encouraged Missionary zealots he labeled "muckrakers." Meanwhile, many midlife women broke free from convention and threw their support behind a budding feminist movement. Kate Chopin, widow and mother of six, wrote *The Awakening,* whose heroine protests the duality of the "outward existence which conforms, the inward life which questions." The last Progressive President, Woodrow Wilson, managed World War I in the complex manner of his generation—surrounded by diplomats, lawyers, journalists, statisticians, and public-private associations.

Afterward, Wilson tried to secure a "peace without victory" in which multilateral process would forever replace violent conflicts of principle. Younger voters showed little interest in his League of Nations proposal, and a 79 percent Missionary Congress buried it for good.

ELDERHOOD: The 1920s did little roaring for those who, like writer Sarah Orne Jewett, were "wracked on the lee shore of age." Poverty remained high among the elderly, but their overall income distribution was more even than among the Gilded, and the younger public grew more willing to discuss their hardships sympathetically, especially the question of what to do with elderly "in-laws." As always, Progressives approached their economic status with foresight and planning (in lieu of the Gilded winner-take-all ethos). Around 1910 they began a vast expansion in private pension plans, and by the time they retired they became the first nonveteran generation to receive significant pension income. Many elder Progressives—like Hall, who admired the young flappers and cultivated "zests" like walking barefoot—continued to watch and emulate the young. "Reversing age-old custom," notes Mark Sullivan, the chronicler of Wilson-era America, "elders strove earnestly to act like their children, in many cases their grandchildren." Their main message to juniors was to stay calm, keep faith in the democratic process, and listen to expertise. The eightyish Elihu Root kept lecturing the young on the importance of a "World Court," while Frank Kellogg promoted an arcane disarmament process (what one senator called "an international kiss") that would later impair America's ability to respond to Hitler. Their senior statesmen issued calls to humanity and fairness that were not always observed—for example, Franz Boas' defense of cultural pluralism against eugenics-minded Missionaries. "The greatest dangers to liberty lurk in insidious encroachment by men of zeal," warned Louis Brandeis, defending "the process of trial and error." Meanwhile, old Florence Kelley called herself "the most unwearied hoper," and old John Dewey unflaggingly pursued "liberalism" as "committed to an end that is at once enduring and flexible." In their final years, the greatest Progressive thinkers lacked final answers about life—and had the humility to admit it.

* * *

"The muddled state is one of the very sharpest of the realities," Henry James once observed. Indeed, his own generation remains saddled with a "muddled" image, often blurred together with the burly Gilded or zealous Missionaries. Combining a belief in fairness, openness, and what Ella Wheeler Wilcox called "just the art of being kind," Progressives gave the Gilded Age its human face and helped make the Missionary Awakening an age of reform and not revolution. Their fascination with process and detail provided a mediating link between their "build big" next-elders and their "think big" next-juniors. Much of their contribution hinged on their ability to see "out of the confusion of life" what James described as "the close connection of bliss and bale, of the things that help with the things that hurt." Yet they also waffled in the face of rapid social change. Vacillating on foreign policy and unwilling to forgo "cheap labor" immigrants, they invited the floodtide of jingoism and racism that swept over America at the turn of the century. Their accommodation of "separate but equal" Jim Crow laws sealed the fate of southern blacks. And their uncertain parental hand left Lost children vulnerable to cruel economic abuse. But their irrepressible belief in human perfectibility gave a powerful boost to the liberal side of the modern American character. Collectively, Progressives shared a quality once affixed to *Uncle Remus* author Joel Chandler Harris: "the seal of good humor . . . and a pleasant outlook on the world."

The Progressives never saw themselves as heroes or prophets. Rather, they saw themselves as a modern cadre of value-free meliorators who could link progress to expertise, improvement to precision. "The science of statistics is the chief instrumentality through which the progress of civilization is now measured," declared Census chief Simon Newton Dexter North in 1902, "and by which its development hereafter will be largely controlled." Late in life, as the world lurched toward chaos, old Progressives sometimes questioned such certainty. In 1914, the 71-year-old Henry James wrote to a friend, "You and I, the ornaments of our generation, should have been spared the wreck of our belief that through the long years we had seen civilization grow and the worst become impossible. The tide that bore us along was then all the while moving to this as its grand Niagara." Yet what few Progressives ever lost—no matter how old— was their urge to stay involved and thereby overcome a feeling that they had missed something early in life. "I don't regret a single 'excess' of my responsive youth," added James. "I only regret, in my chilled age, certain occasions and possibilities I didn't embrace."

Chapter 10

THE GREAT
POWER CYCLE

"The Atomic Age began at exactly 5:30 A.M. Mountain War Time on the morning of July 15th, 1945, on a stretch of semidesert land about 50 airline miles from Alamogordo, New Mexico," wrote *New York Times* reporter William Laurence (age 57) of the first moment "the earth had opened and the skies had split." Another man of blunt and staccato expression, President Harry Truman (age 61), took the news impassively and prepared to order the two remaining bombs dropped on Japan. When 77-year-old Secretary of War Henry Stimson was informed, he dispatched a coded message to Winston Churchill at Potsdam: "Babies satisfactorily born"—to which the like-aged British Prime Minister replied: "This is the Second Coming, in wrath." Standing nearby at the New Mexico test site, meanwhile, was the scientist whose organized mind had orchestrated the first atomic fireball, 41-year-old J. Robert Oppenheimer. Asked for his thoughts, Oppenheimer recalled a Hindu description of deity: "If the radiance of a thousand suns were to burst into the sky, that would be the splendor of the Mighty One." Added another young physicist, "The sun doesn't hold a candle to it!" Several weeks later, 19-year-old Russell Baker was training for a massive and bloody invasion of Japan when he heard of the Nagasaki blast and Japan's sudden capitulation. He wrote to his mother in a mixture of open relief and secret vexation: "It seems like I'm pulling some monstrous joke on myself when I say the war is over, because I really can't believe it." These whirlwind weeks marked the dawn of "Superpower America," the climactic moment of the GREAT POWER CYCLE:

- Henry Stimson's visionary MISSIONARY GENERATION (Idealist, then age 63 to 85) had originally ordered the A-bomb's development. These were the patriarchs of the national struggle, the dark figures in newsreel footages, the stern elder leaders who provided guidance for what seemed to be the very defense of Christian civilization. If the use of atomic weapons raised any moral questions, Americans of all ages trusted this generation to answer them. A couple of years earlier, President Franklin Roosevelt had asked several grayheads—most notably, James Byrnes, George Marshall, and Stimson himself (average age, 70)—to examine the A-bomb "in terms of a new relationship with the universe." While the bombs were being built, only Albert Einstein (age 66) could worry out loud about what the atom might unleash; anyone younger would have been instantly suspected of disloyalty. Afterward, the craggy Douglas MacArthur saw redemptive power in this new and terrible "crucible of war," capable of forcing mankind to face a dilemma that "is theological and involves a spiritual recrudescence." Weeks later, in Tokyo, he administered what he termed history's "first Christian occupation" of an Asian land, bringing to "our vanquished foe the solace and hope and faith of Christian morals."

- Harry Truman's get-it-done LOST GENERATION (Reactive, age 45 to 62) provided the war effort's pragmatic midlife generals, including the gruff careerist Leslie Groves, who managed the Manhattan Project. "The war's over," said Groves after a glance at the test blast. "One or two of those things and Japan will be finished." Truman delighted that America had "spent two billion dollars on the biggest scientific gamble in history—and won." Groves, Truman, and their midlife peers understood that America looked to them less for Roosevelt-like vision than for Patton-like action. "To err is Truman," chided many editorials two months earlier after this relative unknown had become Commander in Chief and had first learned of the A-bomb project (a secret none of FDR's seventyish cabinet had bothered to share with him). Yet unlike his elders, President Truman knew from personal experience what human slaughter might accompany a yard-by-yard conquest of the Japanese mainland. So he "let the buck stop" with him—and ordered Hiroshima bombed. Soon enough, Truman and his peers would cope with further thankless tasks: cleaning up after the debris left by FDR's visionary Yalta plan, eyeballing the Soviets with a gaming "brinksmanship" that younger leaders would deride as irrational, and keeping America on a steady, cautious course while hearing the expressions "old," "tired," and "reactionary" hurled at them. No big deal: The Lost had grown used to such negative judgments.

- Robert Oppenheimer's smart and dutiful G.I. GENERATION (Civic, age 21 to 44) provided the team of scientists responsible for this "Mighty One." Here stood the greatest power man had ever possessed—and they had created it. Without their heroism, the use of the bomb and the subsequent elevation of America to superpower status would not have been possible. Over the past three years, swarms of uniformed young men (average age, 26) had conquered the entire Pacific. Rosie the Riveter women had assembled bombers and battleships to arm them. Seabees had built bases out of jungles and barren reefs, including Tinian, where the *Enola Gay* took off for Hiroshima. The pilot of the first A-bomb-laden bomber, Paul Tibbets, was himself a ribbon-laced 30-year-old. Several years after their "gadget" had humiliated the Tokyo warlords, G.I.s would take it a step further by designing the H-bomb. They would call it "the Super" and the G.I. trio who designed it (Edward Teller, Luis Alvarez, and Oppenheimer) "Supermen"—a fitting image for a generation whose reason and teamwork had unleashed the ultimate energy of pure matter. Later in life, the G.I.s would harness their collective might and labor to fulfill their elders' vision by building a gleaming "Great Society" of peace, prosperity, and friendliness—only to hear their own children attack its spiritual emptiness.

- The eldest among Russell Baker's aspiring SILENT GENERATION (Adaptive, age 3 to 20) knew the A-bomb blasts had spared them from harm—and equally from any chance to match their next-elders in glory and heroism. Although they hadn't invented this monster, henceforth what William Styron called "the almost unimaginable presence of the bomb" would symbolize their coming-of-age sense of powerlessness, irony, and nonjudgmental relativism. Two decades later, while thirtyish Pentagon technicians designed "fail-safe delivery systems" to prevent nuclear weapons from atomizing the very people they were supposed to protect, thirtyish artists would try to release their collective tension in sentimental lyrics and ironic humor. Peter, Paul, and Mary would wistfully sing *Where Have All the Flowers Gone?;* Barry McGuire *Eve of Destruction;* and Tom Lehrer *So Long Mom* ("I'm off to drop the bomb"). In another song, Lehrer quipped of an eminent G.I. scientist: " 'Once the rockets are up, who cares where they come down? / That's not my department,' says Wernher von Braun." It would become the Silent's own "department" to worry about what happens when powerful things "come down" on people—from Carl Sagan warning against "nuclear winter" to Michael Harrington and Martin Luther King, Jr., arguing that money spent on bombs should be spent instead on the poor.

The start of the nuclear age marked the culmination of a generational drama that was by then nearly six decades old. It opened in the late 1880s, when a generation of indulgently raised post–Civil War youths triggered revivalism,

FIGURE 10–1

Great Power Cycle: Age Location in History

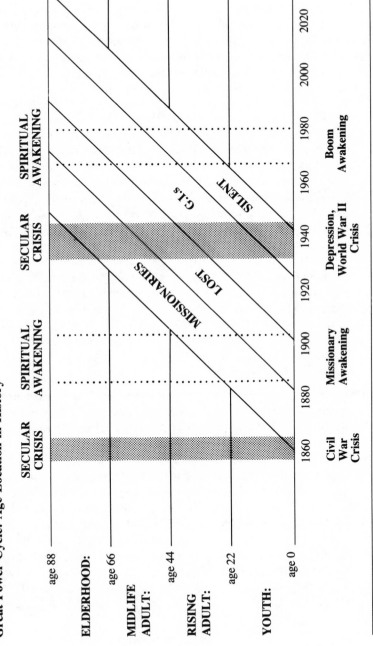

labor unrest, and the "Cross of Gold" paroxysm of William Jennings Bryan. What Roosevelt described as "a mysterious cycle" of generational "destiny" extended into the unrivaled "Pax Americana" of the mid-1960s, right up to LBJ's escalation of the Vietnam War. At the beginning of this ninety-year epoch, the Old World still regarded the United States as a frontier society, at best a minor player in world affairs. By its end, the United States had emerged as a great global power, fueled by the world's most productive economy and armed with the world's most formidable defense establishment.

The Great Power Cycle contained two social moments:

- *The Missionary Awakening* (1886–1903) or "Third Great Awakening" began in 1886 with the Haymarket Riot and the launching of the global student missionary movement. By 1893, a combination of agrarian protests and urban labor violence sparked the tumultuous 1890s, a decade historian Henry Steele Commager considers a "cultural watershed" in American history and historian Richard Hofstadter calls a "searing experience" to those who lived through it. Following Bryan's revivalist run for President in 1896, the awakening pushed a young, excited cadre of "muckraking" writers and reformers into the public eye just after the turn of the century. During Theodore Roosevelt's first term, these youth movements crested, and the awakening ended. As the rising generation lost interest in "progressive" reforms, and especially after the financial panic of 1907, the national mood sobered. Meanwhile, the awakening had given birth to the Bible Belt, to Christian socialism, to Greenwich Village, to Wobblies, and to renascent labor, temperance, and women's suffrage movements. *LOCATION IN HISTORY; Gilded in elderhood; Progressives in midlife; Missionaries in rising adulthood; Lost in youth.*

- *The Great Depression–World War II Crisis* (1932–1945) reached from the economic trough of 1932 through the triumph of VJ-Day in 1945, roughly spanning the thirteen-year Presidential reign of Franklin Roosevelt. It began in a mood of despair and pessimism about the future, stretched through the New Deal ("the Third American Revolution," according to historian Carl Degler), climaxed in a total war against totalitarianism, and ended at the dawn of a new era of power, affluence, and global leadership. One of every eight Americans now alive came of age during this era. Most of them recall how the mid-1940s ushered in an exhilarating sense of collective triumph, feelings those younger than themselves have never known. From the moment the crisis peaked, the rising peer elite began assuming leadership positions, leading ultimately to a "new generation" taking the White House in 1961— a post they still hold three decades later. *LOCATION IN HISTORY: Missionaries in elderhood; Lost in midlife; G.I.s in rising adulthood; Silent in youth.*

MISSIONARY GENERATION

Born 1860–1882
Type: Idealist

Age Location:
Missionary Awakening in rising adulthood
Great Depression–World War II Crisis in elderhood

In 1896—as the aging Gilded elite reeled from labor violence, student evangelism, and agrarian revivals—36-year-old William Jennings Bryan swept to the Democratic Presidential nomination with an exhortation that was as generational as it was partisan: "You shall not press down upon the brow of labor this crown of thorns, you shall not crucify mankind upon a cross of gold." The "Boy Orator of the Platte" then added, in a slap at McKinley's Progressives, "We beg no longer; we entreat no more; we petition no more. We defy them." With these words, Bryan's coming-of-age MISSIONARY GENERATION pushed to a climax its passionate attack on the soulless Darwinism of Gilded elders. George Herron, the 27-year-old "Prophet of Iowa College," challenged "the wicked moral blindness of our industrialism." The thirtyish Jane Addams, "Our Mother Emancipator from Illinois," launched social reforms from Hull House. In *The Octopus, The Jungle,* and *Shame of the Cities,* Frank Norris, Upton Sinclair, and Lincoln Steffens lashed out with a literary venom not seen since the early writings of Whitman and Thoreau. Meanwhile, thousands of their young peers were forming what essayist John Jay Chapman termed a "galaxy and salvation army of militant benevolence" with "an inner life and social atmosphere peculiar to itself, its tone and mission." As some youths summoned forth a "Kingdom of God," others shouted anarchist slogans, threw bombs, lynched blacks, and called for the conquering of heathen lands. The aspiring youth elite simply absorbed the mood, enjoying "the bright college days" of a noisy decade they would afterward remember as the "Gay Nineties"—at Stanford (Herbert Hoover), West Point (Douglas MacArthur), and Harvard (Franklin Roosevelt).

Missionaries first appeared as the welcomed postwar youngsters of the late 1860s and 1870s. Indulgently raised and educated by the midlife Gilded in a world of orderly families and accelerating prosperity, they came of age horrified by what George Cabot Lodge called "a world of machine-guns and machine-everything-else" and what Stephen Crane, gazing at a coal mine, called "this huge and hideous monster . . . grinding its mammoth jaws with unearthly and

MISSIONARY GENERATION (Born 1860 to 1882)

TYPE: Idealist

Total number: 45,000,000
Now alive in U.S.: 1,000
Percent immigrant: 23%
Percent slave: 1%

SAMPLE MEMBERS, birth (death)

1860 William Jennings Bryan (1925)
1860 Jane Addams (1935)
1863 Billy Sunday (1935)
1863 William Randolph Hearst (1951)
1863 Henry Ford (1947)
1868 W.E.B. DuBois (1963)
1869 Frank Lloyd Wright (1959)
1869 Emma Goldman (1940)*
1871 Theodore Dreiser (1945)
1871 Orville Wright (1948)
1875 Mary McLeod Bethune (1955)
1878 Isadora Duncan (1927)
1878 Upton Sinclair (1968)
1879 Albert Einstein (1955)*
1879 Margaret Sanger (1966)
1880 Douglas MacArthur (1964)
1880 John Llewellyn Lewis (1969)
1880 H.L. Mencken (1956)
1880 Helen Keller (1968)
1880 George C. Marshall (1959)
* = immigrant

FAMILY TREE

Typical grandparents: Transcendental
Parents: Gilded and Progressive
Children: Lost and G.I.
Typical grandchildren: Silent

PERIOD OF POLITICAL LEADERSHIP

Plurality in House: 1909–1937
Plurality in Senate: 1917–1943
Majority of Supreme Court: 1925–1943

U.S. PRESIDENTS: 1921–1945

1865 Warren G. Harding (1923)
1872 Calvin Coolidge (1933)
1874 Herbert Hoover (1964)
1882 Franklin D. Roosevelt (1945)

PROMINENT FOREIGN PEERS

1869 Mahatma Gandhi (1948)
1870 V.I. Lenin (1924)
1874 Winston Churchill (1965)
1875 Albert Schweitzer (1965)
1881 Pablo Picasso (1973)

HISTORY AND LIFECYCLE

Age	Date	
0– 2	1862:	Battle of Antietam; Morrill Act grants land for state colleges
0–16	1876:	Hall of Machines featured at Philadelphia Exposition
4–26	1886:	Haymarket Riot; student missionaries organize; *Little Lord Fauntleroy*
10–32	1892:	Homestead Massacre; agrarian populism expands; 161 blacks lynched
14–36	1896:	Bryan wins Democratic nomination; revivalist campaign loses election
16–38	1898:	Spanish-American War; Hearst papers push "jingo" fever
23–45	1905:	Haywood founds IWW; DuBois founds Niagara Movement
38–60	1920:	Palmer raids; women's suffrage; Prohibition begins
51–73	1933:	Roosevelt launches New Deal, scraps antitrust; Prohibition ends
59–81	1941:	Lend-Lease Act; attack on Pearl Harbor; U.S. enters World War II
63–85	1945:	Roosevelt dies; Axis powers surrender; Baruch announces "Cold War"
69–91	1951:	Peak foreign aid under Marshall Plan; MacArthur fired by Truman

SAMPLE CULTURAL ENDOWMENTS: *Intolerance* (film, D. W. Griffith); "Into My Own" (Robert Frost); *Prejudices* (H. L. Mencken); *Sister Carrie* (Theodore Dreiser); syndicated column (Will Rogers); *The Shame of the Cities* (Lincoln Steffens); *Living My Life* (Emma Goldman); "What I Believe" (Albert Einstein); *Women and the New Race* (Margaret Sanger); *Beale Street Blues* (W. C. Handy); *The Souls of Black Folk* (W.E.B. DuBois); "I Am the People, the Mob" (Carl Sandburg); *The Last Puritan* (George Santayana) monotonous uproar.'' This inner rebellion of ''moral'' sons against ''laborious'' fathers, recalled best-selling American novelist Winston Churchill in 1908, triggered ''the springing of a generation of ideals from a generation of commerce.'' Missionary first-wavers, leavened by the first large influx of non–Anglo Saxon white immigrants, entered their twenties as preachy student leaders, rebellious career women, and Haymarket rioters. Last-wavers reached adulthood while the fires of Chautauqua revivalism, muckraking, and labor radicalism still raged. Their tumultuous awakening defined the Missionaries for life as a generation of moral pathfinders, men and women to whom any opinion was a religion once they decided it was right. William Allen White recalls that Bryan's campaign ''was a fanaticism like the Crusades. Indeed the delusion that was working on the people took the form of religious frenzy.'' Unlike their Progressive next-elders, Missionaries were attracted by the specter of purifying confrontation. ''People who love soft words and hate iniquity forget this,'' Chapman wrote in 1898, ''that reform consists in taking a bone away from a dog.'' A fellow student had earlier attributed Chapman's popularity to sheer zeal: ''He is glowing and beautiful like fire . . . destructive like fire, seeking heaven like fire.''

Missionary anger remitted into self-discovery during Theodore Roosevelt's second term. When the economy slumped after the Panic of 1907, they hardly noticed. Instead, reveling in the personal independence of their new automobile age, they shifted their attention from messianic upheaval to the serious task of reshaping self and community. Their lofty-worded movements spread the spectrum from the holy (Billy Sunday's fundamentalism, ''White Angel'' Booth's Salvation Army) to the domestic (Elmer McCollum's fruit faddism, Frank Lloyd Wright's ''Prairie Style'' architecture); from the utopian (Bill Haywood's Wobblies, Emma Goldman's anarchists) to the mean-spirited (William Simmons' reborn Ku Klux Klan, Henry Goddard's eugenics movement); from the uplifting (Jane Addams' settlement houses, Walter Rauschenbusch's ''Social Gospel'') to the sober (Andrew Volstead's crusade against liquor, Francis Harrison's against narcotics). Not least, for rising adults who loudly hailed ''the New Woman,'' was the unprecedented strength of their feminist cadre—including Isadora Duncan (celebrating sexual emancipation by dance), Charlotte Perkins Gilman (assailing *This Man-Made World*), Margaret Sanger (broadcasting birth-control advice in *Woman Rebel*), and countless others in what came to be annual suffrage marches up New York's Fifth Avenue. Whatever their causes, the Missionary mental approach remained a generational constant: a fierce desire to make the world perfect according to standards that welled up from within.

Entering midlife around World War I, this generation often found itself split into opposite camps, rural evangelicals versus urban Social Gospelers (or ''modernists''). Yet growing pessimism about America's future in the hands of their nihilistic Lost juniors brought them together behind a common generational mission: the vindication of social good over social evil. Thus did fiftyish Missionaries transform into enthusiastic circa-1917 ''Crusaders for Democracy,'' and later into the "Decency" enforcers of the 1920s. They pushed through Prohibition, women's suffrage, immigration restriction, Smoot-Hawley, Red deportation, "vice squads," and punitive criminal laws—all in an effort to rekindle higher principles of national community. With the Great Depression and global totalitarianism of the 1930s, this effort matured into a sense of historical imperative. And when the era of crisis culminated in war, a still younger generation (of G.I.s) looked to aging Missionaries for wise leadership, for a fresh definition of national purpose they could dutifully champion against all enemies. "That is the conflict that day and night now pervades our lives," President Franklin Roosevelt proclaimed after the attack on Pearl Harbor, "No compromise can end that conflict. There has never been—there never can be— successful compromise between good and evil. Only total victory can reward the champions of tolerance, and decency, and freedom, and faith." In old age, this generation of moralists—the likes of Roosevelt, MacArthur, Henry Kaiser, and George Marshall—established America as a global beacon of revitalized civilization.

Throughout their lives, Missionaries startled older and younger generations by their fixation on mind and spirit, by their odd detachment from the material realities of life. They championed the inner life, from Jane Addams' "higher conscience" in immigrant neighborhoods, to W.E.B. DuBois' "black consciousness" in race relations, to the "stream of consciousness" novels of Stephen Crane—even to the "primitive consciousness" of Jack London's *Call of the Wild* and Edgar Rice Burroughs' *Tarzan of the Apes.* By the time America was rallying behind this generation's leadership at a moment of national emergency, incoming President Franklin Roosevelt remarked of "our common difficulties" that "they concern, thank God, only material things." Several years later, Roosevelt repeated "the belief I have already affirmed many times that there is not a problem, social, political, or economic, that would not find full solution in the fire of a religious awakening. . . ." In *Confessions of a Reformer,* Frederic Howe explained that "early assumptions as to virtue and vice, goodness and evil remained in my mind long after I had tried to discard them. This is, I think, the most characteristic influence of my generation. It explains the nature of our reforms, . . . our belief in men rather than institutions and our messages to other people. Missionaries and battleships, anti-saloon leagues and Ku Klux Klan . . . are all a part of that evangelistic psychology . . . that seeks a moralistic explanation of social problems and a religious solution to most of them." George Santayana was surely thinking of his fiftyish peers when he observed in 1920: "Americans are eminently prophets. They apply morals to public affairs. . . . They are men of principles, and fond of stating them."

The word "missionary" symbolized this generation's lifelong quest for global reform. The effort began with what Ivy League students proclaimed to be the "missionary crusade" of the 1880s, sealed by an 1886 assembly at Mount Hermon, Massachusetts, at which students proclaimed "the kingdom of God on

earth'' and adopted the motto many would apply into old age: ''The Evangelization of the World in This Generation.'' In vast numbers, these young zealots
built Christian encampments all over Asia. They loved calling themselves ''missionaries,'' the Latin plural derivative of the Greek ''apostle,'' or ''one sent.''
When hundreds of them were massacred during the Chinese Boxer Rebellion of
1900 (some decapitated torsos found with their hands still locked in prayer),
thirtyish peers back home took to heart their role as global martyrs, ''ones sent''
to bring new values to the ''Brotherhood of Man'' by force of their example.
Thirty-three years later, Franklin Roosevelt became the leader whom ''young
men followed''—notes historian Arthur Schlesinger, Jr.—''as they had followed
no American since Lincoln.'' And forty-five years later, FDR became the only
President whose death was universally likened to the martyrdom of Lincoln.
''He was just like a daddy to me always,'' confessed the young G.I. Lyndon
Johnson. ''He was the one person I ever knew, anywhere, who was never afraid.
God, God—how he could take it for us all.'' What they achieved themselves
early in life hardly compared to what others saw in them late in life. Sherwood
Eddy recalled of Robert Speer, his crusading classmate of the 1880s and author
of *Missionary Principles and Practice:* ''What he was, was more important than
what he did.''

This is the first generation to which many living Americans feel a personal
connection. Today's elders recall Missionaries as history saw them last, as the
visionary leaders who guided America through the Great Depression and World
War II. Today's 50-year-old probably remembers at least one Missionary grandparent; today's 75-year-old, a Missionary parent or two. Chances are, those
memories are of stern old Victorian patriarchs and matriarchs, devoted to what
we would now describe as traditional religion. In one respect, Missionaries were
literally the last ''Victorians'': They were the last Americans to come of age
before the grand queen died in 1901. Yet the full story of their lifecycle cannot
possibly be told by invoking the Victorian stereotype, nor indeed by recalling
the steel-willed leaders of the mid-1940s—a cadre of elders now sometimes
remembered as ''the World War II Wise Men.'' Instead, the full story must
include very different images—of youthful indulgence, coming-of-age fury,
rising-adult introspection, and midlife pomposity and intolerance. What finally
emerged late in life, the austere and resolute persona, was largely self-created
by a generation determined (in Edith Wharton's words) ''to build up, little by
little, bit by bit, the precious thing we'd smashed to atoms without knowing it.''

Missionary Facts

- Today's idyllic image of the traditional American Yuletide—Christmas trees,
  jingle bells, sleighrides, chromo cards, and a jolly, present-toting Santa
  (first sketched by Thomas Nast in 1863)—was created mainly by the midlife
  Gilded for the benefit of Missionary children.

- The early Missionary childhood witnessed an unprecedented growth in American primary schooling. During the 1870s alone, the number of high schools more than doubled, and the year 1880 marks the nineteenth century's high-water mark for the share of all Americans under age 20 attending school. During the next couple of decades, secondary education expanded rapidly. From 1884 to 1901, the number of women attending coed colleges rose sevenfold. From 1884 to 1907, the number of college and postgraduate degrees tripled.

- Attending college, Missionaries sparked the greatest wave of campus rebellions since the 1830s. The "settlement movement" (also known as the "New Franciscanism") belongs almost entirely to this generation. Between 1886 and 1911, 17,500 students and recent graduates, mostly from affluent families, joined Jane Addams on her urban crusade—a far higher percentage of the national student body than the circa-1965 Peace Corps.

- Missionaries came of age during a boom era for youthful outdoor sports: golf, tennis, and roller-skating in the 1880s, and amusement parks and the "bicycle craze" of the 1890s. Young women actively participated in looser clothing and reinvented "bloomers" (called "rationals" in 1895) for bicycle riding.

- During the 1890s, Missionaries produced the largest-ever surge of famous authors in their twenties—including Jack London, Frank Norris, Stephen Crane, and Booth Tarkington. Joined a decade later by the like-aged Upton Sinclair, Ray Stannard Baker, William Allen White, and Lincoln Steffens, young Missionaries dominated the ranks of turn-of-the-century "muckrakers." According to historian Louis Filler's composite biography, the typical muckraker—"born in the Eighteen Sixties" and "raised in the shadow of momentous events"—became "radical in his college days," "bloomed" with the rise of Theodore Roosevelt, and "invariably" supported America's entry into World War I.

- After steadily rising from 1880 on, per capita alcohol and drug consumption peaked around 1905—just as last-wave Missionaries were reaching their twenties. Moving into midlife, Missionaries launched their memorable drive to eradicate all forms of substance abuse (as well as crime and pornography), and by the mid-1920s they succeeded in pushing alcohol consumption to its lowest level in American history.

- Having been born the first generation never to know slavery, Missionary blacks came of age just as southern Jim Crow laws were stripping them of their rights as citizens—an era historian Rayford Logan calls "the Nadir" of black history. At least 60 blacks were reported lynched each year between 1885 and 1904 (peaking at 161 in 1892). This generation of American blacks—women especially—became legendary for its principled racial leadership. Journalist Ida Wells chaired the Anti-Lynching League; educator Mary McLeod Bethune organized the black women's movement; and in 1909, W.E.B. DuBois, founder of *The Crisis*, joined James Weldon Johnson in issuing "the call" for a National Association for the Advancement of Colored People.

- "The decades that straddle the turn of the century," writes historian Harvey Levenstein, "constituted a veritable Golden Age of food faddism." As lifelong advocates of "New Nutrition," Missionaries pioneered vegetarian diets, introduced salads and cole slaw, counted calories, and discovered vitamins. After Upton Sinclair published *The Jungle* in 1906, public disgust at the sight and smell of Gilded meatpacking triggered an immediate fall in beef prices—and a long-term decline in protein's role in the American diet. During World War I, while Missionary food crusaders urged "meatless" and "wheatless" Sundays, the verb "to Hooverize" (coined after the 43-year-old director of Wilson's Food Administration) became synonymous with "to do without."

- Missionary women married at a higher average age than women of any other American generation until the Boom. As late as 1915, two of every five 1880s-era women's college graduates remained single. Nine percent of all Missionary women had never married by age 60—the largest share ever recorded for that age. "The 1890s were a boom time for being single," write historians Ruth Freeman and Patricia Klaus of "the first generation of bachelor women" who took pride in calling themselves "spinsters."

- Through their lifecycle, Missionaries entirely redefined the role of women in American public life. Around the turn of the century, Missionary women surged into previously all-male professions (law, theology, medicine, dentistry, journalism), became the first female "secretaries," and began to monopolize primary school teaching. According to historian James McGovern, "the great leap forward in women's participation in economic life came between 1900 and 1910." In politics, moreover, Missionary women stood at the head of their generation's two successful constitutional amendments (women's suffrage and Prohibition). Nineteen Missionary women won election to Congress—versus two women from all prior generations combined.

- When they were combat-age, Missionary men faced a lower risk of dying in war than any other American generation—yet none can match the Missionaries for crusading zeal abroad. In all three wars of their lifecycle—the Spanish-American War, World War I, and World War II—they led the call for intervention, often over resistance from their elders or juniors.

• Elder Missionaries (especially women) achieved unprecedented gains in American longevity. From the 1930s on, mortality rates fell by 20 to 30 percent in all age brackets between 65 and 85 as Missionaries aged through them. This became the first generation in which women outlived men.

• Missionaries also retained elective national office until very late in life. They kept a majority share of Congress and governorships until fifty-five years after their last birthyear (1937) and a 25 percent share until sixty-three years afterward (1945)—both figures unmatched by any other generation before or since. From 1925 to 1945, the age of congressmen, governors, and cabinet members climbed to its highest level in American history.

• Although Missionary political leaders founded Social Security in 1935, fewer than one in twenty of their generation ever received retirement-related benefits from the program. And those who did got an average of $23 per month (about $125 in 1990 dollars), which remained unadjusted for inflation throughout the 1940s. By today's poverty standard, 60 percent of Missionary elders (age 67 to 89) were poor in 1949—versus 34 percent of all Americans between age 15 and 64.

The Missionary Lifecycle

YOUTH: "Children are not generally indulged enough," insisted Jacob Abbott in *Gentle Measures in the Management of the Young,* the leading parental manual of the 1870s. In *Home Treatment for Children,* Mattie Trippe urged parents to let kids "revel in an absolute sense of freedom, feeling only the restraints of affection." Missionaries were the indulged children of the Gilded Age—an age of big constructions, rapid economic expansion, and an adult belief in science and experience over faith. Older generations felt themselves living in a rapidly modernizing era whose main shortcomings were ethical and could someday be remedied by the young. Likening the nurture tone of the 1870s and 1880s to that of the Dr. Spock 1950s, historian Mary Cable described this "long children's picnic" as "a controlled but pleasantly free atmosphere." W.E.B. DuBois remembered his childhood as "a boy's paradise," Jane Addams how her girlfriends had been "sickened with advantages," Henry Canby how families had "more cheerfulness" and "more give and take between parents and children" than the "previous generation" had enjoyed. The Missionaries also benefited from a huge expansion in education, led by rising-adult Progressive teacher-experts and funded by midlife Gilded taxpayers (and, later, by elder Gilded philanthropists). In northern cities, Missionaries included the first American "kindergarten" students—in the South, the first generation of black youngsters to grow up mostly literate.

While Gilded-era science elevated "Mama" in a child's eye, it pushed "Papa" into a world of adult competition outside the home, a world many children would later condemn as spiritually hollow. Inspired by *Little Lord Fauntleroy* and best-selling piano songs like "Always Take Mother's Advice," magazine fiction put unprecedented stress on Mama's central child-rearing role. The link between Missionaries and mothers would last a lifetime. Billy "Rosebud" Hearst was a notorious "mama's boy." Al Smith lived alone with his mother until he married at age 27. Frank Lloyd Wright benefited from a mother who purposely meditated on "fine architecture" while he was still unborn. When the teenage Douglas MacArthur entered West Point, his mother came right along with him and found lodgings outside the gates. Many eminent Missionaries would later credit Mama for their success—or, in the case of Sara Delano Roosevelt, author of *My Boy Franklin,* Mama would make the claim on her own. In this Darwinian age, the most popular children's books (*Black Beauty, Heidi,* and Horatio Alger's *Bound to Rise*) joined Gilded mamas in assuring children that the good-hearted always get rewarded. Churches deemphasized death and damnation, and Sundays became a day for family outings. "The parents left religion to the Church, and the Church left it to the service and the Bible," recalled Canby. "There was a tacit understanding between generations that hellfire had been overdone." Coming of age, however, many Missionaries chose to renege on their side of this "tacit understanding."

COMING OF AGE: In *The Evolution of a College Student,* educator William Hyde described the typical 1890s-era freshman as homesick, the sophomore as arrogant, the junior as socialist, and the senior as religious—with an "ascetic, egotistical" fiancée intent on becoming a settlement house worker. During the decade and a half between 1886 and 1903, in college or out, these youths raised on Santa Claus and Horatio Alger came of age as stern reformers, bellowing prophets, and spiritual explorers. Students accused anxious Progressive teachers of sharing what Ray Stannard Baker called the "enlightened selfishness" of the Gilded era. "As for questions," remembered Lincoln Steffens, "the professors asked them, not the students; and the students, not the teachers, answered them." Young writers flayed the Gilded-built world for "soulless money-getting," "immense banking, roaring industries," and "hugeness and disorder." In the early 1890s, George Herron drew huge crowds to hear his "Message of Jesus to Men of Wealth." While "there may have to be some dying done before our social wrongs are thoroughly righted," Herron exhorted his listeners: "A simple generation of Christians, yea, a single generation of preachers and teachers . . . could regenerate the world." Reflecting back on his twenties, Frederic Howe wrote: "That was the thing that interested me—finding myself; and I wanted to be surrounded by people who were interested in finding themselves, who wanted to understand life and its meanings."

Not content with mere words, many young Missionaries turned to symbolic acts of violence. They founded anarchist communes (including the radical Massachusetts enclave of Emma Goldman and Alexander Berkman), where they contemplated their rage against "bosses"—and then vented it at the Haymarket Riot, Homestead Massacre, and Pullman Strike. They often succeeded in martyring themselves for the workers' revolution. One convicted anarchist, Louis Lingg, blew himself up with a dynamite cap in his mouth rather than go to the gallows. "Perhaps there is no happiness in life so perfect as the martyr's," O. Henry later observed in one of his short stories. Fledgling writers like Stephen Crane strained to mix holiness with gore ("The clang of swords is Thy wisdom/ The wounded make gestures like Thy Son's"), while the headlines of the young "New Journalism" publisher young William Randolph Hearst shrieked of wrecks, fires, and foreign atrocities. "If bad institutions and bad men can be got rid of only by killing them, then the killing must be done." So read an unsigned Hearst editorial not long before 28-year-old anarchist Leon Czolgosz shot and killed President McKinley. Four years later, the public began to hear the singing voice of young Wobblies: "Onward Christian soldiers, rip and tear and smite/ Let the gentle Jesus bless your dynamite." "We shall bear down the opposition," screamed Upton Sinclair at the close of *The Jungle*. "Chicago will be ours! *Chicago will be ours!* CHICAGO WILL BE OURS!"

RISING ADULTHOOD: The bombs and riots triggered by twentyish hotheads during the 1890s later embarrassed this generation as its members moved into their thirties and forties. During the Presidencies of Roosevelt and Taft, late-starting Missionaries shrugged off a souring economy and tried to catch up with their personal lives and careers. Richard Hovey, who had earlier accused the Gilded of being "like an oyster, all stomach," now admitted that he had "no real objection to a bathtub and clean linen." But if their fire turned inward and fragmented into separate channels, it did not extinguish. By degrees, these young men and women entirely reshaped American values and culture. While Christian socialists preached the Social Gospel to urban immigrants, Billy Sunday preached "fundamentalism" to an emerging rural Bible Belt. While poet-guitarist Carl Sandburg, "Ragtime" Scott Joplin, and "Father of the Blues" W. C. Handy enlivened Greenwich Village, new martyrs like Joe Hill ("the man who never died") kept the radical Wobbly fringe alive. Cheering Roosevelt's "Great White Fleet," many young adults asserted a holy creed of white world supremacy—spearheaded by D. W. Griffith's *Birth of a Nation* and by young Senator Albert Beveridge's "Almighty Plan" to rid the world of "savage and senile peoples." Meanwhile, W.E.B. DuBois began rallying his black peers to defy Booker T. Washington's "Tuskegee Machine" and quit apologizing to whites. Insisting that "younger men believed that the Negro problem could not remain a matter of philanthropy," DuBois launched the Niagara Movement, the first national black platform that refused to accept second-class social and political status.

As their spiritual energy split into separate streams, two Missionary-propelled inventions—the Wright brothers' airplane and the automobile of Henry Ford, Alfred Sloan, and Walter Chrysler—joined technology to the individuating of inner aspirations. Migrating and commuting far more than their Progressive elders at like age, Missionary rising adults embraced new social inventions like the "vacation," "motel," "suburb," and "country club." A number of rural-born authors fled eastward (theirs having been the first large generation of western frontier babies), where they criticized what Sherwood Anderson labeled "lives of quiet desperation" in rural small towns. "I loathed you, Spoon River," wrote Edgar Lee Masters, "I tried to rise above you." Avoiding marriage, many thirtyish women ignored popular warnings that "the home is in peril" and wondered along with novelist Ellen Glasgow why they must "sit at home and grow shapeless and have babies galore." Those who did start families rejected the stodgy Victorianism of their parents and sought simpler lives (the "servantless kitchen") and smaller houses (what historian Gwendolyn Wright calls the new "minimalist house"). Self-assured, righteous, and generally intolerant as they approached midlife positions of power, the Missionaries reflected a sublimated sexuality among a generation whose men and women, Canby later admitted, "tacitly agreed to look upon one another as sexless." While the tall, mannish "Gibson Girl" became the symbol of young women invading the male professional world, muckraking and ministerial young men laid claim to a moral pedestal that the Gilded had left to the lady.

MIDLIFE: "There is but one side in a moral question. Which do you take?" prodded William Jennings Bryan, helping to transform what had been the Progressive "temperance" movement into Missionary-style "Prohibition." At last taking over the very institutions they had attacked in their youth, Missionaries now wanted to run them with zeal. In 1917, after pushing yet another Progressive President into war, they used their growing political clout to harness the brief emergency for "moral" purposes: not just the constitutional agendas of rural drys and feminists (both of which quickly triumphed), but more sweeping means of controlling the younger Lost whose hedonism they despised and whose wildness they feared might taint a new generation of G.I. children. General "Black Jack" Pershing took brutal action against doughboy war deserters. Judge Kenesaw Mountain Landis sentenced hundreds of younger (and no longer inspirational) Wobblies to hard time, and then turned his cudgel to cleaning up baseball. Attorney General Mitchell Palmer (the "Fighting Quaker," famous for addressing enemies as "thee") rounded up 4,000 supposed Bolsheviks on a single night and deported a shipful. James Truslow Adams admitted that his peers had found a "scapegoat" and that "the name on its collar is 'The Younger Generation.'"

While President Wilson complained that the war unleashed a "spirit of rising brutality" that made Americans "forget there ever was such a thing as tolerance," many Missionary reformers welcomed how the war effort brought to America "union and communion" (Mary Follett), a "wider and wiser control of the common interests" (Robert Park), and "true national collectivism" (Robert Woods). When Senator Borah and his fellow "irreconcilables" denied Wilson his postwar League of Nations, Americans could sense that the Progressives were at last yielding to a more passionate and less genteel generation of leaders.

As the 1920s wore on, thanks to a well-timed bull market, the midlife urban elite rose at the expense of their rural and evangelical peers. But still the caustic moral tone deepened. Henry Ford offered a "just share" to workers who passed his exam "on the clean and wholesome life." Calvin Coolidge insisted "true business" would bring "moral and spiritual advancement"—making this "Puritan in Babylon" (according to the like-aged William Allen White) a man "wise according to his day and generation." Congress virtually halted immigration; "Czar of the Movies" Will Harrison Hays pushed a "Code of Decency" against sex on camera; Ku Klux Klan leaders tried to "Americanize" the heartland; and the nation's first "vice squads" began to hunt down bootleggers. While even DuBois expressed alarm at the growth in youth crime, a new generation of Missionary judges meted out more executions and longer prison terms, and state health officials began authorizing "eugenical" sterilizations. By now, Missionaries began hearing the younger Lost revile them as "Babbitts" or as "Tired Radicals." An occasional Missionary joined in. Self-proclaimed "debunker" H. L. Mencken gleefully roasted his "homo booboisie" peers. But as the 1920s drew to a close, most of this high-toned generation agreed with Paul Elmer More and Irving Babbitt that America needed a "New Humanism," an austere new ethic of social order and self-discipline. With the rise of Herbert Hoover, renowned as a brilliant humanitarian of global vision, Missionaries hoped that their best man was in position to propel the "Gospel of Business" overseas—to eliminate poverty, promote Christianity, and raise moral standards worldwide.

ELDERHOOD: "This generation has a rendezvous with destiny," announced Franklin Roosevelt in the depths of the Great Depression when his own "generation" ranged in age from its mid-fifties to its late seventies. As crisis approached, the aging and authoritarian Missionaries moved comfortably into place as stewards of social and economic regimentation. With the demise of Prohibition and the rise of the "New Deal coalition," the urban-rural schism expired—partly through cooperation in the face of peril, and partly through the leadership of urban modernists like Al Smith. As the midlife Lost mellowed, they joined Missionary leaders in staking America's future on a rising generation of good-scout G.I.s. "The interest of Roosevelt was with the younger man," recalled his adviser Barbara Armstrong. Most elder Missionaries—including pension activists like Francis Townsend and John McGroarty (dubbed the "Poet

Laureate of California'')—ultimately accepted the intergenerational quid pro quo of Roosevelt's Social Security legislation. The young were promised new jobs, a "family wage," and (in the words of Senator Wagner) "new places available for the strong and eager." The old got a meager and much-delayed pension upon "retiring," but, far more important to them, they retained the moral authority to set national priorities in an era of economic and wartime emergency.

It would have been a cruel "New Deal" for any other generation. Economically, the Missionaries had sacrificed their own interests by directing most available public resources toward youth. But these elders had few complaints. They took too much pride in directing the sacrifices of others. During a decade and a half of crisis, they consolidated their social authority—over ineffective opposition from the Lost and often with the encouragement of G.I.s. In religion, old Missionaries continued to dominate American churches. In politics, they remained the undisputed leaders of now-graying Presidential cabinets, Congressional committees, and state assemblies. In social legislation, they became "the social-work progressive crowd" and academic "Elders"—those whom historian Otis Graham, Jr., describes as "a small ascetic fraternity, the visible saints of twentieth-century reform" (and whom Mencken less respectfully labeled "the New Deal Isaiahs"). In war, they became guiding patriarchs (Secretaries Henry Stimson and Cordell Hull; Admirals "Bull" Halsey and Ernest King; Generals MacArthur and Marshall; industrialists Henry Kaiser and Bernard Baruch; physicist Albert Einstein). Today's older Americans remember the serene self-assurance and unquestioned authority commanded by these elders—and not just in America. During the war, the entire Free World knew Roosevelt as simply "the President" or "Dr. Win-the-War"; after the war, it knew George Marshall as "Europe's Savior." When MacArthur left the Philippines proclaiming "I shall return," his righteous self-esteem energized people of all ages; when he came home from Korea, awestruck younger congressmen likened him to "God Himself." After World War II, though the Lost finally assumed command, eightyish visionaries continued to symbolize what all Americans called their "Great Crusade." They retreated into old age like the global missionary and 1946 Nobel Peace Prize laureate John Mott, who (in the words of a younger admirer) had "something of the mountains and sea" in him and "went away with that calm, unhasty step, with that manner that seemed never ruffled, never excited, . . . very simple and a bit sublime."

* * *

Where the angry spiritualism of Transcendental youth culminated in the apocalypse of the Civil War, the Missionaries demonstrated how a youthful generation of muckrakers, evangelicals, and bomb-throwers could mature into revered and principled elders—wise old men and women capable of leading the young through grave peril to a better world beyond. From the 1880s through the 1940s, the Missionary hand can be seen pushing American ideals and history forward.

Just as we today honor the reforms of the Progressive Era as a testament to fair process, we remember Prohibition, the New Deal, World War II, and the Marshall Plan as a testament to the imperative that "good" must triumph over "bad." Some of what they did in pursuit of morality, of course, they overdid. And when excesses were committed, it was usually the younger, more pragmatic Lost who had to bear the punishment and clean up the mess left behind: from the Palmer Raids to Prohibition, from Hoovervilles to Yalta. By the late 1940s, as younger Americans began yearning for some national purpose less lofty than rectitude, the Missionary star faded at last. Perhaps it was time. "Do not be deceived— we are today in the midst of a cold war," announced 77-year-old Bernard Baruch only two years after VJ-day. These were ominous words from a man and a generation that had always been able to find extra moral stature in every new war and every new crusade.

Without question, Americans today have the Missionaries to thank for lifting America to its present-day status as a great global power. America still lives by the visions they glimpsed. In foreign policy, the very term "foreign aid" was invented by elder Missionaries (Herbert Hoover and Herbert Lehman), perhaps recalling those classmates on Mount Hermon who first set their sights on "The Evangelization of the World in This Generation." At home, the term "Great Society" was similarly popularized by elder Missionaries (James Truslow Adams and Fiorello La Guardia), perhaps recalling that youthful image of Bryan—"the bard and prophet of them all," wrote Vachel Lindsay—who claimed that "a nation can be born in a day if the ideals of the people can be changed." In 1948 at age 83, art critic Bernard Berenson defined "culture" as "the effort to build a House of Life . . . that humanistic society which under the name of Paradise, Elysium, Heaven, City of God, Millennium, has been the craving of all good men these last four thousand years or more." Franklin Roosevelt had something similar in mind when he described his "Four Freedoms" just nine months before leading America to war. "That is no vision of a distant millennium," he explained. "It is a definite basis for a kind of world attainable in our own time and generation."

LOST GENERATION

Born: 1883–1900
Type: Reactive

Age Location:
Missionary Awakening in youth
Great Depression–World War II Crisis in midlife

"There died a myriad . . . / For an old bitch gone in the teeth, / For a botched civilization." That is how the thirtyish Ezra Pound described what Missionaries liked to call America's "Crusade for Democracy." World War I was cruel enough to soldiers in the trenches, but the homecoming was humiliating. In 1919 and 1920, their next-elders meted out the Volstead Act to purge them of liquor, "Red Scare" Palmer Raids to purge them of radicals, and John Sumner's Society for the Suppression of Vice to purge them of pornography. "The season 'tis, my lovely lambs, / of Sumner Volstead Christ and Co.," lampooned 26-year-old e.e. cummings. "Down with the middle-aged!" joined in John Dos Passos, age 24. These literati would soon know themselves as the LOST GENERATION, scrambling survivors in a world of pomposity and danger. As the 1920s dawned, some were already getting into trouble—like John Reed, dying an unrepentant "Red" in Moscow, or Harry Truman, whose clothing store was going bust. But amid this sea of alienation, the post-Armistice years dealt lucky draws to a few who were "Puttin' on the Ritz": Babe Ruth (blasting home runs for the Yankees); "Scarface" Al Capone (setting up "business" in Chicago); Irving Berlin (scavenging in Tin Pan Alley); and young writers like F. Scott Fitzgerald, Sinclair Lewis, and Eugene O'Neill (striking it rich with blockbuster hits). Embittered 30-year-olds fought ideology with pleasure, Babbittry with binges, moral crusades with bathtub gin and opulent sex. "America was going on the greatest, gaudiest spree in history," bubbled Fitzgerald in *This Side of Paradise,* setting the tone for the "Roaring Twenties."

Fitzgerald described his generation as at once "prewar and postwar." With a rowdy childhood and a tired old age as bookends, the Lost lifecycle was divided roughly in thirds by two world wars. ("In the meantime, in between time, *Ain't We Got Fun?*") The story began with streetwise kids who grew up fast—too late to join in the spiritual high of their next-elders, but fast enough to stay one step ahead of Missionary efforts to clean them up later on. They were, wrote Fitzgerald, "a new generation dedicated more than the last to the fear of poverty and the worship of success; grown up to find all gods dead, all wars fought, all

LOST GENERATION (Born 1883 to 1900)

TYPE: Reactive

Total number: 45,000,000
Now alive in U.S.: 1,100,000
Percent immigrant: 21%

FAMILY TREE

Typical grandparents: Gilded
Parents: Progressive and Missionary
Children: G.I. and Silent
Typical grandchildren: Boom

SAMPLE MEMBERS, birth (death)

1885 Sinclair Lewis (1951)
1885 George Patton (1945)
1888 Irving Berlin (1989)*
1889 Walter Lippmann (1974)
1891 Earl Warren (1974)
1891 Nicola Sacco (1927)*
1892 Reinhold Niebuhr (1971)
1892 Mae West (1980)
1893 Dorothy Parker (1967)
1894 Norman Rockwell (1978)
1895 J. Edgar Hoover (1972)
1895 Babe Ruth (1948)
1896 George Burns
1896 F. Scott Fitzgerald (1940)
1898 Paul Robeson (1976)
1899 Humphrey Bogart (1957)
1899 Al Capone (1947)*
1899 Ernest Hemingway (1961)
1900 Louis Armstrong (1971)
1900 Adlai Stevenson (1965)
* = immigrant

PERIOD OF POLITICAL LEADERSHIP

Plurality in House: 1937–1953
Plurality in Senate: 1943–1959
Majority of Supreme Court: 1941–1967

U.S. PRESIDENTS: 1945–1961

1884 Harry S. Truman (1972)
1890 Dwight D. Eisenhower (1969)

PROMINENT FOREIGN PEERS

1883 Benito Mussolini (1945)
1889 Adolf Hitler (1945)
1889 Charles Chaplin (1977)
1890 Charles de Gaulle (1970)
1893 Mao Zedong (1976)

Age	Date	HISTORY AND LIFECYCLE
0–9	1892:	Ellis Island quarantine begins for new flood of poor immigrants
5–22	1905:	First "nickelodeons" and "jelly beans"; word "adolescent" coined
12–29	1912:	Child labor peaks; sinking of *Titanic*
18–35	1918:	Doughboys come home to crackdown on drinking, drugs, crime
29–46	1929:	Valentine's Day gangland massacre; Black Thursday stock crash
32–49	1932:	Bonus Army riot; soup lines and Hoovervilles multiply
35–52	1935:	"Okies" flee dust bowl; Huey Long murdered; anti-FDR Liberty League
41–58	1941:	Vandenberg, Nye abandon isolationism; Congress follows FDR to war
45–62	1945:	Truman becomes President, orders atomic bombs dropped
50–67	1950:	Kefauver Committee grills Lucky Luciano and other mobsters
60–77	1960:	Ike opposes moon shot, warns against "military-industrial complex"
64–81	1964:	Dirksen ends opposition to civil rights laws

SAMPLE CULTURAL ENDOWMENTS: *The Great Gatsby* (F. Scott Fitzgerald); *The Waste Land* (T. S. Eliot); *Babbitt* (Sinclair Lewis); *The Sound and the Fury* (William Faulkner); *Monkey Business* (film, Marx Brothers); *Creed of an Advertising Man* (Bruce Barton); *An American in Paris* (George Gershwin); *Ain't Misbehavin'* (Duke Ellington); *The Maltese Falcon* (Dashiell Hammett); *The Big Sleep* (Raymond Chandler); *The Old Man and the Sea* (Ernest Hemingway); *The View from Eighty* (Malcolm Cowley) faiths in man shaken." So they lashed back at "the lies of old men" and the finger-wagging of grim dowagers. They led America through a dazzling decade, waiting for Hemingway's bell to toll for *them*. When it did—with the stock crash and depression—they fell back exhausted at first, and then stepped forward as clear-eyed managers for their elders and as selfless protectors of their juniors. The Great Depression dealt them its cruelest blow, robbing them of what should have been their peak income years and ushering in public action that ran against their grain. But lacking confidence in their own moral judgments, the Lost joined the national effort, lending what they liked to call "brains"—and what was, in effect, a keen realism about human nature. After providing outstanding gener-alship in World War II, gaining top command by the war's end, the Lost mel-lowed into a cautious old age. Their elder survivors presided as social anchors over an era of strengthening families, warm nurture of the young, and sharply improving economic fortunes for the generations behind them.

"Mama, I have been a bad boy. All my life I have been a bad boy," murmured author Thomas Wolfe just before his death, a burned-out wreck at age 38 after a lifetime of wildness. "I was a bad kid," echoed Babe Ruth, the carousing and hard-drinking Bambino. "I had a rotten start." Such confessions were, in effect, the credo of a demeaned generation. When they were children, the media were obsessed with the problem of "bad boys." Popular magazines featured stories like "Bad Boy of the Streets" and "Making Good Citizens out of Bad Boys." From the decade before to the decade after 1900, while city-dwellers fretted over a rising tide of street crime, the number of published articles on "juvenile delinquency" rose tenfold. By World War I, Missionaries shifted public attention to the vices of young adults—their lust, drunkenness, violence, and "Black Sox" corruptibility. The taint followed them through what Frederick Lewis Allen would later call "the Decade of Bad Manners," an era of gangsters, flappers, expatriates, and real-estate swindlers. By the late 1920s, elders looked upon the Lost as a social time bomb threatening to blow America to pieces. In 1932, Missionary General MacArthur ran his cavalry over their unemployed veterans' march on Washington to public applause—as if their joblessness (and the crash) had somehow been their fault. When a new Missionary President promised a few months later to purge "a generation of self-seekers" from "the temple of our civilization," Americans of all ages knew who those "money changers" were.

"My candle burns at both ends;/ It will not last the night," Edna St. Vincent Millay had earlier predicted. She was right. By Pearl Harbor, virtually every one of their zany cultural heroes of the 1920s and 1930s had hit "The Crack-up," as Fitzgerald named one of his last essays. The glittery Lost veneer evap-orated, but the "bad boy" survivalism lingered on—with "Blood and Guts" Patton and "Give 'Em Hell" Truman. Yet so too did the stigma of selfishness and unreason. Scarred by their youthful encounters with next-elder moralists, many midlife Lost became anti–New Dealers and isolationists. ("**The war fever** is on. New uniforms for soldiers are designed," warned radio star Father Charles Coughlin. "Once more, we must begin hating the 'Hun' and bleeding for Great Britain and France.") Roosevelt, in turn, called them "Copperheads" and in 1944 got his most rousing campaign response by asking entire crowds to join a chant against three Lost isolationists: "MARTIN, BARTON—AND FISH!" Condemning defeatist "Tories" like Ezra Pound and T. S. Eliot, Archibald MacLeish called his peers *The Irresponsibles,* while soon after D-Day the elder Henry Stimson pointedly reminded America that "cynicism is the only mortal sin." Daunted once again, the Lost entered postwar elderhood without fanfare, making way gracefully for an aggressive new batch of scoutlike G.I.s. Still accepting blame in old age, the Lost preserved their pride by refusing to ask for favors. They repeatedly pulled the lever for Republicans who promised *not* to help them in the 1950s and 1960s, feeling inferior to richer and smarter juniors who lacked their fatalism about life.

Gertrude Stein, a sympathetic Missionary, told Hemingway that his was a "lost" generation. He adopted her name at the beginning of *The Sun Also Rises,* a 1926 novel that popularized the European wanderings of Americans his age and persuaded readers that "the Great War" had wasted those whom Fitzgerald called *All the Sad Young Men.* True, the horrors of mustard gas and trenchfoot catalyzed their generational identity. But years before Eddie Rickenbacker "barnstormed" the Siegfried Line, Missionary elders were already finding plenty they didn't like in these smooth, undereducated, daredevil kids. In 1911, Cornelia Comer spoke for many of her prim fortyish peers when she wrote an *Atlantic Monthly* "Letter to the Rising Generation" accusing them of "mental rickets and curvature of the soul," of a *"culte du moi,"* and of growing up "painfully commercialized even in their school days." While admitting that "you are innocent victims of a good many haphazard educational experiments" that "have run amuck for the last twenty-five years," Comer asked: "What excuse have you, anyhow, for turning out flimsy, shallow, amusement-seeking creatures . . . ?" And already the young Lost were taking the message to heart—while groping for a voice of their own. Responding to Comer, 25-year-old Randolph Bourne explained simply that his generation was the logical "reaction" to universal parental neglect. "The modern child from the age of ten is almost his own 'boss,'" he observed, and while "it is true that we do not fuss and fume about our souls . . . we have retained from childhood the propensity to see through things, and to tell the truth with startling frankness."

To the Lost, the greatest human need was a clear head. Existence before essence. Coming of age as America's first existential generation, they often returned to those stark nihilisms which seemed to make sense out of the chaotic world of their childhood: surrealism, Dadaism, expressionism, futurism, Freudian relativism—all overshadowed by pessimistic theories of social entropy and decline. They couldn't fathom their next-elder Missionaries, so busy trying to find meaning in life. They thought they knew better—that behind those loudly trumpeted principles, there was no meaning. "What is moral is what you feel good after," declared Hemingway, "and what is immoral is what you feel bad after." Few of the Lost made effective reformers or preachers. Instead, they became the most stunningly original generation of artists and writers in American history. They never stopped using what they called their "revolution of the word" to pour ice-water realism on their generational neighbors and to express their incorrigible aversion to grandiosity. To "Kingdom of God" Missionaries, the young Hemingway mockingly announced in 1933, "Our nada who art in nada, nada be thy name." To "Great Society" G.I.s, the eightyish Henry Miller quipped in 1974: "It's silly to go on pretending that under the skin we are all brothers. The truth is more likely that under the skin we are all cannibals, assassins, traitors, liars, hypocrites, poltroons."

From Ernest Hemingway to F. Scott Fitzgerald, Mae West to Jimmy Cagney, Paul Tillich to Reinhold Niebuhr, the Lost never expected that anyone would look to them for greatness or goodness. All they asked was the chance to remind their elders and juniors how life really worked, and the opportunity to do what needed doing—quickly, effectively—when nobody else would stoop to the task. Meanwhile, they were content to bear the blame so long as public-spirited crusaders kept their distance. They would make their own amends for their own shortcomings. Most of today's 60-year-olds recall as children the presence of at least one Lost parent, probably the one who embraced them fondly if too frequently during the dark years of the Great Depression. Most of today's 40-year-olds recall as children at least one reclusive Lost grandparent, or maybe just that foreign-born "granny" down the street who scowled (with a twinkle in her eye) whenever a baseball rolled across her yard. You couldn't pull the wool over their eyes. Nor could you make them forget a lifetime brimming with adventure: Ellis Island and sweatshops, sleek Pierce-Arrows and the Battle of the Marne, speakeasies and hangovers, a giddy bull market and a global crash, soup lines and dust-bowl caravans. They hid their early years from those nice-looking, TV-age youngsters they got to know in their old age—most assuredly because they didn't want any kid to try reliving them.

Lost Facts

• Lost children entered the cash labor market at a higher rate than any generation of American children before or since. In 1910, nearly one child in five between age 10 and 14 (three in five between 15 and 19) was gainfully employed. Many worked in "sweatshops" (a word first coined in 1892). In the cities, one Lost child in six worked at some point as a "newsie" hawking the headlines—including Irving Berlin, Jack Dempsey, Al Jolson,

William O. Douglas, Groucho Marx, and Earl Warren. Later on, as rising adults, this generation of grown-up entrepreneurs resisted collective action. Despite a tight labor market, union memberships declined from nearly 5 million in 1921 to under 3.5 million in 1929.

• No other generation of children ever purchased such a large share of its total consumption with self-earned income. Lost pocket cash sustained America's first child-only retailers (candy stores and nickelodeons) and nationally marketed sweets, including jelly beans, Tootsie Rolls, Hershey Bars, and bubble gum. From 1889 to 1922, the Lost sweet tooth propelled a doubling in per capita sugar consumption to about one hundred pounds annually (about where it remains today). In the 1920s, "sugar" became a term of endearment.

• From first cohort to last, Lost youths showed little improvement in rates of illiteracy, absenteeism, dropout, or college entry. From 1880 to 1900, the share of all white children in primary schools dropped from 62 to 54 percent; for black children, from 34 to 31 percent. When Lost young men took the first "I.Q." tests during World War I, the results showed that half the draftees had a "mental age" of under 12. During the 1920s, the so-called "threat of the feeble-minded" turned many midlife voters against immigration and prompted the Missionary psychologist Henry Goddard to invent technical terms ("moron," "idiot," and "imbecile") to identify every gradation of stupidity. After 1950, when the Lost began to reach their midsixties, the learning gap between the elderly and nonelderly rapidly widened. In 1970, the educational disparity between all adults over 25 (who averaged 12.2 years of schooling) and adults over 65 (who averaged 8.7 years) was the largest ever measured in this century.

• The Lost were America's first generation to grow up amid widespread adult-approved narcotics use. In 1900, while opium and chloral hydrate consumption was still rising, many other newly synthesized and unregulated drugs were entering the marketplace, including paraldehyde, sulphonal, veronal, and heroin. Cocaine or coca—a wondrous midlife discovery to Sigmund Freud, "Sherlock Holmes," and many like-aged Progressives in America—was routinely sold in cough syrup, lozenges, and (until 1904) Coca-Cola. Yet when the Missionaries rose to power on the eve of World War I, the Lost took most of the blame for drug-related violence and crime.

• From 1900 to 1920, while the Lost came of age, America's homicide rate rose by 700 percent. Just before it peaked in the early 1930s, Lost street hoodlums had matured into America's biggest-ever crime kingpins: Al Capone, Frank Costello, Lucky Luciano, Dutch Schultz, and Legs Diamond. The Lost coined the word "underworld," as well as "gangster," "mobster," "racketeer," "moll," and "getaway car." Equally inventive with the lexicon of music and sex, they coined "get hep," "jive," "cat," "cathouse," "floozy," "party girl," "trick," "fast" or "loose" woman, "sugar daddy," "boy-crazy," and "hot pants."

- The great influenza of 1918, the deadliest epidemic in American history (and fatal mostly to young adults), killed about 250,000 Lost—five times the number who died in combat during World War I. Decades later, the Lost's unusually high rate of Parkinson's disease in old age has often been attributed to this flu (or, some think, to their early contact with toxic industrial chemicals). From the early 1950s through the 1960s, as Lost replaced Missionaries as elders, old-age mortality rates stopped falling. Last-wave Lost males showed no gain over last-wave Missionary males in life expectancy at age 65.

- At age 20 (in 1910), the Lost were 50 percent more suicide-prone than last-wave Missionaries had been at age 20 (in 1900). From childhood on, moreover, the Lost have thus far been more suicide-prone than the next three generations—G.I.s, Silent, and Boom—at every phase of life. In longitudinal surveys taken in the 1960s and 1970s, the Lost scored higher in "suspicion" and lower in "self-sentiment" than later-born G.I.s at the same age.

- The Lost accounted for the first black "Great Migration" out of the rural South and into the urban North. After growing up during the rise of Jim Crow and coming of age during the Wilson-era job boom, about 1.5 million black Americans emigrated out of the South from 1910 to 1930—nearly three times the prior number of black emigrants since the Civil War.

- With nine million members born abroad, the Lost is (in absolute numbers) America's largest immigrant generation. An unmatched proportion came from Eastern and Southern Europe, many of them Jewish. Of all Americans today over age 85, one in six is a naturalized citizen (one in three in New York and New England)—a far higher share than of any other living generation.

- The Lost attained a majority share of Congressional seats and governorships later in their lifecycle (fifty-eight years after their first birthyear) than any other American generation. On a per-cohort basis, no other generation has been as weakly represented in national leadership posts over its lifetime.

- Throughout their adult lives, the Lost have been the most Republican-leaning of generations. As elected congressmen, they were more likely than elder Missionaries to oppose the New Deal in the late 1930s. As voters, they chose Willkie in 1940, split roughly 50-50 for Goldwater in 1964, and gave

Reagan his biggest generational proportions in 1980 and 1984. As Presidential contenders, they were mostly Republican: Alfred Landon, Wendell Willkie, Dwight Eisenhower, and "Mr. Republican" Robert Taft. Two others were third-party socialists: Norman Thomas and Henry Wallace. Their one incumbent Democrat, Harry Truman, won (barely) once; and their one other Democratic contender, Adlai Stevenson, lost (badly) twice.

• Hit by the Great Depression during their midlife earning years, the Lost occupied the one age bracket never targeted by a New Deal relief program. After the war, as G.I.s built and inhabited sparkling suburbs, the Lost mostly stayed put. Nearly half never lived in a house or apartment with two or more bedrooms and bathroom. In 1985, compared to a typical G.I. retiree in his late sixties, a surviving Lost elder (who was at least twenty years older) had one-third less total income, received one-fifth less in Social Security, was far less likely to have a private pension or own his own home, and was roughly twice as likely to live in poverty.

The Lost Lifecycle

YOUTH: In 1897, 8-year-old Virginia O'Hanlon wrote the *New York Sun* and asked her famous question: "Is there a Santa Claus?" Many in her class, she said, were anti-Santa skeptics—and, chances are, they were unpersuaded by the *Sun*'s reassuring answer. The children of the 1890s were America's most tough-minded ever, growing up fast amid gangs, drugs, saloons, big-city immigration, and an emotional climate raging with evangelical fervor and social reform. Few turn-of-the-century parents knew how to protect their nests. Often they were permissive to the point of near-neglect, following the "Don't drive them" advice of 1890s-era parent counselor Hannah Smith. George Burns recalled that at bedtime his mother "would stand there with the door open. When the house was full she'd close it. Sometimes I made it, sometimes I slept in the hall." The fiftyish Progressive Jacob Riis, stepping into a tenement, noted that "the hall is dark and you might stumble over children pitching pennies back there. Not that it would hurt them; kicks and cuffs are their daily diet. They have little else." Unsupervised by parents or governments, children surged into the labor market—girls as piece-rate "homeworkers," boys as newsies, bootblacks, scavengers, messengers, "cash boys," nonunion cigar-rollers, or ten-hours-a-day coal miners. What they earned (and their parents didn't take away), they spent. A few pennies in the hand became a ticket to a world of playful consumption.

Although Dewey-style "progressive" educational reforms were already in full gear, Lost kids found school irrelevant next to the grim realities of street life. "School was all wrong," complained Harpo Marx. "School simply didn't teach you how to be poor and live from day to day." (Harpo "dropped out" when classroom toughs threw him out the window when the teacher wasn't looking.) When it suited them, Lost children mingled well with adults, but their hardened precocity sat badly with values-focused elders. Addams decried the kids' jaunty consumerism, Bryan their cynicism, Theodore Roosevelt the ruthlessness of their football (eighteen college players died on the field in 1905 alone). Roosevelt's daughter Alice—smoking, swearing, and sipping champagne in the White House—became a headline-grabbing symbol of a child generation growing up "bad." The Progressive G. Stanley Hall was the first to label these unrestrained young savages "adolescents"; he was also the first to ascribe their moral development to sex drives rather than to religion. "Never has youth been exposed to such dangers of both perversion and arrest as in our own land and day," he lamented. Thomas Wolfe soon wondered "what has happened to the spontaneous gaiety of youth"—children who are "without innocence, born old and stale and dull and empty . . . suckled on darkness, and weaned on violence and noise." "They tried to shut their eyes," recalled Mike Gold of the adults he met when he was a hustling street urchin. "We children did not shut our eyes. We saw and knew." Some did well, but a larger number did badly. Living and dying by their new credo "It's up to you," these "kids" were already paying the dues of independence.

COMING OF AGE: "We have in our unregenerate youth . . . been forced to become realists," declared 23-year-old John Carter shortly after the Armistice. "At 17 we were disillusioned and weary," recalled Malcolm Cowley. The Lost came of age hearing sixtyish Progressives describe how civilization must inexorably climb to higher levels of Edwardian refinement and control, but a series of disasters that no one could explain (including the San Francisco earthquake and the sinking of the *Titanic*) made them wonder. They watched Missionaries rise to power pontificating about a society whose seamy and rapacious underside—from sweatshop children and young prostitutes to widespread drug abuse and gang violence—only teenagers could see with clarity. Most 20-year-olds turned a deaf ear toward older, campus-touring radicals like Jack London and Upton Sinclair. "College students are more conservative than their professors because they too often regard college as a back door to big business," observed one disappointed student organizer. Well before World War I, the first signs of alienation surfaced. In 1908, the youthful Van Wyck Brooks wrote *Wine of the Puritans,* his title popularizing a word that fresh Ivy League graduates (in *Seven Arts*) would soon paste on their next-elders. In 1913, magazines proclaimed "Sex O'Clock in America," announcing what soon became known as a "revolution in morals." Then came the "Flapper of 1915," who (reported Mencken) "has forgotten how to simper; she seldom blushes; and it is impossible to shock her."

These youth crosscurrents came together in World War I—a war they would call "the sausage machine," the ultimate evidence of their elders' colossal blindness. Hemingway, Dos Passos, Cowley, and cummings; all volunteered as ambulance drivers, immediate eyewitnesses to the worst carnage. "Abstract words such as glory, honor, courage, or hallow were obscene beside the concrete names of villages, the numbers of roads, the names of rivers, the numbers of regiments and dates," wrote Hemingway. After the war, while many young intellectuals lingered in Paris ("I prefer to starve where the food is good," chided Virgil Thompson), most doughboys returned home to a nation firmly in Missionary control. There, wrote Fitzgerald, "men of fifty had the gall" to tell veterans of 30 how to behave. The Lost "Flaming Youth" instinctively bucked and turned toward pleasure-seeking. Already in 1915, Bruce Barton penned *A Young Man's Jesus,* almost a parody of Missionary evangelism, urging "those of us who are this side of thirty-five to unite and take back our Jesus, . . . a young man glowing with physical strength and the joy of living" and possessing "our bounding pulses, our hot desires." Soon after the war, Sinclair Lewis scored two more salvos in *Main Street* and *Elmer Gantry.* Triggering the "roar" of the Twenties, the Lost prompted Missionaries to roar back about the "Problem of the Younger Generation." The Lost knew they were bad, yet refused to take all the heat. In his 1920 *Atlantic Monthly* article entitled " 'These Wild Young People' By One of Them," Carter observed that "magazines have been crowded with pessimistic descriptions of the younger generation"—but added, "the older generation has certainly pretty well ruined this world before passing it on to us."

RISING ADULTHOOD: "The shows were broader, the buildings were higher, the morals were looser, and the liquor was cheaper," Fitzgerald wrote from New York City in 1926, at the height of the fun, "but all these did not really minister to much delight. Young people wore out early—they were hard and languid. . . . The city was bloated, glutted, stupid with cakes and circuses, and a new expression, 'O yeah?' summed up all the enthusiasm. . . ." Uptown, Lost blacks streaming in from the South touched off a cultural explosion. While "Garveyism" held out new hopes of racial independence and Claude McKay wrote *Home to Harlem,* Alain Locke proclaimed the birth of "the New Negro," free of "cautious moralisms" and "the trammels of Puritanism." DuBois and other older Missionaries did not always approve. "The leaders of the NAACP," explains literary historian Sterling Brown, "felt that the characterization of Harlem sweet-backs and hot mammas did injustice to their propaganda and purposes." But music named after a black idiom for sex—"jazz"—drew crowds of white urbanites and put its stamp on an era of youthful hedonism and what-you-see-is-what-you-get cynicism. As male bootleggers built entrepreneurial empires in defiance of Prohibition, blasé *garçonnes* like Dorothy Parker and Zelda Fitzgerald disappointed older suffragettes. "The Jazz Age . . . had no interest at all in politics," recalled Fitzgerald. But if their ideas were languid, Lost dancing was "jitterbug" kinetic. These 30-year-olds cherished money, leisure, and style—from chromy Art Deco and *Metropolis* futurism to Arabian luxury. Lost-directed movies scorched audiences with what one producer called "neckers, petters, white kisses, red kisses, pleasure-mad daughters, sensation-craving mothers."

By their early forties, Lost entrepreneurs were inventing supermarkets and shopping centers, soda fountains and cafeterias, frozen foods and automats—all for their faster pace of living. "Self-help" experts Dale Carnegie and Norman Vincent Peale knew how to counsel a generation that cared far more about success than expressing any feeling of self-worth. ("Win, win, win . . . but always avoid the pronoun 'I.'") As Fitzgerald declared that "living well is the best revenge" and the Great Gatsby pined after Daisy—"her voice is full of money"—"Kingfish" Huey Long made points with the luckless in Louisiana by declaring "every man a king" and then picking every man's pockets. Like Ty Cobb, sliding spikes high into home plate, the Lost directed their most savage competitive instincts against their own peers. The mood began darkening in 1927 with the execution of Nicola Sacco and Bartolomeo Vanzetti, pathetic victims of Missionary zeal. Wrote Vanzetti bitterly just before his death: "Our words—our lives—our pain: nothing!" "For de little stealin' dey gits you in jail soon or late," wrote Eugene O'Neill in *The Emperor Jones.* "For de big stealin' dey makes you emperor and puts you in de Hall o' Fame when you croaks." Come 1929, the St. Valentine's Day Massacre shocked public opinion ("lousy public relations," admitted Capone). Sinclair Lewis ridiculed the "chilly enthusiasms" of elder New Humanists, but in *A Preface to Morals* Walter Lippmann reflected ominously on his generation's mental and ethical chaos. Fitzgerald kept his room full of calendars and clocks, ticking away toward the collective "crash" his peers could sense was coming. A few (like Joseph Kennedy) sold out just in time, but the typical youngish investor had the bad luck to buy into the market relatively late, making the bust all the more painful.

MIDLIFE: Malcolm Cowley called 1930 a year of "doubt and even defeat" for his generation—a year of broken friendships, sudden poverty, and suicide. It was the start of their collective midlife hangover, the Great Depression. Their party over and their style suddenly repudiated, the Lost faced the future armed only with the courage of despair. "Now once more the belt is tight and we summon the proper expression of horror as we look back at our wasted youth," observed Fitzgerald, though he suspected that his was "a generation with no second acts." The alienation of 1920s-era intellectuals now reached the poor and the rural. Sullen "Hoovervilles" filled with unemployed men approaching the prime of life without hope. Since jobs were scarce, priority went to household heads—narrowing women's horizons and recasting many unemployed husbands as "breadwinner" failures. Assuming the social responsibilities of midlife, the Lost gave the 1930s their gritty quality. "Everything depends on the use to which it is put," explained Reinhold Niebuhr in *Moral Man and Immoral Society,* warning against "poles of foolishness" and setting the moral tone for a generation now bent on doing the right thing with or without faith.

As the 1930s unfolded, midlife veterans watched the German soldier generation they had already met in battle turn into on-the-march fascists. A few joined the call for national preparedness, including the tortoises who began overtaking hares among the Lost elite—from Raymond Moley and his FDR "brain trust" to a new cadre of Jewish and immigrant intellectuals. Knowing firsthand the horror of war, however, most Lost were uninspired by another call to global altruism. Opinion leaders like Senator Gerald Nye feared that a Roosevelt-led crusade might enslave America under what Moley (by now anti-Roosevelt) called the "iron hand of the Government." Still less did they admire the New Deal. Edmund Wilson called it "the warning of a dictatorship." But Missionary leaders knew how to hit back where it hurt. While Harold Ickes ridiculed Huey Long for "halitosis of the intellect," FDR quipped that "Americans are going through a bad case of Huey Long and Father Coughlin influenza." In 1941, when the Lost at last attained a congressional majority, Wendell Willkie and Arthur Vandenberg quashed their peers' truculence in the face of obvious danger. In World War II, the Lost were the charismatic "G.I.s' generals" whose daring (George Patton), warmth (Omar Bradley), and patience (Dwight Eisenhower) energized younger troops. Fiftyish civilians administered the home front with the homely and unpretentious composure suggested in the paintings of the like-aged Norman Rockwell. By war's end, Truman asserted a pragmatism borne of a lifetime of "hard knocks." Doing lonely battle like Hemingway's bullfighter, Truman took "the heat" and ultimately succeeded in showing the door to two pompous old Missionaries: General MacArthur and John L. Lewis.

ELDERHOOD: Hemingway once described "the wisdom of old men" as a great fallacy: "They do not grow wise. They grow careful." Like so many of the Lost literary elite, Hemingway never reached old age himself—but his description was prescient for those who did in the 1950s and 1960s. Recalling a lifetime spent scrambling away from grand public crusades, the old Lost balked at expressions of lofty ideals and hesitated to approve of anything they considered too bold, too daring, too dangerous. Their leaders' grandest national vision was, as Eisenhower described it, to project a "respectable image of American life before the world." Golf-playing "Ike" took few chances abroad, enacted few new programs, and opposed any newfangled "moon rocket." America's last President to resist deficit financing, he also set a stable economic foundation for the Go-Go Sixties (for which G.I. Presidents would later take credit). Midway through only their third elected Presidential term, the Lost learned they had already overstayed their welcome. In the off-year election of 1958, they were annihilated at the voting booth by younger G.I.s (nearly all Democrats), and two years later Eisenhower heard himself attacked by both of the younger Presidential candidates. In return, after musing over the new cult of bigness and energy, he offered a farewell warning against what he labeled the "military-industrial complex."

Their exit from the public eye was sudden and complete. By the time Kennedy was taking "longer strides" in 1961, the Lost already seemed an antediluvian memory: "old whale" mayors and tobacco-chewing "Dixiecrats," fading bureau chiefs like J. Edgar Hoover and Lewis Hershey, grimy mobsters like Lucky Luciano and Truman's Pendergast hacks (squinting under the spotlight glare of G.I. inquisitors). A decade later, a few Lost survivors saw their image revive. Sam Ervin emerged as a national dispenser of country justice, Claude Pepper as a protector of younger G.I.s then on the brink of retirement. The Pepper-advocated expansion of elder benefits came too late for his own peers, most of whom never saw a "COLA" or a Medicare card. Then again, few Lost had ever asked for them. In 1959, when Ethel Andrus founded the American Association of Retired Persons (now a powerful G.I. lobby), she refused "to bewail the hardships of old age . . . nor to stress the potential political strength of older folk, nor to urge governmental subsidy." In 1964, after Barry Goldwater broadly hinted that he would weaken Social Security, he ran far stronger with the Lost than with any other generation. That's how the Lost preferred it: no favors for a generation that always knew, deep down, they were "bad boys." Having grown up in an age of horsecarts and Russian czars, they grew old feeling like aliens in their juniors' space-age world. During the 1950s, while younger G.I. "gerontologists" defined retirement as "permission to disengage," a younger G.I. playwright (Arthur Miller) let the worn-out salesman Willie Loman "fall into his grave like an old dog." Younger audiences winced, but not the Lost. As Dorothy Parker proved—"poor son of a bitch," she said when she saw Fitzgerald's body—this generation never cared much for mincing words.

*   *   *

Virgil Thompson once described his writings as "sassy but classy"—three words that epitomize our memory of his generation. As America's first (and, many say, best) film stars, the Lost left behind a celluloid image of their versatile personality: from physicality (Mae West, Jimmy Cagney), mischief (the Marx Brothers), and evil (Edward G. Robinson, Boris Karloff) to savoir-faire (Rudolph Valentino, Mary Pickford), adventure (Douglas Fairbanks), and keen survivalism (Humphrey Bogart). As the last generation to come of age without electronic media, the Lost stand as America's most gifted cadre of wordsmiths: They won five of America's nine Nobel Prizes for Literature and produced our culture's most memorable song lyrics (Cole Porter, Oscar Hammerstein). Louis Armstrong and Duke Ellington introduced improvisational jazz, America's first naughty-sounding music. These are lasting gifts from a generation for whom, in Dorothy Parker's words, "art is a form of catharsis," an instinctive response to a whirlwind existence. In their entertainment was a no-nonsense lesson about how the individual can maintain his sanity in a harsh and unjust world. "Living is struggle,'' wrote Thornton Wilder in *The Skin of Our Teeth*. "Every good and excellent thing in the world stands moment by moment on the razor-edge of danger and must be fought for—whether it's a field, a home, or a country.'' Paul Tillich explained in his old age: "Our generation has seen the horrors latent in man's being rise to the surface and erupt.''

With little philosophizing, the Lost did history's dirty work: attacking Belleau Wood, mapping D-Day, dropping A-bombs, and containing Stalinism. Whatever they did, they half expected history to someday blame them. In some cases, history has: for Earl Warren's internment of Japanese-Americans, for example, or "Dixiecrat" foot-dragging on civil rights. Yet, mostly, the Lost showed unthanked kindness to other generations. After fighting in two world wars and bearing the brunt of the Great Depression, the peers of Truman and Eisenhower accepted, without complaint, 91 percent marginal tax rates to balance the budget, liquidate war debt, finance the Marshall Plan, and pay out generous G.I. benefits. They demonstrated (as Bruce Barton put it) that "a man may be down but he is never out.'' When it was up to them, they did indeed "play the sap" for their elders and juniors. Such sacrifices made possible an era their children and grand-children now nostalgically recall as the "American High.'' Yet the Lost taught us more than self-effacing goodwill. From George Patton leading G.I.s in the Battle of the Bulge to George Burns tutoring 13ers in *18 Again!*, they showed us something about what they liked to call "guts.'' So too did they remind us how to have a good time by being just a little "bad.'' As Malcolm Cowley put it: "Did other generations ever laugh so hard together, drink and dance so hard, or do crazier things just for the hell of it?''

G.I. GENERATION

Born: 1901–1924
Type: Civic

Age Location:
Great Depression–World War II Crisis in rising adulthood
Boom Awakening in elderhood

With his triumphant transatlantic flight in 1927, 25-year-old Charles Lindbergh heralded the arrival of a new and very special crop of young adults. Landing in Paris, the adopted home of exiled Lost intellectuals, "Lucky Lindy" didn't seem one bit alienated or debauched. President Coolidge dispatched a navy cruiser to bring home the young pilot—to 18,000 tons of confetti, the Congressional Medal of Honor, and the first-ever designation as an "all-American hero." Dutifully modest about his exploits, he startled (and pleased) elders by turning down lucrative movie offers. A decade later, Lindy's depression-era peers were busy planting trees and building dams and bridges—and, a few years after that, Missionary General George Marshall praised the G.I. GENERATION as "the best damned kids in the world." When these "kids" became America's first astronauts, younger generations hailed their "right stuff," *U.S. News and World Report* their "fearless but not reckless" manner. John Kennedy declared his generation's commitment to land a man on the moon by the end of the 1960s. And they did, in what Eric Hoffer proclaimed "the triumph of the squares." Throughout their lives, these G.I.s have been America's confident and rational problem-solvers: victorious soldiers and Rosie the Riveters; Nobel laureates; makers of Minuteman missiles, interstate highways, Apollo rockets, battleships, and miracle vaccines; the creators of Disney's Tomorrowland; "men's men" who have known how to get things done. Whatever they accomplished—whether organizing "big bands," swarming ashore in Normandy, or making "Bible Epic" movies, they always seemed to do it *big,* to do it *together.* Among G.I.s, says the inscription on their Iwo Jima shrine, "uncommon valor was a common virtue."

In his inaugural address, President Kennedy crisply defined his peers as "born in this century"—and, among this history-absorbed generation, many do perceive the twentieth as "their" century. The G.I. first wave (Walt Disney, Arthur Godfrey, Ronald Reagan) had more of the jaunty optimists, the last wave (Lee Iacocca, George Bush, Lloyd Bentsen) more of the clean-cut rationalists. Several scholars have suggested that the 1900 birthyear represents what Leonard Cain

G.I. GENERATION (Born 1901 to 1924)

TYPE: Civic

Total number: 63,000,000
Now alive in U.S.: 29,000,000
Percent immigrant: 9%

FAMILY TREE

Typical grandparents: Progressive
Parents: Missionary and Lost
Children: Silent and Boom
Typical grandchildren: Thirteenth

SAMPLE MEMBERS, birth (death)

1901 Walt Disney (1966)
1902 Charles Lindbergh (1974)
1902 John Steinbeck (1968)
1903 Bob Hope
1904 Robert Oppenheimer (1967)
1907 John Wayne (1979)
1907 Katharine Hepburn
1907 William Levitt
1908 John Kenneth Galbraith
1908 Jimmy Stewart
1912 Tip O'Neill
1914 Joe DiMaggio
1914 William Westmoreland
1916 Robert McNamara
1916 Walter Cronkite
1918 Billy Graham
1918 Ann Landers
1922 Judy Garland (1969)
1924 Sidney Poitier
1924 Lee Iacocca

PERIOD OF POLITICAL LEADERSHIP

Plurality in House: 1953–1975
Plurality in Senate: 1959–1979
Majority in Supreme Court: 1967–

U.S. PRESIDENTS: 1961–

1908 Lyndon B. Johnson (1973)
1911 Ronald Reagan
1913 Richard Nixon
1913 Gerald Ford
1917 John F. Kennedy (1963)
1924 Jimmy Carter
1924 George Bush

PROMINENT FOREIGN PEERS

1903 George Orwell (1950)
1906 Leonid Brezhnev (1982)
1913 Willy Brandt
1917 Ferdinand Marcos (1989)
1919 Shah Riza Pahlavi (1980)

HISTORY AND LIFECYCLE

Age	Date	
0– 9	1910:	Boy Scouts founded, followed by Girl Scouts (1912)
0–22	1923:	Rose Bowl opens; university enrollments rise sharply
3–26	1927:	Charles Lindbergh completes first transatlantic flight
8–31	1932:	Roosevelt elected with 85 percent support from voters under age 30
17–40	1941:	Pearl Harbor Sunday; all men age 20–44 subject to conscription
21–44	1945:	VE- and VJ-Day; G.I. Bill begins paying out benefits
30–53	1954:	McCarthy hearings; anticommunist witchhunt
37–60	1961:	Kennedy brings "best and brightest" into White House
41–64	1965:	LBJ plans "Great Society"; 89th Congress enacts Medicare
45–68	1969:	Apollo 11 puts man on the moon; Vietnam protests peak
50–73	1974:	Watergate scandal; stagflation; Social Security benefit levels surge
65–88	1989:	Bush, Reagan hail spread of democracy in Eastern Europe and USSR

SAMPLE CULTURAL ENDOWMENTS: *The Grapes of Wrath* (John Steinbeck); *Snow White and the Seven Dwarfs* (film, Walt Disney); *In the Mood* (Glenn Miller); *The Honeymooners* (TV show, Jackie Gleason); *The Origins of Totalitarianism* (Hannah Arendt); *West Side Story* (Leonard Bernstein); *The Making of the President: 1960* (Theodore White); *Modern Economic Growth* (Simon Kuznets); *Roots* (Alex Haley); *Profiles in Courage* (John Kennedy); *The Feminine Mystique* (Betty Friedan); *War and Remembrance* (Herman Wouk) calls a "generational watershed." Cain documents how the children born just after 1900 were much more "favored" than those born just before—in families, schools, and jobs—and how that favored treatment led to important personality differences that have lasted a lifetime. First-wave G.I.s were truly "special" kids who grew up in the most carefully shaped of twentieth-century childhoods, thanks to Missionary parents determined to produce kids as good as the Lost had been bad. From youth to old age, the babies of the century's first decade commanded the admiration (and generosity) of older and younger generations. They became America's first Boy and Girl Scouts—and, a half-century later, America's first "senior citizens." At the other boundary, the babies of 1923 and 1924 were just old enough to be drafted, trained, and shipped to Omaha Beach and Iwo Jima in time to join in the heaviest fighting; those born a year or two later were in line to fight battles that never came. That too produced personality differences that have lasted a lifetime. World War II provided last-wave G.I.s with a coming-of-age slingshot, a catharsis more heroic and em-powering than any since the American Revolution. Where World War I had cheated the optimism of youth, this war rewarded it—and implanted an enduring sense of civic virtue and entitlement. The combination of "good-kid" first-wavers and heroic last-wavers produced a generation of enormous economic and political power, what Henry Malcolm describes as a generation of "Prometheus and Adam"—a generation, as one admirer said of James Reston, that has always shared an "implicit belief in progress and in the central role of great men."

The unstoppable energy of G.I.s is well characterized in their most enduring comic strip character: Superman. Conceived by two thirtyish cartoonists, Super-man became famous just before their G.I. peers entered World War II and themselves began showing "powers and abilities beyond those of mortal men." Everything about the Superman story reads like a parable of G.I.s on the move— the special child, the corrupt older (Lost) Lex Luthor, the rocklike manliness and Formica-like blandness, the unvarying success of Supermannish strength used for community good. Can poverty be eradicated, Model Cities built, busi-ness cycles tamed, Nazis and Communists beaten? Step aside, this is a job for Superpower America—and a generation willing, in Kennedy's words, to "bear any burden, pay any price" to accomplish whatever goal it sets. No other generation this century has felt (or been) so Promethean, so godlike in its col-lective, world-bending power. Nor has any been so adept in its aptitude for science and engineering. G.I.s invented, perfected, and stockpiled the atomic bomb, a weapon so muscular it changed history forever. This intensely left-brained generation looked upon their Apollo 11 moon landing as (in Ayn Rand's words) "the embodied concretization of a single faculty of man: his rationality." Rand's peers became the consummate mid-twentieth-century "technocrats" (a word then connoting unrivaled American competence). So too did they become the nation's greatest-ever economists, social engineers, and community planners, producing what Seymour Martin Lipset in 1960 termed "the shift away from ideology toward sociology.'' ''What we need is a technology of behavior,'' urged B. F. Skinner, whose fictive utopia, *Walden Two,* epitomized his peers' lifelong (and entirely unThoreaulike) confidence that they could design and build their way to social bliss. Such a generation has had little thirst for spiritual conversion, no need for transcending to a new consciousness. Their most influential new religion has been L. Ron Hubbard's Scientology. Their most popular definition of God has been the Deity of Isaac Singer who ''speaks in deeds, in events.'' And their most enduring images of prophecy have featured Billy Graham, America's first televangelist, or Charlton Heston throwing bolts of lightning before a cast of thousands. ''We do not need American philosophers,'' remarked Daniel Boorstin in the late 1960s; to G.I.s like Boorstin, the ideology of America is ''implicit in the American way of life.''

Valuing outer life over inner, G.I.s came of age preferring crisp sex-role definitions. Raised under the influence of the strongly pro-feminist Missionaries, G.I.s matured into a father-worshiping and heavily male-fixated generation. As rising adults, they came to disdain womanish influences on public life. ''Gentlemen, mom is a jerk,'' wrote Philip Wylie in his best-selling *Generation of Vipers,* a book published in the same year (1942) that Army psychiatrists were themselves complaining how badly Army recruits had been overmothered in the years before the war. ''It was suddenly discovered that the mother could be blamed for everything,'' Betty Friedan later recalled. After the war, G.I.-authored books like *Modern Woman: The Lost Sex* and *Educating Our Daughters* launched what historian Carl Degler terms ''a frontal assault on all feminist assumptions.'' Before Friedan defrocked the (mostly G.I.) ''Feminine Mystique'' in 1963, her male peers had succeeded in creating a *Father Knows Best* culture and a political vocabulary whose greatest ''witchhunt'' insults (''simpering,'' ''cringing,'' ''slobbering'') were challenges against virility. The G.I.s' rift with their own children arose, in substantial part, from the refusal of Boomer youths to accept the exaggerated masculinity of G.I. fathers. Even through the social calm of the 1980s, G.I. maleness has rankled younger women, provoking a political ''gender gap'' that has been more generational than partisan. Like Ronald Reagan, the classic G.I. man feels little guilt—and like John Kennedy, he believes that ''a man does what he must.'' Consider their Hollywood honor roll: Bob Hope, John Wayne, Bing Crosby, Burt Lancaster, Kirk Douglas, Henry Fonda, Sidney Poitier, Jimmy Stewart, Gregory Peck. Turn on the camera, let a G.I. be a G.I., and—like Robert Mitchum's ''Pug Henry'' in Herman Wouk's *War and Remembrance*—he'll get the job done.

The initials ''G.I.'' can stand for two things—''general issue'' and ''government issue''—and this generation's lifecycle has stood squarely for both. All their lives, G.I.s have placed a high priority on being ''general'' or ''regular'' (as in ''he's a regular guy''), since regularity is a prerequisite for being effective ''team players.'' They developed this instinct young, building in high school and college what historian Paula Fass labels a "peer society"—a harmonious community of group-enforced virtue. As children, they were nurtured to believe that anything standardized and prepackaged was more likely to be wholesome. When they came of age, President Roosevelt remarked with delight how "the very objectives of young people have changed": away from "the dream of the golden ladder—each individual for himself" and toward the dream of "a broad highway on which thousands of your fellow men and women are advancing with you." Later, G.I. collegialism energized America's V-for-victory wartime mood. Highways that had once teemed with frivolous auto traffic now channeled mile-long convoys of powerful, identical-looking military vehicles. After the war, the peer society reached its pinnacle in the postwar suburban society, with its "Wonder Bread" blandness, its "Spic and Span" kitchens, and its borrow-a-mower neighborliness. While the Ozzies and Harriets were busy constructing the most conformist culture of the twentieth century, Richard Nixon and Joe McCarthy launched a purge of Alger Hiss, the Hollywood Ten, and other G.I.s who had earlier espoused a conformist ideology of the wrong (Soviet) variety. "Anticommunism" thus became a post–World War II bugaboo among a generation that, within itself, has always had a strong collectivist reflex. Even during the McCarthy hearings, G.I.s on both sides of the table dressed in the same gray suits—and after each day's adjournment, no doubt went home to watch the same TV shows in houses Malvina Reynolds memorialized as "little boxes . . . made out of ticky-tacky/ And they all look just the same."

Likewise, their personality has carried a strong "government issue" flavor. The G.I. lifecycle has shown an extraordinary association with the growth of modern government activity, much of it directed toward whatever phase of life they occupied. When G.I.s were young, government protected them from people and things that could hurt them. When they were coming of age, government gave them jobs. When they were rising adults, government provided them with numerous preferential advantages in education, employment, and family formation. When they were in midlife, they benefited from tax cuts and an economy run full throttle. When they reached elderhood, they received newly generous pensions and subsidized medical care—and gained more than others from deficit-laden financing schemes that pushed costs far into the future. Not surprisingly, G.I.s have always regarded government as their benefactor, almost like a buddy who has grown up right alongside them. They have been what historian Joseph Goulden describes as "a generation content to put its trust in government and authority," a generation that instinctively abides by the will of the "community," what President Bush describes as "a beautiful word with big meaning." People of other ages have always seen civic virtue in this generation—and, as a consequence, G.I.s have been the beneficiary of an unmatched flow of payments and other kindnesses from people older and younger than they.

G.I.s have regarded their own civic-mindedness as proof of American exceptionalism, a belief (in the words of Daniel Bell) that "having been born free, America would in the trials of history get off scot free." Even in old age, this great generation of "doers" believes (like 73-year-old Ronald Reagan in 1985) that America always stands "on the threshold of a great ability to produce more, do more, be more." Whatever G.I.s together accomplish in the exercise of citizenship, they think, must by definition be good for all generations. In this hubris has come more than a little miscalculation and disappointment, in both public and family lives. But G.I.s have never stopped trying to make things work. From "Lucky Lindy" to "Joltin' Joe," "Happy Hubert" to "the Teflon President," this generation has spent a lifetime personifying the irrepressibility of modern America. "Despair comes hard to us," says Eda LeShan, "for it was unfamiliar in our growing." None can match G.I.s for knowing how to *Ac-Cent-Tchu-Ate the Positive*—for better or worse. In 1988, when 80-year-old physicist Edward Teller testified in support of the Strategic Defense Initiative, younger congressmen asked him whether "Star Wars" would in fact work as intended. This G.I. father of the H-bomb testily answered the nitpickers: "Let me plead guilty to the great crime of optimism."

G.I. Facts

• From first wave to last, the G.I.s have been a generation of trends—always in directions most people (certainly their Missionary elders) thought for the better: lower rates of suicide and crime, higher aptitudes, greater educational attainment, increased voter participation, and rising confidence in government.

• Throughout the G.I. lifecycle, the federal government has directed its attention to whatever age bracket the G.I.s have occupied. The childhood years of first-wave G.I.s were marked by the first White House Conference on Children (1909), the creation of the U.S. Children's Bureau (1912), and the first federal child labor law (1916). The elder years of first-wave G.I.s were marked by the first White House Conference on Aging (1961), the first federal age-discrimination law (1967), and the creation of the National Institute on Aging (1974). The entire modern growth in government spending has coincided with the duration of their adult lifecycle. When a G.I. born in 1910 turned 19, the federal government consumed less than 3 percent of the nation's economic product; when he reached age 70, it consumed over 22 percent.

• The rate of child labor fell by half during the G.I. youth era—the largest one-generation decline ever. These were the first boys and girls whose pin money came from "allowances" for good behavior, not from earnings. They put three-fourths of their allowance money into school supplies, church boxes, or savings. From the mid-1920s to the early 1930s, the proportion of youths doing the family dishes rose from 32 to 52 percent, even as more adults remained at home.

- In most measures of health, the G.I.s have shown a swifter improvement over their next-elders than any other American generation. From the 1900 to 1924 cohorts, infant and child mortality fell by 50 percent, adult height rose by over one inch, and life expectancy at age 65 rose by 20 percent. Raised on pasteurized milk, safely packaged foods, and "vitamins," coming-of-age G.I.s did indeed appear to Missionary and Lost elders as the brawny, world-moving youths shown in WPA murals.

- G.I.s produced by far the largest one-generation jump in educational achievement in American history. From Lost to G.I., the average length of schooling rose from the ninth-grade level to the twelfth, the share of 20-year-olds attending college tripled, and math and science aptitudes rose sharply. Meanwhile, the proportion of high school students taking foreign languages fell from a pre–World War I peak of 83 percent to a World War II–era low of 21 percent. On campus, religious or "missionary" organizations experienced a sharp decline in memberships during the 1920s—and practically disappeared during the 1930s.

- Nearly the entire array of modern scouting organizations were founded by midlife Missionaries just when first-wave G.I.s were reaching puberty: Boy Scouts (1910), Camp Fire Girls (1910), Girl Scouts (1912), and 4-H Clubs (1914). From their scouting days forward, G.I.s have been the most uniformed generation in American history. As young adults, 2.5 million wore the CCC forest green. Nearly half of all G.I. men wore a military uniform in wartime—the highest proportion for any American generation.

- While the best-known Lost heroes were individuals (Eddie Rickenbacker, Jimmy Doolittle), the enduring G.I. heroes have been collective (the flag-raisers at Iwo Jima, the Boys of D-Day, the Seabees). Knute Rockne and George Gipp were Lost, the "Four Horsemen" G.I.s.

- From the 1930s forward, the G.I.s have been the only generation to support the winning candidate in every election. In all three close elections (1948, 1960, and 1968), G.I.s tipped the outcome to their preferred candidate. Surveys show that 80 percent of all first-wave G.I. voters opted for Franklin Roosevelt in 1932 and 85 percent in 1936, the largest single-generation mandates ever recorded. Last-wave G.I.s congealed into the core of the postwar New Deal coalition; by midlife and elderhood, 65 percent of them confirmed an allegiance to the Democratic Party (though they often voted for Republican G.I. Presidents). G.I.s also included the first generation of blacks to abandon the Party of Lincoln: In 1944, 82 percent of Harlem blacks under age 44 voted for FDR, versus only 59 percent over that age.

• G.I.s have held the White House for thirty years, won nine Presidential elections, and run on major-party tickets twelve straight times (spanning the forty-four years between 1944 and 1988). No other generation except the Republicans comes close to any of these numbers.

• G.I.s have won ninety-nine Nobel Prizes, roughly two-thirds of all the Nobels ever awarded to Americans. They have thoroughly dominated the prizes in physics, chemistry, and medicine, and (through 1989) have won all of America's fourteen economics Nobels. However, other generations have eclipsed G.I.s in literature and peace prizes.

• G.I.s have experienced the "American Dream" of upward mobility and rising homeownership more than any other generation this century, and perhaps ever. Six in seven G.I.s report having fared better financially than their parents, the highest proportion ever recorded. In 1940, 46 percent of American houses were owner-occupied; by 1960, the proportion had risen to 64 percent—roughly where it has remained ever since. New houses were never more affordable than in the early 1950s, when the typical 35-year-old's income was $3,000 per year, mortgage rates were 4 percent, and a new Levittown home sold for $7,000 ($350 down and $30 per month).

• Relative to younger generations, G.I.s have been by far the most affluent elders of the twentieth century. Where Lost elders (in 1960) had the highest poverty rate of any age bracket, G.I.s (today) have the lowest, when all public benefits are included as income. G.I. elders tower over younger adults in rates of homeownership and health-insurance coverage, and in average dollars of discretionary income and household net worth. In 1988, 47 percent of G.I.s "almost never" worry about finances, making theirs the least worrying of living generations.

• G.I. first-wavers sparked the modern "senior citizen" movement, and G.I. last-wavers have benefited the most from it. America's first (and now largest) retirement community, Sun City, was founded in 1960. The Social Security retirement age was lowered to age 62 for men in 1962. Medicare was founded in 1965. The largest rise in Social Security benefit levels occurred between 1972 and 1981. The membership of elder organizations (and the circulation of "senior" newspapers) grew sixtyfold between the early 1960s and the late 1970s. By 1990, the American Association of Retired Persons had become the largest and wealthiest advocacy organization in the nation's history.

- Through the 1950s and early 1960s—when the Lost were reaching age 65—federal benefits per elderly person rose less rapidly than the average wage. From 1965 to 1989—as G.I.s have reached age 65—federal benefits per elderly person have risen fifteen times more rapidly than wages (300 percent versus less than 20 percent, in inflation-adjusted dollars). In 1989, total federal benefits averaged over $14,000 per elderly household. Social Security and Medicare benefits have paid back most G.I.s for the entire value of their prior payroll tax contributions (including employer contributions and interest) within four years after retiring. The 1990 deficit reduction law imposed a 1991 maximum of $41 in extra Medicare charges per G.I. beneficiary, and up to $2,137 in extra Medicare taxes per younger worker.

- Entering old age, G.I.s have remained the most upbeat (or, as they would put it, "copacetic") generation of their time. Between 1957 and 1976, the share of elderly scoring "very high" on a psychological scale of anxiety fell from 22 to 15 percent (while the corresponding share for younger age brackets rose sharply). Recent polls show people over age 65 comprising America's "happiest" age bracket. In a 1990 poll taken of the surviving Harvard Class of 1940—whose median net worth is $865,000—88 percent insisted that they were "fairly or very happy." Their happiness was of this world, not the next: 41 percent reported that they were "not religious at all."

The G.I. Lifecycle

YOUTH: In 1904, muckraker John Spargo's *The Bitter Cry of the Children* augured the determination of Missionaries in their thirties and forties to do better for a new generation, to join forces and seal off the child's world from urban danger and adult vice. In government and family life, Missionaries began building what Emmett Holt called "antiseptic" child environments. New vitamin-rich diets and anti-hookworm campaigns promoted the cause of child health. A "milk station" movement culminated in widespread pasteurization, while Little Mothers' Leagues advised parents, "Don't give the baby beer to drink." (Indeed, a major purpose of Prohibition itself was to push alcohol away from the presence of children.) Thanks to the "protective food" movement, capital investment in food processing grew faster than that of any other industry between 1914 and 1929. Businesses that had once exploited children with impunity now found themselves facing public outcry and legal punishment. Missionaries were determined to see their offspring grow up as "clean-cut" as the world being created for them. From *Pollyanna* to *Little Orphan Annie,* popular literature idealized children who were modest, cheerful, and deferential to adults. As the *Literary Digest* demanded "a reassertion of parental authority," Missionary parents proclaimed the first Mother's Day (in 1908) and Father's Day (in 1910), and founded new scouting organizations to redirect the "gang instinct" to useful purpose. Armies of young scouts learned to help others, do things in teams, develop group pride, and show respect to adults—in short, to show virtues seldom seen in the circa-1900 Lost street urchins. Public education showed a parallel interest in instilling the skills of productive citizenship. Most of the "progressive" Lost-era experiments were replaced by a new emphasis on "vocational" education ("home economics" for girls, "industrial education" for boys). For the first time ever, more teens were in class than out, making school an important socializing force. Thus arose the golden era of the high school, well captured in the teen-movie musicals of Mickey Rooney and Judy Garland. The ethos: Work hard, play by the rules, and everybody gets a reward.

Upon reaching adolescence, the new youths began building the peer society they would retain through life. Adults encouraged kids to police themselves, though always under a resolute grip of adult authority that grew tighter with each advancing decade. According to historian Daniel Rodgers, parents "injected a new, explicit insistence on conformity into child life." Starting at a very young age, kids learned to be sharers and helpers. (Two-year-old George Bush acquired the nickname "Have-Half" because he liked to give half his presents to his elder brother.) In an increasingly standardized youth culture, teens watched the same movies, listened to the same radio songs, and packed the Rose Bowl and other new 100,000-seat stadia to cheer the same sporting events. Having "fine friends" and a busy extracurricular life became more important than getting higher grades than other students. Fraternities and sororities imposed rigid pressures on youths to stay within the bounds of the normal, and administered a ritual of "rating and dating" (understood lists of "dos and don'ts") to control the libido. Those who were too forward or too shy faced peer disapproval, as did those who did not engage in "fair play" (a notion the Lost, at like age, would have found bizarre). Youths began taking pride in their ability to achieve as a group, to fulfill the 4-H Club motto and "make the best better." By the mid-1920s, the word "kid" shifted in meaning from a word of elder criticism to one of praise. The Lost Joseph Krutch described his juniors as "not rebellious, or cynical, or even melancholy. They do what they are told, believe what they are told, and hope for the best." The Lost Malcolm Cowley remarked how the "brilliant college graduates" of the 1920s "pictured a future in which everyone would be made secure by collective planning and social discipline."

COMING OF AGE: "Ours was the best generation," Gene Shuford said of the late 1920s, contrasting his circle with Cowley's. "Underneath we really thought we were all right; that man in general was all right." Within a few years, Shuford's "best" found themselves part of what *Harper's* magazine described as the "Locked-Out Generation" of the Great Depression, "all dressed up with no place to go." Even so, the youth spirit stayed high. With its emphasis on planning, optimism, and collective action, Roosevelt's New Deal perfectly suited the mind-set of twentyish men and women. The National Youth Administration and Civilian Conservation Corps kept them busy: marching in formation, never complaining, getting things done, building things that worked, things that have lasted to this day. When President Roosevelt reshuffled the economic deck in favor of the aggressive young over the positioned old, polls showed God running behind FDR in popularity among youths. "I promise as a good American citizen to do my part for the NRA," chanted 100,000 young people on Boston Common in 1933 (at the urging of James Curley, the city's Missionary mayor). "I will help President Roosevelt bring back good times." But the sluggish economy deferred many a career and marriage, prompting rising student interest in an "apple-pie radicalism" more economic than cultural or moral. Even the most committed ideologues agreed with their FDR-backing peers that the main argument was over what system "worked" best. One young communist bulletin defended its members as "no different from other people except that we believe in dialectical materialism."

Collective action flourished, especially among unionizing young workers in assembly-line industries. In the winter and spring of 1936–1937, nearly half a million engaged in sit-down strikes, prodded by the new G.I.-dominated Congress of Industrial Organizations. From Charles Lindbergh's autobiographical *We* to Mary McCarthy's *The Group,* the 1930s became, for budding writers and artists, what historian Warren Susman labeled "the decade of participation and belonging." Young novelists like John Steinbeck (in *Grapes of Wrath*) shunned the Lost cynicism and instead looked forward to solving problems, especially with the aid of big government. In 1938, 37-year-old Walt Disney released a smash box-office hit, *Snow White and the Seven Dwarfs,* that featured innocent maidenhood and cheerful male teamwork ("whistle while you work") defeating the designs of a brooding witch. Lost critic Westbrook Pegler praised the film as "the happiest thing that has happened in this world since the Armistice." But another Lost writer, Sinclair Lewis, suggested in *It Can't Happen Here* how fascism could indeed "happen here" if this new youth mood ever burst from its harness.

Enter World War II. The movie *From Here to Eternity* portrays prewar soldiers evolving into the selfish "lone wolves" despised by most 20-year-olds. Then Japan attacks—and, instantly, the soldiers forget their personal feuds and rally together into machinelike action. That is indeed what Pearl Harbor did for this generation, galvanizing "good kid" ingot into G.I. steel. While G.I. scientists in their late thirties designed the atomic bomb, marines in their twenties swarmed ashore, soon followed by the bulldozers of the Seabees. (Their motto: "The difficult we do at once; the impossible takes a bit longer.") Like-aged Rosie the Riveters comprised the only mostly female industrial workforce in the nation's history. The young generation repeatedly expressed admiration for the elders who were leading them to victory. Roosevelt was "the man we had grown up under,'' said *Yank* magazine of the Missionary "Commander in Chief, not only of the armed forces, but of our generation.'' While Mary Martin sang *My Heart Belongs to Daddy,* Bing Crosby marched with his combat buddies to the tune of "We'll follow the old man wherever he wants to go.'' In the public eye, these kids in khaki could do no wrong. The Lost General Patton's famous slap of a younger soldier caused a huge fuss back home largely because of disbelief that a G.I. might have had it coming. World War II killed 1.5 percent of G.I. men; among the 97 percent who emerged from the war years without serious injury, the experience gave men the chance (as Margaret Mead later put it) to "experience dangers that would test their mettle . . . among their peers.'' Many would never again know such responsibility, excitement, or triumph. Emerging as world conquerors, they laid claim to a heroism that, later in life, would blossom into a sense of entitlement.

RISING ADULTHOOD: "A good job, a mild future, and a little house big enough for me and my wife.'' That was the ambition of a homecoming G.I. in *The Best Years of Our Lives.* Not since the Revolution had war veterans enjoyed such praise and tangible reward from appreciative elders. Thanks to the "G.I. Bill,'' two of every five 1950-era dollars of outstanding housing debt were covered by taxpayers, many of them older and living in housing worse than what young veterans could buy. Capital spending and real wages for young men boomed—while payroll deductions to support Social Security retirees remained miniscule. Returning war heroes brought a mature, no-nonsense attitude wherever they went—to campuses, to workplaces, to politics. Polls showed young adults more stern-minded than elders on such topics as the Japanese occupation, the use of poison gas, and corporal punishment. Those who entered politics in the late 1930s and 1940s felt a scout leader's sense of duty (like Jimmy Stewart in *Mr. Smith Goes to Washington*) to clean up a greasy Lost world and energize the nation. By 1950, one G.I. (Dewey) had twice run for President, two others (Clark Clifford, George Kennan) had become President Truman's top advisers, and several more (John Kennedy, Richard Nixon, Lyndon Johnson, Gerald Ford) had launched promising political careers. In business, their peers brought their wartime confidence and "high hopes'' into the nation's economic life. Everything they made seemed to be the best (and biggest) in the world. Stephen Bechtel's company erected Hoover Dam and the San Francisco–Oakland Bay Bridge, Robert Moses built massive public housing projects, and William Levitt laid down one gleaming suburban tract after another. Bell & Howell's dynamic young president, Charles Percy, symbolized the new breed of smart, get-things-done industrialists, while two brilliant fortyish executives (Bob McNamara, Lee Iacocca) prodded the American auto industry to produce more functional autos. From *Fortune* writers to the Committee on Economic Development, 40-year-olds of both political parties agreed that big government and big business could both "pitch in'' and work together just fine.

In *The Organization Man,* William Whyte catalogued the suburban G.I. "social ethic" that produced neighborhoods noteworthy mainly for their "friendliness." Like Sloan Wilson's hero in *Man in the Gray Flannel Suit,* the ideal male was at once hard-striving and selfless, the ideal female the devoted mother of a flock of Boom kids. Soon no suburban house was complete without television, a new technology that perfectly expressed the G.I. culture: science tamed for man's benefit, unremittingly upbeat, nurturing children, helping adults keep abreast of collegial tastes. A memorable collection of fortyish entertainers— Lucille Ball, Phil Silvers, Jack Paar, Jackie Gleason, Art Linkletter—showed an unrehearsed, on-air comfort that other TV generations have never quite matched. From Hollywood to Levittown, G.I.s were hard at work institutionalizing the most wholesome American culture of the twentieth century. "We do not engage in loose talk about the 'ideals' of the situation and all the other stuff," observed C. Wright Mills in *The Power Elite.* "We get right down to the problem." Declaring the *End to Ideology* (a phrase coined by G.I.s in 1955), Daniel Bell noted how his peers wanted to overcome real-world challenges, not explore differences in fundamental values. George Gallup defined the "average man" in a society more eager to celebrate sameness than differences among people. The rising black intelligentsia (Ralph Ellison, Richard Wright) lent a cool rationalism to race relations; blacks began arguing (and whites agreeing) that "segregation" was economically inefficient. Whatever his color, a G.I. generally considered the "what to dos" well-settled; only the "how to dos" were open to discussion. In 1958, as John Kenneth Galbraith bemoaned "public squalor" amid "private opulence," his generation began its surge to power in a Democratic landslide. As the 1960s approached, G.I.s waited impatiently for their chance to bring the same friendliness, energy, and competence to public life that they had already brought to the economy and family. Their only worry, admitted Lipset in 1960, was "the problem of conformity which troubles so many Americans today"—a G.I. trait already drawing barbs from the younger Silent.

MIDLIFE: The G.I. rise to national leadership was shaped by the mission they recalled from their childhood: to clean up the squalor and decay left behind by the Lost. Maxwell Taylor criticized *The Uncertain Trumpet* of Lost Presidencies, Eric Sevareid accused the "last generation" of "corruptibility" and a "lack of controlled plans," and John Kennedy complained that "what our young men saved, our diplomats and President have frittered away." When the watershed all-G.I. Presidential election of 1960 arrived, a mannish generation in its forties and fifties was determined to apply its "common political faith" to rebuild American "prestige," to make the nation (in Bell's words) "a world power, a paramount power, a hegemonic power." A few surviving Missionaries, like Robert Frost at Kennedy's inaugural, heralded the coming of a new "Augustan Age." Having campaigned with the slogan "Let's Get This Country

Moving Again,'' the new President declared that "the torch has been passed to a new generation . . . tempered by war, disciplined by a hard and bitter peace.'' In office, he brought "vigor" to governance and assembled like-aged advisers whom the younger David Halberstam described as "a new breed of thinker-doers"—men like Bob McNamara ("the can-do man in the can-do society, in the can-do era") and McGeorge Bundy (possessing "a great and almost relentless instinct for power"). Meanwhile, the G.I. literary and media elite joined in as team players (Walter Cronkite, Chet Huntley and David Brinkley, Joseph and Stewart Alsop, Joseph Kraft, William Manchester, Arthur Schlesinger, Jr., Theodore White). In 1962, Richard Rovere christened a new expression, "the establishment,'' to describe the new power of midlife G.I.s. John Kennedy's assassination hardly caused them to break pace. The ebullient Lyndon Johnson promptly declared: "This nation, this generation, in this hour has man's first chance to build a Great Society.'' In the ensuing 1964 landslide, his G.I. peers reached their pinnacle of power. The "Great 89th" Congress (74 percent G.I.) became what Theodore White termed "the Grandfather Congress of Programs and Entitlements.'' G.I. confidence—and hubris—was at an all-time high.

"Americans today bear themselves like victory-addicted champions,'' said *Look* magazine in 1965. "They've won their wars and survived their depressions. They are accustomed to meeting, and beating, tests.'' With America now led by a generation intent on meeting and beating new tests, the word "crisis" (what Richard Nixon termed "exquisite agony") repeatedly energized the task of government. Two years earlier, the Cuban Missile Crisis had climaxed when, in Dean Rusk's words, we were "eyeball to eyeball, and I think the other fellow just blinked.'' Next came Vietnam. Robert McNamara's new "controlled response" strategy replaced what had been known as the (Lost-era) "spasm" response. But Vietnam helped trigger an angry "generation gap" between G.I. parents and coming-of-age Boomers, along with urban riots, a crime wave, substance abuse, eroticism, and ideological passion—in short, everything hateful to the G.I. life mission. By the late 1960s, whatever G.I.s tried (whether "Model Cities'' or "guns and butter" economics) began to sputter. From Johnson and Nixon in the White House to bosses on the job and fathers in families, G.I. men came under constant attack from juniors and, increasingly, women. If the times were euphoric for youth, they were anything but for G.I.s: "Everything seemed to come unhinged" (James MacGregor Burns); "Something has gone sour, in teaching and in learning" (George Wald); "I use the phrase soberly: The nation disintegrates" (John Gardner). In words that revealed his peers' frustration, Richard Nixon despaired that America had become "a pitiful, helpless giant.'' Many (Rusk, William Westmoreland, Walt Rostow) refused to admit error. Others (McNamara, Bundy) came to share Milton Mayer's view that "we were wrong, and the new generation is right"—although, Mayer added, "the young terrify me.''

ELDERHOOD: Ask today's seniors what movie touched them most as youths, and many will answer *Lost Horizon,* a depression-era film with a disturbing message about aging: that it is hideous and ugly, something that shouldn't happen in a civic-minded community. In a 1946 poll, G.I.s showed the highest generational support for human euthanasia. Through the 1950s, G.I.s often looked upon the old Lost as tired, defeatist, and anti-progress. They vowed not to grow old the same way. Later on, when they entered elderhood themselves, they attacked what they termed the "myths" of a lonely, Lost-like old age— and worked hard to be ever-optimistic, ever-energetic "senior citizens." Today, G.I.s rankle at younger people who assume they are unhappy; indeed, a majority insist that their present phase of life is the best. Where Missionaries are remembered for dressing dark (as though in church), G.I.s make a point of dressing bright (as though at play). As they listen to old "swing" music on "Music of Your Life" radio, they dwell in what they freely admit is a "square," even "corny" culture—a culture that admits neither to loneliness nor to suffering. *Modern Maturity* magazine will not accept ads that mention "pain, inflammation, suffer, hurt, ache, and flare-up" because, says a publishing director, "it's pretty hard to present" these things "in an upbeat way."

Under prodding from younger generations, G.I.s have separated into an elder version of the same peer society they first built in their youth. After leaving the labor force at a younger age than any earlier generation, they entered an active and publicly subsidized retirement. Part of the implicit terms under which the G.I.-Boom generation gap eased in the early 1970s was through an understanding by which the post-Vietnam fiscal "peace dividend" was spent almost entirely on G.I. retirees. In 1972, the first election in which gray-lobby activism became critical, candidates Wilbur Mills and Richard Nixon abandoned their prior opposition to COLA inflation indexing. Congress added an extra 20 percent benefit hike, producing a two-year jump in intergenerational transfer payments that dwarfed the total size of Great Society poverty programs. Over the last two decades, while G.I.s have noted the Boomers' weaker commitment to the spirit of community, these seniors have themselves surrendered to much of the self-orientation they see around them. Only a few (like Maggie Kuhn's Gray Panthers) have adopted the confrontational "me first" Boomer tone. Instead, the "we first" senior citizen movement has applied the same patience, organizational know-how, and teamwork that G.I.s have always carried through life—though now with a new agenda and with bottom-line results that few other generations could ever hope for. "You've already paid most of your dues. Now start collecting the benefits," reads a 1988 AARP membership appeal. So they have: Half of all federal spending is now consumed by pensions, other elderly entitlements, and interest on the national debt—the last representing the burden of today's unfunded consumption on tomorrow's taxpayers. During the 1980s, retiree benefits remained the one area of government which no G.I. President or Silent Congress dared to touch. Likewise, deficit spending has become the one fiscal device which finds few visceral critics among the generation that came of age during the New Deal. Where Lost elders once preferred to attack public spending and leave taxes alone, G.I. elders lean the other way and have provided the core of the modern tax revolt, from Ronald Reagan and Howard Jarvis (of California's Proposition 13) to the rank-and-file memberships of national antitax lobbies.

Their rising affluence has enabled them to separate socially into America's first "seniors only" communities, often far away from their grown-up children. There G.I.s show a vigor and cheerfulness that bring to mind the best of their 1950s-era culture. In Sun City, observes Boomer gerontologist Ken Dychtwald, "it's hard to find time to talk to people; they're too active and busy." "Sun City is secure," he concludes. "A resident may stroll the streets without fear of surprise, of unpleasantness, or unsightliness. The streets are uncommonly clean." And, adds one resident, "I don't know where I could go that I could get so involved with the community." Similarly, the G.I.s' material well-being has enabled them to continue in their accustomed roles as trustees of wealth, givers of gifts, accepters of collect phone calls—and providers (or backstops) for their extended families. No elder generation has ever been so relied upon to foot the bill for family indulgences. In 1987 and 1988, grandparents accounted for 25 percent of all toy purchases—and a rapidly growing share of their *grand*-children's educational expenses. Nor has any elder generation made more down payments to enable its grown children to buy houses which, back in the 1950s, G.I.s could easily afford without parental help. (For today's young adults, reports *Time* magazine, the "G.I. benefit" has now come to mean "Good In-laws.") Among elder G.I.s whose children have divorced, 30 percent report that the newly single son or daughter soon arrives on their doorstep. But if Silent and Boom children frequently ask for G.I. assistance with economic problems, they do not seek elder help nearly so often on questions of values or basic life direction.

The G.I. role as powerful stewards of American material life has left them feeling more friendly than wise—more comfortable keeping active themselves than inspiring the young to action. "In our time as children, grandparents were the teachers, advisors, counselors," Eda LeShan remembers of a social function from which her own peers "have been robbed completely." As anthropologist Dorian Apple has found in cultures throughout the world, "indulgent grand-parents are associated with societies . . . where grandparents are dissociated with authority." Erik Erikson's wife and collaborator, Joan, recently observed how "when we looked at the lifecycle in our forties, we looked to old people for wisdom." Now, she laments, "lots of old people don't get wise." Whatever wisdom G.I.s do have to offer, they lack the pulpit to proclaim it, owing to their early retirement and the recent Boom takeover of positions in the media. A 1989 survey found not a single prominent journalist over age 65 at work in an American newsroom.

In public life, the last prominent G.I.s assert power more than principle—
"better with deeds than with plans or words," to use (the Silent) Senator Lautenberg's description of George Bush, then busy ordering ships and planes and
tanks to the Persian Gulf. In family life, their worldly style of grandparenting
leaves them troubled by what Dychtwald describes as a "lack of respect and
appreciation." From the Oval Office to the family dinner table, elder G.I.s often
feel they don't get enough personal deference from young people—certainly not
what they remember offering their own elder Missionary parents.

* * *

"We've done the work of democracy, day by day," George Bush proudly
declared of his generation in 1989. Whatever G.I.s touched, they made bigger—
and, in their eyes, better. Their accomplishments have been colossal. G.I.s
patiently endured an economic despair that might have driven another generation
to revolution. They ably soldiered the one war America could not afford to lose.
Thanks to their powerful work ethic and willingness to invest, they produced a
postwar economic miracle that ultimately outperformed their communist rivals.
Their massive stockpiles of nuclear weapons preserved an enduring if expensive
and unnerving peace. They have been a truly great generation of scientists,
landing men on the moon and cracking the riddles of human longevity. Their
women may have been the most dedicated teachers and most skillful mothers in
American history. In countless ways, from transistors and satellites to spacious
family homes and a buoyant "GNP" (a term they invented), G.I.s gave institutional firmament to the "Brotherhood of Man" envisioned by their beloved
Missionary fathers. In recent years, news of the retirement or death of G.I.
notables has often prompted remarks from Americans of all ages that no one
will be able to replace their competence.

Yet their final ledger will also include colossal debits: unprecedented public
and private liabilities, exported assets, depleted resources, harms to the global
environment. The generation that inherited so much excess economic capacity
and harnessed it to so many public purposes is bequeathing to its successors a
fiscally starved economy unable to afford a new national agenda. The offspring
of the soldiers the G.I.s conquered—Japanese and German—are today outcom-
peting their own children and eclipsing American economic might. The powerful
G.I. sense of exceptionalism makes them think their constructions can last forever, that Reaganomics-style optimism can produce its own reward. But those
early-in-life virtues—selflessness, investment, and community—have given way
to the repetition of old habits without the old purposes and without the old focus
on the future. To G.I.s, Tomorrowland once meant monorails and moonwalks;
now it means space-age medicine in the intensive-care unit. With their time
coming to a close, G.I.s have difficulty articulating what Bush calls "the vision
thing"—setting directions for a new century many will not live to see. From
George Kennan to Lillian Hellman, Eric Sevareid to Theodore White, Ann
Landers to Ronald Reagan, elder G.I.s voice distress over the steady loss in the

American sense of community in the hands of the young. Back when they ran the "general issue" culture, everything in America seemed to fit together constructively. Now, to their eyes, it doesn't. And they worry about how they will be remembered.

In *It's a Wonderful Life,* a Lost-directed testimonial to G.I.s, Jimmy Stewart despairs at the worthlessness of his deeds until an older man shows him how, had he never lived, his town would have sunk to "Pottersville"—a corrupt, pleasure-seeking, Lost-style abyss. Returning home, Stewart saves his government-subsidized savings and loan business thanks to gifts from young and old, repaying him for all the wonderful things he has done over his life. Contrast this with the G.I. image in the Boom-directed *Cocoon:* senior citizens draining the strength of unborn aliens, and then flying off to immortality while leaving their own children behind. Yet *Cocoon* presents G.I.s in such a warm light that this ghastly behavior seems perfectly natural, as though such friendly people deserve special treatment no matter what it costs the young. No one likes to think of today's senior citizens as selfish, least of all themselves. They would rather just stand firm in the "collective positiveness" suggested by Hubert Pryor of *Modern Maturity* in his 1989 essay "Goodbye to Our Century."

On May 5, 1990, Bob Gilbert and other seventyish veterans rode a motorcade down the streets of Plzen past thousands of Czechs waving American flags under a huge banner reading THANK YOU BOYS. As Gilbert's peers leave us one by one, many G.I.s probably wish they didn't have to go that way, but would prefer to go together in some heroic D-Day redux—one last civic ritual to remind everyone what they once did, as a team, for posterity.

SILENT GENERATION

Born: 1925–1942
Type: Adaptive

Age Location:
Great Depression–World War II Crisis in youth
Boom Awakening in midlife

"Forty-nine is taking no chances," *Fortune* magazine's editors wrote of the "gray flannel mentality" of that year's class of college graduates, the first to consist mainly of Americans born after 1924. "They are interested in the system rather than individual enterprise." Only 2 percent wished to be self-employed. Most of the rest wanted to work in big corporations offering job security. "Never had American youth been so withdrawn, cautious, unimaginative, indifferent, unadventurous—and silent," G.I. historian William Manchester later quipped. The SILENT GENERATION was a name these young people didn't especially like, but they knew it fit. "We had no leaders, no program, no sense of our own power, and no culture exclusively our own," admitted Frank Conroy. "Our clothing, manners and lifestyle were unoriginal—scaled-down versions of what we saw in the adults." Like Robert Morse in *How to Succeed in Business Without Really Trying,* these young grads put on their "sincere" ties, looked in the mirror—and didn't see G.I.s. Instead, they saw the date-and-mate romantics of *Peggy Sue Got Married,* sober young adults chided by one older professor as "a generation with strongly middle-aged values." G.I.s David Riesman and Nathan Glazer labeled them the "Lonely Crowd," possessing an "outer-directed" personality and taking cues from others.

Older generations first knew them as Shirley Temple and Jerry Lewis, Roy Cohn and Charles Van Doren, Ralph Nader and Bobby Kennedy—and younger generations met them as Elvis Presley and Ray Charles, Bob Dylan and Gloria Steinem, Abbie Hoffman and the Chicago Seven. In the decades since, they have aged into America's late-twentieth-century facilitators and technocrats, the Walter Mondales and Geraldine Ferraros—a consummate helpmate generation which has so far produced three decades of top Presidential aides—Pierre Salinger (for Kennedy), Bill Moyers (Johnson), John Ehrlichman (Nixon), Dick Cheney (Ford), Stuart Eizenstat (Carter), James Baker III (Reagan), and John Sununu (Bush). And three First Ladies (Jackie Kennedy, Rosalynn Carter, and Barbara Bush). *But no Presidents.*

Jeane Kirkpatrick describes hers as a generation "born twenty years too

SILENT GENERATION (Born 1925 to 1942)

TYPE: Adaptive

Total number: 49,000,000
Now alive in U.S.: 40,000,000
Percent immigrant: 9%

FAMILY TREE

Typical grandparents: Missionary
Parents: Lost and G.I.
Children: Boom and Thirteenth
Typical grandchildren: Millennial

SAMPLE MEMBERS, birth (death)

1925 William F. Buckley, Jr.
1925 Gore Vidal
1926 Marilyn Monroe (1962)
1927 Andy Warhol (1987)
1928 T. Boone Pickens, Jr.
1929 Martin Luther King, Jr. (1968)
1930 James A. Baker III
1930 Sandra Day O'Connor
1930 Clint Eastwood
1931 James Dean (1955)
1932 Andrew Young
1935 Elvis Presley (1977)
1935 Geraldine Ferraro
1935 Woody Allen
1935 Phil Donahue
1936 Abbie Hoffman (1989)
1937 Jack Nicholson
1940 Ted Koppel*
1940 Pat Schroeder
1942 Barbra Streisand
* = immigrant

PERIOD OF POLITICAL LEADERSHIP

Plurality in House: 1975–
Plurality in Senate: 1979–
Majority of Supreme Court: —

U.S. PRESIDENTS: None

PRESIDENTIAL CANDIDATES

1928 Walter Mondale
1933 Michael Dukakis
1935 Jack Kemp
1936 Gary Hart
1941 Jesse Jackson

PROMINENT FOREIGN PEERS

1926 Fidel Castro
1930 Helmut Kohl
1931 Mikhail Gorbachev
1936 Vaclav Havel
1940 John Lennon (1980)

Age	Date	HISTORY AND LIFECYCLE
0–13	1938:	*Snow White* sets box-office records as Great Depression lingers
3–20	1945:	VE-Day, VJ-Day; atomic bombs dropped; older veterans return
8–25	1950:	Korean War (1950–1953) starts; anti-Communist fear surges
12–29	1954:	McCarthyism prompts student anxiety over ''permanent records''
15–32	1957:	Sputnik in orbit; rock and roll popular; ''beat'' movement peaks
19–36	1961:	John Kennedy inaugurated, founds Peace Corps
21–38	1963:	John Kennedy assassinated; *The Feminine Mystique* published
26–43	1968:	Martin Luther King, Jr., and Robert Kennedy assassinated
27–44	1969:	Armstrong lands on moon; Chappaquiddick; divorce epidemic begins
32–49	1974:	Watergate scandal; ''Watergate babies'' elected to Congress
37–54	1979:	Peak of Carter ''malaise''; energy crisis; hostages taken in Iran
46–63	1988:	''Seven Dwarf'' candidates; Michael Dukakis loses to George Bush

SAMPLE CULTURAL ENDOWMENTS: *The Other America* (Michael Harrington);
Portnoy's Complaint (Philip Roth); *One Flew Over the Cuckoo's Nest* (Ken Kesey); *Unsafe at Any Speed* (Ralph Nader); *Cosmos* (TV series, Carl Sagan); *Heartburn* (Nora Ephron); *Ms.* magazine (Gloria Steinem); *Playboy* magazine (Hugh Hefner); *Future Shock* (Alvin Toffler); *Megatrends* (John Naisbitt); *Fatherhood* (Bill Cosby); *Sesame Street* (educational TV, Joan Ganz Cooney)

soon." Or twenty years too late. Admiral William Crowe calls his peers a
"transitional generation," Rose Franzblau a "Middle Generation," the one she
says is forever "betwixt and between." The Silent boundaries are fixed less by
what they did than by what those older and younger did—and what the Silent
themselves just missed. The first wave came of age just too late for war-era
heroism, but in time to encounter a powerful national consensus—against which
young rebels, like James Dean, found themselves "without a cause." The last
wave graduated from college just ahead of what Benita Eisler termed the "great
divide" before the fiery Boomer Class of 1965. Unlike the first Boomers, the
last of the Silent can remember World War II from their childhood, and many
of them look upon the Peace Corps as a generational bond in a way Boomers
never have. Sixteen percent of Harvard's Class of '64 joined the Peace Corps,
Harvard's top postgraduate destination for that year—whereas the next year's
graduates began criticizing the Peace Corps amid the early stirrings of the Boom's
antiestablishment rebellion.

The Silent widely realize they are the generational stuffings of a sandwich
between the get-it-done G.I. and the self-absorbed Boom. Well into their rising
adulthood, they looked to G.I.s for role models—and pursued what then looked
to be a lifetime mission of refining and humanizing the G.I.-built world. Come
the mid-1960s, the Silent found themselves "grown up just as the world's gone
teen-age" (as Howard Junker put it at the time) and fell under the trance of their
free-spirited next-juniors, the Boomers. As songwriters, graduate students, and
young attorneys, they mentored the Boom Awakening, founding several of the
organizations of political dissent their next-juniors would radicalize. "During
the ferment of the 1960s, a period of the famous 'generation gap,' we occupied,
unnoticed as usual, the gap itself," Wade Greene later recounted. "When nobody
over thirty was to be trusted, our age was thirty-something." During the 1970s,
the sexual revolution hit the Silent when most of them were passing forty, decades
after their natural adolescence. Such awkward timing caused immense problems
in their family lives and transformed them, said Franzblau in 1971, into "a
generation of jealousies and role reversals." Through the 1970s, the Silent
completed the shift from an elder-focused rising adulthood to a youth-focused
midlife—feeling, as in the Dylan lyric, "Ah, but I was so much older then / I'm
younger than that now." As women turned to feminism, men assembled a mix-
and-match masculinity out of fragments from G.I. and Boom.

The Silent lifecycle has been an outer blessing but inner curse. In *Birth and
Fortune*, demographer Richard Easterlin labeled his own peer group "the fortunate ones" whose relatively small size (per cohort) has supposedly given them
an edge on life. Yes, the Silent have enjoyed a lifetime of steadily rising affluence,
have suffered relatively few war casualties, and have shown the twentieth century's lowest rates for almost every social pathology of youth (crime, suicide,
illegitimate births, and teen unemployment). Apart from a significant number
of divorced women who never remarried, the Silent lifecycle has been an escalator

of prosperity, offering the maximum reward for the minimum initiative. No other living generation could half-believe in what Ellen Goodman terms "the Woody Allen school of philosophy: 80 percent of life is showing up." But the outward good fortune of their lifecycle has denied them a clear personal connection to the banner headlines that they see, at times enviously, so well connected to others. However much they try, the Silent have never succeeded in experiencing the snap of catharsis felt by G.I.s or Boomers. Where the G.I.s did great things and felt one with history, where Boomers found ravishment within themselves, the Silent have taken great things for granted and looked beyond themselves—while worrying that, somehow, the larger challenges of life are passing them by. And so they have been keen on manufacturing points of lifecycle reference around personal (rather than historical) markers. Whatever phase of life they occupy is fraught with what various Silent authors have labeled "passages," "seasons," "turning points," or other transitions bearing little or no relation to the larger flow of public events.

Well aware of their own deficiencies, the Silent have spent a lifetime plumbing inner wellsprings older G.I.s seldom felt while maintaining a sense of social obligation Boomers haven't shared. Their solutions—fairness, openness, due process, expertise—reflect a lack of surefootedness, but also a keen sense of how and why humans fall short of grand civic plans or ideal moral standards. Silent appeals for change have seldom arisen from power or fury, but rather through a self-conscious humanity and tender social conscience ("Deep in my heart, I do believe / We shall overcome someday"). Lacking an independent voice, they have adopted the moral relativism of the skilled arbitrator, mediating arguments between others—and reaching out to people of all cultures, races, ages, and handicaps. "We don't arrive with ready-made answers so much as a honed capacity to ask and to listen," says Greene, touting his generation's ability "to continue to bridge gaps, at a time of immense, extraordinarily complicated and potentially divisive changes." The tensions the Silent have felt in adapting to a G.I.-and-Boom-dominated society while preserving their own sensitivity have helped them appreciate the crazy twists of life—and become America's greatest generation of comedians, psychiatrists, and songwriters. Yet this very malleability has left the Silent with badly checkered family lives. "If anything has changed in the last generation," admits Ellen Goodman, "it is the erosion of confidence" among parents "openly uncertain about how we are doing."

In *Private Lives,* Benita Eisler labels hers the generation with "a corpse in the trunk"—and the biggest of those corpses is the R-rated decade of the 1970s. That era in which so much seemed to go wrong in America coincided precisely with the Silent surge to influence over national life. In *Future Shock,* the book that keynoted that decade, Alvin Toffler foresaw a forthcoming "historic crisis of adaptation"—and called for "the moderation and regulation of change" with "exact scientific knowledge, expertly applied to the crucial, most sensitive points of social control." But as Toffler's peers began applying this cult of expertise, they encountered their turbulent passage to midlife—and what Toffler labeled the "transience index" began exploding upward. As the Silent broke and remade relationships, families splintered, substance abuse moved past euphoria to social damage, and American society lost its G.I.-era sense of cohesion. As a generation of Daniel Ellsbergs pushed to get secrets out (and take clothes off), their Phil Donahues and Ted Koppels aimed microphones everywhere, hoping more dialogue would somehow build a better society. Meanwhile, productivity stagnated, the economy sputtered, and the nation endured a series of global humiliations. In *Zero-Sum Society,* Lester Thurow suggested that, increasingly, improvement in the condition of any one group came at the expense of another. What Jerry Brown called "the age of limits" became (in William Schneider's words) "the Zeitgeist theme of his generation." By the time the 1970s ended, an elder G.I. won the Presidency in part by ridiculing this midlife mind-set.

Even with Reagan at the helm, the America of the 1980s did in many ways become a Silent-style Tofflerian "ad hocracy" stressing expertise over simplicity, participation over authority, process over result. Corporations began directing more attention to organization and financing than to the products they made. Public over- and under-regulation became hot political issues, prompting *Time* magazine to play off memories of G.I. muscle by making "The Can't Do Government" the subject of a 1989 cover story. Where the word "liberal" had once referred to a G.I.-style energizer with a constructive national agenda, its meaning transformed into a Silent-style enervator attuned to multitudinous special interests. ("Beware of liberals who came of age politically in the 1950s," warns George Will.) Likewise, the definition of "conservative" evolved from a Lost-style cautious stewardship to the faintly hip, high-rolling optimism of the Silent's new supply-side school—which calls upon the nation to undergo the economic equivalent of a liberating midlife passage, full of zest and swagger and dare. As Mike Dukakis and Jack Kemp define these two new Silent credos in politics, Alan Alda and Clint Eastwood (the latter dubbed by one reviewer the "supply-side star") define them in popular culture. Neoliberal to Neoconservative, racial quotas to Laffer curves, this generation lacks a cohesive core—and fears it may be presiding over (in William Raspberry's words) "the unraveling of America."

In 1949, *Fortune* closed its report on the new crop of college graduates by asking whether they will be "so tractable and harmonious as to be incapable, twenty or thirty years hence, of making provocative decisions?" Today, forty years have passed, and many have since rephrased that question in the present tense. The nation still looks to what Greene terms "fiftysomethings" to comment and mediate, but not to lead. Americans of all ages, Silent included, have repeatedly turned back to G.I.s for a steady hand, and forward to Boomers for new values. And so the Silent have arrived on the brink of elderhood—still feeling "out of it," observes Benita Eisler, "sitting ducks for having our bluff called." Although they continue to wait for a turn at the top, they notice how younger leaders have appropriated their call to "conscience" and older leaders their "kinder and gentler" rhetoric. Having given so much to others, the Silent are beginning to wonder whether their own generation may yet have something new to offer. Or whether instead their greatest contributions have already been made.

Silent Facts

• Born mostly during an era of depression and war, the Silent were the product of a birthrate trough. They later became the only American generation to have fewer members per cohort than both the generations born just before it (G.I.) and just after it (Boom). During the 1930s, the U.S. population grew by only 7 percent, the lowest decennial growth rate in American history.

• In economic terms, the Silent lifecycle has been a straight line from a cashless childhood to the cusp of affluent elderhood—the smoothest and fastest-rising path of any generation for which income data are available. In the immediate postwar years, barely 1 percent of youths between 10 and 15 were in the labor force—the lowest child labor force participation rate of the twentieth century. From age 20 to 40, Silent households showed this century's steepest rise in real per capita income and per-household wealth.

• The Silent were the earliest-marrying and earliest-babying generation in American history. Men married at an average age of 23, women at 20. The 1931–1935 female cohorts were the most fertile of the twentieth century; 94 percent of them became mothers, who bore an average of 3.3 children (versus 81 percent of G.I.s born a quarter century earlier, who bore an average of 2.3 children). This was the only American generation whose college-educated women were more fertile than those who did not complete secondary school.

• While Silent men outpaced G.I.s in educational achievement, Silent women showed no gain. Through the 1950s, new women entrants virtually disappeared from fields like engineering and architecture, where G.I. women had made important war-era advances at like age. Two decades later, Silent women accounted for nearly all the nation's prominent feminists.

• The late-twentieth-century "sexual revolution" and "divorce epidemic" have affected the Silent more than any other generation. From the 1950s to the 1970s, they reported a larger age-bracket increase in their frequency of sexual intercourse than any other generation. Similarly, Silent men and women born between the mid-1930s and early 1940s showed the biggest age-bracket jump in the divorce rate. From 1969 through 1975, as the Silent surged into state legislatures, the number of states with "no fault" divorce laws jumped from zero to forty-five.

- Silent professionals account for the 1960s surge in the "helping professions" (teaching, medicine, ministry, government) and the 1970s explosion in "public interest" advocacy groups. From 1969 to 1979, the number of public interest law centers in America grew from 23 to 111; during the 1980s, only nine new centers were established. The era of Silent-dominated juries (1972 through 1989) roughly coincided with the rise of huge damage awards in personal injury cases.

- The Silent Generation has produced virtually every major figure in the modern civil rights movement—from the Little Rock children to the youths at the Greensboro lunch counter, from Martin Luther King, Jr., to Malcolm X, from Cesar Chavez's farmworkers' union to Russell Means' American Indian Movement. By 1989, nineteen black Silent had been elected to Congress, five more than among the three prior generations (Missionary, Lost, G.I.) put together. Nine Silent Hispanics have so far become congressmen, more than the combined number of all prior American generations.

- In politics and business, the Silent have been a proven generation of bureaucratizers. Compared with the G.I.-dominated Congresses of the early 1960s, Silent Congresses in the mid-1980s convened twice as many hearings, debated for twice as many hours, hired four times as many staff, mailed six times as many letters to constituents—and enacted one-third as many laws. Eighty-four committees had oversight responsibility for HUD in the years just prior to its scandal.

- Opinion rules in Silent-led America. In the 1990 election, voters confronted the largest number of citizen-initiated ballot measures since the Progressive-Era election of 1914. (The California ballot alone had 28 initiatives, accompanied by a two-volume, 230-page voter's guide.) But if opinion rules, the Silent hate to admit that any rule is final. From judicial appeals to NFL instant replays, the 1980s marked an all-time high in institutionalized second-guessing.

- The Silent are virtually guaranteed of reaching 1993—sixty-eight years after their first birthyear—without producing a President. That's twelve years later than the average and seven years later than any other generation from the Republicans on. This "I Go Pogo" generation has shown a lifelong bipartisan attraction to Presidential underdogs. It gave Adlai Stevenson his strongest generational percentage and supported the losing candidate in every close modern election: Nixon over Kennedy, Humphrey over Nixon, Ford over Carter.

- The Silent are the only living generation whose members would rather be in some age bracket other than the one they now occupy. A 1985 study found the fiftyish Silent preferring "the twenties" over any other decade of life—

an age many feel they never really enjoyed the first time around. From the
early 1970s on, Silent entering midlife have fueled a booming market in
dietary aids, exercise classes, cosmetic surgery, hair replacements, relax-
ation therapies, and psychiatric treatments.

The Silent Lifecycle

YOUTH: "Overprotective was a word first used to describe our parents,"
Benita Eisler recalls of her depression-era youth. The first American generation
to be born mainly in hospitals, Eisler's peers grew up hearing stern warnings
not to "do that" or "eat this" or "go there" from midlife Lost adults who
regulated the child's world with the heaviest hand of the twentieth century. While
a child's fatal pony fall in *Gone With the Wind* reminded parents to keep a close
watch over their charges, Norman Rockwell depicted the enduring image of
Roosevelt's fourth freedom, "Freedom from Fear," by showing a sleeping child
lovingly guarded by mother and father. The leading parenting books suggested
"total situation" child care and other no-nonsense approaches, including Herman
Bundesen's strict feeding regimen and John B. Watson's behavioral rules that
critics likened to the housebreaking of puppies. Kids read stories about "Tootle"
(a little train that always stayed on the track) and *Paddle to the Sea* (a little boat
that reached its destination by floating safely with the current). At the movies,
they watched Spanky, Alfalfa, and the "Little Rascals" scrupulously mind their
manners whenever they encountered elders. As threats against the national community deepened, children were bluntly told that older generations were making
enormous sacrifices so they could grow up enjoying peace and prosperity. Family
survival took first priority and gave many kids a home life of limited cultural
experience, plus the fear that any day could bring devastating news—a layoff,
a foreclosed home, the combat death of a father. "As a young child," Frank
Conroy remembers asking "what was in the newspapers when there wasn't a
war going on."

In the years after VJ-Day, the Silent "became teenagers when to be a teenager
was nothing, the lowest of the low," as Conroy put it. "Most of us kept quiet,
attempting not to call attention to ourselves." Watching from the sidelines, they
saw the nation celebrate thirtyish war heroes and an indulged new generation of
postwar babies—and reaffirm a social order at once comfortable and imperme-
able. America offered young people peace and jobs, but put them in a social
and cultural no-man's-land. Their worst school discipline problems ranged from
gum chewing to cutting in line. In 1942, adolescent graffiti in New York City
was just about the tamest on record ("Nuts to all the boys on Second Avenue—
except between 68th and 69th Streets!"). The pressure to conform came more
from adults than from peers. Emulating older G.I.s, most teens became strictly

monogamous "steadies"—who then exchanged pins, got engaged, scheduled "June bride" postgraduation weddings, and "tied the knot." ("It's too late now, there's no turnin' back,/You fell in love, you're part of *The Tender Trap*.") In an age when "getting in trouble" meant dropping out of high school to get married, Silent "juvenile delinquents" were less kids who did something bad than kids who did *nothing*, refusing to accept the confident promise of the postwar era. Like Dion DiMucci's "Why must I be *A Teenager in Love*," popular teen songs bespoke a self-pity, a yearning for "someone to tell my troubles to," a fear of "heartbreak." Amid this sentimentality, kids built human relations skills—and felt useful enough to expect a nice personal harvest from the world their elders had created.

COMING OF AGE: "I hated the war ending," Russell Baker later admitted, acknowledging that the A-bomb may have saved his skin. "I wanted desperately to become a death-dealing hero. I wanted the war to go on and on." While a number of first-wave Silent served in World War II, few saw any action before VJ-Day sent them home as might-have-beens rather than as heroes. Just as Herbert T. Gillis lorded it over young Dobie (and Maynard G. Krebs, who ran when he heard the word "work"), G.I.s and Silent knew who had fought "the big one" and who hadn't. After Hiroshima, they also knew who had built "the big one" and who hadn't. Several years later, the Silent had their own war to fight in Korea, but their most memorable troop movements were retreats rather than advances. Where George Bush's peers had conquered large portions of Europe, Africa, and the Pacific, Mike Dukakis' fought to a tie on one small peninsula. Through the late 1940s, meanwhile, young college freshmen found G.I. veterans everywhere, running the clubs, getting more financial aid (and, by most accounts, better grades), and the pick among marriageable women. The first Silent TV stars were goofballs (Jerry Lewis) or daffy sweethearts (Debbie Reynolds) cast alongside confident G.I. "straight men." As young women watched Grace Kelly and Jacqueline Bouvier abandon their careers for life with an older prince, their male peers watched the reputations and careers of prewar G.I. leftists getting chewed to pieces by Nixon and McCarthy. Youths of both sexes avoided the unorthodox and safeguarded their "permanent records" by applying the motto "Don't say, don't write, don't join."

Postwar Silent youths came of age feeling an inner-world tension amid the outer-world calm—not growing up angry (explained the older Paul Goodman), just *Growing up Absurd*. Older generations didn't expect them to achieve anything great, just to calibrate, to become expert at what G.I. economist Walter Heller called "fine tuning" of the hydraulic G.I. wealth machine. Young adults in the 1950s, recalls Manchester, were "content to tinker with techniques and technicalities" and believed that "progress lay in something called problem-solving meetings." The aspiring youth elite compensated for their lack of aggressiveness with a budding intellectualism. In 1951, William Buckley's *God and Man at Yale* sounded the first erudite challenge against G.I. secularism. In 1955, the "Beat Generation" drew first notice, wrote Bruce Cook, at "that famous reading at the Six Gallery in San Francisco when Allen Ginsberg first proclaimed 'Howl' to an astonished, wine-bibbing multitude." As self-proclaimed "nonconformists" led a "bohemian" coffeehouse cult, goateed 20-year-olds sampled foreign cuisines, listened to "offbeat" music, read "hip" poetry, told "sick" jokes, and lampooned the G.I. "Squaresville." In 1958, the G.I. Herb Caen tagged them "beatniks." If the Silent couldn't match Caen's peers in power and virility, then they'd be William Gaines' Alfred E. Neuman. "What, me worry?" You bet they worried—and came of age, like Elvis, *All Shook Up* ("Well, bless my soul, what's wrong with me,/ I'm itchin' like a man on a fuzzy tree"). As they danced to their new rock and roll, Silent youths put up false fronts and used early marriage as a fortress against adult doubts about their maturity. Making babies quickly and frequently, millions of young householders merged unnoticeably into suburban G.I. culture.

RISING ADULTHOOD: In *Passages,* Gail Sheehy refers to the 20-to-30 age bracket as the Silent lifecycle's "transient decade"—a time when her peers felt a need to build the firm, safe "merger self" while exploring a more adventuresome "seeker self." Thirtyish adults sensed that although G.I.s had the power, they brought compassion and refinement to an age short on both. Starting with the Soviets' 1957 Sputnik space shot, they started questioning American exceptionalism. "Hip" ways of thinking moved beyond coffeehouses into the suburbs with a new style John Updike called "half Door Store, half Design Research." Rising theologians challenged the Catholic orthodoxy in Daniel Callahan's "Generation of the Third Eye" (which "looks constantly into itself," and from which "nothing, or almost nothing, is safe from scrutiny"). As Updike and Philip Roth wrote risqué novels with self-doubting heroes, Tom Lehrer and Stan Freberg brought sophistication to satire, and Andy Warhol found "art" in the G.I. soup-can culture. New musical strains slyly shocked elders (Ray Charles' *What'd I Say?*) while reflecting an appetite for "crossover" pluralism.

This other-directedness gradually asserted itself in the modern civil rights movement. Led by the young Reverend Martin Luther King, Jr., Silent "agitators" adhered to a rule of nonviolence and appealed to the G.I.s' sense of fairness. In 1962, when Tom Hayden, Carl Oglesby, and other Silent founded the Students for a Democratic Society—a vehicle for campus dissent yet to be radicalized by Boomers—they affirmed that "in social change, or interchange, we find violence to be abhorrent." From Michael Harrington's *The Other America* to Charles Silberman's *Crisis in the Classroom,* rising authors probed flaws in the G.I.-built order. At the "right wing" of the spectrum, "Young Americans for Freedom" challenged the big-government centrism personified by the G.I. Nelson Rockefeller. Whatever their politics, the rising Silent differed from

Boomers in their implicit acceptance of the permanence of G.I. institutions (booing Rockefeller from inside the arena—not outside, as at Chicago). So too did the Silent acknowledge the greater strength of those next-elders. Peter, Paul, and Mary sang "If I had a hammer, I'd hammer out justice," as if to admit the G.I.s had the hammers—and were busy hammering out interstate highways and ballistic missiles. And cars, those G.I.-friendly machines that Ralph Nader declared *Unsafe at Any Speed,* having brought "death, injury, and the most inestimable sorrow and deprivation to millions of people."

Among the rising elite, young specialists lent their compliant expertise to the institutional order. With Pierre Salinger and Bill Moyers advising G.I. Presidents, legions of jobs opened up in public service. A budding intelligentsia lingered in universities, shepherding creative young Boomers. Silent athletes manned the last clean-cut sports dynasties (Yankees, Packers, Celtics) and provided the lonely precursors of athletes' rights (Curt Flood, John Mackey). In business, a wave of smart, trainable entry-level workers helped set records for growth and productivity. What Silent workers put in, they got back. Whatever their professional field—management, law, civil service, or teaching—Silent men could count on acquiring a house and car, and on raising a family comfortably. Silent women, however, began to resent being trapped at home, and Silent men prepared to break free of a claustrophobia they knew their elders had never felt. Noted William Styron as early as 1968: "I think that the best of my generation—those in their late thirties or early forties—have reversed the customary rules of the game and have grown more radical as they have gotten older—a disconcerting but healthy sign."

MIDLIFE: *It's Hard to Be Hip Over Thirty.* So read the cover of 37-year-old Judith Viorst's 1968 poetry volume—and, in fact, the phrase "never trust anyone over thirty" was coined by a Berkeley postgraduate, Jack Weinberg, himself approaching that age at a time when the Silent came to notice, envy, emulate, and occasionally steer the passions of coming-of-age Boomers. While still craving respect from G.I. elders for their manliness and seriousness of purpose, the Silent were eager to convince Boomers that they understood them, were with them, and could maybe help them channel their anger. Stokely Carmichael and the memory of the assassinated Malcolm X radicalized the black Silent message to suit young Boomers with more of an instinct for violence. From the lyrics of Bob Dylan and Paul Simon to the psychedelic art of Peter Max and the Motown sound of Berry Gordy, Silent performers and artists gave expression to youth. A young attorney, Sam Yasgur, first coaxed his dad to allow use of his pasture and then handled the details of what Sam expected would be a mannerly festival at Woodstock. As last-wavers like Abbie Hoffman and Jerry Rubin became the pied pipers of revolt ("We knew we couldn't get Archie Bunker, so we went for Archie Bunker's kids," Hoffman said later), first-wavers began lamenting their own missed opportunities in youth, rethinking their capitulation to G.I. culture, and becoming the prototype of what G.I. Spiro Agnew derided as "vicars of vacillation" and "nattering nabobs of negativism." Over a two-month span in 1968, the Silent grieved over the killings of two men whom many Silent today still consider their most gifted leaders—Robert Kennedy (then 43) and Martin Luther King, Jr. (39). A year later, the other Silent heir to the Kennedy mystique fell prey to a deadly extramarital entanglement on Chappaquiddick Island—a symptom of his peers' turbulent passage to midlife.

Having trouble meeting the power standard of next-elders or the ethical standard of next-juniors, Silent men built a composite definition of masculinity. Self-styled "liberated" males put their families at risk by pursuing what John Updike called the "Post-Pill Paradise" and by succumbing to what Barbara Gordon called "Jennifer Fever" (a fascination for free-spirited younger women). Midlife impresarios flaunted Boom erotica in Playboy clubs, R-rated movies, and *O Calcutta* stage productions. At one end of the Silent male spectrum lay those who combined the softer features of their generational neighbors: a confident and gentle Merlin Olsen offering floral bouquets, or a rational and sensitive Carl Sagan trying to communicate with extraterrestrials. At the other end lay the reverse mix: Chuck Norris or Clint Eastwood combining G.I. machismo with "Make my day" Boom judgmentalism. Staring at the two ends from a muddled in-between sat the Woody Allens, torn between the available choices—like one of Gail Sheehy's peers who wished "somebody would let me be what I am, tender sometimes, and a dependent, too, but also vain and greedy and jealous and competitive." Others became outspoken, out-of-the-closet gays (Harvey Milk, Barney Frank), even transvestites (Christine Jorgensen, Renée Richards). A female generation nearly all of whom had married young now insisted on being called Gloria Steinem's status-cloaking "Ms.," as their vanguard attacked "man the oppressor" (Kate Millett) for being a "natural predator" (Susan Brownmiller) driven by "metaphysical cannibalism" (Ti-Grace Atkinson). Fortyish women and men asked what Eisler termed "the question that signals the end of every marriage: 'Is this all there is?'" While all generations joined the divorce epidemic, the Silent were by far the most likely to have children in the household—leaving them with the greatest residue of guilt.

APPROACHING ELDERHOOD: In his 1980 book *The Changing of the Guard,* David Broder confidently proclaimed that "America is changing hands" and predicted that what he has more recently called the "Fit Fifties Generation" would soon break out from under the G.I. shadow and attain national leadership. That didn't happen. By the late 1980s, people of all ages still looked to aging G.I.s for leadership and, increasingly, to Boomers for cultural direction. One Silent candidate after another fell prey to a combination of dullness, a media-coined "stature gap," and that generational bugaboo, the "character issue." Two decades earlier, young Silent reporters were neither willing nor able to torpedo G.I. candidates the way the mostly Boom press did the midlife Silent over issues like adultery (Gary Hart), plagiarism (Joe Biden), issue flipflops (Richard Gephardt), misbehavior of family members (Geraldine Ferraro), or technobabble (Michael Dukakis). In 1988, Gary Hart proudly termed his like-aged candidates a "generational revolution." Reagan referred to them as "kids," the press as "the seven dwarfs"—and, yet again, the Silent nominee fell to a G.I. who warned against "the technocrat who makes the gears mesh but doesn't understand the magic of the machine." "If you understand the Silent Generation, you understand Mike Dukakis," quipped one biographer of the governor whose very nickname—"Duke"—reminded voters how unWaynelike (and un-G.I.-like) he was.

As rising adults, the Silent once gazed up at midlife G.I.s they then called "the establishment." Through the 1980s they have come to recognize that *they* are the establishment, at least on their resumés—but, somehow, the faces they see in the mirror or meet at lunch don't exude the powerful confidence they remember of G.I.s. Peering down the age ladder has only added to their feelings of power inadequacy. What especially "chills the blood" of professed liberals like Senator Moynihan is the recollection that in their youth, "the old bastards were the conservatives. Now the young people are becoming the conservatives and we are the old bastards." Liberal or not, the grown-up Lonely Crowd persists in its plasticity—at times yielding to Boomer passions, other times heartily endorsing whatever the system churns out—be it affirmative action, the free market, an incentive tax rate, a UN resolution, or the compromise verdict of some expert panel. On both sides of the political spectrum, the Silent would much prefer to discuss processes than outcomes.

In their hands, America has grown more accustomed to deferring or learning to live with problems than to taking aggressive steps to solve them. Thanks to the size and complexity of the U.S. economy, tenured professors foresee at worst a slow parabola of national descent while Brookings' Henry Aaron remains confident that "the nation can muddle through without absolute decline." Congressional leaders set priorities through decision-avoidance mechanisms like the Gramm-Rudman Act (or its sequel, "Gramm-Rudman III"). The foreign policy trend-setters lean toward James Baker–style multilateralism and a deference to international law, what Joseph Nye has called "soft power, the complex machinery of interdependence." Industrialists have been replaced by technocrats who manage "M-Form" corporations, financial holding companies long on flexibility and short on product identity. Businesses run "cultural audits" of their employees, Ben Wattenberg's "Gross National Spirit" index charts the nation's feelings, and John Naisbitt heralds such "Megatrends" as an "Information Age" of "high-tech/high-touch." Endowed foundations turn their attention to every new personal injustice. Oil companies portray themselves as nice guys, eager to placate their most hostile critics. A Silent-dominated Judiciary Committee rejects a like-aged Supreme Court nominee (Bork) for being too abrasive, while embracing another (Souter) for promising that personal opinions would "play absolutely no role" in his rulings on abortion. The Census Bureau checks bridges and sewers to see that every American is counted, while leaders of industry put up little resistance to a costly new law requiring them to retrofit for the handicapped. Under the Silent elite, America has become a kinder, more communicative place. It has also become culturally fragmented and less globally competitive.

Today's 50- and 60-year-olds have been less successful in forging a sense of national or personal direction than any generation in living memory. Like Robert Bellah in *Habits of the Heart,* many Silent feel disquieted by the lack of connectedness they see in American life. While Kevin Phillips describes an America shadowed by an "End of Empire frustration" and Barbara Ehrenreich a white-collar workforce haunted by a "fear of falling," Jack Kemp foresees exhilarating prosperity and George Gilder "a global community of commerce . . . a global ganglion of electronic and photonic media that leaves all history in its wake." What mostly emerges is fuss and detail, a world view of such enormous complexity that their own contributions often turn out (as one technician described the Hubble telescope mirror) "perfect but wrong." Sensing this, they feel— deep down—a wounded collective ego. Having grown up playing the child's game of Sorry, the Silent cannot abandon what Sheehy calls their "resignation," a vague dissatisfaction with jobs, families, their children, themselves. Approaching their own old age, many still find themselves emotionally obliged to surviving parents and financially obliged to struggling children in what Robert Grossman terms "Parenthood II." Many are opting for early-retirement pension bonanzas that the nation can currently afford simply because (as Easterlin accurately predicted) their generation is relatively small in numbers. Most aging Silent find themselves wealthier, but more confused as to purpose, than they ever imagined they would be at this phase of life. As Toffler suggests in *PowerShift*—and Tom Peters in *Thriving on Chaos*—they sense that the pace of social and economic change has accelerated beyond anyone's ability to control it. The best Americans can do, suggests Toffler, is to run faster themselves. The peers of Gail Sheehy are thus encountering a new mid-fifties "passage" that Daniel Levinson describes as "a silent despair, a pressing fear of becoming irrelevant." Many also feel that endearing if paralyzing quality Ellen Goodman saw in Pat Schroeder's brief run for the Presidency: "a desire to make it to the top" with "a deep concern about how you make it."

Funny, You Don't Look Like a Grandmother, observes the title of Lois Wyse's 1990 book, targeted at Silent first-wavers who are beginning to transform elderhood around a decidedly un-G.I.-like other-directedness. Travel agents report a new boom business in "grandtravel" (grandparent-grandchild trips) and new interest in "Elderhostels" reminiscent of the way the Silent toured Europe as youths. Self-styled "kids over 60" have formed a "SeniorNet" computer network. In 1989, affluent mid-sixtyish Social Security beneficiaries formed a "21st Century Club" whose members will assign their checks to a philanthropic trust fund. The Silent-led Virginia state legislature recently raised revenues by limiting tax breaks for Silent (but not G.I.) retirees. And Ralph Nader is mobilizing "Princeton Project '55" around the "suppressed crusades among the class-mates," many of whom have become financially successful beyond their collegiate imaginings, but who share an eagerness to join Nader in attacking "systemic social problems." Their agenda remains large. In 1986, the Union of International Associations catalogued 10,000 world problems awaiting solution—and the Silent Generation is running out of time.

*   *   *

Nearly four decades after the Korean War, no national memorial exists for its veterans, prompting one fund-raiser to complain how they were being treated "as if they have never lived, never ennobled their time and place, never contributed to destiny." Though their own generation is an easy touch for other people's charities, Silent veterans have been slow to assemble funds to build this one commemoration to themselves. Their memorial, if it is built, will have no Iwo Jima giants doing great deeds, nor will it make any moral statement like the dark walls of the Vietnam Memorial. Instead, it will depict thirty-eight life-size soldiers in two slightly crooked columns, walking through a forest to nowhere in particular.

"The Silent Generation Is Clearing Its Throat," proclaimed Florida newspaper editor Tom Kelly as the 1990s dawned. "All together now, let's hear it (softly, please, but with feeling) for the Silent Generation, those overridiculed and underappreciated people." This modesty is disarming in a generation two of whose members (Neil Armstrong and Martin Luther King, Jr.) will likely remain, in some distant epoch, among the most celebrated Americans. The peers of Armstrong and King may someday be credited as the generation that opened up the dusty closets of contemporary history, diversified the culture, made democracy work for the disadvantaged, and—as one friend eulogized of Jim Henson—struck a Muppet-like balance "between the sacred and the silly." Above all, the generation that took America from grinding bulldozers to user-friendly computers, from the circa-1960 "Nuclear Age" into the circa-1990 "Information Age," has excelled at *personal communication*. The Silent have constantly tried, and often succeeded, in defusing conflict by encouraging people to talk to each other—from therapeutic T-groups on family problems to *Nightline*-style "global town meetings" on issues of major importance. They have thus lent flexibility to a G.I.-built world that otherwise might have split to pieces under Boom attack—and have helped mollify, and ultimately cool, the Boom's coming-of-age passions. Indeed, the Silent have been pathbreakers for much of the 1960s-era "consciousness" (from music to film, civil rights to Vietnam resistance) for which Boomers too often claim credit. From youth forward, this most considerate of living generations has specialized not in grand constructions or lofty ideals, but rather in people, *life-size people* like the statues planned for the Korean War Memorial. Barbra Streisand's agemates would like to believe that "people who need people are the luckiest people in the world.'' But, true to form, they have their doubts.

Much of this doubt might be resolved if America can someday inaugurate *just one* President who wore that 1950s-era ducktail or ponytail, who served in the Peace Corps, who maybe spent a summer with SNCC in Mississippi, and who cried as only 30-year-olds did when Martin and Bobby died. In 1990, when the mostly Silent U.S. Congress wildly cheered the Czech playwright-dissident-President Vaclav Havel, many were no doubt recalling those old coffeehouse days and thinking: Here is exactly the sort of avant-garde President we thought *we'd* someday give the world. Until they do, the story of their own generation will read, to them, like the middle pages of a book written mainly about somebody else.

Chapter 11

THE MILLENNIAL CYCLE

"Suddenly the Woodstock generation was not wonderfully young, but wonderfully old, somehow, full of wisdom, a kind of Druidic savvy signaled by long hair, walking staffs and face paint accompanied by the thousand-yard squint they'd get after smoking marijuana." So wrote the *Washington Post*'s Henry Allen, in one of the many 1989 retrospectives marking the twentieth anniversary of the Woodstock Arts and Music Fair at Bethel, New York. Back in mid-August of 1969, Woodstock had been the largest civilian generational gathering in American history. As a smattering of celebrants returned to the historic marker (dubbed "The Tomb of the Unknown Hippie") on Max Yasgur's field, the Boomer-dominated media published scores of commemoratives to take stock of the prior two decades. Twenty years had passed since the late-1960s days of "generational consciousness"—roughly the span of another generation. Journalists fixated on aging radicals like 45-year-old Grace Slick (whose old Jefferson Airplane slogan "Feed your head" she now reinterpreted to mean "Go home and read a book") and 42-year-old Arlo Guthrie ("Everybody wears suits more than I thought they would, but that's cosmetic"). But with the passing of two decades, Woodstock had already left a legacy for the first three of what history suggests will be a four-generation MILLENNIAL Cycle:

- Grace Slick's self-absorbed BOOM GENERATION (Idealist, then age 29 to 46) included the overwhelming majority of the 400,000 youths in their late teens and twenties who had attended the original event, plus uncounted millions of others who had partaken in the festivals, be-ins, teach-ins, strikes, and assorted other youth gatherings of the Woodstock era. Other notable events of the Boomer coming-of-age years—the Chicago convention riot, People's Park, Altamont, Kent State—had been deadlier and were remembered more soberly, if at all. By now, Boomers were busy trying to keep their own children from replaying their own youthful exuberances. Where the original (Silent) production of *Hair* had stripped a Boomer cast of clothes, a twentieth-anniversary (Boom) reissue stripped the musical of offensive lyrics, turning a song entitled ''Sodomy'' into a saxophone solo. Boomers remained just as ethics-absorbed as always, but Woodstock's ''New Age'' heirs now had to share the generational spotlight with their slightly younger evangelical peers, who had glimpsed the original rock concert as grade school or high school students.

• Wherever Boomers rented old Woodstock videos to celebrate the occasion, the punkish part-timers behind the checkout counter probably belonged to the THIRTEENTH GENERATION (Reactive, age 8 to 28). For the most part, these $6-an-hour youths kept their mouths shut while overhearing 40-year-olds revel in their culture and exude an air of having defined forever what every person should be around age 20. To these kids, rehashing Woodstock was a waste of time: Just look at the mess it left behind—for example, the drug-related deaths of seven festival performers (and who knows how many thousands of participants) over the ensuing two decades. But, never having known anything remotely like Woodstock themselves, they were also aware of the possible Boomer comeback: Okay, so what did you guys ever do together—invade Grenada? Go wilding? Watch the *Challenger* explosion? And they wondered themselves. A few 13ers revealed a rising alienation in their letter-to-the-editor reactions to Boomer commemoratives: like John Cunningham, whose attitude was ''Woodstock—blech,'' and Jeffrey Hoogeveen, who pointedly told Boomers ''the Sixties are history—history that the rest of us don't need repeated and crammed down our throats.'' Hoogeveen's peers had been the forgotten toddlers of the Woodstock era, kids who by now were old enough to check out such hippie-ish videos as *Easy Rider* and *Hair*—and who, like *The Wonder Years'* Olivia D'Abo, knew how to imitate or avoid Boomerisms, whichever came in handy.

• Back in 1969, Boomer festivals had celebrated themselves; twenty years later, their midsummer outings invariably featured the budding MILLENNIAL GENERATION (Civic, age 7 and under). Where many a Boomer had hitchhiked to Woodstock, taking rides from goodness knows whom and ingesting goodness knows what when they got there (no doubt feeding a few 13er babies some mind-expanding leftovers), their tots traveled there

FIGURE 11–1

Millennial Cycle: Age Location in History

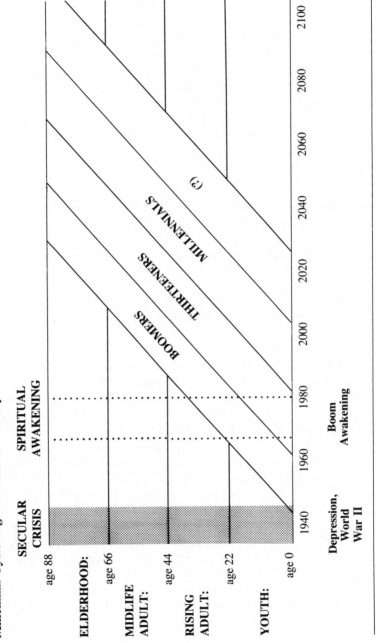

in 1989 strapped into super-safe infant car seats and munching the most wholesome snacks their parents could buy. Already, parents deemed these children special, worth protecting. The eldest had just finished first grade, exposed at home and school to a values-laced list of dos and don'ts unlike anything most 13ers had ever heard. Parents and teachers were carefully recrafting the child's world so this next generation would never go near the dangerous drugs-and-sex environment of the 1970s. Watching those hard-bitten kids behind the video checkout counter, Boom parents redoubled their conviction that their younger tots must never be allowed to grow up like that. No, when these children became old enough to hold summer jobs, they would work in libraries, plant trees, or do something else useful for the community.

Boomers, 13ers, and Millennials are just now beginning to build a generational drama that will continue to unwind for decades to come. To date, this has been a cycle of relative peace and affluence, mixed with growing individualism, cultural fragmentation, moral zealotry, and a sense of political drift and institutional failure. That is to be expected. A sense that the public world is spinning slowly "out of control" is normal for a society moving from an Awakening to an Inner-Driven era.

The Millennial Cycle has completed one exuberant and occasionally violent spiritual awakening, but has yet to encounter a secular crisis. It thus contains just one social moment to date:

• *The Boom Awakening* (1967–1980), best known as the modern "Consciousness Revolution," is what William McLoughlin calls America's "Fourth Awakening." It began in earnest in 1967 with the "Vietnam Summer," inner-city riots, the San Francisco "Summer of Love," and counterculture euphoria. It peaked in 1970, with the Kent State and Jackson State violence, the first "Earth Day," and the "Days of Rage" on university campuses. Throughout the 1970s, it spread under the rubric of the human potential movement, the "Aquarian Conspiracy," a "New Age" transformation of manners, families, lifestyles, and values, and the rise of "Jesus people" and resurgent evangelism. The awakening ebbed sharply in the late 1970s with the growing social and economic pessimism that Boomer Patrick Caddell labeled "malaise," and it ended altogether in 1980—as rates of crime and substance abuse among coming-of-age Americans were reaching their postwar peak. Reagan's election (and his endorsement by the Boom) marked the acceptance of rising-adult social roles by a no-longer-youthful cadre of 1960s kids. *AGE LOCATION: G.I.s in elderhood; Silent in midlife; Boomers in rising adulthood; 13ers in youth.*

BOOM GENERATION

Born: 1943–1960
Type: Idealist

Age Location:
Boom Awakening in rising adulthood

"Anarchist heaven on earth." "Redemption worth fighting for." That's how Todd Gitlin described People's Park—an oblong three-acre patch that Cal-Berkeley's G.I. regents cleared in 1969 so they could put up a new student facility. The kids wanted to keep it a mixture of garden and hangout, a shrine to their budding consciousness. In the ensuing melee, the regents won the battle, but the young rioters won the war. Nothing was built. A year earlier, Columbia students had rebelled against a similar plan to erect a big gymnasium. There too, nothing was built. "You build it up, mother, we gonna tear it down," was Jacob Brackman's motto for his BOOM GENERATION, then triggering America's most furious and violent youth upheaval of the twentieth century. After noticing the powerful inner life underlying the youth anger at Harvard, Erik Erikson remarked that he saw "more of a search for resacralization in the younger than in the older generation." Afterward, to the surprise of many, the Boomer rage cooled. By the mid-1980s, People's Park had become infested with crime and social debris—while a nearby bakery sold $15 tarts iced with the message "Victory to the Sandinistas." The generation that came of age, like Brackman, deriding "banality, irrelevance, and all the uglinesses which conspire to dwarf or extinguish the human personality," seemingly lay exposed (in Gitlin's words) as having gone "from *J'accuse* to Jacuzzi." In 1989, Berkeley's fortyish home-owners began forming neighborhood associations for the purpose of pushing "alcoholics, drug dealers, and wing nuts" out of their parks and out of their lives. Now, it appears, this generation is going from Jacuzzi to cold shower.

As Boomers have charted their life's voyage, they have metamorphosed from Beaver Cleaver to hippie to braneater to yuppie to what some are calling "Neo-Puritan" in a manner quite unlike what anyone, themselves included, ever expected. As The Who and countless others have been unceasingly (and, to some ears, annoyingly) "talkin' 'bout my generation," the Boom has outlived any number of temporary labels: the "Dr. Spock," "Pepsi," "Rock," "Now," "Sixties," "Love," "Protest," "Woodstock," "Vietnam," "Me," "Big Chill," "Yuppie," and "Post-Yuppie" Generation. Boomers were blessed from the beginning with what their chronicler Landon Jones described as "Great Expectations." Their G.I. parents fully expected them to grow up (in William

BOOM GENERATION (Born 1943 to 1960)

TYPE: Idealist

Total number: 79,000,000
Now alive in U.S.: 69,000,000
Percent immigrant: 10%

SAMPLE MEMBERS, birth (death)

1943 Oliver North
1943 Janis Joplin (1970)
1943 Joe Namath
1944 Angela Davis
1945 Steve Martin
1946 David Stockman
1946 Donald Trump
1946 Gilda Radner (1989)
1947 Kareem Abdul-Jabbar
1947 Mark Rudd
1947 David Letterman
1948 Jerry Mathers ("the Beaver")
1950 Jane Pauley
1951 Lee Atwater
1954 Oprah Winfrey
1954 Patty Hearst
1955 Steven Jobs
1955 William Gates
1957 Spike Lee
1959 John McEnroe

FAMILY TREE

Typical grandparents: Lost
Parents: G.I. and Silent
Children: Thirteenth and Millennial
Typical grandchildren: (new Adaptive)

FUTURE PERIOD OF POLITICAL LEADERSHIP

Plurality in Congress: 1995–2015 (proj.)
Term in White House: 2000–2020 (proj.)
Majority of Supreme Court: 2010–2030
   (proj.)

U.S. PRESIDENTS: None

POLITICAL LEADERS

1943 Bill Bradley
1943 William Bennett
1943 Newt Gingrich
1947 Dan Quayle
1948 Albert Gore, Jr.

PROMINENT FOREIGN PEERS

1943 Lech Walesa
1943 Mick Jagger
1945 Daniel Ortega
1948 Prince Charles
1953 Benazir Bhutto

Age	Date	HISTORY AND LIFECYCLE
0– 3	1946:	Spock publishes baby-care book; start of postwar "baby boom"
0– 6	1949:	TV age begins; 1 million sets in U.S.
0–11	1954:	Polio vaccine discovered; *Brown* school desegregation decision
0–14	1957:	Sputnik in orbit; science education becomes a national priority
4–21	1964:	Free Speech Movement at Berkeley; Vietnam War (1964–1973) starts
7–24	1967:	Vietnam Summer; Summer of Love; race riots in over one hundred cities
9–26	1969:	Student strikes; Apollo moon landing; Woodstock festival
10–27	1970:	Kent State and Jackson State massacres; "Days of Rage"; Earth Day
12–29	1972:	McGovern tries to rally youth vote and loses badly; draft ends
14–31	1974:	Woodward and Bernstein help topple Nixon in Watergate scandal
21–38	1981:	Start of Reagan era; first use of word "yuppie"
28–45	1988:	Al Gore runs for President; Dan Quayle elected Vice President

SAMPLE CULTURAL ENDOWMENTS: *Doonesbury* (comic, Garry Trudeau); *All the President's Men* (Bob Woodward, Carl Bernstein); *The Fate of the Earth* (Jonathan Schell); *The Color Purple* (Alice Walker); *Cathy* (comic, Cathy Guisewite); *American Pie* (song, Don McLean); *Saturday Night Live* (TV show); *Close Encounters of the Third Kind* (film, Steven Spielberg); *Strawberry Statement* (James Kunen); *Green Rage* (Christopher Manes); Vietnam Veterans Memorial (Maya Lin); *Do the Right Thing* (film, Spike Lee)

Manchester's words) "adorable as babies, cute as grade school pupils and striking as they entered their teens," after which "their parents would be very, very proud of them." In 1965, *Time* magazine declared teenagers to be "on the fringe of a golden era"—and two years later described collegians as cheerful builders who would "lay out blight-proof, smog-free cities, enrich the underdeveloped world, and, no doubt, write finis to poverty and war." Hardly. As those sunny prophecies collapsed, one by one, Boomers next heard themselves collectively touted as a surly political powerhouse, easily capable of sweeping candidates of their choice to the White House. Not so. Starting with George McGovern in 1972, the Boom has played the role of political siren—first tempting candidates, then luring them to their demise. Meanwhile, the Silent demographer Richard Easterlin predicted that the Boom would feel a lifelong "inadequacy" because of a numbers-fueled peer-on-peer competition. Wrong again. Even if many Boomers have felt pinched by the real estate and job markets, no twentieth-century generation has looked within and seen less "inadequacy" than the smug Boom.

In *Do You Believe in Magic?*, Annie Gottlieb declared the Boom "a tribe with its roots in a time, rather than place or race." First wave or last, Boomers recall that "time" as the 1960s, a decade they remember more fondly than other generations. Their eighteen years of birth began (in 1943) with the first real evidence that G.I. optimism would be rewarded with victory and ended (in 1960) with the first election of a G.I. President. Unlike the Silent, Boomers lack any childhood recollection of World War II. Unlike 13ers, they were all reaching adolescence or lingering in "post-adolescence" (a term coined for them) before the Vietnam War drew to a close. Their first cohort, the 1943 "victory babies," have thus far ranked among the most self-absorbed in American history; their last cohorts are remembered by college faculties as the last (pre-Reagan-era) students to show Boomish streaks of intellectual arrogance and social immaturity. The Boom birthyears precede the demographic "baby boom" by three years at the front edge, four at the back. "I think you could take the baby boom back a few years," agrees Boom pollster Patrick Caddell, noting how those born in the early 1960s "have had different experiences, and their attitudes don't really fit in with those of the baby boomers."

From VJ-Day forward, whatever age bracket Boomers have occupied has been the cultural and spiritual focal point for American society as a whole. Through their childhood, America was child-obsessed; in their youth, youth-obsessed; in their "yuppie" phase, yuppie-obsessed. Always, the Boom has been not just a new generation, but what Brackman has termed "a new notion of generation with new notions of its imperatives." Arriving as the inheritors of G.I. triumph, Boomers have always seen their mission not as constructing a society, but of justifying, purifying, even *sanctifying* it. Where the Missionaries had made G.I.s learn the basics, the G.I.s taught Boomers critical thinking. Kenneth Keniston noted how, even in early childhood, Boomers showed an "orientation to principle." Coming of age, they applied their critical thinking—and new principles—back against the very scientism under which they had been raised. ("We are Bomb Babies," declared 23-year-old Ronald Allison in 1967. "We grew up with fallout in our milk.") Launching the modern "Consciousness Revolution," Boomers found their parents' world in need of a major spiritual overhaul, even of creative destruction. In 1968, a Radcliffe senior declared in her class's commencement prayer: "We do not feel like a cool, swinging generation—we are eaten up by an intensity that we cannot name." In 1980, a dramatic twelve-point October shift among Boom voters turned a slim Reagan lead into a landslide. During the intervening years, Boomers led America through an era of inner fervor unlike any seen since the 1890s.

This Consciousness Revolution was waged across a generation gap between Boomers and G.I.s. It began within families, as a revolt against fathers. Most older Americans who studied young radicals in the late 1960s were struck by their attachment to mothers and their "ambivalence" (Keniston), "oedipal rebellion" (Malcolm), or attitude of "parricide" (Feuer) toward male authority. Youth fury over Vietnam helped spread this patriphobia beyond the family. Many of the most memorable youth symbols of that era were direct affronts against the constructions of G.I. men—from the fury over napalm (whose forerunner, the flamethrower, had enabled G.I.s to overrun enemy pillboxes) and the two-fingered peace taunt (adapted from the old G.I. V-for-victory) to the defiant wearing of khaki (the G.I. color of uniformed teamwork) and the desecration of that very symbol of civic loyalty, the American flag. Several of the most celebrated youth uproars of 1969–1971 had a decided anti-G.I. ring: the hippie invasion of Disneyland, the burning of the Isla Vista Bank of America, the Earth Day burial of an automobile. Even as the society-wide generation gap receded in the 1970s, the Boom ethos remained a deliberate antithesis to everything G.I.: spiritualism over science, gratification over patience, negativism over positivism, fractiousness over conformity, rage over friendliness, *self over community*.

This quest for "self"—what Gitlin has termed "the voyage to the interior" and Christopher Lasch (more critically) the "culture of narcissism"—was a central theme of the Boom lifecycle through rising adulthood. Outwardly, it manifested itself in that distinctly Boom sense of suspended animation, of resisting permanent linkages to mates, children, corporations, and professions. Like Katharine Ross in *The Graduate*, Boomers approached the altar (or nursery, or corporate ladder) and heard something inside scream *"STOP!"* Having jammed the gears of the Silent-era coming-of-age treadmill, Boomers found themselves in a social no-man's-land, unable to satisfy their perfectionist impulses. Many simply grazed, lending no more than casual interest and wry comment to the world around them, applying what sounded to others like a pick-and-choose idealism and showing an apparent lack of interest in building community life. They developed a unique brand of perfectionism in consumption, a desire for *the best* within a very personal (and often financially austere) definition of taste. If a Boomer couldn't afford a house or family, he could at least afford the very best brand of mustard or ice cream—a "zen luxuriousness" with which Katy Butler watched her peers squeeze "the maximum possible enjoyment out of the minimum possible consumption." This mixture of high self-esteem and selective self-indulgence has at once repelled and fascinated other generations, giving Boomers a reputation for grating arrogance—and for transcendent cultural wisdom.

The Boom's fixation on self has forged an instinct to make plans or judgments according to wholly internalized standards, based on immutable principles of right and wrong. This gift for deductive logic over inductive experimentation has made Boomers better philosophers than scientists, better preachers than builders. The highest-testing Boom cohorts, those born in the mid-1940s, have reached the age where scientific achievement ordinarily peaks—yet their rise has coincided with an era of declining American preeminence in engineering and math-and-science fields. Boomers were very late to win a Nobel Prize, Thomas Cech winning their first in 1989. (At the same life phase, the Lost, G.I., and Silent had won two, four, and six, respectively.) Instead, Boomers have excelled in occupations calling for creative independence—the media, especially. Exalting individual conscience over duty to community, Boomers have had difficulty achieving consensus and mobilizing as a unit—making them far weaker than the G.I.s at getting big jobs done. Their sense of generational identity is more a Beatlean "Pepperland"—a zone of parallel play—than a peer society in the G.I. sense. They try to be "together" people not collectively but *individually,* consistent with what David Pielke defines as "the notion that infinite worth resides in each and every one of us." Like Donald Trump, a prototype Boomer sees himself capable of becoming a titan of whatever world he chooses fully to inhabit—providing cover for personal disappointments or (as a Boomer might put it) "deferred" ambitions.

Having come of age with mainly an inner catharsis, Boomers sustain a compelling urge for the perfection of man's religious impulses, and for reducing any dependence on the physical self. In the adolescent years of Boom radicals, Keniston noted the "great intensification of largely self-generated religious feelings, often despite a relatively nonreligious childhood and background." This began, in part, with drugs—what *The Aquarian Conspiracy*'s Marilyn Ferguson described as "a pass to Xanadu" for "spontaneous, imaginative, right-brained" youths. The Boom's drug phase passed after bringing transcendence to the first wave, crime to the last—and, by 1990, has been stripped of its spiritual trappings by Boomers (office-seekers, especially) who now say they didn't enjoy what they repeatedly ingested. In their subsequent search for spiritual euphoria, Boomers flocked from drugs to religion, to "Jesus" movements, evangelicalism, New Age utopianism, and millennialist visions of all sorts. As they did, they spawned the most active era of church formation of the twentieth century.

The Boomers' self-absorption has also lent their generation—male and female—a hermaphroditic, pistil-and-stamen quality. In *The Singular Generation,* Wanda Urbanska exalted their "self-sexuality," their "ability to give pleasure to oneself." Having grown up when sex-role distinctions had reached their 1950s-era zenith, Boomers of both sexes have spent a lifetime narrowing them. Men are intruding into the domain of values nurturance that, in their youth, mainly belonged to G.I. mothers and teachers, while Boomer women are invading the secular roles once reserved for can-do G.I. males. These trends have made Boomers more independent of social bonds, yet also more open to emotional isolation and economic insecurity. Concerned that their male peers may be unreliable providers, Boomer women are the first since the peers of Jane Addams to fear that early marriage and family may actually worsen their future household standard of living.

As Boomers begin entering midlife, a schism has emerged between mostly fortyish modernists and New Agers at one edge, and mostly thirtyish traditionalists and evangelicals at the other. Each side refuses to compromise on matters of principle—believing, like anti-abortionist Bill Tickel, that "it's just easier to have blanket absolutes." This values clash reflects an important bipolarity between the generation's first and last waves, whose differences have been widely noted by pollsters and marketers. At one end, the "victory" and "hello" babies of the middle to late 1940s were born almost entirely to G.I.s, not long after the peak years of parental protectiveness. At the other, the babies of the conformist late 1950s were parented mostly by Silent just as that protectiveness was giving way, and came of age at the point of maximum freedom (some would say chaos) in adolescent life. To date, last-wave Boomers have fared worse than first-wavers in educational aptitude, financial security, and self-destructive behavior; first-wave Boomers have fared worse in marital stability—partly because they married earlier. (G.I. cohorts showed precisely the opposite trends, from first wave to last.) But measured by inner-life standards, the two ends of the Boom feel equally serene.

This generation has a fuse-lit explosiveness well suggested by its name. In 1946, *Fortune* magazine declared the start of "the Great American Boom," a "boom" not just in fertility, but also in economics, education, housing, and science. The robust achievements and optimism of that era left a lasting mark on children. If G.I.s measure their worth objectively, by the works they leave to history, Boomers measure themselves subjectively, by the spiritual strength they see within. Many are having difficulty matching their parents' like-aged achievements in economic and family life. Yet they invariably consider their "consciousness" to be higher—and, by that yardstick, they are doing very well. From urban lofts to rural communes, downwardly mobile Boomers "face the truth about the way they live now with some dignity and grace," Katy Butler reports. "If it's by choice and it's not overwhelming, having no money can be a way of entering more deeply into your life." Many of them are "choosing" not to achieve by any worldly standard. But the American Dream does indeed live on for this generation—in the form of a well-ravished soul.

Boomer Facts

- Demographers attribute roughly half of the postwar "baby boom" to unusual fecundity, the other half to an unusual bunching of family formation. The main bulge, from 1946 to 1957, resulted from the coincident babymaking of late-nesting G.I.s and early-nesting Silent. After 1957, most last-wave Boomers (and first-wave 13ers) were the younger children of large Silent-headed families.

- In training, confidence, and sheer time spent changing bedsheets, no generation of American women can match the G.I.s for the intensity of the nurture they provided their mostly Boom children. Among Boomer preschoolers who had working mothers, four in five were cared for in their own homes, usually by relatives. Only 2 percent attended institutional child care.

- During the Boomer youth, G.I. science made sweeping advances against childhood illness—conquering such once-terrible diseases as diphtheria and polio, and fluoridating the water to protect teeth. Pediatrics reached its height of physical aggressiveness: No generation of kids ever got more shots or had more operations, including millions of circumcisions and tonsillectomies that would not now be performed.

- In his interviews with undergraduate male activists in the late 1960s, Keniston encountered "an unusually strong tie between these young men and their mothers in the first years of life." In 1970, one poll found 32 percent of white Boomers (44 percent of blacks) mentioning their mothers alone as "the one person who cares about me." Only 8 percent of whites (2 percent of blacks) gave the same response about their fathers. A year later, G.I. author Philip Wylie labeled the Boom *The Sons and Daughters of Mom*.

- By almost any standard of social pathology, the Boom is a generation of worsening trends. From first-wave to last-wave teenagers, death rates for every form of accidental death rose sharply—and the rates of drunk driving, suicide, illegitimate births, and teen unemployment all doubled or tripled. Crime rates also mounted with each successive cohort, giving rise after the mid-1960s to "crime waves" that seemed to worsen with each passing year. During the 1970s, the incidence of serious youth crime grew twice as fast as the number of youths. Criminals born in 1958, moreover, were 80 percent more likely than criminals born in 1945 to commit multiple crimes—and 80 percent more likely to send their victims to the hospital or morgue.

- The seventeen-year SAT slide spanned nearly the entire Boom, from the 1946 cohort to the 1963 (13er) cohort—yet the worst years of that slide coincided with the greatest grade inflation ever measured. In 1969, 4 percent of college freshmen claimed to have had a straight-A high school grade average; by 1978, that proportion had nearly tripled, to 11 percent. From 1969 to 1975, the average collegiate grade rose from a C + to a B. By 1971, three-fourths of all colleges offered alternatives to traditional marking systems.

- Within the Boom, the "sexual revolution" was more a women's than a men's movement. Comparing the 1970s with the 1950s, one survey showed Boomer men with only a 3 percent increase in sexual activity over what the Silent did at like age—the smallest increase for any age bracket over that span. Similarly, the proportion of male youths experiencing premarital sex rose only slightly from the Silent to Boom eras. By contrast, Boomer women doubled the rate of premarital sex over the Silent (from 41 percent to 81 percent) and tripled their relative propensity to commit adultery (from one-fourth to three-fourths of the rate for men).

- The effort to avoid service in Vietnam was a more pervasive generational bond than service in the war itself. Only one Boomer man in sixteen ever saw combat. Among all the rest, two-thirds attributed their avoidance to some deliberate dodge. One Boomer in six accelerated marriage or fatherhood (and one in ten juggled jobs) to win a deferment, while one in twenty-five abused his body to flunk a physical. One percent of Boomer men committed draft-law felonies—ten times the percentage killed in combat. Less than one of every hundred offenders was ever jailed. The 1943–1947 cohorts provided the bulk of the draft avoiders, the 1947–1953 cohorts most of the combat troops. The median soldier age during the Vietnam War (19) was the lowest in American history.

- The Boom's only consensus "lesson" about Vietnam was that it was badly handled by G.I. leaders. Before 1970, Boomer opinion split roughly in half over the basic issue of U.S. presence in Southeast Asia. Only after the Kent State shootings and the "Days of Rage" did most college-attending Boomers oppose the war—although non-college Boomers remained more prowar than any elder group (college-educated or not). Today, one Boomer in four considers Vietnam to have been a "noble cause" (the highest proportion for any generation), and the generation splits roughly 50-50 between those who think the United States should have stayed out and those who would have fought to win. Following Iraq's invasion of Kuwait in 1990, Boomers were more inclined than any other generation to believe that sending American troops to the Gulf was "the right thing" to do.

- During the 1980s, rising-adult Boomers migrated out of mainline "established" churches, but surged into New Age and evangelical sects. Through the decade, overall Boom church attendance rose by nearly 30 percent. America's fastest-growing church is the Assembly of God (whose membership quadrupled in the 1980s), its largest branch of Protestantism is the fundamentalist Southern Baptist church, and the number of "charismatic" or "pentecostal" Catholics has quintupled. America now has more Muslims than Episcopalians. Seven Boomers in ten believe in psychic phenomena (versus five in ten among older generations). Within the generation, polls show first-wave Boomers believing more in meditation and reincarnation, last-wavers more in "born-again" conversion, mealtime grace, and the inherent conflict between religion and science.

- In the 1988 Presidential primaries, Boomers gave the greatest generational support to the two reverends in the race: Pat Robertson and Jesse Jackson. (G.I.s gave them the least support.)

- Were it not for employed women (and dual-income households), Boomer family incomes would be well below what the Silent earned at like age. Married Boomer couples are doing slightly better than their next-elders did, single women much better. But the individual Boomer man is not. A 40-year-old first-waver earns about 15 percent more than his G.I. father did at like age, whereas a 30-year-old last-waver has fallen about 10 percent behind his Silent father. Between age 30 and 40, where the typical full-time G.I. worker enjoyed a 63 percent inflation-adjusted rise in income, the first-wave Boom worker suffered a net 1 percent decline.

- Asked to compare themselves economically with their fathers at the same phase of life, Boomers are evenly split over whether they are doing better or worse. Yet they overwhelmingly consider their careers better (by a five-to-one ratio), their personal freedoms greater (by six to one), and their lives more meaningful (by nine to one).

The Boom Lifecycle

YOUTH: "We wanted our children to be inner-directed," recalled G.I. Eda LeShan. "It seemed logical to us that fascism and communism . . . could not really succeed except in countries where children were raised in very authoritarian homes." Boom children enjoyed a hothouse nurture in intensely child-focused households and communities. As G.I. dads worked to pay the bills, G.I. moms applied what LeShan termed "democratic discipline," dealing with children "thoughtfully, reasonably, and kindly." Seeking advice, these moms turned to a like-aged pediatrician, Benjamin Spock, who mixed science with friendliness and instructed his G.I. peers that "we need idealistic children." Coaxing (rather than pulling rank) in the nursery, Spock-guided moms applied his "permissive" feeding schedule to infants. Extending this logic to older kids, my-child-is-my-career moms invested tremendous maternal time and energy in grade-school Boomers. They hosted Cub Scout dens, typed book reports, cleaned children's rooms, and applied what one California psychologist termed the "He'll-clean-up-his-room-when-he's-ready-to-have-a-clean-room" philosophy. First-wave Boomers passed through public schools in their Sputnik-era peak of institutional confidence, thanks in part to a powerful mutual support network between G.I. mothers and teachers. Many a child's life did indeed match the *Happy Days* image preserved in vintage television sit-coms. To the eye of a Boomer kid, any problem seemed fixable by adults, especially once those white-coated scientists came on the scene. To youths like Cheryl Merser, "somebody was always watching over them—God or a saint or a guardian angel or the stars or whatever," and the future looked to be "the way life was on *The Jetsons*—happy, easy, uncomplicated, prosperous." To most middle-class youths, poverty, disease, and crime were invisible—or were, at most, temporary nuisances that would soon succumb to the inexorable advance of affluence. With the outer world looking fine, the inner world became the point of youth focus.

As successive Boom cohorts passed through childhood, the adult nurturing style leaned more toward tolerance than guidance, and parents began second-guessing the sacrifices they were making for the sake of their kids. Meanwhile, the adolescent environment darkened. From sex to politics, circa-1970 campus behavior swiftly filtered down to kids in high school, even junior high. By now reflecting a Silent ethos, public schools began losing the old G.I. mom-to-teacher peer support system. Reform-minded educators began insisting that adults had as much to learn from youths as vice versa. The curricula stressed learning skills over subject matter, social relevance over timeless facts. New student "rights" were litigated, and old extracurricular activities atrophied. Adolescent boy-girl coupling became increasingly tentative and individualized; where the Silent had gone "steady," Boomers went "with" someone. Popular song lyrics gradually shifted from Silentish styles (today remembered as "light" rock) to the more Boom-driven pessimism and defiance associated with "hard" (or "acid") rock. The Silent-era couples-only Saturday-night dance nearly vanished, eclipsed by rock concerts at which dateless teenagers could dance the night away all by themselves if they wanted. The first Boomer cohorts came of sexual age with the Beatles' *I Wanna Hold Your Hand*, middle cohorts with the Rolling Stones' *Let's Spend the Night Together*, late cohorts with Bruce Springsteen's *Dancing in the Dark*. Yet, whether first-wavers asserting a creative role in an idealized future or last-wavers attempting a more defiant withdrawal from the world, adolescents looked within themselves to find solutions to life's problems.

COMING OF AGE: "I Am a Student! Do Not Fold, Spindle, or Mutilate!" read the pickets outside Berkeley's Sproul Hall in 1964, mocking the computer-punch-card treatment the faculty was supposedly giving them. Where student movements had once been the work of a lonely (and polite) few, masses of youths began swarming to angry rallies. Coffeehouse poets gave way to bullhorn-toting radicals, in what Silent ex-activists Peter Collier and David Horowitz recall as a generational shift. "Those of us who had come of age in the fifties" and "were more comfortable thinking or talking about it" gave way to a later-born "second wave of activists" more likely to heed the simple motto: *"Do It!"* With the dawning of the Silent-led but Boom-energized "Free Speech Movement," these undergraduates served first notice of what would, by 1967, become the most emotionally intense and culturally influential youth rebellion in American history. The next four years brought a series of angry youth uprisings in schools, military depots, and inner cities—joined by a mixture of students and like-minded "nonstudents" who hung around campuses. Wealthy kids dressed down, donned unisex styles, and became self-declared "freaks"—as if to reject the affluence and ordered family lives of their parents. As James Kunen put it in *The Strawberry Statement,* "I want everyone to see me and say 'There goes an enemy of the state,' because that's where I'm at, as we say in the revolution biz." "STRIKE!" became the summons, the clenched fist the emblem, T-shirts and jeans the uniform, and "corporate liberalism" the enemy. "Who are these people?" asked the Silent Daniel Moynihan, then on the Harvard faculty. "I suggest to you they are Christians arrived on the scene of Second Century Rome."

Screaming radicals and freaked-out "hippies" represented just 10 to 15 percent of their generation, but the righteous often prevailed in a youth culture where purity of moral position counted most. In sharp contrast to the depression-era days of G.I. student "isms," organization counted for little. Keniston notes how the "young radicals" of the late 1960s, having grown up with "feelings of loneliness, solitude, and isolation," were profoundly mature by measures of ego strength and self-esteem, yet still childlike in their social skills. Collegians could issue "nonnegotiable demands" with little fear of later consequences, in part because of the amnesty they always demanded (and usually received), but also because the supercharged G.I.-built economy offered good jobs to all comers. The arguments of the New Left (led by "red diaper" babies who were waging their own battle against Old Left G.I. fathers) tended to be moral and cultural, with virtually no appeal off-campus. Yet a similar depth of rage welled up among Boomers who showed no affinity with college strikers. Urban black youths sparked deadly riots in American cities; non-college white Boomers were twice as likely as their elders to vote for George Wallace in the 1968 election; and the many town-versus-gown scuffles of that era were, in the main, Boom-on-Boom affairs.

With the economy still purring, the youth frenzy congealed around the Vietnam War—a policy construction almost perfectly designed to create conflict between rationalist elders and spiritualist juniors. Waging it as a limited, scientifically managed form of international pest control, G.I. leaders supported a morally questionable ally and avoided asking for any contribution from noncombatants (LBJ's "guns and butter"). Though not pacifist by nature, Boomers had been raised to question, argue, and ultimately disobey orders not comporting with self-felt standards and ultimate sacrifices. As much as Boomers hated the war, what they hated worse was the draft—its intrusion on privacy, its stated policy of "channeling" their lives in government-approved directions. With help from Silent counsel, Boomers did a good job of bollixing it. Yet the draft's enormous class bias created festering divisions between Boomers who went to Vietnam and those who didn't. For those who came of age in Southeast Asia, war offered little glory and few fond memories. The war's most celebrated heroes were G.I. POWs like Jeremiah Denton (or, in film, the aging "Green Beret" John Wayne), the most famous firefight was the My Lai atrocity, and the most publicized Boom soldier was William Calley. Coming home, Boomer "vets" had a defeat to haunt them, not a victory to empower them.

Vietnam casualties peaked in the same year (1969) that the Boomer rebellion turned bloody, with an eighteen-month spate of radical bombings and shootings—and a surge in street crime. Youths then felt what Gitlin described as "a tolerance, a fascination, even a taste" for violence. According to a Gallup Poll in 1970, 44 percent of all college students (versus only 14 percent of the public at large) believed that violence was justified to bring about social change. Rap Brown called violence "as American as apple pie," Angela Davis used it to great media effect, and the photo of Patty Hearst staging a bank holdup made older generations fear the latent urges in the most normal-looking people her age. From the Boom perspective, the most successful student strikes were those in which force was either threatened by strikers (as at Cornell) or used against them (by G.I. presidents Kerr, Kirk, and Pusey at Berkeley, Columbia, and Harvard). In the end, unwanted violence broke the youth fever. The killing of six students at Kent State and Jackson State briefly mobilized the generation in 1970. Following the "Days of Rage," polls showed campus unrest leading the nation's list of problems, and older generations showed a fixation on youth opinion unlike anything since the days of the young Missionaries. Eighteen-year-olds were awarded the vote, and national political conventions quadrupled the number of under-30 delegates. In 1970, the Silent Charles Reich wrote a rapturous best seller about how the Boom's "Consciousness III" would lead to *The Greening of America.*

Then, as the war wound down and draft calls eased, Boomers began heeding their Beatle mentors' "simple words of wisdom: *Let It Be.*" When the economy went sour in 1973, the youth mood turned to a grinding pessimism. The storm having passed, last-wavers came of age amid a gray generational drizzle of sex, drugs, unemployment, and what Lansing Lamont called a "lost civility" on campus. In politics, the Boom settled in as more apathetic and just plain illiberal than their G.I. parents could ever have imagined. As the Boom showed an air of resignation about government and business, aging G.I.s began acquiescing to the youth cult of self—and America's consumption binge was off and running.

RISING ADULTHOOD: "I have made no plans because I have found no plans worth making," declared the Dartmouth valedictorian in 1971. "All too many people are just waiting for life rather than living," observed the *Berkeley Daily Californian* in that same year. In politics and family lives, Boomers in their twenties remained detached—yet in the smaller strokes of their day-to-day existence, they began testing what they found within on the world without. Many began showing an emotional intensity older generations found strange, even compulsive. As exercise faddists searched for the "runner's high," backpackers with graduate degrees sparked a back-to-nature movement unlike anything seen since the turn of the century, and meditative diet faddists triggered what historian Harvey Levenstein terms "the century's Second Golden Age of Food Quackery." Through the 1970s, people of all ages still looked to Boomers for values guidance, and Boom trends soon blossomed into national attitudes—for example, as consumer brand loyalties weakened and "Made in the U.S.A." became passé among the cognoscenti. But the biggest news came in the workplace. In athletics, the first occupation over which they gained leverage, the likes of Andy Messersmith and Joe Namath proclaimed "free agency," after which sporting life grew more argumentative and less team-oriented. A few years later, a growing flood of late-starting Boomers began to spread these same traits throughout the economy. They insisted on having "meaningful" (read: un-G.I.-like) careers, and by the mid-1970s America's postwar productivity surge came to an abrupt end. Not drawn to industrial or service jobs, cutting-edge Boomers preferred smallish, eclectic businesses. Their homes began bristling with offices, neighborhoods with support services—an infrastructure around which, piece by piece, the economy was retooling to match the Boom's personality.

Thirtyish first-wavers were also actively designing a new concept of self-religion. The Boom heralded the "New Age" with the "Manifesto of the Person," asserting "our sovereign right of self-discovery." In this "Human Potential Movement," self-described as a "reaction to industrialized, mechanized thinking," large numbers of Boomers began dabbling in psychic phenomena and experiments in communal living. Whether immersed in Tai Chi, Zen, beta waves, or other New Age mind states, Boomers built churches in the privacy of their own heads. Urbanska termed this "Sheilaism," naming it after a friend named Sheila who had "this little voice inside" saying "God is whatever I feel." Conversions to "born-again" fundamentalism became more common than at any time in living memory. Boom religion returned the Calvinist notion of "calling" to its original emphasis on the immediate and subjective. A rising adult did not have to spend a lifetime preparing G.I. "works" for salvation. Boomers viewed spiritual life the way Richard Darman later described their consumption: They wanted it all—"NOWWWWW!"

Enter the "yuppie." Literally, the word means "young urban professionals," but that is misleading: Only some 5 percent of the Boom match the demographic (urban, professional, affluent) definition of the word. A much larger proportion, however, fit the subjective definition: self-immersion, an impatient desire for personal satisfaction, and weak civic instincts. Everything a yuppie does—what he eats, drinks, listens to, lives in, and invests for—sends a negative message about G.I.-style culture and institutions, at a time when G.I.s are losing energy to resist. The yuppie spurns organized philanthropies for causes he thinks he has discovered himself. His busiest work occurs in the smallest units: the home, the small business, the PTA, the day-care center, the town zoning board, the "privatized" governing body. His method of achieving social change—unassociated individuals, each acting pursuant to his own compass—is the opposite of the cohesive, peer-pressured G.I. approach at like age. The word "yuppie" first appeared in 1981, just after most Boomers chose Reagan over Carter, and signaled their acceptance of adult social roles. Having finished the task of reforming the inner world, this generation gradually began taking on the outer.

APPROACHING MIDLIFE: Where the Silent once prided themselves on their ability to "grow young" with advancing age, Boomers look upon themselves as "growing up" to a new sense of responsibility and self-denial—what P. J. O'Rourke calls the "new seriousness." One advertising agency labels Boomers "the New Grown-ups" and claims they are launching an "era of less-than-instant gratification." In her thirties, Cheryl Merser discovered that "a grown-up is someone who can buy cookies and not eat the whole package at once." The fastest-track yuppies are showing a growing taste for ascetic self-denial—for example, preferring negative product names (nonfat, noncaffeine, non-aerosol, non-nitrate, even "no-color" mascara) that flaunt what the consumer is *not* consuming. Surveys show that today's Boomers are more apt to believe that patience is necessary to appreciate value and are more likely to buy products that *are* good than products that *taste* or *feel* good. Their aging has a nonapologetic quality—as though now that they're older, they know better.

More in parallel than collectively, Boomers are asserting judgments that reflect the perfect moral order of Pepperland. Although they have grown reasonably comfortable with aging G.I. leaders who adopt their "values" terminology, Boomers still see themselves as the embodiment of moral wisdom. It makes no difference that they have entirely vacated the "youth" age bracket. On matters of right and wrong, in fact, most Boomers now care as little for the opinions of their 13er juniors as they ever cared for the opinions of their G.I. and Silent elders. At the very moment Boomers patched up the rift with their parents, notes journalist Henry Allen, "they saw they still had problems with materialistic Republican reactionaries, except that the reactionaries were twenty years younger." "A generation that when young trusted nobody over 30 today trusts nobody under 30," agrees Pennsylvania history professor Alan Kors, observing how his peers seek to "cleanse the souls of the undergraduates of the political, social, and moral sins" of their youthful upbringing.

A growing chorus of social critics is noticing a Boom-led (and often 13er-targeted) "New Puritanism" in circa-1990 America. Fortyish Americans are beginning to police "politically correct" behavior, pass "anti-ugly" zoning ordinances, punish students for "inappropriately directed laughter," circulate "Green Lifestyle" guides and attach "Green Seals" to products, ban obscene music, promote "chastity," and even support novel forms of corporal punishment and boot-camp incarceration that G.I.s would never have imagined—and that Boomers, two decades ago, would have considered fascist. The abortion debate rages in deadly earnest, mostly Boom-on-Boom, with shades of first-wave pro-choicers against last-wave pro-lifers. Smoking or regular drinking, observes *New York Times* writer Molly O'Neill, are becoming the "new Scarlet Letters" among ex-flower children. When G.I.s were reaching their forties, "Buy you a drink?" and "Have a smoke?" were friendly icebreakers between strangers; now M.A.D.D.'s Candy Lightner attacks social drinking (and Congressman Dick Durbin airborne smoking) as dangerous, even immoral. As one Boom activist puts it, "There is no such thing as being too rude to a smoker."

Now gaining real power, Boomers do not inherently dislike government: The idea of using the state to tell people what to do suits them just fine. Their task is to redirect public institutions toward what they consider a socially redemptive purpose. Casting aside the Silent preoccupation with process and expertise, Boomers (when focused) zero in on the essentials, choose between right and wrong, and act accordingly. Boomers of all ideological stripes, from Oliver North and Fawn Hall to "Animal Rights" lab bombers, can be easily attracted to lawlessness in pursuit of a higher purpose. In Washington, D.C., the memory of Mitch Snyder beckons social activists to invite arrest "in the name of a just and loving God," while in California "Earth First" eco-saboteurs apply the motto "No Compromise in Defense of Mother Earth." New York Reverend Al Sharpton summons blacks to "burn the city down" over alleged injustices, while Shelby Steele calls upon blacks to examine "the content of our character" and reject racial preferences as "kindness that kills." When Boom-driven movements produce legislative enactments—such as Oregon's refusal to spend Medicaid funds on operations considered too expensive or unlikely of success—the budgetary result can be less important than the no-pain-no-gain message to society at large. Addressing America's unmet social needs, from crime and homelessness to health and education, Boomers are far more inclined than other generations to share Karl Zinsmeister's view that "genuine compassion demands that we forego the comfortable, and ever so easier, responses of softness.''

Vanguard Boomers show streaks of severity, the desire for not just an enemy's defeat, but his destruction. Confronted with Saddam Hussein, Boomers at the *Wall Street Journal* call on American forces to "take Baghdad and install a MacArthur Regency"—and drop hints about war-crimes tribunals. Former Secretary of the Navy James Webb proposes "ruthless and overpowering" retaliation against foreign enemies and suggests constructing a "very large, very primitive federal prison in a remote area of Alaska" for drug dealers. As William Bennett unjokingly weighs the advantages of beheading underworld kingpins, his peers show the strongest generational support for capital punishment. Boomers dominate the national ranks of the "Fryers Club," young prosecutors who favor the death penalty (and who confer over how to beat older ACLU defense lawyers). For other generations, support for the death penalty declines if respondents are told to ignore the issue of deterrence—but not for Boomers, who are more likely to see execution as moral retribution.

Boomers are starting to show a fascination for apocalyptic solutions. Unlike their G.I. fathers, who excelled at *overcoming* crisis, Boomers are attracted to the possibility of *fomenting* crisis. Bennett sums up his own approach to governance in two words: "Consequence and Confrontation." The 47-year-old budget director, daring to close down essential federal services if the deficit is not reduced, is dubbed "Apocalypse Darman" by the press. In Congress, Newt Gingrich promises to use "values" as "a way of dividing America," while Marty Russo refuses to go along with a budget process "that stinks and lies." Silent Congressman Byron Dorgan, speaking for many of his House peers, acknowledges how "confrontational" younger colleagues simply "don't respect the old rules and courtesies." The gathering Boom vision of the future is at once dark and bright—with new pronouncements about how denial, even pain, will be necessary today to achieve righteousness tomorrow. The Sierra Club's Dan Becker has openly rooted for "especially bad" weather so "a crisis mentality can take over" about global warming, while *Washington Post* sportswriter Tom Boswell has asked whether the "purification by fire" of a canceled season might be needed to cleanse baseball of greed. James Fallows has declared that "the world economy badly needs a few crises" and that America would benefit from a "7.0 magnitude diplo-economic shock." Whatever the problem, the Boom prescription is not for a sugar-coated cure, but for a purgative tonic.

The "sky will first need to fall" before the world wakes up to its environmental folly, insisted Boomer columnist Christopher Winner just before Earth Day 1990, an event that had a far sterner, less euphoric tone than the original Earth Day in 1970. "And when the dead are counted, when pan-global rules prevent further murder of air and water and all that which sustains and encourages life, the first real Earth Day will bear celebration." Winner's peers, say Collier and Horowitz, are "a destructive generation whose work is not over yet." Peering into the future of the Woodstock Generation, Anthony Casale and Philip Lerman see the prospect of "howling cold, danger, and misery." Yet what some interpret as a belligerent pessimism is, in its present chrysalis, a summons to rekindle a principled vision of national (and global) community. In one jurisdiction after another, Boomers who once voted for Reagan are now starting to push for a more explicit exercise of public authority—more taxes, zoning, schools, or prisons— so long as this authority moves America toward the lofty social standard that Boomers themselves have sanctified. Until that standard is reached, they will distrust any path that doesn't hurt—and they will care less than others about how many feel the "howling cold" along the way.

*   *   *

When Lloyd Bentsen told Dan Quayle, "You are no Jack Kennedy," and Howard Metzenbaum said of William Bennett that "he believes words speak louder than actions," those rockets landed on more than just individual targets. In the G.I. mind's eye, you could replace Quayle or Bennett with any of today's 45-year-olds, and none of them could match a G.I. doer in his prime. Then again, the hubristic Kennedy—the war-hero President of "prestige" and "long strides"—was decidedly no Boomer. Nor did his "best and brightest" share anything like the common thread of consciousness among Boomers (Jody Powell, Hamilton Jordan, David Stockman, Peggy Noonan, Lee Atwater, and Richard Darman) who have visited the White House inner circle during the last two decades. As Quayle, Bennett, Al Gore, Bill Bradley, Bob Kerrey, and others in their mid-forties threaten to push aside the Silent in the generational succession to the Oval Office, their generation already holds one of every four seats in the House of Representatives, fills nearly every important office in George Bush's West Wing, and broadly dominates the media—from Hollywood to National Public Radio to the editorial writers at the *Wall Street Journal*. Whatever their stripe, Boomers are far less interested in tangible constructions (what Metzenbaum calls "actions") than in establishing a fresh moral regime.

Offering themselves as the magistrates of this new order, Boomers are stirring to defend values (monogamy, thrift, abstention from drugs) other generations do not associate with them. Their scorched-earth rhetoric seems misplaced in a generation of onetime draft dodgers. Critics can and do call them smug, narcissistic, self-righteous, intolerant, puritanical. But one commonly heard charge, that of "hypocrite," ill fits a generation that came of age resacralizing and has kept at it. Boomers are in no rush. Always the distracted perfectionists, they first apply a light hand, then (once they start paying attention) a crushingly heavy one. They "graze" on munchies until they figure it's time to diet, and then they don ashes and sackcloth.

"Oh, how I miss the Revolution," wrote the (conservative) Boomer columnist Benjamin Stein in 1988. "I want the Revolution back." Seventeen years earlier, Charles Reich had prophesied how new Boomer values would someday transform civilization "beyond anything in modern history. Beside it," he bubbled, "a mere revolution, such as the French or Russian, seems inconsequential." Reich

misperceived the Boom's readiness to assume power and pandered to its trappings, but he understood its seriousness of purpose. From Jonathan Schell to
Jeremy Rifkin, Charles Murray to Alan Keyes, Steven Jobs to Steven Spielberg,
Boomers are still doing what they have done for decades: giving America its
leading visionaries and "wise men" —or just its preachy didactics— regardless
of the age bracket they occupy.

On December 2, 1989, *Good Housekeeping* magazine published a full-page
ad in the *New York Times,* welcoming America to the 1990s, "the Decency
Decade, the years when the good guys finally win. . . . It will be a very good
decade for the Earth, as New Traditionalists lead an unstoppable environmental
juggernaut that will change and inspire corporate America, and let us all live
healthier, more decent lives" and "make people look for what is real, what is
honest, what is quality, what is valued, what is important." In ways other
generations partly applaud and partly loathe, Boomers today stand midgame in
a many-pronged reworking of American society. The righteous fires of People's
Park are still smoldering.

THIRTEENTH GENERATION

Born: 1961–1981
Type: Reactive

Age Location:
Boom Awakening in youth

In November of 1979, just after an Iranian mob had swarmed into the U.S. Embassy in Tehran, a University of Georgia student center gave a special screening of the movie *Patton*. The students gave the film a standing ovation, hanged an effigy of the Ayatollah, and then ran through the streets chanting anti-Iran slogans. That year, a new breed of college freshman came to America's campuses. Previously, faculty members had lined up to introduce themselves. Suddenly, as a Georgetown campus minister put it, "students began lining up to introduce themselves to us." Meet the smooth opening wedge of the THIRTEENTH GENERATION—what *Washington Post* writer Nancy Smith pointedly calls "the generation after. Born after 1960, after you, after it all happened." These were the babies of 1961, 8-year-olds of Woodstock, 13-year-olds of Watergate, 18-year-olds of energy crisis and hostage humiliation—and 29-year-olds when a 1990 *Time* cover story defined this generation as post-Boom "twenty-somethings." In 1979, just as these kids were making life-pivoting decisions about schools and careers, older generations sank into an eighteen-month abyss of national pessimism. For Silent parents, Thinking Small was a midlife tonic. But never having had their own chance to Think Big, the high school class of 1979 saw this grim mood very differently. From the Vietnam hysteria to Nixon's "Christmas Without Lights" to Three Mile Island—at every turn, these kids sensed that adults were simply not in control of themselves or the country.

Far more than other generations, 13ers feel that the real world is gearing up to punish them down the road. Annual polls of high school seniors show that those born just after 1960 came of age much more fearful of national catastrophe than those born just before. These early 1960s babies (as we saw in Chapter 2) grew up as the kids whose low test scores and high rates of crime, suicide, and substance abuse marked a postwar extreme for American youth. The indicators have not improved much for Americans born in the late 1960s and 1970s. Altogether, writes Felicity Barringer in the *New York Times*, older Americans are coming to perceive them as "a lost generation, an army of aging Bart Simpsons, possibly armed and dangerous."

Unlike the Boomer kids-in-jeans of the 1960s, 13ers present, to elder eyes, a splintered image of brassy sights, caustic sounds, and cool manner. Moviegoers

THIRTEENTH GENERATION (Born 1961 to 1981)

TYPE: Reactive

Total number: 93,000,000
Now alive in U.S.: 79,000,000
Percent immigrant: 11%

FAMILY TREE

Typical grandparents: G.I.
Parents: Silent and Boom
Children: Millennial (and new Adaptive)
Typical grandchildren: (new Idealist)

SAMPLE MEMBERS, birth (death)

1961 Michael J. Fox*
1961 Eddie Murphy
1962 Jon Bon Jovi
1962 Roger Clemens
1962 Tom Cruise
1963 Tatum O'Neal
1963 Michael Jordan
1963 Whitney Houston
1963 Len Bias (1986)
1964 Tracy Chapman
1965 Brooke Shields
1966 Mike Tyson
1967 Lisa Bonet
1967 Jim Abbott
1968 Mary Lou Retton
1968 Moon Unit Zappa
1968 Gary Coleman
1972 "Tiffany" Darwish
1972 Samantha Smith (1985)
1976 Jennifer Capriati

* = immigrant

FUTURE PERIOD OF
POLITICAL LEADERSHIP

Plurality in Congress: 2015–2035 (proj.)
Term of Presidency: 2020–2040 (proj.)
Majority of Supreme Court: 2030–2050 (proj.)

PROMINENT FOREIGN PEERS

1961 Princess Di
1963 Julian Lennon
1967 Boris Becker
1968 Wuer Kaixi
1969 Steffi Graf

Age	Date	HISTORY AND LIFECYCLE
0– 1	1962:	U.S. government approves public sale of birth-control pill
0– 4	1965:	"Baby boom" ends; Supreme Court upholds right to contraceptives
0– 7	1968:	*Rosemary's Baby* begins decade-long popularity of bad-child films
0–12	1973:	*Roe* v. *Wade* abortion case; Christmas Without Lights
0–18	1979:	U.S. hostages seized in Iran; long lines at gas pumps
0–19	1980:	Military enlistments surge; youth vote supports Reagan
2–22	1983:	*A Nation at Risk* sharply criticizes students; Grenada invasion
5–25	1986:	Schoolchildren watch *Challenger* shuttle explode on takeoff
8–28	1989:	Surge in gang killings, "wilding"; Berlin Wall dismantled
9–29	1990:	Rock lyrics censored; U.S. troops go to Persian Gulf

SAMPLE CULTURAL ENDOWMENTS: *Liar's Poker* (Michael Lewis); *sex, lies, and videotape* (film, Steven Soderbergh); *Less Than Zero* (Bret Easton Ellis); *20 Under 30* (Debra Spark); *The Dartmouth Review*; *Slippery When Wet* (album, Jon Bon Jovi); *Short Sharp Shocked* (album, Michelle Shocked); *Fast Car* (song, Tracy Chapman); *As Nasty as They Wanna Be* (album, 2 Live Crew); *Think of One* (album, Wynton Marsalis); *Remote Control* (MTV); *Hangin' Tough* (album, New Kids on the Block); "Too Much Fun" (graffiti art, Brett Cook) know them as Tom Cruise as *Top Gun,* breaking a few rules to win; as *The Breakfast Club,* a film about how teachers try to punish a hopeless and incorrigible "Brat Pack" of teenagers; as Steven Soderbergh's *sex, lies, and videotape;* and as Rob Lowe playing the ultimate *Bad Influence.* In city life, they have become America's kamikaze bicycle messengers, speeding Domino's and Federal Express drivers, murderous inner-city "crack" gangs, computer hackers, and would-be novelists—guys who, as John Schwartz (author of *Bicycle Days*) puts it, like to "live a little faster." In high schools, 13ers are Asian-American valedictorians and Westinghouse science finalists, more than half of them immigrants or the children of immigrants. Fresh from college, they are the Yale class of 1986, 40 percent of whom applied for investment banking jobs with one company (First Boston)—the lucky ones becoming dealmakers who "age like dogs" in Michael Lewis' game of *Liar's Poker.* In athletics, they are young Olympians leading chants of "U-S-A! U-S-A!", or "Air Jordan" and "Neon Deion" Sanders with their "in-your-face" slam dunks and end-zone spikes, or one-armed Jim Abbott winning against impossible odds. In the army, 13ers are the defenders of Saudi oilfields and the invaders of Panama, whose boom boxes may have helped persuade Manuel Noriega to surrender—one of whom said, on receiving a warm goodbye from the Panamanians, that "to them it's everything, to us it's just a battle."

Older generations see them as frenetic, physical, slippery. Like the music many of them listen to, 13ers can appear shocking on the outside, unknowable on the inside. Elders find it hard to suppress feelings of disappointment over how they are turning out—dismissing them as a "lost," "ruined," even "wasted" generation in an unrelenting (and mostly unanswered) flurry of what Ellen Goodman has termed "youth-bashing." Disparaging them as the "dumb" and "numb generation," Russell Baker says "today's youth suffer from herky-jerky brain." Boom evangelists like California's Larry Lea condemn their soullessness and have declared "spiritual warfare" on youth "worship of the devil." Under the headline "Hopes of a Gilded Age: Class of 1987 Bypasses Social Activism to Aim for Million-Dollar Dreams of Life," a *Washington Post* article complains how "the fiery concerns of many of their predecessors over peace and social justice are mementos from a dimming past." *People* magazine has coined the phrase "Rettonization of America" to describe how young stars now sell their names and reputations to the highest bidder. Boomers are shocked by the 13er chemical of choice, steroids (which augment the body and dim the mind, just the opposite of Boom-era psychedelics). Sportswriter Bill Mandel contemptuously dismisses baseball slugger José Canseco as "the perfect athlete" for his era—"pumped up bigger than a steer and completely oblivious to the vital subtext of his sport." The Boomer media often portray 13ers as driven more by appetites than by ideas—as when Jay Leno tells teenage television viewers why they eat Doritos: "We're not talkin' brain cells here. We're talkin' taste buds." Soft-drink commercials do not show 13ers chanting and swaying on some verdant hillside, but instead careening (like Michael J. Fox for Pepsi) through some hellhouse and winding up on a pile of junk. "What he needs," said a recent Ad Council caption of a confused-looking teenager, "is a good swift kick in the pants." "This is the thought that wakes me up in the middle of the night," says one Boomer teacher in *The Breakfast Club*, "that when I get older, these kids are gonna take care of me." "Don't hold your breath," answers another.

Every year through the 1980s, new reports of their academic scores have triggered harsh elder assessments of their schooling and intelligence. The barrage began in 1983 when *A Nation at Risk* despaired of a "rising tide of mediocrity" emerging from America's schools. Allan Bloom's *The Closing of the American Mind* declared the 13ers' minds quite closed, and Diane Ravitch and Chester Finn's *What Do Seventeen-Year-Olds Know?* answered their own question by saying, in effect, not much. Grading 13ers collectively in twenty-nine subjects, Ravitch and Finn dished out twenty F's—and no other grade higher than a C−. The sympathy and indulgence once offered to low-scoring young Boomers has evaporated. Columnist Richard Cohen recently called for "humiliating, embarrassing, mocking—you name it—the dummies who have scored so low on these tests." And "just when you think America's students can't get any dumber," reported Jack Anderson in 1989, out comes another book like Steve Allen's *Dumbth,* or another blue-ribbon report from the Carnegie Foundation, calling them "shallow" and chastising their "uncivil speaking" and "deteriorating" campus culture (all this in an era of campus calm that would have been the envy of any Boom-era dean). Right or wrong, the message sent to 13ers and their would-be employers is clear: that these kids got an inferior education and are equipped with inferior minds—that they are (to quote one Boomer college president) "junky."

Thirteeners find these criticisms overblown. They look upon themselves as pragmatic, quick, sharp-eyed, able to step outside themselves to understand the game of life as it really gets played. And whatever they are, 13ers insist, they *have* to be. Because of the way they were raised. Because of the world into which they are coming of age. To begin with, 13ers see no welcome mat on their economic future: Since the mid-1970s, while the costs of setting out in life (college tuitions and housing) have raced ahead of inflation, the rewards (salaries and fringe benefits for young workers) have steadily fallen behind. They are suffering what economist Robert Kuttner describes as a "remarkable generational economic disease . . . a depression of the young" which makes 13ers feel "uniquely thirsty in a sea of affluence." Money isn't everything—but 13ers find themselves both unprepared for and uninvited to most other avenues of social approval. Money means survival, and for a generation whose earliest life experiences have taught them not to trust others, survival must come first.

Older critics seldom acknowledge the odd twists that have so far plagued the 13er lifecycle. In the early 1970s, Norman Lear produced *All in the Family–*

style television shows that bred child cynicism about the competence of the adult world—then, in the late 1980s, Lear's "People for the American Way" lobby whipsawed the grown-up kids thus nurtured with a stinging report rebuking their "apathy and disengagement from the political process." When 13ers were entering school, they heard gurus (like Charles Rathbone) say there was "no single indispensable body of knowledge that every child should know," so their schools didn't teach it—then, upon finishing school, they heard new gurus (like E. D. Hirsch, in *Cultural Literacy*) say yes, there was such knowledge, and they hadn't learned it. Thirteeners were told, as Rathbone (and many others) had urged, to be "self-reliant, independent, self-actualizing individuals." So they learned to watch adults carefully and emulate how they behave—collectively resembling Tatum O'Neal in *Paper Moon,* the kind of kids adults have a hard time finding adorable.

Imagine coming to a beach at the very end of a long summer of big crowds and wild goings-on. The beach bunch is sunburned, the sand shopworn, hot, and full of debris—no place for walking barefoot. You step on a bottle, and some cop cites you for littering. That's how 13ers feel, following the Boom. Much like River Phoenix in the film *Running on Empty,* first-wave 13ers have had to cope and survive in whatever territory the Boom has left behind, at each phase of life. Their early access to self-expression and independence stripped them of much of the pleasure of discovery and rebellion—leaving them, in Bret Easton Ellis' words, "looking up from the asphalt and being blinded by the sun." By the time Ellis' peers came of age, the symbolic meanings—of sex, drugs, student rights, whatever—had all faded. What they found, instead, were the harsh realities of social pathology. One by one, 13ers have slowed or reversed these trends—the SAT decline, the youth crime, the substance abuse, the early sex—but 13ers have felt the full brunt of them and have borne the ensuing adult criticism.

Thirteeners, not Boomers, were America's true "children of the 1960s." And, especially, the 1970s. An awakening era that seemed euphoric to young adults was, to them, a nightmare of self-immersed parents, disintegrating homes, schools with conflicting missions, confused leaders, a culture shifting from G to R ratings, new public-health dangers, and a "Me Decade" economy that tipped toward the organized old and away from the voiceless young. "Grow up fast" was the adult message. That they did, graduating early to "young adult" realism in literature and film, and turning into what *American Demographics* magazine has termed "proto-adults" in their early teens (where, two decades earlier, Boomers had lingered in "post-adolescence" well into their twenties). At every phase of life, 13ers have encountered a world of more punishing consequence than anything their Silent or Boom elders ever knew. Consider the 13ers' matter-of-fact approach to sexuality, yet another trait that has brought adult complaint. First-wavers were just reaching puberty when adults were emitting highly charged sexual signals in all directions. At the time, sex education was unabashedly value-neutral, empty houses provided easy trysting spots, and their parents were, as Ellen Goodman describes them, "equally uncomfortable with notions that sex is evil and sex is groovy." With adults having removed attitudinal barriers against the libido, 13ers have begun re-erecting age-old defense mechanisms: platonic relationships, group dating, and a youth culture (reminiscent of Lost-era street life) in which kids watch out for their own safety and for the physical integrity of their own circle of friends. Unlike Boomers, 13ers are coming of age knowing where the youth euphoria of the late 1960s actually led. As Redlands College's Kim Blum puts it, "the sexual revolution is over, and everybody lost."

The 13er lifecycle experience has, so far, been the direct inverse of the Silent. Where the Silent passed through childhood in an era of parental suffocation and entered young adulthood just as barriers to youth freedom began to loosen, 13ers have faced exactly the opposite trend. Where the Silent grew up with a childlike awe of powerful elders, 13ers have acquired an adultlike fatalism about the weakness and uncertainty of elders—and question their ability to protect the young from future danger. When the first Silent were children, America was in the skids of depression, but by their twentieth birthday, public confidence was vast and rising. When the first 13ers were born, America was riding high and G.I. leaders seemed to be achieving everything at once—but then, as they reached adolescence, the nation mired itself in doubt. The Silent emerged from their storybook childhood hoping to add some nuance and subtlety to a culture they found oversimple. Thirteeners, by contrast, are growing up in what teacher and author Patrick Welsh describes as "a world of information overload." Hearing others declare everything too complex for yes-or-no answers, 13ers struggle to filter out noise, cut through rhetoric, and isolate the handful of practical truths that really matter. Also unlike the homogeneous young Silent, 13ers are coming of age with sharply diverging personal circumstances (what an economist would call a "spreading bell curve") in education, family economics, and career opportunities. Where their parents once struggled to break free from a tight generational center of gravity, 13ers wonder if they will ever be able to find one.

Confronted with these facts of life, 13ers have built a powerful survival instinct, wrapped around an ethos of personal determinism. In their world, what a person is, what he looks like, and whether or not he succeeds depend less on what a person is inside than on how he behaves. Thirteeners are constantly told that whatever bad things strike people their age—from AIDS to drug addiction, from suicides to homicides—are mainly their own fault. In this sort of youth environment, staying alert to the physical is an assertion of virtue. Unlike Boomers at like age, a low-income 13er probably comes from a world of splintered families and general hopelessness—and has little in common with some "Richie Rich" out in the suburbs. And so kids feel obliged to dress up (at an age when most Boomers dressed down) to preserve a sense of personal honor and to avoid being "disrespected" in a real-life game of king of the mountain.

Doing what they feel they must, knowing it brings adult criticism, 13ers have come to accept, even to take a perverse fun in, what a young rapper would call "attitude," in being "BAAAAD." They tend to agree with their elders that, probably, they *are* a wasted bunch. From the standpoint of an individual 13er, weak peer competition isn't such bad news. Their own cultural artifacts make half-comic reference to their own garbagey quality. Chris Kreski, the 26-year-old lead writer for *Remote Control,* a 13er-designed TV-quiz-show parody, admits his show is "stupid." (In 13er lingo, words like "stupid," "bad," or "random" are words of praise.) The Bon Jovi song *You Give Love a Bad Name* became an instant hit among the teens of the 1980s. In 1990, when a think tank issued yet another negative report on 13ers (documenting their "massive cheating, résumé fraud, assaults on teachers, venereal disease, pregnancies, and materialism"), its authors afterward remarked that 13ers themselves seemed to agree with these findings. In *River's Edge*, a film evoking how many 13ers look at life, one teenager mockingly says to his buddies, "You young people are a disgrace to all living things, to plants even. You shouldn't even be seen in the same room as a cactus."

As they struggle to preserve what optimism and self-esteem they can, 13ers have developed what psychologist David Elkind calls the "patchwork self." Two decades ago, older generations saw great promise in youth. Not now—not these youths, anyway. As first-wavers find themselves elbowed aside by Boomers seemingly at every turn, last-wavers lock their radars onto Nintendo in fantasized quest of fortune or death, or join the Spurtlegurgles in singing the lyric of a missionless childhood ("We're here because we're here because we're here because we're here"). "So many things have already happened in the world that we can't possibly come up with anything else," explains 15-year-old David Peters, a fast-food worker in California. "So why even live?" No other generation in living memory has come of age with such a sense of social distance—of adults doing so little for them and expecting so little from them.

Lacking the ego strength to set agendas for others, 13ers instead react to the world as they find it. They're proud of their ability to poke through the hype and the detail, to understand older people far better (they sense) than older people understand them. They take solace in the privacy that affords them. Many even delight in the most demeaning images of youth ever crafted by the electronic media: Max Headroom, beheaded in an accident, imprisoned within TV sound bites; the Teenage Mutant Ninja Turtles, flushed down the toilet as children, deformed by radiation, nurtured on junk food; and Bart Simpson, the "under-achiever" whose creator likens him to everyone's "disgusting little brother"— the "little Spike-Head" whom William Bennett says he'll "straighten out" with "a couple of soap sandwiches." Beyond low self-esteem and blighted minds, what these pop icons all have in common is that they were created and promoted by Boomers—the 13ers' principal nemeses. Some day, some way, 13ers would love to get those Boomers on life's equivalent of *Remote Control,* swivel their yuppie chairs around, and dump them in a vat of greenish goo.

"My generation was born on Friday the Thirteenth," insists Bowdoin College's Gregg Linburg. "That's a day you can view two ways. You can fear it, or you can face it—and try to make it a great day in spite of the label. That's what my generation is going to do." Counting back to the Awakeners, Linburg's peers are, in point of fact, the thirteenth to call themselves American citizens. Demographers have so far given them a name at once incorrect and insulting: "baby busters." Population is not the issue. Thirteeners outnumber Boomers by ten million in 1990, a gap widening by the year, and their first-wave (1961–1964) cohorts are among the biggest ever. "Baby bust" theorists see in the name some new youth advantage in a world of easing youth competition—but try telling that to collegians born in the smallish late-1960s cohorts. Yet the worst aspect of this "bust" nomer, and why 13ers resent it, is how it plants today's 25-year-olds squarely where they don't want to be: in the shadow of the "boom," and negatively so—as though wonder has been followed by disappointment.

To young Americans uninterested in labels—to those who still remain what Shann Nix calls "the generation with no name"—we assign a number: thirteen. The tag is a little Halloweenish, like the clothes they wear—and slippery, like their culture. It's a name they can see as a gauntlet, a challenge, an obstacle to be overcome. The thirteenth card can be the ace, face down, in a game of high-stakes blackjack. Kings and queens, with their pompous poses and fancy curlicues, always lose to the uncluttered ace, going over or going under. The ace—like this generation—is nothing subtle, but it's nice to have around when you're in a jam.

13er Facts

• The 13th is the most aborted generation in American history. After rising sharply during the late 1960s and early 1970s, the abortion rate climbed by another 80 percent during the first six years (1973 to 1979) after the Supreme Court's *Roe* v. *Wade* decision. Through the birthyears of last-wave 13ers, would-be mothers aborted one fetus in three.

• Parental divorce has struck 13ers harder than any other American generation. In 1962, half of all adult women believed that parents in bad marriages should stay together for the sake of the children; by 1980, only one in five thought so. A 13er child in the 1980s faced twice the risk of parental divorce as a Boomer child in the mid-1960s—and three times the risk a Silent child faced back in 1950. Four-fifths of today's divorced adults profess to being happier afterward, but a majority of their children feel otherwise.

- No other American generation has ever grown up in families of such complexity. In 1980, just 56 percent of all dependent children lived with two once-married parents, another 14 percent with at least one previously married parent, 11 percent with a stepparent, and 19 percent with one parent. One in five had half siblings. The likelihood of children receiving support payments from the noncustodial parent declined from the Boomer to 13er childhood eras.

- No other child generation has witnessed such a dramatic increase in domestic dissatisfaction (and surge to the workplace) on the part of mothers. Between 1960 and 1980, among mothers with children aged 5 or under, the proportion with full- or part-time jobs rose from 20 to 47 percent. Through the 1970s, the number of "latchkey" children under age 14 left alone after school roughly doubled.

- A late-1980s survey of "teen trendsetters" found 48 percent describing their (mostly Silent) parents as "cool"—versus just 7 percent as "strict" and 1 percent as "nosy." According to youth marketer and pollster Irma Zandl, 13ers associate lack of parental authority with family instability. Observes Zandl, "I've never heard any teenager say, 'I wish my father were more sensitive.'"

- When they first reached high school, 13ers encountered much less of the teacher-and-voter indulgence that had greeted their next-elders. The Boomer-era grade inflation came to an abrupt end: Youths born in 1961 received 10 percent fewer high school A's and 10 percent more C's than those born in 1960. At the ballot-box, first-wave 13ers were the targets of the late-1970s "Proposition 13" school-tax revolts in California and other states. Similarly, during the decade after 1978 (that is, after the last Boomers had reached age 18), the purchasing power of both the child-poverty benefit and the federal minimum wage declined steeply and continuously.

- A sampling of teachers who taught Boomers in the mid-1960s and 13ers in the mid-1980s was asked to compare the two, in forty-three measures of aptitude and achievement. The score: Boomers 38, 13ers 4, with one tie. The teachers scored Boomers higher in all academic skills, communications ability, and commitment to learning. Thirteeners outscored Boomers in negotiating skills, consumer awareness, adult-interaction skills, and "defenses to prevent extreme dependency on parents or authorities."

- The 13th is on its way to becoming the first generation since the Gilded to be less college-educated than its next-elders. College completion rates, seven years after high school graduation, fell from 58 percent for the Boomer Class of 1972 to 37 percent for the 13er Class of 1980. Meanwhile, the economic stakes of higher education have risen sharply. From 1973 to 1986, the average inflation-adjusted earnings of young college graduates fell by 6 percent—but for young high school dropouts, they fell by 42 percent.

- By a two-to-one majority, 13er men prefer military to civilian public service—in a sharp turnaround from the Boom youth era. Starting when the first 13er cohort reached age 19, the armed forces began a dramatic three-year rise in the quality of new enlistees. Thirteeners are the best-educated generation of soldiers in American history.

- Much like Michael J. Fox in *Family Ties* (the conservative kid of liberal parents), these are by far the most Republican-leaning youths in the sixty-year history of age-based polling. From Boom to 13th, the partisan tone of young voters has shifted strikingly—from roughly a ten-point Democratic advantage to a Republican edge that, in 1985, reached eighteen points (52 percent to 34 percent). In fifteen of sixteen consecutive polls taken between 1981 and 1988, 13ers gave Ronald Reagan a higher approval rating than any other generation—except the Lost.

- Thirteener teenagers face a much lower risk of dying from disease than did Silent teenagers forty years ago. But this 13er advantage has been almost entirely offset by a much higher risk of dying from accidents, murder, and suicide. Roughly 2,000 minors were murdered in 1988—twice the number killed in 1965 (a year of urban riots when America had 6.5 million more youths under age 18). Homicide is now the dominant cause of youth mortality in America's inner cities. Among black males 15 to 24 years old living in Washington, D.C., murder accounted for 47 percent of all deaths in 1987.

- Fear is a pervasive reality within a generation of urban schoolchildren that brings an estimated 135,000 guns (and six times as many knives) to the classroom each day. Eight percent of urban seventh to twelfth graders say they miss at least one day of school per month because they are physically afraid to go. At the same time, 13ers learn young that the only way to cope with fear is not to show it. Says Bronx junior-high teacher Klaus Bornemann: "The kid who demonstrates fear is raw meat."

- As teenagers, 13ers are committing suicide more frequently than any generation since the Lost. In 1976, the child suicide rate rose above the previous record, set in 1908. Through the 1980s, roughly 5,000 children under age 18 committed suicide each year, the largest number and proportion ever recorded for that age bracket.

- Already, 13ers have become the most heavily incarcerated generation in American history. From Boom to 13th, the proportion of youths in jail rose by roughly one-third—for whites and blacks, women and men. The average length of a sentence has risen by 12 percent during the first half-dozen years in which 13ers have entered the adult criminal justice system. In 1990 (when 13ers attained a majority of the U.S. prison population), one in every four black men between the ages of 20 and 29 was in jail, on probation, or on parole.

• The decade of the 1970s brought a steep decline in the economic fortunes of children. From the 1950s through the early 1970s, the over-65 age bracket showed the highest poverty rate; since 1974, the under-18 bracket has shown the highest. Thus, the distinction of occupying America's poorest age bracket passed directly from Lost to 13th without ever touching G.I., Silent, or Boom along the way. Roughly one 13er in five now lives in poverty. At the same time, 13ers report the most negative generational attitude toward welfare spending—and two-thirds believe that if they ever end up unemployed, it's their own fault.

• Through the 1980s, the 13ers' economic distress has moved right up the age ladder with them. In 1967, male wage earners in their early twenties made 74 percent as much as older males; by 1988, that ratio had fallen to 54 percent. Between 1973 and 1988, the median income of households headed by persons under age 25 (adjusted for inflation and family size) fell by 18 percent. The negative trend was not confined to unmarried 13er mothers; even among married couples with children, the median income fell by 17 percent.

• From the 1960s to the 1980s, the proportion of household heads age 18 to 24 owning their own homes fell by one-third—the steepest decline for any age bracket. In 1990, three out of four young men that age were still living at home, the largest proportion since the Great Depression.

• During the 13er childhood era, America has substantially shifted the federal fiscal burden from the old to the young. Since 1972, older generations have deferred paying for some $2 trillion in current consumption through additional U.S. Treasury debt—a policy five times more expensive (in lifetime interest costs) for the average 15-year-old than for the average 65-year-old. Federal tax policy has shifted in the same direction. In 1990, according to the House Ways and Means Committtee, a young 13er couple with one worker, a baby, and $30,000 in wage income had to pay five times as much ($5,055 in taxes) as the typical retired G.I. couple with the same income from public and private pensions ($1,073 in taxes).

• Before 13ers came along, postwar sociologists generally assumed that hardening cynicism was a function of advancing age. No longer. From 1965 to 1990, the share of all Americans under age 35 who look at a newspaper daily declined from two-thirds to less than one-third—by far the steepest drop of any age bracket. In a late-1980s survey of "Cynical Americans," researchers noted that "the biggest surprise" was how "cynicism now seems to defy the traditional partnership of youth and idealism." Today, cynicism is "hitting hardest among young adolescents—more than half of those age 24 and under. . . . They think it's all bull."

The 13er Lifecycle

YOUTH: The years of the "Consciousness Revolution" were among the most virulently anti-child periods in American history, producing a childhood world Tom Cruise recalls as "kind of scattered." Sacrificing one's own career or conjugal happiness became passé—even, by the logic of the era, bad for kids themselves. As the 1960s wore on, Silent mothers and fathers increasingly looked at their children as hindrances to self-exploration. By the 1970s, they cast an envious eye at young Boomers—who then mainly looked upon babies like headaches, things you take pills not to have. Adults ranked autos ahead of children as necessary for "the good life," and the cost of raising a child (never much at issue when Boomers were born) became a hot topic. A flurry of popular books chronicled the resentment, despair, and physical discomfort women were said to endure when bearing and raising 13er children. In *Ourselves and Our Children* (whose priorities revealed themselves in the juxtaposition of its title), "consider yourself" was ranked ahead of "benefiting our children" as a principle of sound parenting. Popular parental guides emphasized why-to-dos over what-to-dos, concluding that *doing* the right thing was less important than parent and child each *feeling* the right thing. To accomplish that, authors like Thomas Gordon (in *Parental Effectiveness Training*) advised parents to teach children to understand behavioral consequences at very young ages. Popular books by T. Berry Brazelton and Burton White stressed the determinism of the early childhood years, suggesting that a child's lifetime personality might be substantially sealed by the time he entered school. As Marie Winn would later note, "early-childhood determinism appeared to be a gift from gods" for parents with new wanderlust or careerism who could thereby conclude that their 6- or 10-year-old children could cope with family trauma well enough, given how carefully they had been tended as tots.

Divorce, and its attendant confusion and impoverishment, became the central fear of the 13er childhood world. In *It's Not the End of the World,* Judy Blume offered children the tale of a once-happy family disintegrating amid shouting, slapping, and crying. Hearing these messages, even kids in stable families felt vulnerable and reacted by hardening their shells against adversity. While parents tried to persuade themselves (like Kyle Pruett in *The Nurturing Father: Journey Toward the Complete Man*) that family dissolution "freed" parent and child to have "better" and "less constricted" time together, these kids saw things differently. (Asked about his own divorced dad, *Breakfast Club* actor Anthony Michael Hall said: "No comment, but yes, he lives.") Thirteeners knew that where Boomers had been once worth the parental sacrifice of prolonging an unhappy marriage, they were not. Coping with the debris, America's 1970s-era children went from a family culture of *My Three Sons* to one of *My Two Dads,* encountering step-thises, half-thats, significant others, and strangers at the breakfast table beyond what any other child generation ever knew. Reading Norma Klein's *It's OK If You Don't Love Me,* a child could ponder the fate of an adolescent girl who juggled a sex life with two boyfriends while sorting through her feelings about her mother's lover, her mother's former second husband, and her father's second wife and their two children.

"The parent is usually a coordinator without voice or authority," observed Kenneth Keniston in 1977, noting how the moms and dads of that decade "hardly ever have . . . the power to make others listen to them." In homes, schools, and courtrooms, America's style of nurturing children completed a two-decade passage from *Father Knows Best* to the tone of self-doubt in Bill Cosby's *Fatherhood:* "Was I making a mistake now? If so, it would just be mistake number nine thousand seven hundred and sixty-three." Alvin Poussaint noted the dominant media image of the parent as "pal," who was "always understanding; they never get very angry. There are no boundaries or limits set. Parents are shown as bungling, not in charge, floundering as much as the children." This was not inadvertent. Parents who admit to being "many-dimensioned, imperfect human beings," reassured the authors of *Ourselves and Our Children,* "are able to give children a more realistic picture of what being a person is all about." On the one hand, Silent parents were, like Cosby's Cliff Huxtable, gentle and communicative; on the other hand, they expressed ambivalence where children sought clear moral answers, abandoned a positive vision of the future, and required children to respond very young to sophisticated real-world problems. Like father and son in *Close Encounters of the Third Kind,* adults became more childlike and children more adultlike.

Through the 1970s, the media reinforced the growing view among children that adults were not especially virtuous, competent, or powerful. Adult life held no secrets. From TV sit-coms to "breakthrough" youth books, older generations made little effort to shield children from any topic, no matter what the effect on a child's sense of security and comfort. "I hate the idea that you should always protect children," wrote Judy Blume in defense of her books. "They live in the same world we do." *Mad* magazine's Al Feldstein put it more bluntly: "We told them there's a lot of garbage out in the world and you've got to be aware of it." One "Self-Care Guide" for latchkey children advised kids of "ways you can protect yourself from mugging and assault: Always pay attention to what is happening around you when you are on the street." And so 13ers were deliberately encouraged to react to life as you would hack through a jungle: Keep your eyes open, expect the worst, and handle it on your own.

APPROACHING RISING ADULTHOOD: Even as first-wavers reach their late twenties, this generation cannot be said to have "come of age." Nothing yet cements them emotionally. To date, the 13th remains a splintery generation; people can (and do) find almost anything they want in these kids. Far more than older generations, 13ers come with myriads of regional subgroups and ethnic minicultures, each thinking its own thoughts, listening to its own music, laying its own plans, and paying little heed to each other. Yet the first signs of bonding are beginning to appear—a common *alienation* visible in 13er art and writing, and in their growing awareness of their own economic vulnerability. "Sure we're alienated," admits American University student Daniel Ralph. "But who wouldn't be, in our shoes?"

Thirteeners are coming to realize that they bear much of the burden for the Reagan-era prosperity that so enriched the Silent and G.I.s. In inner cities, their impoverishment has caused adult alarm; elsewhere, it has been less noticed, thanks to a veneer of family-subsidized teen affluence. Even in the suburbs, 13ers entering the labor force are bearing much of their nation's new burden of foreign competition and debt. In industries where productivity is stagnant, two-tier wage systems hold elders harmless while making the new hires bear the full cost-cutting burden. Where foreign investors bid up the price of real estate, current homeowners profit, but would-be young homebuyers pay. Even as the 1980s-era spurt of tax reform lowered the tax rate on high-bracket incomes, FICA taxes on after-school wages kept going up.

Spurred by a sense of economic need, youths are working younger, longer, later at night, and at more dangerous jobs than any child generation since the Lost. As federal administrators chart the steady rise in child labor law violations, 13ers carefully hone their survivalist ethic. Two-thirds believe they will have to work harder than earlier generations simply to enjoy the same standard of living. After leaving school, 13ers face tough choices made all the more frustrating by the adult wealth they see around them. Scanning her life's options, one Washington, D.C., youth complained: "The way society presents it, I'll either be strung out on drugs, a manager at McDonald's, or a lawyer." Something resembling her middle course is the most frequent path, as many find themselves doing the low-wage counter, delivery, and cleaning jobs Boomers have always found demeaning—the "McJobs" that Amitai Etzioni describes as "more time-consuming, less character-building" than what talented youths used to look forward to. In most professions—law, medicine, business, the media—13ers are encountering less promising promotion paths than the Boom knew at their age, and a smaller likelihood of ever getting a second chance if they fail the first time.

So far, they have concealed their plight thanks to the distinctly 13er habit of calling as little attention as possible to what they are feeling. In life, as when they walk down the street with their Walkmen and designer shades, they know how to keep others from knowing what they're hearing, watching, or thinking.

They leave their troubles behind when they come to work—and take their minds off the job when they leave. Boomer bosses like ad executive Penny Erikson see them as "not driven from within," best suited for "short-term tasks" and in need of "reinforcement from above." Ask 13ers how they're doing, and as long as life stays reasonably patched together, "No problem" is their answer. They have learned to adjust by moving quickly into and (when they see a dead end) out of jobs. They look for quick strikes ahead of long-term promises, the *Wall Street Journal* describing them as "more willing to gamble their careers than . . . earlier generations." Often, their best chance for success comes from striking out on their own, finding a small market niche, and filling it more cheaply and sensibly than older-run businesses—following the example of such twenty-fiveish entrepreneurs as David Montague (folding bicycles) or Doug Wadsworth (plastics recycling). But for every Darryl Strawberry who hits the jackpot, untold others don't. And those who don't run smack into their deterministic ethos—that failure means something must be wrong with *you*. A rising number are masking their economic problems by "boomeranging" back into the parental house after a few years of trying to make it on their own.

Having no place to "boomerang" to, inner-city 13ers inhabit an especially grim world that does not like them, does not want them, and (as they see it) has nothing to offer them. "There's a growing malaise that young people suffer from," observes Victor Herbert, director of New York City high schools. "They feel they're not to be trusted, they're not good people, and they don't have to follow whatever inhibitions have been built up, especially when they're moving in a crowd." Urban kids have begun reacting with a nihilism that older generations consider proof of their worthless ruin. A new, reactionary style of sexism, racism, and soulless violence has seeped into 13er-penned song lyrics. As "Ice-T" raps about "bitches," young thugs commit what elders call "hate crimes" targeted against gays, women, and high-achieving ethnic groups. A new breed of young criminal shows a remorseless bent toward killing and maiming for no serious reason. Prizefighter Mike Tyson has admitted to having "shot at a lot of people. . . . I liked to see them run. I liked to see them beg." Where Boomer youths who assaulted Silent victims were said to have mitigating reasons for their antisocial behavior, 13ers who attack Boomer victims (as in the Bernhard Goetz and the Central Park jogger cases) are condemned, in the Boom-led media, as "evil" thugs deserving only of execution or, at best, a stiff term in some boot-camp prison. Back in the late 1960s, Boomer crime was associated with rage and betrayed expectations; today, the young 13er criminal strikes elders as emotionally detached—even insensible. William Raspberry accuses them of being a "generation of animals," Stanton Samenow of having "the ability to shut off their conscience." The kids themselves invented the word "wilding" to describe their behavior. Asked why his friends go wilding, one New York City youth explained, "Sometimes they do it for fun, sometimes they do it for money, sometimes they just do it."

"We can arrest them, but jail is no deterrent," reports Washington Long, chief of police in Albany, Georgia. "I've had kids tell me, 'Hell, I ain't got nowhere else to go nohow.' " "For them, it's just a matter of fact," agrees Washington, D.C., police chief Isaac Fulwood. "Oftentimes, they don't say anything. They just sit there and say, 'Officer, do what you gotta do' "—like the 16-year-old "wilder" Yusef Salaam, who asked his sentencing judge to "Give me the max." (He got it.) As Terry Williams describes it in *Cocaine Kids,* what is new about 13er criminals is their all-business attitude: their use of calculated violence to protect inventory (smugglers), market share (competing gangs), customer service (safe houses), accounts receivable (addicts), employee relations (runners), and risk management (cops). A young drug-runner, says Fulwood, "navigates in a world where most of us couldn't function, a world where you've got to be cunning, slick, and mentally and physically tough." And, of course, a world in which other choices seem even more hopeless. "I got no plans I ain't going nowhere," sings Tracy Chapman, "So take your fast car and keep on driving."

"When you get beneath the surface of their cheerfulness," observes Christopher Lasch, "young people in the suburbs are just as hopeless as those in the ghetto . . . living in a state of almost unbearable, though mostly inarticulate, agony. They experience the world only as a source of pleasure and pain." Like a whole generation of Breakfast Clubbers, 13ers face a Boom-driven culture quick to criticize or punish them but slow to take the time to find out what's really going on in their lives. By one count, their ranks include a half-million family "throwaways"—a word coined just for them. A generation of self-perceived throwaways might as well take a few risks. Punkers who blast their ears with boom boxes know what they're doing. "They tell me it will hurt me down the line," explains one 20-year-old Ohioan with a deafening sound system in his car, "but I don't care. I'm young and stupid, I guess." Thirteeners know life holds no special favors, for them at least. "I keep hearing this is the best time of our lives," says Harvard student Mandy Silber. "And I wonder—is it all downhill?" Where the Silent and Boom at like age had every reason to expect someday to nestle into law partnerships, tenured professorships, and seats on the stock exchange, 13ers see very clearly the dead-end traps of a "McJobs" economy. *American Demographics* predicts that the five fastest-growing job fields of the early 1990s will be cashiers, nurses, janitors and maids, waiters and waitresses, and truck drivers. Anytime they see others celebrate (or moralize), 13ers watch their wallets—believing, as in the Bangles lyric, "Trouble is, you can't believe that it's true/When the sun goes down, there's something left for you."

In *Less Than Zero,* an Ellis novel touted by its publisher as heralding a "New Lost" generation, two youths have this exchange: "Where are we going?" "I don't know, just driving." "But this road doesn't go anywhere." "That doesn't matter." "What does?" "Just that we're on it, dude." Hemingway and Fitzgerald would have liked these kids, so open-eyed behind those Ray-Ban Wayfarer sunglasses. "Prewar," Scotty would have called them. Not yet lost, but traveling down that road.

*   *   *

Late in 1989, as East German students poured over the Berlin Wall, a *Washington Post* article described high school kids as "left flat" and "utterly unmoved" by events that brought their teachers tears of joy. The youth attitude that strikes elders as blasé is, from the 13er perspective, unflinching and realistic. They have already tramped through the dirty beach where idealism can lead. Remembering how the "freedom" of open classrooms produced noisy chaos and gave them what others constantly tell them was a bad education, they have learned to be skeptical about what happens whenever barriers are broken down. Maybe there will be new wars, maybe bad economic news—at the very least new competition. These kids were less surprised than their teachers when Iraq shattered the post–Cold War peace. American campuses were hardly fazed— Berkeley freshman Charles Connolly speaking for many when he said, "I think we should go in there and take care of it, full throttle." Meanwhile, thousands of Connolly's peers throttled off in uniform to keep oil flowing from Saudi Arabia to the big American homes and cars that so few 13ers can ever imagine buying at the same age their parents did. Where the Korean War once featured hardboiled, Trumanesque elders and sensitive, *M*A*S*H**-like juniors, the Persian Gulf crisis features the opposite. Silent 60-year-olds assume the complex, polysyllabic tasks: satellite communications, multilateral negotiations, peace-process evaluations. Thirteener 20-year-olds prepare for the brute, one-syllable jobs: sweat, hide, move, hit, and kill.

Amid his Silent peers' euphoria over the end of the Cold War, pollster Peter Hart published a highly critical report about "Democracy's Next Generation," noting that only 12 percent of them mentioned voting as an attribute of good citizenship. Then again, 48 percent mentioned personal generosity. Having grown up in an age of anti-institutional feeling, 13ers look at it this way: When you vote, maybe you'll waste your time—or, worse, later feel tricked. But when you do something real, like bringing food to the homeless, you do something that matters, if only on a small scale. The president of MIT has likened the 13er civic attitude to that of the Lone Ranger: Do a good deed, leave a silver bullet, and move on.

In *The Disappearance of Childhood,* Neil Postman observes that when 13ers were little, adults gave children "answers to questions they never asked." That problem still plagues this generation—except now the questions are, in effect, what made you the way you are, and how can we fix it? Blue-ribbon Silent committeemen (like Paul Volcker) anguish over how to change their attitude about government, and inner-city Boomers (like Washington, D.C., health commissioner Reed Tuckson) "look internally" to understand "how we produced these children." But 13ers consider such efforts a waste of time and energy.

From their angle, there's the temptation to play Max Headroom and say a computer-programmed "I'm sorry-sorry." Mostly, they figure such talk is pointless—like aspiring opera singer Marie Xaviere, who says that "even if you didn't want us, you made us. But we're here, and we're going to make the best of it." They know they are a generation without an elder-perceived mission. Yet "in spite of all the criticism and generally low expectations," Daniel Ralph insists his generation "will make a difference." What 13ers ask of others, maybe hopelessly, is to lend an unjaundiced ear and check out what Nancy Smith calls "our 'attitude,' a coolness, a detachment . . . and the way we speak: ironic, flip, uncommitted, a question mark at the end of every other sentence." "Dial into our style," invites Miles Orkin in his essay "Mucho Slingage by the Pool." "It's not like some fully bent tongue from hell or anything."

Their elders don't yet see it, 13ers themselves only dimly sense it, but this streetwise generation does indeed bring a bag of savvy tricks their elders lack— skills that may come in handy the next time America gets into real trouble. More than anyone, they have developed a seasoned talent for getting the most out of a bad hand. Take note, Beaver Cleaver: Thirteeners may never have glimpsed Nirvana, but they know how to win.

MILLENNIAL GENERATION

Born: 1982–
Type: Civic (?)

In September of 1988 at Burrville Elementary in Washington, D.C., 5- and 6-year-old children arrived for their first day of kindergarten wearing brand-new green-and-yellow coats and ties, blouses and dresses. If Boomer school board member Nate Bush gets his way, these kids will wear school-issued clothes all the way through high school, like it or not: "Parents are going to have to exercise their authority and say, I'm the parent, you're the child, and this is a good idea." A year later, having seen Japanese children in trim blue uniforms, Boomer author James Fallows suggested their use in America "to promote some sense of purpose and fellow-feeling at school." At Burrville Elementary, 13ers in older grades found the uniforms slightly humiliating, but the younger kids hardly seemed to mind. These kids in green coats and yellow blouses are the vanguard of America's MILLENNIAL GENERATION. Cute. Cheerful. Scoutlike. Wanted. Not since the 1910s, when midlife Missionaries dressed child G.I.s in Boy Scout brown, have adults seen such advantage in making kids look alike and work together. Not since the early 1900s have older generations moved so quickly to assert greater adult dominion over the world of childhood—and to implant civic virtue in a new crop of youngsters.

Even the timing of this new generation is historic. Its birthyears will stretch to and probably just beyond the year 2000, the end of the second millennium. As the 1990s begin, the year 2000 is becoming a national target date, much like the 1969 deadline President Kennedy once set for landing a man on the moon—except this time, the goal aims at the nurture of what some are calling a "new generation" whose excellence Americans hope to celebrate when the Millennium arrives. In 1990, the nation's governors set an ambitious agenda of educational goals for the year 2000, including a 90 percent high school graduation rate for the "Class of 2000." President Bush agreed, promising that by the year 2000 "U.S. students will be first in the world in mathematics and science achievement." Also in 1990, investigations into child labor practices found violations at an all-time high, prompting some reformers to set the year 2000 as a goal for removing children from dangerous and exploitive jobs and pushing them back into school and family life. Former Surgeon General Everett Koop has declared the nation's determination to produce the "smoke-free high school Class of 2000." And a Washington, D.C., group describing itself as "Concerned Black Men" has launched "Project 2000" to provide "young black boys with consistent, positive, and literate black role models" in time for the Millennium.

MILLENNIAL GENERATION (Born 1982 to ?)

TYPE: Civic (?)

Projected number: 76,000,000
Now alive in U.S.: 33,000,000
Percent immigrant: 12%

SAMPLE MEMBERS, birth (death)

  1982 Hilary Morgan
  1982 Dooney Waters
c. 1983 Cecilia Chichan
c. 1983 Jebbie Bush
  1985 Jessica McClure
  1985 Tabatha Foster (1988)
  1987 "Baby M"

FAMILY TREE

Typical grandparents: Silent
Parents: Boom and Thirteenth
Children: (new Adaptive and new Idealist)
Typical grandchildren: (new Reactive)

FUTURE PERIOD OF
POLITICAL LEADERSHIP

Plurality in Congress: 2035–2060 (proj.)
Term of Presidency: 2040–2065 (proj.)
Majority of Supreme Court: 2050–2075
  (proj.)

PROMINENT FOREIGN PEERS

1982 Prince William

Age	Date	HISTORY AND LIFECYCLE
0–0	1982:	"Class of 2000" born; flurry of books demand protection for children
0–1	1983:	Cute-baby movie trend begins
0–2	1984:	*Time* cover story proclaiming "The End of the Sexual Revolution"
0–3	1985:	U.S. becomes debtor nation; crying-baby antideficit ads
0–5	1987:	"Everybody's Baby" Jessica McClure rescued; Baby "M" case
0–6	1988:	Surge in "cocooning," celebrity pregnancies, school uniforms
0–7	1989:	*Webster* case limits *Roe* v. *Wade*; antidrug crusade grows
0–8	1990:	Educational goals set for the year 2000; first Children's Summit at UN

Fueling this adult mission toward the Millennial generation is palpable (mainly Boom) disappointment in how the 13th is turning out, and second thoughts about how 13ers were raised. "I'm sorry to say it," observed federal judge Vincent Femia in 1989, "but we've lost a generation of youth to the war on drugs. We have to start with the younger group, concentrate on the kindergartners." The circa-1990 preoccupation with "drugs" reflects a broader anxiety about harms that were done and should not be repeated. In a 1990 *Atlantic* cover story, Boomer Karl Zinsmeister suggests "preventing young criminals from infecting a class of successors" by "putting the full weight of public protection on the side of babies and schoolchildren." Though "it may be too late to save the 'me first' generation from the folly of the new feudalism," notes former New York mayor Edward Koch (also in 1990), a "new generation" could be provided "the experience of working successfully with others." In films like *Parenthood*, the Boom culture has drawn a striking contrast between hardened teenage 13ers and cute Millennial "Babies on Board."

First-wave Millennials are riding a powerful crest of protective concern, dating back to the early 1980s, over the American childhood environment. In 1981, the year before the "Class of 2000" was born, a volley of books assaulted adult mistreatment of children through the 13er birthyears (*Children Without Childhood, The Disappearance of Childhood, Our Endangered Children, All Grown Up and No Place to Go*). Within the next couple of years, other authors began reconsidering the human consequences of divorce, latchkey households, and value-neutral education. In 1984, two kids-as-devils movies (*Children of the Corn, Firestarter*) flopped at the box office, marking the end of a dying genre— and the start of a more positive film depiction of children. Through the mid-1980s, studios released several child-as-victim movies (*The Shining, Cujo*), and in the late 1980s, cuddly-baby movies (*Raising Arizona, Three Men and a Baby, Baby Boom, For Keeps, She's Having a Baby*). The new cinematic children began helping adults—not, like film 13ers, by sharing parental burdens, but by reminding parents to cope with life more responsibly on their own. From 1986 to 1988, polls reported a tripling in the popularity of "staying home with family." From Jane Pauley's twins to Bruce Willis' Lamaze class, the Boom's media elite reinforced the new interest in infant nurture. By 1988, babies were declared a "fad" by the *San Francisco Chronicle*, "the new lovers" in the *New York Times*.

The changing tone of the popular culture coincided with the ebbing of the Consciousness Revolution in the early 1980s. First-wave Millennials arrived in an America awash in moral confidence but in institutional disrepair. Some social changes (deferred marriage, smallish dual-income households) became uncontroversial facts of American life, while others ("open" marriages, mind-altering drugs) were rejected. The rates of abortion, voluntary sterilization, and divorce either plateaued or reversed. A few legislators began criticizing the antichild policy consensus—from unchecked growth in federal borrowing to dwindling health benefits for impoverished mothers. In 1985, while the Grace Corporation sponsored TV public service ads linking the national debt with a crying baby, Congressman John Porter blasted huge budget deficits as "fiscal child abuse." In 1988, *Forbes* magazine ran a cover story entitled "Cry, Baby: The Intergenerational Transfer of Wealth," a new KIDS-PAC lobby was formed around children's interests, and child care surged ahead of foreign policy as the issue of most concern to voters. In 1989, while federal attorneys were filing the first-ever lawsuit against apartment units that banned children, George Bush admitted he was "haunted" by the plight of inner-city children and pointed with hope to the straight-arrow example of one crack-house child—7-year-old Dooney Waters.

"The '60s Generation, Once High on Drugs, Warns Its Children," headlined the *Wall Street Journal* in 1990. As parents, teachers, and prosecutors, fortyish Boomers are setting about to protect children from the social and chemical residue of the euphoric awakening they themselves had launched a quarter century earlier. At dinner tables around the nation, 40-year-old parents are telling small children to stay away from drugs, alcohol, AIDS, teen pregnancy, profanity, TV ads, unchaperoned gatherings, and socially aggressive dress or manners. Likewise, at press conferences, 40-year-old political candidates are trying to persuade the public that although maybe they did experiment a little with drugs, they never really enjoyed it. While Tipper Gore battles lurid rock lyrics, Michigan's "mother lion," Terry Rakolta, campaigns against sex and violence on prime-time television, and Barbie's doll band changes from the old "Rockers" to the cleaned-up "Sensations." Grown-up Boomer radicals who once delighted in shocking their own moms and dads now surprise themselves with their own strictly perfectionist approach to child nurture. In growing numbers, fathers are demanding "daddy-track" work schedules that allow them more time at home to raise their young children. Garry Trudeau, father to young twins, drew a *Doonesbury* strip that showed a Boomer proudly explaining that he had raised his girl "like an Asian child . . . by teaching her the value of discipline, hard work, and respect for others."

In general, Boomer parents are determined to set an unerringly wholesome environment for their Millennial tots. Where Silent parents had brought 13er kids along to see R-rated movies made *about* them, Boomers take their Millennials to see G-rated movies made *for* them. Where the old 13er *Willy Wonka*–style movies had stressed individualism and differences among kids, the new Boom-produced films (*An American Tail, Oliver and Company, The Land Before Time*) stress civic virtues: equality, optimism, cooperation, and community. Where the Disney animation studios laid off cartoonists during the 13er era, they began replenishing their staffs during the Millennial era—and now employ more artists than at any time since the 1937 production of *Snow White*. Boom scriptwriters are crafting plots with stronger moral lessons and less ambivalent messages about drugs, alcohol, and teenage sex. In the late 1980s, even the bellwether *Cosby Show* shifted focus. Mom and dad Huxtable became less pally and more in charge—making punishments stick, and telling little Rudy "you're too young" to do this or know about that. Meanwhile, evangelical Boomers are taking Dr. Dobson's advice in *Dare to Discipline*.

Not since the Teddy Roosevelt–era furor over runaway streetcars have adults made such serious efforts to take danger out of the child's daily life. In 1990, New Yorkers expressed deeper anger over nine stray-bullet killings of small children than they had ever felt about the much larger number of murders among teenage 13ers. In the safer suburbs, a wide assortment of new child-safety devices has recently swamped the market—including the Gerber drawer latches, stove knob covers, furniture corner cushions, toilet locks, I-See-U car mirrors, and Kiddie Kap bicycle helmets (all displayed in a "Perfectly Safe" catalogue). The 1980s decade began with states passing laws requiring infant restraints in automobiles; the decade ended with talk of requiring infant restraints in commercial airplanes—and (in Howard County, Maryland) with the nation's first-ever *bicycle* helmet law.

Ever so gradually, adults of all ages are rediscovering an affection and sense of public responsibility for other people's children. Back in the 1970s, the Boom's "Big Chill" gatherings were all-adult affairs. During the 1980s, they started including babies, then small children, and now bigger children. Infant and toddler seats began appearing in restaurants that had never before had them. In 1987, the whole nation anxiously followed the fate of little girls in distress: "Everybody's Baby," 18-month-old Jessica McClure, saved after being trapped for two days in an abandoned well in Lubbock, Texas; 2-year-old Tabatha Foster, whose five organ transplants were made possible by $350,000 in public donations (much of it from celebrities); and 4-year-old Cecilia Chichan, the sole survivor rescued from the crash of Northwest Flight 255 in Detroit.

This new generation of children is being treated as precious—often, more precious than their parents. A judge in Washington, D.C., recently sentenced a pregnant first-time drug offender to jail for the explicit reason that her behavior put her unborn child at risk. Where the media once urged parents to allow their 13er children plenty of room for self-discovery, adult society (in the media, legislatures, and courts) is now prodding parents to control the child environment and is enforcing its intention with tough new laws that make parents civilly or criminally liable for their children's misbehavior. Commenting on a new California law that incriminates parents for gang vices committed by children, Ellen Goodman observes that lawmakers have "turned the Bible on its head. . . . They've decided that the sins of the sons shall be visited upon the parents." For the first time in living memory, calls are rising for special orphanages, "academies," and Boys Towns for small children whose (mostly 13er) parents are deemed socially unfit—places in which William Bennett says children "will be raised and nurtured" under "strong rules and strong principles." Where 13er kids were best known as latchkeys, throwaways, boomerangs, and other terms implying that adults would just as soon have them disappear, Millennials have so far been perceived very differently—as kids whom adults wish to guard with dutiful care. During the two most famous custody battles of the 1980s, newspaper stories focused less on the parents than on the children: New Jersey's "Baby M" and the District of Columbia's Hilary Morgan. Two decades ago, such baby stories would have seemed bizarre beyond comprehension. Today they attract intense nationwide concern.

As Hilary's peers reach school age, public education is moving toward "new traditionalism," values, and greater adult assertiveness. Kindergartens have become more academic, and elementary schools are stressing "good works"—an emphasis on helping out with family and neighborhood chores. Sex education now includes calls for continence, replacing what had earlier been a carefully nonjudgmental, value-neutral approach. In a series of censorship and search-and-seizure cases, the G.I.-dominated U.S. Supreme Court has reversed a two-decade trend toward student rights and strengthened the hand of school disciplinarians. As Boomers replace Silent as parents and teachers, public schools have started to earn higher approval ratings in public polls. Teachers are rising in public esteem (and pay), and PTAs are flourishing with new membership and purpose. What Chester Finn calls "a seismic shock" has gripped the adult mood toward education, with sharply increasing support for more homework, longer school days, toughened graduation requirements, greater parental involvement in classrooms, and a nationally standardized curriculum. *No way* will perfectionist Boomer parents let *their* tots reach age 17 unable to pass the Ravitch-Finn history and literature test.

Boom parents and teachers have also been slowing down the childhood development clock—unlike the Silent, who sped it up. From 1976 through 1988, the proportion of students held back in elementary school jumped by one-third. In 1989, roughly one of every five kindergarten-eligible children were deliberately kept in preschool programs. The sale of Gesell Test materials, used for determining a child's kindergarten readiness, jumped 67 percent between 1984 and 1987. Meanwhile, publishers of children's literature have reversed the 13er-era emphasis on rushing readers to more sophisticated subject matter. Parents now read babylike cloth and cardboard books to Millennial children—books that, when 13ers were little, had to be imported from Europe if they could be found at all. New story lines (like Oak Tree's *Value Tales*) focus less on family problems than on family virtues.

If the circa-1990 nurturing trends please the Boom, they are in effect a repudiation of the way in which many Silent raised their own kids. "Drown the Berenstain Bears" became Boomer Charles Krauthammer's cry against youth literature that celebrates the parent as pal. At school board and PTA meetings, Boom parents in their thirties often chastise the elder Silent for their permissiveness. Where the Silent would rather give kids complete information and then let them make up their own minds, Boomers are more inclined to establish firm rules, reinforced by adult supervision and careful attention to any transgressions. In angry answer to suggestions that the answer to drugs lies in more information about them, William Bennett said of little crack-house Dooney: "This child does not need drug education. That child needs protection, that child needs order, and that child needs love." Goodman acknowledges that "we are now seeing various attempts to put parents in charge, to shore up authority, to foster at least the image and maybe the reality of a traditional family unit." Many wonder if the offspring of such families will develop the openmindedness we now take for granted in children. "What they're learning is that life is black and white," observes columnist Anna Quindlen, without hearing "the long version of answers to life's questions" and without gaining "a measure of empathy and understanding to shade the primary colors of censure." Admitting that today's third and fourth graders "seem more evolved young citizens than we were" at that age, Quindlen sees them assimilating society's "Shalt Nots" about crime, drugs, pollution, and education with disquieting energy and unanimity.

The Millennials show every sign of being a generation of trends—toward improved education and health care, strengthening families, more adult affection and protection, and a rising sense that youths need a national mission. A two-decade animus against children, of course, cannot reverse itself overnight. Polls in the mid-1980s still showed adults more self- than child-focused in behavior, though less so than a decade earlier. Divorce and abortion rates are stuck at high levels, if down a bit from their early-1980s peak. Thirteeners are delaying parenthood even more than Boomers at like age, but are showing a greater commitment to making marriages last. Sex, violence, and alcohol and cigarette advertising in the media remain accessible to small children, though the proportion of R-rated films has been falling and the standards for PG ratings have stiffened. American elementary schools are still underfunded in comparison with those of other developed nations, but tax revolts against their fiscal base are gradually cooling off. Massive federal budget deficits continue, albeit with more evidence of adult guilt over the burdens they will someday impose on today's children. Overall, the arguments of those who stress more values, more structure, and more protection in the child's world are strengthening, from one year to the next, while the arguments of those who disagree are losing ground.

Millennial Facts

• First-wave Millennials, born after the great 1960s and 1970s plunge in American fertility rates, have the lowest child-to-parent ratio in American history. They arrived at a time when only 2 percent of all kids under age 18 live in families with five or more kids—just one-fourth the proportion of first-wave 13ers.

- In contrast to 13ers—and despite their small number per family—Millennial babies frequently arrive to parents who want them desperately. The abortion rate peaked in 1980 and has since shown a gradual decline. Infertility treatment and "preemie" (premature infant) care have become two of the fastest-growing fields in medicine. From 1986 to 1988, the number of infertility-related doctor visits quadrupled. In 1970, a two-pound baby had only a 5 percent chance of living; in 1990, 90 percent survive—at an average cost of over $100,000 per child.

- The early 1980s marked a decisive turnaround in public attitudes toward public schools: the beginning of "quality education" as a political issue; the first year most parents approved of the performance of their local school districts; and the first of seven straight years in which teacher salaries increased faster than inflation—after seven straight earlier years of real salary decline.

- The poverty rate for children under six peaked in 1983 (at 24.6 percent) and thereafter has gradually declined. The U.S. divorce rate peaked in 1981; the homicide rate against children age 1–4 peaked in 1982.

- Since 1983, an increasing share of children below the poverty line have been made eligible for Medicaid assistance. In 1990, despite pressure to reduce federal spending, Congress expanded Medicaid to cover all poor children under age 18 by the year 2001—starting with everyone born after September 30, 1983, upon reaching 6 years of age. (No 13ers need apply.)

- According to national surveys, the per capita savings rate for children age 4 to 12 held steady at about 15 percent from 1968 to 1984—but by 1989 it had risen sharply, to over 30 percent. In the early 1980s, kids that age saved only one-third as much as they spent on candy, soft drinks, and snacks. Today, with the encouragement of their parents, they save more than they spend on convenience food. Over the last decade, the proportion of child income coming from allowances (rather than job earnings) has risen steadily.

*   *   *

"Only Eight Years Old," headlines an ad in a 1990 issue of the *Atlantic*, "And *He's* Teaching *Me* About Science!" Twenty years ago, such an ad would not have appeared. Or, if it had, no one would have believed it. Now we do. Boomer moms and dads are setting out to produce kids who are smart and powerful and dutiful—kids possessed of rational minds, a positive attitude, and selfless team virtue. Someday, Boomers hope, Millennials will build according to great ideals their parents can only envision, act on vital issues their parents can only ponder. These children are not being raised to explore the inner world (Boomers figure they can handle that arena just fine), but instead to achieve and excel at the outer.

Each day, we see dreams and wonder reappear in adult chatter about these little citizens just now learning to walk, talk, and read. In 1988, NASA official Thomas Paine predicted that "the first Martians are already born and toddling around somewhere here on earth." Others speculate that these smart preschoolers might grow up to be great scientists who can solve the riddle of cancer, great engineers who can protect the environment, and great producers who can put an end to world hunger. If they do, a girl born today can expect to live, on average, into her nineties. That will take her beyond the year 2080, past America's Tricentennial. As Mom and Dad gaze into baby's big beautiful eyes, they wonder—we all wonder—what those eyes will someday see.

Part III
THE FUTURE

Chapter 12

THE PAST
AS PROLOGUE

"Tomorrow Is Another Day." "Somewhere over the Rainbow." The glimmering Futurama at the 1939 New York's World Fair. "There'll Be Bluebirds over the White Cliffs of Dover." During the turning-point years of 1937–1943, in the midst of a CRISIS ERA, these messages reflected how Americans of all ages looked at the future. People felt hope, determination, and total consensus about where society should go: toward material abundance (millions of cars and shoes) and spiritual simplicity (home and apple pie). It was all within reach, but conditioned on a struggle everyone knew would demand total unity from all, total sacrifice from some. There was little debate about right and wrong, only about *how to get the job done.* Americans looked to elders for strategic vision, to midlifers for tactical means, and to rising adults for selfless muscle. All those who today remember this mood—this sense of all-encompassing urgency suffused with childlike innocence—wonder why it has proved so hard to rekindle.

Such moods do not arrive often. But they do arrive from time to time. On three earlier occasions Americans have experienced a similar feeling: in the 1680s, in the 1770s, and (briefly) around 1860. On each of these occasions, Americans braced for a raging storm, urging one another not to lose hope that the sun would shine afterward.

Moving forward a couple of decades, we can see what the future looked like in an OUTER-DRIVEN ERA. Here we find Tomorrowland, a 1950s image of a *friendly* future: moving sidewalks, soft-hued geometric shapes, futuristic Mu-

347

zak, and smiling, well-scrubbed families. In Disney's Carousel of Progress, the "progress" remains fixed, while the "carousel" (what moves) is the audience, sitting in chairs and watching household life get predictably easier, cleaner, and more scientific. Laying out the years to come with all the confident linearity of a monorail, Tomorrowland had what the "crisis" future didn't: specificity and certainty. Yet it also lacked urgency, moral direction, and hope—and today's visitor to the G.I.-Jetson household finds it about as warm as push-button transmission. We sense much the same when we visit the Smithsonian Institution's Hall of Machines, full of huge, perfectly engineered turbines from the 1876 Centennial Exposition (the mechanical future of the midlife Gilded). Or when we page through the geometrical street plans for the District of Columbia and the countless square townships drafted around 1800 (the Palladian future of midlife Republicans). Or when we read the circa-1710 poetic odes to flax and shipping (the worker-bee future of midlife Glorious). During each of these eras, Americans looked into the future and saw Tomorrowland: secure, tangible, comfortable, under control—and distressingly spirit-dead.

Moving forward yet another cycle notch, we arrive in an AWAKENING ERA—and encounter a sudden discontinuity. Sometime between the mid-1960s and the early 1970s, the American vision of the future shifted from Tomorrowland to Pepperland. Erector-set affluence was now a ghastly material cancer, publicly disdained and privately taken for granted. Of course we got to the moon (so Americans thought). In another decade, we would be exploring the outer planets, and in another four or five, shuttlecrafting to Alpha Centauri. But all that *out there* felt trivial compared to what people felt *in here*. Americans searched for soul over science, meanings over things. They explored an inner future without dates or chronology—a euphoric experience, celebrated by coming-of-age youngsters who sensed the Millennium (*Childhood's End*) in what seemed like total holocaust for everything their elders had built (*Soylent Green*). Where have we seen Pepperland before? Try Greenwich Village around 1900. Or the New England communes of the 1840s. Or the Connecticut Valley in the late 1730s. Or the Puritan flagship *Arabella* in 1630. "I see a new heaven and a new earth," cried Jonathan Edwards 250 years ago. Looking toward the future, so have many Americans during each of these eras.

A final step forward lands us roughly in the mid-1990s, somewhere near the middle of an INNER-DRIVEN ERA. To understand how the future will look then, we can reflect on where the mood has been heading over the last several years. According to most 1980s-era opinion polls, Americans of all ages emerged from their "Consciousness Revolution" feeling terrific about their personal, *inner* lives—but never so worried about the disintegrating foundations of their social, *outer* world. By 1990, people came to share a disquieting sense of fragmenting community, of eroding public purpose, of institutions that no longer function, of mounting financial and environmental liabilities that must someday fall due. Three or four decades ago, we knew we could *do* everything but worried we could no longer *feel* anything. Today we sense the reverse. Once again, this mood is nothing new. Recall America on the eve of World War I, steeping in inward satisfaction just when a floodtide of crime, boozing, immigrants, and political corruption threatened to wipe all "decency" off the continent. Or America around 1850, building moral confidence but helpless in the face of implacable sectionalism that (too soon) would trigger war. Or the colonies in the early 1750s, rejuvenated with spirit but reeling from violence, mobs, insurrections, and imperial machinations beyond anyone's control.

These four visions of the future are all component pieces of a broader social mood that accompanies our four successive constellational eras: AWAKENING, INNER-DRIVEN, CRISIS, and OUTER-DRIVEN. In each era, the mood is determined by the unique combination of different generational types at each stage of life. Recognize the Awakening mood of the 1970s? We can't imagine it without "square" Civics entering elderhood, "spoiled" Idealists coming of age, and sensitive, passage-prone Adaptives sandwiched in between. How about the Crisis mood of the 1930s? Unthinkable without Civics and Idealists in reversed positions, and (this time) gritty Reactives sandwiched in between.

Drawing on the American experience, this chapter examines what these patterns say about how the social mood changes, how generations mature, and how the generational cycle helps or hurts the future.

Cycles and futures are not supposed to be a happy mix. When Americans talk of generations, they like to associate them with hopes for progress—in particular, with the American Dream that each successive generation will fare better over time. The very concept of a historical cycle may seem to threaten these hopes and this dream. If history runs in circles, after all, how can it move forward? As the generational biographies have shown, however, our cycle is perfectly compatible with the progress of civilization by any standard normally used to measure it—material, spiritual, social, or cultural. All the cycle explains is *when and why different generations apply different standards in working toward progress.* Wherever we use the word "cycle," the reader may if he wishes replace it with "spiral," with all the opportunity and danger implicit in that word. A spiral turns in a circle while at the same time moving upward—or downward.

Our cycle (or spiral) may offer more reason to be optimistic about the future than the conventional linear view of history. Consider, for example, the perspective of many of today's elder G.I.s, who came of age during the Great Depression and who tend to measure the American Dream by Civic milestones: public order, community purpose, friendly neighborhoods, dutiful families, benign science, and a rapidly ascending standard of living. Take those milestones, assess the trends of the past two or three decades, and reflect on what a linear view of history would conclude about America's future. Now *that's* pessimism. But a cycle offers hope. It suggests, as we have just seen, that the standards by which Americans measure progress shift from one era to the next—from material to spiritual, from community improvement to self-perfection, from basic survival to civilized refinement—and then back again. As the Missionary historian James Truslow Adams bravely wrote during the dark hours of the Great Depression, the American Dream gives every youth "the chance to grow into something bigger and finer, as bigger and finer appeared to him." So too for every new generation.

One lesson of the cycle is that every generational type has its own special vision of the American Dream. Each type can fare well or badly in fulfilling that vision. Likewise, each can leave gifts—or harms—to its heirs. We call these "generational endowments." Looking to the cycle, we can see important differences in the endowments each generational type gives to the future.

To appreciate the connection between generations and progress, we need to build paradigms—first of the four constellational moods, and then of the peer personality and lifecycle of each generational type.

The Cycle of Constellational Moods: A Paradigm

"Those who cannot remember the past are condemned to repeat it." Despite George Santayana's warning, many fundamentals of history do seem to repeat no matter how much we try to remember and learn from them. Indeed, were history purely random, it would be less important—and remembering it would be pointless. Most of us, however, sense that history does leave telltale traces of a certain regularity, that we can learn from parallels between the culture, fashions, politics—or simply the moods—of different periods.

To identify some of these parallels, let's begin by lining up all the constellational eras in American history. There have been as many of these—eighteen—as there have been generations. In Chapter 2, we defined each era as a generation-long birthyear period preceding each aligned constellation (which occurs in the year the last cohort of each new generation is born). We display these eras in Figure 12-1. Notice how the Civil War Cycle had only three eras (including an abbreviated combination of Inner-Driven and Crisis eras), just as it had only three generational types.

Since a constellational era typically lasts about twenty-two years, a four-era cycle lasts roughly eighty to one hundred years, or about the lifespan of a long-lived individual. To calibrate the duration of America's five cycles, in fact, we might compare them with five Idealist lifespans laid end-to-end. Consider the sequential lives of Simon Bradstreet (1603–1697), Benjamin Franklin (1706–1790), Lucretia Mott (1793–1880), Franklin Roosevelt (1882–1945), and Albert Gore, Jr. (1948–   ). Each of these individuals has witnessed (or in the last case

FIGURE 12–1

Constellational Eras,
Dated by Generational Birthyears

CYCLE	AWAKENING ERA	INNER-DRIVEN ERA	CRISIS ERA	OUTER-DRIVEN ERA
PRE-COLONIAL:				Elizabethan Renaissance 1584–1614
COLONIAL:	Puritan Awakening 1615–1647	Religious Intolerance 1648–1673	Glorious Revolution 1674–1700	Age of Enlightenment 1701–1723
REVOLUTIONARY:	Great Awakening 1724–1741	French and Indian War 1742–1766	American Revolution 1767–1791	Era of Good Feeling 1792–1821
CIVIL WAR:	Transcendental Awakening 1822–1842	1843 ——————— 1859	Civil War	Reconstruction, Gilded Age 1860–1882
GREAT POWER:	Missionary Awakening 1883–1900	World War I, Prohibition 1901–1924	Depression, World War II 1925–1942	Superpower America 1943–1960
MILLENNIAL:	Boom Awakening 1961–1981	—— 1982–		

can expect to witness) each constellational era at some point in his or her life. A similar end-to-end exercise could be performed with notable members of other generational types with the same result. *Everyone who lives a normal lifespan experiences every constellational era once.* Of course, each type witnesses each era from a different phase-of-life perspective. Idealists, for example, see an Awakening era as rising adults and a Crisis era in elderhood, while Civics see these two periods from a reversed perspective. Again, we notice how age location governs the two-way interaction between generations and history.

Associated with each type of era is a paradigmatic mood. But what are these moods, and how do we identify them amid the noise of history? How can we say that the mood in the 1950s, for example, was anything like the mood in the 1870s—or, for that matter, in the 1710s?

To identify a mood, we must first strip away the cumulative shape of civilization that every constellation largely inherits from the past—such as affluence, technology, basic social mores and cultural norms, and established political institutions. We must also strip away the chance events and the passing fashions, language, and mannerisms through which a mood expresses itself. Again, it may help to envision a "spiral," where the direction of the spiral indicates the cumulative progress—or, if it happens, decline—of civilization, and where the random perturbations in the spiral indicate era-specific events. What remains— the circle of constellational moods—is driven by the repeating overlap of generational types.

Popular music offers a lively illustration of how cyclical recurrences can be distinguished from linear trends. Clearly, over the past century and a half, we can map out a steady improvement in the technology and marketing of music. Progressives came of age with live ballads and marches performed largely by professionals. Missionaries brought home the first widely marketed song sheets for home piano play. The Lost enjoyed the first Victrolas, with cylindrical records. G.I.s bought the first 78s for songs broadcast on AM radio. The Silent listened to stereos with 33-rpm LPs. Boomers played cassettes in their cars and popularized FM radio. Thirteeners love their compact disks. Today's electronics industry is abuzz with talk of the new digital technology that awaits Millennial teenagers. Yet over this same period, behind the linear improvement, popular music has reflected the mood of each new era and the type of each new peer personality. Over the Great Power Cycle, the most memorable Missionary songs were spirituals and blues, soulful and angry; the Lost had jazz, improvised and naughty; the G.I. invented big-band swing, standardized and upbeat; and the Silent had folk and rock, subversive and infused with social conscience. So far in the Millennial cycle, that pattern has repeated—with Boomer music inward-seeking and tinged with fury (adding the "acid" and "Jesus" to rock) and 13er music punkish, prankish, and diverse.

When we look at history this way, searching for basic patterns in social behavior, we can spot several that coincide with the constellational eras. Figure 12-2 lists them.

Some of the trends shown in Figure 12-2 resist quantification. "Attitude toward institutions" obviously cannot be measured. Few historians would disagree, however, that prevailing attitudes toward government and family in 1740 and 1975 (especially among rising adults) represent an opposite extreme from the prevailing attitudes in 1700 and 1940. Take your choice: the frenzied bonfires of young John Davenport or the crisp "Family Well-Ordered" essays of young Cotton Mather; the hippies of Wheeler Ranch or the Seabees of Guadalcanal. Other trends can be quantified, at least partially. A growing tolerance for personal risk, for instance, usually results in more criminal behavior. The historical record suggests that rates of crime (or public complaints about crime) have risen steeply during every Awakening era since the 1730s and have reached cyclical highs during every Inner-Driven era since the late 1740s. "It seems to be now become dangerous for the good people of this town to go out late at night without being sufficiently well armed," commented the *New York Gazette* in 1749. So have many New Yorkers told each other in the 1840s, the 1910s—and, yes, the 1980s.

Several major social indicators generally track the cycle shown in Figure 12-2. For example:

• Rates of substance abuse tend to rise steeply during an Awakening era, peak near its end, and then fall after last-wave Idealists finish coming of age (and first-wave Idealists enter midlife). The sharpest alcohol-consumption turn-around in American history occurred in the late 1830s (the end of the Transcendental Awakening), followed by a further decline in the 1840s. The second-sharpest occurred between 1900 and 1910 (the end of the Missionary Awakening), followed by a further decline during Prohibition. More recently, per capita alcohol consumption began accelerating around 1960, peaked around 1980 (the end of the Boom Awakening), and has lately been falling. For mind-altering drugs, from opiates to hallucinogens, the pattern is much the same. Each time, young Idealists get most of the euphoria while society looks on indulgently, after which young Reactives get most of the blame when society begins cracking down. Commenting on this long-term cycle, historian David Musto notes that "a person growing up in America in the 1890s and the 1970s would have the image of a drug-using, drug-tolerating society; a person growing up in the 1940s—and perhaps in the 2000s—would have the image of a nation that firmly rejects narcotics."

• Fertility tends to rise during Outer-Driven eras, when Idealists are born. The Puritans, Awakeners, Transcendentals, and Boomers were all the products of birth booms, just as their Adaptive next-elders were all the products of Crisis-era birth dearths. For the Missionaries, the anomalous Civil War Cycle created a somewhat different pattern: the birthrate suddenly fell for war-baby first-wavers (born from 1860 to 1865), but thereafter stabilized until the early 1880s—the only birthrate plateau during an otherwise steady downslope that stretched 130 years from the Gilded through the Silent. Birthrates always ease during Awakening eras, either by stabilizing after earlier growth (for Liberty babies) or by falling sharply (for 13er babies).

• Immigration tends to rise during an Awakening era, peak during an Inner-Driven era, and fall during a Crisis era—each trend reflecting a different social consensus about pluralism and community. Since most immigrants have always ranged in age from their mid-teens to late thirties, Idealist and

FIGURE 12–2
Constellational Moods, by Era

	AWAKENING ERA	INNER-DRIVEN ERA	CRISIS ERA	OUTER-DRIVEN ERA
	(Aligned Constellation at End of Era)			
ELDER:	Civics	Adaptive	Idealists	Reactives
MIDLIFE:	Adaptives	Idealists	Reactives	Civics
RISING:	Idealists	Reactives	Civics	Adaptives
YOUTH:	Reactives	Civics	Adaptives	Idealists
CYCLE CALENDAR:	Year 1-22	Year 23-44	Year 45-66	Year 67-88
NURTURE OF CHILDREN:	under-protective	tightening	over-protective	loosening
SEX ROLE DIVISIONS:	narrowing	narrowest point	widening	widest point
TOLERANCE FOR PERSONAL RISK:	rising	high	falling	low
INDIVIDUALISM VS. COMMUNITY:	rising individualism	maximum individualism	rising community	maximum community
WORLD VIEW:	rising complexity	maximum complexity	rising simplicity	maximum simplicity
BEHAVIOR TOWARD IDEALS:	discover	cultivate	champion	realize
BEHAVIOR TOWARD INSTITUTIONS:	attack	redefine	establish	build
SENSE OF GREATEST NEED:	fix inner world	do what feels right	fix outer world	do what works
VISION OF FUTURE:	euphoric	darkening	urgent	brightening

(especially) Reactive generations have had foreign-born flavors. The Liberty, Transcendental, Gilded, Boom, and 13th comprise, in fact, the only American generations in which the share of immigrants has risen over their next-elders. Civic generations, on the other hand, have always shown a marked decline in their immigrant share. Civics enter rising adulthood during a Crisis era, when immigration is more difficult or less attractive—and when elder Idealist leaders typically take a hard anti-immigrant stance in order to "protect" the national community better than their Adaptive predecessors.

• Economic growth tends to accelerate smoothly during an Outer-Driven era, falter during an Awakening era, proceed irregularly during an Inner-Driven era, and encounter severe setbacks or dislocations during a Crisis era. From 1942 to 1973, for example, U.S. real output per worker grew far more rapidly than during any other comparable period over the last century. (The former year signaled the turning point of a Crisis era, the latter of an Awakening era.) Since 1973, growth in the American standard of living has slowed dramatically. Earlier episodes of robust economic growth follow roughly the same pattern: 1692 to 1735, 1789 to 1837, and 1867 to 1893. Toward the end of each of these periods, the public consensus underlying economic progress disintegrated as America entered an Awakening era. Ultimately, the progress itself either stopped, decelerated, or (at best) fluctuated erratically. At the other end of the cycle, Crisis eras typically include periods of serious material hardship—sometimes directly related to war (1774–1789, 1861–1867), sometimes not (1929–1938).

Readers who reflect on these social indicators (and on the cyclical trends noted in Figure 12-2) will have no problem recognizing where we are today: approaching the middle of an Inner-Driven era. Nor will they have trouble figuring out where we have been over the last several decades and, more important, *where we are headed.*

Let's now summarize the mood of each constellational era:

THE MOOD OF AN AWAKENING ERA reflects society's transition into a spiritual awakening. The focus on inner life grows to maximum intensity, as secular interest in outer life declines. Artistic culture is highly innovative. New social ideals, emerging out of utopian experiments in individual autonomy and perfect fellowship, are used to attack and weaken established institutions. Society has difficulty coalescing around common goals, and any social effort requiring collective discipline encounters withering controversy. Wars are unlikely, and those that occur are controversial when fought and badly remembered afterward. Sex role distinctions narrow, public order deteriorates, and crime and substance abuse rise. A euphoric enthusiasm over near-term spiritual progress eclipses public concern over secular problems, contributing to a high tolerance for risk-prone lifestyles. Child-rearing reaches the cyclical point of minimum protection and structure. The era's defining, two-apart generational dialogue arises between coming-of-age Idealists and aging Civics—a noisy clash that elevates the new values of youth but leaves institutional leadership with the old. *Sample military conflicts:* Spanish-American War, Vietnam War.

THE MOOD OF AN INNER-DRIVEN ERA begins where the fervor of the awakening leaves off. Satisfaction with personal and spiritual life is high, and individualism flourishes. Cultural and social life fragments amid signs of growing socioeconomic inequality. While confidence in established institutions sinks to a cyclical nadir, new efforts arise to redefine or recreate institutions around new ideals. Frenetic and pleasure-seeking lifestyles emerge, side by side with growing seriousness of purpose and a declining public toleration for aberrant personal behavior. Perceptions about society's collective future darken, time horizons shorten, and mounting secular problems are deferred. Wars become more likely—and are fought with moral fervor but without consensus or follow-through. Sex-role distinctions narrow to their thinnest point, families strengthen, and child-rearing begins to move back toward protection and structure. The era's defining, one-apart generational dialogue arises between rising-adult Reactives and midlife Idealists—open hostility between risk-taking adventurers on one side and punitive moralizers on the other. *Sample military conflicts:* King George's War, French and Indian War, Mexican-American War, World War I, the 1989 Panama invasion, the 1990 Persian Gulf deployment.

THE MOOD OF A CRISIS ERA reflects society's transition into a secular crisis. A grim preoccupation with outer-world peril grows to maximum intensity, as spiritual curiosity declines. Artistic culture avoids nuance, often (in the form of propaganda) overtly reinforcing "good" conduct. Worldly problems are no longer deferred, but are allowed to congeal into a struggle requiring total consensus, aggressive public institutions, and personal sacrifice. Wars are very likely, and they are fought with fury and efficacy. Sex role distinctions widen, public and family order strengthen, and personal violence and substance abuse decline. A rush of hopeful confidence in near-term secular progress crowds out worries about questionable public means and contributes to a low tolerance for risk-prone lifestyles. Child-rearing reaches the cyclical point of maximum protection and structure. The era's defining, two-apart generational dialogue arises between coming-of-age Civics and aging Idealists—a friendly alliance that harnesses the worldly energy of the young but leaves values in the hands of the old. *Sample military conflicts:* King Philip's War, colonial Glorious Revolution, American Revolution, Civil War, World War II.

THE MOOD OF AN OUTER-DRIVEN ERA begins where the grim trauma of the recent crisis leaves off. The sense of community reaches its cyclical peak. Individualists are ostracized, and social and cultural life tends toward friendly blandness and homogeneity. The ideals that triumphed in the Crisis era are secularized and institutionalized. The emphasis is on planning, doing, and building—though a few loners begin voicing disquiet over the spiritual cost of rapid economic and scientific progress. Perceptions about the society's collective future brighten, and public time horizons lengthen. Wars tend to be unwanted echoes of the recent crisis—and are fought with consensus but without enthusiasm. Sex-role distinctions widen to their maximum point, but family cohesion begins to weaken, and child-rearing gradually becomes looser and more indulgent. The era's defining, one-apart generational dialogue arises between rising-adult Adaptives and midlife Civics—a low-keyed competition between sensitive doubters on one side and powerful builders on the other. *Sample military conflicts:* Queen Anne's War, War of 1812, Korean War.

The Cycle of Generational Types: A Paradigm

Having built a paradigm for the moods of the constellational cycle, let's do the same for each generational type. To be sure, no individual generation can fit such a paradigm exactly. This is especially true for the two generations most affected by the mistimed crisis during the Civil War Cycle—the Gilded and Progressives. Yet as we have seen in Chapter 5, even this exception offers a powerful normative message for each of today's living generations.

The IDEALIST Lifecycle

Nurtured as children amid secular confidence and coming of age during an awakening, Idealist generations travel a *prophetic* lifecycle. Early in life, Idealists believe themselves closer to God than older generations; late in life, all generations regard them as repositories of lofty values beyond the comprehension of youth. At a distance, we remember Idealists best for their coming-of-age passion (William Tennent, Nat Turner, William Jennings Bryan) and for their principled elder stewardship in times of crisis (Samuel Adams, Abraham Lincoln, Franklin Roosevelt). Their phases of life:

YOUTH: The Idealist generation grows up in a post-crisis era of mellowed Reactive elders, vigorous Civic midlifers, and conformist Adaptive rising adults. Parental protectiveness is high but receding, maintained by the confidence of Civic fathers but gradually subverted by the sympathy of Civic mothers. Children are indulged by parents in a world gripped with secularism, rationalism, and community-spirited conformism. Older generations hope the new children can bring a richer moral dimension to a world needing little additional safety or order, but showing symptoms of cultural sterility.

RISING ADULTHOOD: Having cultivated a strong inner life during childhood, Idealists come of age experiencing a spiritual awakening. They burst forth

FIGURE 12–3
Idealist Lifecycles

	YOUTH	RISING	MIDLIFE	ELDER
PURITAN (born 1584–1614)	Elizabethan Renaissance	Puritan Awakening	Religious Intolerance	Glorious Revolution
AWAKENER (born 1701–1723)	Age of Enlightenment	Great Awakening	French and Indian War	American Revolution
TRANSCENDENTAL (born 1792–1821)	Era of Good Feeling	Transcendental Awakening	Civil War	Reconstruction, Gilded Age
MISSIONARY (born 1860–1882)	Reconstruction, Gilded Age	Missionary Awakening	World War I, Prohibition	Depression, World War II
BOOM (born 1943–1960)	Superpower America	Boom Awakening	____	____

with angry challenges to their elders' public and private behavior, which they regard as intolerably deficient in moral worth. Unable to defend themselves effectively, aging Civics ultimately cede the values agenda to the young. Meanwhile, rising Idealists launch the entire society into a fever of renewal, which typically peaks and is already half forgotten by the time their last wave has entered rising adulthood. Right-brained spiritualists, they encourage individual autonomy, resist social cooperation (except as a means of self-discovery), and erode prevailing distinctions between sex roles.

MIDLIFE: After their coming-of-age outburst, the Idealists' first instinct is to retrench, to concentrate on perfecting the inner life. Entering midlife, they gradually reshape institutions around new values and assume a judgmental stance against what they perceive to be the moral vacuum of the younger Reactives. They come to political power slowly but resolutely, beginning with relatively weak leaders tolerant of their peers' self-immersed impulses. Gradually, splits emerge and deepen between Idealist factions holding competing moral positions—each insisting on applying absolute principles to the outer world, but disagreeing with the other factions over what those principles should be.

ELDERHOOD: One Idealist faction ultimately prevails, setting an agenda for decisive collective action. Producing leaders of great moral authority, Idealists impose their will sternly on people of all ages—calling on younger Reactive and Civic generations to make sacrifices for principled causes. The society now passes through an era of secular crisis—a key historic turning point, possibly a major war. After the crisis, public institutions substantially reflect the inner visions of Idealist elders, who look upon themselves as vital links to culture and civilization. From the young, they seek personal obedience and respect more than public power or reward.

The REACTIVE Lifecycle

Nurtured as children during an awakening and coming of age amid spiritual confidence but secular unease, Reactive generations travel a *picaresque* lifecycle. Early in life, Reactives desperately seek to escape or outwit the judgments of next-elder Idealists; late in life, they make unthanked sacrifices for next-junior Civics. At a distance, we remember Reactives best during their rising-adult years of hell-raising (Paxton Boys, Missouri Raiders, rumrunners) and during their

FIGURE 12–4
Reactive Lifecycles

	YOUTH	RISING	MIDLIFE	ELDER
CAVALIER (born 1615–1647)	Puritan Awakening	Religious Intolerance	Glorious Revolution	Age of Enlightenment
LIBERTY (born 1724–1741)	Great Awakening	French and Indian War	American Revolution	Era of Good Feeling
GILDED (born 1822–1842)	Transcendental Awakening	Civil War	Reconstruction, Gilded Age	Missionary Awakening
LOST (born 1883–1900)	Missionary Awakening	World War I, Prohibition	Depression, World War II	Superpower America
THIRTEENTH (born 1961–1981)	Boom Awakening	——	——	——

midlife years of tough, in-the-fray leadership (George Washington, Ulysses Grant, Harry Truman). Their phases of life:

YOUTH: The Reactive generation is child to an era of still powerful Civic elders, torn Adaptive midlifers, and moralizing Idealist rising adults. With Adaptive approval, children are left free to find their own norms of behavior and adjust to a world of narrowing sex-role distinctions. No longer protective, parents expose children to real-world anxieties and dangers. With a largely self-absorbed adult society immersed in a spiritual awakening, youths are given little sense of mission or direction. Adults tend to view them harshly—at best, as inconvenient; at worst, as disappointing or even wicked.

RISING ADULTHOOD: Reactives come of age with little collective self-esteem. Their early contact with the real world, however, gives them strong survival skills and high hopes for individual success. They perceive midlife Idealists as pompous and judgmental, and are themselves perceived as amoral and devoid of inner life. Defining themselves in cynical opposition to the Idealists, who by now are starting to govern with an increasingly heavy hand, young Reactive adults engage in social and economic entrepreneurship, tinged with pleasure-seeking and other high-risk behavior.

MIDLIFE: Playing to win but half-expecting to lose, Reactives enter midlife accepting wide gaps in personal outcomes—and between sex roles. They regard success or failure as a private matter while they gradually learn to abide, and no longer fight, the Idealist stigma against their generation. They become cautious in family life and gradually mellow in personality. Their ablest peers become society's most cunning, pragmatic, and colorful public figures—military and commercial managers of great realism, effective leaders for the secular crisis congealed by elder Idealists.

ELDERHOOD: Elder Reactives remain undemanding in a new, post-crisis era when society begins praising the energy of Civic midlifers and indulging a new crop of Idealist youths. Aging leaders compensate for their generation's earlier bingelike behavior by shunning risk and encouraging conformism. By instinct, old Reactives are wary conservatives, "not born yesterday," inclined to warn more than guide. They retire into an individualist, if neglected, role.

The CIVIC Lifecycle

Nurtured as children amid spiritual confidence and coming of age during a secular crisis, Civic generations travel a *heroic* lifecycle. Early in life, Civics believe themselves more powerful than older generations; late in life, all gen-

FIGURE 12–5
Civic Lifecycles

	YOUTH	RISING	MIDLIFE	ELDER
GLORIOUS (born 1648–1673)	Religious Intolerance	Glorious Revolution	Era of Enlightenment	Great Awakening
REPUBLICAN (born 1742–1766)	French and Indian War	American Revolution	Era of Good Feeling	Transcendental Awakening
G.I. (born 1901–1924)	World War I, Prohibition	Depression, World War II	Superpower America	Boom Awakening
MILLENNIAL (born 1982–2003?)	—	—	—	—

erations regard them as uniquely optimistic, collegial, and competent. At a distance, we remember Civics best for their collective coming-of-age triumphs (the Glorious Revolution, Yorktown, VJ-Day) and for their crowning midlife achievements (the Peace of Utrecht and slave codes, the Louisiana Purchase and steamboats, the Apollo moon launches and interstate highways). Their phases of life:

YOUTH: The Civic generation spends childhood during a post-awakening era of sensitive Adaptive elders, values-oriented Idealist midlifers, and pleasure-seeking Reactive rising adults. Idealist parents look upon these children as special, an instrument through which their inner visions can be achieved or defended. The child environment, now perceived to be dangerous, is pushed back toward greater protection and structure. Since adults expect children to be dutiful, smart, and potentially powerful, youths develop a clear collective mission and high ambitions for cleaning up and rebuilding the outer world.

RISING ADULTHOOD: Coming of age, Civics develop activity-oriented peer relationships, peer-enforced codes of conduct, and a strong sense of generational community. They band together at a historic moment and—guided by the principled wisdom of elder Idealists and the realistic leadership of midlife Reactives—successfully shoulder a secular crisis. After doing their duty unselfishly, they afterward expect, and receive, generous praise and reward from other generations. Left-brained achievers and instinctive team players, they expect human relationships to be clearly defined and push for wider distinctions between acceptable sex roles.

MIDLIFE: Empowered by the hubris of early success, Civics reach midlife as builders and doers, defenders of a wholesome but conformist culture. After impatiently awaiting their turn atop society, they push aside the aging Reactives and enter leadership roles with vigor, certain of their own ability to make things work. They try to institutionalize and rationalize every sphere of social life, from science to religion, statecraft to the arts. Their midlife hubris, however, often encourages them to overreach and push secular perfection too far. As Civics begin passing out of midlife, they elicit a stormy crusade of moral purification from coming-of-age Idealists.

ELDERHOOD: Old age does not weaken the Civic reputation for unusual energy and collective purpose. As elders, however, they grow frustrated at how the new spiritual agenda saps the strength of their powerful institutions, which they fear may not survive without their special competence. They detach themselves from new cultural trends but retain an active role in public affairs. From the young, Civics seek institutional power and economic reward more than personal respect or obedience.

The ADAPTIVE Lifecycle

Nurtured as children during a crisis and coming of age amid secular confidence but spiritual unease, Adaptive generations travel a *genteel* lifecycle. Early in life, Adaptives try to excel in the subordinate tasks given them by next-elder Civics; late in life, they seek approving judgments from next-junior Idealists. At a distance, we remember them best during their quiet years of rising adulthood (the log-cabin settlers of 1800, the Great Plains farmers of 1880, the young suburbanites of 1960) and during their midlife years of flexible, consensus-seeking leadership (the Whig "compromises" of Henry Clay and Daniel Webster, the "good government" reforms of Theodore Roosevelt and Woodrow Wilson, the budgetary and peace "processes" of Phil Gramm and James Baker III). Their phases of life:

YOUTH: The Adaptive generation enters childhood surrounded by stern Idealist elders, pragmatic Reactive midlifers, and aggressive Civic rising adults. A secular crisis erupts. Reactive-led families surround children with an intensively protective, even suffocating style of nurture. Children are expected to stay out of the way of harm—and of busy adults. Though assured of their collective worth, they are told their individual needs take a low priority as long as the

FIGURE 12-6
Adative Lifecycles

	YOUTH	RISING	MIDLIFE	ELDER
ENLIGHTENMENT (born 1674–1700)	Glorious Revolution	Age of Enlightenment	Great Awakening	French and Indian War
COMPROMISE (born 1767–1791)	American Revolution	Era of Good Feeling	Transcendental Awakening	Civil War
PROGRESSIVE (born 1843–1859)	Civil War	Reconstruction, Gilded Age	Missionary Awakening	World War I, Prohibition
SILENT (born 1925–1942)	Depression, World War II	Superpower America	Boom Awakening	____

community is struggling for its survival. Adaptive youths inherit a world of widening sex-role distinctions. They grow up well behaved, while wondering how (or if) they can live up to the expectations of powerful elders who are sacrificing so much on their behalf.

RISING ADULTHOOD: Taught to pursue acceptance from older generations, Adaptives come of age emulating successful adult behavior. Not old enough to participate in the crisis as adults, they fail to experience a cathartic rite of passage—and fail to acquire the self-confidence of their next-elders. Individually insecure in an era of public optimism, they try conforming to the expectations of elders, which now means playing the ameliorator to the Civics' grand post-crisis edifice. Meanwhile, they probe cautiously for a fresher, more fulfilling role. This effort leads to a cult of professional expertise (beating the Civics at their own game) and to critical gestures of conscience and humanism (exposing the Civics' spiritual shortcomings). Young adults infuse popular culture with new vitality and provide encouraging mentors to new youth movements that hit just too late for them to join.

MIDLIFE: Adaptives enter midlife while coming-of-age Idealists are triggering a spiritual awakening. This new phase of life poses an awkward personal "passage" for a generation forced to choose between the outer mission of older Civics and the inner mission of younger Idealists. Post-passage, still searching for an elusive catharsis, Adaptive midlifers compensate for their earlier confor- mism by engaging in high-risk political and family behavior. In public life, they focus on issues low in substance but rich in personality and drama. Those who reach positions of leadership tend to rely on expertise, process, and pluralism— and, in so doing, tend to postpone unpleasant choices.

ELDERHOOD: Entering old age while a more sober and values-oriented leadership style is emerging, Adaptives remain personally flexible and culturally sensitive. By instinct, elder Adaptives are trusting liberals—believers in the inherent goodness of man and his need for second chances. Just as they once took cues from Civic elders, now they adopt the agenda of younger Idealists while wishing to be accepted as full partners in the new values regime. They preserve a social conscience, show a resilient spirit, and never stop raising new questions.

In Figure 12-7, we summarize the peer personalities of each of the four generational types.

These contrasting peer personalities lead to important contrasts in leadership styles. Figure 12-8 compares the best-remembered American political leaders of each type—listing two from each generation over the first four cycles. We include only those who have held a major office: colonial governorships for the first cycle, the Continental Congress for the Awakeners, and U.S. Presidents (or, for the Silent, Presidential nominees) thereafter.

For each set of eight names in Figure 12-8, reflect on common elements, the outline of a composite peer personality. The following impressions emerge:

• Idealist leaders have been cerebral and principled, summoners of human sac- rifice, wagers of righteous wars. Early in life, none saw combat in uniform; late in life, most came to be revered as much for their words as for their deeds.

• Reactive leaders have been cunning, hard-to-fool realists, taciturn warriors who prefer to meet problems and adversaries one-on-one. They include the only two Presidents who had earlier hanged a man (Washington and Cleve- land), one governor who hanged witches (Stoughton), and several com- manders who had led troops into battle (Bacon, Washington, Grant, Truman, and Eisenhower).

• Civic leaders have been vigorous and rational institution-builders, busy and competent even in old age. All of them, entering midlife, were aggressive advocates of technological progress, economic prosperity, social harmony, and public optimism.

FIGURE 12–7

Peer Personalities, by Generational Type

	IDEALIST	**REACTIVE**	**CIVIC**	**ADAPTIVE**
Lifecycle Type:	prophetic	picaresque	heroic	genteel
Parental Attachment in Youth:	strongest to mother	independent of both	strongest to father	obedient to both
Coming-of-Age Experience:	sanctifying	alienating	empowering	unfulfilling
Principal Focus, Coming-of-Age:	inner-world	whatever works best	outer-world	torn between inner & outer
How Perceived Coming-of-Age:	stormy	bad	good	placid
Preoccupation in Rising Adulthood:	reflecting	competing	building	ameliorating
Attitude Transition in Midlife:	detached to judgmental	risk-seeking to exhausted	energetic to hubristic	conformist to experimental
Preoccupation in Elderhood:	civilization	survival	community	family
How Perceived as Elders:	visionary, wise	lonely, caustic	busy, confident	sensitive, flexible
Style of Leadership:	righteous, austere	pragmatic, cautious	grand, expansive	process-fixated, pluralistic
God is . . .	truth	persuasion	power	love
How It Is Nurtured:	relaxing	underprotective	tightening	overprotective
How It Nurtures:	tightening	overprotective	relaxing	underprotective
Positive Attributes:	principled resolute creative	savvy perceptive practical	rational selfless competent	caring open-minded expert
Negative Attributes:	ruthless selfish arrogant	amoral pecuniary uncultured	overbold unreflective insensitive	indecisive guilt-ridden neurotic

FIGURE 12-8

Political Leaders,
First Four Cycles by Generational Type

DOMINANT GENERATIONS	RECESSIVE GENERATIONS
IDEALISTS	**REACTIVES**
John Winthrop (MA)	Nathaniel Bacon (VA)
William Berkeley (VA)	William Stoughton (MA)
Samuel Adams	George Washington
Benjamin Franklin	John Adams
James Polk	Ulysses Grant
Abraham Lincoln	Grover Cleveland
Herbert Hoover	Harry Truman
Franklin Roosevelt	Dwight Eisenhower
CIVICS	**ADAPTIVES**
Gurdon Saltonstall (CT)	William Shirley (MA)
Robert "King" Carter (VA)	Cadwallader Colden (NY)
Thomas Jefferson	John Quincy Adams
James Madison	Andrew Jackson
——	Theodore Roosevelt
——	Woodrow Wilson
John Kennedy	Walter Mondale
Ronald Reagan	Michael Dukakis

• Adaptive leaders, reflecting a more complicated mixture of passive and aggressive masculinity, have been advocates of fairness and the politics of inclusion, irrepressible in the wake of failure. With the single exception of Andrew Jackson, all those listed in Figure 12-8 rank among the most expert and credentialed of American political figures.

We can extend these analogues beyond national leaders to the broader occupational world. To be sure, each generational type (and each generation) has included many individuals who have made important achievements in every realm of human endeavor. But if we recall the most influential members of our eighteen generations and batch their careers by generational type, striking patterns emerge. As shown in Figure 12-9, certain occupational callings can be linked with the four peer personalities.

We find American history dominated by Idealist thinkers, Reactive risk-takers, Civic doers, and Adaptive improvers. This pattern offers clues about the enduring

FIGURE 12–9
Principal Callings, by Generational Type

DOMINANT GENERATIONS	RECESSIVE GENERATIONS
IDEALISTS	**REACTIVES**
Preachers	Entrepreneurs
Writers	Brigands
Radicals	Industrialists
Publishers	Generals
Teachers	Salesmen
CIVICS	**ADAPTIVES**
Statesmen	Artists
Scientists	Lawyers
Economists	Therapists
Diplomats	Legislators
Builders	Statisticians

legacy that each type leaves behind for its heirs—the legacy we call "generational endowments."

Generational Endowments

Most Americans have always cared deeply about their national destiny and have liked to think they are adding to—not subtracting from—the sum total of civilized progress they pass on to heirs. Over the centuries, however, the way Americans have felt and behaved as societal legators has changed substantially from one era to the next. Each generational type has shown its own special endowment tendencies, good and bad.

Central to a generation's endowment motivation is its awareness of what Auguste Comte termed its "morphology"—its awareness of death. Most social categories are essentially immortal. If we think of ourselves as white or black, Christian or Jew, northerner or southerner, we are not compelled to view the future with special urgency. Any work we leave undone in our lifetime can be completed later by another member of our group. But generations are different. Each has only a limited time to make its mark or otherwise keep its peace.

Individuals also understand that their own time is limited, of course—but most of the 440 million Americans who have ever lived have had trouble recognizing direct links between their own behavior and the progress of civilization.

Thus when people make major sacrifices on behalf of the future, social scientists tend to puzzle over such behavior, seeing it as contrary to self-interest (what economists call the irrational "endowment motive") or as a blind instinctual drive to provide for one's own family (an attempt, say sociobiologists, to ensure the survival of one's own DNA). Nothing loftier seems plausible, however inadequately such motives explain the behavior of great social benefactors, such as an Andrew Carnegie or a Martin Luther King, Jr. Yet as members of generations, we have less difficulty appreciating how we steer the destiny of our society. Just as age location connects our personal biographies with the broad currents of history, so do generations bridge the gap between personal and social goodwill. Whatever other reasons we might have to behave well toward the future, our generational membership prompts us to act now rather than later. Each generation realizes that when it fades, so too will fade *its own way of thinking about the future*.

From Robert Beverley in the 1710s to John Kennedy in the 1960s, Americans have generally agreed that each generation has an obligation to leave behind a more secure and affluent world than it inherits. Around the time of the drafting of the United States Constitution and the absorption of state debts into one national debt, Thomas Jefferson argued that since each generation is "as an independent nation," it is thereby entitled to disclaim any debts from the past (and, presumably, any promises to the future). Madison and Hamilton believed otherwise, and their view prevailed. Indeed, their view has *always* prevailed. Successive American generations have rarely hesitated to bind their heirs through public and private action, producing an impressive record of material and institutional endowments. But this record is not without its peaks and valleys. Over the centuries, the "present versus future" debate has sometimes been resolved in favor of the future, sometimes in favor of the present. Children (and unborn generations) cannot vote, and grand plans for the future often cannot override the urgencies and desires of the moment. This is especially true in an Inner-Driven era, a time when society trusts values more than institutions. In this regard, the circa-1990 policy paralysis over trade and budget deficits has much in common with the circa-1910 stalemate over urbanization.

Many Americans today express doubts about their society's capacity—or willingness—to do anything worthwhile on behalf of future generations. On the one hand, polls indicate that adults worry increasingly (and rather hopelessly) about the harms they are passing on, from massive debts and inadequate schooling to a despoiled environment and crumbling infrastructure. On the other hand, many flaunt a lack of concern in their daily lives. A favorite bumper sticker among G.I.s declares "We're Spending Our Children's Inheritance," while a Boomer favorite trumpets "Whoever Dies with the Most Toys Wins."

Is America abandoning any interest in its own destiny? The cycle suggests it is not. As we have seen, each constellational era has its own vision of what the future needs, and today's vision is consistent with the mood of an Inner-Driven

era. True enough, America's enthusiasm about material and public-order endowments is now quite low. As an aging Civic generation passes from power,
this feeling is (on schedule) sinking to a cyclical nadir. Yet if we think about
other kinds of endowments—such as the retooling of institutions in the direction
of pluralism, compassion, and fair process—it is hard to recall when Americans
have ever been so hard at work. With an Adaptive generation in power, the
country's activity in this area has recently been (again on schedule) energetic
and growing. Just as a society's vision of the future shifts with the constellational
mood, so does the primary focus of its endowment activity. How it shifts depends
on the phase-of-life positioning of peer personalities.

To see how this works, let's look at the link between endowments and generational types:

- *Throughout its lifecycle, each generation's endowment efforts are concentrated*
  in areas closely connected to its peer personality.

Clearly, a generation can endow the future in any number of ways. It can
build airports, establish corporations, write poetry, protect the wilderness, fight
to preserve liberty, expand rights for the handicapped, fund a pension plan, or
teach children how to spell. It can add to the accumulated stock of physical,
natural, or human capital—or add to the ancestral legacy of political, artistic,
and spiritual capital. But since different generations think and feel differently
about life, their preference among kinds of endowment will not be uniform or
random. Idealist generations do not grow up eager to turn beaches into concrete
harbors, nor Civic generations to found spiritual cults. Likewise, young Reactives
seldom daydream about making life failsafe through flowcharts, nor do many
young Adaptives yearn to vanquish competitors in *Top Gun* dogfights. Instead,
each generation concentrates on making endowments expressive of its lifelong
peer personality. Reflect on the types of endowments Americans celebrate on
four major national holidays. On Thanksgiving, we celebrate the spiritual values
of daily life, thanks to the (Idealist) Puritans; on July Fourth, national independence, thanks to the (Reactive) Liberty; on Memorial Day, public heroism,
thanks to the (Civic) G.I.s; and on Martin Luther King's Birthday, cultural
pluralism, thanks to the (Adaptive) Silent.

Looking through the biographies of America's eighteen generations, we can
see that every generation makes at least some mark in every variety of endowment. But, as with so much else, an important pattern emerges. Figure 12-10
summarizes how each generational type shows a special instinct—and talent—
for certain endowment activity.

As a generation matures, its endowment behavior becomes part of its peer
personality—part of its self-image and its image in the eyes of elders and juniors.
Just as each generation (and type) tends to stake out a matching endowment

FIGURE 12–10
Principal Endowment Activities,
by Generational Type

DOMINANT GENERATIONS   **RECESSIVE GENERATIONS**

IDEALISTS	REACTIVES
Principle	Liberty
Religion	Pragmatism
Education	Survival
CIVICS	ADAPTIVES
Community	Pluralism
Technology	Expertise
Affluence	Social Justice

agenda, so do other generations come to defer to that generation (and type) for providing such endowments. Over the past several decades, for example, Americans of all ages have looked to G.I.s for big constructions, to the Silent for fairness, to Boomers for reflection. Similarly, early-nineteenth-century Americans looked to Republicans for institutions, to Compromisers for mediation, to Transcendentals for religion—and, later, to the Gilded for hard-nosed realism.

Whatever its type, a generation works to achieve endowments with an intensity that varies over its lifecycle. In youth, its endowment activity is virtually nil. Coming of age, it begins building a legacy by fulfilling or challenging the endowment expectations of elders. Maturing into midlife leadership, it begins to make major contributions on its own. As its first cohorts enter elderhood—typically attaining the highest leadership posts while realizing its agenda must soon be either completed or abandoned—its activity reaches maximum intensity and then falls off. Moving beyond elderhood (right around the time the next generation of its type is entering youth), a generation typically sees its agenda neglected. Since each type of generation is pushing a certain endowment activity throughout its lifecycle, this dynamic gives endowment behavior a characteristic pattern during each constellational era. Specifically:

• *The endowment behavior of each constellational era reflects the NEW endowment activity of the generational type coming of age; the STRONG and RISING endowment activity of the type entering midlife; the PEAKING, then FALLING activity of the type entering elderhood; and the DORMANT activity of the type moving beyond elderhood (and moving into youth).*

FIGURE 12–11
**Endowment Behavior,
by Constellational Era**

PRINCIPAL ENDOWMENT ACTIVITIES		AWAKENING ERA	INNER-DRIVEN ERA	CRISIS ERA	OUTER-DRIVEN ERA
Modern Example:		1970s	1990s	1930s	1950s
IDEALIST endowments:	Principle Religion Education	new	strong and rising	peaking, then falling	dormant
REACTIVE endowments:	Liberty Pragmatism Survival	dormant	new	strong and rising	peaking, then falling
CIVIC endowments:	Community Technology Affluence	peaking, then falling	dormant	new	strong and rising
ADAPTIVE endowments:	Pluralism Expertise Social Justice	strong and rising	peaking, then falling	dormant	new

We show this dynamic in Figure 12-11, which indicates how society-wide attention to different endowments shifts over time.

Let's summarize the endowment activity of each era:

AN AWAKENING ERA begins with Civic endowment activity in confident overdrive. Society is building big things, exploring new worlds, organizing new institutions. As the moral claims of young Idealists emerge, a spiritual awakening lashes out at society's secular bias—which suddenly halts and frustrates its forward motion. By the end of the era, Civic "progress" is mired, while the fairness- and process-oriented endowments of the Adaptive ameliorators gain favor. The old Reactive focus on prudence and realism now appears stodgy and old-fashioned.

AN INNER-DRIVEN ERA begins with Adaptive endowment activity reaching high tide—pushing pluralism to the limit, infusing justice with process, and making institutions highly professional and complex. Coming-of-age Reactives apply new survival skills to a world they find harsh. The values- and morality-oriented endowments of Idealist moralizers gradually gain popularity. Civic endowments, now seen as gridlocked and unworkable, attract little new interest until near the end of the era.

A CRISIS ERA begins with Idealist endowment activity rising to maximum fury. Society now places total priority on establishing a consensus of good-versus-bad, right-versus-wrong. Sometime near the peak of the secular crisis, this fervor gives way to the sharp-eyed, prudential endowments of midlife Reactives. The energy and teamwork of coming-of-age Civics emerge from a new chrysalis. By now, the old Adaptive sensitivity to process and pluralism is deemed a wasteful, even subversive luxury.

AN OUTER-DRIVEN ERA begins with Reactive endowment activity in great popular demand—emphasizing survival and stability, and consolidating new institutions while preserving families and tradition from encroachment. The more ambitious and collectivist endowments of the Civic builders gradually gain popularity. Coming-of-age Adaptives build expertise. Tired of moral crusades, society turns its back on Idealist endowments until near the end of the era.

Within any era, the most striking pattern is not so much the emergence of a new endowment activity (which is gradual), but the decline of an old activity (which is rapid). Since younger generations have grown accustomed to relying on an older generation to champion its own preferred endowment activity, they are unprepared to fill the gap when that older generation passes on. Like a table with one leg jerked away, therefore, society suffers a ''tilt'' or disequilibrium from the sudden absence of this endowment activity. The implications are clear:

• *In each era, the most noticeable endowment neglect or reversal is likely to occur in the endowment activity associated with the generation currently passing beyond elderhood.*

In a Crisis era, for example, due process and fair play fall into disfavor—not only from the force of events, but also *because the generation that everyone expects to defend them is disappearing.* Think back to the aggressive regimentation of economic and social life during the mid-1930s, or to the mass internment of Japanese-American citizens a few years later. Where were the Adaptives? Where were the Progressive trust-busters and champions of due process? They were, by then, too old to be heard. We could ask similar questions of prior Crisis eras. Where were the Adaptive conciliators during the Civil War or the American Revolution? The Compromisers or Enlighteners were, by this time, too old or discredited.

The same pattern holds for other types of eras. The culturally sterile ''end of ideology'' decade of the 1950s (an Outer-Driven era) could have used a few zealous Idealists to stir things up—but the Missionaries were disappearing. Much the same could be said for the culturally quiescent Jeffersonian era of the early 1800s (then feeling the loss of the Awakeners) or the circa-1880 height of the Gilded Age (when the Transcendentals were fading). The Do-It-Now euphoria that gripped America from the late 1960s through most of the 1970s (an Awakening era) needed something very different: a splash of ice-water realism. Skeptical Reactives might have sobered us up and spared us disappointment later on. But it was too late; by the time of Model Cities and Woodstock, all but a few of the Lost had passed from the scene. Today, America is moving into an Inner-Driven era—with Adaptives adding layers of institutional process and detached Idealists still perfecting new values. Whose endowment activity are we beginning to miss the most? The G.I.s, the only living generation that still knows how to unify the community and get big things done.

The overlapping pattern between generations and endowment behavior leads to a final lifecycle observation:

• *Each generation develops a lifelong endowment agenda pointing toward the endowment activity that society neglected or reversed during its youth.*

The Silent, like every earlier Adaptive generation, grew up in a crisis-gripped world that had little time for refinement, sensitivity, or play-by-the-rules fairness. Their lifelong agenda has pointed toward rectifying such mistakes, toward raising again the banner dropped in old age by the Progressives. (It was, for example, a Silent-dominated Congress that recently awarded $20,000 in damages to every Japanese-American interned during World War II.) Boomers, like every earlier Idealist generation, grew up as children during a cyclical low tide of spiritual curiosity. Their lifelong endowment agenda points toward infusing society with new spiritual energy. Indeed, the Boom is the first generation since the Missionaries to show signs of preparing for late-in-life moral crusades. For 13ers, we should ask what they will someday sense was missing from their childhood environment. Most likely, it will be something all generations have missed since the mid-1960s: the active presence of the pragmatic Lost. As for the newly arriving Millennials, perhaps they will grow up yearning for something Americans are *about* to miss: the active presence of the team-playing G.I.s.

"As is the generation of leaves," wrote Homer, "so it is with the generations of men, which alternately come forth and pass away." Endowment behavior reflects a stabilizing dynamic intrinsic to the generational cycle, which ensures that no one dimension of progress is pushed too long—or lies dormant too long. Like Homer's "leaves," each kind of endowment activity has its own season. This makes the cycle of generations a powerful force for rejuvenation, a balance wheel for human progress, and—if all generations play their roles well—a guarantor of the American Dream.

The past is prologue. Let's turn to the future.

Chapter 13

COMPLETING THE
MILLENNIAL CYCLE

Histtory is full of sparks. Some have blazed for a moment, then died. Others have touched off conflagrations out of all proportion to the sparks themselves.

Suppose authorities seriously suspected that a band of terrorists, linked to a fanatically anti-American nation, had smuggled a nuclear bomb into New York City. How would America respond? To answer this question, we would need to know when this event is taking place—specifically, during which constellational era.

Suppose the terrorist threat had arisen during the last Awakening era, say around 1970. At that time, it would surely have unleashed raging national cross-currents of secular confidence and spiritual rebellion. Almost any official response would have been intensely controversial. G.I. leaders in their fifties, acting as hubristic crisis managers, would have played down the threat by assuring the public that daily life need not be disturbed—while working to control the situation through vigorous technological means. Angry coming-of-age Boomers would have organized behind a variety of symbolic and emotional responses, accusing the U.S. government of lying (one way or the other) and blaming it all on some monstrous institutional plot. Caught in between, the thirtyish Silent would have puzzled for reasons why any foreigner could hate us so much. Evacuation would have taken place in a mood of collective hysteria and disbelief. America would have been at war with itself more than with the perpetrators.

Alternatively, suppose this nuclear terrorism were to happen sometime in the early 1990s, in the middle of the current Inner-Driven era. By then, the span of roughly a quarter century will have entirely reshaped the likely national response—which would now stress caution, conciliation, and deferral. Silent cabinet officers would consult allies, form committees, review options, and invite full public discussion. After initiating multilateral negotiations, leaders would generally try to wait things out. The crisis would frustrate but not anger Boomers (who would trade philosophic remarks about how it was bound to happen sooner or later) and would hardly ruffle young 13ers (many of whom might rush toward the city to sell or volunteer transportation to families wanting to leave). Official evacuation plans would be expensive and overcomplicated and would elicit little public confidence that they would work as intended. Most people would stay calm and simply make their own plans. Chances are, the nation would squeeze by the immediate threat undamaged, but leave its underlying causes either unsolved or, at best, mildly ameliorated.

Finally, suppose the terrorists were to strike during the upcoming Crisis constellation, sometime around the year 2020. Once again, a quarter turn in the generational constellation would prompt a response that, from today's perspective, seems unrecognizable. Boomer leaders in their sixties would neither hide nor ponder the rumor; instead, they would exaggerate the threat (who said there was a bomb in only *one* city?) and tie it to a larger sense of global crisis. Unifying the nation as a community, these leaders would define the enemy broadly and demand its total defeat—regardless of the human and economic sacrifices required. Evacuation would be mannerly, with cooperative Millennial youths seeking and accepting orders from elders and with pragmatic midlife 13ers making sure no time is wasted. The nation would act promptly and decisively as a single organism. For better or for worse, Americans would be far more inclined than in other eras to risk catastrophe to achieve what its leaders would define as a just outcome.

Here we have one hypothetical event, and three hugely contrasting responses. In all likelihood, the impact on history would come less from the act of terrorism itself than from the *response* it would provoke.

In looking ahead to the future, no one can say whether nuclear terrorism will ever strike. Nor can anyone be sure about any number of troubling scenarios often mentioned in predictions about the early twenty-first century: the use of chemical, germ, or nuclear weapons by small nations; revolution in Latin America; belligerent Third World fundamentalism; AIDS; the global warming trend; ozone depletion; exhaustion of fossil fuels; the abuse of high-tech genetics; trade wars; or a debt-fueled financial crisis. Nobody can today predict what specific problems or events America's leaders will face in the 2010s and 2020s. Likewise, around 1745 and 1910, respectively, nobody could have predicted the Boston Tea Party or Pearl Harbor Day—still less the rapid and momentous sequels to those events.

When experts investigate the future, they typically rely on *quantitative* projections. But these same experts acknowledge that they are helpless before the great mysteries of human nature: how people will *respond* to those problems, how they will think, behave, and vote. When energy forecasters probe the long-term future of fossil fuels, for example, they seldom ask whether Americans in the twenty-first century will act any differently than they did during the "Me Decade" 1970s. Implicitly, these forecasters assume people would react to another oil shortage by behaving the same way: government with complex regulation, producers with market chaos, consumers with angry gas lines. Likewise, economists who make long-term Social Security projections tend to assume that persons in pre- and post-retirement age brackets will maintain the same political attitudes that people in these age brackets have shown in the recent past. In other words, they assume that old Silent and Boomers will sustain the "senior citizen" benefits lobby with the same intensity as G.I.s, and that younger 13ers and Millennials will subsidize elder benefits as willingly as the Silent and Boom have in recent decades. Straight-line projections like these can be way off the mark—the equivalent of forecasting how the Civil War would be waged by studying the speeches of Henry Clay. History tells us one thing for certain about social behavior: It never remains the same for long. The realistic question is not whether it will change, but how and when.

That is where the qualitative insight of the generational cycle can help. Through it, we can check out the mysterious wild cards of social behavior and assess what other forecasters normally avoid—*future constellational moods* and *the peer personalities of today's generations as they age into new phases of life.* Using our hypothetical nuclear terrorism as a point of departure, reflect on how America did in fact respond to perceived threats against the national community at analogous moments during the Great Power cycle: at the time of the Chicago Haymarket Riot of 1886 (in an Awakening era); at the time of the sinking of the *Lusitania* in 1915 (an Inner-Driven era); or at the time of the attack on Pearl Harbor in 1941 (a Crisis era). In each of these examples, history was determined less by the sparklike event itself than by the mood of the constellational era in which it occurred.

This is not to say that history is invariant, with predetermined outcomes. Any era can bring forward good or bad leaders, good or bad choices. What we do suggest is that constellational eras and generational lifecycles follow predictable patterns, within which each generation has a limited choice of scripts. During social moments—secular crises especially—those scripts become more fateful, more determinative of history, more likely to result in triumph or tragedy.

Building from the paradigms of the last chapter, we can extend these generational scripts into the future. The Millennial Cycle already began (as all cycles must) with one social moment: the Boom Awakening of the late 1960s and 1970s. The next—what we call the "Crisis of 2020"—is due to begin when the Millennial Cycle has run about halfway through its course. The current cycle is still young, still unfolding. It will surely bring many surprises. Yet, with four centuries as a guide, we should be able to anticipate its major trends and turns.

In the pages that follow, we present a generational itinerary of America's future, from the 1990s through the 2060s. It is a story of hope and worry, of opportunity and danger. Each of today's generations will face the future with its own unique peer personality, its own special mission of endowment. How will they fare? Contemporary readers can speculate. Only our heirs will know for sure.

Completing the Eras of the Millennial Cycle

Somehow the past always seems nearer than the future. World War I started eight decades ago in Europe. That's not so long ago. The year 2069 is the same distance in the future. Just the sound of that year conjures an unfathomable (even, some might think, irrelevant) future. But the Census Bureau predicts that roughly 35 million presently living Americans will live through the 2060s— nearly three times more than today's twelve million surviving Lost and G.I.s who were youngsters in 1914. History records what happened over the past eight decades. Now let's look at what the cycle tells us about the next eight.

We start with an automatic demographic projection, reminding us how old we shall all be at twenty-two-year intervals into the future—from 1981 until the year 2069.

Figure 13-1 starts with 1981 because that was the last cohort year of a new (Reactive) generation and thus marks an aligned Awakening constellation. Moving forward from 1981, using twenty-two-year multiples, we estimate that the next four aligned constellations will occur around 2003 (Inner-Driven), 2025 (Crisis), 2047 (Outer-Driven), and 2069 (Awakening). Notice how, in Figure 13-1, the age brackets of living generations are roughly aligned with the four phases of life in 1981 and at all subsequent twenty-two-year intervals. We cannot project these aligned constellations with precision, of course. For another two or three decades, we cannot even be sure whether 1981 is in fact the last 13er cohort—and beyond that, the boundary years are even less certain. Knowing that generations average twenty-two years in length, however, we can make reliable estimates and project future rhythms with a relatively small margin of error.

Figure 13-2 displays the generational constellations in future aligned years and shows the lifecycle phase of each generation alive in those years.

Here we see the mix of peer personalities America can expect during each era. For the three generations yet to be born, we indicate their probable type. We also add a fifth life phase, "post-elderhood," in recognition of the unprecedented leap in elderly life expectancy over the last half century. In 1940, men

FIGURE 13–1

Completing the Millennial Cycle:
Generational Ages in Aligned Constellation Years

ALIGNED CONSTELLATION:	AWAKEN-ING	INNER-DRIVEN	CRISIS	OUTER-DRIVEN	AWAKEN-ING
YEAR END:	1981	2003	2025	2047	2069
Missionary	Age 99+	—	—	—	—
Lost	81–98	Age 103+	—	—	—
G.I.	57–80	79–102	Age 101+	—	—
Silent	39–56	61–78	83–100	Age 105+	—
Boom	21–38	43–60	65–82	87–104	Age 109+
Thirteenth	0–20	22–42	44–64	66–86	88–108
Millennial	—	0–21	22–43	44–65	66–87
(New Adaptive)	—	—	0–21	22–43	44–65
(New Idealist)	—	—	—	0–21	22–43
(New Reactive)	—	—	—	—	0–21

and women at age 65 were expected to live another twelve and thirteen years, respectively; today, they are expected to live another fifteen and nineteen years, and these numbers may rise further in the decades ahead. Recall how the endowment activity of any generation moving through elderhood crests amid controversy and then declines sharply. The growing presence of post-elders, therefore, could be an important cycle innovation, full of new opportunity and new danger.

Figure 13-2 shows two future social moments—a secular crisis and a spiritual awakening. These moments begin and peak (though they do not always end) sometime during the era preceding an aligned Awakening or Crisis constellation. The cycle indicates that the period 2004–2025 is due to become the next Crisis era, the period 2048–2069 the next Awakening era. Applying the paradigms of Chapter 12, we can forecast how the constellational mood will shift over the next several decades.

Through the late 1980s and 1990s, America has been and will remain in an Inner-Driven mood. On schedule, each of today's generations is maturing in a

FIGURE 13–2
Completing the Millennial Cycle:
Constellational Eras and Phases of Life

	AWAKENING ERA	INNER-DRIVEN ERA	CRISIS ERA	OUTER-DRIVEN ERA	AWAKENING ERA
ALIGNED YEAR	1981	2003	2025	2047	2069
POST-ELDER	Lost (Reactive)	G.I. (Civic)	Silent (Adaptive)	Boom (Idealist)	Thirteenth (Reactive)
ELDER	G.I. (Civic)	Silent (Adaptive)	Boom (Idealist)	Thirteenth (Reactive)	Millennial (Civic)
MIDLIFE	Silent (Adaptive)	Boom (Idealist)	Thirteenth (Reactive)	Millennial (Civic)	(New Adaptive)
RISING	Boom (Idealist)	Thirteenth (Reactive)	Millennial (Civic)	(New Adaptive)	(New Idealist)
YOUTH	Thirteenth (Reactive)	Millennial (Civic)	(New Adaptive)	(New Idealist)	(New Reactive)

predictable direction as it begins to enter a new phase of life. The G.I.s are becoming energetic "post-elders," the Silent sensitive elders, Boomers moralistic midlifers, and 13ers alienated rising adults. Also on schedule, these same generations have emerged from the recent awakening feeling good about their personal lives yet worried that this spiritual afterglow cannot thrive forever on the strength of secular endowments made in pre-awakening decades.

The opening years of this era, the middle to late 1980s, ranked among the less eventful of modern American history. The national mood was calm, with values quite settled in contrast to the awakening 1970s. G.I. leaders stayed on as reliable caretakers at the very top of public institutions increasingly regarded as ineffective. The Silent—now filling most lesser posts, from Congress and Cabinets to state legislatures and corporate directorships—impressed their made-by-committee stamp on political and economic life. Boomers, still wrapped up in young families and new careers, made their yuppie phase of political remission the subject of much wonderment. Thirteener youths showed early signs of economic distress and cultural alienation. And Millennial babies benefited from a rekindled adult affection for infants. Most Americans worried that the country was not facing up to its long-term challenges, but found it very difficult to concentrate attention on an effective response. By the decade's end, talk of a "new world order" felt premature in a society unsure of its own foundations. As the 1990s dawn, the generational constellation—and mood—resemble those of 1910, 1845, 1750, and 1650.

What will the 1990s bring? With the fading presence of G.I.s, public confidence in old institutions will wane even further. Elder Silent leaders will discuss and debate—but never rule out—any perceived institutional inequity. Midlife Boomers will come out of remission trumpeting moral rectitude. Coming-of-age 13ers will game the system without any pretense of higher principle. Meanwhile, public life will become more zealous, less friendly. Social intolerance will grow, respect for privacy decrease. New "values" coalitions will arise while older voting blocks based on economic, class, and racial self-interest weaken. Child nurture will become stricter, and the protective function of schools and neighborhoods will attract growing public support. The senior citizen movement will weaken and the child lobby strengthen. The widening gap between haves and have-nots will be increasingly recognized as a problem—and people at both ends of the economic spectrum (the intractably poor and the greedy rich) will be attacked for lacking acceptable civic virtue. Boomer-retooled justice will punish aberrant behavior with growing severity and overtones of moral retribution; Boomer-retooled institutions will strictly regulate conduct (from drug use to parenting) formerly regarded as matters of personal choice.

During the 1990s, three distinct generational cultures will emerge. At the elder end, the Silent will struggle to buttress and defend their pluralist culture— an emphasis on lifestyle tolerance, economic opportunity, and process-protected fairness. These efforts will peak before the mid-1990s and then decline steeply. Displacing the Silent will be the Boom's moralistic culture—an emphasis on ethical absolutes, community values, and accountability in public and private life. Meanwhile, 13ers will advance into rising adulthood engaged in an alienated culture—an emphasis on getting what you can, without excuses, in a world that (as they will then see it) never cared about giving them much.

When America reaches an aligned Inner-Driven constellation, sometime around 2003, each generation will fully occupy a new phase of life. The surviving G.I.s will be very old, the Silent in elderhood, Boomers in midlife, 13ers in rising adulthood, and Millennials in youth. The generational alignment will match the constellations of 1924, 1855, 1766, and 1673. *At all four of these moments, Americans perceived their social life to be fragmenting into centrifugal and uncontrollable wildness.* The Boomer and 13er cultures will by then be moving into self-contained camps: loud, moralizing aggressors on the older side and atomized, pleasure-seeking victims on the younger—a vindictive age polarization America has not witnessed since the Roaring Twenties. Looking down the age ladder, elder Silent will express dismay at growing signs of tribalism, nativism, social intolerance, and just plain meanness. Boomers will voice exasperation over the ineffective leadership (however well-intentioned) of their next-elders and fury at the help-myself nihilism of their next-juniors. Looking up, 13ers will sense among older generations an utter impracticality, an inability to see the world for what it really is.

As America moves into the ensuing Crisis era, long-deferred secular problems can be expected to reemerge with fearsome immediacy. The aging Silent will participate eagerly in the new search for institutional solutions that *work* while reminding their juniors (something few will then want to hear) that the solutions should be *fair* as well. Boomers, their first-wave cohorts frowning on the "Golden Age" sales brochures beginning to arrive by mail, will turn up their moral megaphones to full blast. If ever there were a time to turn Pepperland into reality, many Boomers will be thinking, that time is nearing. On the brink of midlife and now beginning to tire, 13ers will sense their party boat drifting toward a waterfall—and will start thinking about which way to leap, and when. Millennials, busy transforming college life, will astound and delight elders with their friendly, optimistic, and team-playing attitude.

Moving further ahead, perhaps halfway into the Crisis era, history suggests the mood will calm somewhat. Engulfed in the electric air before a storm and perhaps already buffeted by the first shock, Americans will look toward the future with a new attitude of personal realism and public determination. The sense of community will strengthen, with one set of ideals pulling most political energy into its orbit. As each generation begins to feel the full burden of its next phase of life, each will push for a new social role definition: stewardship for elder Boomers, pragmatic management for midlife 13ers, teamwork for rising-adult Millennials. The generational cycle will approach its moment of maximum opportunity—and danger.

At this point, most likely late in the Crisis era, some spark of history can be expected to ignite a new social moment—a secular crisis—snapping generations into these new roles. Such a crisis will give Boomers a chance to thrust their awakening ideals into the core of a new national (perhaps even global) order, 13ers a chance to redeem themselves while playing for the ultimate stakes, and Millennials a chance to demonstrate civic virtue and triumph over great adversity. Meanwhile, a new generation of child Adaptives, smothered by heavily protective 13er nurture, will cower at the sight of adults doing great deeds.

Enter the "Crisis of 2020."

When will this crisis come? The climactic event may not arrive exactly in the year 2020, but it won't arrive much sooner or later. A cycle is the length of four generations, or roughly eighty-eight years. If we plot a half cycle ahead from the Boom Awakening (and find the forty-fourth anniversaries of Woodstock and the Reagan Revolution), we project a crisis lasting from 2013 to 2024. If we plot a full cycle ahead from the last secular crisis (and find the eighty-eighth anniversaries of the FDR landslide and Pearl Harbor Day), we project a crisis lasting from 2020 to 2029. By either measure, the early 2020s appear fateful.

How old will each generation be when the crisis arrives? On average, history tells us, the crisis begins sixty-two years after the Idealists' middle birthyear and nineteen years after the Civics' middle birthyear. It peaks five or ten years later. Thus, at the peak of the crisis, the surviving Silent will be in their mid-eighties and beyond, the Boomers in elderhood, 13ers in midlife, Millennials in rising adulthood, and a new generation of Adaptives in youth.

What will precipitate this crisis? It could be almost anything, including incidents trumped up by a generation of elderly warrior-priests, gripped with visions of moral triumph. The spark that catches fire may seem accidental, but—as with many past examples (the overthrow of Andros, the Boston Tea Party, Lincoln's election, and Pearl Harbor)—old Idealists may have a hand in stirring events to maximum political effect, mobilizing younger generations into action.

How significant will this crisis be? Recall the parallel eras: the Glorious Revolution, the American Revolution, the Civil War, and the years spanning the Great Depression and World War II. The Crisis of 2020 will be a major turning point in American history and an adrenaline-filled moment of trial. At its climax, Americans will feel that the fate of posterity—for generations to come—hangs in the balance.

What will the national mood be like? This crisis will be a pivotal moment in the lifecycles of all generations alive at the time. The sense of community will be omnipresent. Moral order will be unquestioned, with "rights" and "wrongs" crisply defined and obeyed. Sacrifices will be asked, and given. America will be implacably resolved to do what needs doing, and fix what needs fixing.

How will this crisis end? Three of the four antecedents ended in triumph, the fourth (the Civil War) in a mixture of moral fatigue, vast human tragedy, and a weak and vengeful sense of victory. We can foresee a full range of possible outcomes, from stirring achievement to apocalyptic tragedy.

What happens if the crisis comes early? What if the Millennium—the year 2000 or soon thereafter—provides Boomers with the occasion to impose their "millennial" visions on the nation and world? The generational cycle suggests that the risk of cataclysm would be very high. During the 2000–2009 decade, Boomers will be squarely in midlife and nearing the peak of their political and institutional power. From a lifecycle perspective, they will be exactly where the Transcendentals were when John Brown was planning his raid on Harper's Ferry. Boomers can best serve civilization by restraining themselves (or by letting themselves be restrained by others) until their twilight years, when their spiritual energy would find expression not in midlife leadership, but in elder stewardship.

Let's assume the crisis arrives on schedule, around the year 2020. Once the end is in view, all generations will gaze hopefully toward the milk and honey of the post-crisis world. By the year 2030, American society will settle into an Outer-Driven era. Boomers will start moving on to the old-old rung, 13ers to elderhood, and Millennials to midlife. New Adaptives will quiescently come of age, and an indulged new crop of Idealist children will command adult affections. The decade after the crisis—probably the 2030s—will be a slow-moving period in American history, a time of community and family life, spiritual staleness, and benign confidence about the future. The era will be upbeat but culturally bland, reminiscent of antecedent eras around 1710, 1800, 1880, and 1955. Midlife Millennials will set out on giant secular projects, while the more cautious rising-adult Adaptives will concentrate on smallish, ameliorative agendas. By this point, circa-2000 America will be remembered as socially disorganized, wild but fun, and somewhere on the cusp of what will then be perceived as the "modern" era—much as the 1920s were remembered in the 1950s.

After another quarter century has passed—when 13ers are eightyish curmudgeons and first-wave Millennials on the brink of elderhood—a highly secular culture will be due for resacralization. We can expect that a team-playing cadre of sixtyish Millennials will then provide brittle targets for a rising generation of Idealist zealots. At that point the Millennial Cycle will come to a close, and a new cycle will begin. Past spiritual awakenings have started, on average, about sixty-five years after mid-cohort Civic births, peaking seven years later. This suggests the next awakening—the next era like the late-1960s "Consciousness Revolution"—will heat up sometime in the 2050s. The next cycle moment to match the early Reagan-Bush years (with Civic elders, Adaptive midlifers, Idealist rising adults, and Reactive youths) will occur around the year 2069, the scheduled date for the next aligned Awakening constellation. We stop our chronology there, with today's infants in old age. The 1980s will then be recalled as dimly as Americans today know the decade after 1900—and school history lessons will breeze through the years between 1945 and 1990 much as today's move briskly from 1865 to 1910.

While every era is a drama of many actors, each generation follows its own script. Therefore, the drama is best understood when told actor by actor—along the generational diagonal.

Completing the Missionary and Lost Diagonals

For the roughly one thousand Missionary supercentenarians and the one million surviving Lost (mostly in their nineties), the future holds mainly the remembrance of the past. In 1990, the oldest known American with a confirmable birthdate was 112. The quiet witness borne by these scattered last-wave Missionaries more than 130 years after that generation's first birthyear can remind others how far the lifespans of their last 112-year-old survivors might reach: into the 2030s for G.I.s, the 2050s for the Silent, the 2070s for the Boom, the 2090s for 13ers, the 2110s for Millennials. Centenarians have lately been America's fastest-growing age bracket, a trend that could easily continue through the twenty-first century.

As they live on into the 1990s, the Missionaries and Lost can offer other important reminders for younger generations of their same type. Boomers would do well to reflect on how Missionaries changed from brash young reformers to stern elder "Victorians," and how they transcended the zeal and self-absorption of their youth to produce greatness in old age. Similarly, 13ers can learn important lessons from the Lost: how history dealt them short-term excitement but longer-term pain; how so many "ran on empty" to the point of exhaustion; how life went on and alienation passed; how at a critical hour they exercised practical realism as no other generation could; and how, at life's end, they became risk-averse conservatives. Today's 25-year-olds today exhibit many of the tendencies of what Fitzgerald termed the "prewar" personality of the Lost. Perhaps 13ers can aspire to match the best of what the Lost became—the Nobel-laureate authors, the savvy adventurers, the level-headed pragmatists—with less of the impulse toward self-destruction.

Completing the G.I. Diagonal

Most of the thirty million G.I. survivors believe they have a lot of living yet to do. They are right. Six in ten G.I.s will live another ten years, one in four another twenty. But this generation that hates the word "old" is beginning to realize it is becoming just that. Gradually, G.I.s are drifting beyond what gerontologists (with G.I. blessing) not long ago christened the "young old" phase and into the "old old" phase until recently associated with the Lost. As they coin new names for themselves—maybe something like "Super Seniors"— G.I.s will energize the contemporary image of what it means to be over 80.

Entering Post-Elderhood in an Inner-Driven Era (1991–2003)

Physical decline will come hard to a generation whose definition of self (and virtue) has always been so closely tied to *activity,* to getting things done. Many G.I.s will feel newly depressed, finding a loss of purpose, sensing a loss of respect. Yet the core of this generation will try, as always, to keep spirits up. Many of those in failing health will move from seniors-only condos into member-run "planned care communities," euphemized updates of what the Lost bluntly called "nursing homes." Wherever G.I.s live, their peer society will remain as friendly and collegial as ever.

The mutually supportive relationship between government and G.I.s will continue into the latter's deep old age. Over the next fifteen years, public attention to the needs of senior citizens will shift up the age bracket, away from issues that not long ago were on the minds of 60-year-olds (early retirement, reduced income and property taxes) and toward those of concern to 80-year-olds (long-term custodial care, access to life-extending technologies). The G.I. lobbies will make the case, with Silent support and Boom acquiescence, that their generation is "entitled" to the best-available health care, regardless of income or, more important, *age*. Like the Glorious and Republicans before them, G.I.s will expect to be treated well, and their juniors will generally comply—with any request involving material reward. And, as has always been the case with G.I. benefits, the long-term cost will be initially underestimated.

With the G.I.s alone atop the age ladder, however, this "please–thank you" relationship with government will take an unfamiliar turn. Forty years ago, everyone understood that giving this generation public rewards for public deeds was a form of future-oriented investment. These young G.I.s *were* the future. When they prospered, America prospered—and their Idealist and Reactive neighbors (Missionary and Lost) looked on with approval, even though they shared less in the public largess. During the 1990s, as G.I.s continue to get rewards, their Idealist and Reactive neighbors (Boom and 13th) will again look on with little objection and will again neither receive, nor expect to receive, like treatment. Yet there is one obvious difference: *The G.I.s will no longer be the future.* The generations looking on with noses pressed against the glass will not be older, but younger. The G.I. self-perception will not change at all. They will still see themselves as nice kids getting a public allowance for good deeds. But the same behavior that two life phases ago (in an Outer-Driven era) had the feel of investment will now (in an Inner-Driven era) have the feel of consumption.

G.I.s did not expect their lifecycle story to turn out this way. From the moment they first came of age, they followed their elders' instructions to save, invest, build, and be patient, pursuant to a Social Security "deal" through which G.I.s would be rewarded later in their lifecycle by younger (and presumably wealthier) generations. Through the postwar boom, everyone assumed that these juniors would be able to afford the burden with little trouble—thanks to an expanding workforce, rising levels of savings and investment, and heady rates of productivity growth. Benefit levels kept rising, enabling G.I.s to receive back many times what they and their employers had paid into the trust funds. G.I.s assumed their children and grandchildren would later enjoy the same pyramiding benefits when their own turns came.

But something happened along the way. Sapped by deficits, inflation, and a pro-consumption tax bias, savings rates did not rise. (They fell.) Productivity growth did not speed up. (It slowed down.) Younger generations did not have larger families. (They had smaller ones.) Moreover, the public cost of supporting G.I. elders soared beyond all earlier projections—thanks to a mixture of automatic cost-of-living hikes, earlier retirement, greater longevity, health-care inflation, and the G.I.s' own political muscle. In time, the cost began crowding out most other public resource priorities.

The result? Through the 1980s, generational transfer payments undermined the youth-focused investment activity that G.I.s undertook earlier in their life-cycle, and ushered in a historic reversal of phase-of-life income patterns. From Progressives to Missionaries to Lost, every elder generation the G.I.s knew earlier in life had accepted, in old age, lower per capita incomes and higher (typically much higher) poverty rates than generations in youth or rising adulthood. The G.I.s, by contrast, became America's first generation of elders whose per capita income (after taxes) exceeds the average for all younger people. Today, when all income transfers are considered, America has ten times more 13ers and Millennials than G.I.s living below the poverty line. Even so, the federal government currently spends ten times more per G.I. than it does per 13er and Millennial child. When the G.I.s were young, by contrast, elder Missionaries used government to direct resources in *exactly the opposite direction*—away from elders, and toward youth.

What went wrong, and when? The typical G.I. answer bears the bruises of their old generational battle with the Boom—and shows a clear parallel to the old Republican-Transcendental quarrels of the early nineteenth century. Many G.I.s charge that Boomers have betrayed history—much as the aging Jefferson blamed the young in the 1820s and Albert Gallatin blamed the young in the 1830s and 1840s. *What* went wrong, in the G.I. view, is that America's recent crop of rising adults have lacked the civic virtues G.I.s possessed in their own youth. From the crumbling apartments of Pruitt-Igo to the debt-leveraged buyouts on Wall Street, Boomers have always seemed to grind down more than build—to care about self more than community, about consuming more than saving, about preserving personal independence more than working hard or building families. *When* things went wrong (again in the G.I. view) was during the late 1960s and 1970s. True enough. In their coming-of-age euphoria, Boomers detested the material creations of their G.I. elders and castigated the very concept of deferring current consumption for the sake of future rewards—a concept Boomers considered to be a central pathology of their elders' mind-set. Yet this Boom Awakening clouded the G.I. judgment as well, by subtly egging on their sense of worldly hubris. In effect, Boomers told the G.I.s: "You've made material life effortless, so why bother working at it?" And G.I.s answered: "You're right, we have done rather well. Maybe it *is* time to let go." And so they did.

Much rested on this acquiescence. Despite their 1960s-era criticisms, *the Boom and Silent have always depended on the G.I.s—the generation that in their eyes has always epitomized secular endowment—to defend the ethic of investment.* When the G.I.s indicated it was okay to feed off the future, other generations accepted that decision from the ones who ought to know. From the early 1970s forward, roughly halfway through the G.I. tenure of political leadership, America initiated a fundamental shift in its allocation of resources: from the future to the present, from investment to consumption, from young to old. G.I.s have benefited personally from this shift, while 13ers (and possibly Millennials) stand to bear its biggest cost.

Today's seniors can rest easy on two counts. First, no younger generation will ever take away a significant part of their retirement "deal" against G.I. opposition. Whenever G.I.s claim that their public and private affluence belongs to them because they *earned* it, they will encounter little dissent from the one generation that could challenge them: the Boom. Yes, Boomers will think, you *did* earn it—and, like a Jeffersonian "independent nation" generation, you have the right to take it all with you. Boomers are willing to shell out high Social Security taxes with little expectation they will get the money back, because they themselves gain something immaterial in return: personal independence from their parents and the ability to redefine social values without interference from politically powerful elders. Second, the G.I.s can take some solace in recognizing that they are not the first generation to see their own unique endowment type erode upon moving behind elderhood. That happens to all generations. If the Great Society plan for a well-ordered cornucopia now seems out of reach, G.I.s can nonetheless be proud that much of what they built still endures.

Most of all, as the 1990s progress, G.I.s will notice younger generations start to miss their old "Civic" magic for making things work and start to see in the G.I. peer personality something America badly needs to relearn. Generational monuments like Iwo Jima, once symbols of intimidating G.I. power, will become shrines to a Civic spirit remembered, but increasingly perceived as weak and endangered. Where people of all ages will look to Boomers for values, they will still (Boom included) look to G.I.s for guidance on secular endowments, deep into the latter's "old old" age. Thanks to lengthening lifespans, a significant number of G.I.s will live to see this, and may well be heartened by it.

If these post-elders decide to help America rekindle a sense of teamwork and productive community, then younger generations are likely to follow. If G.I.s themselves suggest that their wealthiest members deserve no health- or nursing-care subsidies or that rank-and-file seniors deserve no discounts below what harder-pressed 13ers must pay in full—for everything from property taxes to bus rides—their example may encourage a new generation of children to start acting as selflessly as G.I.s themselves did in youth. If G.I.s themselves support additional investment in education, Boom and 13er parents may join them in putting the needs of children ahead of their own. If G.I.s stop tolerating trade and budget deficits that are (by simple arithmetic) elder-favoring, younger voters may well agree that, yes, we really *should* stop burdening children with debt.

Will G.I.s relax their collective expectation of late-in-life reward? History says they will not. By the standards of their respective centuries, Glorious and Republican elders died relatively wealthy, but culturally isolated and unhappy about how their heirs were managing public affairs. Yet history has one blind spot: Neither of these Civic predecessors had the G.I.s' opportunity, as the first set of powerful post-elders in American history, to reach all the way across the cycle and help raise a new Civic generation. In the 1990s, the G.I.s will have this chance, with the Millennials.

The power of this G.I.-Millennial bond is the major question mark in the remainder of the G.I. lifecycle and offers the most likely catalyst for a late-in-life repair of senior-citizen endowment behavior. G.I.s know, through their own experience, that Civic generations need a positive relationship with government *starting with childhood*. G.I.s (like Boomers) were able to ignore rising poverty among 13er children—but (also like Boomers) they may find Millennial poverty far less tolerable. Raising the Millennials is mainly the task of Boomers, of course—and this will complicate the G.I. task of helping these children. Today's seniors will never feel comfortable with the Boomer personality—nor the Boom with the G.I. personality. But as the 1990s progress, both generations may begin to realize that much of this antagonism has heretofore rested on their respective phase-of-life positions. Younger Idealists and older Civics collectively repel each other, but older Idealists and younger Civics, just as strongly, attract each other.

In post-elderhood, therefore, G.I.s can make an important discovery about their children: *that Boomers, in midlife, are coming to resemble the G.I.s' own parents*—the righteous Missionaries—whose patriarchal persona today's seniors remember so admiringly. G.I.s know they raised Boomers differently from the way they themselves were brought up. Nonetheless, they expected Boomer "yuppies" to behave as dutifully and collegially as they themselves had in the 1930s and 1940s. Instead, the tempestuous Boomers followed the Missionary-led path through rising adulthood—a phase of life during which G.I.s knew their parents only through a child's undiscerning eye. As custodians of the memory of great Missionary leaders, G.I. senior citizens may come to see in Boomers not the embodiment of Civic-type virtues, but the *factory* of those virtues. The more G.I.s notice this, the less they may feel inclined to opt out of the world of younger generations, or to deplete any more of the endowments they worked so hard for so many decades to build. In return, Boomers may see in G.I. post-elders a living example of the competence and power they envision for their cherished Millennial children. This could prove to be a mutually pleasing finale to the still-simmering G.I.-Boom rift—much as the midlife Awakener Benjamin Franklin finally grew to respect the "Do-Good" memory of Glorious Cotton Mather, the very symbol of Civic order that Franklin had ridiculed as a young man.

Time—and "their" twentieth century—is running out on this generation. Yet at this writing, a G.I. Commander-in-Chief still sits in the Oval Office, and millions of George Bush's peers enjoy a life as healthy and energetic as his. These senior citizens remain politically powerful out of proportion to their numbers, and have ample time left to make an important choice between two currencies of elderhood. Were G.I.s to relinquish some of their claims to secular reward, they might redeem a greater measure of the inner reward available to the elders they knew in their own youth: the confidence that, in their final years, they are doing what they can to endow their heirs with a better world. No generation of younger Americans will dare force this trade-off on the G.I.s. It is a decision only they can make.

Completing the Silent Diagonal

The Silent, like all their Adaptive predecessors, have thus far glided through history. Blessed with economic good fortune, they have been spared both the outer sacrifices of their elders and the inner trauma of their juniors. But they have been denied adventure and have never felt fully comfortable at any age. The Silent have spent a lifetime realizing two important facts: First, they are not G.I.s; second, they are not Boomers. As they grow old, they will *still* be aware of these two facts. At the same time, the aging Silent will grow increasingly worried about the fate of the generation they raised—the young 13ers—whose unromantic outlook on life seems so oddly different from what they recall of their own early years.

Entering Elderhood in an Inner-Driven Era (1991–2003)

As the 1990s proceed, a new breed of American elder will emerge: the "high-tech" senior, running his MacIntosh with software on investments, leisure opportunities, and eligibility rules for this or that special benefit. No American generation has ever entered old age better equipped than the Silent. Today's sixtyish men and women stand at the wealthier edge of America's wealthiest-ever generation, poised to take full advantage of the generous G.I.-built old-age entitlement programs. Armies of merchandisers and seniors-only condo salesmen will pounce on these new young-oldsters as they complete a stunning two-generation rags-to-riches transformation of American elderhood. Where the 1950s-era elder Lost watched their offspring whiz past them in economic life, the 1990s-era elder Silent will tower over the living standards of their children. In 1960, 35-year-olds typically lived in bigger houses and drove better cars than their 65-year-old parents. In the year 2000, the opposite will be the case.

Were this to happen to any other living generation, it would feel like a triumph. *But not for the Silent*. In old age, as always, the Silent will carry what Benita

Eisler calls that "corpse in the trunk." Anxiety. Guilt. The capacity to see drought in sunny weather, flood the minute it starts to shower. No generation has more difficulty enjoying a good thing—or has such keen antennae for sensing the needs of others. Once the Silent perceive that their affluence is *generational* and is unlikely to be exceeded by their own 13er children, they will feel a genuine hurt.

As these high-tech seniors stare at their amber monitors, they will wonder whether they deserve such a long list of late-in-life rewards. The Silent weren't denied jobs in the Great Depression (new toys and second helpings, maybe). The Silent didn't win any war (they tied one). The Silent didn't build grand endowments (they handled the details). The very word "entitlement," so comfortably uttered by G.I.s, will have a newly embarrassing ring. The Silents' core achievements—civil rights, sexual liberation, mainstreaming for the handicapped—are not the sort to make them feel entitled to pecuniary reward. From their perspective, the mere acceptance of reward would call into question the sincerity of the original undertaking. Any Silent doubts will be reinforced by Boomers, who will find ways of saying "No, you're *not* entitled!" if the question is ever asked.

The ascendance of Silent into the "young old" age category will begin a fateful erosion of the political consensus on federal retirement policy—a consensus that has warded off all challenge since the mid-1960s. Throughout their lives, the Silent have been easy targets for scandals. That will not change in the 1990s, as the media begin to expose a growing number of affluent Silent retirees (and ex-officeholders) for alleged abuses of public generosity—stories the media would never attempt (and the public never accept) about G.I. retirees. Meanwhile, long-term forecasts for retirement and health-care programs will become decidedly less sanguine. Old-age benefits will then become negotiable, "on the budget table" in ways unthinkable back in the 1970s and 1980s. Cast on the defensive and equipped with a libertarian sense of equity, the Silent will suggest some sort of compromise—for example, that their nonpoor members get back the Social Security and Medicare money they once paid into the trust funds, maybe with a little interest, but nothing more. Entitlement programs will thus begin moving toward "means testing," targeting benefits on the needy. State and Fortune-500 pension plans that had once looked so attractive to early retirees will begin eroding in purchasing power. Subsidized health care will be subject to new triage regulations disfavoring the old. Civil service and military retirees who can lay no claim to G.I.-style heroism will face new challenges against "double dipping," automatic COLAs, and veterans' benefits for non–service related illnesses. Private pension plans will face public pressure to reduce their enormous (and largely unfunded) retiree health-care liabilities. Gifts and estates will be subject to higher taxes by legislators who will consider Silent wealth less "earned" than the G.I. facsimile. All this will meet with little effective resistance from Silent-run elder organizations, which will back away from aggressive, G.I.-

style lobbying and take a conciliatory new line on young-to-old transfers (*except* those involving the very old G.I.s, which will still be stoutly defended). Like the Silent themselves, their elder lobbies will become more self-doubting, pluralist, other-directed, and compromising.

Silent elders will not share the G.I. instinct for peer-group collegiality. Instead, they will look for social activities that bring them in contact with youth and adventure. An unprecedented number will use their time, money, and talent to help others, at home and overseas. Recalling their Peace Corps days, the Silent will assemble a variety of public-spirited "Senior Corps" to channel elder talent and expertise toward solving social problems. Their generous gifts and bequests will usher in a golden age of private philanthropy. Redirecting Social Security income to charity (or to their own 13er children) will become a popular trend among the wealthy. The Silent will look upon automatic "senior citizen" discounts as unnecessary, even unfair—and younger generations will agree. The Silent will be more reluctant than G.I. elders to say "Read my lips—no new taxes" when private sacrifice is asked to meet a heartfelt public need. This most affluent of living generations may well lead the call for greater progressivity in the tax structure.

Reversing the G.I. trend toward collective separation, these new-breed elders will want to stay actively engaged in an increasingly Boom-dominated society. The postwar trend toward ever-earlier retirement will backtrack. The Silent will insist on the right of 70-year-olds to participate in the world of younger people— to remain useful, help others, and stay employed if they wish. Many early retirees will feel guiltily idle and rejoin the workplace in people-oriented service jobs— whether they need the money or not. The visual and print media will see an increase in the number of old columnists and news anchors, bravely resisting the weakening of their generation's pluralist message. "Seniors Only" living communities will become more uncommon and controversial, perhaps even the objects of legislative or juridical attack. Boomers who were perfectly happy when G.I.s chose to separate will see reprehensible antichild (and anti-Millennial) attitudes in similar Silent behavior. Most Silent will agree.

That powerful, collegial G.I. name "senior citizen" will fit the Silent peer personality awkwardly at best. While perhaps continuing to use the term, the Silent will look for ways to humanize it, to make it more personal and accessible. The Silent will feel less the senior citizen than the senior partner; they may be attracted to the simple noun "senior," a more modest term when standing alone, one that evokes the image of the sympathetic upperclassman. Their nicknames will be quaintly hip, evoking memories of the 1950s and making gentle fun of themselves—perhaps something like "Oldster," "Granddaddio," or "Old Bopper." They will camouflage their new phase-of-life uncertainty in a rich smile of irony, unconcerned about juniors taking over the mantle of power—and powerless to stop it, anyway.

The "Old Bopper" mind-set will combine a denial of age with a better-late-than-never search for catharsis. So far, the Silent have seen a millstone in every age milestone—and around the year 2000, sociologists will discover an unsettling new lifecycle "passage" in the mid-sixties. New-breed elders try thinking, acting, and looking young. To guard against appearing old, the Silent will keep their wardrobes within mainstream fashions, and will undergo many a face-lift and tummy tuck. Seniors-only tours will fall sharply in popularity, supplanted by those catering to grandparents with grandchildren. In the company of younger people, Silent elders will scale mountains, ride rapids, hack through jungles, backpack through deserts, parachute from planes—anything with a little tingle of death-defying risk. Many will keep ambitious checklists of everything they still want to do—for example, to see every great Broadway musical, visit every national park, or traverse every continent. "Senior circuits" of aging Silent athletes will gain in popularity. This nostalgia for youth and romance will extend to music and film as well; Elvis Presley and Marilyn Monroe will remain powerful Silent icons. Aging performers like the Everly Brothers or Peter, Paul, and Mary will stay popular well into their old age, with rock and roll replacing the G.I. fox-trot at senior sock hops. "Wake up Little Susie, Wake up!" will reverberate in even the most formal of ballroom settings.

The elder Silent will be wealthy enough to provide a gold mine for targeted products and services. Marketers will tap into them by appealing to their sense of irony, their earnest sentimentality, and (especially) their thirst for catharsis. Old Boppers will feel an unquenchable yearning to be true individuals, to feel alive, to dabble in slightly juvenile adventures in risk and defiance—even while retaining their lifelong confidence in expertise and attention to detail. They will continue to emulate whatever Boomers happen to be doing or feeling. In electoral politics, the Silent will be slow to make up their minds, and more swayed than others by candidates with high name recognition, impressive credentials, and proven management skills. On the surface they will delight in zany, iconoclastic rhetoric, yet underneath they will insist on genial, flexible temperaments.

The aging Silent will usher in a renaissance of the American extended family. More than at any other time in American history, 65-year-olds will have parents still living. Nor can the Silent count on their own children to leave home once and for all. Run the 13er "boomerang" child syndrome on fast-forward, and picture a continuing stream of young adults abandoning small urban apartments and returning to the large homes of their Silent parents. Sooner or later, many a 13er live-in child will drop the hint, the parent will relent, and the master-bedroom *coup d'état* will occur. The typical G.I. parent, who scrimped long years to afford household comfort, would never give in so easily. But the Silent are a softer touch. Having been empty-nesters rather early, they will attach less value to the privilege of living alone in a big home. Besides, the Silent will be culturally compatible with their children in ways the G.I.s were not. Around the turn of the century, these 65-year-old rock-and-rollers will get along just fine with their 35-year-old post-punk children. Grandparents will welcome the chance to help nurture a new generation of children—a task they realize they performed too young the first time around. Silent authors will do to the "art" of grandparenthood what they once did to the "art" of sex: They will scrutinize it endlessly, making it the subject of countless books, films, plays, songs, and paintings. And they will professionalize it with consultants, seminars, and global conferences.

The Silent will see in extended family life a certain measure of atonement for the damage they did to the family (individually or collectively) back in the years of the Boom Awakening. Many will come to regret the hurried and unprotected upbringing they gave 13ers. But while the Silent confess easily to mistakes, they are loath to admit that any mistake is final. Like old John Crittenden or John Dewey, they will never quit trying to set things right. In the 1990s and beyond, generous help to their adult children will offer the Silent another chance to do just that.

The personal lives of Old Boppers will be more complicated than what we today associate with G.I.s. Their "swinging" will occasionally infuriate their juniors. Like William Byrd II, the Silent will still "play the fool" in their late sixties and beyond, still succumb to sexual dalliances and experimental urges. They will always be drawn to the emotional complexity of life and interested in the daily lives of younger people. Even when their health fails, they will be reluctant to enter a long-term-care facility. Their physical decline will bring a surge in at-home elder care, mostly financed by the Silent themselves. Whatever long-term-care subsidies the G.I.s win in the early 1990s will not be extended to Silent elders above the poverty line.

The Silent spent a lifetime taking cues by looking up and down the age ladder. In youth, they looked entirely up. In old age, they will look entirely down. In government, aging Silent leaders will offer the grayer hues of public administration, deferring rather than solving core problems and only occasionally taking a breakaway risk. Hobbled by locked-in G.I. artifacts—budget deficits, low marginal tax rates, uncancelable defense projects, entitlements programs running on autopilot—the Silent will blame their political indecisiveness on circumstances supposedly beyond their control. Like the Compromiser "Great Triumvirate," they will prefer to ameliorate old policies rather than start over again from scratch. Whatever the problem, their approach will focus on better process (a new budget amendment, a new incentive tax scheme, a new blue-ribbon commission) rather than on the ultimate desired outcome. To Boom critics, Silent leaders will reply that the world is complicated and that aggressive solutions are premature—admitting, at the same time, that all points of view must be considered.

The Silent seem fated to pass from national power with the shortest and weakest tenure since the Enlightener days of Alexander Spotswood. Already leapfrogged by Boomers in the White House and House Republican lines of succession, their zero for six in Presidential campaigns (dating back to 1968) might well end up zero for nine or ten. History suggests that an Adaptive generation gets its best chance to produce a charismatic leader (an Andrew Jackson, Theodore Roosevelt, Robert Kennedy, or Martin Luther King, Jr.) while entering midlife, not while entering elderhood. To win the Presidency, a Silent would have to forget the old G.I.-style New Deal coalition and replace the cult of expertise with the more values-laden campaign style of the Boom— for example, by showing interest in religion, demanding stern punishment for moral miscreants, displaying anger in public, and projecting an empathic sense of community. Silent women may do better than their male peers in presenting such themes. Yet regardless of sex, a Silent candidate's best chance may arise if the American political system feels either "on hold" or deadlocked. The more quickly a sense of social or economic emergency arises, the less likely the Silent will be able to slow their slide from power.

Their slide has already begun. The Silent share of congressmen and governors peaked at 68 percent in 1983 and has been declining gradually ever since, to 65 percent in 1989. Following the usual pattern, this decline will accelerate during the early to middle 1990s and leave the Silent with no more than a 35 percent share after the year-2000 election. At some point in the 1990s, Silent officeholders may well fall victim to Boomer attacks on professionalism, an alienated 13er mood, or their own self-doubts—marking an abrupt end to the enormous electoral success Silent incumbents have enjoyed in recent years.

Silent elders will be of mixed mind about Boom-led social and political trends. They will complain about Boomers and 13ers dismantling their procedural solutions for civil rights, and they will fear for the wounded egos of heavily chaperoned Millennial children. They will try to calm the inner passion of the Boomers and lend sensitivity to Boomer crusades. They may assert new virtue in the word "liberal" to younger generations—who, in turn, will find Silent sentimentality and technobabble increasingly rococo. Like aging Enlighteners, the seventyish Silent elite will dislike the rising trend toward mean-spirited public life. Like aging Compromisers, they will prefer conciliation over crisis. Like aging Progressives, they will trust electoral or judicial or legislative process over principle. And like all three, they will be mostly ignored. As the Inner-Driven era ends, the Silent will age into America's biggest worriers about the future— not exactly pessimists (the Silent believe there's always a second chance), just worriers.

The Silent have never been and never will be collectively powerful, but will continue enriching others with a gentler kind of endowment. Until the next Adaptive generation comes of age—in the 2030s—no other generation will press the case for other-directed social compassion, pluralism, sympathy for the underdog, and procedural fairness. Nor will any other have the Silent capacity for intergenerational understanding. The Silent can mediate the upcoming cultural clash between Boom and 13th. So too can they set the underlying "rules of the game" for the Crisis of 2020. Their success at these tasks will hinge on their ability to separate the fundamental from the aesthetic, to know when to join (and how to mentor) the Boomers, and to realize that the Millennials, unlike the 13ers, require a protective nurture to thrive. Past the year 2000, as the ranks of the Silent begin to thin, other generations will come to miss the politeness, tolerance, and *niceness* that Americans now associate with people in their fifties and early sixties.

Entering Post-Elderhood in a Crisis Era (2004–2025)

As the forces of history amass under Boom leadership, the Silent can remind Boomers of kindness, 13ers of conscience, Millennials of caution. The danger will lie in any attempt by aging Silent leaders to get too much in the way of the thickening forces of history—for example, if an eightyish President (or Supreme Court) insists on scrupulous process at a moment when younger generations begin to coalesce around the need for decisive action. The last time this happened, during the Presidency of old Compromiser James Buchanan, the foot-dragging of elder Adaptives helped foment the most destructive crisis in American history. The same could occur if antiquarian Silent leadership helps usher in the Crisis of 2020.

The Silent will reach their final lifecycle "passage"—death—at a time no less awkward than any of their earlier milestones. Three of every four can expect to depart during the first quarter of the twenty-first century, years when the cycle suggests the skies of history will darken. Some will live on into the midst of crisis. But, like Cadwallader Colden, Roger Taney, and Louis Brandeis (who died in 1776, 1863, and 1941, respectively), their last survivors may have to say farewell at the most unsettling of times: right around the year 2020. They will know what the crisis is, but not how it will turn out. Future events will confirm what the Silent have always sensed is their lot: born at the wrong time, ten years too soon or ten years too late.

Completing the Boom Diagonal

The fate of the Boom is one generational future that has already attracted wide public attention. Thus far, most demographers and social scientists have reached two major conclusions: that the Boom's vast size will alone give it unusual electoral power, and that its collective late-in-life personality will fall somewhere in the spectrum between the hippie and the yuppie. Wrong on both counts.

First, any suggestion that the Boom will dominate the electorate by dint of raw numbers is flat-out mistaken. Its greatest numerical edge occurred in the late 1970s, right around the pre-yuppie peak of its political detachment. That edge shrank gradually in the 1980s and will erode further with each successive decade. In 1990, 13ers outnumbered Boomers by 14 percent. Starting in 1996, 13ers will eclipse Boomers in raw voting clout—and around the year 2016, the Boom will slip behind the Millennials and become America's third-largest generation of eligible voters.

Second, if Boomer fiftysomethings or seventysomethings repeat the behavior pattern of their teens or thirties, theirs would be the first American generation ever to do so. Yes, they will always listen to 1960s music, debate the "lessons" of Vietnam, and show a weakness for granola and mineral water. But while all generations are steered by their coming-of-age experiences, none returns there. History suggests the celebrated Boomer trek from hippie to yuppie will lead to someplace still different—someplace their heirs will find far more memorable.

Entering Midlife in an Inner-Driven Era (1991–2003)

In the early 1990s, some Boomers will look back upon their awakening as a moment of generational trajectory, propelling them on a path of collective destiny. Others will express open contempt for any such pretension. As all Boomers assert their midlife values, they will subject their coming-of-age awakening— what it did and did not accomplish—to growing scrutiny. Along with this scrutiny will come stormy peer-on-peer invective. Boomers should not be surprised to see this happen. They are following the script of every prior Idealist generation entering midlife, dating back to the first charges and countercharges of "hypocrisy" traded among Winthrop's small wilderness gathering in the 1640s.

The 1990s will bring fuller development to several important Boomer trends of the late 1980s. Though yuppies will still be around, Boomer perfectionism will begin to express itself less in the realm of personal fulfillment than in the realm of social virtue. Boom politics will become more intensely values-laden. Like Missionaries in their forties and fifties, Boomers will grow increasingly pompous, intolerant, uncompromising, snoopy, and exacting of others. At the same time, they will become more dutiful, principled, and demanding of themselves.

The Boom's era of political remission will end sometime in the 1990s, perhaps around the time the last G.I. President departs. The "generational politics" touted by so many over the last two decades will finally start bearing results— but it will be linked to *inner-world,* not outer-world, ends. Notwithstanding their current reputation for personal selfishness, Boomers will not mobilize around appeals to collective self-interest—for example, around tax, labor, trade, or retirement issues. Instead, they will look for lofty commitments on matters of principle. To other generations, their moral perfectionism will seem whiny, mean-spirited, even (in the context of the Boomer past) hypocritical. But it will reflect a growing generational commitment to solve the unsolved—an attitude that will help revitalize a sense of national community.

Boomer interest in real-world institutions will assume a new seriousness. As the 1990s progress, a growing share of all school districts, state legislatures, and corporations will emerge entirely retooled around Boom values—while the remainder will seem almost Mesozoic in their pristine G.I.-ness or (more often) their fuzzy Silentized G.I.-ness. Following the path of every other Idealist generation, Boomers will begin with local and grassroots institutions and work their way up to the most powerful bodies of national leadership. Their share of Congress and governorships (now 21 percent) will expand rapidly in the mid-1990s and will probably become a plurality following the 1994 or 1996 election. If Boomers follow the Missionary pattern, they will reach their lifetime peak share of national leadership around the year 2005, just as the Inner-Driven era is ending, sixty-two years after the birth of their first cohort.

Each step of the way, Boomer-retooled institutions will grow teeth. In power, Boomers will scrap Silent process, regard no budget item as "untouchable," and attack political arrangements (from the sugar cartel to sweetheart defense contracts) that, in recent decades, have seemed impenetrable. Seeing new virtue in community, they may see advantage in taxes (on consumption), regulation (on speculative investment and pleasure-seeking leisure), and public intrusions into what others will consider matters of personal and business privacy. Regional planning and consumer groups will propel their causes by asserting ethical values ahead of individual self-interest. An antidrug and pro-environmental alliance may well emerge as the nation's most potent lobby, at all levels of government. And as the Boom moves beyond the age of procreation and begins to equate sexual freedom with 13er license, the balance of power in the abortion debate may well turn toward the evangelical last-wavers. Growing numbers of Boom feminists may shift their focus away from self and toward progeny—perhaps acquiring the view of aging Transcendental Susan B. Anthony that abortion is "degrading to women" because it encourages them to "treat our children as property to be disposed of." If so, a decade of abortion prohibition could be for Boomers what a decade of alcohol prohibition was for Missionaries.

Whatever righteous causes Boomers have in mind, they will remain a hard sell for political and commercial marketers. At the voting booth, fiftyish Boomers will show all the perversity of the fiftyish Silent—with more of the independence and less of the niceness. They will disdain party allegiances, argue at fundraisers, hang up on telemarketers, and generally take far less interest in flesh-and-blood candidates than in abstract issues. To reach them, aspiring politicians will have to demonstrate candor, simplicity, moral rectitude, serenity of soul, even a hint of detachment. The appealing air of the minister will be more effective than the polished air of the expert. Product marketers will have to take much the same tack. Boomers will seek high purpose in what they buy: quality over quantity, uniqueness over comfort, inner satisfaction over outer popularity. The perfect Boomer product will, like the perfect health food, allow a gesture of austerity in the very act of consumption. Boomers will seek ways to express their defiance of material urges while still indulging in them—for example, by using mail-order and home-delivery services that allow them to buy without stooping to shop.

Boomer-run corporations will keep relentless focus on the "bottom line"— not just profits, but *principles* about what companies should mean to their owners, employees, customers, and neighbors. Like Henry Ford, Boomer manager-owners will try to turn firms into agents of public and private virtue. Even well-performing companies will downsize staffs, defer dividends, or shift marketing strategies to achieve values-related goals. This managerial style will strike 13ers as ruthless, even "puritanical"—but in return for this added moral authority, Boom executives will be prepared to accept a narrowed pay gap between themselves and their workers.

In contrast to credentialed Silent careerists, the midlife Boom elite will have highly eclectic backgrounds. A growing number of nonlawyers will enter politics, non-Ph.D.s publish in academic journals, nonpriests give sermons, even non-doctors give medical advice. Some of the most promising Boomer politicians (and Presidential candidates) will spring from outside the ranks of law, government, and party politics. The Boom elite will assiduously maintain individual identities apart from institutions. Many a Boomer will work for a corporation and have a business (or profit-making hobby) on the side. The Boomers' high-tech home offices will have the same individuating effect on the American workplace that the Missionaries' automobiles had on the American community. Feeling in control of their choices, midlifers will make career switches easily. Turnover will rise in top-level jobs. In Congress, resignations over matters of principle will become more common, Silent-style PACs will weaken, and name recognition and incumbency will lose much of their present-day advantage. Throughout the top echelons of government and business, interest in philosophy, literature, and the arts will rise—and interest in "how-to" manuals will fall.

Midlife Boomers will concentrate less on infusing perfectionism into their personal lives (today's effete yuppie stereotype) and more on infusing it into their family and public lives. They will openly insist on enforcing a new sense of local (and, gradually, national) community—and will battle against vestiges of Silent-style pluralism and rights-protected fairness. Many of today's media experts are predicting that the official "Millennial"—the year 2000—will trigger a tidal outpouring of Aquarian weirdness from fiftyish Boomers, from bacchanals serving homemade wine and Yugoslavian brie to Vedic mantras hummed on mountain tops at sunset. The experts will be disappointed. By then "into" their new institutional roles, Boomers will no longer be satisfied with cultural ephemera; instead, they will push an austere and stripped-down version of their New Age morality (an update of what midlife Missionaries called "Decency") straight into mainstream social life. The culture war between the Boom and 13th can be expected to heat up for precisely this reason. Most of today's 13ers are quite content to see Boomers pass their leisure hours among their own peers, in retreat from the real world. All 13ers have to do is stay out of the way. But when Boomers decide to stay home on weekends and tell 13ers how to behave, *that's* when the battles will begin. Americans who have lately grown accustomed to looking upon (Silent) 50-year-olds as a nice, open-minded bunch will sense a new and cold wind as first-wave Boomers pass the half-century mark.

Around the year 2000, Boomers will settle in as a more cerebral "older" generation. They will seek the classic and the enduring over the faddishly popular. They will challenge sex, profanity, and violence in the media—and will get results. Like all Idealist generations entering midlife, Boomers will mount a relentless attack on all forms of substance abuse. They will strike blow after blow against tobacco—taxing, restricting, and humiliating anyone involved in its production and use. The alcohol industry can expect its sternest challenge since Prohibition. The firearms industry will fare better thanks to the fact that the Boom will not dislike violence per se, just *meaningless* (read: "13er") violence. Boom opinions will be nitpicked (but emulated) by the Silent, resented (but coped with) by the 13th.

In inner cities, Boomer civic and religious leaders will reestablish moral principles and police the world of youth activities with far greater attention to ends than means. Sharing the Boom cult of community, the midlife black elite will assert moral leadership in troubled neighborhoods that (in their view) need them. Inner-city religious leaders will become sharply intolerant of youth misbehavior. The black Boom elite will back away from procedural mechanisms like affirmative action—and will instead force younger people to build "character" and accept more responsibility for their own condition. When black Boomers call attention to white racism, their purpose will not be (as it was for Progressives and Silent) to galvanize the white establishment to act, but rather (as it was for Transcendentals and Missionaries) to galvanize the black community to act on its own. In the tradition of Frederick Douglass and W.E.B. DuBois, black Boomers may ultimately make their most enduring contributions in letters and cultural leadership.

Like prior Idealist generations, the Boom will produce an explosion of women into public life. By the year 2000, midlife women will surge into boardrooms, media anchor booths, university presidencies, and Congress—and will begin making plausible runs for the White House. Aging Boom women may see in their own peers the apogee of their lifelong struggle for equality with men in public life. Like Lucy Stone and Elizabeth Cady Stanton, they will rage against the growing willingness of younger generations to abandon the feminist cause, rewiden sex role distinctions, and push women back toward the pedestal of family life.

Boomer judgmentalism will land heavily on the criminal justice system. In contrast to the Silent, midlife Boomers will find it easier to condemn individuals and harder to condemn "society"—a word that for them will now mean "Boom society," whereas for the like-aged Silent it had meant "G.I. society." Boomers will define new crimes, from limitations on freedom of speech to new vagrancy statutes for panhandlers who refuse to live in austere shelters. Criminal juries will be unrelievedly harsh, appeals shortened, sentences lengthened, parole boards weakened, prison life regimented, and the worst offenders executed with a grim efficiency not seen since the stern tenure of Missionary judges. Boomers will develop new "shaming" approaches to punishment, emphasizing confession, humiliation, and personal reform where the Silent always thought it fairer to stick to rules. This will be a sore point for 13ers, destined to become the leading objects of the harsh new Boom penology.

In civil law, similarly, Boom judges and juries will show a new sternness. Inquiring into culpability rather than "deep pockets," they will be more inclined to grant "punitive" damages than to compensate for pain and suffering. Litigation will be streamlined and made less costly—and more final. Private industry will find in moral rectitude an effective strategy for winning (or avoiding) lawsuits. After recasting the insurance industry in line with new values, Boomers will treat insurance assets as community resources and limit plaintiffs to stingier awards. A Boomer jury will resist making the community pick up the tab where it deems an individual to be at fault.

As demanding as this generation will be of others, the Boom will be no less demanding of its own members. Grumpy midlifers will frown on nontraditional sexual behavior, especially where it appears to threaten the family. Divorce will become more stigmatic. Boomers will not tolerate impure behavior in public life, and will expiate their own youthful excesses through the occasional pillaging of public figures with hippieish pasts. Those who persist in Awakening era behavior patterns deep into midlife (in the mold of the wayfaring Transcendentals John Humphrey Noyes and Henry Ward Beecher) will suffer the opprobrium of their peers. Meanwhile, just as the Transcendental elite disdained Millard Fillmore and the Missionary elite ignored Warren Harding, Boomers may well be disappointed with their first cadre to achieve national political prominence. Their collective power will be stymied by high individual self-esteem (the notion that "I" could do better than anybody who might be on the ballot). The "debunkers"—the Boom's Mencken-like challengers from within—will chip away at any early effort to energize the generation into an aggressive political consensus.

As Boomers pass through their forties and fifties, two trends bear watching. The first is the grace with which they accept their advancing years. So far,

Boomers have not much noticed the aging process. In part, this reflects a strengthening focus on the spiritual and cerebral over the physical—but also an urge to remain forever the youngish generation while appearing not to care about it. If Boomers cling to a youth-fixated narcissism into their forties and fifties, America will be heading for trouble. When the Silent emulated the mannerisms and physique of youth, Boomers did not feel at all bothered; if anything, they felt flattered. But when the older generation has higher collective self-esteem, any midlife "fountain of youth" poses a direct threat to the social role of rising adults. If fiftyish Boomers try too hard to look and act thirty, they will endanger an effective late-in-life partnership with 13ers and increase the risk that any later crisis could turn out badly. History's best relationships between midlife Idealists and rising-adult Reactives (Landon Carter with George Washington, or Gertrude Stein with Ernest Hemingway) have all featured the Idealist who played the repository of culture, the reminder of stable, deeply rooted values—not the youthful sprite. Like a Bradstreet, Franklin, Longfellow, or Sandburg, Idealist generations have the capacity to age elegantly, in their own eyes and in the eyes of others.

The second trend to watch will be the strength and behavior of midlife Boomer factions, especially the split between the New Age (modernist) and evangelical (traditionalist) camps, whose major 1980s-era battles focused on abortion and sex education. The search for a Boom values consensus will hinge, in part, on the nation's economic performance. With modernism emanating largely from the generation's better-off first-wavers and traditionalism more from worse-off last-wavers, any further widening of this economic gap will aggravate values conflicts. The Boom may split along geographical lines—for example, with urban, bicoastal New Agers squaring off against heartland evangelicals. This could prompt talk of regional secessions. Yet if the Transcendentals demonstrated how sectionalism can rapidly grow into implacable hatred, the Puritans, Awakeners, and Missionaries proved that an Idealist generation, however fragmented early in life, retains the capacity to find common principle in times of approaching crisis. If Boomers unify, the initial evidence will be the coexistence of divergent values in the same communities, and the emergence of new and seemingly odd alliances like the Missionaries' pre–World War I "reform trinity" of fundamentalists, feminists, and western agrarians. If Boomers reach a midlife consensus in support of cleaning up the world of the Millennial child, that will bode well for the decades to follow.

Entering Elderhood in a Crisis Era (2004–2025)

Picture a holiday parade one decade into the next century. Will there be any crisply marching, eyes-ahead, flag-carrying war veterans, followed by purple-fezzed Shriners driving silly cars in tight formations? Hardly. In their place will be bearded old vets in ragtag khaki, their step defiantly out of sync with younger drummers, their eyes piercing the crowd with moral authority. In 2004, thirty-five years after Woodstock, Boomers will range in age from 43 to 60. By 2026, the youngest Boomer will be 65, the oldest 82. In the intervening era, as this generation passes through its life phase of maximum power, history suggests it will encounter a secular crisis comparable to the greatest moments in American history. Meet the old Boom, the next embodiment of Hawthorne's "Gray Champions," combining "the leader and the saint" to show the descendants of the Puritans "the spirit of their sires." Boom principle—or righteous fury—will cast a long shadow over the entire twenty-first century. If the future follows the cycle, old Boomers will bring world history to a decisive turning point. Whatever the outcome, younger generations will later remember, in black-and-white, the stern Boom sense of moral imperative—decades after the floral hippie and pin-striped yuppie images have been forgotten to all but the historian.

One rather safe prediction experts often make about elderly Boomers is that they will collide with underfunded federal pension and health-care systems, starting in the mid-2010s. This is one issue where the unprecedented size of the Boom Generation does matter. A straight-line extrapolation of recent productivity, fertility, and longevity trends indicates that by the year 2025, younger workers would have to hand over 30 to 40 percent of their payroll to provide old Boomers with G.I.-style public support. To extract such taxes, Boomers would have to wage and win a furious political war against 13ers and Millennials, a war that would surely sap their moral authority. Perhaps it is a war old Boomers could win. History says it is not a war they will wage.

All their lives, Boomers have been bracing themselves for an old age of diminished material dependence. As the 1990s dawn, more than seven of every ten Boomers do not think Social Security will help them when they are old. For G.I.s at like age, any doubts about their future public reward would have triggered prompt and effective political action. But for inner-fixated Boomers, this negative expectation simply requires an adjustment to karma and is not a great cause for alarm. No matter how hard life gets, no matter how serious the world's problems, Boom self-esteem will remain unconquerable. Old Aquarians will consider themselves "together" people. Sensing their physical mortality and their susceptibility to the fourth dimension (time), Boomers will turn focus to the fifth—the spiritual. Other generations will find this attitude peculiar, even frightening. But thanks to this inner fixation, Boomers will cope with harsh economic realities gracefully, without wasting resources they would rather direct toward loftier community goals.

In what they demand from the young, old Boomers will be utterly unlike elder G.I.s, who gave their juniors full reign over their society's values and demanded economic benefits in return. Social Security originated seventy-five years after the birth of the first Missionary cohort and was, at that time, primarily a *youth-oriented* program. For a pittance of support, Missionary elders vacated jobs for younger breadwinners—in return for retaining the moral authority to guide the young through an era of great trial. During the darkest hours of crisis, old Missionaries accepted declining living standards in order to help see America through to triumph—and, thereafter, to reward young G.I. heroes. That, in Missionary eyes, was the proper ethical arrangement.

The Boom will do much the same. In national politics, with the G.I.s by then almost entirely gone and the Silent weakening, Boomers will force a dramatic turn in the politics of Social Security. In the 2010s, they will lay the terms for an entirely new intergenerational "deal," snapping the chain of ever-rising benefits that G.I.s insisted would never end. Boom leaders will thoroughly recast—and probably rename—Social Security and Medicare. To avoid raising the burdens on younger generations, they will leave their peers with a purchasing power below what the G.I.s and Silent will have enjoyed, exempting only the "deserving" poor from the new regime of old-age austerity. Affluent Boomers will receive little economic recompense from a lifetime of payroll taxes paid to support others. Yet in a turnabout from the G.I. entitlement ethic, Boomers will derive self-esteem from knowing they are *not* receiving rewards from the community.

Thanks to Boomer asceticism, the proportion of circa-2020 national income spent on elder medical care may rise little if at all above what it is today—despite their larger numbers, their longer lifespans, and (very likely) the huge variety of expensive medical technologies then available. Driven by personality as much as economics, Boomers will widely prefer less costly "self-care" to hospital care wherever feasible. Elder use of chemical medications will decline, offset by a growing reliance on alternative medical approaches—from New Age homeopathy to evangelical faith-healing. Federal health policy will dispense with the G.I.-era notion that elder beneficiaries can privately decide with their doctors how much of the younger taxpayers' income they want to spend on health care. Instead, the type and extent of health-care assistance old Boomers receive will be a tightly regulated social decision.

This intergenerational deal will be two-sided. In return for an austere elderhood, Boomers will demand sweeping moral authority—and, in all likelihood, will retain national leadership until they reach advanced old age and see their values firmly locked in place. The Boom share of Congress and governors, though peaking before 2010, will remain a dominant plurality into the 2020s. Like their Awakener and Missionary predecessors, *Boom leaders will exercise their greatest political influence unusually late in life*. Even after their governmental tenure expires, moreover, they will still insist on setting America's cultural and intellectual tone. Occupations that today are associated with the Boom—education, media, the arts—will gray with them. From university lecterns to news anchor booths to the Oval Office, America circa 2020 will value the visionary over the pragmatic, the learned over the energetic, the resolute over the yielding—in short, the old over the young (which in that era will mean Boomers over 13ers). Throughout American society, elders will be looked upon as titans—not especially competent in practical matters, but unquestioned chieftains of national purpose. Boom women will attain a level of public power that will seem unprecedented then, legendary afterward.

This two-sided deal will reverberate throughout America's economic and family life. To elder Boomers, "retirement" will arrive gradually and be of little social consequence. The very concept of a fixed retirement age will blur, late-in-life career changes will be encouraged, and Boomers who retire early to a life of pure consumption will suffer the disapproval of their peers. Many will reach elderhood in an independent mind-set: self-employed, gripped with creative visions, and (by today's standards) nearly pensionless.

The typical old Boomer will be not a busy "senior citizen," but a meditative patriarch. Not a pie-baking grandma or hook-baiting grampa, but a steel-willed Grand Mother or Grand Father. Not a "Golden Ager" squeezing consumption out of a debt-fueled economy, but an ascetic elder glowering down from Sinai, looking upon himself as a critical link in human civilization, without whose guidance the young might sink into Philistinism. Old Boomers will still listen to their "classic rock" music—but what Boomers hear and what grandchildren overhear will be entirely different. The same "Can't buy me love" lyric that may remind an old Boomer of carefree self-exploration will come across to a 15-year-old in the year 2025 as a severe, even smug message of self-denial. Boomers will study history and reread literature dimly remembered from youth. Those with time and money will travel solo (or in small groups) in search of self-discovery and wisdom: to a Shakespearean festival, an Israeli kibbutz, maybe an archaeological dig. Looking old (and surrounding oneself with old things) will become fashionable. Just as high self-esteem was linked with the appearance of youth when Boomers were young, so will it be linked with the appearance of age when Boomers are old. The very word "old" will possess a new grace, making age-denying euphemisms ring odd. "Senior citizen" may even become a term of derision, bringing to mind discredited images of G.I.-style Sun City.

As Old Aquarians flock to cathedrals of twenty-first-century spiritualism, they will break from the young more than the circa-2000 elder Silent. In contrast to G.I.s, however, this will be more an inner than outer separation. Regional communities now associated with Boom culture—northern California, Colorado, Oregon, and Massachusetts (a focal point for every earlier Idealist generation in old age)—will age with this generation and assume an air of stuffy principle, off-putting to fun-loving younger adults. Many an old Boomer will relocate to university communities, especially those combining high-quality scholarship with pleasant climates (Palo Alto, Austin, Westwood, the Carolina Triangle). On campus, they will be part professor and part pupil in an almost Woodstockian redefinition of university life.

Small towns and rural life will acquire the same appeal to evangelical Boomers they once had to Bible Belt Missionaries, as repositories of enduring values. The circa-1990 New Age camps scattered throughout the American countryside will age in place and grow in size, offering final homes to flower-child wayfarers. New Age or not, communal living will enable those of modest means to share expenses in an era of reduced pensions, providing emotional support for the very large share of elders who will never have prepared for retirement and who will lack spouses, children, or both. This time, the Boom's Pepperland will not bring the social rejuvenescence of a spiritual awakening; rather, it will represent a collective ratification of Boom values that, increasingly, will seem old to others.

By the 2010s, this aging generation will feel its collective mortality, along with a sense of urgency about unsolved (and previously deferred) problems in the outer world. Events that earlier would have elicited compromise or stalemate will now bring aggressive action pursuant to Boom principle. The Crisis of 2020—the Gray Champion's hour of "darkness, and adversity, and peril"— will be at hand.

Whatever the crisis turns out to be, old Boomers may be inclined to attribute it to "mistakes" America made when it turned its back on the future during the Inner-Driven era of the 1980s and 1990s. Responding to domestic and international challenges in ways unimaginable today, Boom leaders will be policy perfectionists, inclined to enforce principle even at the risk of toppling the existing order. These elders will see in themselves a global mission—ethical, ecological, economic, and quite possibly military. This generation's quest for righteousness—having been local through rising adulthood and national in midlife—will extend globally in elderhood. They will define the acceptable behavior of other nations narrowly and the appropriate use of American arms broadly. Like other old Idealists, Boomers will not instinctively dislike authoritarian regimes; indeed, they will be quite authoritarian themselves. The question they will ask is whether such authority is exercised for good or for evil. Boomers will find enemies, most likely in new places. Unlike their G.I. fathers, Boomers will have little interest in a continued U.S.-Soviet rivalry. They may even find a second superpower useful in helping to maintain order in an ethically disheveled world. Instead, the old Boom is far more likely to direct its global wrath at the Third World. Their quest for environmental asceticism may put them on a collision course with developing societies whose first priority is to enjoy a higher material standard of living—no matter what air is polluted or how many forests slashed. Terrorists and drug traders may or may not still be major problems by the 2010s, but Boomers will have grown accustomed to blaming this ilk for whatever goes wrong overseas. Most Third World leaders, moreover, will be a generation younger than the Boom, who by then will associate men in their forties with a roguish amorality.

Great peril might arise if Boomers find themselves confronting old religious fundamentalists whose inner zeal matches their own. The most terrible war in

American history featured Idealist leaders on both sides (Lincoln and Davis, and their respective Congresses). All the other crises have pitted elder Idealist leaders against younger, less godly opponents (Puritans against Bacon, Andros, and King James II; Awakeners against General Howe and King George III; Missionaries against Hitler and Tōjō). Picture a 70-year-old William Bennett delivering a "Confrontation and Consequence" missive to a twenty-first-century Ayatollah. Then imagine the aftermath.

Whatever the circumstance and whoever the adversary, the Crisis of the 2020s will transform Boomers into America's next Gray Champions, the principled elders to whom younger generations will turn for determination and vision. The time will be right for a great leader to emerge, some elder man or woman with "the eye, the face, the attitude of command" of an Abraham Lincoln or Franklin Roosevelt.

The major question—indeed, the one whose answer may decide whether Boom leadership will end in triumph or tragedy—will hinge on this generation's capacity to restrain (or let others restrain) its latent ruthlessness. Like William Berkeley or Joseph Bellamy, William Sherman or Douglas MacArthur, elder Idealists seek total victory by whatever means available. Historically, aging Idealists have been attracted to words like "exterminate" and "eradicate," words of apocalyptic finality. If the purpose of crisis is inner principle, the degree of outer-world destruction needed for those ideals to triumph will be of secondary consideration. Make no mistake: Faced with crisis, this generation of onetime draft resisters will not hesitate, as elder warrior-priests, to conscript young soldiers to fight and die for righteous purpose. This stop-at-nothing zeal is already apparent in the first Boomer cohorts to reach their mid-forties, from Elliott Abrams and Oliver North at one ideological edge to Mitch Snyder and Denis Hayes at the other. Picture these individuals as national elders, uncalmed by anyone older—and then realize they represent their generation's *moderate* first wave, whose youth was marked by relatively few (but increasing) social pathologies. Add in the fiery passion of the more evangelical last-wavers, sharpen everyone's moral conviction, reduce everyone's level of tolerance, subtract the active presence of any adult Adaptives—and that is the leadership awaiting America, circa 2020. It is easy to picture aging Boomers as noble, self-sacrificing patriarchs—but just as easy to see these righteous Old Aquarians as the worst nightmare that could ever happen to the world.

Other generations of spiritualist elders have had visions of apocalypse; this one will have the *methods*. Had the Transcendentals discovered an immensely destructive weapon, they no doubt would have used it to destroy Richmond (or Washington). Lacking such a weapon, the Missionaries set loose a smart young Civic generation to invent and build one—which the country was in a mood to use, as events showed. The Boom will be the first Idealist generation to enter a crisis with the weapons of Armageddon at its immediate command. Will the

Boom do what the G.I.s haven't (and the Silent almost surely won't) and use nuclear weapons in anger, willing to risk annihilation to vindicate truth and justice? If a Doomsday Machine appears to aging leaders as a path toward generational Valhalla, the temptation could be strong.

While the era presided over by Boomer Gray Champions will be a time of extreme danger, so too will it be a time of historic opportunity. Boomers will enter old age during an era of looming challenges that would seem insurmountable by the incrementalist standards of the 1980s and 1990s. From unsustainable entitlements to insufficient investment, from decaying infrastructure to an American economy controlled by foreign creditors, from Third World revolution to nuclear proliferation, from depleted fossil fuels to a poisoned atmosphere— Boom elders will be in position to guide the nation, and perhaps the world, across several painful thresholds. If Boomers fail at this mission, history suggests that no other American generation will be commensurately empowered for the remainder of the twenty-first century.

Let us hope that old Boomers will look within themselves and find something richer than apocalypse. If they see (and assert) themselves as beacons of civilization, younger Americans may well look up to them as G.I.s did to the great Missionary leaders: as elders wise beyond the comprehension of youth. If the Gray Champions among them can seize this historic opportunity, they can guide a unified national community through the gates of history to a better world beyond.

Entering Post-Elderhood in an Outer-Driven Era (2026–2047)

Boomers will grasp the reins of power until around the peak of the crisis, at which time they will either exit heroically (Missionary-style) or be tossed out (Transcendental-style). Having gathered around the drumbeat of Boomer principle going into the crisis, younger generations will now want to escape from the stern Boom shadow. They will want to taste something material, practical, friendly—in short, something non-Boom. As they face this inevitable reaction, old Boomers will also face a temptation that has confronted every aging Idealist generation since the Puritans: to take their church with them (just as Civics are tempted to take their community with them) as they pass beyond their tenure of power. It is the temptation to believe, like the elder Missionary poet Wallace Stevens in *Opus Posthumous,* that "God is in me, or else is not at all."

The Boomers will also do what all generations must: They will die. If the end comes easy to no generation, Idealists are at least able to see in death a form of spiritual transcendence. The preferred Boomer departure will be one with a reason, with a *meaning.* Here and there, a few Don Quixotes will deliberately link their death to one final stand for principle. Driven by a mixture of economics, ecological concern, and moral assertion, Boomers will redefine the ethics of comforting the dying—and of hallowing the dead. Many Boom authors will (like Stevens) publish posthumously, in an effort to extend their cultural reach as far as possible into the future. In some circa-2020 equivalent of the New Deal or Marshall Plan, old Boomers may succeed in defining core principles that their Millennial children will then cement into place through the middle of the twenty-first century.

When the year 2030 dawns, Boomers will range in age from 69 to 87. Assuming the crisis has turned out well, eightyish first-wavers will then reflect back on a well-timed lifecycle. A person born in the late 1940s will recall growing up indulged, coming of age at an exciting if hazardous time to leave home, and passing through rising adulthood in an era that prized consumption and careerism. Among Boomers lucky enough to last eight decades (more than half of those alive today), the second forty years will be just as memorable. Boomers will have spent midlife in an era well suited to the sober realizations of mature parents and community leaders, entered old age just as elder wisdom was newly venerated, and reached their collective deathbeds knowing the necessary deeds had been done, allowing heirs to live happily ever after (or so it may seem at the time). If this all comes to pass, this generation may be eulogized as Franklin Roosevelt was by Churchill, for having died ''an enviable death.''

By the year 2050, America will have a few very old Boomer survivors, the twenty-first-century equivalents of Susan B. Anthony or Robert Frost. These celebrated elders will join others in rejoicing over the enormous secular power of their midlife Millennial children. By the mid-2050s, as the next Idealist generation comes of age, three or four million old Aquarians will remain alive. More than a few will be on university faculties somewhere, telling tittering young audiences what the Woodstock 1960s were like, and finally—around age 100—getting a chance to see them happen again.

Completing the 13er Diagonal

The generational cycle is a sneaky fortune wheel for a Reactive generation. It spins, it turns—and just when it lets you think you've lost, it tantalizes. Just when you think you've won, it clicks again, and you've lost. So will it be for 13ers.

Entering Rising Adulthood in an Inner-Driven Era (1991–2003)

The ''Society for the Acceleration of Time'' calls upon Boomers to hurry up, get old, and get out of the way. Organized fleetingly in 1989, this mock-serious 13er lobby articulates the feeling of many of today's 25-year-olds: an anxiety about whether young adults can ever rise out of the shadow of the domineering Boom. The nation's next great generational rivalry is brewing, on the edge of bubbling over.

Throughout American history, the nastiest one-apart generational feuds have been between midlife Idealists and rising Reactives. This has happened every time—between Puritans and Cavaliers; Awakeners and Liberty; Transcendentals and Gilded; Missionaries and Lost. Idealists invariably come to look upon younger Reactives as a wild, soulless, and "bad" generation—while Reactives see older Idealists as pompous, authoritarian, and (in power) more than a little dangerous. Thirteeners and Boomers are already beginning to regard each other this way. During the 1990s, this mutual suspicion will harden. The last skirmish between these two oil-and-water types arose just before World War I, grew mean after the Armistice, and contributed mightily to the "roar" of the 1920s. Something like this "roar" lies in America's near-term future.

The cycle suggests that 13ers will suffer an *alienating event* when their first cohorts are in their thirties. This nasty stroke of history will convince them that theirs is indeed a luckless lifecycle. It could be AIDS; this epidemic, which has thus far mainly struck the Boom, will ravage the 13th if it expands unchecked. Or it could be a diplomat-directed but youth-scourging military campaign— something on par with the Progressive-led intervention against Kaiser Wilhelm II or the Enlightener-led war against French Canada. (Lining up the 13er lifecycle with those of the Liberty and Lost, such a campaign would occur sometime in the early 1990s.) But most likely, the alienating event will take the form of an economic downturn. Even a brief one will serve the purpose.

Economic threats loom heavy on the 13er horizon. To begin with, their first class graduated from college in 1983—which means that this generation's aspiring elite has yet to confront even mildly harsh conditions in the national economy. Second, never before in American history have public-benefit "safety nets" been tilted so heavily toward retired elders (no matter how affluent) and away from rising adults (no matter how poor). The great majority of 13ers in poverty, for example, are not eligible for a penny in subsidized health care. Finally, many are coming of age with unprecedented financial burdens. No previous American generation has arrived in the workforce paying such high tax rates on their first dollar of earnings, bearing such large high-interest student loans, facing so many anti-youth "two-tier" wage and benefit scales, or encountering such high housing costs relative to income.

If the economy weakens, 13ers will feel stranded as a generation, sensing little of the elder goodwill G.I.s enjoyed through the Great Depression, nor the public exaltation of youth that buoyed Boomers through the stagflated 1970s. To their regret, 13ers will find themselves paying a price for the generational criticism they endured (but did not answer) through the 1980s. Young workers will find themselves perceived, and treated, as the most expendable employees. To keep their jobs, they will have to show not just promise, but bottom-line *results*. In sharp contrast to the 1950s-era experience of the rising Silent, many 13ers will pass through their twenties unable to sustain the quality of life—and, especially, the level of consumption—they enjoyed as adolescents. Many of those from affluent families will "boomerang" back to parental homes, dragging out their child-era dependency. Those from harder-pressed families will fall into an unsupported poverty. As the year 2000 approaches, the worries of circa-1990 youth will crystallize into a bleak adult reality: Theirs may be America's first generation since the Gilded to reach age 40 with a lower standard of living than their parents had enjoyed at like age.

These setbacks will send shock waves through the most market-oriented rising generation since the circa-1920 Lost. Unlike the Silent and Boom, 13er self-esteem rests heavily on hopes for economic success—a fact confirmed by count-less youth polls over the past decade. Once they perceive themselves failing in the marketplace—amid continuing criticism of their cultural and moral defi-ciencies—13ers are likely to react in the same hard-bitten manner as the Lost did when they encountered the Missionary vice squads. Many will quietly blame themselves. Others will lash out against midlife Boomers, who will remain contemptuous of 13er ideas and aspirations (in stark contrast with how rising-adult Boomers were treated by their own next-elders). Boomers, by then standing in the way of the jobs, pay, and promotions, will require 13ers to prove them-selves in a hotly contested marketplace—in effect, forcing them to move in what Boomers will consider the "wrong" direction in order to survive. The Boom's midlife quest to impose moral judgments on grown-up Breakfast Clubbers will strike a growing chorus of 30-year-olds as pitiless and Scrooge-like.

Once alienation sets in, 13ers will accentuate behavior patterns that today strike older generations as frenetic, soulless, and physically shocking—confirm-ing elder judgments that this truly is a "wasted" generation. Thirteeners will then put their own stamp on the American mood. There will be no mass move-ments or organized plans; instead, they will burst forth with a hedonistic cross-culture that will look, taste, smell, sound, and feel anti-Boom. It will be defiantly noncerebral, probing the physical devil where the like-aged Boom once probed the spiritual sublime, seeking pleasure where next-elders once sought beatitude, evoking the black prankishness of Halloween where the hippie culture once evoked the image of a spring rainbow. Young novelists, filmmakers, songwriters, and columnists will produce works that will seem interesting if puzzling to the aging Silent, wholly inarticulate to Boomers, and keenly expressive to 13ers themselves. This clash of jaundiced rising adults with righteous midlifers will resemble the 1920s—not the 1960s.

By the late 1990s, professional athletics will offer an exaggerated example of what will be happening to 13ers throughout the economy and culture. Pay will be increasingly market-driven and disconnected from the bargaining power of organized labor. Year-to-year results will be rewarded more than lifetime achievement. The stars who can win, show Ruthian bravado, and fill arenas will make fantastic sums (enhanced by international bidding). At the other edge, nonstar journeymen will lose ground and attract little public sympathy when they fail. The fun in sports will have a brassy quality, more akin to pure entertainment than civic ritual. Boomers will look upon 13er athletes as gladiators and will pointedly urge Millennial children to look elsewhere for role models.

Throughout the economy, the 13ers' preoccupation, indeed their *need,* will be personal economic survival. For many, the clearest path to success may be to leave elder-led institutions and strike out on their own. They will seek market niches where quick deals matter more than big words, and will take care of tasks Boomers may find useful if a bit distasteful (delivery services or solid waste disposal, for instance). Such businesses will bring fortunes to a lucky few, but most of those engaged in them will be poorly paid. Looking for a lightning strike at success, 13ers will dart from job to job. Their mobility will discourage employers from investing in job training—or from offering pensions to new hires.

The international marketplace will provide this generation with its most promising economic frontier—and a way to take advantage of its underappreciated linguistic and computer skills. At times, young entrepreneurs will engage in global business activities their elders will look upon as piratical, opportunist, even traitorous. Many will seek their fortune in the service of America's creditors, helping them purchase, manage, or liquidate American assets. Lucrative opportunities may arise in nations with fledgling capitalist economies—in enterprises like fast food, fashion, and entertainment. Boomers will regard video stores in Prague as a symptom of decadence, and the Silent will despairingly contrast their own Peace Corps days spent teaching English to Nigerians with young McDonald's employees teaching Hamburger 101 to Muscovites. Thirteeners will never be widely attracted to public service or the nurturing professions (teaching, medicine, the ministry) in the manner of the G.I.s, Silent, or Boom. Instead, whatever their careers, they will aim for opportunities with a bottom line. Their economic realism will strike many elders as unfeeling, selfish, even reactionary. But, over time, 13ers will shrug off these complaints. Like all rising-adult Reactives before them, they will see themselves as nomads driven by necessity in a world whose economic harshness is not their fault.

Even as they scramble after new opportunities, 13ers will react with skepticism to world events that elders may hail as promoting human freedom. Any further euphoria of elder Silent over "breaking down barriers" will remind them of their chaotic childhood—something that felt good to every generation but their own. If chaos brings new ethnic or economic unrest, and if that leads to conflict, it will be their job, not their elders', to fight any war necessary to clean up the mess left behind—the sort of "modern war" (as Hemingway put it) in which "you die like a dog for no good reason." Reminiscent of the doughboy Lost, any homecoming celebration for 13er soldiers will be tinged with elder criticism—and will heighten feelings of alienation. In war or out, 13ers will find themselves bearing a major share of the burden for any economic or social transitions. But they won't be easily suckered. Like the "Don't Tread on Me" Liberty of the 1760s, life's hard knocks will have taught these 30-year-olds to stay away from the complicated abstractions of the aging Silent and the high-minded crusades of midlife Boomers. As the Boom rises to power, 13er voters will turn even more antigovernment than they are today. As Boomers begin endorsing global crusades, 13ers will turn toward isolationism—and, like the 1920s-era Lost, will take pleasure in revealing elder "lies." In families, communities, and national politics, 13ers will press to simplify the complex, narrow the bloated, and eliminate the unworkable. They will be drawn to blunt, no-nonsense candidates.

Thirteener culture will be far more ethnically diverse than the Boom's. Where the Lost catapulted Eastern and Southern Europeans to prominence, 13ers will do the same for Hispanics and Asians. The Chinese democracy movement and political controversies in Latin America will provide the grist for poignant intra-generational clashes. With this new ethnic diversity will come a new, youth-propelled racism and a propensity for "hate crimes." Lacking a cultural center of gravity, 13ers of all backgrounds—including the white middle class—will feel at risk in ways their Boomer and Silent parents did not. The most stellar young ethnic achievers will encounter a festering racial hostility from their own peers, much as the Jewish Lost did in the 1920s.

Most of the children allowed to grow up poor or unskilled in the 1970s and 1980s will carry their incapacities and pathologies with them into adulthood. Through the 1990s, unmarried mothers and the undereducated of both sexes will remain just as unemployable (and dependent) in their thirties as they were in their teens. Efforts at adult remedial education will be halfhearted and ineffectual. Worse, many of today's youth gangsters will ripen into their adult facsimile, waging Capone-style wars with police (most of whom, by then, will be canny 13ers themselves). Older generations will blame the nation's problems of crime, drugs, and disintegrating inner cities on their attitude of treating life as a game. By the late 1990s, as 13ers wholly fill the crime-prone phase of life, street crime will be perceived as evil, and the criminal beyond rehabilitation except through the sternest of regimens. Once Boomer judges go to work, this will almost surely become the most permanently warehoused (and executed) generation in American history. Nor will many 13ers rise to defend their criminal peers. By their ethos, if you're bad and are caught, you don't complain about your punishment.

Rising 13ers will sense they will never gain much collective esteem from others. Americans who today look upon 25-year-olds as a wasted bunch will, a decade from now, look upon 35-year-olds in much the same way. Any stroke of luck they enjoy in the marketplace—whether lower housing prices or wage inflation in the service sector—will be proclaimed "bad news" by older generations. Their greatest skills will go relatively unnoticed: the capacity to observe, to identify unmet needs, to be "smooth" and conceal feelings when necessary, to move quickly when the moment is right, and to make sure that whatever people try does in fact work as intended. Likewise, 13ers will come to believe that the best way to win individually is by taking incredible risks. They will figure that those who play by the (mostly Boom) rules probably won't get anywhere—so why play by the rules? Many will thus embrace what might be called the "lottery ticket" mentality: A 13er will be prepared to risk a loss (since he'll already be losing) for a tiny chance to win big. Their career paths will take on a kinetic frenzy. Thirty-year-olds will jump at opportunities their elders will find inconsequential and take on long odds their elders will find incomprehensible. Their greatest successes will come in small businesses that outhustle and (thanks to low wages and benefits) underprice elder-dominated rivals. The U.S. Postal Service may well come under ruinous attack from new enterprises run by piece-rate 13ers who—as veteran bicycle messengers, delivery drivers, and computer hackers—will know how to move information more cheaply and reliably than tenured civil servants.

Economic risk-taking and cultural alienation will drive 13ers to seek stability in family life. First-wavers may continue the Boom trend toward late marriage—not out of any quest for postadolescent self-discovery, but rather out of economic necessity and an unwillingness to repeat the mistakes of their early-marrying, heavily divorcing Silent parents. Seeing the dual-income household as a necessary condition for affluence while knowing from personal experience the perils of a latchkey childhood, 13ers of both sexes will look upon working motherhood as a temporary necessity to be overcome later in life when income permits. Many will begin marriage and parenthood in Silent homes, enabling them to receive substantial elder help with child care. Once they begin to tire of risk-taking (as did the Lost in the late 1920s), 13ers will become more conservative in their private lives. Turning away from marital infidelity and divorce, they will make a great effort to shield their offspring from the less pleasant facts of life.

Despite their economic problems, 13ers will blossom into America's leading generation of shoppers, thanks largely to purchases they will make for others (in extended families, or in new shopping services). Accordingly, they will have a huge influence on products, styles, and advertising—much as the Lost had in the 1920s. Once marketers realize this, the American media will be barraged with messages stressing bluntness over subtlety, action over words, the physical over the cerebral. The most successful of these messages will hint at 13er alienation and appeal to a sense of dark humor. Many ads that effectively target 13ers will be pointedly anti-Boom. For example, Pepsi might hit back at the 1990 Coca-Cola ad showing fortyish jeans-clad Boomers on a verdant hillside, teaching their Millennial children the Woodstockian chant "I'd like to teach the world to sing in perfect harmony." A retaliatory ad might run a clip of that blissful scene, jerk it fast forward to an image of old hippies, and end with a metallic clang and a message (draped in black): "Drink Pepsi. The Anti-Coke."

Two sets of questions will haunt their rising adulthood. First, will their Silent and (especially) Boom elders learn to appreciate that this generation does indeed offer a pragmatic sensibility that America will find important, even essential, in the decades ahead? Will the Silent stop despairing over how 13ers are turning out so unlike what they had envisioned—and will they instead see young adults who know how to compensate for some of the Silent's own worst mistakes? Will Boomers come to realize that the 13ers' very different childhood environment has endowed them with valuable antidotes to the Boom's own worst tendencies—or will Boomers continue to look on them not just as juniors, but as inferiors? The answers to those questions will affect the depth of 13er alienation and the surliness of this forthcoming generational clash.

The second set of questions has more to do with 13ers themselves. By the spin of the cycle, whatever phase of life they happen to occupy will be (as it has already been) tempest-tossed, laden with perhaps the wrong kind of adventure for people their age. Over four centuries, Reactive generations have been assigned the thankless job of yanking American history back on a stable course—and, afterward, have gotten few rewards for their sacrifices. Will this realization prompt 13ers to burn out young—or will it harden a gritty self-confidence around an important generational mission? As America's most perceptive living generation, 13ers can recognize a few crucial facts of life that Boomers will not—for example, that without a little "bad" pragmatism, even the most noble Boomer dreams will never get off the ground. More to the point: Without a few black sheep to slow the shepherd, those aging Boomers might really do something crazy.

Entering Midlife in a Crisis Era (2004–2025)

Early in the new century, as fortyish 13ers watch graying Aquarians get "into" national leadership, they will appreciate that whatever bad hand history dealt them, they at least grew up with clear heads. Their pleasure-seeking era will draw to a close—along with the worst of the Idealist-Reactive tussle. Boomers might then start discerning in them the rough-hewn tools needed to achieve lofty Boom visions—and, in return, 13ers might see in Boomers the leadership without which they might never find larger purpose in their own lives.

Sometime around the year 2010, this generation will hit a hangover mood like that of the Lost in the early 1930s and the Liberty in the late 1760s: a feeling of personal exhaustion mixed with a new public seriousness. Forty- and fifty-year-olds will fan out across an unusually wide distribution of personal outcomes, reminiscent of a night at the bingo table. A few will be wildly successful, others totally ruined, while the largest number will have lost a little ground since the days of Boomer midlife. Many of the early-rising stars will now be replaced in the limelight by steadier peers—the equivalent of Lost "brains"—in what may seem like a twenty-first-century *Revenge of the Nerds*. Midlife Asian-Americans will establish their ethnic group as a major cultural and intellectual force, akin to the midlife German Gilded or midlife Jewish Lost.

Thirteeners will make near-perfect 50-year-olds. On the one hand, they will be nobody's fools. If you really need something done, and you don't especially mind how it's done, these will be the guys to hire. On the other hand, they will be nice to be around. More experienced than their elders in the stark reality of pleasure and pain, 13ers will have that Twainlike twinkle in the eye, that Trumanesque capacity to distinguish between mistakes that matter and those that don't. In business, they will excel at cunning, flexibility, and deft timing—a far cry from the ponderous, principles-first Boomer style. In sports, the combination of 13er coaches and Millennial players may well produce a new golden era of athletic teamwork. In the military, 13ers will blossom into the kind of generals young Millennial soldiers would follow off a cliff. Their leading politicians may strike old Boomers as uncerebral, yet plainspoken, sensible, quick on their feet—and more inclined to deal than to argue.

In the early twenty-first century, 13ers will make their most enduring mark on the national culture. Their now-mature keenness of observation and their capacity to step outside themselves will kick off exciting innovations in literature and filmmaking. The "Brat Pack" will expand and mature into the best on-screen generation since the Lost. As parents of growing children, 13ers will by now be too affectionate, too physical—too eager to prevent teenagers from suffering the same overdose of reality they will recall from their own youth. In so doing, they will tip the scales toward overprotection of children—much as the Liberty did in the 1780s, the Gilded in the 1860s, and the Lost in the 1930s. Midlife parents, mothers especially, may hear themselves criticized by Millennials for "momming" a pliant new generation of Adaptives.

Thirteeners will see, and evaluate, the Crisis of 2020 with the sharpest eye of all living generations. By lifecycle position and peer personality, they will have the most capacity for maneuver and can be expected to produce the Crisis era's most colorful leaders and stigmatized traitors—reminiscent of how the Cavaliers produced the courageous rebels as well as the Stuart collaborators; the Liberty, the rugged Patriots as well as the raging Tories; the Gilded, the blue and gray commanders as well as the Copperheads and bandits; and the Lost, the managers of D-Day as well as the isolationists and fascists. Some untamed 13er factions may try to pitch the national mood toward dangerous adventure (like the pre–Civil War Gilded) or toward dangerous isolationism (like the pre–World

War II Lost). If so, their own peers will be best positioned to resist—and, like Arthur Vandenberg in 1941, to call their bluff. Midlife 13ers will have little ability to influence the nature and timing of whatever crisis the Boom will congeal, but will instead provide able on-site managers and behind-the-scenes facilitators, the ones whose quick decisions could spell the difference between triumph and tragedy.

Controlling the Boom may indeed emerge as the 13ers' most fateful lifecycle mission. This will be the generation best able to deflect any Boomer drift toward apocalyptic visions. In an age of rising social intolerance, the very incorrigibility of midlife 13ers will at times be a national blessing. The task of preventing disaster may well fall to life- and liberty-loving 50-year-olds, pockmarked by hard experience, to tell zealous Boomers to "get real," to find cannier solutions that pose fewer risks or that do less to erode personal liberty. A 13er may someday be the general or Presidential adviser who prevents some righteous old Aquarian from "loosing the fateful lightning" and turning the world's lights out.

Those who sustain their alienation into midlife may find themselves the targets of a Boom-Millennial alliance to root out 13er pessimism, fear, or greed from public life—much as Franklin Roosevelt rallied the G.I.s against the Lost trio of "Martin, Barton, and Fish," or as Samuel Adams rallied the Republicans against Liberty Tories. The capacity of circa-2020 50-year-olds to mellow the national mood, and their success in being heard by old Boomers, will hinge on the ability of these two generations to calm their earlier quarrels and build mutual respect. As they age in place, they will, like siblings, half remember and half forget how they behaved toward each other in earlier years.

Whatever goes wrong in the crisis, 13ers will get more than their share of the blame; whatever goes right, they will get less than their share of the credit. Even now, as 25-year-olds, they know the feeling. They had better get used to it. When you're Reactive, it comes with the territory.

Entering Elderhood in an Outer-Driven Era (2026–2047)

The end of the crisis era will hit this generation on the opening cusp of its era of national leadership—and the beginning of its physical decline. In 2025, the oldest 13ers will be 64, the youngest 44. The crisis will have interrupted their peak earning years. Many will be a bit too young to be spared personal sacrifice, a bit too old to start life over again.

History suggests 13ers will suffer a rough and neglected old age. Those who fail to provide for themselves will end up poor, by the standard of the era. When Boom leaders introduce a new youth focus into public benefits programs, 13ers can expect to find themselves passed over in the transition. Those who were counting on large inheritances from affluent Silent parents may find them substantially taxed away by Boom-run legislatures. Older generations will take little interest (and may indeed see waste) in letting 13ers get something for nothing. Even self-earned, private investments may prove hazardous, thanks to some twenty-first-century equivalent of the Liberty's Continental dollars and the Gilded's Confederate dollars. Old Boom leaders eager to reward young Millennials for their public service may resort to huge doses of inflation—in effect, wiping out the accumulated private wealth claims of midlife 13ers. Unlike Boomers, 13ers will not have spent a lifetime preparing themselves psychologically for an ascetic old age. Material well-being will matter deeply to them, and they will cherish whatever remains of their economic and social independence. Yet, as they age, they will feel warmly toward younger generations they will mostly admire—and will not seek to improve their own standard of living at the expense of youth. Rather, like the elder Gilded and Lost, 13ers will take a wistful pleasure in seeing their children shoot past them economically.

The men and women who were once such wild risk-takers will settle into a reclusive old age, engaging in pursuits that will be seen at the time as conventional, even fogyish. As has been true for all their Reactive predecessors, the 13th will be the last generation to have fully come of age before a history-bending crisis. Thus, they will be perceived as (and feel like) relics from the past, with habits and values still rooted in some repudiated "old regime." They will be crusty old conservatives, restraining the young from misjudging human nature through naive overconfidence.

Sometime around the mid-2020s, 13er candidates will win a clear majority of national leadership posts. Their post-crisis Presidents might well be jockish heroes like Washington, Grant, and Eisenhower—admired more for personality than for vision. Like the Gilded and Lost, 13er leaders will distrust debt and inflation as instruments of public policy. Indeed, they may be inclined to keep tax rates high to force the nation to produce more than it consumes—exactly the opposite of the national choices they will remember from their own youth. Under their leadership, America will turn its energy toward building the outer world, not toward cultural depth or spiritual fervor. But that won't be held against 13ers. In time, the maturing Millennials will fault them for a very different reason: for being do-nothing obstructionists, barriers to the execution of the unfinished moral agenda of the now-lionized Boomers.

Like Increase Mather, Patrick Henry, and Mark Twain, the most popular 13er elders will warn against the danger of pushing too far and too fast in a cruel world rigged with pitfalls. But younger generations will not listen. In an Outer-Driven era, the can-do Millennials will be too busy coaxing smiles out of their oh-so-adorable Idealist babies.

Completing the Millennial Diagonal

Watching today's little kindergartners at play focuses the mind on what these children might someday accomplish. We wonder whether the tiny boys and girls now playing with Lego blocks might become great twenty-first-century architects and builders. Whether the tykes out capturing lightning bugs might grow up as the nation's next great generation of Nobel-laureate scientists. Whether the first-graders now reciting the Pledge of Allegiance might someday show an extraordinary talent for teamwork and public service. Whether the children now being taught to say "please" and "thank you" will remember those lessons. The generational cycle tells us not just to wonder, but to *expect* such a destiny from these kids. America's mothers and fathers are today giving birth to the nation's next great Civic generation, inheritors of the tradition of Cotton Mather, Thomas Jefferson, and John Kennedy. History suggests there is but one condition: The crisis they encounter as rising adults must turn out well. For this reason, these children have the most riding on the post-1990 endowment behavior of the G.I., Silent, and Boom Generations.

Entering Youth in an Inner-Driven Era (1991–2003)

To elders disappointed in 13ers, the onset of Millennial youth will bring unremitting good news. As these kids pass through school, they will sail smoothly behind a debris-clearing insistence on quality education and good behavior. The first impact of midlife Boomer nurture will be felt in day care and the primary grades. Throughout the nation's public schools, Boom teachers and administrators will join the Transcendentals and Missionaries as renowned midlife educators. Silent elders will be far less inclined than G.I. elders to mount "Proposition 13" rebellions against school taxes. In its twilight years of Silent leadership, Congress will repair the "safety net" for the benefit of infants and small children. The ambitious educational goals set in 1990 for the year 2000 will be substantially achieved: From suburbs to inner cities, schools will show rising aptitude scores, and American children will gradually improve their ranking vis-à-vis the Japanese, Europeans, and others who have consistently outscored 13ers.

By the late 1990s, the social environment for American adolescents will show huge contrasts from what it was during the late 1970s. By degrees, the child's world will move toward greater protection. In and out of school, Millennials will hear a sterner, more resolute adult message than 13ers ever knew. Boomers will crisply define right and wrong, caring less about a child's opinion than their own (G.I.) parents had cared about the Beaver's back in the 1950s. Thanks to the active presence of family-focused 13ers, home-employed Boomers, and live-in Silent grandparents, the quality of home child care will improve, and neighborhoods will retain more daytime adults. Parents or not, adults of all ages will show far less tolerance for criminal behavior by and against children and will push the unruly remnants of the 13er youth era beyond the fringe of family life. Boomers will try to guard Millennials against 13er wildness. And, even when they fail, that wildness will serve the same purpose that Lost wildness served for G.I.s: It will show child Millennials *what to avoid*—a negative standard by which elders and kids can together take pride in the civic virtue of the new generation. Millennials will become a generation of trends, from a less protected and still rambunctious first wave to a highly protected, purposeful, and unusually smart last wave. The Millennial Walt Disneys are already in elementary school; the Millennial George Bushes will be born just after the year 2000.

The Millennial youth culture will be more clean-cut and homogeneous than any seen since that of the circa-1930 G.I.s. By the first decade of the twenty-first century, schools will at last be fully computer-equipped and the learning style of students will shift from an MTV-ish "parallel" thinking back to a more logical "serial" thinking. Where Boomers and 13ers had once seen computers as a force for social individuation, Millennials will see them as a force for social homogenization. Teen peer leaders will express a growing interest in community affairs and a growing enthusiasm for collective action. Under the Boom regime of get-tough laws and no-kidding moral standards, teen pathologies—truancy, substance abuse, crime, suicide, unwed pregnancy—will all decline. Adults will welcome a change in teen sex, which will become less matter-of-fact and starkly physical, more romantic and friendly. These trends will be apparent not just in affluent suburbs, but also in inner cities where peer-pressured boys will show more responsibility toward their sexual (and parental) relationships. Teen music will become more ballad-like, wholesome, and singable, with top tunes appealing to all generations. (To Millennial ears, on the other hand, 13er music will sound chaotic—and old Boomer classics will sound oddly ethereal and unpleasantly androgynous.) From music to fashion to cinema, the adolescent culture will accentuate, even celebrate, sexual distinctions.

When the first Millennials come of age in the early twenty-first century, 13ers will begin mellowing—just in time for these young Civics to develop a positive impression of the Reactive peer personality. The G.I. recollection of their 1920s-era fun-loving (Lost) and strict (Missionary) teachers offers an illustration of what may lie in store. Where Millennials will respect Boomers as beacons for the "should-dos" of life, they will rely on 13ers as avuncular guides to the "want-to-dos." Millennials will see their next-elders as daring, puckish, and full of mischief. In return, 13ers will see these kids as extremely smart but naive—a bit too optimistic for their own good and in need of a lesson or two about real life. College-age Millennials will be fascinated by 13er cultural trends, occasionally joining in 13er naughtiness—but will try to do so discreetly, so as not to disappoint the high Boomer standard. Later, 13ers will show a continuing kindness toward a younger generation getting a better deal out of life (though maybe a bit less fun) than they ever got at the same age.

While still in their youth, Millennials will be called upon to perform civic deeds. Community institutions (schools, libraries, churches, police) will become increasingly important in a child's life. Scout programs will be revitalized, and new ones formed. Boomers will prod Millennial adolescents to spend more time studying, practicing, and organizing with some socially useful purpose in view. By law and family fiat, teen employment will be sharply curtailed. Child television viewing will decline, and what programs Millennials do watch will be sanitized and laden with moral lessons. Universities will provide new government-aided forms of tuition finance, linked to the performance of public service before, during, or after college. Around the year 2000, a wave of very different freshmen will descend on America's campuses, showing a great talent for student politics, for athletic teamwork, and—in the classroom—for math and science.

Through adolescence, Millennials will look upon government as a more benign and reliable means of providing for their age bracket than a helter-skelter marketplace increasingly shaped by rising 13ers. A Boom-enacted program of mandatory national service will put millions of youths in uniform—a compulsion Millennials will not mind nearly as much as Boomers did (or 13ers would) at like age. Instead, they will see in it the opportunity to prove their civic virtue and earn public adulation. Whatever practical agenda comes their way, Millennials will figure out a solution, organize, cooperate, share burdens, and get the job done—all with an effectiveness and cheerfulness that will stun their elders. For all their excellence, the first Millennials to come of age will also seem a bit bland. They won't waste their time reflecting on values or following spiritual impulses—nor will Boomers ask them to do so.

Aging Boomers will gradually realize their style of nurture is producing better doers than feelers, better rationalists than spiritualists. In short, these kids will bear an eerie resemblance to the G.I.s against whom Boomers rebelled in the late 1960s. But that likeness won't bother most Boom midlifers, who will see in Millennials precisely what the country needs to overcome adversity. Like the old Awakeners, who loved their Republican kids while lamenting the Liberty, Boomers will develop far better lifelong friendships with Millennials than with 13ers. Indeed, the relationships between older Idealists and younger Civics have ranked among the warmest intergenerational bonds in American history.

Entering Rising Adulthood in a Crisis Era (2004–2025)

Early in the Crisis era, rising-adult Millennials (especially the first wave) will encounter economic and social hardship. Unlike 13ers, however, they will emerge undaunted—thanks to their patience, confidence, and powerful instinct for community. Around the time their last wave is reaching its late teens, a secular crisis will peak, just as it did for the Glorious, Republicans, and G.I.s. This cathartic moment will seal the Millennials as a generation, distinguishing them forever from midlife 13ers and younger Adaptives, and fixing their cohort boundaries. For now, we locate the former boundary between the 1981–1982 cohorts and the latter between the 2003–2004 cohorts. Both locations are estimates. Most likely, we will have to wait another four decades before drawing the Millennial end-year with any precision, just as in 1910 we would have had to wait until the late 1940s to draw it for G.I.s.

The Millennials' Civic peer personality is not preordained. If the crisis comes too soon or (worse) unfolds badly, the Millennials will mirror the Progressives, a smart but hobbled generation that was later unable to realize the agenda of its Idealist elders. But if the crisis allows the Millennials to coalesce as a genuine Civic type, this generation will show more teamlike spirit and more likemindedness in action than most Americans then alive will recall ever having seen in young people. Before the crisis, many Millennials may be attracted to global ideologies that promise material utopias through collective action. As the nation unifies, new voters will coalesce politically and may produce an electoral landslide, perhaps even a sudden party realignment, that will strengthen the mandate of aging Boom leaders.

Elderly Boomers will see in this generation an effective instrument for saving the world. Having themselves screamed against duty and discipline when young, Boomers will now demand duty and discipline from post-adolescents. They will get both. In return, old Boomers (joined by midlife 13ers) will shower youthful heroes and heroines with praise and reward. Inevitably, rising Millennials will start feeling the intoxication of hubris. They will resist elders—Boomers included—whom they perceive as unwilling to relinquish private and material privilege. Just as young Republicans muzzled the Tory Awakeners and young G.I.s voted the laissez-faire Missionaries out of office, so too will Millennials rise up against whomever they perceive to be enemies of community solidarity and public action.

Millennials will carry out whatever crisis mission they are assigned—as long as they can connect it with their own secular blueprint for progress. If crisis brings war, soldiers will obey orders without complaint. If it involves environmental danger or natural resource depletion, young scientists will make historic breakthroughs. If the crisis is mostly economic, the youthful labor force will be a mighty engine of renewed American prosperity. Whatever their elder-bestowed mission, these rising youths will not disappoint. Assuming the crisis turns out well, Millennials will be forever honored as a generation of civic achievers.

Entering Midlife in an Outer-Driven Era (2026–2047)

When the crisis is past and a new Outer-Driven era is dawning, the age bias of public institutions will tilt far (perhaps too far) in the direction of Millennials, a generation that people of all ages will by then equate with investment in the long-term future—much as government tilted in favor of Republicans in the 1790s and G.I.s in the late 1940s. In politics, as a sense of national community builds, Millennial voters may well congeal into an "end of ideology" generation whose political parties will show little difference in style. Meanwhile, they will take steps to solidify their peer conformity by unmasking radicals who embraced the wrong "ism" in their eager youth (the early-twenty-first-century equivalent of Republican Jacobinism or G.I. communism). The political culture of fortyish Millennials in the 2030s will be highly conformist. Only team players will be invited.

By manner more than conviction, Millennials will construct a circa-2030 national mood reminiscent of the post–World War II "American High." Rising leaders will feel an obligation to complete the unfinished agenda of revered Boom elders. Institutions will strengthen, construction will boom, and American society will substantially change its outward appearance. In churches, ministers will emphasize social fellowship over spiritual self-discovery. In universities, brilliant minds will feel in godlike control over nature. Scientists will design (and taxpayers will fund) grand projects that glorify the thinker-doer-builder. "Right-stuff" Millennials will command (and younger technicians will copilot) manned space flights to the nearest planets. Midlife parents and their children (with old-fashioned 13ers looking on) will perceive themselves as distinctly "modern." The days of V-8 engines and vacuum tubes will seem as quaint in the 2030s as the days of steam turbines and telegraph lines did in the 1950s.

Like earlier Civic generations, fiftyish Millennials will feel most comfortable with widely separated sex roles. They may begin to view the assertive moral posturing of very old Idealist women as anachronistic—and look upon the suspicious self-sufficiency of aging 13er women as antisocial and possibly dangerous. To the chagrin of old feminists, Millennials will exalt the masculine and criticize the feminine influence on public life—and do the reverse in private life. This resurgent sexism will limit the life options of rising Adaptive women, thereby planting the seeds of a mid-twenty-first-century feminist renaissance.

Thanks to the Millennial team orientation, ethnic loyalties will weaken relative to the sense of national community. Applying the circa-1990 definition, this is far and away the most "minority" generation in American history. But by the middle of the twenty-first century, the very word "minority" will have an odd ring to a generation more inclined to homogenize than pluralize. Racial integration will again be a public goal. This will give historic opportunity for Millennial blacks and Hispanics to achieve a far greater measure of social and political equality than their Silent grandparents ever knew. As Millennials try to rid the nation of racial and ethnic distinctions, however, they will be opposed by rising Adaptives who will see advantage in preserving pluralism.

Entering Elderhood in an Awakening Era (2048–2069)

Sometime in the 2040s, vigorous veterans in their fifties may well march down Pennsylvania Avenue, accompanied by parade floats carrying their instruments of valor. They will celebrate the inauguration of America's first Millennial President. The message to other generations will be much the same as it was back in 1961: the arrival in power of a great and heroic Civic generation.

Watching from the sidelines will be a new (and probably "boom") crop of kids, raised indulgently and scientifically by Millennial moms and dads. These kids will notice something a bit stale, a bit unreflective in the veterans' parade. Beyond that, watch out: Within a few years, just as busy Millennials are undertaking their grandest-ever projects, the fury of youth will erupt. By the 2050s, sixtyish Millennials can expect to find themselves on the wrong side of a two-apart "generation gap" reminiscent of the late 1960s. They will think back on what good children they were back in the 1990s and puzzle over why their children cannot afford them the same respect they once showed their own Boom parents. After the fires of a new awakening have cooled, and after a series of outer-world disappointments, Millennials will retreat together into a comfortable old age—wondering with each other if their lifetime constructions can survive a rising generation of narcissists.

As a Bushlike President stages his generation's final inaugural—this could happen on January 20, 2069—old Millennial heroes, by now in their seventies, will march down Pennsylvania Avenue for the last time. The next President will come to power knowing about the Crisis of 2020 only through a child's eye, or from film clips. When that happens, Americans of all ages will feel something missing.

By our present-day capacity to reckon the future, the Millennial Generation will have an unfathomably long reach. Perhaps a million will live to see the twenty-second century. Some will be around to celebrate the arrival of babies who will live into *the twenty-third century,* babies who will grow up looking upon John Kennedy as distantly as Kennedy looked upon Thomas Jefferson. Those of us born in a year that will then seem ancient—in 1910, 1930, 1950, or 1970—can hardly imagine what world these future children might inherit, and what world they might pass on in their turn. We can only guess at the great wonders they will see, the great deeds they will accomplish, the great truths they will grasp. They too will play their role in the drama of American generations.

It has been a vast and magnificent pageant, with so many acts and so many actors since John Winthrop first felt the hand of God. Yet surely one with even more acts and actors yet to come.

Chapter 14

THE BEGINNING
OF HISTORY

Most of us, as individuals, feel a rather limited connection with the larger story of human progress. Few are lucky (or unlucky) enough to participate in great events, fewer still with any sense that our own personal acts make any appreciable difference. But through our generational membership, we all take part in history-bending moments. And, through our cross-generational relationships, we communicate across eras of mind-bending length.

Each person stands at the apex of an unfolding generational drama, heir to the past and ancestor to the future. Charles Francis Adams, U.S. ambassador to England during the Civil War, stood at the center of an extraordinary family tree. He published a ten-volume biography of his grandfather (a U.S. President), compiled a twelve-volume diary of the notes of his father (also a President), and then saw one of his sons (a celebrated author) write a biography of him. Consider the lifespan of his extended family: Charles' grandfather John was born in 1735, and his grandson Charles Francis III died in 1954. Both their lives overlapped his by roughly two decades. Thus, Charles Francis Adams was nurtured by an ancestor and gave nurture to an heir whose combined lifespans extended 220 years.

Setting aside its unique career portfolio, the Adams family tree resembles that of most Americans today. Picture a Boomer woman, age 40 in 1990, whose grandmother was age 70 when she was born, and who has a 5-year-old daughter in kindergarten. Suppose that child will also, at age 35, give birth to a daughter who will live to age 85. Consider the lifespan of this Boomer's extended family: Her grandmother was born in 1880, and her granddaughter will survive until the year 2105. If this Boomer woman lives to age 80, she will—much like Charles Francis Adams—be nurtured by or herself nurture family members whose combined lifecycles extend 225 years. That span includes parts of four centuries, reaching from the days of Civil War widowhood to an era in which (who knows?) women astronauts might explore the moons of Jupiter.

We ask our reader to make this same calculation about the reach of your own lifecycle. Think of the oldest family ancestor (or mentor) you knew as a child, and the youngest heir (or protégé) you expect you will know at age 80. That is the span of generational history you occupy. Chances are, your span will roughly match the current length of the history of the American nation, the 214 years from 1776 to 1990. In an age when a "long-term" weather forecast stretches a few months and a "long-term" budget forecast a few years, this two-century epoch demonstrates what "long-term" does in fact mean. And why we should care about it. No generation is the first; surely, none wishes to be the last. The reader should think of himself and his generation as lying nowhere near the end of our story, but somewhere in the middle, or even toward the beginning.

In their perspective on history, Americans alive today have much in common with their ancestors. The generations alive in 1910, 1845, 1750, or 1650 all saw themselves living at the edge of the future. They felt pride and regret about days gone by, hope and anxiety about days to come. Some current trends pleased them, others not. They were learning what they could from the old, teaching what they could to the young. Each generation had its own "diagonal" connection with the events of its time, its own glimpse of the cycle, its own vision of the future. Each encountered a crisis at some phase of life. We have every reason to expect this pattern to continue into the twenty-first century—except, next time, any crisis with a bad ending could bring unprecedented tragedy. The cycle teaches us that bad endings can take decades to build and in their early phases can be hard to foresee—hinging, as do all great episodes in history, on how small children are nurtured, and whether elder generations offer the young a constructive mission upon coming of age.

Mankind's rejuvenative capacity is no less remarkable than the genesis of life itself. If the cycle has any central lesson, it is that each generational type makes its own unique contribution to human progress—something its members alone, among the living, can provide in sufficient measure to keep civilization from veering toward disaster. In the 1990s no less than in decades gone by, the cycle will look to each living generation for something special. From surviving G.I.s, the cycle will ask civic example and protection against erosion of worldly endowments. From the elder Silent, it will ask an other-directed kindness. From midlife Boomers, vision and values. From rising-adult 13ers, pragmatism and defense of individual liberty. From young Millennials, new civic energy and devotion to community.

Two generations have especially important roles in the drama ahead. With the G.I.s having mostly made their mark and the Silent running out of time to make theirs, the vortex of history is inexorably moving toward the Boom and 13th. No less is riding on them than once rode on Franklin and Washington, Lincoln and Grant, or Roosevelt and Eisenhower. As these examples make clear, the scripts awaiting both generations are markedly at odds with what Americans now associate with their recent phases of life. Future generations of Americans must rely on aging Boomers to build a very unyuppielike ethic of community responsibility and principled self-sacrifice. Where their G.I. parents were heroes young, history warns Boomers to expect their greatest test in old age. Similarly, future generations are counting on 13ers to graduate from *Liar's Poker* and mellow into midlife cautionaries, guardians of family life, and protectors against Idealist excess. Where the Silent hedged their bets in youth and took their chances in midlife, history warns 13ers to prepare for the opposite. If Boomers and 13ers pursue their respective missions well, the cycle of generations will also be a cycle of progress for those who follow.

"For ourselves and our posterity." The Preamble to the United States Constitution includes these five words, a summons to treat the present and future as partners in human destiny. When reading (or writing) history, we naturally digress from remembrances of others to imagine future remembrances of ourselves. Just as we are all heirs of ancestors we mostly admire, so too are we all ancestors to heirs whose admiration we should wish to earn. Reflecting on the story of America's eighteen generations, we realize that all of us alive today were once "posterity" in the dim vision of times gone by. And, perhaps, we will remind ourselves of our sacred obligation to act as kindly toward the future as ancestral generations once did toward us.

GLOSSARY

COHORT: All persons born in the same year.

COHORT-GROUP: All persons born in a limited span of consecutive years.

AGE LOCATION: The age of a cohort-group at a particular moment or era in history.

PHASES OF LIFE: Twenty-two-year age brackets defined according to central social role:

Elderhood: Age 66 and over; central role: stewardship.

Midlife: Age 44–65; central role: leadership.

Rising Adulthood: Age 22–43; central role: activity.

Youth: Age 0–21; central role: dependence.

GENERATION: A cohort-group whose length approximates the span of a phase of life and whose boundaries are fixed by peer personality.

PEER PERSONALITY: A generational persona recognized and determined by (1) common age location; (2) common beliefs and behavior; and (3) perceived membership in a common generation.

GENERATIONAL DIAGONAL: The diagonal formed by any generation when age is plotted on the vertical axis and the date on the horizontal axis.

FIRST WAVE and LAST WAVE: "First wave" refers to a generation's early-born cohorts, more likely to be children of the second-prior generation; "last wave'' refers to a generation's late-born cohorts, more likely to be children of the first-prior generation.

SOCIAL MOMENT: A brief era (typically about a decade) when people perceive that historic events are radically altering their social environment. There are two types of social moments:

Secular Crisis: When society focuses on reordering the outer world of institutions and public behavior.

Spiritual Awakening: When society focuses on changing the inner world of values and private behavior.

DOMINANT and **RECESSIVE GENERATION:** A dominant generation (Idealist or Civic) encounters social moments while entering rising adulthood and again while entering elderhood; a recessive generation (Adaptive or Reactive) encounters social moments while entering youth and again while entering midlife.

GENERATIONAL TYPES: Four basic types of peer personalities and lifecycles, determined by age location relative to social moments; they normally recur in the following fixed order:

An Idealist generation encounters a spiritual awakening entering rising adulthood and a secular crisis entering elderhood.

A Reactive generation encounters a spiritual awakening entering youth and a secular crisis entering midlife.

A Civic generation encounters a secular crisis entering rising adulthood and a spiritual awakening entering elderhood.

An Adaptive generation encounters a secular crisis entering youth and a spiritual awakening entering midlife.

GENERATIONAL CYCLE: A set of consecutive generations beginning with an Idealist-type and ending with an Adaptive-type; alternatively, a set of constellational eras, beginning with an Awakening era and ending with an Outer-Driven era.

GENERATIONAL CONSTELLATION: The relative age location of all four generational types at any single moment in history.

ALIGNED CONSTELLATION: The special constellation that arrives (roughly every twenty-two years) when the last cohort of a new generation is born and when every generation is aligned with a single phase of life. There are four aligned constellations, and they normally recur in fixed order:

Awakening constellation: Idealist rising adults, Civic elders.

Inner-Driven constellation: Reactive rising adults, Adaptive elders.

Crises constellation: Civic rising adults, Idealist elders.

Outer-Driven constellation: Adaptive rising adults, Reactive elders.

CONSTELLATIONAL ERA: The era, roughly twenty-two years long, preceding each aligned constellation and sharing the same name.

CONSTELLATIONAL MOOD: The social mood characteristic of any given constellation or constellational era.

ENDOWMENT: Any enduring social legacy, helpful or hurtful, that an older generation passes on to younger generations.

ENDOWMENT ACTIVITY: The sphere of social life in which each type of generation tends to concentrate its lifelong endowment efforts.

Appendix A

A THEORY
OF GENERATIONS

As is the generation of leaves, so too of men:
At one time the wind shakes the leaves to the ground
   but then the flourishing woods
Gives birth, and the season of spring comes
   into existence;
So it is with the generations of men, which
   alternately come forth and pass away.

—Homer, *Iliad*, Sixth Book

One generation passeth away, and another generation cometh:
   but the earth abideth forever.

—Ecclesiastes 1:4

At the dawn of recorded history, the standard measure of cosmic time in nearly all Indo-European cultures was not the year or the century, but the *generation*.

When transcribing myths of prehistoric Aegea into verse in the eighth century B.C., Hesiod rarely used any other concept to measure time's passage. His sequential "generations" marked not only the appearance of the gods—Gaea, Uranus, Cronus, and Zeus—but also the five sequential ages or generations of mankind (Gold, Silver, Bronze, Heroic, and Iron). Philo, writing of the legendary founding of Phoenicia, originated his story with "Genos," the first ruling male god. The Old Testament begins with "Genesis," the godly act of begetting the universe, and measures time ever afterward with a seemingly

433

endless series of generations "begetting" one another. With Homer, the generation appears in a more specifically historical context. Though rarely mentioning years, Homer tells us that Nestor, patriarch of Pilos, had seen "two generations of men die" prior to the Trojan War and presently "ruled over a third." Herodotus and Thucydides routinely measured the age of a civilization by counting its generations. The myths and legends of the Egyptians, Babylonians, Persians, Celts, Teutons, Slavs, and Hindus reveal a similar taste for generational clockwork.

What exactly do these narratives mean by a "generation"? Etymology, unfortunately, does not help us much. In Indo-European languages, the word nearly always derives from the root stem *gen-,* which (in its verb form) means nothing more specific than "to come or bring into being." In modern English, we retain this entirely abstract meaning in our verb "to generate." But bring *what* into being? If we think literally of parents and children, of course, we arrive at one basic definition, the *family generation:* the set of all children "brought into being" by a father or mother. Modern English preserves this meaning in special words such as "genealogy" (the record of parent-to-child lineage) and expressions such as "third-generation immigrant" or "ten generations of kings." The family definition is sometimes perfectly adequate for interpreting myth and history. When we learn, for example, that Zeus belongs to the second-generation descendants of Uranus, we know precisely what is meant—that Zeus is the grandchild of Uranus.

As the abstract root implies, however, "generation" has always been used in a very different sense as well. *Genus* can also refer anything new that the cosmos or society at large "brings into being" at a single moment in time. That can include what we call a "cohort generation"—a cohort-group sharing an age location in history and therefore a common peer personality. When Hesiod described the five generations of mankind, he was making no implicit reference to parentage. Rather, he was emphasizing that each new *genos* (translated variously as "race" or "age") lives at about the same time and possesses a distinct way of life and set of values. When Homer's like-aged Achaean heroes, having sailed home in triumph after sacking Troy, later acknowledge each other as members of "the same generation," genealogy is likewise irrelevant. They were all shaped in the same way, at the same time, and at the same stage of life. Today, of course, we still use this meaning. Sometimes we apply it to things: a "new generation" of cars, computers, or ideas. More often, we apply it to people: "my generation" versus "your generation." Yet many age-old expressions like "a generation of peace" have meanings that are perfectly ambiguous. Rather than specify whether they mean family lineages or cohort-groups, most writers—modern as well as ancient—have leaned on the nuances of both.

For millennia, poets and philosophers have sensed that the generation, however defined, connotes the ebb and flow of life, of families, and of historical time. Over the last couple of centuries, many writers have grown specifically interested in what we call a "cohort" generation. But so malleable a concept still eludes most efforts to understand it. The central questions remain unanswered: *what* exactly is a generation, *how* does it develop a distinct peer personality, and *why* do peer personalities tend to arrive in cycles? We have already summarized our theory of generations in Part I. This appendix, retracing that ground in more detail, is intended for the reader interested in our theory's intellectual roots and core logic.

We begin by distinguishing the "cohort" from the "family" generation and by looking at the mixed record of modern writers who have grappled with the generations approach before us. Since a consensus theory of cohort generations has yet to step forward, we offer our own. For this, we journey to a mythical "Cohortia," a traditional society with an invariant lifecycle. There we see how a social moment can establish well-defined cohort generations of similar length. We also see how a modern Cohortia can establish a continuous sequence of cohort generations alternating between dominant and recessive types. Finally, we explain where and why we can expect a four-stroke generational cycle to emerge—precisely the cycle confirmed by our examination of American history.

The Cohort Generation

In 1970, historian Philip Greven, Jr., wrote a pathbreaking account of seventeenth- and eighteenth-century family life in a small New England farming town. Entitled *Four Generations: Population, Land, and Family in Colonial Andover, Massachusetts*, the book makes skillful use of town records to draw a detailed portrait of early New England social life: births, deaths, migration, occupations, property, wills, and households. Greven organizes his presentation of chapters and data according to four generations. He defines the first as the group of (mostly) 25-to-45-year-olds who originally settled the town in the 1640s and 1650s. He defines the others strictly in terms of genealogy. The second generation consists of the first generation's children; the third, of its grandchildren; and the fourth, of its great-grandchildren.

When Greven wants to look at life in a purely familial context, his generational scheme is logical and convenient. He can always be certain that each member of one group is exactly one parent-child link removed from the previous group. Should he discover, for example, that members of the second Andover generation all share some trait (say, parental strictness) that may influence their children, he can examine the consequences in the third generation: the set of all their sons and daughters. When Greven wants to look at life in a historical context, on the other hand, the scheme becomes useless. Since women give birth over a spread of many years (ordinarily, from their late teens to their mid-forties), each successive generation of children has lifespans that begin and end over ever-longer periods. Greven's first generation was born mostly within a two-decade span. But by the fourth generation, he finds births stretched out over more than a century. Several fourth-generation Andoverans were already married by 1715, sixty years before the American Revolution. Several others did not marry until the late 1780s, when Madison was hammering out the U.S. Constitution.

What if we wanted to focus on another sort of generation—say, the young Andoverans that fought in the French and Indian War? Fortunately, Greven has this contingency in mind. Scattered throughout his book, he tabulates the same data by cohort-group, and somewhere among these tables we could examine the 1725–1740 war-fighting cohorts. Not surprisingly, most scholars who cite Greven also prefer the birthyear rather than the family numbers. Most historians want to locate people in history, not in genealogies.

The example of colonial Andover brings us back to the basic distinction between family and cohort generations—and the confusion between the two meanings that has plagued the word since Homer and Hesiod. Is one type of "generation" better than the other? Not necessarily. It all depends on the object of the inquiry.

The *family generation* is important when we want to examine the link between a specific group of parents and all of their children (or vice versa). For most other purposes, however, the concept is treacherous. Except in a few specialized cases (inheritance and dynastic titles, for example), genealogical ties rarely carry much force beyond the third generation. More important, family generations live only in "family" time, a rhythm of births unique to each lineage and having no lasting connection to historical or "social" time. There is no intelligible way to apply the concept to an entire society. Where would we begin? Even if we could trace everyone back to his society's original Adam and Eve, the result would be senseless. Many schoolmates would find themselves ten generations removed from each other.

We could, of course, just select the Adams and Eves arbitrarily. This is what Greven does by applying a "first generation" tag on all of the first Andover settlers—a natural choice since, after all, they did found a new colony. Ordinarily, the tagging would not be so simple: Imagine the problem if we wanted to study Columbus, Ohio, starting in the year 1900. Selecting the first generation, moreover, only delays the inevitable. Before long, the ever-diverging threads of family time will come back to haunt us. Assume that our first generation is born over a twenty-year period and that the distribution of births by age is the same as that of modern-day America—relatively narrow by historical standards. The result, shown in Figure A-1, would remind us of Andover. The second generation would be born over a period of about fifty years, the third over eighty-five years, the fourth over more than a century, and so on. Alternatively, our reader might imagine a simple experiment. Suppose you invited all your cousins to a family reunion. Then, in a variation on the old St. Ives riddle, suppose you asked your grandparents to invite the grandchildren of all their cousins. Chances are, some of those invitees will be newborn infants, while others will have died of old age. Everyone coming to the party will belong to the same family generation. But what else will you and your guests all have in common? Surely, far less than the people you meet at a high school or college reunion.

The *cohort generation,* by contrast, has no direct connection with genealogy or lineage. It is defined, instead, as everyone who is "brought into being" at the same historical moment—that is, everyone who belongs to the same cohort-group. Fathers and mothers or brothers and sisters in the same family generation do not necessarily belong to the same cohort generation. But unlike the family generation, all members of the same cohort

FIGURE A–1
Distribution of Family Generations

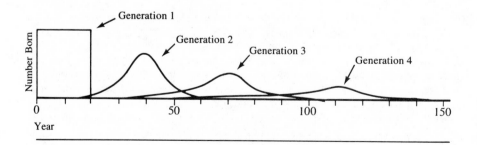

generation live in the same social or historical time. At any given moment, members of a cohort generation can all be found in a common age bracket. They all share both a special history and a special type of personality and behavior shaped by that history. And cohort generations can follow each other, consecutively, without any loss of historical definition over time.

In fact, *cohort generations are to societies what family generations are to families.* In both cases, the earlier generation is always older than the next and normally exercises authority over those that follow—the cohort type in a public setting, the family type in a private setting. In both cases, several distinct generations will appear to layer themselves at any one moment, creating the patterns we call "generational constellations." Looking up the constellation of family generations, for instance, a child sees the roles of parent, grandparent, and great-grandparent each filled by people having distinct individual personalities. Likewise, looking up the ladder of cohort generations, a youth sees older life phases—rising adulthood, midlife, and elderhood—each filled by cohort-groups having distinct peer personalities. But again, there remains a crucial difference: Genealogy creates a separate time thread of family time for each lineage; only the cohort-group binds all the threads together into a single rope of social time.

Modern Efforts to Define the Generation

For centuries after Homer, hardly any western mind bothered to distinguish between family and cohort generations. In the context of family life (especially when "generation" had a number attached), judges, clerics, and philosophers assumed without hesitation that the word referred to lineage: the "third generation of daughters," the "fourth-generation owner," the "fifth-generation legacy," and so on. Yet in the context of social life the meaning could abruptly shift to the cohort-group. Chroniclers used "rising generation" to refer, at any given moment, to everyone approaching adulthood, "declining generation" to refer to everyone approaching old age. The translators of the King James Bible wrote of great events affecting "this" or "that" generation of Hebrews and of specific groups of adults similarly praised ("a chosen generation") or damned ("a generation of vipers"). Linked to a personal pronoun, the meaning depended entirely on the idiom. To curse a neighbor "and all his generation" was to speak ill of his family and his children. To observe that David "served his own generation" was to speak of his peers.

Why so little effort to distinguish between meanings? For the same reason there was scant interest in the underlying concept of the birth cohort: the power of tradition. Until the eighteenth century, even the most educated westerners rarely doubted that history moved at a glacial pace, that seasonal rhythms were timeless, and that phases of life passed down unaltered from parent to child. All evidence indicated that the lifecycle was indeed universal. At special moments—a Trojan War or an Old Testament prophecy— one could notice a distinct cohort generation emerge, but there seemed little need to insist on a rigorous definition. As time passed on, so too would "that generation," and then all would be as before. Special interest in the cohort generation awaited a new world view, a new belief that history had speed and direction and that frequent Trojan War–like moments could be expected. Such a belief arrived in the late eighteenth and early nineteenth centuries, along with democratic revolutions, the early stirrings of industrial-ization, and the modern dogmas of rationalism and progress.

The first westerners to attach a modern significance to generations were the propa-gandists supporting the French Revolution in the 1780s and 1790s. No coincidence here. Just as these *philosophes* liked to call themselves a unique generation, pushing mankind into a wondrous age of improvement, so too did they ponder how elites, in any age, set new rules for society. Although their interest was limited to "political" generations of like-aged leaders, many took great care to define generations and locate them in history. Thomas Jefferson, writing home from the salons of Paris in 1789, concluded that a generation must be a cohort-group precisely thirty-four years long. (He later revised it to 18.2 years.) Similarly, in 1809, the scholar Jean-Louis Giraud sliced up centuries of French history into fifteen-year generations. These early definitions were crude and me-chanical, but gradually lent the word ominous new overtones. After Robespierre and Napoleon (European peers of Thomas Jefferson and Andrew Jackson, respectively), the western public needed little help in understanding how suddenly a special generation could arise—and how thoroughly it could change the world.

In the mid-nineteenth century, a new Victorian cadre of scientists and philosophers touched off a more serious wave of interest in generations. For Auguste Comte, John Stuart Mill, and Émile Littré, the basic question remained what it had been for the earlier Parisians: how generations determine the pace of civilized progress. But now the focus widened beyond mere politics. Comte saw generational change as the causal dynamic behind all social change. Littré agreed, suggesting that the character of each generation is no less complex than that of each stage of human life or historical evolution. (In 1863, he coined the word "cohort" to explain personality contrasts between French leaders then in power.) Mill defined a generation broadly as "a new set of human beings" who "have been educated, have grown up from childhood, and have taken possession of society." Like the others, Mill rejected the notion that successive "political generations" can influence each other independently of culture, science, manners, and mores. "In the filiation of one generation to another," he noted, "it is the whole which produces the whole, rather than any part a part."

The cohort generation remained a live subject for the rest of the nineteenth century—mostly because few writers could resist guessing its length. Antoine Cournot and Ottokar Lorenz, for example, talked about a "three-generation century." Few writers, however, had much that was new to say on the subject. One important exception was the Italian historian Giuseppe Ferrari, who developed a penetrating model of generational cycles in the 1860s and 1870s (to which we shall return). Another exception was Wilhelm Dilthey, whose writings—little known until decades after his death—addressed the confusion still clouding the meaning of "generation." The word, Dilthey insisted, has two separate definitions. The first is a "span of time" that "lasts from birth until that age when, on the average, a new ring of life is added to the generational tree." However, "a generation is *also* a term applied to a relationship of contemporaneity between individuals, that is, between those who had a common childhood, a common adolescence, and whose years of greatest manly vigor partially overlap. We say that such men belong to the same generation."

During the two decades following the cataclysm of World War I, the generation entered yet another vogue, again from a new perspective. To the rising social thinkers of the

1920s, the link between generations and progress seemed a waste of time. Far more interesting in that decade of relativism was how each generation creates its own subjective reality, its own psychology, emotions, values, art. To François Mentré, who coined the term "social generations" in a book by that name in 1920, a generation was "a state of collective mind embodied in a human group that endures for a certain time." To José Ortega y Gasset, a generation represented the "vital sensitivity" of a society, "a pulsation of its historical energy." Like many others, Ortega noticed an alternation between generations that are historically "decisive" and those that are not. During the interwar years, art historians like Wilhelm Pinder and Julius Peterson popularized the notion of a "cultural" generation. Karl Mannheim puzzled over what he called the "Generations Problem" from exile, a safe distance from his increasingly dangerous German peers. Oddly, despite the rise of fascism (and Stalinism) throughout Europe, most scholars regarded the "political generation" as a tired subject.

Attempts to solve this "generations problem" became one of the many intellectual casualties of global war, and the problem remained dormant for the first two decades of the postwar era. At the height of student activism in the late 1960s, it briefly resurfaced in response to the counterculture movement of American Boomers and their "Generation of 1968" European agemates. When the political fuss died down, however, so did the interest—after producing memorable song lyrics, but far less innovative social thinking than in earlier eras.

The "Generations Problem" Today

We can now look back over two centuries of generational writing. Setting aside their many differences of opinion, nearly all of the authors in this modern school have struggled to define "generation" in explicitly *cohort*—as opposed to *family*—terms and to bring this definition to the attention of the western world. Where have their efforts been successful? And where have they failed?

Among successes, one stands out: The cohort "generation" has entirely reshaped our popular understanding of the word. The new meaning has crept into our intuitive vocabulary, into the daily parlance of several languages, and into our basic perception of historical change. Since the 1920s, for example, no 20-to-25-year cohort-group has come fully of age in America without encountering at least one determined attempt to name it. Nor do we any longer confuse such terms with family lineage. Four centuries ago, we would have thought that a young person "talkin' 'bout my generation" had a story to share about his grandfather or grandchildren. Today we know otherwise—that he has a story to share about his peers, about how they all came of age and have come to see life. Nowhere in recent years has the cohort generation gained such unprecedented legitimacy as in the polling and marketing industries. For thousands of professionals, the "Baby Boom Generation" has become synonymous with a cohort-group whose tastes marketers are willing to pay millions to understand. Gradually and almost by default, we have watched a precise and infant science (the study of cohorts) merge with popular idiom (the generation).

Triumphant in popular culture, the cohort generation has been confined by experts to the shadow world of unproven hypothesis. This remains the great failure of generations writing. Present-day historians mention a "generation" only in passing. Academics discussing aging, lifecycles, sociology, and politics hardly touch the word. Most of the blame for this unfriendly reception can be directed at the generations writers themselves. From Comte through Mannheim and beyond, their writings have been sometimes colorful, eloquent, and painstakingly empirical—but seldom explanatory. Three obvious and related questions can be asked of cohort generations. How do they arise? Why should they change personality at any particular cohort boundary? And why should they have any particular length? You can read endless tomes of generations literature looking for answers to these questions. You won't find any.

Over the years, the expected length of a cohort generation has vexed many a writer. Clearly, to be a usable concept, we need to know approximately how long it is. Why not three years? Why not ninety years? Responding to these queries, however, generations writers have typically resorted to evasion or nonsense. A few—Mill and Mannheim, for example—finesse the issue by refusing to speculate on length. They tell us how to find out, in effect, but they won't get their own hands dirty. Most other writers go to the other extreme, telling us exactly how long every generation must be. The magic number, they insist, is "precisely" thirty-three years (Lorenz, Cournot), or thirty years (Comte, Dilthey), or twenty-five years (Littré), or 18.2 years (Jefferson), or fifteen years (Ortega).

Not a single writer justifies either the precision or absolute regularity of these time spans. Worse, many fail to defend even the approximate number—a failure revealed by their vague reference to the average length (or half-length) of a family generation, reinforcing the age-old confusion surrounding the very meaning of the concept. As recently as 1946, Johan Huizinga believed it was a fair criticism of the entire generations school to observe that "the generation, biologically speaking, is and always will be a completely arbitrary period of time." Small wonder that skeptics have regarded the cohort generation, like astrology, as a provocative idea searching blindly for a reason. Or that Bob Dylan might seem to offer the last word on the subject.

In the remainder of this Appendix, we offer the specifics we see lacking in the writings of others. Our approach is consistent with the conclusions of the best generations writers—including Littré, Ferrari, Dilthey, Mentré, and Ortega—who agree that the length of a cohort generation must be linked to the length of a phase of life, not to family genealogy. It also leads us to the basic dynamic of the recurring cycle we have identified in American history.

A Journey to Cohortia

Join us on a journey to the mythical land of Cohortia.

Cohortia is a traditional society, largely free from the most serious kinds of historical shocks. From time to time, Cohortians encounter bloody wars, deadly famines, and charismatic shamans. But not often.

Traditional Cohortia

Let us make two initial assumptions about Cohortians. First, we assume *their social behavior is governed by a well-defined and relatively unchanging lifecycle.* In each life phase, a "good Cohortian" is expected to fulfill a cluster of age-based social roles. Second, we assume *the Cohortian lifecycle includes four basic life phases, each based on a multiple of the span between birth and coming of age.* Let's assume the same twenty-two-year life phases we described in Chapter 2:

• ELDERS (age 66–87). Central role: *stewardship* (supervising, mentoring, channeling endowments, passing on values).

• MIDLIFE ADULTS (age 44–65). Central role: *leadership* (parenting, teaching, directing institutions, using values).

• RISING ADULTS (age 22–43). Central role: *activity* (working, starting families and livelihoods, serving institutions, testing values).

• YOUTH (age 0–21). Central role: *dependence* (growing, learning, accepting protection and nurture, avoiding harm, acquiring values).

These phase-of-life role descriptions are suggestive only. All the first assumption requires is that each role be basically different and that the age-borders be reasonably well defined. Cohortians are quite ordinary in this respect. Every society recognizes lifecycle passage points, and practically every society acknowledges a sharp "coming-of-age" separation between the roles of youth and rising adulthood. It does not matter how many live into midlife and elderhood, since these central roles can be performed (if lifespans are short) by only a few people.

Now imagine a sudden shock—a "social moment"—such as a major war or revolution. And add a third assumption: *Any social moment affects an individual's personality differently according to his current phase of life.* It does so by triggering a behavior response conditioned by the phase-of-life role. For youths, the response might be dependence (keeping out of the way); for rising adults, activity (arming to meet the challenge); for midlifers, leadership (organizing the troops); and for elders, stewardship (establishing the purpose of the war). The stress of responding to the social moment leaves a different emotional imprint and memory with each group according to the role it is called upon to play. These differences, furthermore, are reinforced by the social interaction within each group. Youths might mirror each other's dread and anxiety, for example, while rising adults might collectively encourage each other's valor and sense of duty. With this social moment, four adjacent cohort-groups separately coalesce into generations, each with a distinct peer personality. The more serious the trauma, the sharper the contrasts between peer personalities. The length of these generations depends on the length of the phases of life, assumed here to be twenty-two years.

Letting time pass after the war is over, we notice the continuing influence of the social moment. Twenty-two years after the social moment, when each generation has risen one phase-of-life notch, four distinctly different peer personalities still exist. Those who were elders during the war have passed on, but a new crop of youths (all born after the war) has arrived. Having no firsthand memory of the trauma, these youths develop a peer personality unlike that of any of the elder generations. Assume, for now, that nothing else happens thereafter. When forty-four years have passed, the number of distinct generations falls to three: elders and midlifers (who remember the war as rising adults and youths) and everyone younger than age 44. After sixty-six years, only two discrete generations are left: elders and everyone younger than age 66. By the eighty-eighth year— that is, by the fourth postwar constellation—the "war-touched" generations vanish entirely. All living Cohortians are, once again, products of the traditional lifecycle.

Figure A-2 illustrates this dynamic. As in Chapter 2, we show time horizontally and phases of life vertically, revealing cohort-group lifecycles along the diagonal. Time is measured in years, with the "0" for the first aligned constellation, "22" for the next, and so on. Each cohort-group is given a letter in order of its birth. Notice that social moments are shown starting before the aligned constellation. Suppose, as is likely, the social moment is not a brief cataclysm, but something akin to the ten-year Trojan War. In this case, the social moment would start earlier than "Year 0"—and, as it rages, would mark each cohort as it enters each phase of life. Youth cohorts, for example, would come of age during the war as they go off to fight in it. The catalyzing moment would then arrive, as it certainly did for Troy's conquerors, near the end of the social moment.

To understand how this interaction of generations and history might work, imagine Cohortia literally re-enacting the Trojan War. For purposes of illustration, let's introduce Homer's cast of characters, each representing a generation:

COHORTIAN GENERATION	HOMERIC CHARACTER	PHASE OF LIFE DURING SOCIAL MOMENT	PHASE-OF-LIFE ROLE DURING SOCIAL MOMENT
B	Nestor	Elderhood	Stewardship
C	Agamemnon	Midlife	Leadership
D	Odysseus	Rising Adulthood	Activity
E	Telemachus	Youth	Dependence

A little background may help the reader locate these characters. In the *Iliad,* we learn through flashbacks about the prewar constellation (year −22). Nestor (B), ruler of Pilos, is somewhere in midlife; Agamemnon (C) is the rising-adult chief of the House of Atreus; Odysseus (D) is a child in Ithaca; and Telemachus (E) is not yet born. The war itself, the central drama of the *Iliad,* begins near the year −10 and ends in year 0. Odysseus and his coming-of-age peers Ajax and Diomedes are forged by war into collective giants, a triumphant and heroic cohort-group; Agamemnon, now a haunted figure entering midlife, leads the troops; and Nestor, in old age, presides with his wisdom over the Achaean alliance. Meanwhile, back in Ithaca, Odysseus' wife Penelope manages on her own to raise their only child, Telemachus. Like most of his (cohort E) peers, Telemachus reflects the personality of what the British call their "air raid generation": sensitive and eloquent, yet insecure and cautious.

In the dramatic climax of the *Odyssey,* Homer takes us ahead one more step: almost exactly a generation further to year 22. Agamemnon would now be an old man, had he not been treacherously murdered by his wife for his own sins. In midlife, Odysseus finally makes it back to Penelope in Ithaca, where he once again plays the hero and saves the kingdom. Telemachus comes of age—obediently and with his father's help—and looks forward to inheriting the kingship in an era of sweet peace. There the saga ends. What will happen in years 44, 66, or 88? Homer does not say. As Telemachus moves into midlife and Odysseus into elderhood, the number of identifiable generations will begin to narrow. Presumably, the "dark ages" will reclaim the Greek kingdoms and the lifecycle will return to gray tradition. It is not a story that would interest the epic poet, at least not until a new social moment arrives.

And yet, reflecting on the last scenes of the *Odyssey,* we cannot help wondering how these postwar cohort-groups (F, G, H, and I in Figure A-2) could revert so quickly to Cohortia's traditional lifecycle and personality. Consider the scenario. Cohort F youths grow up while the midlife leadership role is filled by the heroic peers of Odysseus (D). But cohort G youths grow up (and cohort F fills rising adulthood) while that same role is played by the far less confident peers of Telemachus (E). Given the different nurturing and leadership styles of these two postwar constellations, it seems likely that the peer personalities of these two younger groups will also differ—from each other and from the traditional lifecycle. And if they differ, so might cohorts H and I, and so on.

Thus far, traditional Cohortia does not allow for this possibility. We implicitly assume

FIGURE A–2
Traditional Cohortia

	Social Moment					
Time in Years	**Yr −22**	**Yr 0**	**Yr 22**	**Yr 44**	**Yr 66**	**Yr 88**
Phase of Life						
ELDER, age 66–87	A	Ⓑ	C	D	E	F
MIDLIFE, age 44–65	B	Ⓒ	D	E	F	G
RISING, age 22–43	C	Ⓓ	E	F	G	H
YOUTH, age 0–21	D	Ⓔ	F	G	H	I

Note: Circle marks cohort-group in or entering that phase of life during social moment.

that each phase of life, together with its role definition, is forever fixed by custom—regardless of the peer personality passing through it. A social moment merely puts a personality mark on a cohort-group, but otherwise has no lasting influence. But that raises a provocative question: What happens when the power of tradition is removed? To answer this question, let's drag Cohortia into modernity. Here we find the impact of a social moment to be more far-reaching.

Modern Cohortia

In modern Cohortia, we ease the power of tradition by making two new assumptions. First:

• *A social moment not only shapes personality according to current phase-of-life roles, but also forges an enduring bond of identity between each cohort-group and its role—an acquired style that redefines both how each group will later regard itself and how it will later be regarded by others.*

In modern Cohortia, in other words, a phase-of-life role is no longer totally rigid, but can now be modified by the generational personality passing through it. If a social moment shapes an active peer personality among rising adults, for example, this cohort-group will take an active role and self-image with it as it ages. With apologies to Homer, let's go back and modernize the Trojan War. A modern Odysseus would not simply return to Ithaca in midlife with the personality of a war hero. He and his peers would modify the very definition of midlife according to the same role—by projecting heroic activity into political, cultural, and family behavior. (Dante and many later writers amended Homer's account in precisely this fashion, by depicting an aging, hubristic Odysseus organizing new missions and voyages.) A modern Telemachus and his peers might very well let this happen, since their role during the war—dependence and emulation—will continue to shape their later behavior and self-image.

Our second new assumption about modern Cohortia puts a biological and social limit on how long any generation can modify phase-of-life roles:

• *A central role acquired during a social moment can extend into the next life phase—but not into the life phase after that.*

If the central role of rising adulthood is activity, a generation shaped by that role can transfer it to midlife, but not to elderhood. Even a modern Odysseus cannot, in old age, sustain society's active role in the face of physiological decline and his approaching awareness of his own mortality. Nor, eventually, would society permit him to do so. The dependent role of childhood can likewise be transferred to rising adulthood, but not to midlife. The time would come when the modern Telemachus would have to abandon dependence for the role of leadership, by necessity if not by choice.

Now let's retrace the story depicted in Figure A-2, recast for modern Cohortia. In year 0, the story begins unchanged: We see the same social moment hitting all four cohort-groups and shaping each into a distinct generation. In year 22, the generations all move up a lifecycle notch—but this time, each one takes its war-defined role or style along with it. Here is where we notice the pliable rising adult (Telemachus), the heroic midlifer (Odysseus), and perhaps the too-cunning elder (Agamemnon). In year 44, each generation moves up a second lifecycle notch. But now, at last, the two surviving event-shaped generations (D and E) must abandon their acquired central roles.

This will not happen by free choice, since the roles have become wedded to each group's underlying personality—nor by social design, since modern Cohortia lacks firmly prescribed behavior. Thus, the reshuffling of central roles is not likely to happen gradually. Far more likely, *it will happen suddenly through a new social moment—triggered, in effect, by the new generational constellation.* The time will arrive when the social tension between original and acquired roles (in midlife and elderhood) becomes intolerable. The time will also arrive when a new, coming-of-age cohort-group—postwar babies who never knew the sixtyish Odysseuses as heroic young warriors nor the fortyish Telemachuses as deferential children—will insist on claiming an active social role.

At this point, we cannot say what type of new event to expect, except to point out that it will depend upon the external and domestic circumstances of modern Cohortia. It need not be another war. All we require somewhere near year 44 is a new and distinct social moment that will reidentify each cohort-group with the original central role associated with its new phase of life. In particular, we can expect the new event to thrust some new active role on the now-rising adults (F) and some new dependent role on the new crop of children (G). The generational dynamics of modern Cohortia are illustrated in Figure A-3.

Modernity does not alter the way in which Cohortia shapes generational personalities during social moments. It does, however, trigger the arrival of new social moments timed to shape a new array of distinct generations at two-constellation intervals. Notice that in each constellation, there are always four distinct personalities. Notice, as well, that the two-constellation (or forty-four-year) rhythm creates two basic types of generational lifecycles. Generations D, F, and H encounter social moments in or entering rising adulthood (coming of age) and later in or entering elderhood. Because they tend to transfer their active rising-adult role into midlife, their style always dominates major social and cultural change in Cohortia. That is why we call these generations "dominant." Generations E, G, and I encounter social moments in youth and later in or entering midlife. Their styles tend to be overshadowed by the more potent personalities of their next-elders or next-juniors. That is why we call these generations "recessive."

So far, we have assumed that every social moment creates a positive association between each generation and its expected social role. But this may not always happen. In particular, an unsuccessful experience for a dominant, rising-adult generation may prevent it from forging any meaningful bond with its role during the social moment. Thus:

• *A society must resolve a social moment successfully in order to shape the coming-of-age generation as dominant; otherwise, it will shape the coming-of-age generation as recessive, unable or unwilling to take its active role with it into midlife.*

FIGURE A-3
Modern Cohortia

	Social Moment			Social Moment			Social Moment
Time in Years	Yr −22	Yr 0	Yr 22	Yr 44	Yr 66	Yr 88
Phase of Life						
ELDER, age 66–87	A	ⓑ	C	ⓓ	E	ⓕ
MIDLIFE, age 44–65	B	ⓒ	D	ⓔ	F	ⓖ
RISING, age 22–43	C	ⓓ	E	ⓕ	G	ⓗ
YOUTH, age 0–21	D	ⓔ	F	ⓖ	H	ⓘ

Note: Circle marks cohort-group in or entering that phase of life during social moment.

As we have seen, this happened once in America, when the Progressives emerged from the Civil War with few positive associations with their coming-of-age role—partly because this anomalous social moment arrived ahead of schedule. From the American experience alone, of course, we cannot say just how often this might happen. The possibility that social moments may frequently arrive off-schedule and end in tragedy may explain, aside from the stronger force of tradition, why modern Europe has failed to produce dominant generational types of the same power, color, and variety as those of the New World (to the American eye, at least).

From a Two-Stroke Rhythm to a Four-Type Cycle

The regenerative quality of peer groups—their capacity to grow, wither, fall, and then renew themselves—has fascinated philosophers, historians, and dramatists since the beginning of time. The very structure of Greek tragedy, as in the plays of Aeschylus, centers on the concept of age-related hubris. This combination of blindness and over-reaching inevitably has generational consequences (''visit the sins of the father on the sons'') and, by implication, teaches generational lessons. But the simple fact that one generation's tragic excesses do not lead to a permanent cycle of destruction and decay reflects the capacity of successor generations to learn from, and compensate for, the mistakes of their elders. These successors, in turn, then make their own mistakes. Over the last two centuries, cross-generational rejuvenation has been a recurring theme in story and song, from Ivan Turgenev's *Fathers and Sons* to Graham Nash's *Teach Your Children*.

Even where tradition is strong, we can observe this dynamic in individual families: the parents who unknowingly err in raising their children and the children who rise above the setback but later compensate by erring in the opposite direction with their own children. Where tradition is weak and life phases can be redefined by distinct peer personalities, we can observe it happening across entire societies. In a social context, the "parents" and "children" refer not to families but to cohort generations. Returning to the dynamics of social moments in modern Cohortia, let's assume the following:

• *During a new social moment, each generation will redefine the central role of the phase of life it is entering in a direction that reverses the perceived excesses of that role since the last social moment.*

The premise here is that generation-specific styles forged during a social moment will later become dysfunctional as time passes and that most people will sense this fact. Given the opportunity—that is, given a new social moment—each generation will seek a new style, appropriate for its phase of life, that compensates for past excesses and steers society back on the right course. For example, over the forty-four long years that modern Odysseus and his peers have been busy redefining Cohortian adulthood in terms of endless martial projects, we could imagine a growing consensus that a different sort of style is called for—perhaps a search for values and principles that would give such projects a fresh sense of purpose. When the next social moment arrives, therefore, each generation will not only reclaim its generic life-phase role, but will shift its style in a compensatory direction. Sometime near year 44 in modern Cohortia, we might witness an old Odysseus relinquishing at last his worldly agendas; a midlife Telemachus stepping gently into power, careful to avoid his father's swagger and hubris; a coming-of-age cohort-group of zealous Dionysians more keen on inner than outer discovery; and a new crop of hardscrabble youths whom no one expects to be obedient.

This impulse to compensate for excess shows up not only in the desire of adults to correct past mistakes, but also in the hope of adults to spare their own children from such mistakes. In short:

• *Each generation has a formative, nurturing relationship primarily with other two-apart generations (dominant with dominant, recessive with recessive); each tries to cultivate in the second-younger generation a peer personality it perceives as complementary to its own.*

Any generation's children (using 20-to-25-year cohort-groups) typically fall into both of the two next-younger generations. Yet for the entire period that any generation is situated mostly in midlife—the life phase in which it combines its influence as parents with norm-setting leadership in public life—the generation then situated mostly in youth will be exactly two generations removed. The elder generation of parents, therefore, will set the nurturing tone for any generation of children. As we noted in Chapter 3, recent

American history offers some familiar illustrations: the G.I.s (not Silent) set the parental tone for Boom children; the Silent (not Boom) for 13er children; and, it appears, the Boom (not 13ers) for Millennial children—even though the biological link splits about evenly in all three cases.

This two-apart nurturing relationship reinforces the pendular swing in social direction. Dominant (or recessive) parents in midlife set the parental tone for dominant (or recessive) children who will later assume the same lifecycle role in modern Cohortia's two-stroke rhythm. Tacitly or explicitly, a parental generation will encourage its younger counterpart to acquire a style that compensates for the self-perceived imbalance in the elder peer personality. Around the year 22, for example, the dominant midlife peers of modern Odysseus will try to coax something different from discipline and valor out of the dominant postwar youth, perhaps by encouraging a bit more spirit and demanding a bit less duty. Around the year 44 (overlapping with the next social moment), the recessive midlife peers of modern Telemachus will do the same for the recessive generation then in youth, perhaps by loosening family authority. The sequel that we have here conceived—coming-of-age prophets and self-sufficient children—shows how occupants of the two younger life phases can take an active role in the next social moment.

By year 44, once again, a new two-stroke rhythm is underway—but with a new twist. Rather than simply revert to where everything stood forty-four years earlier, the society now turns toward an array of phase-of-life styles that reverses the direction in which the society was moving before. If we assume that these directions are bipolar, then the two-stroke rhythm begins to look more like a four-stroke cycle. Even in Homer's traditional Cohortia, we can glimpse hints of such a dynamic. Reflect on Nestor (the wise elder) and Agamemnon (the cunning midlifer), and try to imagine a social moment forty-four years prior to the sack of Troy that might have shaped these two personalities. Nestor would then have been a rising adult (dominant) and Agamemnon a child (recessive). Now compare them to another pair at year 0, Odysseus and Telemachus: same ages, same dominant-recessive types, yet an entirely unlike pair of personalities. One social moment made the coming-of-age Nestor wise, the child Agamemnon opportunistic; the next made the coming-of-age Odysseus heroic, the child Telemachus deferential.

The recurrence of compensating peer personalities is an important force for *regeneration and balance* in human civilization. What is it, in man, that makes this cycle a gravitational orbit around timeless norms of human behavior, with successor generations moderating the excesses of their elders? Why is the cycle not a centrifugal spiral, with successor generations lunging toward ever more dangerous extremes? We do not know. The answer may be rooted in a basic social instinct for balance between risk and caution, between reflection and activity, between passion and reason, or between the emulation of mothers versus fathers. We leave such questions to anthropologists and psychologists. Whatever the reason, this instinct has worked to mankind's benefit in the past and enhances the prospects for survival and progress in the future.

The Four-Part Generational Cycle

From the Hebrew tribes' flight from Egypt to their founding of a new society in Canaan, the early books of the Old Testament tell the most dramatic story of unfolding cohort generations known to the West. Examining this story schematically, we have little trouble identifying—in choreographed succession—four distinct peer personalities.

- *First,* the holy peers of Aaron and mother-protected Moses: the young adults who awakened their people to the spirit of their one true God ("I am who I am"), defied the authority of the most powerful institution on earth (Pharaoh's Egypt), and later on—during midlife and old age—led the Hebrews through the wilderness to the threshold of Canaan (their "promised land").

- *Second,* a tough generation of "stiff-necked" backsliders: the worshipers of the golden calf, "murmurers" and "men of little faith"—for whose sins God punished the Hebrews with extra trials and tribulations. Possessed of divided loyalties and split timing, they were too young to have been exalted by Moses' spiritual awakening, but too old not to remember the enticing fleshpots of Egypt.

- *Third,* the dutiful soldier-peers of Joshua: the children who were nearly all born after Exodus and who first came of age in victorious battles in the wilderness; the young adults whom the patriarch Moses anointed for leadership (none older was allowed to enter Canaan); and the midlifers of martial unity and discipline who succeeded in conquering the natives of Canaan through decades of warfare.

- *Fourth,* the original generation of Judges: the invisible children whose births were overshadowed by war; the obliging young adults who served the mighty Joshua; and the midlifers whose exercise of power was marked by political fragmentation, petty feuds, and uncertainty about the future.

Setting aside the gigantic lifespans of a few major actors, we can recognize the rhythm pulsing through this story. It is the generational calendar of Cohortia. Using twenty years as the length of a Hebrew life phase (Numbers informs us that all Hebrew males age 20 and older were normally "able to go to war"), we count double that span to take us from one social moment to the next. Exactly forty years pass between the Moses-led Exodus and the Joshua-led invasion of Canaan. Another forty years take us to the death of Joshua and his peers. Only then, as the story fades in the absence of new social moments, do the first Judges climb to leadership ("and there arose another generation after them, which knew not the Lord, nor yet the works which he had done for Israel").

Perfectly in time with this rhythm, we also notice the familiar oscillation between Cohortia's two basic generational types, dominant and recessive:

- *Moses' peers.* Type: dominant. Social moment (year 0) as rising adults and again (year 40) as elders.

- *Golden Calf peers.* Type: recessive. Social moment (year 0) as children and again (year 40) as midlifers.

- *Joshua's peers.* Type: dominant. Social moment (year 40) as rising adults and story end (year 80) as elders.

- *First Judges' peers.* Type: recessive. Social moment (year 40) as children and story end (year 80) as midlifers.

Clearly, a two-stroke cycle does not do justice to the range of personalities that emerges in this story. Although both dominant generations (of Moses and Joshua) are shaped as rising adults by social moments, we cannot help noticing how much these two moments differ from each other. Moses' peers encounter a spiritual, inner-driven crisis: an urgent need to inspire heart-felt values, even if it means defying the world. The Golden Calf generation is later perceived (by the standards of its next-elders) to be unprincipled and sinful. Joshua's peers, on the other hand, encounter a secular, outer-driven crisis: an urgent need to establish a new world, even if it means neglecting the heart. Similarly, the First Judges' peers are later perceived (by the standards of their next-elders) to be weak and ineffective.

The dynamic of Exodus is a four-type cycle: the first two-part beat triggered by prophecies and other-world agendas, the next two-part beat by emergencies and this-world agendas. In lifecycle timing, these successive dominant or recessive generations have much in common. Yet in outlook and behavior, their personalities appear to be diametrically opposed.

This four-type cycle illustrates a fundamental pattern that arises most distinctly when, as in America, generations are left free to develop and express their own personalities. Why? Think back to the lessons of Cohortia. Picture a generation that has been shaped young by an inner-driven event and has spent two constellations redefining the adult role in spiritual terms. As this peer group enters old age, it will likely leave behind it a society well stoked in moral conviction, but imperiled by mounting and unsolved practical problems. Or picture the reverse: a generation shaped young by outer-driven event—leaving behind, as it enters old age, a rational and secularized world crying out for spiritual rebirth.

As we learned in Cohortia, cohort generations do not happen often in traditional societies. A four-type generational cycle would be rare indeed. That is what makes the Exodus cycle so striking. To begin, it needed a providential moment, the Hebrews' spiritual awakening. And to propel itself thereafter, it needed a successful outcome and a temporary loosening of lifecycle traditions, perhaps brought about by the dislocation of wandering and war.

The Tradition of the Four-Type Cycle

We should not expect a well-defined, four-type cycle of generations to be characteristic of premodern societies. Nor, Exodus aside, has it been. Yet we need not look far to find provocative bits and pieces of such a cycle. On the one hand, the great classical historians—Homer, Virgil, Thucydides, Livy, and Polybius—often identify cycles launched by heroic, Joshua-like generations. On the other hand, ancient religious chronicles more often focus on cycles launched by spiritual, Moses-like generations (such as those beginning with Abraham, Samuel, Christ, or Mohammed). Apparently, premodern observers knew of two basic types of dominant generations: one martial or institutions-founding, the other spiritual or values-founding.

Whenever these observers discuss a lengthy sequence of generations, moreover, it is significant that the number four is most often cited as a cyclical endpoint. The Old

Testament often refers to curses and punishments reaching "unto the fourth generation," rarely three and never five. The poetry and prose of the classical era took for granted that human history traveled through cycles of four "ages"—where "ages" could refer to anything from millennial epochs to generations. (Hesiod's belief in five never became popular.) So too in the Islamic world. "Prestige lasts only four generations in the best of cases," Ibn Khaldun wrote in the fourteenth century, observing how political dynasties seem to follow a four-generational pattern. The first builds. The second has personal contact with the builder. The third sustains what was built as a matter of tradition. The fourth destroys. The fifth builds again, and so forth.

Whatever may have prompted each version of the four-generation formula, ancient and medieval cycle theorists apparently agreed on one thing: that the fifth generation— or the first generation of the next cycle—would bring with it redemption and a new beginning. A termination to old curses. A new Golden Age. A purging of inherited tragedy. In religious terms, this four-generation span reaches from one generation of prophet-redeemers to the next—in secular terms, from one generation of hero-builders to the next.

In the nineteenth century, the four-type cycle again attracted attention. Among the early generations writers, Comte, Littré, and Ferrari separately suggested that generations can plausibly be arranged in a fourfold morphology. Littré's categories reflect vivid and distinct personality types: scientific, aesthetic, moral, and industrial. Begin with the third, and his sequence parallels Exodus. Writing a few years later, Ferrari identified a cycle even closer to that ancient example. In *Teoria dei periodi politici,* published in 1874, Ferrari claimed that social and political change—the "ebb and flow of history," as he put it—is driven by a repeating cycle of four generational types. Each of his four types reflects a distinct personality, with opposite personalities appearing two generations apart. The first is preparatory; the second, revolutionary; the third, reactionary; and the fourth, harmonizing. The leadership style of each successive type lines up with a parallel sequence in history: a subversive period, a solution, a struggle against the solution, and a final victory that confirms the solution.

Now let's combine Ferrari's "ebb and flow" with Littré's morphology. Starting with Ferrari's second type and Littré's third, and adding a brief summary of the role played by each, we create what we might call the "Littré-Ferrari cycle." Note how closely it matches the four-generation drama of Exodus.

- First, a *"revolutionary"* (Ferrari) or *"moral"* (Littré) generation forges an entirely new array of feelings and values, and works to fulfill its implicit agenda.

- Second, a *"reactionary"* (Ferrari) or *"industrial"* (Littré) generation struggles against the values emphasis of its elders, and prefers pragmatism and independence.

- Third, a *"harmonizing"* (Ferrari) or *"scientific"* (Littré) generation identifies problems, builds a social consensus, agrees on rational solutions, and works effectively to achieve them.

- Fourth, a *"preparatory"* (Ferrari) or *"aesthetic"* (Littré) generation perfects and embellishes the solution, yet undermines the consensus and provides lone forerunners for the next values revolution. (Then the cycle repeats.)

Within the past quarter century, Julián Marías (a Spanish sociologist-philosopher) and Samuel Huntington (a Harvard professor of government) have separately proposed a four-part generational cycle. Marías published his paradigm in 1967 in an effort to clarify and explain Ortega's original two-stroke oscillation between "polemic" and "cumulative" types (roughly, what we call "dominant" and "recessive"). In Marías' cycle, the first generation creates and initiates, the second fabricates a stereotyped personality, the third reflects and theorizes, and the fourth stylistically challenges forms and customs.

In 1981, Huntington developed a similar model based on social and political change in American history. He notes an alternating pattern between inner- and outer-driven behavior: a period of newly conceived values and "creedal passion," followed by a period of effective public action that institutionalizes these ideals. Huntington calls this the "IvI" ("Institutions versus Ideals") cycle—a cycle of four parts. In it, "moralism eventually elicits cynicism, cynicism produces complacency, complacency leads to hypocrisy, and hypocrisy in due course reinvigorates moralism." Between the polarities of inner- and outer-driven behavior, Huntington finds "gaps" roughly the same length as two life phases. He lines up American social moments—what we call spiritual awakenings and secular crises—almost exactly as we do.

In his earlier writings, Huntington acknowledges that a generation is an "experiential and attitudinal group" and that American history can be interpreted in terms of a cycle in which "major struggles" take place "between the advance guard of the new generation and the rear guard of its predecessor." "There certainly is an extraordinary tendency to interpret American politics in terms of cycles," he concludes. "I think we can relate cycles to generational analysis." Curiously, however, his 1981 model hardly mentions generations. As such, his theory is incomplete. But when we combine Huntington's rhythm of history with Marías' generational alternation, a very useful composite emerges. Lining up Marías' third phase with Huntington's first, we create what we might call the "Marías-Huntington cycle":

- First, an inner-driven, moralistic generation reflects and theorizes, distills new values and ideas, and begins a period of "creedal passion"—that is, a society-wide effort to close the gap between ideals and reality.

- Second, a cynical generation stylistically challenges forms and customs.

- Third, an outer-driven, morally complacent generation institutionalizes the ideals identified earlier.

- Fourth, a hypocritical generation fabricates a stereotyped personality. (Then the cycle repeats.)

In its fundamentals, this Marías-Huntington cycle is very similar to the Littré-Ferrari cycle identified a century earlier, to the cycle of Exodus, and even to the hints of a full cycle we found in Homer's *Iliad*. Figure A-4 summarizes the correspondence of generational types between our own four-part cycle and the earlier paradigms.

As we recall from Chapter 4, each of these four types has a distinct lifecycle and a special relationship to spiritual awakenings and secular crises. Each shapes and is shaped

FIGURE A–4
Five Generational Cycles Compared

OUR CYCLE	MARÍAS-HUNTINGTON	LITTRÉ-FERRARI	EXODUS	THE ILIAD
IDEALIST	inner-driven moralist	revolutionary moral	Aaron, Moses prophetic	Nestor wise
REACTIVE	anticustom cynical	reactionary industrial	Golden Calf sinful	Agamemnon cunning
CIVIC	outer-driven institutionalizing	harmonizing scientific	Joshua heroic	Odysseus hubristic
ADAPTIVE	stereotyped hypocritical	preparatory aesthetic	Judges fragmented	Telemachus deferential

by history. Altogether, these types order themselves into four parallel types of constellations, each with a matching era and mood.

Figure A-4 summarizes a remarkable set of correspondences that has fascinated the West in theory and myth over the span of three millennia. The four-part generational cycle refuses to expire. Like the concept of the generation itself, it has never fully emerged from shadowy speculation and established itself as a legitimate intellectual tradition. Perhaps, in time, it will.

Appendix B

AMERICAN POLITICAL LEADERSHIP BY GENERATION

For reference, we offer the following three tables as summary indicators of American political participation by generation.

- *Figure B-1* shows generational participation in several key political events before the swearing-in of the first U.S. Congress in 1789: colonial delegates to the Stamp Act Congress (1765); known members of the Boston Tea Party riot (1773); signers of the Declaration of Independence (1776) and Constitution (1787); and state governors and delegates to the Continental Congress (every odd-numbered year from 1775 to 1787, omitting delegates whose birthdates are unknown).

- *Figure B-2* lists American Presidents (including presidents of the Continental Congress) by generation, lifespan, party, term, and age.

- *Figure B-3* computes each generation's "national leadership share" for every odd-numbered year since 1775. From 1789 through 1989, this is a simple average of each generation's percentage share of all House members, all senators, and all governors. From 1775 through 1787, it is a simple average of each generation's percentage share of delegates to the Continental Congress and state governors. (For these years, the share with unknown birthdates is designated "NA" to make the known shares easier to interpret.) House members, senators, and delegates are counted if they are officially in office at the end of the listed calendar year; governors are counted if they serve at least six months of the listed year, whether or not they are in office at the end of the year. The table was calculated from a database containing about 15,000 names: all congressmen and governors from 1787 through 1989 and all delegates to the Continental Congress from 1774 through 1788.

TABLE B–1
Political Leadership Before 1789, by Generation

	AWAKENING	LIBERTY	REPUBLICAN	TOTAL
COLONIAL DELEGATES TO THE STAMP ACT CONGRESS (New York City; October 7–25, 1765)	14 52%	13 48%	0 0%	27 100%
[average age]	[51]	[36]	[NA]	[44]
KNOWN MEMBERS OF THE BOSTON TEA PARTY RIOT (Boston; December 16, 1773)	1 1%	15 19%	62 79%	78 100%
[average age]	[57]	[39]	[23]	[27]
SIGNERS OF THE DECLARATION OF INDEPENDENCE (Philadelphia; July–August, 1776)	11 20%	35 63%	10 18%	56 100%
[average age]	[61]	[44]	[32]	[45]
SIGNERS OF THE U.S. CONSTITUTION (Philadelphia; September 17, 1787)	4 10%	13 33%	22 56%	39 100%
[average age]	[69]	[52]	[37]	[46]

TABLE B–1 (continued)

Political Leadership Before 1789, by Generation

	AWAKENING	LIBERTY	REPUBLICAN	TOTAL
REVOLUTIONARY OR STATE GOVERNORS AT END OF YEAR (percentages only)				
1775.........	80%	10%	10%	100%
1777.........	33%	67%	0%	100%
1779.........	25%	50%	25%	100%
1781.........	23%	62%	15%	100%
1783.........	23%	77%	0%	100%
1785.........	23%	77%	0%	100%
1787.........	23%	62%	15%	100%
DELEGATES TO THE CONTINENTAL CONGRESS AT END OF YEAR (percentages only)				
1775.........	22%	66%	12%	100%
1777.........	17%	58%	25%	100%
1779.........	16%	61%	22%	100%
1781.........	13%	53%	34%	100%
1783.........	5%	47%	48%	100%
1785.........	0%	43%	57%	100%
1787.........	2%	24%	75%	100%

TABLE B–2

American Presidents, 1774–1989, by Generation

PRESIDENT	GENERATION	LIFESPAN	STATE	TERM	AGE DURING TERM
CONTINENTAL CONGRESS					
Peyton Randolph	AWAKENING	1721–1775	VA	1774, 1775	53, 54
Henry Middleton	AWAKENING	1717–1784	SC	1774–1775	57–58
John Hancock	LIBERTY	1737–1793	MA	1775–1777	38–40
Henry Laurens	LIBERTY	1724–1792	SC	1777–1778	53–54
John Jay	REPUBLICAN	1745–1829	NY	1778–1779	33–34
Samuel Huntington	LIBERTY	1731–1796	CT	1779–1781	48–50
Thomas McKean	LIBERTY	1734–1817	DE	1781	47
John Hanson	AWAKENING	1721–1783	MD	1781–1782	60–61
Elias Boudinot	LIBERTY	1740–1821	NJ	1782–1783	42–43
Thomas Mifflin	REPUBLICAN	1744–1800	PA	1783–1784	39–40
Richard Henry Lee	LIBERTY	1732–1794	VA	1784–1786	52–54
Nathaniel Gorham	LIBERTY	1738–1796	MA	1786–1787	48–49
Arthur St. Clair	LIBERTY	1736–1818	PA	1787–1788	51–52
Cyrus Griffin	REPUBLICAN	1748–1810	VA	1788–1789	40–41

UNITED STATES

PRESIDENT	GENERATION	LIFESPAN	PARTY	TERM	AGE DURING TERM
George Washington	LIBERTY	1732–1799	Federalist	1789–1797	57–65
John Adams	LIBERTY	1735–1826	Federalist	1797–1801	61–65
Thomas Jefferson	REPUBLICAN	1743–1826	Dem-Republican	1801–1809	57–65
James Madison	REPUBLICAN	1751–1836	Dem-Republican	1809–1817	57–65
James Monroe	REPUBLICAN	1758–1831	Dem-Republican	1817–1825	58–67
John Quincy Adams	COMPROMISE	1767–1848	Dem-Republican	1825–1829	57–61
Andrew Jackson	COMPROMISE	1767–1845	Democrat	1829–1837	61–69
Martin Van Buren	COMPROMISE	1782–1862	Democrat	1837–1841	54–58
William Henry Harrison	COMPROMISE	1773–1841	Whig	1841	68
John Tyler	COMPROMISE	1790–1862	Whig	1841–1845	51–54
James Polk	TRANSCENDENTAL	1795–1849	Democrat	1845–1849	49–53
Zachary Taylor	COMPROMISE	1784–1850	Whig	1849–1850	64–65
Millard Fillmore	TRANSCENDENTAL	1800–1874	Whig	1850–1853	50–53
Franklin Pierce	TRANSCENDENTAL	1804–1869	Democrat	1853–1857	48–52
James Buchanan	COMPROMISE	1791–1868	Democrat	1857–1861	65–69
Abraham Lincoln	TRANSCENDENTAL	1809–1865	Republican	1861–1865	52–56
Andrew Johnson	TRANSCENDENTAL	1808–1875	Republican	1865–1869	56–60
Ulysses S. Grant	GILDED	1822–1885	Republican	1869–1877	46–54
Rutherford B. Hayes	GILDED	1822–1893	Republican	1877–1881	54–58
James A. Garfield	GILDED	1831–1881	Republican	1881	49

PRESIDENT	GENERATION	LIFESPAN	PARTY	TERM	AGE DURING TERM
Chester A. Arthur	GILDED	1830–1886	Republican	1881–1885	50–54
Grover Cleveland	GILDED	1837–1908	Democrat	1885–1889	47–51
Benjamin Harrison	GILDED	1833–1901	Republican	1889–1893	55–59
Grover Cleveland	GILDED	1837–1908	Democrat	1893–1897	55–59
William McKinley	PROGRESSIVE	1843–1901	Republican	1897–1901	54–58
Theodore Roosevelt	PROGRESSIVE	1858–1919	Republican	1901–1909	42–50
William H. Taft	PROGRESSIVE	1857–1930	Republican	1909–1913	51–55
Woodrow Wilson	PROGRESSIVE	1856–1924	Democrat	1913–1921	56–64
Warren G. Harding	MISSIONARY	1865–1923	Republican	1921–1923	55–57
Calvin Coolidge	MISSIONARY	1872–1933	Republican	1923–1929	51–56
Herbert Hoover	MISSIONARY	1874–1964	Republican	1929–1933	54–58
Franklin D. Roosevelt	MISSIONARY	1882–1945	Democrat	1933–1945	51–63
Harry S. Truman	LOST	1884–1972	Democrat	1945–1953	60–68
Dwight D. Eisenhower	LOST	1890–1969	Republican	1953–1961	62–70
John F. Kennedy	G.I.	1917–1963	Democrat	1961–1963	43–46
Lyndon B. Johnson	G.I.	1908–1973	Democrat	1963–1969	55–60
Richard M. Nixon	G.I.	1913–	Republican	1969–1974	56–61
Gerald R. Ford	G.I.	1913–	Republican	1974–1977	61–63
Jimmy Carter	G.I.	1924–	Democrat	1977–1981	52–56
Ronald Reagan	G.I.	1911–	Republican	1981–1989	69–77
George Bush	G.I.	1924–	Republican	1989–	64–

TABLE B–3

National Leadership Share, 1775–1989, by Generation

END OF YEAR	BIRTH YEAR UNKNOWN	AWAKENING	LIBERTY	REPUBLICAN	COMPROMISE	TRANSCENDENTAL	GILDED	PROGRESSIVE	MISSIONARY	LOST	G.I.	SILENT	BOOM
1775	NA	51%	38%	11%	—	—	—	—	—	—	—	—	—
1777	NA	25%	62%	12%	—	—	—	—	—	—	—	—	—
1779	NA	21%	56%	24%	—	—	—	—	—	—	—	—	—
1781	NA	18%	57%	25%	—	—	—	—	—	—	—	—	—
1783	NA	14%	62%	24%	—	—	—	—	—	—	—	—	—
1785	NA	12%	60%	29%	—	—	—	—	—	—	—	—	—
1787	NA	12%	43%	45%	—	—	—	—	—	—	—	—	—
1789	1%	3%	41%	55%	—	—	—	—	—	—	—	—	—
1791	1%	1%	34%	64%	—	—	—	—	—	—	—	—	—
1793	1%	—	28%	69%	—	—	—	—	—	—	—	—	—
1795	1%	2%	17%	79%	—	—	—	—	—	—	—	—	—
1797	2%	—	16%	77%	4%	—	—	—	—	—	—	—	—
1799	1%	—	10%	83%	6%	—	—	—	—	—	—	—	—
1801	1%	—	12%	73%	14%	—	—	—	—	—	—	—	—
1803	2%	—	12%	70%	16%	—	—	—	—	—	—	—	—
1805	2%	—	11%	71%	16%	—	—	—	—	—	—	—	—
1807	3%	—	10%	64%	23%	—	—	—	—	—	—	—	—
1809	3%	—	6%	59%	32%	—	—	—	—	—	—	—	—
1811	2%	—	5%	52%	42%	—	—	—	—	—	—	—	—
1813	1%	—	—	47%	51%	—	—	—	—	—	—	—	—
1815	2%	—	—	37%	60%	—	—	—	—	—	—	—	—
1817	2%	—	—	32%	66%	—	—	—	—	—	—	—	—
1819	1%	—	—	25%	73%	1%	—	—	—	—	—	—	—
1821	2%	—	—	20%	77%	1%	—	—	—	—	—	—	—
1823	2%	—	—	15%	80%	2%	—	—	—	—	—	—	—
1825	1%	—	—	7%	85%	6%	—	—	—	—	—	—	—
1827	1%	—	—	8%	82%	9%	—	—	—	—	—	—	—
1829	1%	—	—	6%	81%	12%	—	—	—	—	—	—	—
1831	1%	—	—	4%	76%	18%	—	—	—	—	—	—	—
1833	2%	—	—	4%	67%	27%	—	—	—	—	—	—	—
1835	1%	—	—	2%	61%	35%	—	—	—	—	—	—	—
1837	1%	—	—	1%	55%	43%	—	—	—	—	—	—	—
1839	1%	—	—	—	47%	52%	—	—	—	—	—	—	—

END OF YEAR	BIRTH YEAR UNKNOWN	AWAKENING	LIBERTY	REPUBLICAN	COMPROMISE	TRANSCENDENTAL	GILDED	PROGRESSIVE	MISSIONARY	LOST	G.I.	SILENT	BOOM
1841	1%	—	—	—	35%	64%	—	—	—	—	—	—	—
1843	1%	—	—	—	25%	75%	—	—	—	—	—	—	—
1845	—	—	—	—	22%	78%	—	—	—	—	—	—	—
1847	—	—	—	—	17%	83%	—	—	—	—	—	—	—
1849	—	—	—	—	14%	85%	—	—	—	—	—	—	—
1851	—	—	—	—	13%	86%	1%	—	—	—	—	—	—
1853	—	—	—	—	8%	88%	3%	—	—	—	—	—	—
1855	—	—	—	—	7%	88%	4%	—	—	—	—	—	—
1857	—	—	—	—	4%	90%	6%	—	—	—	—	—	—
1859	—	—	—	—	2%	90%	9%	—	—	—	—	—	—
1861	—	—	—	—	1%	87%	12%	—	—	—	—	—	—
1863	—	—	—	—	1%	78%	21%	—	—	—	—	—	—
1865	—	—	—	—	1%	73%	27%	—	—	—	—	—	—
1867	—	—	—	—	—	63%	37%	—	—	—	—	—	—
1869	—	—	—	—	—	44%	56%	—	—	—	—	—	—
1871	—	—	—	—	—	40%	60%	—	—	—	—	—	—
1873	—	—	—	—	—	39%	60%	1%	—	—	—	—	—
1875	—	—	—	—	—	33%	66%	1%	—	—	—	—	—
1877	—	—	—	—	—	26%	73%	1%	—	—	—	—	—
1879	—	—	—	—	—	21%	76%	3%	—	—	—	—	—
1881	—	—	—	—	—	16%	79%	5%	—	—	—	—	—
1883	—	—	—	—	—	14%	74%	12%	—	—	—	—	—
1885	—	—	—	—	—	11%	74%	15%	—	—	—	—	—
1887	—	—	—	—	—	10%	71%	19%	—	—	—	—	—
1889	—	—	—	—	—	9%	63%	27%	—	—	—	—	—
1891	—	—	—	—	—	5%	60%	34%	1%	—	—	—	—
1893	—	—	—	—	—	2%	58%	39%	1%	—	—	—	—
1895	—	—	—	—	—	2%	46%	48%	4%	—	—	—	—
1897	—	—	—	—	—	1%	36%	57%	7%	—	—	—	—
1899	—	—	—	—	—	—	30%	61%	9%	—	—	—	—
1901	—	—	—	—	—	—	26%	60%	13%	—	—	—	—
1903	—	—	—	—	—	—	23%	57%	20%	—	—	—	—
1905	—	—	—	—	—	—	16%	57%	27%	—	—	—	—
1907	—	—	—	—	—	—	13%	50%	36%	—	—	—	—
1909	—	—	—	—	—	—	10%	50%	40%	—	—	—	—
1911	—	—	—	—	—	—	5%	47%	48%	—	—	—	—
1913	—	—	—	—	—	—	4%	40%	56%	—	—	—	—
1915	—	—	—	—	—	—	3%	36%	60%	1%	—	—	—

END OF YEAR	BIRTH YEAR UNKNOWN	AWAKENING	LIBERTY	REPUBLICAN	COMPROMISE	TRANSCENDENTAL	GILDED	PROGRESSIVE	MISSIONARY	LOST	G.I.	SILENT	BOOM
1917	—	—	—	—	—	—	1%	27%	70%	2%	—	—	—
1919	—	—	—	—	—	—	1%	22%	76%	2%	—	—	—
1921	—	—	—	—	—	—	—	21%	77%	2%	—	—	—
1923	—	—	—	—	—	—	—	13%	83%	4%	—	—	—
1925	—	—	—	—	—	—	—	10%	81%	9%	—	—	—
1927	—	—	—	—	—	—	—	11%	78%	12%	—	—	—
1929	—	—	—	—	—	—	—	7%	77%	16%	—	—	—
1931	—	—	—	—	—	—	—	3%	77%	20%	—	—	—
1933	—	—	—	—	—	—	—	2%	72%	26%	1%	—	—
1935	—	—	—	—	—	—	—	1%	62%	35%	2%	—	—
1937	—	—	—	—	—	—	—	—	52%	44%	3%	—	—
1939	—	—	—	—	—	—	—	1%	42%	50%	6%	—	—
1941	—	—	—	—	—	—	—	—	35%	57%	8%	—	—
1943	—	—	—	—	—	—	—	—	31%	59%	10%	—	—
1945	—	—	—	—	—	—	—	—	25%	58%	16%	—	—
1947	—	—	—	—	—	—	—	—	18%	57%	26%	—	—
1949	—	—	—	—	—	—	—	—	13%	55%	32%	—	—
1951	—	—	—	—	—	—	—	—	10%	49%	40%	—	—
1953	—	—	—	—	—	—	—	—	8%	44%	48%	—	—
1955	—	—	—	—	—	—	—	—	6%	42%	52%	—	—
1957	—	—	—	—	—	—	—	—	4%	37%	59%	—	—
1959	—	—	—	—	—	—	—	—	2%	31%	66%	2%	—
1961	—	—	—	—	—	—	—	—	1%	26%	69%	4%	—
1963	—	—	—	—	—	—	—	—	1%	20%	75%	5%	—
1965	—	—	—	—	—	—	—	—	—	14%	76%	9%	—
1967	—	—	—	—	—	—	—	—	—	11%	74%	14%	—
1969	—	—	—	—	—	—	—	—	—	8%	72%	19%	—
1971	—	—	—	—	—	—	—	—	—	7%	68%	26%	—
1973	—	—	—	—	—	—	—	—	—	4%	63%	33%	—
1975	—	—	—	—	—	—	—	—	—	2%	54%	43%	1%
1977	—	—	—	—	—	—	—	—	—	1%	47%	50%	2%
1979	—	—	—	—	—	—	—	—	—	—	37%	58%	4%
1981	—	—	—	—	—	—	—	—	—	—	30%	63%	6%
1983	—	—	—	—	—	—	—	—	—	—	21%	68%	11%
1985	—	—	—	—	—	—	—	—	—	—	20%	68%	12%
1987	—	—	—	—	—	—	—	—	—	—	18%	66%	16%
1989	—	—	—	—	—	—	—	—	—	—	14%	65%	21%

NOTES ON SOURCES

Birthyears and Ages. For birthyear and other biographical information used throughout this book, we relied on Gale Research Company, *Biography Almanac* (1987); Charles Scribner's Sons, *Dictionary of American Biography* (1930); C. & G. Merriam Co., *Webster's Biographical Dictionary* (1969); R. R. Bowker, *Who's Who in American Politics* (12th ed., 1989–90); Michael Barone and Grant Ujifusa (eds.), *The Almanac of American Politics* (National Journal, various editions); Congressional Quarterly, Inc., *American Leaders, 1789–1987: A Biographical Summary* (1987); John W. Raimo, *Biographical Directory of American Colonial and Revolutionary Governors, 1607–1789* (Meckler Books, 1980); U.S. Congress, *Biographical Directory of the American Congress, 1774–1927* (1928); and Greenwood Press, *American Writers Before 1800: A Biographical and Critical Dictionary* (1983). Where an exact year is unknown, we note "c." (for "circa") before an approximate year often cited by historians. Except in special cases (for instance, in Appendix B, where we list the ages of Presidents), we generally assume that an individual was born on January 1 when we refer to his or her age at a given historical moment, even if this means we sometimes overshoot an age by one year. Thus, we might claim that James Madison was 37 years old on the first Fourth of July, even though Madison (born on August 27, 1749) was actually 36 years old. All Old Style (Julian) calendar dates before 1752 have been converted to New Style (Gregorian) dates.
Political Leaders. Where we refer, in a given year, to the collective age or generation of colonial governors, Continental Congress delegates, congressmen, Supreme Court Justices, or Presidents of the United States, we relied upon information provided by the above sources. To derive the numbers, we used a computer database (described in Appendix B).

Source Abbreviations

Abs	=	Bureau of the Census, *Statistical Abstract of the United States* (annual), by table
AD	=	*American Demographics*
AHR	=	*American Historical Review*
AmB	=	Charles Scribner's Sons, *Dictionary of American Biography* (1930)
AmW	=	Greenwood Press, *American Writers Before 1800: A Biographical and Critical Dictionary* (1983)
AQ	=	*American Quarterly*
CLH	=	Emory Elliott (ed.), *Columbia Literary History of the United States* (1988)
CPR	=	Bureau of the Census, *Current Population Reports* (various series and years)
EnE	=	Glenn Porter (ed.), *Encyclopedia of American Economic History* (1980)
EnS	=	David L. Sills (ed.), *International Encyclopedia of the Social Sciences* (1968)
EPr	=	U.S. Executive Office of the President, *Economic Report of the President* (annual)
HSt	=	Bureau of the Census, *Historical Statistics of the United States, Colonial Times to 1970* (1975), by data series
Hth	=	National Center for Health Statistics, *Health, United States, 1987* (1988), by table
JAH	=	*Journal of American History*
JEH	=	*Journal of Economic History*
JFH	=	*Journal of Family History*
JIH	=	*Journal of Interdisciplinary History*
JSH	=	*Journal of Social History*
OxA	=	Samuel Eliot Morison, *The Oxford History of the American People* (1965)
PO	=	*Public Opinion*
POQ	=	*Public Opinion Quarterly*
NYT	=	*New York Times*
SHG	=	Clifford K. Shipton, *Sibley's Harvard Graduates* (1958), by vol. and class year
SSP	=	Social Security Administration, *Social Security Area Population Projections, 1989* (Actuarial Study No. 105, 1989)
VM	=	*Virginia Magazine*
VSt	=	National Center for Health Statistics, *Vital Statistics of the United States* (1990), volume, part, and table.
WMQ	=	*William and Mary Quarterly*
WP	=	*Washington Post*
WSJ	=	*Wall Street Journal*
Yth	=	U.S. Department of Education, *Youth Indicators, 1988: Trends in the Well-Being of American Youth* (1988)

Population Data. Unless otherwise noted, all numbers referring to population, deaths, births, fertility rates, family size, households, immigration, and population by age and race since 1790 were derived from publications of the Bureau of the Census. Through 1970, most of these data are available in *HSt*, chs. A-C; since 1970, they are available in *CPR*, series P-25, in *Abs*, and in *VSt* (annual). Before 1790, we relied on the non-Census data and sources published in "Colonial and pre-Federal Statistics" in *HSt*, ch. Z. All projections of generational populations into the future (1988–2080) have been derived from the "Middle Series" fertility, mortality, and immigration assumptions in Gregory Spencer, *Projections of the Population of the United States, by Age, Sex, and Race: 1988 to 2080* (Bureau of the Census, 1989). **Population and Immigration by Generation.** Through 1790 (roughly, through the last Compromiser birthyear) the population figures calculated for each generation are an estimate of all non-Indian births within the non-Canadian British colonies of North America plus all permanent net immigration to these territories. After 1790, they include all births within all territories under jurisdiction of the United States plus all permanent net immigration. Since even rudimentary birth data are not available before 1909, nor official immigration data before 1820, many of these figures include estimates. Before the twentieth century, we ordinarily proceeded by (1) interpolating the population at the last cohort birthyear of each generation, (2) estimating the share of the population born since the last cohort birthyear of the previous generation, and (3) adjusting the growth for estimated infant and child mortality. We then further adjusted this "native-born and youth-immigrant" total by adding an estimate of the foreign-born population in this cohort-group that immigrated at older ages. Before 1790, although most demographers and historians agree on approximate population data (total and by age) and on approximate child mortality rates, little is known about overall colonial fertility and immigration. In general, our approach was to combine approximate estimates from various sources (e.g., New England passenger lists, Virginia "headright" registrations, and anecdotal evidence from Philadelphia and New York City) with plausible fertility and mortality estimates to generate numbers consistent with overall population. Our estimate of total immigration from 1620 to 1700 (about 150,000 whites, plus 25,000 blacks) is roughly consistent with other estimates. See, for instance, Wesley Frank Craven, *White, Red, and Black: The Seventeenth-Century Virginian* (1971); review of Craven by Edmund S. Morgan (*VM*, Jul 1972); James Horn, "Servant Immigration to the Chesapeake in the Seventeenth Century," in Thad W. Tate and David L. Ammerman (eds.), *The Chesapeake in the Seventeenth Century* (1979); and David Hackett Fischer, *Albion's Seed: Four British Folkways in North America* (1989). Our immigration estimates from 1700 to 1790 (about 480,000 whites, plus 250,000 blacks) are somewhere in the middle range of most estimates. See J. Potter, "The Growth of Population in America, 1700–1860," in D. V. Glass and D.E.C. Everley (eds.), *Population in History* (1965).

Spelling and Notation. All citations from seventeenth- and eighteenth-century documents have been conformed to modern spelling and punctuation conventions. Lengthy book or pamphlet titles have been abbreviated where convenient. In the references that follow, every source is noted in full the first time it is mentioned under a chapter heading; thereafter, it is noted only by author's last name and date. In Chapters 7 to 11, "Cycle Background" notes cover sources important to two or more generations in the cycle. The "Backgrounds" to individual generations tend to cover sources important to that generation alone.

PREFACE

For a survey of attitudes toward history, see "DemoMemo" (*AD*, Dec 1985); 68% of recent college graduates reported using history "rarely" or "never," the highest percentage for any of the twenty subjects covered (versus, for example, 19% for mathematics, 28% for physical education, 35% for English, and 41% for art). Gail Sheehy, *Passages: Predictable Crises of Adult Life* (1976); Benita Eisler, *Private Lives: Men and Women of the Fifties* (1986). Previous books coauthored by current authors: Lawrence M. Baskir and William Strauss, *Chance and Circumstance: The Draft, the War and the Vietnam Generation* (1978), and *Reconciliation After Vietnam* (1978); Peter G. Peterson and Neil Howe, *On Borrowed Time: How the Growth in Entitlement Spending Threatens America's Future* (1988). On "falsifiability," see Karl R. Popper, *The Logic of Scientific Discovery* (1959), ch. 4. The Schlesinger cycle is most fully presented in Arthur Schlesinger, Jr., *The Cycles of American History* (1984). Leopold von Ranke, *Über die Epochen der neueren Geschichte* (1910), 529–31.

CHAPTER 1: PEOPLE MOVING THROUGH TIME

Thompson, in a speech nominating George Bush for President (Aug 17, 1988), during the Republican National Convention. For references to polls and other data about the Lost, G.I., Silent, Boom, and 13th Generations, see the text and source notes for Chapters 10 and 11. We reserve our brief summary of the "generations school"—its authors and writings—to the Appendix A text and source notes. "Among democratic nations, each generation is a new people" appears in Tocqueville, *Democracy in America* (1835; Random House translation, 1945), 62. On p. 105 appears Tocqueville's more famous remark: "Among democratic nations new families are constantly springing up, others are constantly falling away, and all that remain change their condition; the woof of time is every instant broken and the track of generations effaced. Those who went before are soon forgotten; of those who will come after, no one has any idea. . . ." On Gorbachev's peers, see Ludmilla Alexeyeva and Paul Goldberg, *The Thaw Generation: Coming of Age in the Post-Stalin Era* (1990). For outstanding analyses of generational dynamics abroad since the French Revolution, see the various writings of Anthony Esler, Lewis S. Feuer, Yves Renouard, John Eros, Louis Mazoyer, William J. McGrath, Sigmund Neumann, Julian Peterson, and Peter Loewenberg (Western Europe); Daniel R. Brower, and Abbott Gleason (Russia); Marvin Rintala (Finland); Marvin Zeitlin (Cuba); S. N. Eisenstadt (Africa, Israel); William Quandt (Arab world); and William Preston (Canada). For an excellent bibliography on the subject of foreign generations, see Anthony Esler, *Generations in History: An Introduction to the Concept* (1982), and Alan B. Spitzer, "The Historical Problem of Generations" (*AHR*, Dec 1973). Four reasons why the United States should exhibit sharper generational cleavages than Old World societies are offered in Samuel Huntington, "Generations, Cycles, and Their Role in American Development," in Richard J. Samuels (ed.), *Political Generations and Political Development*

(1976). Samples of Daniel Webster's oratory appear in Paul D. Erickson, *The Poetry of Events: Daniel Webster's Rhetoric of the Constitution and Union* (1986). Francis Fukuyama, "The End of History" (*The National Interest*, Summer 1989).

CHAPTER 2: LIFE ALONG THE GENERATIONAL DIAGONAL

The books cited at the beginning of Chapter 2 all rank among the best generational writings of their respective cohort-groups: Gail Sheehy, *Passages* (1976), 18–19, 101, 344; Cheryl Merser, *"Grown-Ups": A Generation in Search of Adulthood* (1987), 19, 21; Daniel Levinson, *The Seasons of a Man's Life* (1978), ch. 6; Erik Erikson, *Childhood and Society* (1950) and *The Life Cycle Completed* (1982); Erikson (1950), 413. Malcolm Cowley, *Exile's Return* (1934); Ellen Lagemann, *A Generation of Women* (1979). **The Cohort-Group Biography.** The "life-course fallacy" and "fallacy of cohort-centrism" are elegantly defined in Matilda White Riley, "Aging, Social Change, and the Power of Ideas," in Stephen R. Graubard (ed.), *Generations* (1979); see also Riley, "Aging and Cohort Succession: Interpretations and Misinterpretations" (*POQ*, Spring 1973). The third fallacy, what we refer to as the "age-bracket fallacy," Riley (1979) calls the "fallacy of age reification." Sheehy (1976) quotes Borges at the opening of part 1; Levinson (1978), 322. In 1863, Littré first defined the word "cohort" as everyone born at the same time—according to Annie Kriegel, "Generational Difference: The History of an Idea," in Graubard (1979). **The Generational Diagonal.** "Aging seems to produce . . ." is the conclusion of John Crittenden, "Aging and Party Affiliation" (*POQ*, 1962). Nearly a decade later, rebuttals to Crittenden sparked a lively debate: see Neal E. Cutler, "Generation, Maturation, and Party Affiliation," Crittenden, "Reply to Cutler," and Cutler, "Comment" (all in *ibid.*, 1969–70); see also Norval D. Glenn and Ted Hefner, "Further Evidence on Aging and Party Identification" (*ibid.*, Spring 1972). During the 1980s, the simple aging-Republicanism model at last gave way to the alternative hypothesis—perhaps first offered (but little noticed) in A. Campbell et al., *The American Voter* (1960)—that the events of the early 1930s forged a tie between young adults and the Democratic Party strong enough to withstand the test of advancing age. Virtually every age-graded political survey taken during the 1980s showed persons over age 65 leaning more Democratic than the rest of the electorate and persons under age 30 leaning more Republican. See *PO* for the best year-by-year summaries of these findings; see also source notes for Chapters 10 and 11. The pathbreaking results of the Seattle Longitudinal Survey have appeared in Schaie, *Longitudinal Studies of Adult Psychological Development* (1983), "Late Life Potential and Cohort Differences in Mental Abilities," in Marion Perlmutter (ed.), *Late Life Potentials* (Special Publication Series of the Gerontological Society of America, undated), and, with Iris Parham, "Social Responsibility in Adulthood: Ontogenetic and Sociocultural Change" (*Journal of Personality and Social Psychology*, 1974). On the SAT-score decline and the Wirtz Commission findings, see the report of the Advisory Panel on the Scholastic Aptitude Test Score Decline, *On Further Examination* (College Entrance Examination Board, 1977). For the Congressional Budget Office (CBO) cohort analysis of SATs and other aptitude test scores, see CBO, *Educational Achievement: Explanations and Implications of Recent Trends* (Aug 1987) and *Trends in Educational Achievement* (Apr 1986). For the best bibliography on cohort differences in aptitude test scores since World War I, see Brian Waters, *The Test Score Decline* (Human Research Resources Organization, 1981). **Sources for Figure 2-1.** Grade-school aptitude data are taken from CBO (1987); the 17-year-olds' alcohol consumption data from Jerald Bachman, Lloyd Johnson, and Patrick O'Malley, *Monitoring the Future* (Institute for Social Research, Survey Research Center, University of Michigan; annual); the 18-year-olds' alcohol consumption data from the American Council of Education's Cooperative Institutional Research Program at UCLA (directed by Alexander Astin et al.; annual); the arrest rates for arson, robbery, and assault from U.S. Department of Justice, *Age-Specific Arrest Rates, 1965-85* (FBI Crime Reporting Program, 1986); and the "driving while intoxicated" arrest rates from U.S. Department of Justice, *Special Report: Drunk Driving* (Bureau of Justice Statistics, Feb 1988). For suggestive age-bracketed data on suicide, see René Diekstra and Keith Hawton, *Suicide in Adolescence* (1987), and Howard S. Sudak, Amase B. Ford, and Norman B. Rush (eds.), *Suicide in the Young* (1984); see also source notes for Chapter 11. **From Cohorts to Generations.** In the cohort samples ranging from 1633 to 1970, the political leadership data were calculated from the authors' own database (see above and Appendix B); most of the other data are indirectly referenced in the source notes for Chapters 7 through 11. Contemporaneous news reports indicated that seventeen of the twenty-five American soldiers killed in Panama were born between 1967 and 1970.

CHAPTER 3: BELONGING TO A "GENERATION"

"You belong to it . . ." is a statement by Hunt Conroy, a character in Thomas Wolfe, *You Can't Go Home Again* (1934), 715. The 1946–1964 cohort definition of "the Baby Boom" arose simply because demographers observed, in retrospect, that 1946 and 1964 marked an especially large rise and fall in the total fertility rate of American women. That this definition adequately identifies "Baby Boomers" as a behavioral and attitudinal "generation" has since become a standard working assumption among many journalists and social scientists. See Richard Easterlin, *Birth and Fortune* (1980); Landon Jones, *Great Expectations: America and the Baby Boom Generation* (1980); and Cheryl Russell, *100 Predictions for the Baby Boom* (1987). Marías, *Generations: A Historical Method* (1967; University of Alabama Press translation, 1970), 101–2. Alan Spitzer, "The Historical Problem of Generations" (*AHR*, Dec 1973). For a description of the sharp age-graded differences in Vietnam-era draft eligibility, see Lawrence Baskir and William Strauss, *Chance and Circumstance* (1978). Ortega, *The Modern Theme* (1923; Harper and Row translation, 1961), 14–15; Mannheim, "The Problem of Generations," in Paul Kecskemeti (ed.), *Essays on the Sociology of Knowledge* (1952); Ferrari, *Teoria dei periodi politici* (1874), 7–15. **Chronology: Common Age Location in History.** Mannheim (1952); Ortega, in Marías (1970), 84, 98; Pinder, *The Problem of Generation in the History of European Art* (1928), cited in Marías (1970), 114, 117. Merser, *"Grown-Ups": A Generation in Search of Adulthood* (1987), 98. **Attributes: Common Beliefs and Behavior.** Comte, *Cours de philosophie positive* (1838), cited in Marías (1970), 24; Dilthey, various sources, paraphrased in Marías (1970), 52–7; Ortega (1961), 14–15; Julius Peterson, "Literary Generations," in Ermatinger (ed.), *The Philosophy of Literary Science* (1930), cited in Marías (1970), 122. The surveys of college freshmen have been published annually since 1966 by the American Council on Education's Cooperative

Institutional Research Program at the University of California at Los Angeles (directed by Alexander Astin, et al). For marriage data from the early 1700s, see Daniel Scott Smith, "The Demographic History of Colonial New England," in Maris A. Vinovskis (ed.), *Studies in American Historical Demography* (1979), and the summary of historical research presented in Vinovskis, *Fertility in Massachusetts from the Revolution to the Civil War* (1981), 42–9; see also Chapter 7 source notes. **Awareness: Perceived Membership in a Common Generation.** Marías (1970), 106; F. Scott Fitzgerald, "Echoes of the Jazz Age" (1931), in Malcolm and Robert Cowley (eds.), *Fitzgerald and the Jazz Age* (1966). On the 1942–1943 cohort division between Silent and Boom generations, see source notes for Chapters 10 and 11. Ortega, in Marías (1970), 94; Mannheim (1952).

CHAPTER 4: THE FOUR-PART CYCLE

Nixon, in "Footprints in the Cosmic Sand," *WP* 7/20/89; Lewis, in Michael L. Smith, "Selling the Moon," in Richard Fox and T. Jackson Lears (eds.), *The Culture of Consumption* (1983); Reagan, last televised address as President (Jan 1989); Sheehy, *Passages* (1976). For a fuller explanation of the four-part cycle, see Appendix A.

CHAPTER 5: THE CYCLE IN AMERICA

For the complete story of "The Gray Champion," see Nathaniel Hawthorne, *Twice-Told Tales* (first series, 1837). **Eighteen American Generations.** For evidence on the mortality and fecundity of pre-Puritan cohorts, see Chapter 7 source notes. Ortega, in Marías, *Generations: A Historical Method* (1967; University of Alabama Press translation, 1970), 158–9. Arthur Schlesinger, *New Viewpoints in American History* (1925, 1948), ch. 5; Daniel Elazar, *The Generational Rhythm of American Politics* (monograph presented to the Center for the Study of Federalism, Temple University, 1976); Samuel Huntington, "Paradigms of American Politics: Beyond the One, the Two, and the Many" (*Political Science Quarterly*, Mar 1974); and Morton Keller, "Reflections on Politics and Generations in America," in Stephen Graubard (ed.), *Generations* (1979). Merser, *"Grown-Ups": A Generation in Search of Adulthood* (1987), 98. **Spiritual Awakenings.** McLoughlin, *Revivals, Awakenings, and Reform* (1978), ch. 1; see also two works that helped inspire McLoughlin: Anthony F. C. Wallace, "Revitalization Movements" (*American Anthropology*, 1956); and Robert Bellah, *The Broken Covenant* (1975). After describing the "Puritan Awakening" of the early seventeenth century, McLoughlin begins his count with the "First Great Awakening" of the 1730s and 1740s and reaches the "Fourth Great Awakening" by the late 1960s and 1970s.

CHAPTER 6: FROM PURITANS TO MILLENNIALS AND BEYOND

Films: *Rosemary's Baby* (1968); *The Exorcist* (1973); *Exorcist II* (1977); *The Omen* (1976); *Damien-Omen II* (1978); *The Final Conflict* (third in "Omen" series, 1981); *It's Alive!* (1974); *It Lives Again* (1978); *Demon Seed* (1977); *Paper Moon* (1973); *Taxi Driver* (1976); *Bugsy Malone* (1976); *Carrie* (1976); *Willy Wonka and the Chocolate*

Factory (1971); *Kramer vs. Kramer* (1979); *The Shaggy Dog* (1959); *Raising Arizona* (1987); *Three Men and a Baby* (1987); *Baby Boom* (1987); and *Parenthood* (1989). For an excellent analysis of this spate of "bad-child" movies, see Kathy Merlock Jackson, *Images of Children in American Films: A Sociocultural Analysis* (1986). Rental apartments: Vance Packard, *Our Endangered Children* (1983), 44–5. Child abuse: U.S. House of Representatives, *U.S. Children and Their Families* (Report of the Select Committee on Children, Youth and Families; Mar 1987), 74. Homicide rate against children: *Hth*, table 30. Sterilizations: Battelle Memorial Institute, *Cosmopolitan Report: The Changing Life Course of American Women* (1986), vol. 1, 7.36–7. Legal abortions: *Hth*, table 10; for data before 1973, see Battelle Memorial Institute (1986), vol. 1, 7.38. Tax rates: U.S. Treasury analyst Eugene Steuerle, cited in Allan Carlson, "What Happened to the 'Family Wage'?" (*Public Interest*, Spring 1986). Poverty by age bracket: *CPR*, series P-60. R-rated movies: survey cited in Cobbett Steinberg, *Real Facts: The Movie Book of Records* (1981), 41. Teacher salaries: see Chapter 11 source notes. For sources on Cavalier, Liberty, Gilded, and Lost children, see source notes for Chapters 7, 8, 9, and 10, respectively. A lucid account of the early-twentieth-century reversal in adult attitudes toward child safety is available in David Nasaw, *Children of the City: At Work and at Play* (1985), and Vivian A. Zelizer, *Pricing the Priceless Child: The Changing Social Value of Children* (1985). The most striking "great man" accounts of oedipal bonding between son and mother (or hostility between son and father) have featured leaders of what we would call "Idealist" generations. For example: Martin Luther in Erik H. Erikson, *Young Man Luther: A Study in Psychoanalysis and History* (1958); Oliver Cromwell in Antonia Fraser, *Cromwell: Lord Protector* (1974); Jonathan Edwards in Richard L. Bushman, "Jonathan Edwards as Great Man: Identity, Conversion, and Leadership in the Great Awakening," in Robert J. Brugger (ed.), *Our Selves/Our Past: Psychological Approaches to History* (1981); Abraham Lincoln in L. Pierce Clark, *Lincoln: A Psycho-Biography* (1933); Franklin Roosevelt in Noel F. Busch, *What Manner of Man?* (1944). For suggestive insights into the mother (or father) focus of Idealist (or Civic) youths as generational peer groups, see source notes for Chapters 7 through 11— especially, on the (Idealist) Puritans, David Leverenz, *The Language of Puritan Feeling: An Exploration in Literature, Psychology, and Social History* (1980); on the (Idealist) Awakeners, "The Evangelicals," in Philip Greven, *The Protestant Temperament* (1977); on the (Civic) Republicans, Catherine Albanese, *Sons of the Fathers* (1976); on the (Idealist) Transcendentals, George B. Forgie, *Patricide in the House Divided: A Psychological Interpretation of Lincoln and His Age* (1979); on the (Civic) G.I.s, Betty Friedan, *The Feminine Mystique* (1963); and on the (Idealist) Boomers, Kenneth Keniston, *Young Radicals* (1968), Lewis Feuer, *The Conflict of Generations: The Character and Significance of Student Movements* (1969), and Henry Malcolm, *Generation of Narcissus* (1971). Works by the cited leaders of "Civic" generations: James I of England (pre-Colonial "generation of 1560"), *Daemonology* (1597); Cotton Mather (Glorious), *The Wonders of the Invisible World* (1692); and Philip Wylie (G.I.), *Generation of Vipers* (1942). **Cycle Theories of American History.** Frank Klingberg, "The Historical Alternation of Moods in American Foreign Policy" (*World Politics*, Vol. 4, 1951–52). For the Schlesingers' cycle theory, see Arthur Schlesinger, *Paths to the Present* (1949), and Arthur Schlesinger, Jr., *The Cycles of American History* (1986). On Schlesinger Jr.'s forecast on the 1988 election, see Schlesinger, Jr., "Wake Up, Liberals, Your Time Has

Come," *WP 5/1/88;* see also discussion in *"Conventional Wisdom" (Newsweek,* Nov 21, 1988), and "Letters to the Editor" *(Newsweek, Dec* 19, 1988). "It is the generational experience . . ." appears in Schlesinger, Jr. (1986), 29. For a discussion of the "political generation" concept, see Marvin Rintala, "Generations" article in *EnS.* We summarize the tradition of "generations" writing—including the pioneers of the four-part cycle mentioned here—in Appendix A text and source notes. **The Predictive Record of the Generational Cycle.** Richard Cohen of the *Washington Post* (Oct 1989) was the first to coax Joan Quigley to admit that her astrological charts failed to predict "the Big One" in her own hometown. **Looking for Analogues.** Mentré, in Marías (1970), 155; Pinder, in *ibid.,* 115–16. Esler, *Generations in History: An Introduction to the Concept* (1982), 152.

CHAPTER 7: THE COLONIAL CYCLE

COLONIAL CYCLE BACKGROUND. See Daniel J. Boorstin, *The Americans: The Colonial Experience* (1958); David Hackett Fischer, *Albion's Seed: Four British Folkways in America* (1989); "Transfer of Culture," in T. H. Breen, *Puritans and Adventurers* (1980). On New England: James Truslow Adams, *The Founding of New England* (1921); and Samuel Eliot Morison, *Builders of the Bay Colony* (1930). On the southern colonies: Sigmund Diamond, "Virginia in the Seventeenth Century" *(American Journal of Sociology,* 1958); and Bernard Bailyn, "Politics and Social Structure in Virginia," in James M. Smith (ed.), *Seventeenth-Century America* (1959). On family life: Edmund Morgan, *The Puritan Family* (1944); John Demos, *A Little Commonwealth: Family Life in Plymouth Colony* (1970); and Gerald F. Moran and Maris A. Vinovskis, "The Puritan Family and Religion: A Critical Reappraisal" *(WMQ,* Jan 1982). On community life: Philip J. Greven, Jr., *Four Generations: Population, Land, and Family in Colonial Andover, Massachusetts* (1970); Kenneth A. Lockridge, *A New England Town: The First Hundred Years: Dedham, Massachusetts, 1636–1736* (1970); Sumner Chilton Powell, *Puritan Village* (1965); and Edward M. Cook, Jr., *The Fathers of the Towns: Leadership and Community Structure in Eighteenth-Century New England* (1976). On the role of women: Laurel Thatcher Ulrich, *Good Wives: Image and Reality in the Lives of Women in Northern New England, 1650–1750* (1982); Lyle Koehler, *A Search for Power: The "Weaker Sex" in Seventeenth-Century New England* (1980); and Julia Cherry Spruill, *Women's Life and Work in the Southern Colonies* (1938). On education and intellectual life: Samuel Eliot Morison, *The Intellectual Life of Colonial New England* (1936); Bernard Bailyn, *Education in the Forming of American Society* (1960); Kenneth A. Lockridge, *Literacy in Colonial New England* (1974); and Perry Miller, *The New England Mind: The Seventeenth Century* (1939) and *The New England Mind: From Colony to Province* (1953). On religion: David Hall, *The Faithful Shepherd: A History of the New England Ministry in the Seventeenth Century* (1972); and David Lovejoy, *Religious Enthusiasm in the New World* (1985). On old age: David E. Stannard, *The Puritan Way of Death* (1977); John Demos, "Old Age in Early New England," in John Demos and Sarane Spence Boocock (eds.), *Turning Points: Historical and Sociological Essays on the Family* (1978); and David Hackett Fischer, *Growing Old in America* (1977). On the economy and demographics: Gary M.

Walton, "The Colonial Economy," in *EnE;* James A. Henretta, *The Evolution of American Society, 1700–1815* (1973); and essays in Maris A. Vinovskis (ed.), *Studies in American Historical Demography* (1979).

COLONIAL CYCLE REFERENCES. Shakespeare, *Hamlet* (c. 1600); Foxe, *Book of Martyrs* (first English edition, 1563). On James I's notorious campaign against witchcraft, see H. R. Trevor-Roper, "The European Witch-Craze of the Sixteenth and Seventeenth Centuries," in *Religion, the Reformation, and Social Change* (1967). **Preparing for the Puritans: The Reformation Cycle.** Countless historians have referred to the "Reformation generation"; for a thorough tour through every stripe of spiritual leader and extremist sect (and a discussion of the Reformation's generational dimension), see George Williams, *The Radical Reformation* (1967). Anthony Esler, *The Aspiring Mind of the Elizabethan Younger Generation* (1966), 4–5, 66, 68, 185, 240–2. **The Colonial Cycle.** Aside from the afflicted girls and several local magistrates, we do not know for certain who joined the large crowd that watched the September 22 executions at Salem. We know that Stoughton and both Mathers had been present at previous executions and that the New England elite—including Leverett, the Brattles, and the ailing Bradstreet in Boston—took an avid interest in the trials. William Drummond (one of Bacon's rebel leaders, executed in 1676 by William Berkeley), cited in Clifford Dowdey, *The Virginia Dynasties: The Emergence of "King" Carter and the Golden Age* (1969), 85–6. Thomas Brattle had already been commended by Isaac Newton for his observations (at age 22) on Halley's Comet in 1680. Quote on Leverett is from a eulogy by Nathaniel Appleton, *A Great Man Fallen in Israel* (1724).

PURITAN BACKGROUND. For an overview of the Puritan peer personality: Edmund Morgan, *The Puritan Dilemma: The Story of John Winthrop* (1958); John Adair, *Founding Fathers: The Puritans in England and America* (1982); David Leverenz, *The Language of Puritan Feeling* (1980); Michael Walzer, *The Revolution of the Saints* (1968); Edmund Morgan, *Visible Saints: The History of a Puritan Idea* (1963); Miller (1939); Larzer Ziff, *Puritanism in America* (1973); Francis J. Bremer, *The Puritan Experiment* (1976); Andrew Delbanco, *The Puritan Ordeal* (1989); and T. H. Breen and Stephen Foster, "The Puritans' Greatest Achievement: A Study of Social Cohesion in Seventeenth-Century Massachusetts" (*JAH,* Jun 1973). On the sad story of the Puritan Chesapeake settlers: "Looking Out for Number One," in Breen (1980); and Carville V. Earle, "Environment, Disease, and Mortality in Early Virginia," in Thad W. Tate and David L. Ammerman (eds.), *The Chesapeake in the Seventeenth Century* (1979). On the Puritans' European background: Lawrence Stone, *The Causes of the English Revolution* (1972) and "Social Mobility in England, 1500–1700" (*Past and Present,* Apr 1966); H. R. Trevor-Roper, "Religion, the Reformation, and Social Change" and "The General Crisis of the Seventeenth Century," in Trevor-Roper (1967); Esler (1966); and Christopher Hill, *Society and Puritanism in Pre-Revolutionary England* (1967).

PURITAN REFERENCES. Winthrop, "A Model of Christian Charity" (1630), in Edmund Morgan, *Puritan Political Ideas* (1965), doc. 5. On age of New England settlers, see "Moving to the New World," in Breen (1980). On age and mortality of Virginia settlers, see Diamond (1958), and Irene W. D. Hecht, "The Virginia Muster of 1624/5 as a Source for Demographic History" (*WMQ,* Jan 1973). Mayflower passengers quoted by Francis

Higginson, in A. L. Rowse, *The Elizabethans in America* (1959), 129–30. Cotton, *God's Promise to His Plantations* (1634). **Facts.** Education: By 1640, there were 114 university men in New England; for family ratio, see Morison (1930), 184. Hobbes, in Mark H. Curtis, "The Alienated Intellectuals of Early Stuart England" (*Past and Present,* 1962). Age of M.P.s: Stone (1972), 133. Women: Keith Thomas, "Women and the Civil War Sects" (*Past and Present,* 1958); Lovejoy (1985), chs. 1–3; and Emery Battis, *Saints and Sectaries: Anne Hutchinson and the Antinomian Controversy in the Massachusetts Bay Colony* (1962). Longevity: Fischer, (1977), 42–7; and John Demos, "Notes on Life in Plymouth Colony" (*WMQ,* Apr 1965). **Youth.** George Herbert, *Doomsday* (pub. posthumously, 1633). Joseph Hall, "A Puritane," in *Characters of Virtues and Vices* (1608); see also "Malvolio" in William Shakespeare, *Twelfth Night* (c. 1601), and "Zeal-of-the-Land Busy" in Ben Jonson, *Bartholomew Fair* (1614). Leverenz (1980), 3–4; see also Delbanco (1989). **Coming of Age.** Herbert, in Lovejoy (1985), 9; Winthrop, in Morgan (1958), 12, 29. **Rising Adulthood.** On "love," see Hall (1972), 87, Breen and Foster (1973), and Lockridge (1970). Cotton, in Morison (1930), 116; Wheelwright, in Lovejoy (1985), 84. **Midlife.** Morgan (1963), 129–30. Winthrop's famous "little speech" (1645), in Richard S. Dunn, *Puritans and Yankees: The Winthrop Dynasty of New England, 1630–1717* (1962), 24. **Elderhood.** "Cosmic optimism" appears in Miller, *The New England Mind: The Seventeenth Century* (1961), 37–8; comment on John Eliot, in Adair (1982), 248; Shepard, in *ibid.,* 128.

CAVALIER BACKGROUND. For an outstanding analysis of the negative generational self-image of New England Cavaliers, see Emory Elliott, *Power and the Pulpit in Puritan New England* (1975). See also Leverenz (1980), ch. 7; Delbanco (1989), ch. 7; and Perry Miller, "Declension in a Bible Commonwealth," in *Nature's Nation* (1967). On the Cavalier "literature of self-condemnation": Miller, *Errand into the Wilderness* (1956). On the southern Cavalier: the excellent essays in Thad W. Tate and David L. Ammerman (eds.), *The Chesapeake in the Seventeenth Century* (1979); Warren M. Billings (ed.), *The Old Dominion in the Seventeenth Century: A Documentary History of Virginia, 1606–1689* (1975); and Dowdey (1969). On Cavalier adventure: Alan Vance Briceland, *Westward from Virginia: The Exploration of the Virginia-Carolina Frontier, 1650–1710* (1987); Frank Sherry, *Raiders and Rebels: The Golden Age of Piracy* (1986); and Cyrus H. Karraker, *Piracy Was a Business* (1953). On the significance of King Philip's war to midlife New Englanders: Richard Slotkin and James K. Folsom, *So Dreadful a Judgment* (1978); Douglas Leach, *Flintlock and Tomahawk: New England in King Philip's War* (1958); and Peter N. Carroll, *Puritanism and the Wilderness: The Intellectual Significance of the New England Frontier, 1629–1700* (1969). On Bacon's Rebellion: Wilcomb E. Washburn, *The Governor and the Rebel* (1957).

CAVALIER REFERENCES. Josiah Coale, in Lovejoy (1985), 116; most of Lovejoy's "Quakers of the First Generation" were Cavaliers. On vital statistics in the Chesapeake: Darrett B. and Anita H. Rutman, " 'Now-Wives and Sons-in-Law': Parental Death in a Seventeenth-Century Virginia County," in Tate and Ammerman (1979). Berkeley, in Breen (1980), 128. Stone (1972), 133; he adds, "The unexpected conservatism of the young is still puzzling." On the age and timing of the servant migration to the Chesapeake: Wesley Frank Craven, *White, Red, and Black: The Seventeenth-Century Virginian* (1971), and review by Edmund Morgan (*VM,* Jul 1972). Fischer (1989); Richard S. Dunn,

Puritans and Yankees: The Winthrop Dynasty of New England, 1630–1717 (1962), vi,
191–2; Bernard Bailyn, *The New England Merchants in the Seventeenth Century* (1955),
109. **Facts.** Odds for Maryland servant: Russell R. Menard, "From Servant to Freeholder:
Status Mobility and Property Accumulation in Seventeenth-Century Maryland" (*WMQ*,
Jan 1973). Regional differences: Fischer (1989); and "Transfer of Culture," in T. H.
Breen (1980). Educational decline: the consensus of historians on New England's second
generation is summarized in Elliott (1975), 45–51. Harvard graduates: Morison (1930),
211. **Youth.** On Chesapeake servants: see Peter Wilson Coldham, "The 'Spiriting' of
London Children to Virginia: 1648–1685" (*VM*, Jul 1975); Marcus W. Jernegan, *Laboring
and Dependent Classes in Colonial America, 1607–1783* (1931); and Lois Green Carr
and Lorena S. Walsh, "The Planter's Wife: The Experiences of White Women in Seventeenth-Century Maryland" (*WMQ*, Oct 1977). Revel, in Billings (1975), 137; Wigglesworth, in Richard M. Gummere, *Seven Wise Men of America* (1967), 32; Eleazar
Mather, in Elliott (1975), 18. **Coming of Age.** Miller (1953), 11; Richard Mather, in
ibid., 28. For a sampling of "the bitter charges of the aging first-generation settlers
against their sons," see Elliott (1975); mayor of Bristol, in James Horn, "Servant Emigration to the Chesapeake in the Seventeenth Century," in Tate and Ammerman (1969);
Berkeley, in Dowdey (1969), ch. 2; Stoughton, *New England's True Interest* (1670);
Handlin, "The Significance of the Seventeenth Century," in Paul Goodman (ed.), *Essays
in American Colonial History* (1967). **Rising Adulthood.** Winthrop, in Dunn (1962),
199–200; Mather, *An Earnest Exhortation* (1676). **Midlife.** On Cavalier collaboration
with James II's new regime, see Theodore B. Lewis, "Land Speculation and the Dudley
Council of 1686" (*WMQ*, Apr 1974). At least fifteen of the nineteen "witch" suspects
(two men, thirteen women) executed in Salem in 1692 appear to have been Cavaliers;
most of the accusers were younger. See John Demos, *Entertaining Satan: Witchcraft and
the Culture of Early New England* (1982); and Carol Karlsen, *The Devil in the Shape of
a Woman* (1987). From the 1660s on, the average age of witch suspects had been rising—
apparently tracking this cohort group over time. According to Demos, all fourteen Salem
suspects who had previously been accused of witchcraft were Cavaliers; in personality,
they were "abrasive in style, contentious in character—and stubbornly resilient in the
face of adversity." **Elderhood.** Selyns, in *AmW;* Mather, *Pray for the Rising Generation*
(1679); Tompson, *New England's Crisis* (1676), in Slotkin and Folsom (1978), 215;
Scottow, *Old Men's Tears for Their Own Declensions* (1691); Burt, *A Lamentation* (pub.
posthumously, 1720); Wigglesworth, *God's Controversy with New England* (1662); Demos (1978).

GLORIOUS BACKGROUND. On the history-shaping event that united them as a generation:
David S. Lovejoy, *The Glorious Revolution in America* (1972). On the first (King William's) war against France: Howard Peckham, *The Colonial Wars 1689–1762* (1964).
On the social achievements of southern Glorious: "Horses and Gentlemen," in Breen
(1980); Carole Shammas, "English-Born and Creole Elites in Turn-of-the-Century Virginia," and David W. Jordan, "Political Stability and the Emergence of a Native Elite
in Maryland," both in Tate and Ammerman (1979); Jack P. Greene, "Foundations of
Political Power in the Virginia House of Burgesses, 1720–1750," in T. H. Breen (ed.),
Shaping Southern Society: The Colonial Experience (1976); and Virginia Bernhard, "Poverty and the Social Order in Seventeenth-Century Virginia" (*VM*, Apr 1977). For New
England: Philip S. Haffenden, *New England in the English Nation, 1689–1715* (1974);

and "War, Taxes, and Political Brokers," in Breen (1980). On the tightening trend in childhood and adolescence: Roger Thompson, "Adolescent Culture in Colonial Massachusetts" (*JFH*, Summer 1984); and Lorena S. Walsh, " 'Till Death Us Do Part': Marriage and Family in Seventeenth-Century Maryland," in Tate and Ammerman (1979). On changing attitudes toward sex roles: Spruill (1938); Ulrich, (1982), and "Vertuous Women Found: New England Ministerial Literature, 1668–1735" (*AQ*, Winter 1976); and Margaret W. Masson, "The Typology of the Female as a Model for the Regenerate: Puritan Preaching, 1690–1730" (*Signs*, Winter 1976). On important parallels between the world views of Cotton Mather and Robert Beverley: Richard S. Dunn, "Seventeenth-Century English Historians of America," in Smith (1959).

GLORIOUS REFERENCES. Colman, in Miller (1953), 414; Thomas Shepard, Jr., *Eye Salve* (1673); Wadsworth, in Miller (1953), 463; Mather, in *ibid.*, 440, 410; Colman, in *AmW;* Carter, in Dowdey (1969), 220; Wadsworth, in Ulrich (1976). For the best description of this elevation of "reason" and "good works," see Miller (1953), chs. 14–16. On the compatibility of science and witchcraft: Sanford Fox, *Science and Justice: The Massachusetts Witchcraft Trials* (1968); and Kenneth Silverman, *The Life and Times of Cotton Mather* (1984). **Facts.** Election to town offices: Cook, Jr. (1976), 105–7. Virginia House of Burgesses: Henretta (1973), 91. **Youth.** Virginia and Massachusetts statutes, cited in Bailyn (1960), 26; Increase Mather, *The Divine Right of Infant Baptism* (1690); Oakes, *New England Pleaded With* (1673). On the new attitude toward conversion: "Beyond Conversionism," in Hall (1972); Perry Miller, " 'Preparation for Salvation' in Seventeenth-Century New England" (*Journal of the History of Ideas,* 1943); Robert G. Pope, *The Half-Way Covenant: Church Membership in Puritan New England* (1969); and Perry Miller, "The Half-Way Covenant" (*New England Quarterly,* Dec 1933). Oakes, *The Unconquerable . . . Soldier* (1674); John Carter, in Dowdey (1969), 101. **Coming of Age.** See Lovejoy (1972); Mather, in Miller (1953), 159; "War, Taxes, and Political Brokers," in Breen (1980); Mather, *Addresses to Old Men and Young Men and Little Children* (1690). **Rising Adulthood.** Cotton, *A Meet Help* (1699); Budd, *Good Order Established* (1685). **Midlife.** Wise, *A Word of Comfort* (1721). On economic progress: Walton (1980); Henretta (1973); Terry L. Anderson, "Economic Growth in Colonial New England" (*JEH,* Mar 1979); and David H. Flaherty, *Privacy in Colonial New England* (1972). On the establishment of slavery: Winthrop D. Jordan, *White Over Black: American Attitudes Toward the Negro, 1550–1812* (1968); "A Changing Labor Force and Race Relations in Virginia, 1660–1710," in Breen (1980); Paul C. Palmer, "Servant into Slave: The Evolution of the Legal Status of the Negro Laborer in Colonial Virginia" (*South Atlantic Quarterly,* Summer 1966); and James H. Brewer, "Negro Property Owners in Seventeenth-Century Virginia" (*WMQ,* Oct 1955). Sewall, *The Selling of Joseph* (1700); Sewall, in Arthur Zilversmit, *The First Emancipation: The Abolition of Slavery in the North* (1967), 60. **Elderhood.** Colman, in Miller (1953), 400; sumptuary laws, Stannard (1977), 115; Mather, in Stannard (1977), 150, and in Demos (1978). Colman, *Sermon after the Funerals of Brattle and Pemberton* (1717); Carter, in Dowdey (1969), 154.

ENLIGHTENMENT BACKGROUND. For two skillful portraits of the Enlightener peer personality—in two regions—see Peter N. Carroll, *The Other Samuel Johnson: A Psychohistory of Early New England* (1978), and Kenneth A. Lockridge, *The Diary, and Life, of William Byrd II of Virginia, 1674–1744;* see also "The Generations of the Golden Age" and "Life in Thrall," in Clifford Dowdey, *The Golden Age: A Climate for Greatness, Virginia 1732–1775* (1970). On the Enlighteners' impact on political life: William Pencak, *War, Politics, and Revolution in Provincial Massachusetts* (1981); Kenneth A. Lockridge and Alan Kreider, "The Evolution of Massachusetts Town Government, 1640 to 1740" (*WMQ,* Oct 1966); Edward M. Cook, Jr., "Social Behavior and Changing Values in Dedham, Massachusetts, 1700–1775" (*WMQ,* Oct 1970); and Jack P. Greene, "The Growth of Political Stability," in John Parker and Carol Urness (eds.), *The American Revolution: A Heritage of Change* (1973). On their impact on cultural and religious life: James Truslow Adams, *Provincial Society, 1690–1763* (1927); Thomas J. Wertenbaker, *The Golden Age of Colonial Culture* (1949); and J. William T. Youngs, Jr., "Congregational Clericalism: New England Ordinations Before the Great Awakening" (*WMQ,* Jul 1974). On slavery: Allan Kulikoff, "The Beginnings of the Afro-American Family in Maryland," in Land, Carr, and Papenfuse (eds.), *Law, Society, and Politics in Early Maryland* (1977).

ENLIGHTENMENT REFERENCES. "Speeches of the Students of the College of William and Mary Delivered May 1, 1699" (*WMQ,* Oct 1930); Pencak (1981), 61; Foxcroft, in Miller (1953), 449; Appleton, *Faithful Ministers* (1743). **Facts.** Mobility in New England: "Migration and the Family in Colonial New England: The View from Genealogies" (*JFH,* 1984). Marriages in the South: Walsh (1979). Royal Society memberships: see list in Morison (1936), 274–5. **Youth.** On Johnson's "tame and pliable" youth, see Carroll (1978); on his later, critical reference to "bogeymen," see *ibid.,* 159. Willard, *A Child's Portion* (1684); Mather, *The Young Man's Preservative* (1701). On the implosion of family life in New England, see "Puritan Tribalism," in Morgan (1944). **Coming of Age.** Miller (1953), 335. On coming-of-age behavior: Dowdey (1970) and Carl Bridenbaugh, *Cities in the Wilderness: The First Century of Urban Life in America, 1625–1742* (1968). **Rising Adulthood.** *Gazette,* cited in *ibid.,* 466; Paine (father of Constitution signer Robert Treat Paine), in Miller (1953), 321; Henry Peacham, *The Complete Gentleman* (1622); on Byrd II, see Lockridge (1987), 21. Greene (1973). **Midlife.** Wigglesworth, in Miller (1953), 454; Niles, *Tristitiae Ecclesiarum* (1745); Doolittle, *A Short Narrative* (1750); Henry Flynt on Appleton, in *SHG,* vol. V, Class of 1712; Dexter, in William T. Youngs, Jr., *God's Messengers: Religious Leadership in Colonial New England, 1700–1750* (1976), 128. **Elderhood.** Chauncy, in Miller (1953), 420; Johnson, in Carroll (1978), 140; Gay's acquaintance, in *SHG,* vol. VI, Class of 1714; Perkins' letter in *ibid.,* vol. VI, Class of 1717; Greaves and Appleton, in *ibid.,* vol. V, Class of 1703 and 1712; the (self-written) epitaph of Byrd II, in Alden Hatch, *The Byrds of Virginia* (1969), 174–5. The courtroom victory of printer Peter Zenger is commonly cited as a pioneering victory for "freedom of the press."

CHAPTER 8: THE REVOLUTIONARY CYCLE

REVOLUTIONARY CYCLE BACKGROUND. See Boorstin (1958); Fischer (1989); Dowdey (1970); John C. Miller, *Origins of the American Revolution* (1943); Rhys Isaac, *The Transformation of Virginia, 1740–1790* (1982); Gary B. Nash, *The Urban Crucible: Social Change, Political Consciousness, and the Origins of the American Revolution*

(1979); Marcus Cunliffe, *The Nation Takes Shape: 1789–1837* (1959). On political leadership: Cook (1976); James Kirby Martin, *Men in Rebellion* (1973); Jackson Turner Main, *Political Parties Before the Constitution* (1973); and H. and James Henderson, *Party Politics in the Continental Congress* (1974). On family life and generational themes: Edwin G. Burroughs and Michael Wallace, "The American Revolution: The Ideology and Psychology of National Liberation" (*Perspectives in American History*, 1972); Jay Fliegelman, *Prodigals and Pilgrims: The American Revolution Against Patriarchal Authority, 1750–1800* (1982); Peter Shaw, *American Patriots and the Rituals of Revolution* (1981); Michael Kammen, *A Season of Youth: The American Revolution and the Historical Imagination* (1978); Melvin Yazawa, *From Colonies to Commonwealth: Familial Ideology and the Beginnings of the American Republic* (1985); Daniel Blake Smith, "The Study of the Family in Early America: Trends, Problems, and Prospects" (*WMQ*, Jan 82); and Rhys Isaac, "Order and Growth, Authority and Meaning in Colonial New England" (*AHR*, Feb-Jun 1971). On community life: Richard L. Bushman, *From Puritan to Yankee: Character and the Social Order in Connecticut, 1690–1765* (1970); Greven (1970); Daniel Blake Smith, *Inside the Great House: Planter Life in Eighteenth-Century Chesapeake Society* (1980); Carl Bridenbaugh, *Cities in the Wilderness* (1968) and *Cities in Revolt: Urban Life in America, 1743–1776* (1955); Michael Zuckerman, *Peaceable Kingdoms: New England Towns in the Eighteenth Century* (1970); Christine Leigh Heyrman, *Commerce and Culture: The Maritime Communities of Colonial Massachusetts, 1690–1750* (1984); Douglas Lamar Jones, *Village and Seaport: Migration and Society in Eighteenth-Century Massachusetts* (1981); Gregory H. Nobles, *Divisions Throughout the Whole: Politics and Society in Hampshire County, Massachusetts, 1740–1775* (1983); and Robert A. Gross, *The Minutemen and Their World* (1976). On the role of women: Mary Beth Norton, *Liberty's Daughters: The Revolutionary Experience of American Women, 1750–1800* (1980); Elaine F. Crane, "Dependence in the Era of Independence: The Role of Women in a Republican Society," in Jack P. Greene (ed.), *The American Revolution* (1987); Joan Hoff Wilson, "The Illusion of Change: Women and the American Revolution," in Alfred F. Young (ed.), *The American Revolution* (1976); and Linda K. Kerber, *Women of the Republic: Intellect and Ideology in Revolutionary America* (1980). On childhood and education: Philip Greven, *The Protestant Temperament: Patterns of Child-Rearing, Religious Experience, and the Self in Early America* (1977); Edward Shorter, *The Making of the Modern Family* (1975); Lockridge (1974); Lawrence A. Cremin, *American Education: The Colonial Experience, 1607–1783* (1970); James Axtell, *The School upon a Hill: Education and Society in Colonial New England* (1974); Peter Gregg Slater, *Children in the New England Mind* (1977); John F. Roche, *The Colonial Colleges in the War for American Independence* (1986); and Melvin Yazawa, "Creating a Republican Citizenry," in Green (1987). On religion: Lovejoy (1985); William G. McLoughlin, "The Role of Religion in the Revolution," in Stephen G. Kurtz and James H. Hutson, *Essays on the American Revolution* (1973); Cushing Strout, *The New Heavens and New Earth: Political Religion in America* (1973); John F. Berens, *Providence and Patriotism in Early America, 1640–1815* (1978); and Nathan O. Hatch, *The Sacred Cause of Liberty: Republican Thought and the Millennium in Revolutionary New England* (1977).

REVOLUTIONARY CYCLE REFERENCES. Langdon, *Government Corrupted by Vice, and Recovered by Righteousness* (delivered in Watertown, May 31, 1775). The exact text of Langdon's sermon in Cambridge sixteen days later has not survived, but we can safely assume it was (if possible) even more vehement; the next day, Langdon visited and prayed with the wounded. Prescott, in *AmB*. Chauncy, *Seasonable Thoughts on the State of Religion in New England* (1743). Bellamy in Heimert (1966), 471; Hawley, in *ibid.*, 470; Morgan, in North Callahan, *Daniel Morgan, Ranger of the Revolution* (1961), 25. Cecilia M. Kenyon, "Men of Little Faith: The Anti-Federalists on the Nature of Representative Government" (*WMQ*, 1955). Brackenridge portion of Brackenridge and Philip Freneau, *The Rising Glory of America* (1771); Evans, *A Discourse Delivered in New York* (1784), in Royster (1979), 246; John Adams to Jefferson (Aug 24, 1815), in Lester J. Cappon (ed.), *The Adams-Jefferson Letters* (1959); Rush, *An Address to the People of the United States* (1787); Dwight, *America* (1772); Morgan, "The American Revolution Considered as an Intellectual Movement," in Arthur M. Schlesinger, Jr., and Morton White (eds.), *Paths of American Thought* (1963). Adams, in Samuel Flagg Bemis, *John Quincy Adams and the Foundations of American Foreign Policy* (1949), 28; Jackson, "Announcement to His Soldiers" (1812), cited in Michael Paul Rogin, *Fathers and Children* (1975), 14; Webster, in Merrill D. Peterson, *The Great Triumvirate* (1987), 35.

AWAKENING BACKGROUND. Any effort to understand this generation must begin with the event that shaped them as rising adults. For the big picture: McLoughlin (1979), ch. 3; J. M. Bumsted and John E. Van de Wetering, *What Must I Do to Be Saved?: The Great Awakening in Colonial America* (1976); and Cedric B. Cowing, *The Great Awakening and the American Revolution* (1971). For finer detail: Bushman (1970); Nobles (1981); Heyrmann (1984); Nash (1979); Harry S. Stout, "The Great Awakening in New England Reconsidered: The New England Clergy" (*JSH*, Fall 1974); James Walsh, "The Great Awakening in the First Congregational Church of Woodbury, Connecticut" (*WMQ*, Oct 1971); J. M. Bumsted, "Religion, Finance, and Democracy in Massachusetts: The Town of Norton as a Case Study" (*JAH*, Mar 1971); and Cowing, "Sex and Preaching in the Great Awakening" (*AQ*, Fall 1968). The definitive description of the evangelical (and, implicitly, generational) link between the Great Awakening and the Revolution is Alan Heimert, *Religion and the American Mind: From the Great Awakening to the Revolution* (1966); see also McLoughlin (1973); Strout (1973); Behrens (1978); Hatch (1977); Miller, "From the Covenant to the Revival," in *Nature's Nation* (1967); Morgan, "The Puritan Ethic and the American Revolution" (*WMQ*, 1967); and Harry S. Stout, "Religion, Communications, and the Ideological Origins of the American Revolution" (*WMQ*, Oct 1967). For the best biographical prototype of the Awakener peer personality, see Christopher M. Jedrey, *The World of John Cleaveland: Family and Community in Eighteenth-Century New England* (1979).

AWAKENING REFERENCES. *Post* on Davenport, cited in Nash (1979), 210; Salem minister, in *ibid.*, 212; Bushman (1970), 187, and (ed.) *The Great Awakening* (1970), xi. French diplomat Barbe Marbois on Benezet during the Revolution, in *AmW;* for preaching "hate" and much more, see "Samuel Adams," in *SHG*, vol. X, Class of 1740; Franklin, entry for c. 1721 in *Autobiography* (1790). Edward Everett (1835) on Adams in Pauline Maier, *The Old Revolutionaries* (1980), 47; John Adams on Sherman, in *AmB;* for Edwards, see Heimert (1966); Bernard Bailyn, *The Ordeal of Thomas Hutchinson* (1974). Mayhew, *A Discourse Concerning Unlimited Submission* (1750); Hawley, in Shaw

(1981), 145; Trumbell, in *AmB;* Oliver, esp. in *Origin and Progress of the American Revolution: A Tory View* (unpublished until 1961); Curwen and Auchmuty, both cited in *AmW*. **Facts.** New churches, and numbers and ages of conversions: Cowing (1971), 1; Bumsted and Wetering (1976), ch. 7; Walsh (1971); and Strout (1973), 41. "Age of Presbyterians: Research of William H. Kenney," in *ibid.,* 39. College students: *SHG*. Publications: Hatch (1977), 39; and Ruth H. Bloch, *Visionary Republic: Millennial Themes in American Thought, 1756–1800* (1985), 22. Women: see Rosemary R. Ruether and Rosemary S. Keller, *Women and Religion in America,* vol. 2: *The Colonial and Revolutionary Periods* (1981). Age of office-holding: Cook, Jr. (1976), 185–6; and Gross (1976), 62–3. Witherspoon: Cremin (1970), 301. **Youth.** Cotton Mather, *A Family Well-Ordered* (1699). On the attachment of many young Awakeners—especially evangelicals—to their mothers, see Greven (1977), part 2; Whitefield, in *ibid.,* 24; Adams, in *AmB* and in Ralph Volney Harlow, *Samuel Adams, Promoter of the American Revolution: A Study in Psychology and Politics* (1975). Edwards, in Richard L. Bushman, "Jonathan Edwards as Great Man," in Robert J. Brugger (ed.), *Our Selves/Our Past: Psychological Approaches to History* (1981); Woolman, in Edwin H. Cady, *John Woolman* (1965), 27. Boston press, cited in Bridenbaugh (1968), 388–9; Nash (1979), 133. **Coming of Age.** Edwards, *Faithful Narrative* (1737); Chauncy (1743); Tennent, *The Danger of an Unconverted Ministry* (1740); Finley, in Greven (1977), 116–7; Edwards, in Heimert (1966), 62; Franklin, in Nash (1979), 220. **Rising Adulthood.** Adams, in Maier (1980), 34; Livingston, *Philosophic Solitude* (1747); Carter, in "Introduction" to Jack P. Greene (ed.), *The Diary of Colonel Landon Carter* (1965); Pemberton, in Heimert (1966), 30; Bland, *A Modest and True State of the Case* (1753); Fothergill, in Peter Brock, *Pioneers of the Peaceable Kingdom* (1968), 128. **Midlife.** Bellamy, in Heimert (1966), 344–5. Analogy between "Committees" and "communion of colonies" made by Mayhew in 1766; see Strout (1973), 70–71. On "college enthusiasm," see Beverly McAnear, "College Founding in the American Colonies, 1745–1775" (*Mississippi Valley Historical Review,* 1955); on "civic enthusiasm," see Max Savelle, *Seeds of Liberty: The Genesis of the American Mind* (1948), and Richard L. Merritt, *Symbols of American Community, 1735–1775* (1966). Witherspoon, in Roche (1986), 29; Parsons, in Heimert (1966), 421; Hawley, in *ibid.,* 472. **Elderhood.** Adams, in Gordon S. Wood, *The Creation of the American Republic, 1776–1787* (1972), 123–4, and in Maier (1980). On Calvinistic piety in the Continental Congress, see Strout (1973), 67–8. Bellamy, in Heimert (1966), 471. Sherman, *A Short Sermon on the Duty of Self-Examination* (1789); Adams, in Maier (1980); Carter, in Greene (1965). On the Awakener role in the slavery question, see Arthur Zilversmit, *The First Emancipation: The Abolition of Slavery in the North* (1967); on the new Awakener attitude toward death, see Stannard (1977). Hatch, "The Origins of Civil Millennialism in America: New England Clergymen, War with France, and the Revolution" (*WMQ,* Jul 1974); Heimert (1966), 12; Edwards, in *ibid.,* 59. Franklin on seal: see Berens (1978), 107.

LIBERTY BACKGROUND. For insights into the Liberty's basic connection to history, see "On Faith and Generations in Revolutionary Politics," in Maier (1980); Kenyon (1955); Jack P. Greene, "Search for Identity" (*JSH,* Winter 1969–70); C. A. Weslager, *The Stamp Act Congress* (1976); Robert M. Weir, "Who Shall Rule at Home: The American Revolution as a Crisis of Legitimacy for the Colonial Elite" (*JIH,* Spring 1976); John

W. Tyler, *Smugglers and Patriots* (1986); Jackson Turner Main, *The Anti-Federalists* (1961); and J. E. Crowley, *This Sheba, Self: Conceptualization of Economic Life in Eighteenth Century America* (1974). On their coming-of-age experience with war: Fred Anderson, *A People's Army: Massachusetts Soldiers and Society in the Seven Years' War* (1984); James G. Lydon, *Pirates, Privateers, and Profits* (1970); and John Ferling, "Soldiers for Virginia: Who Served in the French and Indian War" (*VM,* Jul 1986). On their reputation for riot and violence: Richard Maxwell Brown, "Violence and the American Revolution," in Stephen G. Kurtz and James H. Hutson, *Essays on the American Revolution* (1973), and "Back Country Rebellions and the Homestead Ethic in America, 1740–1799," in Brown and Don E. Fehrenbacher (eds.), *Tradition, Conflict, and Modernization: Perspectives on the American Revolution* (1977); Maier, "Popular Uprisings and Civil Authority in Eighteenth-Century America" (*WMQ,* Jan 1970); Douglas Greenberg, *Crime and Law Enforcement in the Colony of New York, 1691–1776* (1976); and Jesse Lemisch, "Jack Tar in the Streets: Merchant Seamen in the Politics of Revolutionary America" (*WMQ,* Jul 1968).

LIBERTY REFERENCES. Washington, in John E. Ferling, *The First of Men: A Life of George Washington* (1988), 26, 54; Adams' diary, in Greven (1977), 251; Wolfe to Lord George Sackville (1759), in Weir (1976); Awakener chaplain was John Cleaveland, cited in Anderson (1984), 217. For historian on Sears, see Maier (1980), 64. Landon Carter, in Greene (1965); Benjamin Franklin, in Sheila L. Skemp, "William Franklin: His Father's Son" (*Pennsylvania Magazine of History and Biography,* Apr 1985); Bartlett, in Charles Royster, *A Revolutionary People at War* (1979), 272; Adams' diary, in Weir (1976); Adams to Jefferson, in Donald E. Cooke, *Fathers of America's Freedom* (1969), 15. On new words for the elderly, see Fischer (1978), ch. 2. Henry, in Robert Douthat Meade, *Patrick Henry, Patriot in the Making* (1969), vol. 2, 35. Dickinson, *The American Liberty Song* (1768); Warren, *The Massachusetts Song of Liberty* (1770); Hopkinson, *My Days Have Been So Wondrous Free* (1759). For "Liberty" theme in rioting, see Shaw (1981). **Facts.** Diphtheria and child mortality rate: Greven (1970), ch. 7; Axtell (1974), 73–5; Maris A. Vinovskis, "Angels Heads and Weeping Willows: Death in Early America," in Vinovskis (1979); and John Duffy, *Epidemics in Colonial America* (1953). War casualties: Nash (1979), 245; Anderson (1984); and Lydon (1970), ch. 9. Drinking and crime: Bridenbaugh (1955) and (1968); and W. J. Rorabaugh, *The Alcoholic Republic* (1979). Riots: Brown (1973); and Maier (1970). The six Continental Congress delegates accused of treason were Robert Alexander, Andrew Allen, Isaac Low, John Joachim Zubly, William Samuel Johnson, and Silas Deane; the last two were later acquitted (Johnson soon enough to become a Constitution signer, Deane over fifty years after his death). "Localism": Main (1973), esp. Appendix. **Youth.** Johnson, *Elementa Philosophica* (1752); Chauncy (1743). Edwards, *Conversions and Revival in New England* (1740); Edwards' aggressive campaign against "immoral books" in the hands of youth led directly to his resignation from Northampton's church in 1750. Eliot, *An Evil and Adulterous Generation* (1753), which dealt mostly with youth vices; Franklin, *Poor Richard's Almanac* (1733–58). See Douglas Lamar Jones, "The Strolling Poor: Transiency in Eighteenth-Century Massachusetts" (*JSH,* Spring 1975). For the unprecedented erosion of family authority over children during this period, see "A Note on the Historical Family," in Burroughs and Wallace (1972), Moran and Vinovskis (1982), Isaac (1971), Greven (1970), Bushman (1970), Lockridge (1970), and Smith (1980). **Coming of Age.**

DeLancey, in Nash (1979), 237; British officers, in Anderson (1984) and Ferling (1986); William Pencak, *War, Politics, and Revolution in Provincial Massachusetts* (1981), 122. **Rising Adulthood.** Colden, in Arthur M. Schlesinger, "The Aristocracy in Colonial America," in Goodman (1967); Carter, in Greene (1965); Franklin, in Nash (1979), 283; John Eliot on Samuel Adams, in Maier (1980), 6. See Emory G. Evans, "Planter Indebtedness and the Coming of the Revolution in Virginia" (*WMQ*, Oct 1962). "Virginians are . . . ," cited by Rhys Isaac, "Preachers and Patriots: Popular Culture and the Revolution in Virginia," in Alfred F. Young (ed.), *The American Revolution* (1976); Boone, in Appendix to John Filson, *Discovery, Settlement, and Present State of Kentucky* (1784). **Midlife.** Harrison, in Cooke (1969), 54; Washington to Lund Washington (Dec 17, 1776), in Ferling (1988), 181; Mason, Virginia "Declaration of Rights" (1776); Banastre Tarleton on Francis Marion ("as for this damned old fox, the Devil himself could not catch him"), cited in Hugh F. Rankin, *Francis Marion: The Swamp Fox* (1973), 113; ". . . like a Christian or a gentleman" appears in David C. Whitney, *The Colonial Spirit of '76* (1974), 296; Henry, in Maier (1980), 289; see also Kenyon (1955) and Main (1973). **Elderhood.** Jefferson on Washington, in David C. Whitney, *The American Presidents* (1967), 3. Washington, Farewell Address (1796); Fischer (1977), 93, 88; Adams to Benjamin Rush (1809), in Zoltan Haraszti, *John Adams and the Prophets of Progress* (1952), 1; Adams on "great men," in Andrew Achenbaum, *Old Age in the New Land: The American Experience since 1790* (1978), 32; Stiles, in Edwin Gaustad, "Society and the Great Awakening in New England" (*WMQ*, Oct 1954); see also Darline Shapiro, "Ethan Allen: Philosopher-Theologian to a Generation of American Revolutionaries" (*WMQ*, Apr 1964). Emerson, in Kammen (1978), 104.

REPUBLICAN BACKGROUND. For a penetrating lifecycle analysis of this generation, see Peter Charles Hoffer, *Revolution and Regeneration: Life Cycle and the Historical Vision of the Generation of 1776* (1983). For other central themes in the Republican peer personality: title essay of Trevor Colbourn (ed.), *Fame and the Founding Fathers: Essays by Douglass Adair* (1974); Catherine Albanese, *Sons of the Fathers: The Civil Religion of the American Revolution* (1976); Stanley Elkins and Eric McKitrick, "The Founding Fathers: Young Men of the Revolution" (*Political Science Quarterly*, Jun 1961); John M. Murrin, "Self-Interest Conquers Patriotism: Republicans, Liberals, and Indians Reshape the Nation," in Jack P. Greene (ed.), *The American Revolution* (1987); Garry Wills, *Inventing America* (1978); and Jan Lewis, "Domestic Tranquillity and the Management of Emotion among the Gentry of Pre-Revolutionary Virginia" (*WMQ*, Jan 1982). On their participation in war and victory: Charles Royster, *A Revolutionary People at War: The Continental Army and American Character, 1775–1783* (1979); the excellent essays in John Ferling (ed.), *The World Turned Upside Down: The American Victory in the War of Independence* (1988); and John R. Van Atta, "Conscription in Revolutionary Virginia" (*VM*, Jul 1984). On their generational achievements in politics and culture: Henry F. May, *The Enlightenment in America* (1976), parts 3–4; David Lundberg and Henry F. May, "The Enlightened Reader in America" (*AQ*, Summer 1976); Richard Buel, Jr., *Securing the Republic: Ideology in American Politics, 1789–1815* (1972); Russel Blaine Nye, *The Cultural Life of the New Nation, 1776–1830* (1960); Lester H. Cohen, "Creating a Usable Future: The Revolutionary Historians and the National Past," in Greene (1987); and David H. Fischer, "The Myth of the Essex Junto" (*WMQ*, Apr 1964).

REPUBLICAN REFERENCES. Humphreys, *The Glory of America* (1783); song of New York recruits, in Royster (1979), 8; *ibid.,* 8; see Julian P. Boyd, "Thomas Jefferson's 'Empire of Liberty' " (*Virginia Quarterly Review,* Autumn 1948); Morgan (1967); Jay to John Lowell (1796), in David Hackett Fischer, *The Revolution of American Conservatism* (1965), 9; Madison and Gallatin, in *AmB;* Hamilton, in Vernon L. Parrington, *The Colonial Mind* (1927; 1954, vol. 1), 309–10; William Wirt on Marshall, in *AmB;* Barlow, *The Canal: A Poem on the Application of Physical Science to Political Economy* (1802); Boorstin, *The Lost World of Thomas Jefferson* (1960), 29; see "Roman Virtue," in Howard Mumford Jones, *O Strange New World* (1952); Knox, in *AmB;* Hale, in *ibid.;* Jefferson to Baron von Humboldt (1804), in George Seldes (ed.), *The Great Thoughts* (1985), 209; see John P. Diggins, "Slavery, Race, and Equality: Jefferson and the Pathos of the Enlightenment" (*AQ,* Summer 1976). **Facts.** Nutrition and height: Robert W. Fogel, Stanley L. Engerman, and James Trussel, "Exploring the Uses of Data on Height," and Kenneth L. Sokoloff and Georgia C. Villaflor, "The Early Achievement of Modern Stature in America" (*Social Science History,* Fall 1982); and S. F. McMahon, "Provisions Laid Up for the Family: Toward a History of Diet in New England, 1650–1850" (*Historical Methods,* Winter 1981). Colleges and clerical callings: Roche (1986), 9. Freemasonry: Albanese (1976), ch. 4; and Philip Davidson, *Propaganda and the American Revolution, 1763–1783* (1941), 100–1. Town offices: Cook (1976), 105–7, 191. Age of "Federalists": Elkins and McKitrick (1961). Hamilton, in Albanese (1976), 203. "Veneration": Webster, *An American Dictionary of the English Language* (1828). On Samuel Wilson, alias "Uncle Sam," see *AmB.* **Youth.** Fliegelman (1982), 22. On sudden rise in numbers of tutors in New York City and Philadelphia, see Cremin (1970), 539; on domestic colleges, see McAnear (1955) and Smith (1980). Witherspoon, in Cremin (1970), 300; Marshall, in *AmB;* on Jefferson, see Dowdey (1970), 197, 241–2; Kenneth S. Lynn, *A Divided People* (1977), 68. **Coming of Age.** Dwight, *Columbia* (final version appeared in 1783); ballad in 1779, cited in Albanese (1976), 56; Rush to William Peterkin (1784), in Yazawa (1987); Randolph, in Maier (1980), 289; *The Federalist* (Mar–May, 1788): seventy-seven essays, of which Hamilton wrote fifty-one, Madison twenty-nine, and Jay five. **Rising Adulthood.** "Caesar," "Lycurgus," and "Publius" were popular pamphlet pseudonyms; "mechanical courage," in Royster (1979), 227. Webster, in Norman Risjord, *Forging the American Republic, 1760–1815* (1973), 245. On "female" monarchism and "male" republicanism, see Greven (1977), part 5; Federalists on Jefferson and France, in Fliegelman (1982), 234; Jefferson on Adams' Presidency, in Merrill D. Peterson, *Adams and Jefferson: A Revolutionary Dialogue* (1976), 82; historian Crane (1987) on Jefferson; Hitchcock, *An Oration: Delivered July 4, 1788,* cited in Albanese (1976), 209. **Midlife.** Jefferson, first inaugural address (Mar 4, 1801); Joel Barlow, *The Columbiad* (1807); Livingston, in *AmB.* **Elderhood.** Marshall, in *ibid.;* Madison, in Marshall Smelser, *The Democratic Republic, 1801–1850* (1968), 187; Jefferson, in Nye (1960), 31; and in Peterson (1987), 128; Jefferson to Martha Jefferson (1787), in Morgan (1967); Freneau, in Hoffer (1983), 129; Humphreys, in *ibid.,* 121; Gallatin (at age 88), in Page Smith, *The Nation Comes of Age* (1981), 227; Jefferson, in Hoffer (1983), 123; Hamilton, in *The Federalist* (1788), no. 15; Pickering, in Hoffer (1983), 87; "happify," in Webster, *The American Spelling Book* (1798), cited in Fliegelman (1982), 161; Webster's "empire of reason" (1789), in Hoffer (1983), 58; Rush, in Jacqueline S. Reinier, "Rearing the Republican Child: Attitudes and Practices in Post-Revolutionary Philadelphia" (*WMQ,* Jan 82).

COMPROMISE BACKGROUND. Except perhaps for the unconventional approach of Michael Paul Rogin, *Andrew Jackson and the Subjugation of the American Indian* (1975), no major efforts have been made to describe the overall Compromiser lifecycle and peer personality. For penetrating biographical insights: Merrill D. Peterson, *The Great Triumvirate: Webster, Clay, and Calhoun* (1987); Irving H. Bartlett, *Daniel Webster* (1978); Samuel Flagg Bemis, *John Quincy Adams and the Foundations of American Foreign Policy* (1949); and Burke Davis, *Old Hickory: A Life of Andrew Jackson* (1977). On the Compromiser "second-generation" approach to politics: Cunliffe (1959); Leonard D. White, *The Jeffersonians* (1951); David Hackett Fischer, *The Revolution of American Conservatism* (1965); Robert V. Remini, *The Revolutionary Age of Andrew Jackson* (1976); and Matthew A. Crensen, *The Federal Machine: Beginnings of Bureaucracy in Jacksonian America* (1975). Changes in their attitudes toward family, culture, religion, and sex roles are addressed by Fliegelman (1982); Smith (1980); Norton (1980); Kerber (1980); Barbara Welter, "The Cult of True Womanhood: 1820–1860" (*AQ*, Summer 1966); Claudia Goldin, "The Economic Status of Women in the Early Republic" (*Journal of Interdisciplinary Studies*, Winter 1980); Ann Douglas, *The Feminization of American Culture* (1977); Jan Lewis, *The Pursuit of Happiness: Family and Values in Jefferson's Virginia* (1983); Daniel Walker Howe, *The Unitarian Conscience: Harvard Moral Philosophy, 1805–1861* (1970); and David J. Rothman, *The Discovery of the Asylum: Social Order and Disorder in the New Republic* (1971). For their social environment during midlife and beyond, see source notes for Chapter 9, esp. Arthur Schlesinger, Jr., *The Age of Jackson* (1945); Edward Pessen, *Jacksonian America: Society, Personality, and Politics* (1985); and Page Smith, *The Nation Comes of Age* (1981).

COMPROMISE REFERENCES. Webster, Bunker Hill Monument speech (1825), cited in Kammen (1978), 17; Jefferson, in Meriwether Lewis, *The Expedition of Lewis and Clark* (1814, 1966), xiv, vii; for references to "post-heroic" and "second" generation, see Rogin (1975), Kammen (1978), Lewis (1983), Fischer (1965), and Remini (1976); Beecher, in Hatch (1977), 174. Jackson on the Tariff of 1828, in Robert Remini, *Andrew Jackson* (1966), 118; Crenson (1975), 159; Walter Channing (William's brother) suggested that "the blame" for poverty "goes to society itself"—cited in Rothman (1971), 173. John William Ward, *Andrew Jackson: Symbol for an Age* (1953), 49–50. John Randolph, Gregg's Motion to Annex Florida (House of Representatives; Mar 6, 1806); Rogin (1975), 50; Channing, *The Union* (1829); Garrison, in Vernon L. Parrington, *The Romantic Revolution in America* (1927; 1954, vol. 2), 325. Clay, in Peterson (1987), 469; Webster, in Bartlett (1978), 33; Taylor, in Silas Bent McKinley and Silas Bent, *Old Rough and Ready: The Life and Times of Zachary Taylor* (1946), 286. **Facts.** Romantic themes in magazines: Herman R. Lantz et al., "Pre-Industrial Patterns in the Colonial Family in America: A Content Analysis of Colonial Magazines" (*American Sociological Review*, Jun 1968), and "The Preindustrial Family in America: A Further Examination of Early Magazines" (*American Journal of Sociology*, Nov 1973). Romantic novels: Nye (1960), 247–58; and Lawrence Stone, *The Family, Sex, and Marriage in England, 1500–1800* (1977), 318, 284. Age of generals in War of 1812: Smelser (1968), 227, 319. Wise (1834), in Kammen (1978), 15. Women's education: Norton (1980), 268, 287–9; see also Linda K. Kerber, "Daughters of Columbia: Educating Women for the Republic, 1787–1805," in Stanley Elkins and Eric McKitrick (eds.), *The Hofstadter Aegis* (1974). Political lexicon: Cunliffe (1959), 178–9. Workforce engaged in farming:

Paul David, "The Growth of Real Product in the United States Before 1840: New Evidence, Controlled Conjectures" (*JEH*, Jun 1965). Fertility and divorce: evidence summarized in Steven Mintz and Susan Kellogg, *Domestic Revolutions* (1988), 51–2, 61. Relative wealth as elders: evidence summarized in Fischer (1977), 229. **Youth.** Clay, in Peterson (1987), 8–9; on the new importance of "respectability," see Jeannette Mirsky and Allan Nevins, *The World of Eli Whitney* (1952), 3–4. **Coming of Age.** Randolph, in *OxA*, 367; Adams in letter to *Columbian Centinel* (1793), in Bemis (1949), 36; Webster, in Bartlett (1978), 33. On "old maids," see Pessen (1985), 47; Southgate, in Mary Cable, *The Little Darlings* (1972), 64. On Webster, see Bartlett (1978), 38. Clay, in Clement Eaton, *Henry Clay* (1957), 61. **Rising Adulthood.** Webster, in George B. Forgie, *Patricide in the House Divided: A Psychological Interpretation of Lincoln and His Age* (1979), 82; Wirt, in White (1951), 346; on "standing" versus "running" for office, see Fischer (1965); on "the cult of true womanhood," see Welter (1966). **Midlife.** Irving, in Parrington (1927; 1954, vol. 2), 201; Tocqueville (1835, 1945), vol. 2, 275–8, 35; Cooper (1837), in Eaton (1957), 137; Emerson (1837), in Nye (1960), 293; Stevens, in Alphonse Miller, *Thaddeus Stevens* (1939), 97–8; Morison, in *OxA*, 574; Hale et al., in Douglas (1977), 52–5. **Elderhood.** Clay, in Remini (1976), 159; Scott, letter to W. H. Seward (Mar 3, 1861); Hone, in Smith (1981), 1079; Buchanan, in Kenneth M. Stampp (ed.), *The Causes of the Civil War* (1986), 84. Richard Henry Dana on Webster, in Smith (1981), 1088.

CHAPTER 9: THE CIVIL WAR CYCLE

CIVIL WAR CYCLE BACKGROUND. See Page Smith, *The Nation Comes of Age: A People's History of the Ante-Bellum Years* (1981), and *Trial by Fire: A People's History of the Civil War and Reconstruction* (1982); James MacGregor Burns, *The Workshop of Democracy* (1986); J. C. Furnas, *The Americans: A Social History of the United States* (1969); Edward Pessen, *Jacksonian America: Society, Personality, and Politics* (1985); Arthur M. Schlesinger, Jr., *The Age of Jackson* (1945); Richard Hofstadter, *The American Political Tradition* (1948), chs. 5–7; Robert V. Remini, *The Revolutionary Age of Andrew Jackson* (1987); Clement Eaton (ed.), *The Leaven of Democracy* (1963); David Brion Davis (ed.), *Antebellum American Culture: An Interpretive Anthology* (1979); essays in Kenneth M. Stampp, *The Causes of the Civil War* (1974); James M. McPherson, *Battle Cry of Freedom* (1988); Albert K. Weinberg, *Manifest Destiny* (1935); Daniel Boorstin, *The Americans: The Democratic Experience* (1973); John Chamberlain, *The Enterprising Americans: A Business History of the United States* (1961); John Hope Franklin, *From Slavery to Freedom: A History of Negro Americans* (1980); C. Vann Woodward, *The Burden of Southern History* (1960); and Francis Simkins and Charles Rowland, *A History of the South* (1972). On political leadership: essays in James L. Bugg, Jr., and Peter C. Stewart (eds.), *Jacksonian Democracy* (1976); Dumas Malone and Basil Rauch, *Crisis of the Union, 1841–1877* (1960); John L. Hammond, *The Politics of Benevolence: Revival Religion and American Voting Behavior* (1979); and W. R. Brock, *An American Crisis: Congress and Reconstruction, 1865–1867* (1963). On family, community life, and the role of women: Mary P. Ryan, *Cradle of the Middle Class: The Family in Oneida, New York, 1790–1865* (1981); Steven Mintz and Susan Kellogg, *Domestic Revolutions: A*

Social History of American Family Life (1988); Michael Grossberg, *Governing the Hearth: Law and Family in Nineteenth Century America* (1985); Carl Degler, *At Odds: Women and the Family in America from the Revolution to the Present* (1980); Ann Douglas, *The Feminization of American Culture* (1977); essays in Michael Gordon (ed.), *The American Family in Socio-Historical Perspective* (2nd ed., 1978); and Herbert G. Gutman, *The Black Family in Slavery and Freedom, 1750–1925* (1976). On childhood and education: Mary Cable, *The Little Darlings* (1975); Joseph Hawes and Ray Hiner, *Growing Up in America: Children in Historical Perspective* (1985); Joseph Kett, *Rites of Passage: Adolescence in America, 1790 to the Present* (1977); Robert M. Mennel, *Thorns and Thistles: Juvenile Delinquents in the United States, 1825–1940* (1973); Oscar Handlin, *Facing Life: Youth and the Family in American History* (1971); essays in Harvey J. Graff (ed.), *Growing Up in America* (1987); Carl F. Kaestle, *Pillars of the Republic: Common Schools and American Society, 1780–1860* (1983); David Nasaw, *Schooled to Order* (1979); Frederick Rudolph, *The American College and University: A History* (1962); and Lewis Feuer, *The Conflict of Generations: The Character and Significance of Student Movements* (1969), ch. 7. On religion: Sydney E. Ahlstrom, *A Religious History of the American People* (1975); Ernest Lee Tuveson, *Redeemer Nation: The Idea of America's Millennial Role* (1968); Cushing Strout, *The New Heavens and New Earth: Political Religion in America* (1973); and essays in William O'Neill (ed.), *Insights and Parallels: Problems and Issues of American Social History* (1973). On old age: Andrew Achenbaum, *Old Age in the New Land: The American Experience since 1790* (1978); David Hackett Fischer, *Growing Old in America* (1977), William Graebner, *A History of Retirement* (1980); and Daniel Scott Smith, "Old Age and the 'Great Transformation': A New England Case Study," in Stuart F. Spicker et al. (eds.), *Aging and the Elderly* (1978).

CIVIL WAR CYCLE REFERENCES. "Corkscrew sensation" appears in McPherson (1988), 344; Riddle, in *ibid.*, 345; on expression "baptism of blood," see Charles Reagan Wilson, *Baptized in Blood: The Religion of the Lost Cause, 1865–1920* (1980); Jackson, in McPherson (1988), 455; Holmes, in T. Jackson Lears, *No Place of Grace* (1981), 124. Pessen (1985), 70; Charles and Mary Beard, *The Rise of American Civilization* (1927, 1933 ed.), vol. II, ch. 18.

TRANSCENDENTAL BACKGROUND. For the best overall portraits of the Transcendental peer personality: George B. Forgie, *Patricide in the House Divided: A Psychological Interpretation of Lincoln and His Age* (1979); Peter Walker, *Moral Choices: Memory, Desire, and Imagination in Nineteenth-Century Abolition* (1978); Lois Banner, "Religion and Reform in the Early Republic" (*AQ*, Dec 1971); William G. McLoughlin, "The Second Great Awakening," in *Revivals, Awakenings, and Reforms* (1978); James Moorhead, *American Apocalypse: Yankee Protestants and the Civil War, 1860–1869* (1978); Tuveson (1968); O'Neill (1973); Strout (1973); see also Stanley M. Elkins, *Slavery: A Problem in American Institutional Life* (2nd ed., 1968), and J. G. Randall, "The Blundering Generation" (*Mississippi Valley Historical Review*, Jun 1940). For revealing biographies: Carl Sandburg, *Abraham Lincoln: The Prairie Years and the War Years* (one-vol. ed., 1954); Charles Sellers, *James K. Polk: Jacksonian, 1795–1843* (1957); Robert H. Abzug, *Passionate Liberator: Theodore Dwight Weld and the Dilemma of Reform* (1980); Alphonse B. Miller, *Thaddeus Stevens* (1939); Clifford Clark, Jr., *Henry*

Ward Beecher (1978); and Julius Silberger, Jr., *Mary Baker Eddy* (1981). On social, religious, and literary movements: John M. Whitworth, *God's Blueprints: A Sociological Study of Three Utopian Sects* (1975); Anne C. Rose, *Transcendentalism as a Social Movement, 1830–1850* (1981); Laurence Veysey (ed.), *The Perfectionists: Radical Social Thought in the North, 1815–1860* (1973); David Rothman, *The Discovery of the Asylum* (1971); Frederick Merk, *Manifest Destiny and Mission in American History* (1963); Stephen Nissenbaum, *Sex, Diet, and Debility in Jacksonian America: Sylvester Graham and Health Reform* (1980); Vernon L. Parrington, *The Romantic Revolution in America, 1800–1860* (1927; 1954, vol. 2); Van Wyck Brooks, *The Flowering of New England* (1936); Perry Miller (ed.), *The American Transcendentalists* (1957); and essays by Nina Baym and Lawrence Buell in *CLH*. On feminism: Miriam Gurko, *The Ladies of Seneca Falls: The Birth of the Woman's Rights Movement* (1974); Rosemary R. Ruether and Rosemary S. Keller, *Women and Religion in America*, vol. 1; Margo Horn, " 'Sisters Worthy of Respect': Family Dynamics and Women's Roles in the Blackwell Family" (*JFH;* vol. 8, 1983); and Irene Quenzler Brown, "Death, Friendship, and Female Identity During New England's Second Great Awakening" (*JFH;* vol. 12, 1987).

TRANSCENDENTAL REFERENCES. Emerson, *Life and Letters in New England* (1867); "madmen . . . ," in Parrington (1927; 1954, vol. 2), 337; Poe, in Van Wyck Brooks, *The World of Washington Irving* (1944), 453. "Hair parted in the middle . . ." is from George William Curtis (born 1824), cited in Smith (1981), 675–6; of all the early Brook Farm members with known birthdates, Curtis was the only one not born between 1797 and 1820—see Rose (1981), Appendix C. Hawthorne, *Blithesdale Romance* (1852) and Hawthorne, in Smith (1981), 986–7. Emerson, "Circles," in *Essays, First Series* (1841); Emerson, *Journals,* in Randall (1940); Emerson's "not a book . . . ," in Russel Blaine Nye, *The Cultural Life of the New Nation* (1960), 111; Seward, speech at Rochester, New York (Oct 25, 1858), in Stampp (1959), 105; Sherman, in Sandburg (1954), 661; Garrison, in Strout (1973), 163; Emerson, "Fate," in *Conduct of Life* (1860); Thoreau, in Forgie (1979), 95; Parker, in *ibid.,* 89; Herndon, letter to Charles Sumner (1860), in Stampp (1959), 106; Emerson, "The Transcendentalist" (1842 lecture, first published in *The Dial* in Jan 1843); Holmes, in Brooks Atkinson (ed.), *The Selected Writings of Ralph Waldo Emerson* (1940), xv; Seward, Senate speech (Mar 11, 1850), in Stampp (1959), 103; Garrison, in Smith (1981), 637; Melville, in Smith (1981), 1160; Stowe, *Uncle Tom's Cabin* (1852); Garrison (1837), in Strout (1973), 164; Emerson, "Self Reliance," in *Essays, First Series* (1841); Thoreau, *On the Duty of Civil Disobedience* (1849); Whitman, "Song of Myself" (1855); Poe, "A Dream Within a Dream" (1827); Tocqueville, *Democracy in America* (1835; Random House translation, 1945), 142; Trollope, in Smith (1981), 245–6; Stowe, in Smith (1981), 660; Emerson, "On the Uses of Great Men," in *Representative Men* (1850); description of Lincoln by his friend William Herndon, cited in Smith (1982), 577; Howe, *Battle Hymn of the Republic* (1862); Lincoln, address (Apr 11, 1865); Holmes, in Parrington (1927; 1954, vol. 2), 445–6; Melville, in Smith (1982), 950; Adams, cited in Ken Burns (director), *The Civil War* (documentary film, 1990). **Facts.** Childbearing: Catherine M. Scholten, " 'On the Importance of the Obstetrick Art': Changing Customs of Childbirth in America, 1760 to 1825" (*WMQ,* Jul 1977). Birthnames: David Hackett Fischer, "Forenames and the Family in New England," in Robert Taylor and Ralph Crandall (eds.), *Generations and Change* (1986); see also

Mintz and Kellogg (1988), 49. Student unrest: Rudolph (1962), 118; Feuer (1969), 321–3; and Kett (1977), 47–59. Nye (1960), 232. Ann Braude, *Radical Spirits: Spiritualism and Women's Rights* (1989), chs. 1, 3. Opium: Smith (1981), 687; and David T. Courtwright, *Dark Paradise: Opiate Addiction in America Before 1940* (1972), ch. 1. Alcohol: W. J. Rorabaugh, *The Alcoholic Republic* (1979), Appendix 1; Pessen (1985), 20; and Chapter 12 source notes. Noyes, *History of American Socialisms* (1870). Beards: Alison Lurie, *The Language of Clothes* (1981), 65–8. The sixteen leading Republican Radicals are identified in Brock (1963), ch. 1. **Youth.** Ramsay, in Peter Gay, *The Enlightenment: The Science of Freedom* (1969), 23; Kett (1977), 60; British visitor William Faux, in Furnas (1969), 591; Bushnell, "The Age of Homespun" (1851), cited in Douglas (1977), 60; Kett (1977), 37; Harriet Martineau's comments on the Lowell factory girls, discussed in Furnas (1969), 477; Beecher, in Banner (1971); Emerson, "The Transcendentalist" (1842). **Coming of Age.** Polk, in Sellers (1960), 47; Garrison, "The Liberator's Principles," Jan 1, 1831; Fuller, in Smith (1981), 727; Emerson on Longfellow, in *OxA,* 528; Longfellow, "The Warning," cited in Smith (1981), 623–4. **Rising Adulthood.** Whitman, in Jerome Loving, "Walt Whitman," in *CLH;* Emerson, "The Poet," *Essays, Second Series* (1844); Thoreau, *A Week on the Concord and Merrimack Rivers* (1849); "the unfolding . . ." appeared in *The Dial* (1841), cited in Parrington (1927; 1954, vol. 2), 340; Ahlstrom (1975), vol. 1, 574. On the Gothic revival, see Clifford Clark, Jr., "Domestic Architecture as an Index to Social History" (*JIH,* Summer 1976). Foreign visitors Captain Marryat, Frances Trollope, and Captain Basil Hall, all cited in Smith (1981), 249, 914, and in Pessen (1985), 27–8; Parker, in Miller (1957), 357–9. **Midlife.** Whittier, "Lines Inscribed to Friends Under Arrest for Treason Against the Slave Power" (1856); Stowe (1852). The caning was administered in 1856 by South Carolina's "exterminating angel," Congressman Preston Brooks (age 37), against Massachusetts Senator Charles Sumner (age 45). Phillips, in Woodward (1960), 52; Thoreau, in *ibid.,* 52; Whitman, *Years of the Modern* (1860, first pub. 1865); "Redeemer President" appears in Whitman, *The Eighteenth Presidency!* (1856); Lincoln, in Forgie (1979), 287; Garrison, in Smith (1981), 609; Phillips, in Hofstadter (1948), 144; Stevens, in Miller (1939), 182; Melville, in Smith (1982), 563–4. **Elderhood.** Longfellow, *Elegaic Verse* and *Morituri Salutamus* (1875); Longfellow described by the younger Carl Schurz, in Smith (1981), 977; Parker, in Fischer (1977), 114; Fisher, in Smith (1862), 951; Stevens as described in a contemporary press account, in Miller (1939), 353; Barnes, *The Peaceful Death of the Righteous* (1858); Child, in Fischer (1977), 121; Holmes, "On His Eightieth Birthday" (1887). Tarkenton, in Furnas (1969), 550; Phillips, in Hofstadter (1948), 163; Anthony, "The Solitude of Self" (1892); Brown, in Sandburg (1954), 158–9; Garrison, in Strout (1973), 164; Eddy, *Science and Health with Key to the Scriptures* (1875).

GILDED BACKGROUND. The Gilded lifecycle is best approached through the words of those who lived it: Mark Twain, *Roughing It* (1872), and, with Charles Dudley Warner, *The Gilded Age: A Tale of Today* (1873); Henry Adams, *The Education of Henry Adams* (1906); George Armstrong Custer, *My Life on the Plains* (1874); Ednah D. Cheney (ed.), *Louisa May Alcott: Her Life, Letters, and Journals* (1889); Ulysses S. Grant, *Personal Memoirs* (1885); Andrew Carnegie, *Triumphant Democracy* (1886); William James, *Pragmatism* (1907); and John D. Rockefeller, *Random Reminiscences of Men and Events* (1909). For other accounts of the age they shaped and their leading personality types: H.

Wayne Morgan (ed.), *The Gilded Age* (1963); John G. Sproat, *"The Best Men"*: *Liberal Reformers in the Gilded Age* (1968); Paul A. Carter, *The Spiritual Crisis of the Gilded Age* (1971); Sean Dennis Cashman, *America in the Gilded Age* (1988); Milton Rugoff, *America's Gilded Age: Intimate Portraits from an Era of Extravagance and Change, 1850–1890* (1989); Seymour J. Mandelbaum, *Boss Tweed's New York* (1965); Samuel Carter, *The Last Cavaliers: Confederate and Union Cavalry in the Civil War* (1979); Richard O'Connor, *Wild Bill Hickok* (1959); and Matthew Josephson, *The Robber Barons: The Great American Capitalists, 1861–1901* (1934). For the meaning of war and the far West to their lives: Ralph Abrahamson, *The American Home Front* (1983); Reid Mitchell, *Civil War Soldiers* (1988); McPherson (1988); John Mack Faragher, *Women and Men on the Overland Trail* (1979); Rodman Paul, *The Far West and the Great Plains in Transition, 1859–1900* (1988); and "The Western Hero," in Henry Nash Smith, *Virgin Land: The American West as Symbol and Myth* (1950). For their midlife impact on society and culture: essays in Daniel Walker Howe (ed.), *Victorian America* (1976); Richard Hofstadter, *Social Darwinism in American Thought, 1860–1915* (1945); Vernon L. Parrington, *The Beginnings of Critical Realism, 1860–1920* (1930); Robert Green McCloskey, *American Conservatism in the Age of Enterprise, 1865–1910* (1951); "A Chromo Civilization," in Furnas (1969); and David J. Pivar, *Purity Crusade: Sexual Morality and Social Control, 1868–1900* (1973).

GILDED REFERENCES. Twain (1872); on estimated age breakdown on 49ers, see *HSt*, series A-204 to A-209, for California in 1850; Mann (1846), in Furnas (1969), 550; on youth gangs named "Roach Guards," "Little Dead Rabbits," etc., see Kett (1977), 89, 92; Brooks, "The Younger Generation of 1870," in *New England: Indian Summer, 1865–1915* (1940), 438; Adams, in McPherson (1988), viii; Boorstin (1973), Part I; Blaine, in Hofstadter (1948), 176; Hofstadter, *ibid.*, 176; Conkling, Nominating Speech for Grant (Jun 5, 1880); Sumner, in Burns (1986), 159; Mann, in Maurice Wolfthal, "Johnny Couldn't Read in 1905 Either," *WP* 2/24/90; Strong, in Smith (1981); Whitman, in Malone and Rauch (1960); Longfellow, in *OxA*, 732–3; James, *What Maisie Knew* (preface, 1907–9). Beard, in Morgan (1963), 1; Cram, in Harvey Wish, *Society and Thought in Modern America* (1952), 372; Parrington, in Morgan (1963), 257; Morison, in *OxA*, 732; Dickinson, *No. 288* (c. 1861); James, *The Will to Believe* (1897) and *The Meaning of Truth* (1909); Carnegie, *The Gospel of Wealth* (1900); Twain (1872). **Facts.** For evidence that the Gilded suffered higher child mortality rates than their next-elders, see Yasuki Yasuba, *Birth Rates of the White Population in the United States, 1800–1860* (1962), 86–96; for rising-adult mortality, see casualty figures for Civil War below; for elderly mortality, see also below. In the Confederate states, higher rates of extreme poverty due to the war are well documented; elsewhere, they can be inferred from anecdotal accounts of the new urban poor, of the plains settlers, of the new wave of immigrants, and of the social dislocation after the war. Mills, "The American Business Elite: A Collective Portrait" (*JEH*, Dec 1945, Supplement V). Kett (1977), 132. Nutrition and height: Robert W. Fogel, Stanley L. Engerman, and James Trussel, "Exploring the Uses of Data on Height" (*Social Science History*, Fall 1982). Life expectancy at age 65: see data for 1900–7 in *SSP*, Table 10; for evidence that the numbers are higher for earlier-born (Transcendental) cohorts, see Warren S. Thompson and P. K. Whelpton, *Population Trends in the United States* (1969), 239–40. War casualties: McPherson (1988), 285,

818, 854–6; Malone and Rauch (1960), 263; and Randall (1940). Rates of gross capital formation: Robert E. Gallman, "Gross National Product in the United States, 1834–1909," in National Bureau of Economic Research, *Output, Employment, and Productivity in the United States after 1800, Studies in Income and Wealth* (vol. 30, 1966). Wholesale prices: *HSt*, E-40, E-52. **Youth.** Macrae, in Smith (1981), 914; Howells, in Furnas (1969), 922; Police Chief George Matsell, in Christine Stansell, "Women, Children, and the Uses of the Streets," in Graff (1987); Charles L. Brace, *The Dangerous Classes of New York and Twenty Years' Work Among Them* (1872). On term "self-dependence," first urged for children in the 1830s, see Brown, (1987). Alcott, "My Kingdom" (written at age 13). On early childhood independence, see Kett (1977), 103–8; on dropping college enrollment, see Rudolph (1962), 218–40; on student reactions to elder Transcendental lecturers, see Feuer (1969), 321. Rudolph (1962), 76; Brown student, in Handlin (1971), 132. **Coming of Age.** Cincinnati newspaper, cited in McPherson (1988), 29; Irving, "The Creole Village," in *Wolfert's Roost* (1855); Emerson, in Kett (1977), 94; Greeley, editorial in the *New York Tribune;* on "Lincoln shouters" and "hurrah boys," see Sandburg (1954), 173; on "Deeds not words!" see Furnas (1969), 128; Sherman, in Smith (1982), 336–7; Twain, in Tuveson (1968), 208; Holmes, Jr., in Lears (1981), 118. **Rising Adulthood.** Timrod, in Wish (1952), 13; Hayes, in Burns (1986), 201. **Midlife.** See "American Intellectuals and the Victorian Crisis of Faith," in Howe (1976); Norton, in Morgan (1963), 81; Twain, in Wish (1952), 395. **Elderhood.** Norton, in Sara Norton and M. A. De Wolfe Howe (eds.), *Letters of Charles Eliot Norton* (1913), vol. II, 272–3; Achenbaum (1978), 54, 39; Osler, "The Fixed Period" (Johns Hopkins Valedictory Address, 1905), in Graebner (1980), 4–5; Adams, *The Education of Henry Adams* (1907); Hale, *Cosmopolitan* (1903), cited in Fischer (1977), 158; Twain, "Seventieth Birthday" (Dec 5, 1905). Holmes, in Cushing Strout, "Three Faithful Skeptics at the Gate of Modernity," in Howard H. Quint and Milton Cantor, *Men, Women, and Issues in American History* (1975); James' "bitch-goddess," in letter to H. G. Wells (1906); James' "cyclone," in Burns (1986), 292; Twain, "By Order of the Author," in *Huckleberry Finn* (1884).

PROGRESSIVE BACKGROUND. The Progressives are best understood by starting with their innovative mood in midlife and then working outward: Richard Hofstadter (1948), chs. 9–10, and *The Age of Reform* (1955); Hofstadter (ed.), *The Progressive Movement: 1900 to 1915* (1963); Robert S. Wiebe, *The Search for Order, 1877–1920* (1967); Morton Keller, *Affairs of State: Public Life in Late Nineteenth Century America* (1977); Mary O. Furner, *Advocacy and Objectivity: A Crisis in the Professionalization of American Science, 1865–1905* (1975); Samuel Haber, *Efficiency and Uplift: Scientific Management in the Progressive Era, 1890–1920* (1964); Nathan G. Hale, Jr., *Freud and the Americans: The Beginnings of Psychoanalysis in the United States, 1876–1917* (1971); Jackson Lears, *No Place of Grace: Antimodernism and the Transformation of American Culture, 1880–1920* (1981); Alfred D. Chandler, Jr., *The Visible Hand: The Managerial Revolution in American Business* (1977), and "The Beginnings of 'Big Business' in American Industry" (*Business History Review*, Spring 1959); and William L. O'Neill, *Divorce in the Progressive Era* (1967). For biographical insights: Dorothy Ross, *G. Stanley Hall: The Psychologist as Prophet* (1972); Sudhir Kakar, *Frederick Taylor: A Study in Personality and Innovation* (1970); John Morton Blum, *Woodrow Wilson* (1956); Theodore Roosevelt,

The Strenuous Life (1900); and Hugh Hawkins (ed.), *Booker T. Washington and His Critics* (1962). For youth and coming-of-age experiences: Kett (1977), chs. 5–6; George Winston Smith and Charles Judah, *Life in the North During the Civil War* (1966); and Roger Lane, *Violent Death in the City* (1979). For the Progressive influence on cultural and social life: David W. Noble, *The Progressive Mind, 1870–1917* (1970); George E. Mowry, *The Era of Theodore Roosevelt, 1900–1912* (1958); James Weinstein, *The Corporate Ideal in the Liberal State, 1900–1918* (1968); Arthur Mann, *Yankee Reformers in the Urban Age: Social Reform in Boston, 1880–1900* (1954); Donald Pizer (ed.), *American Thought and Writing in the 1890s* (1972); Louis Filler (ed.), *Late Nineteenth Century Liberalism* (1962); Morton White, *Social Thought in America: The Revolt Against Formalism* (1947); and C. Vann Woodward, *The Strange Career of Jim Crow* (1955).

PROGRESSIVE REFERENCES. Taylor, *The Principles of Scientific Management* (1911); Wilson, in Blum (1956), 64; LaFollette, in Boorstin (1973), 567; Roosevelt, in Burns (1986), 349. Wilson, in Hofstadter (1955), 230; T. J. Jackson Lears, "From Salvation to Self-Realization," in Richard Fox and Lears (eds.), *The Culture of Consumption* (1983); Adams, *The Law of Civilization and Decay* (1895); Hall, in Lears (1983); Hall, in Hale, Jr. (1971), 372. "Professor Tweetzers" and "Doctors of Dullness," discussed in Rudolph (1962), 401; "goo-goos" and "Miss Nancys," in Morgan (1963), 56, and in Filler (1962), xxxii. Fels, in Mowry (1958), 94; Hearst, in Burns (1986), 369; Howells, in Lears (1981), 48; Adams, in *ibid.*, 291; Sheldon, *In His Steps* (1897). Wilson, Message to the U.S. Senate (Aug 19, 1914); Morison, in *OxA*, 811; Wiebe (1967), 166; Roosevelt, in Andrew Sinclair, *Prohibition: The Era of Excess* (1962), 139; Wilson's "opinion," Address to the Associated Press (Apr 20, 1915), and "what's right," cited in Blum (1956), 161. **Facts.** Rotundity: Levenstein (1988), 12–14. Bellamy, "Pledge of Allegiance" (1892); Bates, *America the Beautiful* (1893); Sousa, *Semper Fidelis* (1888); Lazarus, "The New Colossus" (inscription for the Statue of Liberty, written in 1886). Certification: Kett (1977), 157. Law schools: Boorstin (1973), 62–4. Brookings, in *ibid.*, 213. Articles on "middle age": Kett (1977), 162. Hale, Jr. (1971), 29. Divorce rates: Degler (1980), 166; and O'Neill (1967), 19–20. Drug abuse: H. Wayne Morgan, *Drugs in America: A Social History, 1800–1980* (1981); and Chapter 12 source notes. "Somatic remedies" to female hysteria: G. J. Barker-Benfield, "The Spermatic Economy: A Nineteenth-Century View of Sexuality," and Carl N. Degler, "What Ought to Be and What Was: Women's Sexuality in the Nineteenth Century," both in Gordon (1978). *Atlantic Monthly*, cited in Lears (1983). **Youth.** French visitor Georges Fisch, in Smith and Judah (1966), 309–11. On compulsory school attendance and the high school movement, see Furnas (1969), 749–50, and Kett (1977), 122–31; on report cards, see *ibid.*, 116. Bushnell, in *ibid.*, 114. Kett, in *ibid.*, 116; for a similar conclusion, see Ryan (1981), 145–85; Beecher, in Kett (1977), 124. **Coming of Age.** Sunday school spokesman was Daniel Wise, in *ibid.*, 120; YMCA official, in *ibid.*, 119; Kett, in *ibid.*, 119; Roosevelt, in Paul (1988), 197. On general decline in violence, see Eric H. Monkkonen, "The Organized Response to Crime in Nineteenth- and Twentieth-Century America" (*JIH*, Summer 1983) and Lane (1979). Roosevelt, in Hale, Jr. (1971), 46. **Rising Adulthood.** Gompers, in Page Smith, *The Rise of Industrial America: A People's History of the Post-Reconstruction Era* (1984), 237; Lloyd, *Wealth Against Commonwealth* (1894); Riis, *How the Other Half Lives* (1890); Cable, *The Silent South* (1885); Bellamy, *Looking*

Backward (1888); Blodgett, in Morgan (1963), 56. **Midlife.** McKinley, in *ibid.*, 168; Michelson, at dedication ceremony for University of Chicago physics lab (1894). Roosevelt, *The Strenuous Life* (1900); on origin of the word "muckrakers," see Roosevelt (1906), in Hofstadter (1963), doc. 2. Chopin, *The Awakening* (1899); Wilson, in Blum (1956), 127. **Elderhood.** Jewett, *The Country of the Pointed Firs* (1896); Hall, in Hale, Jr. (1971), 5; Sullivan, cited in Calvin B. T. Lee, *The Campus Scene: 1900–1970* (1970), 23; "international kiss," cited in Burns (1986). Brandeis' "Men of zeal" appears in *Olmstead v. United States* (1928); "trial and error," in *Burnet v. Coronado Oil and Gas* (1932); Kelley, according to Felix Frankfurter, in Otis L. Graham, Jr., *An Encore for Reform: The Old Progressives and the New Deal* (1967), 171. Dewey, in Wish (1952), 519; James, *What Maisie Knew* (preface, 1907–9); James, *ibid.*; Ray Stannard Baker on Harris, in Smith (1984), 749; North, in Boorstin (1973), 172; James (Aug 10, 1914), in Leon Edel (ed.), *Henry James: Selected Letters* (1987), 713; James, letter to Hugh Walpole (1913).

CHAPTER 10: THE GREAT POWER CYCLE

GREAT POWER CYCLE BACKGROUND. See James MacGregor Burns, *The Workshop of Democracy* (1986); Page Smith, *The Rise of Industrial America: A People's History of the Post-Reconstruction Era* (1984), and *Redeeming the Time: A People's History of the 1920s and the New Deal* (1987); William Manchester, *The Glory and the Dream: A Narrative History of America, 1932–1972* (1974); and J. C. Furnas, *The Americans: A Social History of the United States, 1587–1914* (1969), and *Great Times: An Informal Social History of the United States, 1914–1929* (1974). For social histories of specific periods and topics: Walter Lord, *The Good Years: From 1900 to the First World War* (1960); Frederick Lewis Allen, *Only Yesterday* (1931), and *Since Yesterday* (1940); Joseph Goulden, *The Best Years: 1945–1950* (1976); William O'Neill, *The American High: The Years of Confidence, 1945–1960* (1986); Harvey Levenstein, *Revolution at the Table: The Transformation of the American Diet* (1988); H. Wayne Morgan, *Drugs in America: A Social History, 1800–1980* (1981), and Morgan (ed.), *Yesterday's Addicts: American Society and Drug Abuse* (1974); Daniel Boorstin, *The Americans: The Democratic Experience* (1973); C. Vann Woodward, *The Strange Career of Jim Crow* (1955); Robert and Helen Lynd, *Middletown: A Study in American Culture* (1929), and *Middletown in Transition* (1937); and Andrew Gallagher, Jr., *Plainville Fifteen Years Later* (1961). For excellent anthologies chronicling the American mood at three specific moments, see Robert Sklar (ed.), *The Plastic Age (1917–1930)* (1970); Harold Stearns (ed.), *America Now* (1938); André Siegfried, *America at Mid-Century* (1955); and Huston Smith (ed.), *The Search for America* (1959). On youth: Mary Cable, *The Little Darlings* (1975); Joseph Kett, *Rites of Passage: Adolescence in America, 1790 to the Present* (1977); Margaret Steinfels, *Who's Minding the Children: The History and Politics of Day Care in America* (1976); David Nasaw, *Schooled to Order* (1979); Vivian Zelizer, *Pricing the Priceless Child: The Changing Social Value of Children* (1985); Joseph Hawes and Ray Hiner, *Growing Up in America: Children in Historical Perspective* (1985); essays in Harvey J. Graff (ed.), *Growing Up in America* (1987); essays in Michael Katz (ed.), *Education in American History* (1973); John Folger and Charles Nam, *Education of the*

American Population (Census Monograph, 1960); Frederick Rudolph, *The American College and University: A History* (1962); Lewis F. Feuer, *The Conflict of Generations: The Character and Significance of Student Movements* (1969), ch. 7; Helen Horowitz, *Campus Life* (1987); Paula Fass, *The Damned and the Beautiful: American Youth in the 1920s* (1977); and Calvin B. T. Lee, *The Campus Scene: 1900–1970* (1970). On family life: Carl Degler, *At Odds: Women and the Family in America from the Revolution to the Present* (1980); Steven Mintz and Susan Kellogg, *Domestic Revolutions: A Social History of American Family Life* (1988); essays in Tamara K. Hareven (ed.), *Transitions: The Family and the Life Course in Historical Perspective* (1978); Battelle Memorial Institute, *The Cosmopolitan Report: The Changing Life Course of American Women* (1986); Mary P. Ryan, *Womanhood in America* (1979); essays in Michael Gordon (ed.), *The American Family in Social-Historical Perspective* (2nd ed., 1978), esp. Daniel Scott Smith, "The Dating of the American Sexual Revolution: Interpretation and Evidence"; Alfred Kinsey, *Sexual Behavior in the Human Male* (1948), and *Sexual Behavior in the Human Female* (1953); John Demos, *Past, Present, and Personal: The Family and the Life Course in American History* (1986); Mary E. Cookingham, "Combining Marriage, Motherhood, and Jobs Before World War II: Women College Graduates, Classes of 1905–1935" (*JFH,* Summer 1984); and John Modell, "Normative Aspects of American Marriage Timing Since World War II" (*JFH,* Summer 1980). On cultural life: Warren I. Susman, *Culture as History: The Transformation of American Society in the Twentieth Century* (1984); and Lewis Perry, *Intellectual Life in America: A History* (1984). On politics: Warren Miller, *American National Election Studies Data Sourcebook, 1952–1978* (1980); Anthony Orum (ed.), *The Seeds of Politics: Youth and Politics in America* (1972); Norman H. Nie et al., *The Changing American Voter* (1976); and Angus Campbell et al., *The American Voter* (1960). On old age: David Hackett Fischer, *Growing Old in America* (1977); Harvey Lehman, *Age and Achievement* (1953); Andrew Achenbaum, *Old Age in the New Land: The American Experience since 1790* (1978); essays in Bernice Neugarten (ed.), *Middle Age and Aging* (1968); William Graebner, *A History of Retirement: The Meaning and Function of an American Institution, 1885–1978* (1980); and U.S. House of Representatives, *Retirement Income for an Aging Population* (Committee on Ways and Means, Aug 25, 1987), and *Overview of Entitlement Programs, 1990 Green Book* (Committee on Ways and Means, Jun 5, 1990) sections 1, 3–4, and appendices H and I.

GREAT POWER CYCLE REFERENCES. Laurence, in George Seldes (ed.), *The Great Thoughts* (1985); Stimson, Churchill, Oppenheimer, and "another young physicist," all cited in Manchester (1974), 378–9; Baker, *Growing Up* (1982), 230. On the "interim committee" on the A-bomb, see Manchester (1974), 375; MacArthur, in *OxA,* 1045, 1062–3. Groves, in Manchester (1974), 379; Truman, in *ibid.,* 382, 367. For average age of World War II combat troops, see John Morton Blum, *V Was for Victory* (1976), 339. Styron, in "My Generation" (*Esquire,* Oct 1968). Songs: Peter, Paul, and Mary, *Where Have All the Flowers Gone?* (written by Pete Seeger, 1961); Barry McGuire, *Eve of Destruction* (1965); Tom Lehrer, *So Long Mom* (1965) and *Wernher von Braun* (1965). Roosevelt's reference to a "mysterious cycle" of "generational destiny" appears in his acceptance speech to the 1936 Democratic National Convention; Henry Steele Commager, *The American Mind: An Interpretation of American Thought and Character Since the 1880s* (1950), 42; Hofstadter, *Age of Reform* (1955), 166; Degler, "The Third American

Revolution,'' in *Out of Our Past* (1970); the "new generation" was John Kennedy's reference to his own (G.I.) peers in his inaugural address (Jan 20, 1961).

MISSIONARY BACKGROUND. For a lifecycle overview of the Missionaries, beginning with their formative experiences as rising adults, see John Higham, "The Reorientation of American Culture in the 1890s," in *Writing American History* (1970); William McLoughlin, "The Third Great Awakening," in *Revivals, Awakenings, and Reforms* (1978); Lawrence Goodwyn, *Democratic Promise: The Populist Moment in America* (1976); Louis Filler, *The Muckrakers* (1968), and *Appointment at Armageddon: Muckraking and Progressivism in the American Tradition* (1976); Henry David, *The History of the Haymarket Affair* (1936); and Patrick Renshaw, *The Wobblies: The Story of Syndicalism in the United States* (1967). On the broader Missionary impact on society and culture: Jean B. Quandt, *From the Small Town to the Great Community: The Social Thought of Progressive Intellectuals* (1970); Christopher Lasch, *The New Radicalism in America, 1889–1963: The Intellectual as a Social Type* (1965); Henry F. May, *The End of American Innocence* (1979); William O'Neill, *Feminism in America: A History* (1989); James R. McGovern, "The American Woman's Pre–World War I Freedom in Manners and Morals" (*JAH,* Sep 1968); Harvey Wish, *Society and Thought in Modern America* (1952); Commager (1950); Andrew Sinclair, *Prohibition: The Era of Excess* (1962); Kenneth T. Jackson, *The Ku Klux Klan in the City, 1915–1930* (1967); John Hicks, *Republican Ascendancy, 1921–1933* (1960); Arthur M. Schlesinger, Jr., *The Coming of the New Deal* (1959); Otis L. Graham, Jr., *An Encore for Reform: The Old Progressives and the New Deal* (1967), and *The Great Campaigns: Reform and War in America, 1900–1928* (1971); Arthur Ekirch, Jr., *Ideologies and Utopias: The Impact of the New Deal on American Thought* (1969); and Eric F. Goldman, *Rendezvous with Destiny: A History of Modern American Reform* (1956). See also sources that overlap with the Progressives: Richard Hofstadter, *The Age of Reform* (1955); Donald Pizer (ed.), *American Thought and Writing in the 1890s* (1972); Morton White, *Social Thought in America: The Revolt Against Formalism* (1957); and T. Jackson Lears, *No Place of Grace: Antimodernism and the Transformation of American Culture, 1880–1920* (1981). For biographical insights: Ellen Lagemann, *A Generation of Women* (1979); Mercedes M. Randall, *Improper Bostonian: Emily Greene Balch* (1964); Jane Addams, *Twenty Years at Hull House* (1910); Sherwood Eddy, *Pathfinders of the World's Missionary Crusade* (1945); James Weldon Johnson, *The Autobiography of an Ex-Colored Man* (1912); Walter William Liggett, *The Rise of Herbert Hoover* (1932); William Allen White, *Puritan in Babylon* (1938); and Douglas MacArthur, *Reminiscences* (1964).

MISSIONARY REFERENCES. Bryan, speech at the 1896 Democratic National Convention, in Pizer (1972), 380, 375; Herron, in Smith (1984), 483. Norris, *The Octopus* (1901); Sinclair, *The Jungle* (1906); Steffens, *Shame of the Cities* (1904). Descriptions of Addams appear in G. J. Barker-Benfield, "Mother Emancipator" (*JFH,* Winter 1979). Chapman, in Smith (1984), 715; Lodge, in Lears (1981), 239; Crane, "In the Depths of a Coal Mine" (*McClure's,* 1894). "A generation of ideals," in Winston Churchill, *Mr. Crewe's Career* (1908); see also Richard and Beatrice Hofstadter, "Winston Churchill: A Study in the Popular Novel" (*AQ,* Spring 1950); White, in Samuel Eliot Morison and Henry Steele Commager, *The Growth of the American Republic* (1950), 262; saying attributed to Chapman, in John Bartlett, *Familiar Quotations* (1968), 863; fellow student on Chapman, in Smith (1984), 712. Gilman, *This Man-Made World* (1911); Jack London, *Call of the Wild* (1903); Edgar Rice Burroughs, *Tarzan of the Apes* (1914). Roosevelt, State of the Union message (Jan 6, 1942), in E. Taylor Parks and Lois F. Parks (eds.), *Memorable Quotations of Franklin D. Roosevelt* (1965), 227; Roosevelt, first inaugural address (Mar 4, 1933) and speech (Jan 17, 1938), in *ibid.*, 257, 55–56. Howe, *Confessions of a Reformer* (1925), cited in Susman (1984), 89; Santayana, *Character and Opinion in the United States* (1920); the Mount Hermon crusade and "Evangelization of the World" motto is described in Eddy (1945); 43; Arthur M. Schlesinger, Jr., *The Crisis of the Old Order, 1919–1933* (1957), 19; Johnson, in Manchester (1974), 355; the Speer description appears in Eddy (1945), 269; Speer, *Missionary Principles and Practice* (1902); "World War II Wise Men" appears in "The New American Establishment" (*U.S. News and World Report*, Feb 8, 1988); Wharton, in Cheryl Merser, *"Grown-Ups"* (1987), preface. **Facts.** Christmas: Boorstin (1973), 158–62. High schools: Edwin Dexter, *A History of Education in the United States* (1906), 173. Share of all youths attending school: *HSt*, H-433. Coed colleges: Dexter (1906), 448. College degrees: *HSt*, H-751; see also Huston Smith (1959), 91; Page Smith (1984), 589–90; Kett (1977), 178. College unrest: Horowitz (1987), ch. 2; and Feuer (1969), 332–6. Settlement movement: *ibid.*, 339; and John P. Rousmanière, "Cultural Hybrid in the Slums: The College Woman and the Settlement House, 1889–94," in Katz (1973). Filler (1968), 3–7. Alcohol and drug abuse: Chapter 12 source notes; and J. C. Burnham, "New Perspectives on the Prohibition 'Experiment' of the 1920's" (*JSH*, Fall 1968). "Nadir" of black history: Rayford Logan, *The Negro in American Life and Thought: The Nadir, 1877–1901* (1954); and Woodward (1955). Lynching of blacks: *HSt*, H-1170. Diet revolution: Levenstein (1988), 86. Marriage age: Fass (1977), 66–9; Peter Uhlenberg, "Changing Configurations of the Life Course," in Hareven (1978); Warren S. Thompson and P. K. Whelpton, *Population Trends in the United States* (1969), 203–6; and Ruth Freeman and Patricia Klaus, "Blessed or Not? The New Spinster in England and the United States in the Late Nineteenth and Early Twentieth Centuries" (*JFH*, 1984). McGovern (1968). Age of cabinet members: Harvey Lehman, "The Age of Eminent Leaders, Then and Now" (*American Journal of Sociology*, 1947). Falling mortality, age 65 to 85: *HSt*, B-190, B-191; on rising life expectancy at age 65, see *SSP*, table 10. Poverty by age bracket in 1949: Eugene Smolensky, Sheldon Danziger, and Peter Gottschalk, "The Declining Significance of Age in the United States: Trends in the Well-Being of Children and the Elderly since 1939" (Institute for Research on Poverty, University of Wisconsin-Madison, 1987). **Youth.** Abbott, *Gentle Measures in the Management of the Young* (1871), cited in Cable (1975), 100–1; Trippe, *Home Treatment for Children* (1881), cited in *ibid.;* Cable, *ibid.*, 105; DuBois, in Smith (1984), 626; Addams (1910). On the importance given to the mother's role during the 1890s, see Martin U. Martel, "Age-Sex Roles in American Magazine Fiction (1890–1955)," in Neugarten (1968). Mrs. James Roosevelt, *My Boy Franklin* (1933); Anna Sewell, *Black Beauty* (1877); Johanna Spyri, *Heidi* (English translation, 1884); Alger, *Bound to Rise* (1873); Canby, in Cable (1975), 104. **Coming of Age.** Hyde, *The Evolution of a College Student* (1898), cited in Kett (1977), 177; Baker, in Smith (1984), 596; Steffens, in Horowitz (1987), 51–2; Herron, "Message of Jesus to Men of Wealth" (1891); Herron, *Between Caesar and Jesus* (1899); Howe (1925), in Susman (1984), 89; O. Henry, *The Trimmed Lamp* (1907); Crane, "The Blue Battalions," in Pizer (1972), 31; Hearst editorial, in Furnas (1969), 864; "Gentle Jesus . . . ," in Joe

Hill, *I.W.W. Songbook;* Sinclair, *The Jungle* (1906). **Rising Adulthood.** Hovey, in Lears (1981), 115, 119; Griffith, *Birth of a Nation* (film, 1915); Beveridge, in Wish (1952), 393, and in Lord (1960), 8; DuBois, *Dusk of Dawn: An Essay Toward an Autobiography of a Race Concept* (1940); Anderson, *Winesburg, Ohio* (1919); Masters, *Spoon River Anthology* (1915). "The home is in peril" is discussed in McGovern (1968); fictional southern belle in Glasgow, *Phases of an Inferior Planet* (1898). On "servantless kitchen," see Levenstein (1988), 60–71; on "minimalist house," see Gwendolyn Wright, *Moralism and the Model Home: Domestic Architecture and Cultural Conflict in Chicago, 1873–1913* (1980). Canby, in Fass (1977), 73. **Midlife.** Bryan, in Sinclair (1962), 16–17; Adams (1926), in Fass (1977), 17; Wilson, in Furnas (1974), 236; Follett and Park, in Quandt (1970), 141; Woods, in Graham, Jr. (1971), 99. Ford, in Susman (1984), 137–9; White, *A Puritan in Babylon* (1938). On rising imprisonment rates during the 1920s, see discussion in Eric H. Monkkonen, "The Organized Response to Crime in Nineteenth- and Twentieth-Century America" (*JIH,* Summer 1983). On the number of executions (which doubled between 1910 and 1920), see Margaret Callahan, *Historical Corrections Statistics in the United States, 1850–1984* (U.S. Department of Justice, 1986), 217. **Elderhood.** Roosevelt, Speech to the 1936 Democratic National Convention, in Parks and Parks (1965), 147; Armstrong, in Graebner, (1980), 186; Wagner, in *ibid.,* 185; Graham, Jr. (1967), 108–9; for contemporary labels, see *ibid.,* 168; Mencken, "The New Deal Mentality" (1936); Congressman Dewey Short likened MacArthur to "God Himself," in Manchester (1974), 563; Mott described by Eddy (1945), 310. Baruch, speech (Apr 16, 1947), in Seldes (1985), 35. On origin of term "foreign aid," see Boorstin (1973), 568–79. "The Great Society" was first coined by British social scientist Graham Wallas (born 1858) in 1914; for its growing use among American Missionaries, see Adams, *Epic of America* (1931). Lindsay on Bryan, in "Bryan, Bryan, Bryan, Bryan," *Collected Works* (1925); Bryan, in Richard Hofstadter, *The American Political Tradition* (1948), 186; Berenson, *Aesthetics and History* (1948); Roosevelt, State of the Union speech (Jan 6, 1941).

LOST BACKGROUND. For the Lost peer personality, the unmatched source is the lifetime writing of Malcolm Cowley, esp. *Exile's Return* (1934), *A Second Flowering: Works and Days of the Lost Generation* (1956), with Robert Cowley (eds.), *Fitzgerald and the Jazz Age* (1966), and *The View from Eighty* (1981). See also F. Scott Fitzgerald, "My Generation" (*Esquire,* Oct 1968); Edmund Wilson (ed.), *The Crack-Up* (1945); and George Burns, *The Third Time Around* (1980). No other generation expressed its peer personality so vividly in literature and music; see esp. F. Scott Fitzgerald, *This Side of Paradise* (1920); Thomas Wolfe, *You Can't Go Home Again* (1940); Ernest Hemingway, *A Farewell to Arms* (1929) and *The Old Man and the Sea* (1952); Gunther Schuller, *The History of Jazz* (1968); and Ronald Morris, *Wait Until Dark: Jazz and the Underworld* (1980). For the youth and rising adulthood of the Lost: Jacob Riis, *How the Other Half Lives* (1890); Jane Addams, *The Spirit of Youth and the City Streets* (1909); Selwyn K. Troen, "The Discovery of the Adolescent by American Educational Reformers, 1900–1920: An Economic Perspective," in Graff (1987); *Boyhood and Lawlessness* (Survey Associates, 1914); Anthony Platt, *The Child Savers: The Invention of Delinquency* (1969); David Nasaw, *Children of the City: At Work and at Play* (1985); G. Stanley Hall, *Adolescence: Its Psychology and Its Relations to Physiology, Anthropology, Sociology,*

Sex, Crime, Religion and Education (1905); Van Wyck Brooks, "The Culture of Industrialism" *(Seven Arts,* 1917); Greer Collin, *The Great School Legend* (1973); S. E. Ellacott, *Conscripts on the March* (1965); Robert Liston, *Greeting: You Are Hereby Reported for Induction* (1970); Quincy Wright, *A Study of War* (1965); Fass (1977); Furnas (1974); Sklar (1970); F. J. Hoffman, *The Twenties: American Writing in the Postwar Decade* (1955); and Sara Alpern and Dale Baum, "Female Ballots: The Impact of the Nineteenth Amendment" *(JIH,* Summer 1985). On their trials in midlife and old age: Winona Morgan, *The Family Meets the Depression* (1939); Niebuhr, *Moral Man in Immoral Society* (1932); Robert Sobel, *The Origins of Interventionism* (1960); James Abrahamson, *The American Home Front* (1983); Donald Rogers, *Since You Went Away* (1943); Clay Blair, *The Forgotten War* (1987); Reuben Hill, *Family Development in Three Generations* (1970); Martha Riche, "The Nursing Home Dilemma" *(AD,* Oct 1985); and Riche, "The Oldest Old" *(AD,* Nov 1985).

LOST REFERENCES. Pound, *Hugh Selwyn Mauberley* (1920); cummings, in Cowley (1956), 14; Dos Passos, in *ibid.,* 12; Fitzgerald, *This Side of Paradise* (1920); Richard Whiting, *Ain't We Got Fun?* (1920); Fitzgerald (1920); "the lies of old men" appears in Pound (1920); last words of Wolfe according to Max Perkins, in Cowley (1956), 185; Ruth's autobiography, cited in Susman (1984), 143–4. On articles on juvenile delinquency, see Nasaw (1979), 90; Allen (1931), ch. 5; Missionary President was Franklin Roosevelt in his first inaugural address (Mar 4, 1933); Millay, *A Few Figs from Thistles* (1920); Fitzgerald, "The Crack-Up" *(Esquire,* Feb 1936), later included in Edmund Wilson (ed.), *The Crack-Up* (1945); Coughlin, radio address (Feb 5, 1939), in *Why Leave Our Own?* (1939); Roosevelt during 1944 campaign, in Manchester (1974), 320; MacLeish, *The Irresponsibles* (1940); Stimson, *On Active Service in Peace and War* (1948); Hemingway, *The Sun Also Rises* (1926); Fitzgerald, *All the Sad Young Men* (1926); Comer, "A Letter to the Rising Generation," and Bourne, "The Two Generations" *(Atlantic Monthly,* Feb and May, 1911); Hemingway, *Death in the Afternoon* (1932) and "A Clean Well-Lighted Place" (1933); Miller, op-ed essay, *NYT* 9/7/74. **Facts.** Child labor: Degler (1980), 70; Lord (1960), 299; and *HSt,* series D-31, D-80. Newsies: Nasaw (1985), ch. 5. Unionism: Burns (1986), 534. Sugar Consumption: *HSt,* G-911. Education: Folger and Nam (1960), chs. 1–2, 4–5; and *HSt,* H-433, H-707, H-755, H-764. First I.Q. tests: Boorstin (1973), 220–3. Years of schooling, 1952 and 1970: Stephen Crystal, *America's Old Age Crisis* (1982), 33. Drug abuse: Morgan (1981). Homicide: *HSt,* H-972. Vocabulary: Stuart Berg Flexner, *Listening to America* (1982). Influenza: Alfred Crosby, *Epidemic and Peace* (1976). Mortality rates in elderhood: *HSt,* B-190, B-191; on stagnant life expectancy at age 65, see *SSP,* table 10. Suicide: Herbert Hendin, *Suicide in America* (1982), ch. 2; and Morton Kramer et al., *Mental Disorders/ Suicide* (1972), 207. Longitudinal surveys: K. Warner Schaie and Iris Parham, "Stability of Adult Personality Traits: Fact or Fable?" *(Journal of Personality and Social Psychology,* 1976). Black "Great Migration": Reynolds Farley, "The Urbanization of Negroes in the United States" *(JSH,* Spring 1968). Share of elder Lost who are naturalized citizens: "A State by State Look at the Oldest Americans" *(AD,* Nov 1986). Party affiliation: Miller (1980); "Opinion Roundup" *(PO,* May–Jun 1985 and Nov–Dec 1986); and Alan Spitzer, "The Historical Problem of Generations" *(AHR,* Dec 1973). Housing of elder Lost: Hill (1970), p. 108. Income of elder Lost: Riche (1985); and G. Lawrence

Atkins, "The Economic Status of the Oldest Old" (*Milbank Memorial Fund Quarterly,* Spring 1985). Social Security benefit level by cohort, and poverty and pension coverage by age bracket: U.S. House of Representatives (1990), 116–21, 1001, 1011. **Youth.** O'Hanlon, in "Virginia, Santa Can't Find Your House," *WP* 12/24/89; Smith, *The Science of Motherhood* (1894), in Cable (1975), 102; Burns (1980), 9–10; Riis (1890); Marx, in Nasaw (1985), 26. On football player deaths, see Lee (1970), 7; Hall (1905); Wolfe, *You Can't Go Home Again* (1940). Mike Gold, *Jews Without Money* (1930), in Nasaw (1985), 141. **Coming of Age.** Carter, in Cowley and Cowley (1966), 48–9; Cowley (1934), 18; student organizer, Harry Laidler (1925), in Feuer (1969), 344; Brooks, *Wine of the Puritans* (1908); "Sex O'Clock," discussed in Nasaw (1985), 140; Mencken, in Lee (1970), 12; Hemingway, *A Farewell to Arms* (1929); Thompson, in "Virgil Thompson . . . ," *NYT* 10/1/89; Fitzgerald (1968); Barton, *A Young Man's Jesus* (1914), cited in T. J. Jackson Lears, "From Salvation to Self-Realization," in Richard Wrightman Fox and Lears (eds.), *The Culture of Consumption* (1983); Lewis, *Main Street* (1920) and *Elmer Gantry* (1927); Carter (*Atlantic Monthly,* Sep 1920). **Rising Adulthood.** Fitzgerald, in Andrew Trumbull, *Scott Fitzgerald* (1962), 183; McKay, *Home to Harlem* (1928); Locke (1925); Brown, "A Century of Negro Portraiture in American Literature," in Abraham Chapman (ed.), *Black Voices* (1968); Fitzgerald, "Echoes of the Jazz Age" (1931), in Cowley and Cowley (1966); producer on "neckers . . . ," cited in Lewis (1931), 101–2; Carnegie's "always avoid . . ." appears in "At 75, Carnegie's Message Lives On," *NYT* 12/18/87; Fitzgerald first heard "living well . . ." from his friend Gerald Murphy, according to Calvin Thomas, *Living Well Is the Best Revenge* (1962), 141; Fitzgerald, *The Great Gatsby* (1925); Vanzetti, letter to his son (1927), in Seldes (1985), 429; O'Neill, *The Emperor Jones* (1920); Lewis, in Daniel Aaron, "Literary Scenes and Literary Movements" in *CLH;* Lippmann, *A Preface to Morals* (1929). **Midlife.** Cowley (1934), 306; Fitzgerald (1931), in Frederick J. Hoffman, "Some Perspectives on the 1920s," in Sidney Fine and Gerald S. Brown (eds.), *The American Past* (1970); Niebuhr (1932); Wilson, in Manchester (1974), 77; Ickes and Roosevelt, *ibid.,* 115, 114. **Elderhood.** Hemingway (1929); Eisenhower's "respectable image," in letter to Henry Luce, cited in Fred Greenstein and Robert Wright, "Reagan . . . Another Ike?" (*PO,* Dec–Jan 1981), and "military-industrial complex" (Jan 1961), in Manchester (1974), 877; Kennedy to Congress (May 25, 1961), in "Looking Back at Apollo," *WSJ* 7/20/89. Andrus (1965), in "AARP's Catastrophe," *WSJ* 10/2/89; on "disengagement" theory of retirement, see Graebner (1980), 233, 241; Miller, *Death of a Salesman* (1949); Parker, in Manchester (1974), 246. Thompson, "Virgil Thompson . . . ," *NYT* 10/1/89; Parker, in Seldes (1985), 321; Wilder, *The Skin of Our Teeth* (1942); Tillich, in Paul Tillich and Huston Smith, "Human Fulfillment," in Smith (1959); Barton, in Susman (1984), 126; "play the sap" appears in Dashiell Hammett, *The Maltese Falcon* (1929)—later immortalized by Humphrey Bogart on camera (1931); for "American High," see O'Neill (1986); *18 Again!* (film, 1988); Cowley (1956), 248.

G.I. BACKGROUND. Despite crisp cohort boundaries and a peer culture of exceptional solidarity, fewer histories or biographies have been written about this generation than about the Lost, Silent, or Boom. See Manchester (1974); O'Neill (1986); Alfred Kazin, *Starting Out in the Thirties* (1965); Caroline Bird, *The Invisible Scar* (1966); Betty Friedan, *The Feminine Mystique* (1963); and Eda LeShan, *The Wonderful Crisis of Middle*

Age (1973). For revealing data on the G.I. peer personality: Leonard Cain, "Age Status and Generational Phenomena" (*Gerontologist*, Sep 6, 1987); and Schaie and Parham (1976). On the transition from protected children to heroic young adults: Nasaw (1985); Zelizer (1985); Robert Paul Smith, *"Where Did You Go?" "Out" "What Did You Do?" "Nothing"* (1957); Dominick Cavallo, *Muscles and Morals: Organized Playgrounds and Urban Reform, 1880–1920* (1981); David MacLeod, *Building Character in the American Boy: The Boy Scouts, YMCA, and Their Forerunners, 1870–1920* (1983), and "Act Your Age: Boyhood, Adolescence, and the Rise of the Boy Scouts of America," in Graff (1987); Fass (1977); Sheila Bennett and Glen Elder, Jr., "Women's Work in the Family Economy" (*JFH*, Summer 1979); David Katzman, *Seven Days a Week: Women and Domestic Service in Industrializing America* (1978); Philip Wylie, *Generation of Vipers* (1942); Richard Tregaskis, *Guadalcanal Diary* (1943); David Brinkley, *Washington Goes to War* (1988); and S. E. Ellacott, *Conscripts on the March* (1965). For the G.I. perspective on postwar America at midlife and beyond: William Whyte, *The Organization Man* (1956); C. Wright Mills, *The Power Elite* (1959); Ralph Ellison, *The Invisible Man* (1952); Daniel Bell, *The End of Ideology* (1960); Richard Rovere, *The American Establishment* (1962); Alistair Cooke, *Generation on Trial: U.S.A. v. Alger Hiss* (1952); John Kenneth Galbraith, *The Affluent Society* (1958); John Howard Griffin, *Black Like Me* (1961); Arthur M. Schlesinger, *A Thousand Days: John F. Kennedy in the White House* (1965); David Halberstam, *The Best and the Brightest* (1969); Seymour Martin Lipset, *Political Man* (1960); Richard Nixon, *Six Crises* (1962); Eric Sevareid, *This Is Eric Sevareid* (1964); Stewart Alsop, *The Center: People and Power in Political Washington* (1968); Theodore White, *The Making of the President* (1961 through 1973) and *America in Search of Itself: The Making of the President, 1956–1980* (1982); Kenneth Keniston, *Youth and Dissent: The Rise of a New Opposition* (1971), and Lee Iacocca, *Iacocca: An Autobiography* (1984). For elderhood: Henry Pratt, *The Gray Lobby* (1976); Alan Pifer and Lydia Bronte (eds.), *Our Aging Society* (1986); Henry Fairlie, "Talkin' 'Bout My Generation" (*New Republic*, Mar 28, 1988); Samuel Preston, "Children and the Elderly: Divergent Paths for America's Dependents" (*Demography*, Nov 1984); Beatrice Gross and Sylvia Seidman (eds.), *The New Old: Struggling for a Decent Aging* (1978); Erik Erikson, Joan Erikson, and Helen Kivnick, *Vital Involvement in Old Age* (1986); and Ken Dychtwald and Joe Flower, *Age Wave: The Challenges and Opportunities of an Aging America* (1989).

G.I. REFERENCES. Marshall, cited by Ronald Reagan, speech to Republican National Convention (Sep 15, 1988); *U.S. News & World Report*, cited in Michael L. Smith, "Selling the Moon," in Fox and Lears (1983); Hoffer, in *ibid.;* "born in this century . . ." appears in Kennedy's inaugural address (Jan 20, 1961); for discussion of "generational watershed," see Lola Irelan, "Retirement History Study: Introduction" (*Social Security Bulletin*, Nov 1972); Cain (1987); interviewer on Reston, in "Reston, Retiring at 80 . . . ," *NYT* 11/5/89; Henry Malcolm, *Generation of Narcissus* (1971), 43; the Superman cartoonists (both G.I.s) were Jerry Siegel and Joe Schuster; Kennedy (1961); Rand, "Apollo 11," in Leonard Peikoff (ed.), *Voice of Reason* (1988). "What we need . . . ," in Skinner, *Beyond Freedom and Dignity* (1971); Skinner, *Walden Two* (1948). Lipset (1960); Singer, in "Isaac Singer's Perspective on God and Man," *NYT* 10/23/68; Boorstin, *The Genius of American Politics* (1953); Wylie (1942); Friedan (1963); Ferdinand Lundberg and Marynia Farnham, *Modern Woman: The Lost Sex* (1947); Lynn White, Jr., *Educating*

Our Daughters (1950); Degler (1980), 440; on "witchhunt" vocabulary, see Manchester (1974), 492; Kennedy, *Profiles in Courage* (1956); Fass (1977), ch. 3; Roosevelt, radio message to the Young Democratic Clubs of America (1935), in Parks and Parks (1965), 41; Malvina Reynolds, in *Little Boxes and Other Handmade Songs* (1964); Goulden (1976), 427; Bush, in biographic film, televised (Aug 17, 1988) during the Republican National Convention; Bell, in Everett Ladd, "205 and Going Strong" (*PO*, Jun–Jul 1981); Reagan, 1985 State of the Union Message; LeShan (1973), 21; Harold Arlen and Johnny Mercer, *Ac-Cent-Tchu-Ate the Positive* (song, 1944); Teller, in "Star Wars . . . ," *NYT* 2/13/90. **Facts.** Federal spending as a share of GNP, in 1929 and 1980: *EPr* (1990), tables C-1, C-79. Child labor: Degler (1980), 70; Cain (1987); and *HSt*, series D-31, D-80. On "allowances," see Morgan (1939), 82–3. Figures on "doing the dishes": *ibid.*, 35. Infant and child mortality: *HSt*, B-182 to B-184, B-202 to B-205; and Levenstein (1988), ch. 10. Adult height: Robert W. Fogel, Stanley L. Engerman, and James Trussel, "Exploring the Uses of Data on Height" (*Social Science History*, Fall 1982); and John Kieran, "Sports," in Stearns (1938). Mortality: *HSt*, B-182 to B-189. Life expectancy at age 65: *SSP*, table 10. Education and schooling: Cain (1987), 85; Fass (1977), 123– 6; Christian Gauss, "Education," in Stearns (1938); *HSt*, H-433, H-707, H-755; and Folger and Nam (1960), chs. 1–2, 4–5. Foreign-language achievement: O'Neill (1986), 35. On-campus religious organizations: Burns (1986), 515; and Fass (1977), 45–6, 137–8. Voting data: Miller (1980); Nie (1976), 85–7; Campbell (1960), 148; Michael Nelson (ed.), *The Elections of 1984* (1985), 99; Burns (1986), 514; and various surveys published in *PO* through the 1980s. Black G.I. voters: research by John Morsell, in Lipset (1960), 281. G.I.s faring better than parents: "Opinion Roundup" (*PO*, Nov–Dec 1986). Homeownership data: Ben Wattenberg, *The Real America: A Surprising Examination of the State of the Union* (1974), 347; and O'Neill (1986), 12–20. Poverty rates by age bracket: *CPR*, series P-60. On age-bracket comparisons of homeownership, health-insurance coverage, discretionary income, household net worth, and other measures of economic well-being: U.S. House of Representatives (1987), part II, chs. 5, 10; Preston (1984); Peter G. Peterson and Neil Howe, *On Borrowed Time* (1988), chs. 2, 5; "Economic Status of the Elderly," in *EPr* (1985), ch. 5; and American Council of Life Insurance, *Datatrack No. 16: Household Income and Wealth* (Dec 1986). See also Martha Riche, "Big Spenders" (*AD*, Apr 1986); Greg Duncan et al., "The Changing Fortunes of Young and Old" (*AD*, Aug 1986); Blayne Cutler, "Mature Audiences Only" and Charles Longino and William Crown, "The Migration of Old Money" (*AD*, Oct 1989); Leslie Lenkowsky, "Why Growing Old Is Growing Better" (*PO*, May–Jun 1987); "Greener Era for Gray America" (*Insight*, Mar 2, 1987); and "The Booming Business of Aging," *WP* 4/22/88. On financial "worry" by age bracket: "Opinion Roundup" (*PO*, Feb–Mar 1985). On "senior" lobby members and newspapers: Gross and Seidman (1978), 147; Peterson and Howe (1988), 20, 72; "Gray Power" (*Time*, Jan 4, 1988); "AARP Flexes Its Muscles," *WP* 4/18/88; and "Old Money, New Power," *NYT* 10/23/88. Growth in federal benefits to the elderly, 1965–1989: U.S. House of Representatives (1990), 1058–68; and Peterson and Howe (1988), 154. Social Security payback: *ibid.*, 108–9; for a similar finding, see Michael Boskin, *Too Many Promises: The Uncertain Future of Social Security* (1986), ch. 4. Surveys on anxiety: "Opinion Roundup" (*PO*, Feb– Mar 1985); and polls cited in Preston (1984). "Happiest" generation data: "Opinion Roundup" (*PO*, Feb–Mar 1985); see also "Elderly Belie Old Stereotypes," *WP* 3/9/86. Harvard Class of '40: "The Graying of the Class of '40," *WP* 4/25/90. **Youth.** Spargo,

The Bitter Cry of the Children (1904); on rage over child nutrition, see Levenstein (1988), chs. 8–10; on Little Mothers' Leagues, see Hawes and Hiner (1985), 285; Eleanor Porter, *Pollyanna* (1913); Harold Gray, *Little Orphan Annie* (cartoon strip, from 1924); *Literary Digest,* cited in Fass (1977), 37. On "gang instinct" and scouting, see MacLeod (1983) and (1987); on vocationalism, see Edward Krug, *The Shaping of the American High School, 1880–1920* (1964). Rodgers, in Hawes and Hiner (1985), 130; Bush, in Nicholas King, *George Bush: A Biography* (1980), 14; "fine friends" appears in *Cornell Sun* article (1920), cited in Fass (1977), 248; for "rating and dating," see *ibid.,* ch. 4; "fair play" was a standard set by Joan Crawford, in Sklar (1970), 49; Krutch, in Lee (1970), 70; Cowley, *Exile's Return* (1951 ed.), 294. **Coming of Age.** Shuford, in Lee (1970), 36; *Harper's,* cited in *ibid.,* 48, and in Orum (1972), 25; poll comparing God and FDR, in Manchester (1974), 83; NRA pledge, in *ibid.,* 89; young communist bulletin, cited in Orum (1972), 39; Susman (1984), 172; Steinbeck, *Grapes of Wrath* (1939); *Snow White and the Seven Dwarfs* (film, 1938); Pegler, in Allen (1939), 232; Lewis, *It Can't Happen Here* (1935); *From Here to Eternity* (film, 1953); *Yank* editor, in Manchester (1974), 355; Mary Martin, *My Heart Belongs to Daddy* (song, 1937); Bing Crosby, in *Holiday Inn* (film, 1942; later remade into *White Christmas,* 1954); Mead, in Smith (1959), 116–7. **Rising Adulthood.** *The Best Years of Our Lives* (film, 1946). Opinion data, in American Institute of Public Opinion, *Gallup Poll* (1972), poll of 5/28/45 on poison gas, of 10/19/45 on Japan, and of 11/19/54 on corporal punishment. *Mr. Smith Goes to Washington* (film, 1939); Whyte (1956); Sloan Wilson, *Man in the Gray Flannel Suit* (1955); Mills (1959); Bell (1960); Galbraith (1958); Lipset (1960), 448. **Midlife.** Taylor, *The Uncertain Trumpet* (1960); Sevareid (1964), 12; Kennedy, in Manchester (1974), 491; Bell, in Ladd (1981); Frost, speech at Kennedy inaugural (Jan 20, 1961), cited in Halberstam (1969), 38; Kennedy campaign slogan, in *ibid.,* 43; Halberstam on "thinker-doers" McNamara and Bundy, in *ibid.,* 215, 43; Rovere, *The Establishment* (1962); Johnson, Democratic Party nomination speech (Aug 1964); White (1982), 125; "America's Mood Today" (*Look,* Jun 29, 1965); Nixon (1962), xvi; Rusk, in Alsop (1968), 120; McNamara, in *ibid.,* 150; Burns, Wald, and Gardner are all cited in Wattenberg (1974), 15, 18, 22; Nixon, in address to the nation on the situation in Southeast Asia (Apr 30, 1970); Mayer, in "Children's Crusade: A Search for Light," *Los Angeles Times* 11/16/69. **Elderhood.** *Lost Horizon* (film, 1937); for opinion data on euthanasia, see American Institute of Public Opinion (1972), poll of 6/21/47; Robert E. Wood of *Modern Maturity,* in "When Ads Don't Fit the Image" (*Newsweek,* Jan 22, 1990). For the politics of Social Security in the early 1970s, see Martha Derthick, *Policymaking for Social Security* (1979), chs. 17–18, and Michael Boskin (ed.), *The Crisis in Social Security* (1977); for the fiscal consequences of the 1972 Social Security benefit hike and "double-indexing," see Peterson and Howe (1988), chs. 6–7. AARP membership appeal, from a mailing received by authors (on Sep 6, 1988). Dychtwald and Flower (1989), 134–5; Sun City resident, in *ibid.,* 135; for figures on toy purchases, on educational expenses paid by grandparents, and on parents of divorced children, see *ibid.,* 256, 255, 254; "G.I. benefit," in "The Baby Boomers Turn 40" (*Time,* May 19, 1986). For poll data comparing feeling "wise" with feeling "friendly," see Gross and Seidman (1978), 102–9; LeShan (1973), 279; Apple, in Fischer (1977), 156; Joan Erikson, in "Erikson, in His Own Old Age, Expands His View of Life," *NYT* 6/14/88; for 1989 newsroom survey, see Richard Harwood, "Boomers in the Newsroom," *WP* 7/30/89. Lautenberg, in "With Saudi Oil Fields Secured, Bush Now Needs to Define Long-Term U.S. Objectives in the Gulf" *WSJ*

8/30/90; Dychtwald, in "Today's Grandparents Get Fed Up with Baby-Sitting," *San Francisco Chronicle* 8/23/90. Bush, inaugural address (Jan 20, 1989). The "Gross National Product" concept was first defined by Simon Kuznets in 1946. *It's a Wonderful Life* (film directed by Frank Capra, 1946); *Cocoon* (film directed by Ron Howard, 1985); Pryor, "Goodbye to Our Century" (*Modern Maturity,* Jan 1989).

SILENT BACKGROUND. For the Silent peer personality: Gail Sheehy, *Passages: Predictable Crises of Adult Life* (1976); Benita Eisler, *Private Lives: Men and Women of the Fifties* (1986); Howard Junker, "Resume of the Young Man as a Non-Generation" (*Esquire,* Dec 1965); the two "My Generation" essays by first-waver William Styron and last-waver Frank Conroy, *Esquire* (Oct 1968); Daniel Levinson, *The Seasons of a Man's Life* (1978); and Rose N. Franzblau, *The Middle Generation* (1971). For youth and coming-of-age experiences: Glen Elder, *The Children of the Great Depression* (1974); Ernie Anastos, *'Twixt: Teens Yesterday and Today* (1983); Russell Baker, *Growing Up* (1982); James Bryant Conant, *The American High School Today* (1959); Clay Blair, *The Forgotten War: America in Korea, 1950–1953* (1987); Max Hastings, *The Korean War* (1989); Paul Goodman, *Growing Up Absurd* (1960); Bruce Cook, *The Beat Generation* (1971); Malcolm X (with Alex Haley), *The Autobiography of Malcolm X* (1965); LeRoi Jones, *Blues People* (1963); Whyte (1956); David Riesman and Nathan Glazer, *The Lonely Crowd* (1950); David Riesman, *Faces in the Crowd* (1952); Jack Newfield, *A Prophetic Minority: The American New Left* (1967); James Gordon, "The Class of '62," WP 6/14/87; Daniel Callahan, *Generation of the Third Eye* (1965); and Otto Butz, "Unsilent Generation" (*Life,* Feb 17, 1958). For rising adulthood and midlife: Victoria Secunda, *By Youth Possessed* (1984); Robert and Joan Morrison, *From Camelot to Kent State* (1987); Andrew Cherlin, *Marriage Divorce Remarriage* (1981); Morton Hunt, *Sexual Behavior in the 1970s* (1974); Linda Sexton, *Between Two Worlds: Young Women in Crisis* (1979); Ellen Goodman, *Turning Points* (1979); and Ralph Abernathy, *And the Walls Came Tumbling Down: An Autobiography* (1989). For data on income, wealth, and career paths: Richard Easterlin, *Birth and Fortune: The Impact of Numbers on Personal Welfare* (1980); and American Council of Life Insurance, *The Prime Life Generation* (1985). For the Silent perspective on culture and society: Alvin Toffler, *Future Shock* (1970); Ben Wattenberg (1974) and *The Good News Is the Bad News Is Wrong* (1984); Daniel Yankelovich, *New Rules: Searching for Self-Fulfillment in a World Turned Upside Down* (1981); Barbara Gordon, *Jennifer Fever: Older Men and Younger Women* (1988); Bill Cosby, *Fatherhood* (1986); Kate Millett, *Sexual Politics* (1970); Charles Reich, *The Sorcerer of Bolinas Reef* (1976); Thomas Peters, *In Search of Excellence: Lessons from America's Best-Run Companies* (1982); David Broder, *The Changing of the Guard: Power and Leadership in America* (1980); Robert Reich, *The Next American Frontier* (1983) and *The Resurgent Liberal (and Other Unfashionable Prophecies)* (1989); Marvin Harris, *America Now: The Anthropology of a Changing Culture* (1982); John Naisbitt, *Megatrends* (1982), and with Patricia Aburdene, *Megatrends 2000* (1989); Paula Brown Doress (Boston Women's Health Collective), *Ourselves, Growing Older* (1987); and Robert Bellah et al., *Habits of the Heart* (1985).

SILENT REFERENCES. "The Class of '49" (*Fortune,* Jun 1949); on average age of class of '49, see *ibid.;* Manchester (1974), 576; Conroy (1968); *How to Succeed in Business Without Really Trying* (film, 1967); *Peggy Sue Got Married* (film, 1986); William O'Neill, cited in Manchester (1974), 577; Riesman and Glazer (1950); Kirkpatrick, "On Moving into a High-Tech House," *WP* 6/27/88; Crowe, in "From Cold War to Odd Couple" (*Newsweek,* Jul 31, 1989); Franzblau (1971), x; Eisler (1986), 18; for age of Peace Corps volunteers, see "Yesterday's New" (*Harvard Magazine,* Jul–Aug 1989); Junker (1965); Greene, "Fiftysomething—and in Charge," *NYT* 1/2/90; Franzblau (1971), x; Dylan, *My Back Pages* (song, 1964, later popularized by The Byrds); Easterlin (1980). On youth crime: see, during 1940s and 1950s, drop in murder rate, in *HSt,* H-971, and drop in youth incarceration rate, in Callahan (1986), 136. On youth suicide rate: *Hth,* table 31; Hendin (1982), ch. 2; and Kramer (1972), 207. On illegitimate births since 1940: *HSt,* B-30, B-31. On teen unemployment rate: *EPr* (1990), table C-39; see also discussion of cohorts and employment in Charles Murray, *Losing Ground: American Social Policy, 1950–1980* (1984), ch. 5. "Woody Allen school," in Goodman, "Some Advice for the 80's," *San Francisco Chronicle* 9/10/88; "erosion of confidence," in Goodman, "Consent and Compromise," *WP* 10/3/89; Eisler (1986), 304; Toffler (1970), 230, 283, 430; Schneider, "JFK's Children: The Class of '74" (*Atlantic,* Mar 1989); "The Can't Do Government," in cover story "Is Government Dead?" (*Time,* Oct 23, 1989); Will, in "Another Muddy Message" (*Newsweek,* Nov 21, 1988); "supply-side star," description of Eastwood in *Eastern Review* (Jan 1989), citing *New York Review of Books* in 1982; Raspberry, "The Unraveling of America," *WP* 10/11/90; *Fortune* (Jun 1949); "fifty-somethings" appears in Greene (1990); Eisler (1986), 356. **Facts.** Child labor: Degler (1980), 70; and *HSt,* series D-31. Per capita income growth from age 20 to 40: Sheldon Danziger and Peter Gottschalk, "Families with Children Have Fared Worst" (*Challenge,* Mar-Apr 1986); see also American Council of Life Insurance (1985), and "The (P)lucky Generation" (*AD,* Jan 1983). Household wealth and cohorts born in the 1930s: Frank Levy and Richard C. Michel, *Economic Status Across Generations: Prospects for the Future* (Urban Institute, 1990), 91, 162. Fertility: Battelle Memorial Institute (1986), ch. 7; and Jeane Clare Ridley et al., paper presented at annual meeting of Population Association of America (Apr 1987). Women's education: Folger and Nam (1960), 143–4. Sex: Hunt (1974), 190; see also Kinsey (1948) and (1953). Divorce: Robert T. Michael, "The Rise in Divorce Rates, 1950–1974: Age-Specific Components" (*Demography,* May 1978). Surge in "helping professions": Otto Butz, "Defense of the Class of '58," *NYT Magazine* 5/25/58. Public interest groups: "Public Interest Law Groups: Prospering Amid Adversity," *WP* 11/17/88. Charity: "Who Gives to Charity" (*AD,* Nov 1986). Congressional bureaucracy: Norman Ornstein et al., *Vital Statistics on Congress* (1984), chs. 1, 6–7; and "What Is Congress Trying to Hide?" *WSJ* 8/15/89. Voting behavior: Miller (1980); and "Opinion Roundup" (*PO,* Dec–Jan, 1981). Age preference of today's 55-year-olds: "Opinion Roundup" (*PO,* Feb–Mar 1985). **Youth.** Eisler (1986), 29; *Gone With the Wind* (film, 1939); for "total situation" parenting, see Hawes and Hiner (1985), 502; Bundeson, *The Baby Book* (1927); Watson, *Psychological Care of Infant and Child* (1928); "Tootle," in Hawes and Hiner (1985), 400; Holling C. Holling, *Paddle to the Sea* (1941); Conroy (1968); "Most of us kept quiet..." appears in *ibid.;* graffiti, in George F. Will, "Giuliani: He's No Fiorello," *WP* 10/26/89. *The Tender Trap* (film and song, 1955); Dion DiMucci, *A Teenager in Love* (song, 1959). **Coming of Age.** Baker (1982), 230, 228; "Don't say..." motto, cited in Lee (1970), 92; for Silent youth attitudes toward politics, see "Anti-Democratic Attitudes of High School Seniors in the Orwell Year" (*Phi Delta Kappan,* Jan 1984);

Goodman (1960); Heller, in Herbert Stein, *Presidential Economics* (1985), 95; Manchester (1974), 578–9; Buckley, *God and Man at Yale* (1951); Cook (1971), 40; Herb Caen, in "Baghdad-by-the-Bay" column in *San Francisco Chronicle* 4/2/58; Elvis Presley, *All Shook Up* (song, 1957). **Rising Adulthood.** Sheehy (1976), 39, 123–4; Updike, in Eisler (1986), 187; Callahan (1965), 13; Ray Charles, *What'd I Say?* (song, 1959); Port Huron Statement (1962), cited in Garry Wills, *Nixon Agonistes* (1969), 327; Harrington, *The Other America: Poverty in the United States* (1962); Silberman, *Crisis in the Classroom: The Remaking of American Education* (1970); Peter, Paul, and Mary, *If I Had a Hammer* (song written by Pete Seeger and Lee Hayes, 1962); Nader, *Unsafe at Any Speed* (1965); Styron (1968). **Midlife.** Viorst, *It's Hard to Be Hip Over Thirty, and Other Tragedies of Married Life* (1968); Weinberg, in Morrison and Morrison (1987), 231; Hoffman, in *ibid.*, 293; Agnew, in Manchester (1974), 1220; Updike, *Couples* (1968); Gordon (1984); "tender sometimes . . ." appears in Sheehy (1976), 170; Millett, Brownmiller, Atkinson, all cited in Betty Friedan, *The Second Stage* (1981), 48; Eisler (1986), 308. **Approaching Elderhood.** Broder (1980), 12; Broder's "Fit Fifties Generation," *WP* 8/15/89; Hart, in Schneider (1989); Reagan, in *WP* 2/25/88; "the magic of the machine" appears in George Bush, biographic film, televised (Aug 17, 1988) during the Republican National Convention; Richard Gaines on Dukakis, cited in "The Silent Generation's Candidate," *WP* 6/5/88; Moynihan, "What Chills the Blood of Liberals," *WP* 9/24/89; Aaron (and others), cited in Hobart Rowan, "America's Divided But Strong," *WP* 5/17/90; Nye, "The Misleading Metaphor of Decline" (*Atlantic,* Mar 1990); Wattenberg, "Opinion Roundup" (*PO,* Aug–Sep 1983); Naisbitt (1982), 39; Souter, in "Souter: 'I Have Not Made Up My Mind' on Roe," *WP* 9/15/90; Bellah (1985); Phillips, *Post-Conservative America* (1982); Ehrenreich, *Fear of Falling* (1989); Gilder, "The Message of the Microcosm" (*American Spectator,* Dec 1987); "Hubble Probe Opens as Scientists Reassess Mission," *WP* 6/29/89; Sheehy (1978), 45; Grossman, in "Parenthood II: The Nest Won't Stay Empty," *NYT* 3/12/89; Toffler, *PowerShift* (1990); Peters, *Thriving on Chaos* (1987); Levinson, in "For Many, Turmoil of Aging Erupts in the 50's, Studies Find," *NYT* 2/7/89; Goodman on Schroeder, in "She Couldn't Repackage Herself," *WP* 9/29/87. Lois Wyse, *Funny, You Don't Look Like a Grandmother* (1990); for "21st Century Club," see "Using Social Security Checks for Greater Need," *NYT* 9/24/89. Nader, referring to the Center for Civic Leadership in Princeton, New Jersey, in "Alumni Cross 34 Years, Arrive at a Decision," *WP* 12/17/89; Union of International Associations, in "What's in Store for the 1990s?" *WP* 2/1/90; Korean War Memorial fund-raising pamphlet, "The Last Battle," received by author in 1988; Kelly, "Listen Up, You Baby Boomers: The Silent Generation Is Clearing Its Throat," *Fort Lauderdale Sun-Sentinel* 12/29/89; Jule Styne and Bob Merrill, *People* (song, 1963).

CHAPTER 11: THE MILLENNIAL CYCLE

MILLENNIAL CYCLE BACKGROUND. For an overview of the awakening years, see William Manchester, *The Glory and the Dream: A Narrative History of America, 1932–1972* (1974), parts IV–V; Todd Gitlin, *The Sixties: Years of Hope, Days of Rage* (1987); U.S. Riot (Kerner) Commission, *Report of the National Advisory Commission on Civil Dis-*

orders (1968); National (Eisenhower) Commission on the Causes and Prevention of Violence, *Violence in America* (1969); Christopher Lasch, *The Culture of Narcissism: American Life in an Age of Diminishing Expectations* (1979); and Marvin Harris, *America Now: The Anthropology of a Changing Culture* (1981). For social overviews of the post-Awakening years, see Robert Bellah et al., *Habits of the Heart: Individualism and Commitment in American Life* (1985); Richard Reeves, *American Journey: Traveling with Tocqueville in Search of Democracy in America* (1982); Charles Murray, *Losing Ground: American Social Policy, 1950–1980* (1984); Jann Wenner, *Twenty Years of Rolling Stone: What a Long, Strange Trip It's Been* (1987); Arnold Mitchell, *The Nine American Lifestyles: Who We Are & Where We Are Going* (1983); John Naisbitt, *Mega-trends: Ten New Directions Transforming Our Lives* (1982); and Kevin Phillips, *Post-Conservative America: People, Politics, & Ideology in a Time of Crisis* (1982). For the private and public economics of emerging and maturing generations: Easterlin (1980); Peter Peterson and Neil Howe, *On Borrowed Time: How the Growth in Entitlement Spending Threatens America's Future* (1988); Americans for Generational Equity, *The Generational Journal* (1988–89, various editions); Congressional Budget Office, *Trends in Family Income: 1970–1986* (1988); Jerry Gerber et al., *Lifetrends: The Future of Baby Boomers and Other Aging Americans* (1989); and American Council of Life Insurance, *Datatrack* and *Trend Analysis Program* reports (1982–87, various editions). For changes in the education and social environment of youth: Bureau of the Census, *Characteristics of American Children and Youth* (various editions); U.S. Department of Education, *The Condition of Education: A Statistical Report* (1986); report of the (Wirtz Commission) Advisory Panel on the Scholastic Aptitude Test Score Decline, *On Further Examination* (College Entrance Examination Board, 1977); David Bromley, Mary Crow, and Martha Gibson, "Grade Inflation: Trends, Causes, and Implications" (*Phi Delta Kappan,* Jun 1978); Michael Gose, "Students of the 1960s Versus 1980s: A Report of Teacher Per-ceptions" (*High School Journal,* Feb 1986); on testing data, see bibliography in Brian Waters, *The Test Score Decline* (Human Research Resources Corporation, 1981); Diane Ravitch, *The Troubled Crusade: American Education, 1945–1980* (1983); Calvin Lee, *The Campus Scene, 1900–1970* (1970); Helen Horowitz, *Campus Life: Undergraduate Cultures from the End of the Eighteenth Century to the Present* (1987); Alexander Astin, Kenneth Green, and William Korn, *The American Freshman: Twenty Year Trends, 1966–1985* (1987); Jerald Bachman, Lloyd Johnston, and Patrick O'Malley, *Monitoring the Future: Questionnaire Responses from the Nation's High School Seniors* (1976–89, var-ious editions); Margaret Steinfels, *Who's Minding the Children?: The History and Politics of Day Care in America* (1973); Joseph Hawes and Ray Hiner, *American Childhood* (1985); and Ernie Anastos, *'Twixt: Teens Yesterday and Today* (1983). For crime data, see Marvin Wolfgang and Neil Weiner (eds.), *Criminal Violence* (1982); and Bureau of Justice Statistics, *Report to the Nation on Crime and Justice* (1983), *Criminal Victimi-zation in the United States* (1985), and other bulletins and special reports. For other social and political data, see Warren Miller, *American National Election Studies Data Source-book, 1952–1978* (1980); *AD* (1979–90, various issues); Louis Harris, *Inside America* (1987); Anthony Casale, *Tracking Tomorrow's Trends: What We Think About Our Lives and Our Future* (1986); and Department of Defense, *Population Representation in the Military Services* (various years). For the changing experience of women, see Betty Friedan, *The Second Stage* (1981); and Battelle Memorial Institute, *The Cosmopolitan Report: The Changing Life Course of American Women* (1986).

MILLENNIAL CYCLE REFERENCES. Allen, "Woodstock, for What It's Worth," *WP* 8/15/89; Slick, in "Overheard" (*Newsweek,* Sep 4, 1989); Guthrie, in "Woodstock" (*Life,* Aug 1989); *Hair* (musical, 1968; film, 1979); Cunningham, Letter to the Editor: "Who Cares About the '60s," *WP* 8/24/89; Hoogeveen, Letter to the Editor: "Rose-Colored History," *WP* 9/9/89; *Easy Rider* (film, 1969); William McLoughlin, "The Fourth Awakening," in *Revivals, Awakenings, and Reforms* (1978).

BOOM BACKGROUND. The best single generational biography is Landon Jones, *Great Expectations: America and the Baby Boom Generation* (1980). For the first-wave Boom self-image, see Annie Gottlieb, *Do You Believe in Magic? The Second Coming of the Sixties Generation* (1987); Ralph Whitehead, *Glory Days: The Baby Boom Generation and the American Dream* (Center for National Policy, 1986); Joyce Maynard, *Looking Back* (1973); Michael Medved and David Wallechinsky, *What Really Happened to the Class of '65?* (1976); and Joel Makower, *Boom: Talkin' About Our Generation* (1985). For the last-wave self-image, see Gottlieb (1987); Cheryl Merser, *Grown-Ups* (1987); Wanda Urbanska: *The Singular Generation: Young Americans in the 1980s* (1986); Lansing Lamont, *Campus Shock* (1979); Benjamin Hart, *The Third Generation: Young Conservative Leaders Look to the Future* (1987); and Arthur Levine, *When Dreams and Heroes Die* (1980). For data profiles: *The Baby Boom Generation: A Report Describing the Characteristics and Attitudes of America's Largest Generation and Its Impact on Society* (American Council on Life Insurance, 1983); Daniel Yankelovich et al., *The Sixties Generation: A Profile* (1986); Cheryl Russell, *100 Predictions for the Baby Boom* (1987); U.S. Department of Justice, *Delinquency in Two Birth Cohorts* (1985); Morton Hunt, *Sexual Behavior in the 1970s* (1974); and Rex Weiner and Deanne Stillman, *Woodstock Census: The Nationwide Survey of the Sixties Generation* (1979). For Boomers and economics: Phillip Longman, *Born to Pay: The New Politics of Aging in America* (1987); Louise Russell, *The Baby Boom Generation and the Economy* (1982); and U.S. Congress, Joint Economic Committee, *Working Mothers Are Preserving Family Living Standards* (staff study, 1986). For the Boom Awakening and youth culture: Kenneth Keniston (1971) and *Young Radicals: Notes on Committed Youth* (1968); Lewis Feuer, *The Conflict of Generations* (1969), chs. 8–9; Victoria Secunda, *By Youth Possessed* (1987); Jacob Brackman, "My Generation," *Esquire* (Oct 1968); Joan and Robert Morrison, *From Camelot to Kent State: The Sixties Experience in the Words of Those Who Lived It* (1987); Otto Butz (ed.), *To Make a Difference: A Student Look at America* (1967); James Simon Kunen, *Strawberry Statement: Notes of a College Revolutionary* (1969); Jeffrey Hadden, "The Private Generation" (*Psychology Today,* Sep 3, 1969); Susan Littwin, *The Postponed Generation: Why American Youth Are Growing Up Later* (1986); Charles Reich, *The Greening of America* (1970); Mitchell Goodman (ed.), *The Movement Toward a New America: The Beginning of a Long Revolution* (1970); Robert Pielke, *You Say You Want a Revolution: Rock Music in American Culture* (1986); and Herbert London, *Closing the Circle: A Cultural History of the Rock Revolution* (1984). For the Boom-G.I. "generation gap" and its legacy: Alexander Klein (ed.), *Natural Enemies: Youth and the Clash of Generations* (1969); Edgar Friedenberg (ed.), *The Anti-American Generation* (1971); James DiGiacomo and Edwart Wakin, *We Were Never Their Age* (1972); Henry Malcolm, *Generation of Narcissus* (1971); K. Ross Toole, "I'm Tired of the Tyranny of Spoiled Brats" (*Reader's Digest,* Jun 1970); Anthony M. Casale and Philip Lerman, *Where Have All the Flowers Gone? The Fall and Rise of the Woodstock*

Generation (1989); and Peter Collier and David Horowitz, *Destructive Generation: Second Thoughts About the Sixties* (1989). For the Vietnam dimension: Lawrence Baskir and William Strauss, *Chance and Circumstance: The Draft, the War, and the Vietnam Generation* (1978); Center for the New Leadership, *Enduring Legacies: Expressions from the Hearts and Minds of the Vietnam Generation* (1987); and John Wheeler, *Touched with Fire: The Future of the Vietnam Generation* (1984). For "New Age" and related religious movements: Marilyn Ferguson, *The Aquarian Conspiracy: Personal and Social Transformation in the 1980s* (1980); R. T. Gribbon, *Thirty-Year-Olds and the Church: Ministry with the Baby Boom Generation* (1981); Howard Means, "God Is Back: Washingtonians, Especially Baby Boomers, Are Returning to Religion in Increasing Numbers," *Washingtonian* (Dec 1986); and "For Young Baby Boomers, Deeper Faith," *Atlanta Journal* 3/3/90. For the "yuppie" era: Frank Levy and Robert Michel, "Are Baby Boomers Selfish?" (*AD,* Apr 1985); "The Baby Boomers Turn 40" (*Time* cover story, May 19, 1986); "Baby Boomers Have Sixties Heritage, but Charities Say They're Cheap," *WSJ* 9/11/86; and Quinn Mills, *Not Like Our Parents: A New Look at How the Baby Boom Generation Is Changing America* (1987).

BOOM REFERENCES. Gitlin (1987), 355; Brackman (1968); Erikson, "Toward the Year 2000" (*Daedalus,* Summer 1967); Brackman (1968); Gitlin (1987), 433; on "alcoholics, drug dealers...," see "Take Back the Park," *San Francisco Chronicle* 8/26/90; Abigail Truffaut, "The Rise of the Neo-Puritans," *WP* 7/8/90. The Who, *My Generation* (song, 1965); Jones (1980), book title; Manchester (1974), 287; *Time,* 1965 article cited in Medved and Wallechinsky (1976), 3; *Time,* cover story, 1/6/67; Easterlin (1980), 147; Gottlieb (1987), 8; Caddell, "The Politics of the Baby Boom," in David Boaz (ed.), *Left, Right, and Baby Boom* (1986); Brackman (1968); Keniston (1968), 73; Allison, in *Time,* "Let It Be Vivid, Let It Be Now!" in Klein (1969); Radcliffe speaker, in Arthur M. Schlesinger, Jr., "Students and the Velocity of History," in *ibid.* For Boom opinion surge toward Reagan in 1980, see Richard Wirthlin et al., "Campaign Chronicle" (*PO,* Feb–Mar 1981). Keniston (1968), 55; Malcolm (1971), 56; Feuer (1969), 470. Gitlin (1987), 426; Lasch (1979), book title; *The Graduate* (film, 1967); Katy Butler, "The Great Boomer Bust" (*Mother Jones,* Jun 1989); Pielke (1986), 181; Keniston (1968), 80; Ferguson (1980), 87; Urbanska (1986), 82; Tickel, in "Reluctant Couple Converts to Activism," *WP* 2/2/89. For the shift in economic well-being from first wave to last, see income data by age bracket since 1960 in *CPR,* series P-60; see also " '50s Baby Boom Losing Ground in Economic Race," *WP* 9/8/84, Mills (1987), 16, and "New Arguments About America's New Jobs" (*PO,* Jul–Aug 1987). Rise in marriage age from first to last cohorts: *HSt,* A-158, A-159, and *Abs,* no. 126; see also Willard L. Rodgers and Arland Thornton, "Changing Patterns of First Marriage in the United States" (*Demography,* May 1985). "The Great American Boom" (*Fortune,* Jun 1946); see also Jones (1980), 20; Butler (1989). **Facts.** Demographic "Baby Boom": see summary in Jones (1980), 19–35. Day care: Steinfels (1973), 72–3. Aggressive medicine: Carol Foster (ed.), *Growing Up in America* (1989), 36; see also Phyllis McGinley, "The New Breed of Parents," in Klein (1969); and "Penicillin Losing Some Punch," *San Francisco Chronicle* 2/23/89. Keniston (1968), 51. Poll on attachment to mothers: Barbara Bryant, "High School Students Look at Their World" (Ohio State Department of Education, 1970). Wylie, *The Sons and Daughters of Mom* (1971). Accidental deaths: *Yth,* 102. Drunk driving: U.S. Department of Justice, *Special Report: Drunk Driving* (Bureau of Justice Statistics, Feb 1988). Suicide: *Hth,* table 31; Herbert Hendin, *Suicide in America* (1982), ch. 2; and René F. W. Diekstra and Keith Hawton, *Suicide in Adolescence* (1987), ch. 1. Illegitimate births: *Abs,* no. 87. SAT slide: Wirtz Commission Report (1977). Grade inflation: Astin et al. (1987), 85; and Bromley et al. (1978). Nontraditional grading: "Downgrading No-Grade" (*Time,* Feb 4, 1974). Diminishing academic requirements: Ravitch (1983), 225. Educational achievement: Russell (1987), 47; and data published in *CPR,* series P-20. Crime: U.S. Department of Justice (1985); and Wolfgang and Weiner (1982), 193. Sexual behavior: Hunt (1974), 152–3, 190, 258–61, 315. Vietnam combat and draft experience: Baskir and Strauss (1978), 5, 30–1, 69. Opinions on Vietnam: Yankelovich et al. (1986). Opinions among noncollege Boomers: Seymour Martin Lipset and Everett Carll Ladd, Jr., "The Political Future of Activist Generations," in Philip G. Altbach and Robert S. Laufer (eds.), *The New Pilgrims: Youth Protest in Transition* (1972). Boom opinion on American response to Iraq: CBS News-*New York Times* poll, cited in "Opponents to U.S. Move Have Poverty in Common," *NYT* 9/8/90. Religion: Naisbitt (1990), 275–88; "For Young Baby Boomers, Deeper Faith," *Atlanta Constitution* 3/3/90; and (on first- versus last-wave contrasts) CBS News-*New York Times* "48 hours" poll (Dec 5–8, 1989). Boomer vote for Jackson and Robertson: CBS News-*New York Times* poll (2/8/88, Iowa Caucus); ABC News exit poll, in *WP* 2/17/88 (NH primary); CBS News-*New York Times* poll, in "Portrait of the Super Tuesday Voters," *NYT* 3/10/88; and CBS News-*New York Times* poll (6/7/88, CA and NJ primaries). Income: Frank S. Levy and Richard C. Michel, "The Economic Future of the Baby Boom" (paper presented at conference of Americans for Generational Equity on Apr 10–11, 1986); in these figures, "G.I. father" was born in 1919, "Silent father" in 1929, and "first-wave Boomer" in 1943. Boomer lifestyle comparisons with their parents: Whitehead (1986). **Youth.** LeShan (1973), 116–7; Spock, in "When a Generation Turns 40" (*U.S. News and World Report,* Mar 10, 1986); California psychologist, Dr. Leo Pirojnikoff, in Littwin (1986), 20; Merser (1987), 106, 88; the Beatles, *I Want to Hold Your Hand* (song, 1964); The Rolling Stones, *Let's Spend the Night Together* (song, 1967); Bruce Springsteen, *Dancing in the Dark* (song, 1984). **Coming of Age.** On Sproul Hall pickets, see Ravitch (1983), 196; Collier and Horowitz (1989), 319; Kunen (1969); Moynihan, "Nirvana Now" (*American Scholar,* Autumn 1967); on the proportion of Boomers who were radicals, see Ravitch (1983), 223; Keniston (1968), 81; poll on noncollegiate support for Wallace, cited in Lipset and Ladd (1972); Gitlin (1987), 318; 1970 Gallup Poll, cited in Lipset and Ladd (1972); Brown, *ibid.,* 318; Reich (1970), 217; the Beatles, *Let It Be* (song, 1970); Lamont, in Horowitz (1987), 255. **Rising Adulthood.** Dartmouth student, in LeShan (1973), 128; *Daily Californian* (graduation issue, 1971); Levenstein (1988), 204; "Manifesto of the Person," by Theodore Roszak, cited in Ferguson (1980), 36; Urbanska (1986), 211; Darman, in "Darman's Soft Shoe," *WP* 8/10/89. For data defining the yuppie, see "The Big Chill (Revisited) or Whatever Happened to the Baby Boom?" (*AD,* Sep 1985); and "Played Out: The Going Gets Tough and Madison Avenue Dumps the Yuppies," *WSJ* 12/9/87. **Approaching Midlife.** O'Rourke, "What Next for the Boomers? The New Seriousness?" *WP* 3/8/88; Grey Advertising Agency, cited in "Sponsors' New Message: Buy It, But Have Patience," *NYT* 8/27/90; Merser (1987), 49; Allen, "Star Athletes and the Aging of Aquarius," *WP* 6/20/90; Kors, "It's Speech, Not Sex, the Dean Bans Now," *WSJ*

10/12/89. On "New Puritanism," see "Do as I Do: The New Puritanism," *Washington Times* 5/11/89; for "inappropriately directed laughter," see George Will, "Liberal Censorship," *WP* 11/5/89; for "Green" theme, see "Mother Nature's Guilt Trip," *WP* 4/22/90; for "chastity," see "Chastity Organization: Starting Over in Purity," *NYT* 1/28/90; O'Neill, "Words to Survive Life With: None of This, None of That," *NYT* 5/27/90; Snyder, in Letter to the Editor, *WP* 1/4/89; "Earth First" motto, in "Environmentalists Hurt, Then Held in Blast," *NYT* 5/26/90; Sharpton, in "The Black Man's Burden," *WSJ* 8/20/90; Steele, in George Will, "The Stab of Racial Doubt" (*Newsweek*, Sep 24, 1990); Zinsmeister, "Growing Up Scared" (*Atlantic*, Jun 1990); *WSJ*, cited in George Will, "Stuck in the Sand—for Good," WP 9/9/90; Webb's "ruthless," in "At Least the Navy Knows What It's Doing in the Gulf," *WP* 4/20/88; Webb's "prisons," in "Don't Call on the Guard," *WP* 4/13/89; on Boomer attitudes toward capital punishment, see U.S. Department of Justice, *Sourcebook of Criminal Justice Statistics* (Bureau of Justice Statistics; 1986), 102–3; "The Fryers Club Convention" (*Newsweek*, Aug 27, 1990); antismoker activist, in Victoria Sackett, "Discriminating Tastes: The Prejudice of Personal Preference" (*PO*, Jul–Aug 1987); Bennett, in Richard Cohen, "Czar William at the Winter Palace," *WP* 2/23/90; Gingrich, in Thomas Edsall, "The Great Divider," *WP* 3/23/89; "Apocalypse Darman," coined in Paul A. Gigot, "Potomac Watch," *WSJ* 9/28/90; Russo, in "Democrats Vent Rage at Darman," *WP* 1/31/90; Dorgan, in "Degree of Acrimony in Recent Political Battles Worries Analysts Who Say Worse Is Yet to Come," *WSJ* 6/12/89; Becker, in "Environmentalists Hope for Scorcher," *WP* 6/21/89; Boswell, "This Game of Arrogance Needs Heavy Humbling," *WP* 3/16/90; Fallows, "We Need a Good, Healthy Trade Crisis," *WP* 3/4/90; Winner, "In Third World, Earth-Day's a Cruel Joke," *Fairfax Journal* 4/27/90; Collier and Horowitz (1989), 335; Casale and Lerman (1989), 211. Bentsen, in 1988 Vice-Presidential debate; Metzenbaum on Bennett, in Mary McGrory, "Drug Czar's First Stop: D.C.," *WP* 3/9/89; Stein, "Oh, I Miss the Revolution," *NYT* 4/4/88; Reich (1970), 350; *Good Housekeeping*, "The 'Decency Decade' Begins Today," *NYT* 1/2/90.

THIRTEENTH BACKGROUND. For good examples of the 13er peer personality and style: Nancy Smith, "Twenty-five and Pending: A Lost Generation Wants to Get Out of the Baby-Boom Shadow," *WP* 7/2/89; David M. Gross and Sophronia Scott, "Twentysomething" (*Time*, Jul 16, 1990); Miles Orkin, "Mucho Slingage by the Pool," *NYT* 10/5/89; Brett Easton Ellis, *Less Than Zero* (1985); and assorted 13er biographies in Peter Gareffa (ed.), *Contemporary Newsmakers: The People Behind Today's Headlines* (1985 and subsequent years). For 13er lifecycle experiences: Neil Postman, *The Disappearance of Childhood* (1982); Marie Winn, *Children Without Childhood* (1983); Vance Packard, *Our Endangered Children: Growing Up in a Changing World* (1983); David Elkind, *All Grown Up and No Place to Go: Teenagers in Crisis* (1984); "Born in the '60s," *WP* (four-part series, May 27–30, 1986); Burton Pines, *Back to Basics* (1982); and Victoria Secunda (1987). For attitudes shown toward 13er youths in popular culture: Mary DeMarr and Jane Bakerman, *The Adolescent in the American Novel Since 1960* (1986); Kathy Merlock Jackson, *Images of Children in American Film: A Sociocultural Analysis* (1986); and Judy Blume, *Letters to Judy: What Your Kids Wish They Could Tell You* (1986). For elder criticism of 13ers: Benjamin Stein, "Valley Girls View the World" (*PO*, Aug–Sep 1983); Allan Bloom, *The Closing of the American Mind: How Higher Education*

Has Failed Democracy and Impoverished the Souls of Today's Students (1987); Diane Ravitch and Chester Finn, Jr., *What Do 17-Year-Olds Know?: A Report on the First National Assessment of History and Literature* (1987); Lynne Cheney, *50 Hours: A Core Curriculum for College Students* (1989); U.S. Department of Education, *A Nation at Risk: The Imperative for Educational Reform* (National Commission on Excellence in Education, 1983); Steve Allen, *Dumbth and 81 Ways to Make America Smarter* (1985); E. D. Hirsch, Jr., *Cultural Literacy: What Every American Needs to Know* (1987); and Peter Hart, "Democracy's Next Generation" Report (People for the American Way, 1990). For data profiles: "The Sparse Generation" (*National Journal,* special issue; March 8, 1986); Children's Defense Fund, *A Children's Defense Budget: An Analysis of Our Nation's Investment in Children* (1987); Leonard Ramist and Solomon Arbeiter, *Profiles, College-Bound Seniors* (College Board, 1983); Reho Thorum, "The High School Student of the Seventies" (*High School Journal,* Oct 1977); and Allan Ornstein, "The Changing High School Student Culture" (*High School Journal,* Oct 1981). For 13er family nurture: Jean Okimoto and Phyllis Jackson Stegall, *Boomerang Kids: How to Live with Adult Children Who Return Home* (1987); Helen Swan and Victoria Houston, *Alone After School: A Self-Care Guide for Latchkey Children and Their Parents* (1985); Lynette Long and Thomas Long, *The Handbook for Latchkey Children and Their Parents* (1983); Sheila Kamerman, *Parenting in an Unresponsive Society* (1980); Kyle Pruett, *The Nurturing Father: Journey Toward the Complete Man* (1987); Boston Women's Health Book Collective, *Ourselves and Our Children: A Book by and for Parents* (1978); Lenore Weitzman, *The Divorce Revolution* (1985); Bill Cosby, *Fatherhood* (1986); and Andrew Cherlin, *Marriage Divorce Remarriage* (1981). For education: Ivan Illich's *Deschooling Society* (1971); Charles Silberman, *Crisis in the Classroom: The Remaking of American Education* (1970); C. H. Rathbone, *The Informal Classroom* (1971); Nancy Dearman (ed.), *The Condition of Education* (1982); and Patrick Welsh, *Tales Out of School: A Teacher's Candid Account from the Front Lines of the American High School* (1986). For the economic and social hardships of 13er youths: Danziger and Gottschalk (1986); National Association of State Boards of Education, *Code Blue: Uniting for Healthier Youth* (1990); Blayne Cutler, "Up the Down Staircase" (*AD,* Apr 1989); Howard Sudak, Amasa Ford, and Norman Rushforth (eds.), *Suicide in the Young* (1984); Terry Williams, *Cocaine Kids: The Inside Story of a Teenage Drug Ring* (1989); Cheryl Hayes (ed.), *Risking the Future: Adolescent Sexuality, Pregnancy, and Childbearing* (1987); Nicholas Lemann, "The Origins of the Underclass" (*Atlantic,* Jun 1986); U.S. Bureau of Justice Statistics, *Teenage Victims* (1986); and Lawrence Greenfeld and Patrick Lawson, "Trends in Prison Populations," presented at the National Conference on Punishment for Criminal Offenses (1987). For youth opinion: *Yth;* National Association of Secondary School Principals, *The Mood of American Youth* (1984); and Roper Organization, *The American Chicle Youth Poll* (1987).

THIRTEENTH REFERENCES. For Patton screening, see Hart (1987), 67–9; the Georgetown University minister is Father Lawrence Madden, in Pines (1982), 237; Smith (1989); "Twentysomething" (*Time,* Jul 16, 1990); for polls of high school seniors on fear of national catastrophe, see National Association of Secondary School Principals (1984), 42–4; Felicity Barringer, "What IS Youth Coming to?" *NYT* 8/19/90; *Top Gun* (film, 1986); *The Breakfast Club* (film, 1985); *sex, lies, and videotape* (film, 1989); *Bad*

Influence (film, 1989); Schwartz, *Bicycle Days* (1989); Schwartz, in "John Burnham Schwartz, in Early Bloom," *WP* 5/23/89; Lewis, *Liar's Poker* (1989); U.S. soldier in Panama, in *WP* 1/4/90; Goodman, "Why Kids Tune Out Politics," *WP* 12/2/89; Baker, "Herky-Jerky Bang Bang," *NYT* 6/30/90; Lea, in "God's Green Beret," *San Francisco Chronicle* 9/1/90; "Hopes of a Gilded Age," *WP* 6/14/86; "Rettonization," in Gareffa (1985), no. 2; Mandel, "Canseco: A Schmuck for Our Times," *San Francisco Chronicle* 2/26/90; Ad Council poster, in "Depression" (*Newsweek*, May 4, 1987); U.S. Department of Education (1983); Bloom (1987); Ravitch and Finn, Jr. (1987), 261–2; Cohen, "Johnny's Miserable SATs," *WP* 9/4/90; Anderson, "Fighting the Dumbness Trend," *WP* 1/21/90; Allen (1989); Carnegie report, in "Colleges Lack a Value System, Report Says," *San Francisco Examiner* (4/30/90); "junky," quoting the president of Bradford College, in William Raspberry, "Getting Kids Ready for School," *WP* 5/9/88; Kuttner, "Our Sheltered Political Class," *WP* 8/31/90; People for the American Way, cited in "A Frivolous Decade," *WP* 1/3/90; Rathbone, in Ravitch (1983), 249; Hirsch (1987); Rathbone, in Ravitch (1983), 249; *Paper Moon* (film, 1973); Ellis (1985); "proto-adults" appears in "Teens: On the Road to Grown-Up Cares," *WSJ* 2/7/90; Goodman, in Elkind (1984), 13; Blum, in statement given to author; Welsh (1986), 15; Kreski, in "MTV's Game Show Tries to Be Dumb and Finally Succeeds," *WSJ* 8/11/89; Bon Jovi, *You Give Love a Bad Name* (song, 1986); the think tank study is "The Ethics of American Youth," The Josephson Institute, cited in William Raspberry, "Values from the Good Old Days," *WP* 11/7/90; *River's Edge* (film, 1986); Elkind (1984), 17; Peters, quoted in "Time to Toast the Post-Posties," *San Francisco Chronicle* 4/8/90; Matt Groening on Bart Simpson, in "An Animated Conversation with Bart's Creator" (*Rolling Stone*, Jun 28, 1990); Bennett on Bart Simpson, in "Personalities," *WP* 5/28/90; Linburg, in statement given to author; for rising college tuitions, see Terry Hartle, "Are College Costs a Problem?" (*PO*, May–Jun 1987); Nix, in "The Posties," *San Francisco Chronicle* 3/9/90. **Facts.** Legal abortions per 100 live births: *Hth*, table 10; for data before 1973, see Battelle Memorial Institute (1986), vol. 1, 7–38. Rise in divorce rate per 1,000 married women: for 1920–1970, *HSt*, B-217; since 1970, *Abs*, no. 126. Surveys on bad marriages: cited in Preston (1984). Risk of parental divorce: National Center for Health Statistics, *Supplements to the Monthly Vital Statistics Report* (series 24, no. 1, May 1989). Feeling happier after divorce: Winn (1983), 139. Family complexity: "Children Stepping Out" (*AD*, May 1985); and Cherlin (1981), 86. Working mothers: "Family Crises" (*National Journal*, Apr 16, 1988); and *Yth*, 38–41. Latchkey children: Long and Long (1983), 23. "Cool" parents: Sunkist Teen Trendset Survey (1989). Zandl, in "Check It Out!" *WP* 9/23/90. Average grades: published annually in Astin et al. (1978 and later years). Trend in family-assistance benefits per recipient: U.S. House of Representatives, *Children in Poverty* (Committee on Ways and Means, May 22, 1985), 189–219; and *Overview of Entitlement Programs, 1990 Green Book* (Committee on Ways and Means, Jun 5, 1990), section 7. Trend in minimum wage: "Minimum Wage: Bulwark of the Privileged," *WSJ* 6/15/89. Boom versus 13th teacher survey: Gose (1986). College completion: "College Completion Rates Are Said to Decline Sharply," *WSJ* 7/28/89; and "Drop in Black Enrollment Traced Partly to Military Service," *WP* 1/15/90. Earnings by educational background: Joe Schwartz, "The Forgotten Market" (*AD*, May 1988). Military enlistment: U.S. Department of Defense (1987). Republican leanings: "Opinion Roundup" (*PO*, Nov–Dec 1986); and *National Journal* (1986). Mortality rates: *VSt*, vol. II, part

A, section 1 and part B, table 8-6; *Hth,* tables 21–31; and *Yth,* 102–3. Youth violence and fear: see Zinsmeister (1990); and Bornemann, in *ibid.;* see also National Association of State Boards of Education (1990). Suicide: *Hth,* table 31; Sudak (1984); Diekstra and Hawton (1987), ch. 1; and Hendin (1982), ch. 2. Incarceration: U.S. Department of Justice, *Historical Corrections Statistics in the United States, 1850–1984* (Bureau of Justice Statistics; 1986), 34; and U.S. Department of Justice (1986), 399–401; see also "Young Law Breakers Jamming Country's Detention Centers," *NYT* 7/17/88, and "Study: 1 in 4 Young Black Men Is in Jail or Court-Supervised," *WP* 2/27/90. Poverty by age bracket: *CPR,* series P-60 (annual); see also Congressional Budget Office (1988), 38. Attitudes toward welfare and unemployment: "The Age of Conservatism" (*AD,* Nov 1986). Male wage-earners by age bracket: U.S. Bureau of Labor Statistics data compiled in Children's Defense Fund (1987), 257; see also Cutler (1989), and "To Be Young, Male, and Black," *WP* 12/28/89. Household median income: Congressional Budget Office (1988), 94, 96. Homeownership by age bracket: Census survey data updated yearly since 1972 by National Association of Home Builders; see also "Home Ownership Found to Decline," *NYT* 10/8/89. Youths living at home: "Twentysomething" (*Time,* Jul 16, 1990); Okimoto and Stegall (1987), 5; and "Parenthood II: The Nest Won't Stay Empty," *NYT* 3/12/89. Tax comparison: Ways and Means (1990), 1148. Newspaper readers by age bracket: *Times Mirror* survey, cited in "Profiles of Today's Youth: They Couldn't Care Less," *NYT* 6/28/90. "Cynical Americans" survey: "Cynical? So Who's Cynical?" *WP* 6/23/89; survey author Phillip Mirvis, quoted in *ibid.,* wrote *The Cynical Americans: Living and Working in an Age of Discontent and Disillusion* (1989). **Youth.** Cruise, in Gareffa (1985), no. 4; "good life" survey, in Harris (1981), 114; Boston Women's Health Book Collective (1978), 5; Thomas Gordon, *Parental Effectiveness Training* (1970); T. Berry Brazelton, *Infants and Mothers: Differences in Development* (1969); Burton White, *The First Three Years of Life* (1975); Winn (1983), 24–5; Kyle Pruett, *The Nurturing Father: Journey Toward the Complete Man* (1987); Hall, in Gareffa (1985), no. 3; Norma Klein, *It's OK If You Don't Love Me* (1977); Keniston, *All Our Children* (1977), 18; Cosby (1986), 93; Poussaint, in "Here's What Most Parents Look Like to Kids Watching TV" (ad), *NYT* 9/27/88; Boston Women's Health Book Collective (1978), 5; *Close Encounters of the Third Kind* (film, 1977). For "breakthrough" youth books, see DeMarr and Bakerman (1986); for children in films, see Jackson (1986); Blume (1986), 273; Feldstein, in Winn (1983), 64; Long (1983). **Approaching Rising Adulthood.** Ralph, in statement given to author; on rising child labor law violations, see "Secretary Dole: Stiffer Child Labor Penalties," *WP* 6/29/90. On perceptions about working harder and living standards, see "Twentysomething" (*Time,* Jul 16, 1990); see also CBS News poll, 2/23/89. "The way society presents it . . ." appears in Jill Nelson, "After Graduation?" *WP* 5/6/90; Etzioni, in "Teens Overemployed," *Cleveland Plain Dealer* 11/2/87. For youths as shoppers, see "Teens: On the Road to Grown-Up Cares," *NYT* 2/7/90, and Cutler (1989); Erikson, in "Twentysomething" (*Time,* Jul 16, 1990); "The Baby-Busters: New Generation Asks More Than Its Elders of Corporate World," *WSJ* 10/26/88; on 13er entrepreneurs, see "The Year in Start-Ups," (*INC,* Nov 1989). Herbert, in "Schools See Empty Desks at Halloween," *NYT* 11/1/89; Ice-T, cited in "Fighting Words," *WP* 10/15/89; Tyson, in "Tyson's Sensational Punch Lines," *WSJ* 6/23/89; Raspberry, "Living and Dying Like Animals," *WP* 11/2/89; Samenow, "The Wilding of Central Park," *WP* 5/2/89; New York City youth on "wilding," quoted on

ABC World News Tonight 4/24/89. Long, in "Hard Crime, Hard Times Hit 'Breadbasket of the Confederacy,'" *WP* 8/19/89; Fulwood, in "Washington's Year of Shame," *WP* 1/1/89; Salaam, in "N.Y. Jogger's Assailants Given Maximum Sentences," *WP* 9/12/90; Williams (1989); Fulwood, in *op. cit.;* Chapman, *Fast Car* (song, 1988); Lasch, "The I's Have It for Another Decade," *NYT* 12/27/89. For "throwaways," see "Somebody Else's Kids" (*Newsweek,* Apr 25, 1988), and "Discarded Population Put at Nearly 500,000," *WP* 12/12/89. Youth with "Boom" cars, in "Laws Aim to Turn Off Ear-Splitting 'Boom' Cars," *NYT* 1/17/90; Silber, in "Grads Going for Gold," *San Francisco Examiner* 6/11/89; job predictions, in *AD* marketing brochure, mailed to public (1990); Bangles lyric, in Debbi Peterson and Susanna Hoffs, *Angels Don't Fall in Love* (song, 1986); Ellis (1985); "U.S. Students Left Flat by Sweep of History," *WP* 12/2/89; Connolly, in "Berkeley Feels Mideast Storm as a Ripple of Fear," *NYT* 8/29/90; Hart (1990); president of M.I.T. is M. Richard Rose, in "Silver Bullets for the Needy" (*Time,* Mar 16, 1987); Postman (1982), 90; Tuckson, in "Growing Up in D.C., What Went Wrong?" *WP* 5/7/89; Xaviere and Ralph, in statements given to author; Smith (1989); Orkin (1989).

MILLENNIAL BACKGROUND. For examples of the early-1980s shift in child nurture and elder attitudes toward children: Daniel Patrick Moynihan, *Family and Nation* (1986); Lisbeth Schorr, *Within Our Reach: Breaking the Cycle of Disadvantage* (1988); Karl Zinsmeister, "The Rising Threat to American Children" (unpublished, American Enterprise Institute, 1987); "Through the Eyes of Children: Growing Up in America Today" (*Time* cover story, Aug 8, 1988); Tipper Gore, *Raising PG Kids in an X-Rated Society* (1987); and Lester Brown et al., "The Children's Fate," *Natural History* (1986). For data: U.S. House of Representatives, Select Committee on Children, Youth, and Families, *U.S. Children and Their Families: Current Conditions and Recent Trends* (1987); Children's Defense Fund (1987); and Joe Schwartz and Thomas Exter, "All Our Children" (*AD,* May 1989).

MILLENNIAL REFERENCES. Nate Bush, in "D.C. Students' Uniform Response: 'No Way' to Dressing Alike," *WP* 9/22/88; see also "School Uniform Idea Catching On in D.C.," *WP* 9/3/88; Fallows, "A Few Pointers" (*Atlantic,* Nov 1989). President Bush on "mathematics and science," cited in William Raspberry, "No. 1 in Math—the Wrong Goal," *WP* 3/23/90; on child labor investigations, "Why Business Turns to Teen-Agers," *NYT* 3/26/89; Koop, in "Class of 2000 Vows to Be 'Smoke-Free,' " *Boston Herald* 8/31/88; on "Project 2000," see "Adding Gentle but Firm Persuasion," *WP* 2/8/90; Femia, in "P.G. Youths in Drug Cases Increasingly Tried as Adults," *WP* 11/9/89; Zinsmeister (1990); Koch, in "A New Age of New Feudalism," *NYT* 12/26/89; *Parenthood* (film, 1989). New wave of books on childhood: Winn (1983); Postman (1982); Packard (1983); Elkind (1984). New wave of books on divorce, latchkey kids, and value-neutral education: Weitzman (1985); Diane Medved, *The Case Against Divorce* (1988); Judith Wallerstein, *Second Chances: Men, Women, and Children a Decade After Divorce* (1989); Bloom (1987); Ravitch and Finn, Jr. (1987). Films: *Children of the Corn* (1984); *Firestarter* (1984); *The Shining* (1980); *Cujo* (1983); *Raising Arizona* (1987); *Three Men and a Baby* (1987); *Baby Boom* (1987); *For Keeps* (1988); *She's Having a Baby* (1988). Poll on "staying home with the family," in "The Eighties Are Over" (*Newsweek,* Jan 4, 1988); "Boomers Give Birth to a Fad," *San Francisco Chronicle* 8/2/88; "In This

Year's Movies, Baby Knows Best,'' *NYT* 3/13/88. Porter (*Congressional Record,* Apr 4, 1985); *Forbes* (Sep 14, 1988); Bush, in ''Bush Urges Teen-Agers to Help Ghetto Dwellers,'' *WP* 10/5/88; ''The 60s Generation, Once High on Drugs, Warns Its Children,'' *WSJ* 1/29/90; Gore (1987); on Rakolta, see ''The Mother Who Took On Trash TV,'' *WP* 10/10/89; Trudeau in *Doonesbury* (syndicated comic strip, undated). Films: *Willy Wonka and the Chocolate Factory* (1971); *An American Tail* (1986); *Oliver and Company* (1989); *The Land Before Time* (1988). On number of Disney cartoonists, see p. B6, *Fairfax Journal* 11/17/88. James Dobson, *Dare to Discipline* (1970); see ''Pater Familias of Family Values,'' *WSJ* 10/17/88. See ''Jessica McClure: For 58 Hours She Was Everybody's Baby,'' *WP* 5/27/89; Goodman, ''Sins of the Kids: Should Parents Pay . . . ,'' *WP* 5/9/89. Bennett, in ''Bennett Suggests Orphanages as Drug Refuge,'' *WP* 4/28/90; for approval ratings on teachers, see U.S. Department of Education (1986), 90–1; see also ''Opinion Roundup'' (*PO,* Summer 1986); Finn, ''A Seismic Shock for Education,'' *NYT* 9/3/89; for hold-back data, see ''Debate Intensifying on Screening Tests Before Kindergarten,'' *NYT* 5/11/89, and ''Schools Start Flunking Many More Students in Drive on Mediocrity,'' *WSJ* 11/30/88; for sale of Gesell Test materials, see ''Debate Intensifying on Screening Tests Before Kindergarten,'' *NYT* 5/11/89; Krauthammer, ''Drown the Berenstain Bears,'' *WP* 5/8/89; Bennett, in ''President Promises: 'Dooney Doesn't Have to Sell Drugs,' '' *WP* 9/7/89; Quindlen, ''The Shalt Nots,'' *NYT* 10/14/90. **Facts.** Fertility and family size: *National Journal* (1986). Legal abortions per 100 live births: *Hth,* table 10. On cost and survival of ''preemies'': ''Whose Baby Is It, Anyway,'' *WP* 4/22/88; Mary Semander, ''Don't Give Up on Premature Babies,'' *USA Today* 5/22/90; and *Parade* 5/28/89. Attitudes toward public schools: U.S. Department of Education (1986), 90–1. Trend in teacher salaries: *ibid.,* 68. Child poverty rate: *CPR,* series P-60. Divorce rate per 1,000 married women: since 1970, *Abs,* no. 126. Homicide rate against children: *Hth,* table 30. Medicaid eligibility: Congressional Research Service, *Medicaid Source Book: Background Data and Analysis* (1988); and ''Deficit or No Deficit, Unlikely Allies Bring About Expansion in Medicaid,'' *NYT* 11/4/90. Advertisement (*Atlantic,* Jan 1990); Paine, on ABC-Nightline (Sep 29, 1988).

CHAPTER 12: THE PAST AS PROLOGUE

The opening ''Crisis era'' lines come from *Gone With the Wind* (film, 1939), and the songs *Over the Rainbow* (Harold Arlen, 1939) and *The White Cliffs of Dover* (Nat Burton and Walter Kent, 1939). ''The chance to grow . . .'' is from Henry Truslow Adams, in Arthur Ekirch, Jr., *Ideologies and Utopias* (1969), 6. For discussion of 1980s-era polls showing contentment with inner life running ahead of contentment with the outer world, see *PO* (various issues); for a current look at this mix of ''personal optimism and social pessimism,'' see ''90's, in Poll: A Good Life Amid Old Ills,'' *NYT* 1/1/90, and ''Introspective Electorate Views Future Darkly,'' *WP* 1/21/90. **The Cycle of Generational Moods: A Paradigm.** Santayana, *The Life of Reason* (1905–6), vol. I. The *New York Gazette* in 1749, cited in Carl Bridenbaugh, *Cities in Revolt: Urban Life in America, 1743–1776* (1955), 113. Available data on per capita U.S. alcohol consumption indicate that cyclical peaks were reached in 1980–1981, in 1906–1910, and in 1830–1840. See the *First Statistical Compendium on Alcohol and Health* (National Institute on

Alcohol Abuse and Alcoholism, Feb 1981); *NIAAA Quick Facts* (CSR, Inc., periodic); J. C. Burnham, "New Perspectives on the Prohibition 'Experiment' of the 1920s" (*JSH*, Fall 1968); Jack S. Blocker, Jr., *American Temperance Movements: Cycles of Reform* (1989); and Chapter 10 source notes. Although the data are spotty for the 1700s, the low price of alcoholic beverages and the growing number of drinking establishments (per capita) suggest that consumption during the late 1740s and 1750s was certainly unprecedented in the American colonies—and probably not again equaled until the next century. See Chapter 1 and the statistical appendix to W. J. Rorabaugh, *The Alcoholic Republic: An American Tradition* (1979), and Bridenbaugh (1955), ch. 3. For similar trends in narcotics consumption, see H. Wayne Morgan, *Drugs in America: A Social History, 1800–1980* (1981), and David T. Courtwright, *Dark Paradise: Opiate Addiction in America Before 1940* (1972). Musto, cited in "Drug Use? Americans Can't Seem to Remember When," *WP* 8/27/90. For data on trends in total fertility rates since 1800, see Ansley J. Coale and Melvin Zelnick, *New Estimates of Fertility and Population in the United States* (1963) and *SSP*, table 3. For earlier years, see source notes for Chapters 7 and 8. According to Coale and Zelnick, fertility rates remained steady at roughly 4.3 from 1863 to 1885—the only two-decade period between the 1810s and the 1930s when fertility did *not* decline appreciably. For data on immigration, see the beginning of the source notes. For data on standard of living growth (changes in real output per person employed) since 1929, see *EPr* or the National Income and Product Account Statistics, published in U.S. Bureau of Economic Analysis, *Survey of Current Business* (annual). Before 1929, see writings of Simon Kuznets, John W. Kendrick, Robert E. Gallman, Paul David et al., described in article bibliographies in *EnE*. **Generational Endowments.** Comte and Ferrari, both cited in Marías (1970); see source notes for Chapter 3. "Each generation is . . . as an independent nation" appears in a letter (Sep 6, 1789) from Jefferson in Paris to James Madison in New York; see "The Earth Belongs in Usufruct to the Living," in Julian P. Boyd (ed.), *The Papers of Thomas Jefferson*, vol. 15 (1958), 384–99. See also Madison's objections in his response (Feb 4, 1790), in Marvin Meyers (ed.), *The Mind of the Founder: Sources of the Political Thought of James Madison* (1973), 176–9. Hamilton's objections can be inferred from his contributions to *The Federalist* (1788). Later in life, Jefferson himself seldom raised his earlier arguments against long-term public indebtedness. "As is the generation of leaves" appears in Homer, *Iliad*, book 6.

CHAPTER 13: COMPLETING THE MILLENNIAL CYCLE

Completing the Eras of the Millennial Cycle. For historical data on life expectancy at age 65, see *SSP*, table 9. For the most recent future projections, see Social Security Administration, *Annual Report of the Board of Trustees of the Federal Old-Age and Survivors' Insurance and the Federal Disability Insurance Trust Funds* (1990), and Gregory Spencer, *Projections of the Population of the United States, by Age, Sex, and Race: 1988 to 2080* (Bureau of the Census, 1989). According to the Census "Middle Series" projections, life expectancy for men and women at age 65 will rise from 15.1 and 19.4 years (today) to 16.6 and 21.4 years (in 2020) to 18.1 and 23.1 years (in 2060). **Completing the Missionary and Lost Diagonals.** For data and estimates on the number of Americans over age 100, see *CPR*, series P-23, no. 153, "America's Centenarians" (Sep 1987); approximate estimate of 1,000 Americans age 109 and over in 1991 was obtained from Gregory Spencer, U.S. Bureau of the Census. **Completing the G.I. Diagonal.** On the rising material affluence of today's G.I. elders relative to youth and rising adults, see source notes for Chapters 11 and 12. For a quantitative discussion of trends in per capita income, public benefits dollars received, and numbers of Americans in poverty—all by age group—see Peter G. Peterson and Neil Howe, *On Borrowed Time* (1988), ch. 2. In 1722, as a boy of 16, Benjamin Franklin helped his elder brother James lampoon Cotton Mather by writing several famous essays under the sarcastic pseudonym "Silence Do-Good." In 1784, at the age of 78, Franklin expressed his sincere appreciation of Cotton Mather's efforts as a "doer of good" in a kind letter to a fellow elderly Awakener—Cotton's own son Samuel; the letter is cited in Cedric B. Cowing, *The Great Awakening and the American Revolution: Colonial Thought in the 18th Century* (1971), 126. **Completing the Boom Diagonal.** Susan B. Anthony, cited in "Not Every Feminist Is in Pro-Choice Camp," *Washington Times* 7/23/90. The Social Security Administration makes annual projections of the long-term future cost of Social Security cash benefits and Hospital Insurance (Medicare, Part A) according to several economic, demographic, and health-care-cost scenarios. Using the scenario that comes closest to actual American experience over the last couple of decades, the Social Security Administration now projects that the annual cost of Social Security cash benefits and Hospital Insurance (Medicare, Part A) will exceed 30 percent of total worker payroll by the year 2025 and 40 percent by the year 2050. See "Alternative III" in Social Security Administration, *Annual Report of the Board of Trustees of the Federal Old-Age and Survivors' Insurance and the Federal Disability Insurance Trust Funds* (1990). Even this projection assumes that health-care cost inflation will slow dramatically over the next ten years and does not include the tax cost of other underfunded federal pension plans (military and civil service retirement) and health-care benefit programs (Medicaid long-term care and Medicare, Part B). The total burden could be considerably greater. See Peterson and Howe (1988), and John L. Palmer and Barbara Boyle Torrey, "Health Care Financing and Pension Programs," in Gregory B. Mills and Palmer (eds.), *Federal Budget Policy in the 1980s* (1984). The "seven in ten" Boomers who doubt Social Security will help them comes from a poll cited in "Opinion Roundup" (*PO*, Aug–Sep 1981) and a CBS News–*New York Times* poll (Jan 20, 1990). In a survey conducted by the Daniel Yankelovich Group for IDS Financial Services in 1989, people were asked whether they agreed with the statement "I really don't think Social Security will amount to much by the time I retire." Of Silent respondents (age 45–64), 36 percent agreed; of Boomer respondents (age 35–44), 60 percent agreed—the largest generational disparity among all responses to questions about retirement. "God is in me . . ." appears in Wallace Stevens, *Opus Posthumous* (1957); "enviable death . . ." from Winston Churchill, speech before the House of Commons (Apr 17, 1945). **Completing the Thirteener Diagonal.** On polls showing that 13ers place much more importance on financial success than their next-elders at like age, see the UCLA poll cited in Chapter 3 source notes; see also the survey data presented in National Association of Secondary School Principals, *The Mood of American Youth* (1984), 58–60; the Roper Organization Inc., *The American Chicle Youth Poll* (1987), 18; and *Yth*, 122. "But in modern war there is nothing sweet or fitting in your dying. You will die like a dog for no good reason" appears in Ernest Hemingway, "Notes on the Next War," in George Seldes (ed.), *The Great Thoughts* (1985), 180. *Revenge of the Nerds* (film, 1984).

APPENDIX A: A THEORY OF GENERATIONS

On how "generations" were understood by the ancient Greeks, see Laura L. Nash, "Concepts of Existence: Greek Origins of Generational Thought," in Stephen R. Graubard, *Generations* (1979), and Robert Graves, *The Greek Myths*, (1957); in nonwestern mythology, see the *New Larousse Encyclopedia of Mythology* (1968). Classical sources by name and ascribed title: Hesiod (eighth century B.C.), *Theogony;* Philo (c. 20 B.C.– c. A.D. 50), *Cosmogony;* Homer (eighth century B.C.?), *Iliad;* Herodotus (c. 484–c. 425 B.C.), *History;* and Thucydides (c. 460–c. 400 B.C.), *History of the Peloponnesian War.* On Nestor, see *Iliad,* book 1. **The Cohort Generation.** Philip J. Greven, Jr., *Four Generations: Population, Land, and Family in Colonial Andover, Massachusetts* (1970). "A chosen generation" appears in New Testament, 1 Peter 2:9; "A generation of vipers" in *ibid.*, Matthew 3:7; "served his own generation" in *ibid.*, Acts 13:36. See also the historical usage of the word "generation" in modern English in the *Oxford English Dictionary* (1928).

Especially over the last twenty years, an excellent literature has appeared on the major themes and problems of the "generations" approach to social and cultural change. For an introduction, see Julián Marías, "Generations: The Concept," in *EnS,* and *Generations: A Historical Method* (1967, University of Alabama Press translation, 1970); Anthony Esler, *Generations in History* (1982); Alan B. Spitzer, "The Historical Problem of Generations" (*AHR,* Dec 1973); essays (esp. by Laura L. Nash, Annie Kriegel, Matilda White Riley, and Morton Keller) in Graubard (1979); and Yves Renouard, "La notion de génération en histoire," *Revue Historique* (Jan–Mar 1953). On what many social scientists call "political generations," see essays (esp. by Richard J. Samuels and Samuel Huntington) in Samuels (ed.), *Political Generations and Political Development* (1976); Marvin Rintala, "Political Generations," in *EnS,* and "A Generation in Politics: A Definition" (*Review of Politics,* Oct 1963); and Lewis S. Feuer, "Generations and the Theory of Revolution" (*Survey,* 1972). On cohort analysis and generations, see Vern L. Bengtson et al., "Generations, Cohorts, and Relations Between Age Groups," in Robert H. Binstock and Ethel Shanas, *Handbook of Aging and the Social Sciences* (1985); and Norman B. Ryder, "Cohort Analysis," in *EnS.*

Our summary of generations writing since the French Revolution owes much to the excellent treatment of Marías, and we urge the reader to refer to Marías (1970) or to Esler (1982) for fuller citations or translations. Thomas Jefferson, see source notes for Chapter 12; Jean-Louis Giraud or "Soulavie," *Tableau de l'histoire* (1803) and *Pièces inédites sur les règnes de Louis XIV, Louis XV, et Louis XVI* (1809); Auguste Comte, *Cours de philosophie positive* (1830–42) and *Le système de politique positive* (1851–54); John Stuart Mill, *A System of Logic* (1843); Émile Littré, *Paroles de philosophie positive* (1860); Antoine Cournot, *Considération sur la marche des idées et des événements dans les temps modernes* (1872); Ottokar Lorenz, *Die Geschichtswissenschaft in Hauptrichtungen und Aufgaben kritisch erörtert* (1886); Giuseppe Ferrari, *Teoria dei periodi politici* (1872); Wilhelm Dilthey, various essays (written 1865–75); François Mentré, *Les générations sociales* (1920); José Ortega y Gasset, *El tema de nuestro tiempo* (1923); Wilhelm Pinder, *Das Problem der Generationen in der Kunstgeschichte Europas* (1926, 1928);

Julius Peterson, *Die Literarischen Generationen* (1930); Karl Mannheim, "Das Problem der Generationen" (1928). The flurry of interest in the "generation gap" during the early 1970s resulted in one issue of *Daedalus* (no. 4, 1978) and two issues of *Journal of Social Issues* (nos. 2 and 3, 1974) devoted entirely to topical articles on "generations." Johan Huizinga, "The Problem of Cultural History" (1946), in Marías (1970), 132.

A Journey to Cohortia. S. N. Eisenstadt, *From Generation to Generation: Age Groups and Social Structure* (1956), offers a model of "age groups," based on research on societies throughout the world (past and present), which supports our basic distinction between "traditional" and "modern" societies. In most of the premodern societies cited by Eisenstadt, social roles are rigidly and concretely prescribed by an individual's age-group membership. The increasing "specialization" and "differentiation" that accompany life in modernizing societies, however, steadily weaken the institutional link between age and social roles. Rather than prescribe behavior, age groups become a more voluntaristic means of preparing individuals "psychologically" to make their own choices. Thus, in modern societies, younger age groups are more apt to change their tone, aims, and objectives according to the unique cohort-group currently passing through them— even to the extent of manifesting "deviant" or "revolutionary" hostility against the social roles recommended by older age groups currently in power. See also an insightful commentary on Eisenstadt: Philip Abrams, "Rites of Passage: The Conflict of Generations in Industrial Society" (*Journal of Contemporary History,* 1970).

Many medieval authors—most notably Dante (*Inferno,* canto 26)—condemned Odysseus for his ceaseless efforts to lead glorious expeditions later in life. "The gods visit the sins of the fathers upon the children" appears in Euripides (fragments); Ivan Turgenev, *Fathers and Sons* (1862); Graham Nash, *Teach Your Children* (song, 1970). Remarkably (in *Iliad,* book 1), Nestor recalls from his boyhood that his warrior elders were "a godlike race of heroes" and that "in my youth, even these esteem'd me wise." The childhood of Agamemnon (the name means "very resolute") was a gallery of horrors: Agamemnon's father (Atreus) killed one of Agamemnon's brothers (Pleisthenes), killed two of Agamemnon's cousins and served them to their father (Thyestes) in a soup, and was killed by another cousin (Aegisthus); as an infant, Agamemnon narrowly escaped death himself. See Graves (1957), vol. 2, 43–51.

The Four-Part Generational Cycle. See Old Testament, Exodus (ch. 1) through Judges (ch. 2). "From twenty years old and upward, all that are able to go forth to war . . ." appears in Numbers 1:3; "and there arose . . ." in Judges 2:10. Ibn Khaldun, *The Muqaddimah* (written in the 1370s), cited in Marías (1970), 198–207. See Auguste Comte, Émile Littré, and Giuseppe Ferrari, *op. cit.;* Julián Marías (1970), 170–88; and Samuel Huntington, *American Politics: The Promise of Disharmony* (1981). Huntington's description of his "IvI" cycle appears in *ibid.,* 147; his earlier remarks on "generational" cycles appear in Huntington (1977) and Huntington, "Paradigms of American Politics: Beyond the One, the Two, and the Many" (*Political Science Quarterly,* Mar 74).

INDEX OF NAMES

This index includes only the proper names of persons. Following each American name, we indicate generational membership by an abbreviation within parentheses. An occasional "?" following the abbreviation means that we were unable to verify the birthyear and generation exactly. Following each foreign name, we indicate nationality and the generation of the American cohort born in the same year. We use the designational "Reformation Cycle" for birthyears between 1483 and 1583, and "Medieval" or "Ancient" for earlier birthyears.

538 INDEX